Italy For Dummies, 1st Edition

Rome Transit

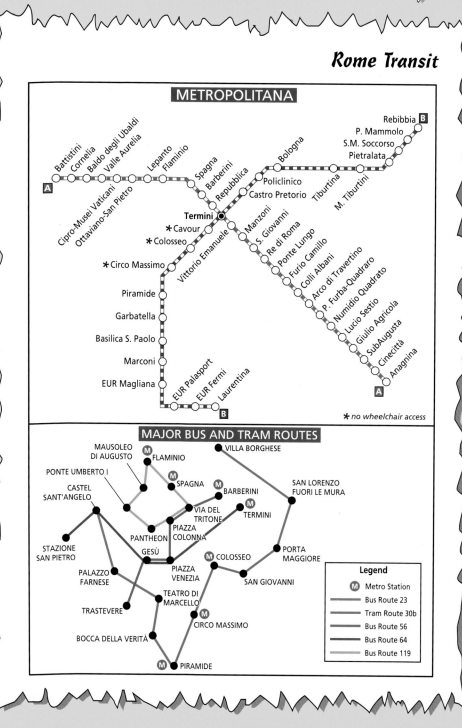

METROPOLITANA

Battistini
Cornelia
Baldo degli Ubaldi
Valle Aurelia
Cipro-Musei Vaticani
Ottaviano-San Pietro
Lepanto
Flaminio
Spagna
Barberini
Repubblica
Bologna
Policlinico
Castro Pretorio
Tiburtina
M. Tiburtini
Rebibbia
P. Mammolo
S.M. Soccorso
Pietralata

A

B

Termini
*Cavour
*Colosseo
Vittorio Emanuele
Manzoni
S. Giovanni
Re di Roma
Ponte Lungo
Furio Camillo
Colli Albani
Arco di Travertino
P. Furba-Quadraro
Numidio Quadrato
Lucio Sestio
Giulio Agricola
SubAugusta
Cinecittà
Anagnina

*Circo Massimo
Piramide
Garbatella
Basilica S. Paolo
Marconi
EUR Magliana
EUR Palasport
EUR Fermi
Laurentina

A

B

*no wheelchair access

MAJOR BUS AND TRAM ROUTES

MAUSOLEO DI AUGUSTO
Ⓜ FLAMINIO
VILLA BORGHESE
PONTE UMBERTO I
Ⓜ SPAGNA
CASTEL SANT'ANGELO
Ⓜ BARBERINI
SAN LORENZO FUORI LE MURA
VIA DEL TRITONE
Ⓜ TERMINI
PIAZZA COLONNA
PANTHEON
GESÙ
STAZIONE SAN PIETRO
PALAZZO FARNESE
PIAZZA VENEZIA
Ⓜ COLOSSEO
PORTA MAGGIORE
TEATRO DI MARCELLO
SAN GIOVANNI
TRASTEVERE
Ⓜ CIRCO MASSIMO
BOCCA DELLA VERITÀ
Ⓜ PIRAMIDE

Legend

Ⓜ	Metro Station
	Bus Route 23
	Tram Route 30b
	Bus Route 56
	Bus Route 64
	Bus Route 119

For Dummies®: Bestselling Book Series for Beginners

Italy For Dummies,
1st Edition

Cheat Sheet

Venice Vaporetto System

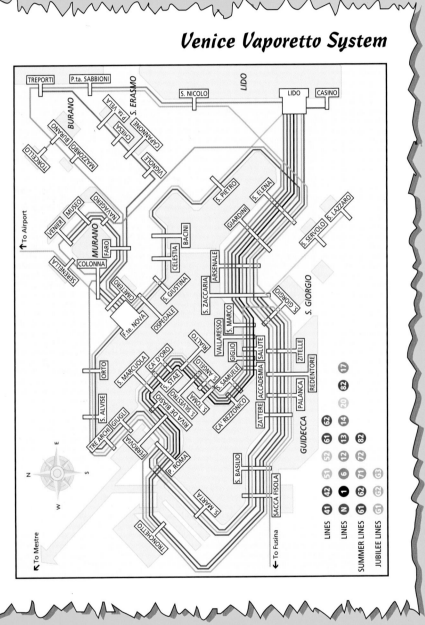

For Dummies®: Bestselling Book Series for Beginners

 TM

References for the Rest of Us!™

BESTSELLING BOOK SERIES

Do you find that traditional reference books are overloaded with technical details and advice you'll never use? Do you postpone important life decisions because you just don't want to deal with them? Then our *...For Dummies®* business and general reference book series is for you.

...For Dummies business and general reference books are written for those frustrated and hard-working souls who know they aren't dumb, but find that the myriad of personal and business issues and the accompanying horror stories make them feel helpless. *...For Dummies* books use a lighthearted approach, a down-to-earth style, and even cartoons and humorous icons to dispel fears and build confidence. Lighthearted but not lightweight, these books are perfect survival guides to solve your everyday personal and business problems.

"More than a publishing phenomenon, 'Dummies' is a sign of the times."

— The New York Times

"A world of detailed and authoritative information is packed into them..."

— U.S. News and World Report

"...you won't go wrong buying them."

— Walter Mossberg, Wall Street Journal, on IDG Books' ...For Dummies books

Already, millions of satisfied readers agree. They have made *...For Dummies* the #1 introductory level computer book series and a best-selling business book series. They have written asking for more. So, if you're looking for the best and easiest way to learn about business and other general reference topics, look to *...For Dummies* to give you a helping hand.

IDG BOOKS WORLDWIDE

1/99

Italy
FOR
DUMMIES®
1ST EDITION

Italy
FOR
DUMMIES®
1ST EDITION

by Bruce Murphy and
Alessandra de Rosa

IDG
BOOKS
WORLDWIDE

IDG Books Worldwide, Inc.
An International Data Group Company

Foster City, CA ✦ Chicago, IL ✦ Indianapolis, IN ✦ New York, NY

Italy For Dummies,® 1st Edition

Published by
IDG Books Worldwide, Inc.
An International Data Group Company
919 E. Hillsdale Blvd.
Suite 300
Foster City, CA 94404
`www.idgbooks.com` (IDG Books Worldwide Web Site)
`www.dummies.com` (Dummies Press Web Site)

Library of Congress Control Number: 00-109408

ISBN: 0-7645-6198-7

ISSN: 1531-1805

Printed in the United States of America

10 9 8 7 6 5 4 3 2 1

1B/RV/RR/QQ/IN

Distributed in the United States by IDG Books Worldwide, Inc.

Distributed by CDG Books Canada Inc. for Canada; by Transworld Publishers Limited in the United Kingdom; by IDG Norge Books for Norway; by IDG Sweden Books for Sweden; by IDG Books Australia Publishing Corporation Pty. Ltd. for Australia and New Zealand; by TransQuest Publishers Pte Ltd. for Singapore, Malaysia, Thailand, Indonesia, and Hong Kong; by Gotop Information Inc. for Taiwan; by ICG Muse, Inc. for Japan; by Intersoft for South Africa; by Eyrolles for France; by International Thomson Publishing for Germany, Austria and Switzerland; by Distribuidora Cuspide for Argentina; by LR International for Brazil; by Galileo Libros for Chile; by Ediciones ZETA S.C.R. Ltda. for Peru; by WS Computer Publishing Corporation, Inc., for the Philippines; by Contemporanea de Ediciones for Venezuela; by Express Computer Distributors for the Caribbean and West Indies; by Micronesia Media Distributor, Inc. for Micronesia; by Chips Computadoras S.A. de C.V. for Mexico; by Editorial Norma de Panama S.A. for Panama; by American Bookshops for Finland.

For general information on IDG Books Worldwide's books in the U.S., please call our Consumer Customer Service department at 800-762-2974. For reseller information, including discounts and premium sales, please call our Reseller Customer Service department at 800-434-3422.

For information on where to purchase IDG Books Worldwide's books outside the U.S., please contact our International Sales department at 317-572-3993 or fax 317-572-4002.

For consumer information on foreign language translations, please contact our Customer Service department at 800-434-3422, fax 317-572-4002, or e-mail `rights@idgbooks.com`.

For information on licensing foreign or domestic rights, please phone 650-653-7098.

For sales inquiries and special prices for bulk quantities, please contact our Order Services department at 800-434-4322 or write to the address above.

For information on using IDG Books Worldwide's books in the classroom or for ordering examination copies, please contact our Educational Sales department at 800-434-2086 or fax 317-572-4005.

For press review copies, author interviews, or other publicity information, please contact our Public Relations department at 650-653-7000 or fax 650-653-7500.

For authorization to photocopy items for corporate, personal, or educational use, please contact Copyright Clearance Center, 222 Rosewood Drive, Danvers, MA 01923, or fax 978-750-4470.

is a registered trademark under exclusive
license to IDG Books Worldwide, Inc., from
International Data Group, Inc.

About the Authors

Bruce Murphy was born in New York City, where he continues to live when not traveling and working on projects as a freelance writer. **Alessandra de Rosa** is a world traveler and professional tourist who has also worked for the United Nations. Bruce and Alessandra also collaborated on *New York City For Dummies*.

Dedication

This book is dedicated to everyone who has dreamed of going to Italy and longs to get to know this beautiful land, its people, and its culture.

ABOUT IDG BOOKS WORLDWIDE

Welcome to the world of IDG Books Worldwide.

IDG Books Worldwide, Inc., is a subsidiary of International Data Group, the world's largest publisher of computer-related information and the leading global provider of information services on information technology. IDG was founded more than 30 years ago by Patrick J. McGovern and now employs more than 9,000 people worldwide. IDG publishes more than 290 computer publications in over 75 countries. More than 90 million people read one or more IDG publications each month.

Launched in 1990, IDG Books Worldwide is today the #1 publisher of best-selling computer books in the United States. We are proud to have received eight awards from the Computer Press Association in recognition of editorial excellence and three from Computer Currents' First Annual Readers' Choice Awards. Our best-selling ...For Dummies® series has more than 50 million copies in print with translations in 31 languages. IDG Books Worldwide, through a joint venture with IDG's Hi-Tech Beijing, became the first U.S. publisher to publish a computer book in the People's Republic of China. In record time, IDG Books Worldwide has become the first choice for millions of readers around the world who want to learn how to better manage their businesses.

Our mission is simple: Every one of our books is designed to bring extra value and skill-building instructions to the reader. Our books are written by experts who understand and care about our readers. The knowledge base of our editorial staff comes from years of experience in publishing, education, and journalism — experience we use to produce books to carry us into the new millennium. In short, we care about books, so we attract the best people. We devote special attention to details such as audience, interior design, use of icons, and illustrations. And because we use an efficient process of authoring, editing, and desktop publishing our books electronically, we can spend more time ensuring superior content and less time on the technicalities of making books.

You can count on our commitment to deliver high-quality books at competitive prices on topics you want to read about. At IDG Books Worldwide, we continue in the IDG tradition of delivering quality for more than 30 years. You'll find no better book on a subject than one from IDG Books Worldwide.

John Kilcullen
Chairman and CEO
IDG Books Worldwide, Inc.

Eighth Annual Computer Press Awards≥1992 *Ninth Annual Computer Press Awards≥1993* *Tenth Annual Computer Press Awards≥1994* *Eleventh Annual Computer Press Awards≥1995*

Publisher's Acknowledgments

We're proud of this book; please send us your comments through our IDG Books Worldwide Online Registration Form located at http://my2cents.dummies.com.

Some of the people who helped bring this book to market include the following:

Editorial

Editors: Ron Boudreau, Linda Brandon

Copy Editor: Billie Williams

Cartographer: Roberta Stockwell

Editorial Manager: Christine Beck

Editorial Assistant: Carol Strickland

Senior Photo Editor: Richard Fox

Assistant Photo Editor: Michael Ross

Production

Project Coordinator: Nancee Reeves

Layout and Graphics: Karl Brandt, Beth Brooks, LeAndra Johnson, Jill Piscitelli, Julie Trippetti

Proofreaders: David Faust, Nancy Price, Linda Quigley, Christine Sabooni

Indexer: Liz Cunningham

Special Help
Robert Annis, Rowena Rappaport

General and Administrative

IDG Books Worldwide, Inc.: John Kilcullen, CEO; Bill Barry, President and COO;

IDG Books Consumer Reference Group

 Business: Kathleen A. Welton, Vice President and Publisher; Kevin Thornton, Acquisitions Manager

 Cooking/Gardening: Jennifer Feldman, Associate Vice President and Publisher

 Education/Reference: Diane Graves Steele, Vice President and Publisher; Greg Tubach, Publishing Director

 Lifestyles: Kathleen Nebenhaus, Vice President and Publisher; Tracy Boggier, Managing Editor

 Pets: Dominique DeVito, Associate Vice President and Publisher; Tracy Boggier, Managing Editor

 Travel: Michael Spring, Vice President and Publisher; Suzanne Jannetta, Editorial Director; Brice Gosnell, Managing Editor

IDG Books Consumer Editorial Services: Kathleen Nebenhaus, Vice President and Publisher; Kristin A. Cocks, Editorial Director; Cindy Kitchel, Editorial Director

IDG Books Consumer Production: Debbie Stailey, Production Director

IDG Books Packaging: Marc J. Mikulich, Vice President, Brand Strategy and Research

◆

The publisher would like to give special thanks to Patrick J. McGovern, without whom this book would not have been possible.

◆

Contents at a Glance

Cartoons at a Glance

By Rich Tennant

"I insisted they learn some Italian. I couldn't stand the idea of standing in front of the Trevi Fountain and hearing, 'gosh', 'wow', and 'far out.'"

page 5

"And how shall I book your flight to Italy – First Class, Coach, or Medieval?"

page 51

"It says, children are forbidden from running, touching objects, or appearing bored during the tour."

page 99

"I know *how* to ask for directions to a McDonald's in Italian, I'm just afraid to."

page 183

"Funny—I just assumed it would be Carreras too."

page 309

"He had it made after our trip to Italy. I give you the Fontana di Clifford."

page 381

"I appreciate that our room looks out onto several baroque fountains, but I had to get up 6 times last night to go to the bathroom."

page 425

"So far you've called a rickshaw, a unicyclist, and a Zamboni. I really wish you'd learn the Italian word for taxicab."

page 479

Fax: 978-546-7747
E-mail: richtennant@the5thwave.com
World Wide Web: www.the5thwave.com

Maps at a Glance

Table of Contents

Introduction

So you've decided to go to Italy. *Molto bene!* But where will you visit? The Eternal City of Rome? The Serene Republic of Venice? The Renaissance glory of Florence? The charming hill towns of Tuscany? The dramatic island of Sicily? What interests you most — paintings, sculptures, frescoes, ancient ruins, baroque churches, beaches, vineyards, food, fashion, grand palazzi, natural beauty, opera? As you can see, you've really created a job for yourself by deciding to visit Italy.

The problem with visiting Italy is that you always have far too many wonderful choices. Italians are very individualistic, and each region has its own particular character and flavor. This applies to each city within each region, each neighborhood within each city, and so on. Italy seems to be the country that everyone wants to visit these days, especially because of the tremendous efforts (both public and private) to restore, refurbish, and modernize the country for Papal Jubilee 2000. In 2001 and beyond, you'll find that these efforts have saved monuments from years of neglect and made Italy even more beautiful. In addition, you'll find an even greater awareness of the needs of visitors, with many attractions staying open late in summer and offering more services. A language barrier remains, of course — unless you know Italian — but nevertheless, you'll find the Italian people warm and welcoming.

About This Book

With a history stretching from the dawn of time through the Roman Empire, the Middle Ages, the Renaissance, and up to the new Europe, Italy offers too much to see in one visit, unless your visit is *long*. Whether you're a first-timer or a visitor who has seen Rome and Florence and now wants to see Venice and Verona or you've seen the north and now want to head south (or vice versa), *Italy For Dummies* is designed to give you all the information you need. We know that you're not really a dummy, so we don't insult your intelligence, but we do cover everything comprehensively and precisely. Some people spend more time planning their trip than they do taking it. However, we assume that you want to enjoy your trip and make the most of it, which includes planning your trip, so in this book, we cut to the chase.

We've written this book to ease you painlessly into your Italian vacation. Unlike some guides, we don't make you work as if you were reading a college textbook. Consult the Table of Contents to select any topic related to your trip, and you can find assistance. Likewise, you don't need to read the book from beginning to end, but you can do so if you wish, of course. This book is a reference work as well as a guidebook — the place where you can look up information as you travel and not just a piece of ballast for the bottom of your suitcase.

Conventions Used in This Book

The structure of this book is nonlinear: You can open it at any point and delve into the subject at hand. The information is concentrated, not spread out all over the map, and we use icons to guide you toward particular kinds of tips and advice (see "Icons Used in This Book" for a full list).

We list the hotels, restaurants, and sights alphabetically, not jumbled up by area, with prices and our frank evaluations. We use this series of abbreviations for credit cards in our hotel and restaurant reviews:

AE: American Express

DC: Diners Club

MC: MasterCard

V: Visa

Note that Discover isn't listed. The Discover card is unknown in Italy, so having one or more of the big three — American Express, Visa, and MasterCard — is best.

How This Book Is Organized

The book is broken down into eight parts. The first two parts cover everything you need to consider to plan your trip and get organized. The other parts of the book concern the several regions of Italy that we've chosen to cover, which are the major tourist destinations and their environs, as well as the island of Sicily. You can read each of these parts independently if you want to zero in right away on the areas that attract you. Following are brief summaries of each of the parts.

Part I: Getting Started

Part I gives you a preview of your choices in Italy. Think of it as our rundown of the best of Italy. In this part, we give you a flavor of the country, climate, special events, and the particular aspects that make traveling in Italy unlike traveling elsewhere. We also suggest some itineraries in case you don't want the hassle of working out your own. Likewise, we help you come up with a workable budget and provide some advice on cutting costs.

Part II: Ironing Out the Details

This part takes you through the nuts-and-bolts of your journey — making the travel arrangements — that you can do through an agent, on the Internet, or on your own. We help you decide if an escorted or a guided tour is right for you and address the special concerns of families, seniors, travelers with special needs, and gays and lesbians. We also cover details like getting a passport, making reservations, and money.

Part III: The Eternal City: Rome

The Eternal City has been renewed magnificently for the Papal Jubilee, and we guide you through its wonderful maze of ancient and modern treasures. We also take you on side trips to Tivoli and its villas, the ancient seaport of Ostia Antica, and the Castelli Romani.

Part IV: Florence and the Best of Tuscany and Umbria

Tuscany is currently Italy's most popular region. Ask just about anyone where he or she would like to have a little hideaway, and you can bet the answer will be "Tuscany!" Part IV deals with the cultural and artistic treasures of Renaissance Florence as well as the most appealing aspects of the surrounding Tuscan towns, such as Lucca, Pisa, Siena, and San Gimignano. It also introduces you to the beauties of Umbria, a small green neighboring region highlighted by such famous towns as Assisi, Spoleto, and Perugia.

Part V: Venice and the Best of the Veneto

La Serenissima (the Serene Republic, the old nickname of the Republic of Venice) is the serene, mysterious, and seemingly impossible city of canals that's sinking slowly year after year. Part V takes you through Venice, perhaps the most magical and strange place in the world, as well as to the top cities of the surrounding region of the Veneto, nearby Verona and Padua.

Part VI: Naples, Pompeii, and the Amalfi Coast

Part VI covers one of the most diverse corners of the country. Naples is as frenetic and fascinating as ever, chock-full of wonderful art, food, and people. Pompeii and Herculaneum are centers of ancient history, while the Amalfi Coast and Capri are part of one of Italy's most beautiful natural areas and most visited resorts.

Part VII: Sicily

To many, Sicily is the heart of Italy. In fact, Goethe called it the "key to everything." Part VII shows you how this intense land has changed recently and how it proudly retains the past. From the region's capital, Palermo, we take you around the island to Taormina, Syracuse, and Agrigento, as well as to some smaller destinations such as Segesta and Cefalù.

Part VIII: The Part of Tens

This special section is part handy reference, part troubleshooting guide, part summary of key points, and part signpost for where to go for more information.

Icons Used in This Book

Throughout this book, you'll notice these four icons intended as signposts and flags for facts and information of a particular nature or interest:

This icon signals advice on dos and don'ts, shortcuts, and how to make the most of your time.

With the Heads Up icon, we tell you about tourist traps, pitfalls, ripoffs, and things and places to avoid.

If you're bringing your children along, look for the Kid Friendly icon to read about venues that families love. When the icon is used in conjunction with a restaurant listing it means that high chairs and *mezza porzione* (half portions) are available. When it's used with a hotel listing, it means that the staff is ready to meet your children's special needs.

This icon signals a way to save money, as well as special deals that you shouldn't overlook.

Where to Go from Here

As we said, now you can dig in, basically wherever you want. If you've already decided which cities you're going to visit (maybe you've even bought your plane tickets), you can go ahead and get down to selecting hotels, sights, and restaurants. But if you're planning to go to Italy and you first need to decide where, the first chapter is dead ahead: Discovering the Best of Italy.

Part I
Getting Started

The 5th Wave   By Rich Tennant

Magnifico!

Molto bello!

"I insisted they learn some Italian.
I couldn't stand the idea of standing
in front of the Trevi Fountain and
hearing, 'gosh', 'wow', and 'far out'."

In this part . . .

So you know you want to go to Italy, but exactly when and exactly where? What sort of weather are you hoping for? Do you want to see the major destinations and have to deal with tourist hordes? Or are you looking for off-the-beaten-path places where you can relax in relative solitude? How much can you afford to spend? In this part, we sort through your options, showing the advantages and drawbacks of each choice and mentioning special considerations. Italy is a relatively expensive destination, but you can make smart choices to reduce the cost and enjoy your trip even more. (We also list less expensive hotels and restaurants throughout the book and offer tips for pinching a lira here and there without sacrificing.)

In Chapter 1, we highlight Italy's most interesting features so you can choose what you like the most. In Chapter 2, we describe the characteristics of each region covered in this book and the best season in which to travel. We also give you a calendar of the most important festivals and events and tips on planning your itinerary. However, if you don't want to plan your own trip, you can follow one of the five itineraries we provide in Chapter 3. In Chapter 4, we deal with budget-related questions, and in Chapter 5, we list some tips for travelers with special interests and needs.

Chapter 1

Discovering the Best of Italy

. . . .

In This Chapter

▶ Gaining an Italian perspective

▶ Enjoying Italy's culture and cuisine

▶ Shopping through Italy

▶ Seeking Italy's natural beauty

▶ Reviewing a brief history of Italy

. . . .

*I*taly has an almost mythical status in the minds of many people, whether it's for reasons of religion, art, architecture, natural beauty, food, people, or any combination of these. Italy was probably the first place in the world to become a tourist destination (beyond being a pilgrimage site). Back in the fifteenth century, artists and scholars of the northern Renaissance came to Italy, drawn to its burgeoning centers of art and learning, and disseminated a new way of thinking — humanism — to the rest of Europe. In the nineteenth century, Americans came to Europe to do the "Grand Tour" (the classic European tour undertaken by the well-to-do and satirized by Mark Twain in *The Innocents Abroad*) and made more stops in Italy than any place else (that's why some people took years to see it, lucky them!).

Italy today is a giant cultural and religious pilgrimage site, drawing millions of visitors every year, and never more than in 2000 for the Papal Jubilee. Stretching from the Dolomites (part of the Alps) in the north and almost to Africa in the south — Tunisia is only 60 miles from Sicily — Italy offers a fantastic variety of natural and cultural attractions. Selecting your destinations from among these riches is a real challenge, whether you're a first-timer or a regular. Therefore, we've put together this run-down of the best Italy has to offer.

Visiting the Sites of Modern Civilization's Beginnings

In Italy, history is present in everyday life everywhere you go, but the remains of the Roman civilization are probably the most striking. In **Rome** you'll find the **Colosseo (Colosseum),** the ancient theater of cruelty in which hundreds of men fought with lions and other ferocious animals to amuse the crowds. You can take a stroll in the **Foro Romano (Roman Forum),** in the **Fori Imperiali (Imperial Forums),** and on the **Palatino (Palatine Hill),** an archaeological park covering much of the ancient center, its main street and temples, its marketplace, and its most exclusive residential area. The **Pantheon** is a still-perfect Roman temple that was transformed into a church during Christian times. And nearby Rome is **Ostia Antica,** the ancient seaport that's now a massive archaeological site.

In **Verona,** you can attend an opera in the **Anfiteatro Romano (Roman Amphitheater),** one of the finest venues for opera today, showing that the ruins are alive and well and still in use. The cities of **Ercolano (Herculaneum)** and **Pompei (Pompeii),** on the other hand, are monuments to a flowering culture that was smothered by volcanic ash and pumice stone during the A.D. 79 eruption of Vesuvius; you can admire these cities today in their eerie completeness. **Sicily** boasts even more Roman and Greek sites, paramount among them the magnificent **Greek temples** of **Agrigento.** In **Siracusa (Syracuse)** and **Segesta,** Greek tragedies are still performed in the amphitheaters where Greek colonists who founded these cities saw them more than 2,000 years ago. Performances are also mounted in **Taormina** in a fabulous ancient theater overlooking the sea and with views of Mt. Etna.

Seeing the Masters: From Cimabue to Michelangelo to Veronese

There's something wonderful about seeing paintings in their original setting and land, rather than in an institution in a faraway city. If you gave each truly great painting and fresco and mosaic and sculpture in Italy your full attention, you'd return home without a spot of color from the glorious Italian sun — you could spend your entire trip indoors, marveling at some of the world's finest art collections. Even though collectors pillaged Italy for centuries, carrying off its treasures to remote points, it's amazing that the country is still so full of fabulous masterpieces.

Begin your tour of masterpieces by abusing your neck in the Vatican's **Cappella Sistina (Sistine Chapel),** whose breathtaking ceiling frescoes by Michelangelo were freshly (and controversially) restored in the 1990s and now glow with vivid color. Likewise, you can see other great works in the **Musei Vaticani (Vatican Museums).** In the **Basilica di San Pietro (St. Peter's Basilica),** you can't miss the unearthly beauty of Michelangelo's *Pietà.*

In Rome, there are dozens of churches full of wonderful paintings that never travel to foreign museums or shows, such as **Santa Maria sopra Minerva** and **Santa Maria del Popolo,** and the country is full of hundreds more. For example, Padua's **Cappella degli Scrovegni** contains a cycle of marvelous Giotto frescoes (though the chapel closed in 2001 for renovations), and Assisi's **Basilica di San Francesco (Basilica of**

St. Francis) — reopened after the restoration of earthquake damage — boasts Giotto's celebrated fresco cycle on the life of St. Francis.

During high season, you may have to grit your teeth and stand in long lines at Florence's **Galleria degli Uffizi** and Venice's **Gallerie dell'Accademia** (thanks to a new system at the Uffizi, however, you can reserve tickets ahead), but the treasures inside are more than worth the wait. These galleries boast more canvas than a tall ship, and virtually every Italian master of the Renaissance onward is represented (Titian, Veronese, Tintoretto, Andrea del Sarto, Raphael, Leonardo, Perugino, Cimabue, Botticelli, and Bellini are a few). Likewise, the star of Florence's **Galleria dell'Accademia** is Michelangelo's unsurpassed *David.*

Italian rules for lining up at museums differ from what you may be used to. You may think that people are packed together, trying to push their way through, but each person is more or less aware of who was there first. Even if the mass of people doesn't look like a line, it's sort of structured like one. Note the faces of who's around you when you arrive so you know where you stand, and be ready to slightly modify your posture so the person behind you knows that *you* know when it's your turn. (Get used to the fact that body language is important in Italy!)

Viewing the Art of Italy's Architecture

When you think about seeing the sights in Italy, you think about the country's wide and wonderful range of architecture — from Roman and Greek ruins to the finest examples of the Romanesque, medieval, Gothic, Renaissance, and baroque styles.

In a country full of spectacular *duomo*s (cathedrals), *basilicas,* and *chiese* (churches), Rome's majestic **Basilica di San Pietro (St. Peter's Basilica)** is the largest and most imposing, crowned by Michelangelo's dome. The marble beauty of Florence's **Duomo** (with its dome by Brunelleschi), **Battistero (Baptistry),** and **Campanile (Bell Tower)** by Giotto rival Siena's **Duomo** and **Battistero** as the top must-sees in Tuscany. In addition to ancient monuments and ruins, many Italian cities boast monumental *piazze* **(squares),** with beautiful buildings surrounding a fountain or ruin and denying the passage of time. A few of the best are Rome's **Piazza San Pietro, Piazza di Spagna,** and **Piazza Navona**; Florence's **Piazza della Signoria**; and Venice's **Piazza San Marco**.

If you don't know a baptistry from a basilica or a loggia from a lozenge, see "Knowing Your Apse from Your Ambone: A Glossary of Architectural Terms" in the Appendix.

Every Italian city seems to have a famous symbolic landmark, like Rome's **Colosseo (Colosseum)** and Florence's and Siena's **Duomos.** In Pisa, of course, it's the **Leaning Tower,** the delicate marble bell tower that has been tipping for centuries. The 13 noble towers of

San Gimignano (remaining from the original 70 or so) are the source of its nickname, the Manhattan of Tuscany. Venice's **Piazza San Marco** and its fantastical **Basilica di San Marco** are among the most recognizable public spaces in the world. And Naples's **Castel dell'Ovo** rises against the surrounding gulf, one of the most scenic large harbors in Italy.

The variety of Italy's architecture from region to region is amazing. Venice has a style all its own, including the delicate and almost mystical **Venetian Gothic** — reflected in the water, the buildings are even more magical. You can also see the explosive **Barocco Siciliano (Sicilian Barocco),** a captivating ornate style that blesses many cities in Sicily and also contrasts with the stark beauty of Norman architecture in Palermo. And in Tuscany and Umbria, the picturesque hill towns are like works of sculpture.

Enjoying the Bounty of the Cucina Italiana

Food and drink are integral parts of all cultures, but Italian cuisine deserves a special status of its own. Variations of Italian traditional dishes have become fundamental parts of other cultures as well. What would the world be like without pizza, that specialty of Naples; pasta in its many forms and sauces; espressos and cappuccinos; gelati; and Chianti Classico, Lambrusco, and Asti Spumante?

To satisfy your hunger in Italy, stop into one of the innumerable *pizzerie, trattorie,* and *osterie.* Italians talk about food the way other people talk about . . . well, other things. You can have a bad meal in any country, but in Italy you really have to work hard to find one. Even so, throughout this book we give you sure-fire restaurants where, for a reasonable amount of lire, you can satisfy your hunger and quench your thirst with vino. From the world-famous Chianti to crisp Frascati to Lachrymae Christi (Tears of Christ), which is made from grapes grown on the slopes of the Vesuvian volcano, you're sure to find food that pleases your palate.

Enjoying regional cuisine

Italian cuisine is really a mix of regional fares: Roman, Tuscan, Venetian, Neapolitan, Sicilian, and so on. Here are some highlights:

- ✔ The Tuscan *bistecca alla fiorentina* is probably the best steak you'll ever have, even if you're from Montana.

- ✔ Neapolitan pizza, the *real* thing, the original from which all other pizzas have descended (and we mean *descended*), is covered with fresh tomato, buffalo-milk mozzarella, and anchovies (if you like them). This pizza will also make you hate your local pizzeria back home.

✔ Of course, you'll find spaghetti, penne, tagliatelle, and other varieties of pasta everywhere in Italy — with *vongole* (clams) in the
south, *cinghiale* (wild boar sauce) in Tuscany, sardines in Sicily,
and an abundance of seafood in Venice and many other places.
You can also find filled fresh pasta, such as tortellini, ravioli, and
lasagne — the richest pasta specialties of all. For Italians, filled
fresh pasta is reserved for special days, but as a visitor you enjoy
special status and can indulge every day you choose.

As for dessert, how about *gelato* (ice cream that surpasses any other
ice cream), *granita* (frozen coffee or lemon ice and, in Sicily, almond
ice), creamy *zabaglione* (made with sugar, egg yolks, and marsala
wine), or *tiramisù* (layers of mascarpone cheese and espresso-soaked
lady fingers).

Even a trip to an Italian supermarket yields a feast: the finest olive oil
you've ever tasted; *parmigiano reggiano* (the original parmesan
cheese), which makes the commercial stuff seem like sawdust; the
tastiest tomatoes you'll ever have; mozzarella, including the famous
mozzarella di bufala (buffalo mozzarella); and fresh local wines.

Quenching your thirst

Italy is also the homeland of some of the best wines in the world (sur-
passing even the French!). In the introduction to the restaurant section
in each chapter, we give you suggestions for some of the best local
wines.

Don't expect to order a martini before dinner. In restaurants, but more
particularly in trattorie, osterie, and pizzerie, you probably won't find a
full bar, because Italians don't drink liquor before dinner. And unless
they're in a pub, Italians don't drink alcohol at all without eating something. More touristy restaurants may be more used to foreign customs,
so if you ask for a scotch and water, they won't stare at you in perplex-
ity. Elsewhere, follow the "when in Rome" rule: Try having *grappa* (a
clear brandy) or an *amaro* (a 60 to 80 proof bitter drink, made with
herbs), which Italians drink *after* a meal.

Check out "From Antipasti to Zuppa Inglese: A Glossary of Italian Menu
Terms" in the Appendix if you can't tell cannelloni from calzone or
pesto from polenta.

Shopping Italian Style

"Made in Italy" seems to have a special ring for shoppers. Italy is
famous for its style, and not only Armani suits and Gucci loafers. You
can find many big fashion and accessories brands (Dolce e Gabbana,
Fendi, Ferragamo, Valentino, Versace, and so on) in the United States
and other countries, but you may save some money buying them in
Italy because of the exchange rates.

Getting the goods

Although you can find many Italian-designer goods in the United States, there are a lot of things that never make it out of Italy or Europe. An example is housewares: Alessi and other manufacturers produce an incredible range of cool-looking coffeemakers, corkscrews, kitchen implements, and every conceivable device you may need. Glassware is similarly varied. You can find these items in pretty much any major Italian city and most minor ones. Italians are also crazy about accessories — look for a big range of fountain pens, watches, sunglasses, gloves, and other tools of personal style building.

You can certainly save some money buying Italian clothes in Italy, but you can really save on Italian shoes — a nice pair of good-quality leather-soled shoes for under $100 is a great deal.

Enjoying regional specialties

Alas, one of Italy's greatest products — food — isn't something you can bring home given most customs regulations. But there are many other specialties from which to choose. Venice is known for blown glass, Florence for leather goods, and both for beautiful paper and lace. All roads lead to Rome, and there you can find just about anything. Rome also has many shops that sell antique furniture, prints, paintings, glassware, and china. Hand-painted ceramics are also an Italian specialty. Deruta in Umbria; Vietri in Campania; Santo Stefano, Sciacca, and Caltagirone in Sicily; and Faenza in Emilia-Romagna (famed for *faïence/majolica*) produce colorful ceramics of every shape and size. At each of the major shopping points, we help steer you toward the good deals and away from the tourist traps; so if you buy a glow-in-the-dark plastic gondola, it's because you really want one!

Italians offer a salutation whenever they enter shops, so follow suit and say *Buon giorno* (bwon *jawr*-know; Good day) as you enter. Doing so gives you the double advantage of making your presence known (you're given attention as soon as it's your turn) and making the shop owner well disposed toward you. If you change your mind, just say *Grazie* (*grah*-tzieh; Thank you) and exit.

Enjoying Italy's Natural Beauty

Italy has been a settled, cultivated, civilized land for thousands of years, so there isn't much wilderness left. However, you can still find natural beauty in abundance, as well as lovely places where human constructions fit harmoniously with the land.

You feel this beauty when you inhale the enigmatic calm of the **Venetian lagoon** from the abandoned island of Torcello or from the tip of the slim, sandy island of the Lido. (It's balanced by the infamous smell and humidity of Venice in summer — and that shiny stuff reflecting the basilica after the high water has abated is mud.) You instantly fall in love with the landscapes of **Tuscany** and **Umbria,** whose rolling green plains, cypress trees, olive groves, walled hill towns, and rich vine-yards look as if they were just lifted from a Renaissance painting. And who can resist the **Costiera Amalfitana (Amalfi Coast),** the gorgeous terraced coastline south of Naples rising at breathtaking height above the sea? The coastline is cut by deep gorges, where towns like Positano and Amalfi nest on the steep rocks. Just 4.8 km (3 miles) off the Amalfi Coast is the island of **Capri,** where Roman emperors like Tiberius once sought amusement. The star of Capri is the stunning **Grotta Azzurra (Blue Grotto).**

If your interest in nature is truly elemental, note that Italy boasts two major volcanoes, one apparently sleeping and the other very much alive. You can climb eerie **Vesuvio (Mt. Vesuvius),** towering over Naples, to admire the view and wonder what's happening in the depth of its cavities. You won't find a single tree on the upper slopes, and you'll be hot and thirsty, but it's an awesome experience. In Sicily you can find the imposing beauty of **Etna (Mt. Etna),** smoking under the snow on its summit (it's three times the height of Vesuvius). When you see this volcano, you'll know why the Greeks believed Hephaestus, the god of fire, lived under it.

Don't forget that all around this long peninsula are beautiful beaches and the perfect waters of the Mediterranean!

Getting a History Lesson — in Brief

If Mesopotamia is the cradle of civilization, Italy is the cradle of Western culture (well, there was Greece too, but that's another book). The Roman Empire borrowed heavily from both Mesopotamia and Greece as well as from every other culture that it absorbed. The princi-ples of Roman civilization and the Renaissance still play a great role in our modern ways of thinking, our values, and our institutions. Summarizing Italy's history in anything less than a book-length study is impossible, but you'll need at least a taste of it in order to understand what you're looking at as you explore the country.

Around 1000 B.C., Italy began developing into the vital cultural center it became in the following 3,000 years. The **Etruscans**, a people later con-quered by Rome, had already developed a sophisticated culture when Rome was still a collection of shepherd's huts. The **Roman Republic,** founded in 509 B.C., was headed by two consuls and a senate, all con-trolled by the upper or patrician (aristocratic) class. The plebeians (working class) later obtained their own council and were represented by tribunes. The Romans have been called the "Prussians of the ancient world" for their militarism, and they first showed their might in two decades of bloody war against Carthage and Hannibal over posses-sion of Sicily. After defeating Carthage, Rome spread its influence across the Mediterranean.

The end of the Roman Republic occurred largely through the antagonism of two great generals, **Pompey** and **Julius Caesar,** who became a tyrant after his defeat of Pompey. Following Caesar's murder on the Ides of March in 44 B.C., civil war ensued and was won by Caesar's grandnephew and adopted son, Octavian, who became the first emperor, **Caesar Augustus.** His regime turned Rome into a glowing marble city the likes of which the world had never seen, but he was followed by a string of mostly debauched and even insane rulers: **Tiberius, Caligula, Claudius** (an exception, even though his third wife, Nero's mother, was also his niece), and **Nero.**

In the early years of the first millennium, the growth of Christianity and other factors ate away at the foundations, yet at the same time, the empire reached its greatest extent — from the Caspian Sea in the east to Scotland in the west. However, a chaotic period of war, plague, barbarian advances, and inflation was the beginning of the bitter end. As **Emperor Constantine** converted to Christianity and founded Constantinople in A.D. 330, Rome's wealth shifted east, and then the **Goths** sacked Rome in A.D. 410. The Huns came next under **Attila,** and were followed by the **Vandals** of North Africa. In A.D. 476, the German chief Odoacer deposed the western Roman emperor, signing the effective end of the once invincible Roman Empire.

Charlemagne tried to revive the Western Empire in A.D. 800 when the pope crowned him emperor, but instead, what he accomplished was to found the forerunner of the **Holy Roman Empire.** This historical oddity profoundly affected Italy's history during the Middle Ages and Renaissance. The German emperor was elected by the German princes, but only the pope could crown him Holy Roman Emperor. For the next 1,000 years, Italian politics were defined by the struggle among the Holy Roman Emperor (who was German), the Papal States (the area of central Italy ruled by the worldly popes), Spain, and France. During the height of the **Renaissance,** city-states like Florence and Siena sought the help of these powerful large states in their local wars, thus inviting foreign intervention in Italy.

In the thirteenth century, the Renaissance began in Italy, which was then the crossroads of the Mediterranean, a banking and commercial culture, with the great seafaring empires of **Venice** and **Genoa.** The result was an explosion of magnificent art and the spread of *humanism,* a new philosophy promoting the dignity of the human individual and developing secularism. Only in the south and in **Sicily,** where the **Normans** (Viking descendants) founded a kingdom in the eleventh century, did medieval feudalism take root. Later, the Spanish rulers used feudalism for their own political aims and induced it to hang on — one of the causes of north-south cultural and economic disparities that still persist.

The **Risorgimento** (resurgence) movement, secret societies such as the Carbonari, and revolutionaries such as Giuseppe Mazzini and Giuseppe Garibaldi brought about Italian unification in the nineteenth century (completed 1870). A liberal state was formed around the House of Savoy, rulers of Piedmont and Sardinia. Between 1870 and World War I, Italy saw massive emigration to the United States and Argentina. Italy was tempted by promises to join the Allies in 1915 mainly in order to get Venice back from the Austrians. However, discontent and economic depression helped Mussolini rise to power in 1922 after his march on Rome. Mussolini's imperialist adventures abroad were matched by repression at home, and his alliance with the Nazis was disastrous. Italians turned against him in 1943 and continued in World War II on the Allied side while suffering under German occupation.

Italy rebuilt after the war and became a modern democratic state. Unemployment is a persistent problem, and many Italians — even those educated in such professions as law, academics, and architecture — work for free for years just to get a foot on the employment ladder. Corruption has also been a persistent problem, but in the 1990s, a series of scandals and dramatic Mafia trials led to a major house cleaning and announcement of a New Italy. Italy is famous for its numerous changes of government in the postwar period. The ramifications of the upcoming European unification are yet to be seen.

Chapter 2

Deciding When and Where to Go

● ●

In This Chapter

▶ Exploring Italy's main areas of interest

▶ Knowing the right time to visit

▶ Scanning a calendar of the best festivals and events

● ●

*Y*our trip to Italy doesn't have to have a single focus. In this book, we give you lots of options from which to choose, taking you through the various and varied regions, cities and towns, attractions and distractions, cuisines, and subcultures, as well as giving you the lowdown on the best times of the year to travel.

The year 2000 was declared a Papal Jubilee, bringing with it many special celebrations and floods of visitors, but now that it's over, your trip can be even more exciting (everything is still spruced up for the event, minus the millions of extra celebrants). You have some delightful win-win choices ahead of you — a cup of espresso on Venice's Piazza San Marco or a glass of Chianti in a *trattoria* in Florence, a visit to the Galleria degli Uffizi in Florence or the Cappella Sistina in Rome, a performance in the Greek-Roman theater in Taormina or a day on the isle of Capri. Wherever you go, you'll meet a friendly and fascinating culture in which you'll never starve and never find yourself bored.

Checking Out Italy's Points of Interest

To show you exactly what this guidebook offers and give you some hints about how to organize your trip, check out the following quick sketch of each area that we include between the covers of this book. (*Italy For Dummies* is a book of highlights, so you won't find all of Italy's regions.)

To view the makeup of Italy by region, check out the map on the inside front cover.

Romancing Rome: From the Colosseum to Vatican City

Roma (Rome) is the capital of modern Italy, as it was the capital of the vast Empire in ancient times. It's completely saturated with fantastic things to see, most of which are world famous: the **Colosseo (Colosseum), Foro Romano (Roman Forum)** and **Fori Imperiali (Imperial Forums), Basilica di San Pietro (St. Peter's Basilica)** and **Musei Vaticani (Vatican Museums), Pantheon** . . . the list goes on and on. There are even things to see underground, like the **Catacombs** (including the famous ones on the **Appian Way**).

At one time or another, you've probably used the expression "When in Rome, do as the Romans do." Well, there are many fun things you can do that Romans have been doing for centuries. For example, you can explore the **Castelli Romani** (hill towns around Rome), where it's pleasurably cool in summer. To enjoy a nice meal with some great local wine, visit the cool gardens of Tivoli's **Villa d'Este,** or immerse yourself in ancient times at **Ostia Antica**'s ruins or the remains of Tivoli's **Villa Adriana (Hadrian's Villa).**

The traffic in Rome is as eternal as the Eternal City itself, and as a major modern city, it has crowded buses and metros at rush hour, as well as thousands of screaming motorbikes and pedestrians. However, it also boasts some of the nicer aspects of modernity too, like varied and exciting nightlife, a huge selection of restaurants, plentiful comfortable hotels, and famous shops. Best of all, Rome's position makes it easy to use as a base for a visit either farther south to Naples and the Amalfi Coast (Sicily is a bit of a stretch) or farther north to Tuscany and Umbria (Venice is a bit of a stretch). See Chapters 11 to 13 for our coverage of Rome and its environs.

Exploring Florence and the best of Tuscany and Umbria

Toscana (Tuscany) is *the* destination for Americans attracted to the lush Italian countryside where most people would love to own a villa. **Firenze (Florence),** with its beautiful **Duomo (cathedral)** and over-abundance of art treasures in the **Galleria degli Uffizi (Uffizi Gallery)** and elsewhere, is the main city in Tuscany and has been drawing visitors for centuries. Tuscany also boasts the **Leaning Tower of Pisa,** where Galileo made his experiments with gravity; the smaller cities of **Siena** (where the Palio delle Contrade horse race occurs twice a year); **San Gimignano** and **Lucca,** which are like medieval or Renaissance jewels; and the region of **Chianti,** renowned for its food, wine, and beautiful hill towns. A little farther afield are the **Cinque Terre (Five Lands),** five ancient fishing/farming villages nestled along a stretch of coast that rivals the more famous **Costiera Amalfitana (Amalfi Coast)** in steepness and natural beauty. Neighboring Tuscany is the smaller region of **Umbria.** Its attractions include the monuments and chocolate of **Perugia,** a city famous for its medieval architecture and culinary traditions; the churches and monasteries of **Assisi,** with the famous frescoes by Giotto celebrating the life of St. Francis; and the medieval town of **Spoleto,** famous for its music-and-art Festival di Spoleto.

Although you may not find the climate of Tuscany and Umbria ideal (baking hot in summer and chilly and damp in winter), its main attractions are hardly a secret, so you have to vie for space with masses of people from all over the planet. However, most people prefer to give up almost anything else in Italy before they cut this region from their itinerary. See Chapters 14 to 17 for our coverage of Florence, Tuscany, and Umbria.

Viewing Venice and the best of the Veneto

Imagine riding along the Canal Grande in a gondola maneuvered by a skilled oarsman, passing beneath bridge after bridge, watching the medieval splendor of the palazzi and other buildings slowly sinking into the lagoon. No place promotes dreaming like **Venezia (Venice).** The **Palazzo Ducale (Doge's Palace), Basilica di San Marco (St. Mark's Basilica),** and **Piazza San Marco (St. Mark's Square)** are magical, and the **Gallerie dell'Accademia** offers countless art treasures. Many artists and writers have been utterly smitten by **La Serenissima (the Serene Republic).**

Although the smell of the canals, the summer humidity, and the crowds (which completely block the narrow streets on weekends and in high season) can be a little much, Venice is always captivating. If you're planning an especially romantic vacation, don't miss Venice.

The surrounding **Veneto** region is full of interesting sights too. **Verona** is a delightful romantic town where (supposedly) Romeo and Juliet lived out their tragic affair. Speaking of tragedy, you can also see an opera in the Roman amphitheater in Verona. While you're in the area, visit nearby **Padova (Padua),** featuring Giotto's most celebrated frescoes in the **Cappella degli Scrovegni** (however, the chapel closed in 2001 for renovations). See Chapters 18 and 19 for our coverage of Venice and the Veneto.

Visiting Naples, Pompeii, and the Amalfi Coast

Napoli (Naples) seems more Italian than the rest of Italy, if such a thing is possible. It's an intense city, perhaps too much so for some people. The bad reputation of Naples has improved markedly in recent years, and the city is full of often overlooked art and cultural treasures, particularly the **Museo Archeologico Nazionale (National Archaeological Museum).** Naples is also the jumping-off point for exploring some of Italy's most popular sites.

The **Costiera Amalfitana (Amalfi Coast)** is a scenic area with beautiful water and seaside resorts, such as Positano and Amalfi, nestled along plunging cliffs. Closer to Naples, **Ercolano (Herculaneum)** and **Pompei (Pompeii)**, Roman cities wiped out by Vesuvius in A.D. 79, are among the country's most important archaeological attractions. And, of course, there's **Vesuvio (Mt. Vesuvius)** itself, the eerie presence towering over Naples.

Off the coast of Naples — less than an hour away — is one of the most famous islands in Italy. **Capri,** a green hill that rises steeply from the sea, has been a trendy resort since the Roman Empire, when Tiberius and Caligula sought "amusement" there. See Chapters 20 to 22 for our coverage of Naples and the Amalfi Coast.

Seeing Sicily

The farther south you go, the more intense and lively Italy becomes. **Sicily** has a reputation as a passionate land, and its rugged beauty, bountiful waters, and rich soils have been fought over for millennia. Early settlers left behind the magnificent Greek temples in **Agrigento,** the **Valle dei Templi (Valley of the Temples),** and **Segesta.** The Normans (a name that comes from Norsemen) created a uniquely beautiful style of art in the capital of **Palermo** as well as all over the island. You can also admire the splendors of the Sicilian baroque and Liberty (art nouveau) styles in Palermo. Towering snow-capped **Etna (Mt. Etna)** dominates the island, and particularly the fashionable city of **Taormina,** which combines well-preserved ancient sites with beaches and a modern resort. Down the coast is **Siracusa (Syracuse),** with its dark and fascinating history — the early part of which is still visible in the excavations of the **Zona Archeologica (Archaeological Zone)** and on the island of **Ortigia.**

Sicily's reputation as headquarters of the Mafia and its bloody vendettas used to scare people away, but a government crackdown has spawned a Sicilian renaissance. Getting to Sicily may take extra time, but it's worth the trip. You won't find such an exciting and pleasing mix of sights, cultures, and flavors anywhere else in Italy. See Chapters 23 to 25 for our coverage of mysterious Sicily.

Knowing the Secret of the Seasons

When planning your trip to Italy, you certainly have to consider the weather at each time of year, and then determine the best time for you to schedule your vacation.

Considering Italy's climate

In general, Italy has a hot, dry climate, with well-defined seasons. Spring and fall are the most pleasant, with mild weather and moderate temperatures; summer is quite hot, especially in the south; and winter can get quite cold in the north.

Of course, because the peninsula is 700 miles long, the weather can vary greatly between north and south, from the rugged limestone Dolomites to Sicily's sirocco-swept fields. Because the Apennine mountains run down the middle of Italy, the weather also varies between the coast and inland areas.

You know your limits, so if you find waiting in line for two hours in the hot sun to get into the Musei Vaticani unendurable, don't come to Italy in July or August. Make sure that you check the average temperatures we list in Table 2-1.

Table 2-1:	Italy's Average High and Low Temperatures							
Region	*Winter* Average Low/Average High				*Summer* Average Low/Average High			
	°C	*°F*	*°C*	*°F*	*°C*	*°F*	*°C*	*°F*
Florence	2.5	36.5	11	52	16.4	61.5	29.7	85
Naples	4.9	41	13.2	56	17.6	64	28.5	83
Palermo	10.6	51	15.4	60	22	71	27.7	82
Rome	3	37	13	55	16.1	61	29.9	86
Venice	1.5	35	8.3	47	15.4	60	24.5	79

Remember that official temperatures are taken at the airports, so the temperatures in towns are higher. Places near the sea (such as Naples), even if farther south, are sometimes cooler than places farther north. For example, Florence, which sits in a valley, is notorious for the summer heat that reverberates off the stone palazzi. Nearby Siena sits atop a hill, so you won't find much shade there. The sea cools Venice somewhat, but the summers there are famous for the stink of the canals and the large crowds. And, after June, Sicily is truly sunstroke territory unless you're used to such conditions.

Italians beat the heat in one of two ways: One is going to the beach and soaking in the water, and the other is not going anywhere. Generally speaking, everything in Italy closes between lunchtime and about 4 p.m., when nobody does anything. Therefore, you may find it hard to shop, but you can still find a museum to prowl through. Restaurants, of course, are open at lunchtime. This custom is changing, slowly, as tourism-driven businesses adopt to visitors' schedules and expectations of longer hours and to their increased volume.

Humidity in Italy isn't nearly as bad as parts of the United States, such as the Mid-Atlantic and Midwest. However, remember that enduring the summer in your air-conditioned office and apartment in Chicago or New York is a lot different from spending a few weeks in a (mostly) unairconditioned country, living out of a suitcase in a rented room.

In our opinion, the best times to visit Italy are April to June and late September to October. The worst times to visit Italy are July and August.

Avoiding the crowds

Italy's off-season was winter, but there isn't much of an off-season anymore. The good thing about the off-season is that you get lower prices, you receive often better and more attentive service, and you don't have to compete so aggressively for a place in line. (Consider that the wait to get into Florence's Uffizi in summer can last as long as three hours — if you don't reserve your tickets ahead.) However, during the off-season, you may have less lodging choices in some areas because of seasonal closures.

Venice, for instance, hasn't really had a low season at all in the past few years. The reason: Global interest in Italy has intensified, fueled by the anticipation of the celebrations for 2000 and the Papal Jubilee. In 2001 and 2002, you may also run into all those people who thought they'd be smart and wait out the Jubilee and go afterward. As a result, predictions are that Italy will be crowded more than usual for some time to come.

Despite the doomsayers, we still think that Italy has a midwinter lull (February). However, around **Easter** there is usually a big influx — not only Catholic pilgrims but also large school groups from around Europe who often take trips (mainly to Florence and Rome) around this time. One strategy for avoiding crowds is to choose destinations away from Rome. Sicily, for example, seemed untouched by the Jubilee fever.

In general, August is one of the least attractive months to visit Italy. Many businesses take their vacation in this month, and the heat is at its peak. However, if August is the only time that you can travel, remember that the seashore will be crowded, but you may find cooler temperatures and less crowding in the mountains.

Labor Day (Festa del Lavoro) is celebrated in Italy and Europe on May 1. Be prepared for businesses to be closed all across the country. Also, **Ferragosto,** which takes place on August 15, is a good holiday to know about, though it's for Italians, not visitors. The Italians, like the French, go on holiday en masse, and many shops and businesses close.

Getting the Lowdown on Italy's Special Events

Festivals, whether celebrated across the country or in individual cities and towns, may play an important role in your decision about when to travel, making your consideration about Italy's climate an academic one. Do you long to attend Venice's Carnevale or Siena's Palio so badly that you're prepared to face the onslaught of revelers? Or, do you want to know when all the big events are held so you can schedule your trip around them? Here's a rundown of Italy's primary festivals and events (plus a few unusual ones).

January

- ✔ **Regata sull'Arno (Regatta on the Arno).** January 1; Florence. Celebrate the new year in Firenze with a boat race. ☎ **055-23320.**

- ✔ **Epifania (Feast of the Epiphany).** January 6; countrywide. This religious holiday is very important for children, because they receive their Christmas gifts on this day, not on December 25. On the days preceding Epiphany, many children's toy and gift markets are held. Full of carts and stands selling gifts and sweets, the one on Rome's Piazza Navona stays open till dawn on feast day.

February

- ✔ **Carnevale.** The week before Ash Wednesday, culminating on Fat Tuesday or *Martedi Grasso;* countrywide. You can best observe this well-established holiday (formerly a pagan rite of the coming of spring) in Venice, where there are spectacular costumes, masked balls, and many events (music, concerts, fireworks, and so on) organized by the city. Contact the Venetian Tourist Office, *A.P.T. Venezia,* Castello 4421, 30100 Venezia (☎ **041-529-8711;** Fax: 041-523-0399) for a calendar of events. Every town in Italy celebrates Carnevale to one degree or another — at least by making *frappe,* thin slices of crunchy fried dough with powdered sugar, and *castagnole,* deep-fried balls of dough, often filled with custard. In Viareggio in Tuscany, the celebration occurs for a whole month, complete with a parade of floats. ☎ **0584-47-503.** In Rome, you can find concerts and organized events, as well as lots of people parading around the city (particularly along Via Veneto) in costume. Check www.comune.roma.it for details.

March/April

- ✔ **Venerdì Santo (Good Friday).** Friday before Easter Sunday; countrywide. The Catholic rite of the procession of the stations of the cross (*Via Crucis*) is presented in many towns as a reenactment with costumes. In Rome, the procession takes place at night, led by the pope, between the Colosseum and Palatine Hill. The processions are spectacular, especially in Assisi and in Sicily.

- ✔ **Pasqua (Easter Benediction).** Sunday, usually at the end of March or beginning of April; countrywide. In Rome, the pope gives his traditional benediction in Piazza San Pietro.

- ✔ **Scoppio del Carro (Explosion of the Cart).** Easter Sunday. Florentines celebrate Easter with a bang. During morning mass, a cart laden with fireworks covered with flowers and led by white oxen is blown up by an effigy of a dove that slides down a wire from the Duomo. ☎ **055-290-832.**

✔ **Mostra delle Azalee (Exhibition of Azaleas).** A week in mid-April, weather dependent; Rome. During this exhibition, more than 3,000 azalea plants are exhibited on the Spanish Steps to celebrate the beginning of spring. Concerts are held in Trinità dei Monti at the head of the steps. ☎ 06-4889-9253.

✔ **Anniversario della Liberazione (Anniversary of the 1944 Liberation of Rome).** April 25; Rome. This event commemorates the massacre in the Fosse Ardeatine on Via Appia perpetrated by the German occupiers: Hundreds of randomly captured Italians (including women and children) were executed in reprisal for a partisan attack. The event is commemorated by a gathering on the site. ☎ 06-4889-9253.

✔ **Festa di San Marco (Festival of St. Mark).** April 25; Venice. This religious holiday is marked by a procession to the Basilica of San Marco in honor of the patron saint of Venezia. Also, the Venetian men mark the day by giving women a red rose.

May

✔ **Calendimaggio.** First weekend after May 1; Assisi. This pagan celebration of spring includes singing, dancing, medieval costumes, and competitions. ☎ 075-812-534.

✔ **Concorso Ippico Internazionale (International Horse Show).** Near the end of May; Rome. For this horse show, the best riders and mounts from Italy, Europe, and beyond compete in the Villa Borghese's beautiful Piazza di Siena for over 100,000,000L ($60,000) in prizes. At the gate, you can buy tickets, which start at 20,000L ($11) For details, contact the Federazione Italiana Sport Equestri at ☎ 06-3630-8547 or www.fise.it.

✔ **International Rose Show.** A week in mid-May — weather dependent; Rome. As many as 5,000 roses of more than 1,000 varieties, many very rare, serve as the background to this international competition among new varieties. The show takes place in the Roseto Comunale di Valle Murcia all'Aventino. ☎ 06-4889-9253.

✔ **Maggio Musicale Fiorentino (Florentine Musical May).** May into June; Florence. Italy's oldest and most prestigious music festival, this concert and dance series includes famous performers and world premiers. ☎ 055-211-158.

✔ **Regata delle Grandi Repubbliche Marinare (Regatta of the Great Maritime Republics).** Second or third weekend in May; each year by turns in Venice, Amalfi, Genoa, or Pisa. These four cities take turns hosting this competition between the great Medieval Maritime Republics. For details, call the tourist office of Pisa at ☎ 050-42-291, Venice at ☎ 041-529-8711, or Amalfi at ☎ 089-871-107.

✔ **Vogalonga.** Second half of May; Venice. Rowers train year-round for this "long row," a major competition. ☎ 041-529-8711.

June

✔ **Festival di Spoleto (Spoleto Festival).** All month; Spoleto. This program of concerts, opera, dance and theater (formerly called the Festival dei Due Mondi) is now in its fourth decade. For details, contact the Associazione Spoleto Festival at ☎ **0743-44-325;** Fax: 0743-40-696; Internet: www.spoletofestival.net.

✔ **Arena di Verona (Verona Amphitheater).** Beginning of June to September; Verona. This festival features opera performed in the city's well-preserved Roman arena. For details, call ☎ **045-800-5151** or check the Web at www.arena.it.

✔ **Gioco di Calcio.** Begins June 16; Florence. For the feast of San Giovanni, patron saint of Firenze, Florentines hold a tournament of rough-and-tumble Renaissance soccer among the city's four traditional neighborhoods, played on Piazza della Signoria and Piazza di Santa Croce (packed with dirt). Fireworks are set off on the Arno River at night. ☎ **055-290-832.**

✔ **Estate Romana (Roman Summer).** Mid- to late June to August; Rome. The Roman Summer is a program of concerts, theater, special exhibits, and other events. Some performances are held inside Roman ruins and are particularly dramatic. For details, call ☎ **06-4889-9253** or check on the Web at www.comune.roma.it.

✔ **Biennale di Venezia/Venice Biennial.** June to October; Venice. One of the premier art expositions in the world, the Biennial takes place in odd-numbered years (2001, 2003, and so on) in the Giardini, Venezia's public park.

July

✔ **Palio delle Contrade.** July 2; Siena. The first of the two palios, this is one of Italy's most famous spectacles: Horses and riders wearing the colors of their Sienese neighborhoods ride around Piazza del Campo in a wild, dangerous race. The event is preceded by much fanfare and pageantry lasting for days, including a giant costume party all over the city the night before. ☎ **0577-280-551.**

✔ **Festa di Santa Rosalia (Festival of St. Rosalia).** July 11–15; Palermo. This festival celebrates the anniversary of the rediscovery of the saint's remains in 1624. Niece of King Guglielmo II, Santa Rosalia abandoned the palace for a cave on Mt. Pellegrino, and her remains were discovered during a plague, which miraculously stopped. A religious procession with a decorated triumphal carriage carrying an orchestra parades through the city, and a candlelight procession ascends the mountain.

✔ **Umbria Jazz.** Mid- to late July; Perugia. This is one of Europe's top jazz events. Call the Associazone Umbria Jazz at ☎ **075-573-2432;** Fax: 075-572-2656; Internet: www.umbriajazz.com.

✔ **Festa del Redentore (Feast of the Redeemer).** Third Saturday and Sunday of July; Venice. The Feast of the Redeemer includes boating and fireworks in Venezia's lagoon to mark the lifting of the plague in 1571.

August

✔ **Palio delle Contrade.** August 16; Siena. This second *palio* is held between the finalists of the previous palio in July. ☎ **0577-280-551.**

September

✔ **Venice International Film Festival.** First 2 weeks of the month; Venice. Held at the Palazzo del Cinema on the Lido, this is one of the top film festivals in the world. Despite the proliferation of big-wigs, hangers-on, and wannabes, you can actually get tickets to screenings. Getting a room in town is another matter, however — book early. ☎ **041-521-8838;** Internet: www. labiennale.it.

✔ **Regata Storica (Historic Regatta).** First Sunday of September; Venice. This rowing event is held in the Grand Canal, and you need tickets to see it. ☎ **041-529-8711.**

✔ **Settembre Lucchese.** The whole month of September; Lucca. This opera festival celebrates the memory of Puccini in his hometown, and all his operas are performed in the original theater where they were first shown. ☎ **0583-419-689;** Fax: 0583-442-505; E-mail: luccadgt@tin.it.

October

✔ **Festa di San Francesco d'Assisi (Feast of St. Francis of Assisi).** October 5; countrywide. This celebration for the patron saint of Italy is observed in various towns and cities, notably Rome and Assisi, with processions, special masses, and other religious events.

November

✔ **Presentation of Mary in the Temple.** November 21; Venice. This religious holiday is celebrated with a procession that crosses the city, including a bridge made of boats strung across the Canal Grande at La Salute.

December

✔ **Crèche Exhibit.** The three weeks before Christmas; Rome. For this event, more than 50 nativity scenes are displayed in the Villa Giulia, and many others are on view in churches around Rome, particularly Santa Maria Maggiore, Santa Maria del Popolo, Santa Maria d'Aracoeli, and Chiesa del Gesù.

✔ **Christmas Blessing.** December 25; Rome. On Christmas Day, the pope blesses Rome and the world from Piazza di San Pietro at noon. The event is broadcast all over the world.

✔ **New Year's Eve.** December 31; countrywide. Italians love New Year's Eve, the occasion for a big celebration all over Italy and especially the capital. Partying reaches its climax at midnight when the capital city explodes — literally — with fireworks. There's no central, publicly funded display — everybody gets into the act, shooting fireworks from every window and roof. By tradition, fireworks are accompanied by the symbolic throwing away of something old to mark the end of the old year (some people get carried away — in the past, items like old TVs and refrigerators have been thrown from upper-story windows).

Trip-Planning Tips

It's tempting when visiting Italy to try to cram too much into your trip. That's because of the wealth of things to see and do. There are, however, ways to make your trip more comfortable and enjoyable. Here are a few tips to help you decide your itinerary for Italy:

✔ **Be realistic.** You know your stamina, aversion/tolerance for crowds and hot weather, level of interest in culture (just how many museums *can* you walk through before burnout?), and budget. Don't overextend yourself (or your kids if they're coming along) and possibly ruin your trip.

✔ **Limit the distance you cover.** If money is not an object, fly to Venice and stay a few days, fly off to Naples and see Capri and the towns on the Amalfi Coast, and then fly down to Sicily for the final leg of your trip. If you don't have unlimited funds and you try getting to all of these cities by car or train, you'll need unlimited time. Especially for your first trip to Italy, keep your exploring limited — perhaps only Tuscany/Umbria or Rome/Florence or Florence/Venice. Doing so will be more practical and probably a lot more fun, while also cutting travel hours, costs, and hassles.

✔ **Park and ride.** Throughout this book, we remind you that driving in the major cities and finding a place to park can be a major pain. Don't do it. Public transportation is highly developed in the big cities, and you don't need a car. If you happen to arrive in a big city by car, either return it to the rental agency (because you won't need it anymore) or garage it if you want to use it again when you leave. For example, you can pick up a car at Pisa's airport, drive through Tuscany's hill towns for several days, and then continue on to Florence, where you can immediately drop off the car.

✔ **Allow time for delays and serendipitous discoveries.** Italy has a reputation for being disorganized, which is partly undeserved. A positive way to look at it is that the Italians have a high tolerance for change — of bus schedules, museum hours, prices, arrangements, you name it. Don't set a schedule in which you *must* get from Florence to Venice in 5 hours, because traffic or a railroad delay may intervene. Likewise, hassles aren't the only things that make tight schedules a bore: You may see a villa, a vineyard, a *trattoria*, a ruin, or a hill town that you just have to investigate along the way. Give yourself permission to take a little extra time out to go with the flow. Traveling is about enjoyment, not accomplishment.

✔ **Remember that quality is more important than quantity.** A quality trip is far more memorable than a quantity trip. Don't try to cram in so many sights and sounds that everything blurs in your mind. One way to think about your itinerary is in terms of what you've seen versus what you've gotten to *know*. Perhaps you've heard someone say about a trip, "I was there once but don't remember much," or you've looked at a vacation picture from years ago and said, "I know I saw this, but I forget what it is." If so, you know the gap that exists between simply seeing something or clicking the shutter so you have a picture to stuff in an album and really *knowing* that you've been there and seen the sight, recalling the sight's history and what it meant to you to stand there and experience it.

✔ **Be honest with yourself.** Perhaps our most heretical advice is this: Don't force yourself to see things you're not really interested in just because everybody (including us) says that they're important. If you're blown away by the first five rooms of Florence's Uffizi, impressed by the next five, and really dazed by the next five, leave and get some yummy *gelato*. Or, if you want to see only the 10 most famous artworks and don't want a course in art history, see those works and then go do something else. It's your trip, your money, and your life.

Chapter 3

Five Great Itineraries

● ●

In This Chapter

▶ Touring Italy in one or two weeks: sample itineraries

▶ Visiting Italy with your kids: a suggested itinerary

▶ Reviewing two special-interest itineraries

● ●

*M*any guidebooks take a connect-the-dots approach to tourism: Here are a thousand hotels and restaurants, a ton of important and secondary sights to see, and a stack of maps, now go figure out your trip. This approach can leave many first-time or time-pressed travelers feeling overwhelmed and frustrated, especially with a country like Italy. Because Italy offers so much, you may find it difficult to put all the disjointed pieces together and come up with a doable, enjoyable itinerary.

Where you should go in Italy depends, above all, upon your interests. Sometimes being self-indulgent is also being smart: If you don't like the beach, don't go there; if you get bored in museums, spend more of your time strolling in parks and gardens and lounging in cafes. One thing you'll learn is that, as D. H. Lawrence observed, "Italy does not judge." Choose what you like from the endless banquet that Italy provides.

Okay, so you're just like everyone else and want to see all of Italy *anyway,* even though your time is limited. You still have to make choices, such as how many hours you can stand in a museum (if you're zonked out from the last one, you're just wasting your time in the next, regardless of how good the art is), how much walking and standing in line in hot sun you can take, and how many breaks you'd like for sitting and thinking about what you've seen, having a drink, and resting your feet. You decide.

In this chapter, we give you some sample itineraries that work and won't break your budget or your back. You may want to develop a tour to fit your special interests, and we give you a couple of suggestions for that too. If you're wild about Renaissance painting but bored by broken columns, you can see more of Rome's museums and skip the Foro Romano. If you're a gourmet, you can visit the country and sample local foods and spend more time in the cities exploring their specialties (and avoid that museum pallor).

Exploring Italy in One Week

Use the following itinerary to make the most of your week in Italy, but be aware that you'll see only the highlights of this rich country: Fly in to Rome as early in the day as possible, get to Termini train station from the airport and then take the three-hour **ATAC bus tour** to get a general city orientation (see Chapter 12 for details). The bus makes slightly extended stops at **San Pietro (St. Peter's)** and the **Colosseum.** Following the tour, enjoy a leisurely dinner in the funky medieval neighborhood of Trastevere and call it a day; you'll be jet-lagged and need to get to bed early. On each of Days Two and Three, see one major and two minor sights (check out Chapter 12 for detailed information on Rome's sights). Major sights include the **Musei Vaticani/Cappella Sistina (Vatican Museums/Sistine Chapel), Foro Romano/Fori Imperiali/Palatino (Roman Forum/Imperial Forums/Palatine Hill),** and **Galleria Borghese (Borghese Gallery).** Minor attractions (in terms of time commitment, not importance) include the **Scalinata di Spagna (Spanish Steps)** and **Piazza di Spagna (Spanish Square), Fontana di Trevi (Trevi Fountain), Pantheon,** and **Piazza Navona.** You can work in other piazze (squares) at night using our restaurant choices in Chapter 11.

On Day Four, take an early train to **Florence** (which takes about two hours, so leaving by 8 or 9 a.m. would be good), and then head for the **Duomo (Cathedral), Giotto's Campanile (Bell Tower),** the **Battistero (Baptistry),** and the **Museo dell'Opera del Duomo (Duomo Museum).** On Day Five, get up early and run to the **Galleria degli Uffizi (Uffizi Gallery)** — of course, you've reserved tickets in advance so you won't have to stand in line for hours (see Chapter 14 for details). In the afternoon, go to the **Galleria dell'Accademia (Accademia Gallery)** — make sure that you reserve tickets here as well — to see Michelangelo's *David,* and then stop by the leather market and test your bargaining skills. Take a predinner stroll on the **Ponte Vecchio (Vecchio Bridge)** and don't forget to see the **Palazzo Vecchio** (from the outside only) and **Piazza della Signoria** on the way back (see Chapter 14 for information on Florence sights, hotels, and restaurants).

On Day Six, take an early train to Venice (2½ hours) and catch vaporetto no. 1 (see Chapter 18 for details on public transportation in Venice) for a slow cruise down the **Canal Grande (Grand Canal),** noting the *palazzi* (palaces) lining the canal and the **Ponte di Rialto (Rialto Bridge)** as you pass under it. Get off to explore **Piazza San Marco (St. Mark's Square)** and the **Basilica di San Marco (St. Mark's Basilica).** In the afternoon, go to the **Gallerie dell'Accademia (Accademia Galleries)** for a tour of several hundred years of Venetian art. On the morning of Day Seven, visit **Santa Maria Gloriosa dei Frari** and the nearby **Scuola di San Rocco.** After lunch, see the **Palazzo Ducale (Doge's Palace)** and the **Bridge of Sighs.** (For more details, see Chapter 18.) You can then either head back to Rome by train that night (about five hours) and fly out the next day or spend your last night in Venice and fly home from there the next morning. If you don't have that extra day, just skip Day Seven.

Seeing Italy in Two Weeks

With two weeks to explore Italy, you'll be able to breathe a little and have the luxury of free time (when you can meet people and have unforgettable experiences). For the whirlwind two-week tour, you can tack another day each onto Rome, Florence, and Venice (see "Exploring Italy in One Week," earlier in this chapter). Doing so allows you to see more of the sites that we list throughout the book, sample more of the great food, and walk around more to get a feel of the cities.

Spend Days One to Four in Rome (see "Exploring Italy in One Week" in this chapter). In Rome, you can also take a side trip to see the **Villa Adriana (Hadrian's Villa)** and **Villa d'Este** or go to **Ostia Antica** to see the ruins of Rome's ancient seaport (see Chapter 13). Early on Day Five, take a train from Rome to Naples (about 2½ hours). Transfer to the train to **Pompeii** (45 minutes away), which you can see in the late morning and early afternoon. Returning to Naples, spend the rest of the afternoon strolling the waterfront and historic neighborhood nearby, seeing the **Castel dell'Ovo (Castle of the Egg), Riviera di Chiaia, Castel Nuovo (New Castle),** and **Palazzo Reale (Royal Palace)** before the ferry's departure for Sicily. (For more details, see Chapters 20 and 21.) The night ferry to Sicily will arrive the next morning in Palermo. Spend the morning of Day Six seeing Palermo's **Palazzo Reale (Royal Palace), Cappella Palatina (Palatine Chapel),** and the **Duomo** (outside only). After lunch, take the bus to the **Duomo di Monreale** and the **Cloister,** where you can see some of the world's most incredible mosaics. Return to Palermo for a family-style Sicilian dinner and crash early.

On the morning of Day Seven, take a train to **Agrigento** and the **Valle dei Templi (Valley of the Temples),** some of the finest Greek ruins anywhere. If you have a rental car, you can drive and make a detour to see the Doric temple in **Segesta** as well. On Day Eight, fly directly from Palermo to Florence on an early flight. Alternatively, you can catch a ferry back to Naples (four hours with the morning fast ferry) and the train to Florence (about five hours). If you choose this option, you may want to break up the trip with a visit to Naples or Rome, spending the afternoon and evening there and catching an early train for Florence. If you choose this option, you may want to delay your departure for Venice from Florence by half a day.

Spend Days Eight and Nine visiting Florence (see Chapter 14). On Day Ten, explore one of the charming towns of Tuscany — **Siena** is an excellent choice (see Chapter 16 for tour companies). On Day Eleven, take an early train to Venice (or an early afternoon train if you arrived in Florence later on Day Eight) and spend the next three days there (see Chapter 18). On Day Thirteen, journey beyond the city to visit **Murano, Torcello,** and the **Lido.** On Day Fourteen, mourn the end of your vacation and get ready to take an afternoon flight home.

Enjoying Italy with Kids

Italy offers many attractions and sights that kids will enjoy. One of the big issues that surfaces while traveling with children through Italy is knowing how much museum time you can or want to have. In general, we think that Rome and Venice are better destinations than Florence for families with children. Why? Rome is a bustling modern city that offers your kids all the stuff they like to do at home, and both Rome and Venice have ample outdoor space to let kids get rid of a little steam. For example, your kids can run off some energy at the **Foro Romano, Fori Imperiali,** and **Palatino;** the **Villa Borghese; Piazza di Spagna;** and the **Scalinata di Spagna** in Rome, as well as the **Piazza San Marco** and the **lagoon** in Venice. In addition, the **Rolling Venice** program is designed especially for teenagers (see Chapter 18 for more details).

One suggestion is to take the itinerary that we mention in "Seeing Italy in Two Weeks," earlier in the chapter, but cut out the trip to Sicily. Instead, while based in Naples, show your kids the **Costiera Amalfitana (Amalfi Coast),** where you can spend some time playing on the beach and enjoying the warm Mediterranean. Alternatively, you can use some of your time in Tuscany to visit the **Cinque Terre (Five Towns),** another place to take a break by the sea. (If you rent a car from Rome, you can drive through **Siena** on the way.)

Taking the Ancient History Tour

If ancient history and culture are your thing, focus on southern Italy, where the main intersection of Etruscan, Greek, Carthaginian, Roman, Norman, and Arab influences took place.

To begin this week-long itinerary of ancient history sights, fly into Rome as covered previously, but during your three-day stay, make sure you see the **Museo Nazionale Romano (Roman National Museum)** in the Palazzo Massimo, the **Palazzo Altemps** for Greek and Roman sculpture, and the **Museo Etrusco di Villa Giulia (Etruscan Museum),** skipping the Galleria Borghese (Borghese Gallery) and San Pietro (St. Peter's Basilica). You may also want to take the side trip to **Ostia Antica,** Rome's ancient seaport. If you absolutely need to see Florence, you can go for two days to get a glimpse of the Tuscan Renaissance, but you'll lose two days' worth of antiquity. Definitely skip Venice.

Assuming you've skipped Florence, take the train south to **Naples,** and then catch another train to **Pompeii.** Make sure that you add a day to see **Herculaneum** as well as the sights in Naples (or, like Tiberius, you can holiday on **Capri**). You can then take the night ferry to **Sicily.** Your first two days in Sicily are the same as in the two-week itinerary that we mention earlier in the chapter, but after **Agrigento** continue to **Syracuse,** the Greek colony that became as powerful as the city-states of the motherland. From there, head to **Taormina** and its beautifully preserved Greek/Roman theater, which hangs over an azure sea in the shadow of **Etna** (into which the philosopher Empedocles is said to have thrown himself). After that it's back to Palermo to catch the ferry to Naples, where you can catch your flight to Rome (see Chapter 23) or home.

Taking the Art Buff's Tour of Italy

If you're an art buff and want an itinerary that highlights the master-pieces of Italy, follow the "Doing Italy in One Week" itinerary (earlier in this chapter), except instead of spending half a day in the Foro Romano, go to the **Palazzo Altemps** or the **Palazzo Barberini** in Rome. In Florence, you can shorten your tour of the Duomo and spend an hour or two at the **Palazzo Pitti.** When you get to Venice, curtail your visit to the Palazzo Ducale (skip the New Prisons and the nonart parts) to make time to go to the **Collezione Peggy Guggenheim (Peggy Guggenheim Collection).**

If you have two weeks, use your extra day in Rome to see the **Caravaggios** in some of the churches, such as **San Luigi dei Francesi.** Plus, you can see both the **Palazzo Altemps** and the **Palazzo Barberini.** Spend your extra time in Florence seeing the paintings by Fra Angelico in the **Museo San Marco (St. Mark's Museum)** and the Masaccio in the church of **Santa Maria del Carmine.** On the way to Venice, stop in **Padua** to see Giotto's masterpiece, the **Cappella degli Scrovegni (Scrovegni Chapel)** (note, though, that it'll be closed for restoration starting in 2001). In Venice, use your extra day to visit the city's churches, like the **Madonna del'Orto** and **La Salute,** filled with masterpieces by Tintoretto, Tiziano, and other Venetian masters. When you head to Sicily, you may give up San Giovanni degli Eremiti in order to make room for a visit to the **Palazzo Abbatellis,** which contains, among other things, the famous *Madonna* by Antonello da Messina.

Chapter 4

Planning Your Budget

● ●

In This Chapter

▶ Devising a realistic budget

▶ Determining traveling, lodging, and dining expenses

▶ Remembering the extras — shopping and entertainment

▶ Saving money

● ●

*B*udgeting your trip isn't always easy. In this chapter, we give you some pointers on being realistic and keeping track of all the costs that you'll have to bear in mind.

Adding Up the Elements

When it comes to planning a trip, you usually deal with two different numbers: what you'd *like* to spend and what you *can* spend. Your budget will have a lot of variables. By deciding what's most important to you, you can trim here and there on the incidentals and splurge on the things that really matter. Airfare, of course, is one of the biggest components, so if your budget is limited, follow the money-saving tips we give you at the end of this chapter and in Chapter 6. If you think ahead and examine the range of choices that we offer in dining, lodging, and so on, you can work out a budget that's right for you. Use the worksheets at the end of this book to help you get an idea of what your trip will cost.

Getting to and around Italy

Chances are that your airfare to Italy is one of the largest items in your budget, but the actual cost depends on the time that you travel. In high season, you're lucky to find a round-trip ticket for less than $800, but at other times, you may find tickets for as low as $350. Airfare is the least flexible of your budget's elements, unless your traveling time is very flexible. Make sure that you check out our money-saving tips before you buy an airline ticket (see Chapter 6).

Transportation within Italy offers many more choices. To explore cities in the United States and many other countries, you either absolutely *shouldn't* rent a car (in New York City, for example) or absolutely *have* to rent one (in the wilds of the U.S. West). In Italy, renting a car is more ambiguous. Because the country's train and bus systems are highly developed and because gas is so expensive, about $4.50 per gallon, you don't save much by driving. (There are other issues that may keep you from driving abroad as well, such as high speeds and hair-raising curves.)

Without a car, you don't have the hassle of trying to find parking and paying for it. And, if you arrive in Venice, Florence, or Rome with a car, you have to keep it garaged during your entire stay: One city has no roads, the second is small and bans cars from the historic center, and the third has too many roads and drivers for you to want to deal with *and* it bans nonresidents from the historic center. Taking public transportation can definitely save you money and trouble. Think how much more you'll enjoy looking out the window at the countryside instead of the cars speeding around you.

The only time you may want to have a car in Italy is when you have the time to see more than just the highlights (see Chapter 7 for the details on renting). For example, say you're a return visitor to Italy and want to spend your 10-day vacation exploring the nooks and crannies of Tuscany/Umbria or Sicily. In this case, a car gives you further flexibility and scope. Otherwise, renting a car is more of a drawback than an advantage

Finding lodging

Most likely, finding a place to stay in Italy isn't the same as finding a hotel or motel where you live. For one thing, your lodging in Italy may be in a building that went up when your hometown was still a big empty spot on the map. And originally, the building may have been a princely palazzo, a grand townhouse, or a spartan monastery. We list many renovated hotels in this book, but space is at a premium in Italy. For a detailed discussion of what you can expect in Italy's hotel rooms, see Chapter 8.

Here's something that may surprise you: Hotel bathrooms in Italy are often tiny. The idea of a private bathroom in every guest room is a relatively new concept, too. In preparation for Papal Jubilee 2000, many older hotels renovated to conform with the new standard of private bathrooms, but sometimes the result — bathrooms crammed into already small guest rooms — may not thrill you. And be aware that rooms still exist with a shared bath down the hall and just a sink (or nothing) in the rooms. If you absolutely want a nice bathroom, be willing to fork over extra lire for a more expensive hotel. On the other hand, you can save a lot of money if you don't mind going down the hall for a shower.

Generally speaking, Italy is an expensive country, but there are regional variations in hotel rates: Florence and Venice are pricier than Rome, but Naples, and even more so Sicily, are cheaper. Figure that 180,000L ($95) buys you a decent double room with private bath anywhere (though a much better room in the south than in the north), but 300,000L ($160) buys you a nice room anywhere. From 400,000L ($215) and up, you're buying a luxury room. Of course, the amount that these estimates represent in dollars (or pounds) always changes.

Consider that you can save money if you renounce the breakfast that your hotel serves, unless it's included with your room rate. Breakfast is worth paying for only at the more expensive hotels ($$$ and above), where you find a buffet with a variety of foods, usually including eggs, sausages, cheese, cold cuts, yogurt, fruit, and cereals. This kind of breakfast may run about 30,000L ($16), so you have to decide if what you get is worth the money.

In all of our hotel reviews in this guide, we supply the *rack rates* (the off-the-shelf rate that hotels quote you, including a range from low to high season) and use a specific number of dollar signs to indicate the prices of hotels. The dollar signs correspond to the following amounts:

$ Up to 150,000L ($80)

$$ 150,000–250,000L ($80–$135)

$$$ 250,000–350,000L ($135–$190)

$$$$ 350,000–450,000L ($190–$240)

$$$$$ More than 450,000L ($240 and up)

Take these amounts with a grain of salt, however, because of exchange rates: A hotel that costs $$$$ at press time may be $$$ when you get to Italy if the dollar is worth more, or $$$$$, if the dollar is worth less. In addition, what was $$$ at press time may be $$$$ when you get to Italy because the hotel may have completed a substantial renovation. Tables 4-1 and 4-2 give you a sampling of costs that you may encounter on your trip.

Table 4-1	What Things Cost in Rome
A metro or city bus ride	1,500L (80¢)
Can of soda	1,500L/2,000L (80¢/$1.10)
Pay phone call	200L (10¢)
Movie ticket	12,000L ($6.50)
Caffè lungo (American-style espresso)	1,200–1,500L (65¢–80¢)
Cappuccino (or something similar)	2,100L ($1.14)
Ticket to the Galleria Borghese	12,000L ($6.50)
Gallon of gasoline	2,100L *per liter* ($1.14)
Average hotel room	200,000L ($110)
Liter of house wine in a restaurant	8,000L ($4.30)
Individual pizza in a pizzeria	10,000–16,000L ($5.40–$8.60)
First-class letter or postcard to U.S.	1,300L (70¢)

Table 4-2	What Things Cost in Greve in Chianti
A subway or city bus ride	1,200L (65¢)
Can of soda	1,200L/1,800L (65¢–$1)
Pay phone call	200L (10¢)
Caffè lungo (American-style espresso)	1,000L (55¢)
Cappuccino (or something similar)	1,600L (85¢)
Gallon of gasoline	2,100L *per liter* ($1.14)
Average hotel room	130,000L ($70)
Liter of house wine in a restaurant	7,000L ($3.80)
Individual pizza in a pizzeria	8,000–14,000L ($4.30–$7.60)
First-class letter or postcard to U.S.	1,300L (70¢)

Eating out

Similar to most places in the world, you can spend a lot or a little in restaurants in Italy. However, there are several levels of restaurant, including *pizzerie, trattorie,* and *rosticcerie,* which are all "below" *ristorante* in terms of formality. Often, *pizzerie, trattorie,* and *rosticcerie* are not only lower-priced options where you can save a little on lunch and dinner but also the best places to eat for quality food.

Although things are changing, *pranzo* (lunch) used to be the big meal in Italy, where lunch hour is more like 1½ to 2 hours. Lunch prices may also be cheaper, so in most cities two people can eat a nice lunch with a half-liter of wine for 46,000L to 74,000L ($25 to $40) if they don't eat in a touristy *piazza* or a glitzy restaurant. Dinner in the same kind of place will be 80,000L ($45) and up for two.

Most restaurants impose a basic table-and-bread charge, called *pane e coperto,* of about 3,000L to 8,000L ($2 to $5), and you'll probably have to drink mineral water (fizzy or not, it's much cheaper than in the United States — but you'll probably like it better than tap water). On the other hand, service is usually included unless otherwise noted (check the menu when you sit down), and we recommend you leave a few thousand lire as an appreciation.

If your budget is limited, take advantage of Italy's great markets, which sell fresh vegetables, meats, cold cuts, cheeses, wine, mineral water, and so on. You can save a lot by making a few meals of your own this way, especially lunch. (Bring your pocket knife!) We like to take a splurge-and-save approach to dining in order to even out our costs. If there's an expensive place we really want to try, we make up for the extra lire outlay by eating a lunch or dinner of fresh bread, prosciutto, sausage, raw or cooked vegetables (from a *rosticceria*), and local wine or mineral water. Our idea doesn't have a patent, so you can do the same if it suits you. Having a picnic lunch is also a great way to visit some of the outdoor sights.

Discovering What Italy Has to Offer

Museums and other sights cost anywhere from 4,000L to 18,000L ($2 to $10) for admission. Most churches are free (though avoid visiting during services unless you're devout). Consider that some of these sights are exhausting, so splitting up your visit makes sense. Sightseeing isn't an area where you can save a lot of money, and you'll probably be sorry if you try.

In the specific destination chapters, we note whenever you can find special combo discount tickets and special discount cards. (In Venice, for instance, youth under 30 can receive a discount for shopping, accommodation, and sightseeing with the Rolling Venice pass.)

Beware that many special discounts are available to non-nationals only, based on reciprocity between countries. Therefore, many discounts — senior and children discounts especially — aren't available to Americans but are available to Brits and other residents of EU countries.

Because of the long, long lines associated with Italy's top museums, you can now make reservations at several museums, thus bypassing waits of up to three hours. The list of museums for which you can make reservations includes Rome's Galleria Borghese (see Chapter 12) and Florence's Galleria degli Uffizi and Galleria dell'Accademia (see Chapter 14).

In many of Italy's churches, you find *light boxes.* When you insert a coin or two, a light pops on to illuminate a painting, fresco, or sculpture for a limited amount of time. Therefore, carrying a pocketful of coins is always a good idea.

Shopping to your heart's content

Italy is famous for its artwork, design, and crafts — art glass, pottery, leather, gold, lace, and so on. Italian fashion isn't too bad either — Versace, Dolce e Gabbana, and Armani are some of the world-famous Italian firms. Shopping is the most personal and flexible part of your budget's bottom line. You can spend hundreds on a full-length leather coat for yourself or for a friend or loved one, or you can skip shopping completely. Throughout this book, we give you our recommendations for the best shops and items that each city offers.

On the other hand, if you have an irresistible craving for something — say a Murano chandelier, a pair of leather boots, a Gucci handbag, or even a Ferrari — you can use your trip as a chance to pick it up. You can save some money (but not tons of it) buying Italian things in Italy. You can also find a much bigger selection than in your hometown.

Italy's *value-added tax* (known as the *IVA*) is a steep 19 percent, but you can get a refund (see "Keeping a Lid on Hidden Expenses," later in this chapter) for purchases costing more than 300,000L ($160).

Experiencing the Italian nightlife

Visiting the opera, going out for a drink, listening to music in a jazz club, and dancing the night away are all extras that make your time in Italy more memorable and pleasant. You can spend big bucks in this area of entertainment, or you can cut your costs down to things that are free or nearly so, such as people watching on a beautiful floodlit *piazza* or ordering a coffee or drink in a classic caffè and soaking in the atmosphere.

If you want to attend a performance of an ancient Greek tragedy or a Verdi opera, we give you the best options for getting tickets at each venue and tips for saving money at the same time. Nightclubs in Italy are about as expensive as anywhere else, but you may be able to avoid a cover charge by sitting or standing at the bar rather than taking a table or by arriving before a certain hour. If you arrive during a public holiday or festival, you may find abundant free entertainment, much of it in the streets.

Be aware that any time you sit down in a caffè or bar in Italy, things cost more. Coffee at an outside table in Piazza del Popolo or Piazza San Marco may cost the same as lunch anywhere else. Most Italians stand at the bar while they have a coffee or a beer.

Keeping a Lid on Hidden Expenses

Italy's *value-added tax* (known as the *IVA*) of 19 percent is included in all the prices that you're quoted. The good news is that, as a visitor, if you spend over 300,000L ($160) in a single store, you can receive a tax rebate. Stores displaying a *Tax Free* insignia can give you an invoice that you can cash at the airport's customs office as you leave Italy. Otherwise, you have to take the invoice from the store, have it stamped at the airport by customs, and then mail it back to the store, which will then send you a check or credit your charge account.

Renting a car might be more expensive than you're used to back home. Because of car theft, some agencies may demand that you take theft insurance, regardless of what your credit card may cover. However, although you may find touring Tuscany or Sicily by car appealing, we recommend traveling by train or bus, because you avoid worries and save money, too.

Tipping, on the other hand, isn't a big extra cost in Italy the way it is in some places. Because waiters are better paid and employers can't wriggle out of paying them a wage by assuming they'll get tips, gratuities aren't a big part of their income. People usually leave a few thousand lire as a token of appreciation and as a polite gesture. However, if you eat in the restaurants of big glitzy hotels in major cities, check the menu: Such places may expect you to fork over the usual American 15 to 20 percent. You do, however, have to tip bellhops who carry your bags, while cab drivers receive a small tip like waiters.

Getting the most bang for your buck

Remember *Frommer's Europe on $5 a Day*? Do you also remember how long ago that book came out? Well, these days the title is *Frommer's Europe from $70 a Day*.

In Europe generally, and in Italy particularly, count on a rock-bottom cost (without transportation) of $50 to $75 per day per person. If you shoot for $50, you'll probably hit $75. Of course, prices have skyrocketed (especially as hotels and restaurants spruced themselves up for the Papal Jubilee), but you can save some money here and there if you follow the tips we give you in this section and throughout the book.

Note, though, that we aren't of the save-a-buck-at-any-cost school. Sometimes paying more makes sense. For example, if you're facing sightseeing overload and are dead tired, you may not want to take an hour-long bus ride to the other side of town to your hotel, so why not take a cab instead? And why not grab a bite to eat in the slightly expensive cafe near where you are rather than deal with crossing town to an extra-cheap restaurant? Only you know what's most important to you and where to splurge or save.

There are many ways to trim your budget down to a size that you can stand. You can also save for your trip. One place to start is your plane ticket. If you buy a relatively expensive ticket, you already start your trip in the hole, and you'll have to sacrifice in other areas to make up for the extra expense. We like the idea of saving a big chunk of change by reserving your ticket early and traveling off peak, and then spreading the saved money around to make the rest of your trip more enjoyable.

Another thing that you can do to save money is to start thinking like an Italian. Italians have relatively less disposable income than Americans. The closer you mirror the way Italians live and travel, the cheaper your trip will be — and the closer you get to the Italians themselves. Staying in a huge hotel designed for tourists with all the fixings will cost you a lot. The luxury of renting a big car will cost you too. Likewise, eating in five-star restaurants instead of exploring local eateries costs you. You can live for a week without a private bath, you can make big healthy sandwiches from stuff that you bought in a market, and you can pass on the postcards, trinkets, and things that you pick up just to say that you've been to Italy. As the management gurus say, don't think of cost cutting as a limitation but as an opportunity.

Cutting costs, not sights

However, there are areas where you shouldn't make cuts, because they'll kill your trip. Not seeing Florence's Uffizi, Venice's Accademia, Rome's Vatican Museums and Sistine Chapel, or some other major sights, just because they cost more, would be a tragedy. We'd rather skip lunch and take the opportunity to go to one of these must-sees twice. Who knows when you'll be back that way again?

Throughout this book, you can find Bargain Alert icons that highlight money-saving tips and/or great deals. Here are some additional cost-cutting strategies:

- ✔ **Visit during the off-season.** If you can travel at nonpeak times (usually winter, with the exception of the Christmas/New Year's holidays), you can find airfares and hotel prices as much as 20 percent less than during peak months.

- ✔ **Travel during off days of the week.** Airfares vary depending not only on the time of the year but also on the day of the week. In Italy, weekend rates are often cheaper than weekday rates. When you inquire about airfares, ask if you can obtain a cheaper rate by flying on a different day.

- ✔ **Try a package tour.** For popular destinations like Italy, you can book airfare, hotel, ground transportation, and even some sight-seeing by making just one call to a travel agent or packager, and you may pay a lot less than if you tried to put the trip together yourself. But always work out the prices that you'd pay if you arranged the pieces of your trip yourself just to double check. See the section on package tours in Chapter 6 for specific suggestions.

- ✔ **Pack light.** Packing light enables you to carry your own bags and not worry about finding a porter (don't forget to tip yourself). Likewise, you can take a bus or train rather than a cab from the airport if you pack light, saving you a few more lire.

- ✔ **Always ask for discount rates.** Membership in AAA, frequent-flyer plans, trade unions, AARP, or other groups may qualify you for discounts on plane tickets, hotel rooms, or even meals. Ask about everything — you may be pleasantly surprised with the answer you receive.

- ✔ **Get out of town.** In many places, you may find that staying in hotels just outside the city or across the river aren't quite as convenient but are a great bargain. You may only need to do a little more walking or take a short commute. See the chapter on each destination for hotel information.

- ✔ **Ask if your kids can stay in your room with you.** Many hotels won't charge you the additional person rate if your extra person is pint-sized and related to you. You can save much more if you don't take two rooms, even if you have to pay some extra lire for a roll-away bed.

- ✔ **Try expensive restaurants at lunch instead of dinner.** At most top restaurants, prices at lunch are usually considerably less than those at dinner, and the menu often boasts many of the same specialties.

- ✔ **Have a picnic.** You can put together some delicious and inexpensive meals at an Italian grocery store, and then enjoy your feast in a garden or park.

✓ **Don't rent a car.** Unless you're planning to drive around Tuscany or Sicily, travel by public transportation. Cars are more trouble than they're worth.

✓ **Study up on the public transportation system.** In Italy, moving from one destination to another by train is cheap and easy. (We include a map of Italy's train system on the inside front cover of this book to get you started.) Using the local bus system in large cities like Venice and Rome is a little more complicated, but it's also a great way to visit the city.

✓ **Walk.** A good pair of walking shoes can save you money in taxis and other local transportation. Remember that the historic center of most cities and towns is pretty small, so you can actually walk almost anywhere you need to go. You'll save money, get your exercise for the day, and get to know the city more intimately.

✓ **Skip the souvenirs.** Your photographs and memories make the best mementos of your trip. Don't waste money on unnecessary trinkets.

Chapter 5

Planning Ahead for Special Travel Needs

Do you want to bring your kids with you on your trip to Italy? Are you a single woman traveling alone and concerned about safety? Are you worried about wheelchair accessibility? Are you interested in special programs and activities for seniors? Do you have concerns about attitudes toward gays and lesbians? In this chapter, we discuss the challenges — and opportunities — that travelers with special needs may encounter in Italy.

Traveling with Kids

Italy has a very family-oriented culture, so you shouldn't have any qualms about traveling with your kids. In fact, Italians love children, and you'll find that people will often talk and play with your child on public transportation and in public areas. However, the Italian society is also a more traditional one. Italians, in general, believe that children should be well behaved (act politely like little adults in museums and other public places), and they aren't afraid that disciplining their children will give the kids a complex. Tantrums, whining, and other such behavioral outbursts are frowned upon.

Opting for child care

Child care in Italy is also handled in a traditional way. Members of the extended family — grandparents and other relatives — often help care for children during the day if both parents work. And it's more common in Italy than in the United States for one parent to stay home taking care of the kids (usually the mother). As a result, Italy doesn't have a major infrastructure of day care and child care. In fact, finding a hotel with day-care service is rare. However, many hotels can arrange for a sitter from a baby-sitting service, and in a few small family-run places, a daughter or son may pitch in and watch your kids. You can find standard day-care service only at the more expensive, larger hotels in the big urban areas. Thus, if you have a very small child, you may find that you wind up paying more for lodging simply because you need the amenities of the higher-priced hotels.

Keeping kids in the know

Kids can have a great time in Italy, and if they know some of the special things in store for them they can show as much excitement about the trip as you. Before you leave, sit down with your children and plan a family strategy. Go over the list of sights and activities in the cities and areas that you plan to visit, particularly noting those with the Kid Friendly icon. Let your kids list a few of the things they'd like to see and do, in order of preference, and make a similar list of your own. You may also want to let your older children research Italy on the Internet (see the Appendix for a list of Web sites). Together, you can then plot out a day-by-day schedule that strikes a balance between your desires and those of your offspring. Following are several resources to consider when traveling with kids:

- ✔ **Check out some books that offer tips to help you travel with kids.** Most of these books concentrate on travel in the United States, but *Family Travel* (Lanier Publishing International) and *How to Take Great Trips with Your Kids* (Harvard Common Press) are full of good general advice that can apply to travel anywhere. Another reliable book with a worldwide focus is *Adventuring with Children* (Foghorn Press).

- ✔ **Consider a special magazine subscription.** *Family Travel Times,* published six times a year by TWYCH (Travel with Your Children; ☎ 888-822-4388 or 212-477-5524), includes a weekly call-in service for subscribers. Subscriptions are $40 per year for quarterly editions. Call to receive a free publication list and a sample issue.

- ✔ **Try out a university-sponsored program abroad.** The University of New Hampshire runs **Familyhostel** (☎ 800-733-9753; www. learn.unh.edu), an intergenerational alternative to standard guided tours. In Italy, the affiliated university is the Art Institute of Florence, Lorenzo de Medici. There are two- or three-week programs during which you attend lectures and seminars, take lots of field trips, and sightsee with a team of experts and academics. The program is designed for children 8 to 15, parents, and grandparents.

Seeing Italy in Senior Style

In general, Italy accords older people a great deal of respect, probably because of the continued existence of the extended family as well as the nature of the Italian language (there are polite forms of address you use when talking to someone older than yourself). Therefore, it's unlikely that you'll encounter ageism.

People older than 60 travel more than ever before, and being a senior entitles you to some terrific travel bargains. If you're not already a member of **AARP** (American Association of Retired Persons), 601 E St. NW, Washington, DC 20049 (☎ **800-424-3410** or 202-434-2277; www.aarp.org), do yourself a favor and join ($8 per year or $20 for 3 years) to receive discounts on car rentals and hotels. The nonprofit **National Council of Senior Citizens,** 8403 Colesville Rd., Suite 1200, Silver Spring, MD 20910 (☎ **301-578-8800**), offers memberships ($12 per couple) that include a bimonthly magazine and discounts on hotels, car rentals, and pharmacy purchases.

If you're faced with traveling alone and would rather tour Italy with a friend, **Golden Companions,** P.O. Box 5249, Reno, NV 89513 (☎ **702-324-2227**), offers a confidential network that helps you find a travel partner.

Most major domestic airlines, such as American, United, Continental, US Airways, and TWA, offer discount programs for seniors. Make sure that you ask whenever booking a flight.

In most cities, seniors receive reduced admission at theaters, museums, and other attractions, as well as discount fares on public transportation. However, the situation in Italy is more complicated. If you're a citizen of a European Union country, you receive a discount. If you're a U.S. resident, however, be aware that because the United States hasn't signed the bilateral agreement (you discount us and we'll discount you), you aren't eligible for senior discounts in Italy. The same rule applies to the under 17 discount.

The Mature Traveler, a valuable monthly 12-page newsletter concerning senior travel, is available by subscription ($30 per year) from GEM Publishing Group, Box 50400, Reno, NV, 89513-0400. And, you can find *101 Tips for the Mature Traveler* from **Grand Circle Travel,** 347 Congress St., Suite 3A, Boston, MA 02210 (☎ **800-221-2610** or 617-350-7500; Fax: 617-350-6206; Internet: www.gct.com).

Grand Circle Travel is also one of the literally hundreds of travel agencies specializing in vacations for seniors. But beware: Many agencies are of the tour-bus variety, with free trips thrown in for those who organize groups of 20 or more. If you're a senior seeking more independent travel, consult a regular travel agent. **SAGA International Holidays,** 222 Berkeley St., Boston, MA 02116 (☎ **800-343-0273**; Internet: www.sagaholidays.com), offers inclusive tours for people 50 and older.

Traveling Without Barriers

A disability shouldn't stop anybody from traveling, and there are more options and resources available than ever before. However, Italy isn't as advanced as some other countries in its accessibility. Part of the problem is the age of the housing stock and the difficulty of retrofitting medieval buildings with elevators or ramps. Some of the major buildings and institutions have been converted; others have not. Calling ahead is always best, especially because special entrances may exist for the disabled. Legislative action has been taken to make Italy more accessible, but application is proceeding slowly (remember that Rome wasn't built in a day). Public transportation reserves spaces for the disabled, but getting in and out of the train or bus can prove difficult. Kneeling buses (buses that lower themselves so passengers can board more easily) have started appearing, but whether you get one depends on the luck of the draw.

For additional information, consider *A World of Options,* a 658-page book of resources for disabled travelers, covering everything from biking trips to scuba outfitters. It costs $45 and is available from Mobility International USA, P.O. Box 10767, Eugene, OR, 97440 (☎ **541-343-1284,** voice and TDD; Internet: www.miusa.org). For more personal assistance, call the **Travel Information Service** at ☎ **215-456-9603** or 215-456-9602 (TTY).

If you're a traveler with a disability, you may also want to consider joining a tour that caters specifically to your needs. One of the best operators is **Flying Wheels Travel,** 143 West Bridge (P.O. Box 382), Owatonna, MN 55060 (☎] **800-535-6790**); it offers various escorted tours and cruises, as well as private tours in minivans with lifts. The **Society for the Advancement of Travel for the Handicapped,** 347 Fifth Ave., Suite 610, New York, NY 10016 (☎ **212-447-7284;** Internet: www.sath.org), can give you the names and addresses of other tour operators. Annual membership is $45 ($30 for seniors and students).

Vision-impaired travelers should contact the **American Foundation for the Blind,** 11 Penn Plaza, Suite 300, New York, NY 10001 (☎ **800-232-5463;** Internet: www.afb.org), for information on traveling with seeing-eye dogs.

Advice for Gay and Lesbian Travelers

Italy is a fairly tolerant country, and violent displays of intolerance such as gay bashing are unusual. If you're polite to people, they'll generally be polite to you, regardless of your orientation, color, beliefs, or sex. All major towns and cities have an active gay life, especially Florence, Rome, and Milan, which considers itself the gay capital of Italy and is the headquarters of **ARCI Gay,** the country's leading gay organization with branches throughout Italy. Capri is the gay resort of Italy, rivaled only by the gay beaches of Venice and Taormina on Sicily.

In preparation for the first-ever World Pride event held in July 2000, the mayor of Rome assumed all responsibility for the planned festivities against the wishes of various religious organizations that wanted things limited in consideration of the Jubilee. The religious organizations based their requests on the fact that during 1999's regular Gay Pride Parade, there had been anti-Catholic demonstrations on church property. To understand the importance of this, remember that the Holy

See (the court of the Pople) is in Rome and that churches are part of that state's territory; therefore, there was a risk of creating a diplomatic incident between the Italian government and the Holy See. In spite of all this, the mayor took a clear position and went out of his way to defend the rights of homosexuals.

The **International Gay & Lesbian Travel Association** (☎ **800-448-8550** or 954-776-2626; Fax: 954-776-3303; Internet: www.iglta.org) links travelers with the appropriate gay-friendly service organization or tour specialist. With approximately 1,200 members, the IGLTA offers quarterly newsletters, marketing mailings, and a membership directory that's updated quarterly. Membership often includes gay or lesbian businesses but is open to individuals for $150 yearly, plus a $100 administration fee for new members. Members are kept informed of gay and gay-friendly hoteliers, tour operators, and airline and cruise-line representatives. Contact the IGLTA for a list of its member agencies, who are tied into its information resources.

General gay and lesbian travel agencies include **Family Abroad** (☎ **800-999-5500** or 212-459-1800; www.familyabroad.com) and **Above and Beyond Tours** (☎ **800-397-2681**; Internet: www.abovebeyondtours.com).

If you're looking for a guidebook written specifically for you, you can't do better than *Frommer's Gay & Lesbian Europe* (IDG Books Worldwide, Inc.), with fabulous chapters on Rome, Florence, and Venice (as well as many other European cities). Two biannual English-language books, focusing on gays but also including information for lesbians, are the *Spartacus International Gay Guide* (Bruno Gmünder Verlag) and the *Odysseus* guide (Odysseus Enterprises LTD.). Both lesbians and gays may want to pick up a copy of *Gay Travel A to Z* (Ferrari Guides). You can order these four from most gay and lesbian bookstores, like **Giovanni's Room** (☎ **215-923-2960**) and **A Different Light Bookstore** (☎ **800-343-4002** or 212-989-4850; Internet: www.adlbooks.com).

Out and About, 8 W. 19th St., Suite 401, New York, NY 10011 (☎ **800-929-2268** or 212-645-6922), offers guidebooks and a monthly newsletter packed with information on the global gay and lesbian scene. A year's subscription is $49. *Our World,* 1104 North Nova Rd., Suite 251, Daytona Beach, FL 32117 (☎ **904-441-5367**; Internet: www.gayweb.com/208/ourworld.html), is a monthly magazine promoting and highlighting gay travel bargains. Annual subscription rates are $35 in the U.S. and $45 outside the States.

Traveling Tips for Women

If you're a woman traveling alone in Italy — especially if you're young and fair-haired — you'll attract young Italian men. In fact, they'll approach you and try to charm you; however, it's unlikely that someone would touch you, let alone harm you. Guidebooks tend to exaggerate pinching, groping, and the like (though on crowded buses these occurrences aren't unheard of). Conditions aren't the same as 20 or 30 years ago, and the younger generation of Italians is less prone to this kind of behavior.

Wearing the proper outfit generally will help you avoid annoying situations. Italians have a stricter dressing code than Americans do, and, although women can generally wear more casual clothing than men, only dressy and longish shorts are accepted. And the farther south you go, the more traditional the society is. In Sicily, men may bother you if you go around in short shorts and revealing tops because Sicilian women don't dress this way. You have two choices in such situations: One is to say, "I'm not Sicilian, and I'll dress however I feel like dressing." The other is to say, "I'm a foreigner in this country, and I'll adapt my mode of dress to fit in with local traditions, even if I don't agree with them." The choice is yours.

Several Web sites offer women advice on traveling safely and happily. The **Executive Woman's Travel Network** (www.delta-air.com/prog_serv/exec_womans_travel/) is the official women's travel site of Delta airlines and offers tips on staying fit while traveling, eating well, finding special airfares, and dealing with many other feminine issues. **WomanTraveler** (www.womantraveler.com) is an excellent guide that suggests places where women can stay and eat at various destinations. The site is authored by women and includes listings of women-owned businesses such as hotels and hostels.

Going It Alone

Many people prefer traveling alone, except for the relatively steep cost of booking a single room, which is usually well over half the price of a double.

Travel Companion (☎ 516-454-0880) is one of the oldest roommate finders for single travelers. Register with them and find a trustworthy travel mate who'll split the cost of the room with you and be around as little, or as often, as you like during the day.

Several tour organizers cater to solo travelers as well. **Experience Plus** (☎ 800-685-4565; Fax: 907-484-8489) offers an interesting selection of singles-only trips.

Travel Buddies (☎ 800-998-9099 or 604-533-2483) runs single-friendly tours with no extra charge because you're traveling solo. And the **Single Gourmet Club,** 133 E. 58th St., New York, NY 10022 (☎ 212-980-8788; Fax: 212-980-3138), is an international social, dining, and travel club for singles, with offices in 21 cities in the U.S. and Canada and one in London.

Part II
Ironing Out the Details

The 5th Wave   By Rich Tennant

"And how shall I book your flight to Italy – First Class, Coach, or Medieval?"

In this part . . .

*P*art 1 covers the basics, but in this part we get down to the nuts and bolts of booking your trip. Chapter 6 concerns the various ways of getting to Italy and saving some money, and Chapter 7 gives you information about getting around Italy after you arrive. Chapter 8 covers hotel options and booking your room. Chapter 9 discusses money — there are more options than ever before concerning how you handle your cash and pay your expenses. Chapter 10 takes care of the details that you too often leave to the last minute, such as getting a passport, thinking about medical and travel insurance, and packing.

Chapter 6

Getting to Italy

· ·

· ·

Getting to Italy may not be half the fun, but it's necessary, and the process can seem fairly complicated. Getting to your destination is probably the biggest part of your budget and of your decision making. Airfares to Italy are significantly higher than those to other European countries, such as England, because it's farther east and south. If you can find a high-season fare for under $800, you're doing well. Of course, with the cutthroat competition among airlines, you may lock-in a much better deal. Similarly, if you wait until the last minute to make your reservations, you may pay through the nose — though even at that point, all is not lost. You may find a last-minute ticket at a reasonable price on the Internet.

Using a Travel Agent

Any travel agent can help you find bargain airfares, a hotel room, or a rental car. A good agent stops you from ruining your vacation if you go overboard trying to save a few dollars. However, the best travel agents can tell you how much time you need to budget for a destination, find a cheap flight that doesn't require you to change planes in Atlanta and Chicago, book you a better hotel room for about the same price as an average room, and give recommendations on restaurants.

The best way to find a good travel agent is to do so the same way you find a good plumber, mechanic, or doctor — by word of mouth. Check with any family members, neighbors, or friends who've had good experiences with travel agents. Also make sure that you pick an agent who knows Italy.

Travel agents work on commission. The good news is that *you* don't pay the commission; the airlines, accommodations, and tour companies do. The bad news is that unscrupulous travel agents try to persuade you to book the vacations that give them the most money in commissions.

To make sure you get the most out of your travel agent, do a little homework. Read about Italy (you've already made a sound decision by buying this book) and pick out some hotels and attractions that you think you'll like. If necessary, get a more comprehensive guide like *Frommer's Rome, Frommer's Portable Venice, Frommer's Italy, Frommer's Italy from $70 a Day, Hanging Out in Italy, Frommer's Tuscany & Umbria,* or the new-in-2001 *Frommer's Northern Italy.* If you have access to the Internet, check prices on the Web in advance (see "Tips for Getting the Best Airfare," later in this chapter) so you can do a little prodding. Then take your guidebook and Web information to a travel agent and ask him or her to make the arrangements for you. Because he or she has access to more resources than even the most complete Web travel site, the agent should be able to get you a better price than you can get by yourself. And he or she can issue your tickets and vouchers before you leave. If the agent can't get you into the hotel of your choice, he or she can recommend an alternative, and you can look for an objective review in your guidebook in the agent's office.

In the past couple of years, some airlines and resorts have started limiting or eliminating travel agent commissions altogether. The immediate result has been that agents don't bother booking these services unless the customer specifically requests them. But some travel industry analysts predict that if other airlines and accommodations throughout the industry follow suit, travel agents may start charging customers for their services. When that day arrives, finding the best agents may prove even harder.

Discovering the Ins and Outs of Escorted and Package Tours

The two main types of tours are escorted and package tours. Escorted tours are where you fly as a group, stay as a group, and tour around as a group with some kind of guide. Package tours are where a packager puts together pieces of a trip and sells them. After you buy the package tour, you're on your own.

Do you like letting your bus driver worry about traffic while you sit in comfort and listen to a tour guide explain everything that you see? Or, do you prefer renting a car and following your nose, even if you don't catch all the highlights? Do you like having lots of events planned for each day, or would you rather improvise as you go along? The answers to these questions will help you determine whether you should choose an escorted tour or travel à la carte.

Escorted tours

Some people love escorted tours. Escorted tours free travelers from spending lots of time behind the wheel; they take care of all the details, and they tell you what to expect at each attraction. You know your costs up front, so you don't experience many surprises. Escorted tours can take you to the maximum number of sights in the minimum amount of time with the least amount of hassle. But many other people need more freedom and spontaneity — they can't stand guided tours, they prefer to discover a destination by themselves, and they don't mind getting caught in a thunderstorm without an umbrella or finding that a recommended restaurant is no longer in business. They consider such things part of travel's adventure.

If you choose an escorted tour, ask the following questions before you buy:

✔ **What is the cancellation policy?** Do I have to place a deposit? Can the tour organizers cancel the trip if they don't secure enough people? How late can I cancel if I'm unable to go? When do I pay? Do I receive a refund if I cancel? If they cancel?

✔ **How jam-packed is the schedule?** Do tour organizers try to fit 25 hours into a 24-hour day, or is there ample time for relaxing and/or shopping? If you don't enjoy waking at 7 a.m. every day and not returning to your hotel until 6 or 7 p.m., you may not enjoy certain escorted tours.

✔ **How big is the group?** The smaller the group, the more flexible the schedule and the less time you'll spend waiting for people to enter and exit the bus. Tour operators may be evasive about this, because they may not know the exact size of the group until everybody makes their reservations, but they should be able to give you a rough estimate. Some tours have a minimum group size and may cancel the tour if they don't book enough people.

✔ **What is included in the package?** Don't assume that anything's included. For example, you may have to pay to get yourself to and from the airport. Or, an excursion may include a box lunch, but drinks may cost extra, or the meal may include beer but not wine. How much choice do you have? Can you opt out of certain activities, or does the bus leave once a day, with no exceptions? Are all your meals planned in advance? Can you choose your entree at dinner, or does everybody get the same chicken cutlet?

With an escorted tour, think strongly about purchasing travel insurance, especially if the tour operator asks you to pay up front. But don't buy insurance from the tour operator! If they don't fulfill their obligation to provide you with the vacation that you've paid for, don't expect them to fulfill their insurance obligations either. Buy travel insurance through an independent agency.

Some companies specialize in escorted Italian tours. Here's a brief list:

✔ **Perillo Tours,** 577 Chestnut Ridge Rd., Woodcliff Lake, NJ 07675-9888 (☎ **800-431-1515** or 201-307-1234; Internet: www. perillotours.com), has been in business for more than half a century. Its itineraries range from 8 to 15 days and are very diverse. From April to October, you can choose among nine itineraries. In the off-season, Perillo Tours visits only the big cities — Rome, Florence, and Venice.

✔ **Central Holidays** (☎ **800-611-1139**; Internet: www.
centralholidays.com) offers fully escorted tours in
addition to their packages.

✔ **Italiatour** (☎ **800-845-3365** or 212-675-2183; Internet: www.
italiatour.com) is associated with Alitalia (Italy's national
airline) and offers many different tours as well.

✔ **Insight International Tours,** 745 Atlantic Ave., Suite 720, Boston,
MA 02111 (☎ **800-582-8380**), runs luxury motor-coach tours lasting from a week to a month.

✔ If you're interested in luxurious, classy tours of Italy, you
can also try **Abercrombie and Kent**, 1520 Kensington Rd.,
Oak Brook, IL 60523 (☎ **800-323-7308**), and Sloan Square
House, Holbein Place, London SW1W 8NS (☎ **020-7730-9600**;
Internet: www.abercrombiekent.com).

You can also check out Italian companies that specialize in one
region. For example, **CST, Compagnia Siciliana Turismo**, Via E.
Amari 124, 90139 Palermo (☎ **091-582-294**; Fax: 091-582-218; Internet:
http://web.tin.it/cst; E-mail: cstmail@tin.it), offers a number
of organized tours of Sicily, lasting from a few days to two weeks.

Package tours

Doing some research and comparing your options when deciding on
a package tour is important, and the best place to start looking is the
travel section of your local Sunday newspaper, as well as the ads in
the back of national travel magazines like *Travel & Leisure, National
Geographic Traveler*, and C*ondé Nast Traveler*. **Liberty Travel** (many
locations; check your local directory — there's not a central toll-free
number) is one of the biggest packagers in the Northeast United States
and usually boasts a full-page ad in Sunday papers. You won't find
much in the way of service but you will get a good deal. **American
Express Vacations** (☎ **800-241-1700**) is another option.

Two other reliable packagers are **Kemwell** (☎ **800-678-0678**; Internet:
www.kemwell.com) and **Central Holidays** (☎ **800-611-1139**; Internet:
www.centralholidays.com). **Italiatour** (☎ **800-845-3365** or 212-
675-2183; Internet: www.italiatour.com), associated with Alitalia, the
Italian state airline, specializes in tours for independent travelers who
take a car or train between destinations for which Italiatour books
accommodation.

Large hotel chains and resorts also offer packages. Call the resort
directly and ask if it offers land/air packages.

Airlines are another good resource for package tours because they
often package their flights together with accommodations. And
although disreputable packagers are uncommon, they do exist; but, if
you buy your package through the airline, you can be pretty sure that
the company will still be in business when your departure date arrives.

Among airline packages, your options include **American Airlines FlyAway Vacations** (☎ 800-321-2121), **Delta Dream Vacations** (☎ 800-872-7786), and **US Airways Vacations** (☎ 800-455-0123).

Making Your Own Arrangements

Whether you're committed to going it alone and planning your trip yourself, or you're just pricing out the pieces to see how much of a deal you're really getting with a package tour (see "Discovering the Ins and Outs of Escorted and Package Tours," earlier in this chapter), making your own travel arrangements is a step-by-step process. First, of course, you need to know what airlines fly to Italy from where you are.

Finding a suitable flight

Rome and Milan are the only two Italian cities to which you can fly non-stop from North America. For Florence, Venice, Naples, or Sicily, you have to take a connecting flight in Rome or Milan. This lack of choice makes it easy to decide into which city you want to fly: Go to Milan if you're focusing on northern Italy, and fly to Rome if you're focusing on southern Italy.

If you have only a week or two in Italy, you can fly into one city and out of another. For example, if you landed in Milan, you could drive down through Tuscany, loop around the near south taking in Rome and some other sites, and then fly out of Rome. The only problem is, airlines really gouge you for this type of itinerary, especially because it often involves two airlines. However, the airline business changes constantly, and it never hurts to check. For the right price, this plan may save you hundreds of miles of driving or sitting on the train.

The Italian national airline, **Alitalia**, offers flights from every major city in the world to every destination in Italy by way of Rome or Milan (☎ 800-223-5730 in the U.S., 800-361-8336 in Canada, 0990-448-259 in the U.K. or 020-7602-7111 in London, 1300-653-747 or 1300-653-757 in Australia, toll free 1478-65-643 or 06-65643 in Italy; Internet: www. alitalia.it or www.alitaliausa.com). Alitalia also offers daily flights to all European capitals. Direct daily flights are scheduled from a number of cities in the United States and from Toronto and Montreal in Canada. Likewise, Alitalia offers direct service between Sydney and Melbourne and Italy, but not every day. At press time, there are three flights a week from Sydney to Rome and three to Milan, as well as one flight a week from Melbourne to Milan and Melbourne to Rome.

In addition to Alitalia, from the United States, **American Airlines** (☎ 800-433-7300; Internet: www.americanair.com) runs nonstop flights to Italy out of Chicago. **Delta** (☎ 800-241-4141; Internet: www. delta-air.com) flies from New York City to Italy, as does **TWA** (☎ 800-221-2000; Internet: www.twa.com). **United** (☎ 800-538-2929; Internet: www.ual.com) flies to Milan from Washington, D.C. **U.S. Airways** (☎ 800-428-4322; Internet: www.usairways.com) flies from

Philadelphia to Rome; **Continental** (☎ **800-525-0280**; Internet: www. flycontinental.com) flies to Rome from Newark, NJ; and **Northwest Airlines** (☎ **800-447-4747**; Internet: www.nwa.com) flies from its hub in Detroit.

In Canada, you can fly **Alitalia** (☎ **800-361-8336**; Internet: www. alitalia.it) from Montreal or Toronto. In addition, you can also fly **Canadian Airlines International** (☎ **800-426-7000**; Internet: www.cdnair.ca) and **Air Canada** (☎ **888-247-2262**; Internet: www. aircanada.ca).

From Britain, your best bet other than Alitalia is **British Airways** (☎ **0345-222-7111** in the U.K.; Internet: www.britishairways.com), though smaller charter companies also offer flights.

From Australia and New Zealand, **Cathay Pacific** (☎ **131-747** toll-free in Australia, 0508-800454 in New Zealand; Internet: www.cathaypacific. com) offers three flights a week to Rome from Melbourne and Sydney, connecting through Hong Kong. The airline also offers two flights from Perth and Cairns, connecting through Hong Kong, and one flight from Brisbaine connecting through Hong Kong. Auckland is also served thrice weekly, also with a connection through Hong Kong. Another option is **Qantas** (☎ **13-13-13**; Internet: www.qantas.com), which offers some direct flights — daily from Melbourne to Rome and several days a week from Sydney. **Air New Zealand** (☎ **800-737-000**; Internet: www. airnz.com) doesn't fly directly to Italy. You have to change in another European city to a national carrier — most likely in London or Frankfurt.

On any day of the week, you can get a connecting flight through a major European capital, where you switch to the national carrier — connecting through London with British Airways or through Paris with Air France. European airlines include **British Airways** (☎ **800-247-297**; Internet: www.britishairways.com), **Air France** (☎ **800-237-2747**; www.airfrance.com), **KLM** (☎ **800-374-7747**; Internet: www.klm.nl), and **Lufthansa** (☎ **800-645-3880**; Internet: www.lufthansa-usa.com).

 All European carriers will make you stop over in their own country before you fly on to Italy. You may not want to add this extra step to your flight if it's already long. However, you may want to take advantage of the stop by checking out Buckingham Palace and catching a show in London or seeing the Eiffel Tower and enjoying a brasserie meal in Paris before heading to Italy.

Getting the best airfare

Airline deregulation has led to some pretty funny situations. The person sitting next to you on the plane probably paid less or more than you paid for your seat. Business travelers who require the flexibility to buy their tickets at the last minute, change their itinerary at a moment's notice, or need to get home before the weekend pay the premium rate, known as full fare. Passengers who can book their tickets long in advance, who don't mind staying over Saturday night, or are willing to travel on Tuesday, Wednesday, or Thursday pay the least, usually a fraction of the full fare. Obviously, planning ahead pays.

Airlines also periodically hold sales. These fares have advance-purchase requirements and date of travel restrictions, but you can't beat the price: usually no more than $500 for a cross-Atlantic flight. Keep your eyes open for these sales as you're planning your vacation, and then pounce on them. (These sales tend to take place in seasons of low travel volume.) You almost never see a sale in the peak months of July and August or around Thanksgiving or Christmas when people have to fly, regardless of the cost of fare.

For Italy, the high season is long and getting longer. For example, in the Jubilee year of 2000, there wasn't a low season. You may be lucky just to get on *any* plane heading for Italy. Another thing to keep in mind is that European national airlines (Alitalia, Lufthansa, Air France, and so on) tend to cost more, but they also seem to have more leg room and better service. This may be an important consideration, given that the flight from New York to Rome is about eight hours compared with five hours to London.

Comparison shopping for airfare is vital, so definitely check with *consolidators* (also known as bucket shops) like **Cheap Tickets** (☎ 800-377-1000), **Cheap Seats** (☎ 800-451-7200), **1-800-FLY-4-LESS** (☎ 800-359-4537), and **1-800-FLY-CHEAP** (☎ 800-359-2432). Consolidators buy blocks of unsold seats directly from the airlines, and then pass some of the savings on to you. Their prices are much better than the fares you can get yourself, and they're often lower than the prices your travel agent can find. You can find their ads in the small boxes at the bottom of the page in your Sunday travel section. Another good choice, **Council Travel** (☎ 800-226-8624; Internet: www.counciltravel.com), caters especially to young travelers, but their bargain-basement prices are available to people of all ages.

Booking your tickets online

Another way to find the cheapest airfare is using the Internet. After all, that's what computers do best — search through millions of pieces of data and return information in rank order. The number of virtual travel agents on the Net has increased exponentially in recent years. Agencies now compete the way locksmiths do in the phone book for the first alphabetical listing. Prepare to spend some hours online in pursuit of a great airfare to Italy; you'll probably have to page through dozens of options. The Internet contains too many companies to mention them all, but a few of the better-respected sites are **Travelocity** (www.travelocity.com; www.frommers.travelocity.com; www.previewtravel.com), **Microsoft Expedia** (www.expedia.com), and **Yahoo!** (http://travel.yahoo.com/travel). Each site has its quirks, but they all provide variations of the same service. Simply enter the dates that you want to fly and the cities that you want to visit, and the computer looks for the lowest fares. The Yahoo! site offers a feature called *Fare Beater,* which checks flights on other airlines or at different times or dates in hopes of finding you an even cheaper fare. Expedia's site e-mails you the best airfare deal once a week if you so choose.

Travelocity is Frommer's online travel planning/booking partner. It offers reservations and tickets for more than 400 airlines, plus reservations and purchase capabilities for more than 45,000 hotels and 50 car-rental companies. An exclusive feature of the system is its *Low Fare Search Engine,* which automatically searches for the three lowest-priced itineraries based on your criteria. Last-minute deals and consolidator fares are included in the search too. If you book with Travelocity, you can select specific seats for your flights with online seat maps and also view diagrams of the most popular commercial aircraft. Its hotel finder provides street-level location maps and photos of selected hotels. With the Fare Watcher e-mail feature, you can select up to five routes and receive e-mail notices when the fare changes by $25 or more. Travelocity's Destination Guide includes updated information on some 260 destinations worldwide — supplied by Frommer's.

At **Priceline.com**, you bid for a ticket (as you would at an auction), and you can get tickets for hundreds of dollars less this way. Type in the destination and various other parameters, such as the number of connections you're willing to make (there's a minimum of one, so forget nonstop flights), and then give the price you'd like to pay and your credit card number. Once you submit the request, you're committed. Within an hour, they send you an e-mail letting you know if your bid has been accepted. Here's the catch: If it *has* been accepted, you're credit card is automatically charged for the tickets and you have no way to back out (we know — we tried once).

Priceline has changed its rules recently: You can no longer endlessly submit requests, starting say at $100 round-trip to Rome and ratcheting up $25 every time. You now have to change one of the other parameters too when you resubmit — the days, the number of connections, and so on. As a result, you have to start the process with a fairly realistic price.

Great last-minute deals are also available directly from the airlines through a free e-mail service called **E-savers**. Each week, the airline sends you a list of discounted flights, usually leaving the upcoming Friday or Saturday and returning the following Monday or Tuesday. See "Finding a suitable flight," earlier in this chapter for each airline's Web site.

Finding Other Ways to Get There

If you're coming to Italy from continental Europe and don't want to fly, taking a **train** is your best alternative. Italy has an excellent rail system, and there are several long-distance trains to and from everywhere in Europe. You can even take the Orient Express to Venice!

Paris is connected by high-speed TGV trains to Torino-Novara-Milan. From Paris, you can also take the famous Palatino, the overnight train to Rome. You can also catch overnight trains from Germany (Hanover, Düsseldorf, Köln, Bonn, and Frankfurt).

Another way to arrive in Italy from continental Europe is by **ferry.** There are several ferry services to Genoa from France (for example, from Sête), from Patras in Greece to Brindisi and Ancona, and from Croatia to Ancona.

If you love driving very long distances and have plenty of time, you can also drive to Italy. Crossing the Alps is quite an experience. The highway takes you through one of the major passes, depending on where you're coming from, or you can take the famous tunnel under Mont Blanc. You then arrive at one of three main cities: Milan (central Italy), Genoa (western coastal), or Venice (eastern coastal). All roads headed south converge in Florence and Rome.

Chapter 7

Getting Around Italy

- -

- -

*T*he first thing that you notice in Italy is that everybody speaks *Italiano.* Luckily, signs are often nonlingual (using international symbols) and bilingual in major tourist areas. Among the most common signs are the italic *i,* usually black on a yellow background, indicating a tourist information office, and the skirted and panted stick figures indicating men's and women's rest rooms.

As a land of tourism, Italy has developed a set of special signs that indicate sights, which are different from the regular road signs. These signs are white lettering on brown or black lettering on yellow, and they often have a little picture (a box with a cross on it for a church, two columns and one lying down for a ruin, and so on). Likewise, they may even include the distance to the attraction in meters.

In this chapter, we give you the information you need to maneuver throughout Italy. Your best bet for getting around the country is via the fast and cheap train system. If you're pressed for time and need to cover a large distance, then opt for a plane. And if you have lots of time, you can rent a car and tour the countryside while getting from one destination to the next. See Table 7-1 for travel times between cities using different modes of transportation.

Traveling by Plane

The Italian national airline is **Alitalia** (☎ **800-223-5730** in the U.S., 800-361-8336 in Canada, 0990-448-259 in the U.K. and 020-7602-7111 in London, 1300-653-747 or 1300-653-757 in Australia, and toll-free 1478- 65643 or 06-65643 in Italy; Internet: www.alitalia.it or www.alitaliausa.com). Alitalia offers flights to every destination in Italy.

However, you can choose from regional airlines as well. **Air Sicilia** (☎ **06-6501-71046**) flies to Sicily from other Italian cities and sometimes offers better rates than Alitalia. Other private airlines include

Air One (☎ toll free **1478-48-880** or 06-488-800 in Italy; Internet: www.flyairone.it), which flies to several destinations in Italy, including between Venice and Rome, and **Meridiana** (☎ **06-874-081** or 199-111-333 in Italy; www.meridiana.it), which also flies to several destinations in Italy and Europe, including from Palermo to Milan, Florence, Pisa, and Verona and from Verona to Catania, Naples, Palermo, and Rome.

When traveling on domestic flights in Italy, you can receive a 30 percent fare reduction if you take a flight that departs at night.

Table 7-1   Travel Times Between the Major Cities

Cities	Distance	Air Travel Time	Train Travel Time	Driving Time
Florence to Milan	298km/185 mi	55 min.	2½ hrs.	3½ hrs.
Florence to Venice	281km/174 mi	2 hrs., 5 min.	4 hrs.	3 hrs., 15 min.
Milan to Venice	267km/166 mi	50 min.	3½ hrs.	3 hrs., 10 min.
Rome to Florence	277km/172 mi	1 hr., 10 min.	2½ hrs.	3 hrs., 20 min.
Rome to Milan	572km/355 mi	1 hr., 5 min.	5 hrs.	6 hrs., 30 min.
Rome to Naples	219km/136 mi	50 min.	2½ hrs.	2½ hrs.
Rome to Venice	528km/327 mi	1 hr., 5 min.	5 hrs., 15 min.	6 hrs.
Venice to Naples	747km/463mi	1 hr., 45 min.	7 hrs., 45 min.	8 hrs., 30 min.

Taking the Train

Train travel in Italy is a bargain. The network is large, the distances are relatively small, the express trains are fast and comfortable, and it's not very expensive. See the Italian train routes map on the inside back cover of this guide.

One train-travel option is buying a pass from the **Rail Europe Group** (☎ **800-438-7245** in the U.S. and 800-361-7245 in Canada for info; 877-456-7245 in the U.S. and 800-361-7245 in Canada for tickets; Internet: www.raileurope.com). The Rail Europe Group offers several choices based on how many days you want to travel and if you want to travel consecutively for several days or stop in between. For example, the **eight-consecutive-day pass** is $199 (second class) and gives you unlimited travel all over Italy for those eight days. Another possibility is the **flexipass,** which allows you to travel on a specific number of days within a month; for example, you can get a four-day flexipass for $159 and have the right to unlimited travel during any four days of your choice. You can also choose other options for longer periods of time. Rail Europe also offers an interesting **Rail 'n Drive pass.** For $420, you get an automatic Hertz car rental for two days (unlimited mileage) as well as three days of unlimited rail travel within a month for two people. Not bad!

Another train-travel option is buying the special **kilometric ticket** directly from the FS (Ferrovia dello Stato, Italy's national rail company). With a kilometric ticket, you buy a number of kilometers that you can use as you wish. Several amounts are available; for example, you can buy 3,000 km for 206,000L ($117). You can use as many kilometers as you want at a time and use the ticket for 2 months; shorter distances are available too. Using the kilometric ticket, you save about 15 percent over what you'd spend buying individual tickets. You can also sign more than one person onto the ticket, so you don't have to buy one for each person in your party. If you're a couple traveling from Rome to Venice (528 km), you'll use up a little over a third of your ticket. Each time you travel, go to the train station window and have the pass validated. The teller will calculate the distance and write down how much mileage (or rather kilometerage) you have left. You can also ask the teller to write "Roma to Venezia, via Firenze" so you don't have to go to the ticket booth at your through-stops. However, you do have to complete the trip within four days. Surcharges apply to the super-fast Eurostar trains, and in the high travel season, you have to reserve your seat (at a slight extra charge).

You can buy kilometric tickets and rail passes at train stations in Italy. Likewise, you can also buy rail passes before you leave the United States through a travel agent or Rail Europe (see contact information, earlier in this section). In the United States, you can buy kilometric tickets from the official U.S. representative of the FS (Ferrovia dello Stato, Italy's national rail company) — **CIT Tours,** 15 W. 44th St., Suite 104, New York, NY 10036 (☎ **800-243-8687** or 212-730-2121; Fax: 212-730-4544). You can also find FS rail info or buy tickets online at www.fs-on-line.com.

Getting Around by Bus

Where the train system stops, you can take a bus and really get out into the middle of nowhere. For example, **SITA,** Viale del Cadorna 105, Firenze (☎ **055-47821**), operates an extensive bus network in central Italy. You often see people from the countryside taking the bus to and from Florence, Siena, and other major centers. In this book, we list other companies for each destination where taking a bus makes sense and is a better way of transportation. You won't see too many tourists on buses, however, which is good if you want to meet real Italians and get a feeling for what life is really like in Italy.

If you're interested in taking a bus, call the company in advance and inquire about the schedules, which change frequently. Tickets must be bought at the bus station in advance as drivers don't have cash to make change.

Floating by Ferry

The only ferries you're likely to use in Italy are those to Capri (see Chapters 21 and 22) and Sicily (Chapter 23). They leave from Naples (for Sicily, you can also take a ferry from Villa San Giovanni near Reggio

Calabria if you drive all the way to the southern tip of Italy), and the ferries to Sicily take cars. For more information, see the relevant chapters.

If you want to bring your car on a ferry, you must make a reservation well in advance to make sure that there's room — especially in high season. Taking your car on a ferry also means that you'll have to pay more. In some cases, you may save money renting your car on arrival rather than taking it on a ferry.

Driving Around in a Car

In order to drive in Italy, you need to get an **International Driver's License** before leaving the United States. Any branch of the **American Automobile Association** (☎ **800-222-4357** in the U.S. or 613-247-0117 in Canada) issues International Driver's Licenses. You have to fill in the AAA application form and provide a 2-inch by 2-inch photograph, a photocopy of your U.S. driver's license, and $10. Don't forget to bring your U.S. license with you in Italy, though, because the International license is valid only in combination with your regular license. An alternative to the International Driver's License is to take an Italian translation of your U.S. license (prepared by AAA or another organization) to an office of the **Automobile Club d'Italia** (☎ **06-4477** for 24-hour information and assistance) in Italy to receive a special driving permit.

Likewise, if you're planning to drive in Italy, make sure that you have a good road map. The map that your rental company gives you isn't good enough. The best maps are published by the **Automobile Club d'Italia** and the **Italian Touring Club** and are widely available in bookstores and at newsstands in Italy. A lot of highway building is going on in Italy, so maps change often.

Knowing the rules of the road

There are two very important rules to know when driving in Italy:

> **Rule 1:** Drive defensively.

> **Rule 2:** Always be ready to get out of the way.

It's a myth that Italians drive badly or at least worse than anyone else. For one thing, you won't see (as you often do in the United States) someone driving along a major highway reading a book or newspaper or putting on makeup. (If you tried that in Italy you'd be killed.) Italians *love* to drive, but they drive *fast* and aren't very patient. If you're going 90 kmh and passing a car going 80 kmh, someone may zoom up behind you going 140 kmh and flashing their lights (a perfect time to apply Rule 2). People do, however, follow the rules of the road (even at 120 kmh), because the penalty for doing something dumb at that speed is often dire (at the very least, people yell and make obscene gestures).

Road signs in Italy for the *autostrada* (limited access, national or international toll road) are white on green; signs for local roads are white on blue. A white-on-blue sign saying "SS119" means that you're on the *strada statale* (state road) number 119.

A puzzling sign placed close to the ground is the white arrow on a blue circle; it points you to the lane that you should enter or the correct way around an obstacle, a traffic island, and so forth. Another important sign is **No Parking** — a blue-and-red circle with a diagonal stripe pointing to the side of the street where you can't park. If the sign shows two stripes (an "X"), you can't park on either side of the street. **Senso Unico** written on a white arrow on blue background means a "one way" street, and the white-on-red stop sign is obvious. Another useful sign to know is **Stazione** or **Stazione FS** or only **FS**, indicating the direction of the local train station (the sign may also include the name of the station).

Keep your eyes peeled for **exits** (each marked *Uscita*). They're often indicated on the highway far in advance and then right on top of the ramp — not a few hundred yards in advance where it's helpful.

The following two rules are rigidly obeyed on the highway in Italy (again, unlike in the States):

> **Rule 1:** Pass only on the left.

> **Rule 2:** *Never* stay in the passing lane unless you're going faster than everybody else. Just pull out, pass, and get back in the slow lane with dispatch. The person on the right always has the right of way at intersections, except in traffic circles, where the cars already in the circle have priority over those trying to enter.

 Naples deserves special mention with respect to driving — even other Italians won't drive there. Consider that on our first visit, in one block we saw a motorcyclist riding a wheelie the length of the street and a tiny car that drove up on the sidewalk and around the signal pole to avoid a red light! If you arrive in Naples by car, find a garage or parking space fast, and then walk and/or take the bus.

If you're from America's Midwest or West and are used to highways that run in straight lines and city streets that follow neat grids, prepare yourself for twisting roads (plunging cliffs optional), paved ancient Roman roads, city streets with kidney-shattering cobblestones, big broad piazzas without lines indicating lanes, and streets only as wide as one *Italian* car. (We once saw a Corvette with New York plates plug up a small street in Rome.) In Italian cities, you also find swarms of *motorini* — what Americans call mopeds (but theirs are much faster). If you're first at a stoplight, a swarm of 15 can easily surround you by the time the light changes. Look out for *motorini,* because they certainly aren't looking out for you.

The driving situation in Italy probably isn't as bad as we've made it sound. But, we will go against the other guidebooks and make the following claim: Unless you're really going to spend time getting way off the beaten track, don't rent a car. If the focus of your trip is the big three cities (Rome, Florence, and Venice), you don't need one. Even if you want to explore the Tuscan countryside, a large fleet of buses serves the territory between Florence and Siena, for example, and you can take trains to smaller cities like Perugia and Assisi in Umbria.

If you aren't in shape or very mobile, however, a car makes sense. But if you want a car just to carry all your luggage, it's a better idea just to bring less luggage. Here's a good compromise: Plan your itinerary so that you can either spend a few days in a city, and then pick up your car when you're ready to leave (not at the airport upon your arrival), or plan your rural driving first, and then dump your car as soon as you get to the city where you'll spend the most time.

In Italy, driving a car is often more expensive than traveling by train or bus, because tolls are high and gas is very expensive (about 9,000L/ $5 per gallon). Driving from Rome to Florence and back, for example, can cost you two tanks of gas ($80 plus) and another $10 to $20 in tolls depending on how much of the *autostrada* you use. Therefore, there's certainly no reason to rent a car just to drive among Rome, Florence, and Venice. Traveling by train is faster, less stressful, and cheaper.

If, after our warnings, you still can't wait to load up a Cadillac with your steamer trunks and do the Amalfi Coast, think again. Italian cars are *small.* Keep your luggage to a minimum (you don't want to drive around and park with your extra suitcase sitting in the back seat), or rent a big-gish car, which, however, is never larger than an American midsize.

If you don't know how to drive a standard shift car (that is, with a manual transmission), consider learning how before leaving for Italy. Most Italian cars are standard. The country is very mountainous, and a car with an automatic shift is often a pain. Likewise, automatics cost more to rent, and rental agencies may run out of them sooner. Standard cars also get better gas mileage, especially crawling up and down steep grades.

Here are some ways to make driving in Italy more manageable and safe:

- ✔ Don't drive much at night.

- ✔ Don't let your gas gauge get too low (under a quarter of a tank), because gas stations often close for lunch and all day on Sunday, except along the *autostrada.*

- ✔ Change drivers frequently and make stops every couple of hours (at least) for some rest, food, and water.

Understanding the rules of renting

Car-rental rates vary more than airline fares. The price you pay depends on the size of the car, the length of time you keep it, where and when you pick it up and drop it off, where you take it, as well as a host of other factors. It's always best to reserve the car before leaving home.

When renting a car, asking a few key questions can save you hundreds of dollars. Are weekend rates lower than weekday rates? Is the rate the same for pickup Friday morning as it is for Thursday night? If you're keeping the car five or more days, you may find that a weekly rate is cheaper than the daily rate. Does the company assess a drop-off charge if you don't return the car to the same renting location? Is the rate cheaper if you pick up the car at the airport or at a location in town? Does the rate include a set number of miles you're allotted to drive? What happens if you go over?

If you see an advertised price in your local newspaper, make sure that you ask for that specific rate; otherwise, the company may charge you the standard (higher) rate. And don't forget to mention membership in AAA, AARP, frequent-flyer programs, and trade unions. These memberships usually entitle you to discounts of 5 to 30 percent. Ask your travel agent to check any and all of these rates. And remember: Most car rentals are worth at least 500 miles on your frequent-flyer account!

Internet resources can make comparison shopping for rental cars easier. For example, Yahoo's partnership with Flifo Global travel agency allows you to look up rental prices for any size car at more than a dozen companies in hundreds of cities. Simply enter the size of car you want, the rental and return dates, and the city where you want to rent, and the server returns a price. It will even make your reservation for you, if you choose. Point your browser to `http://travel.yahoo.com/travel` and choose "Reserve car" from the options. Travelocity.com also offers a car-rental component, and on Priceline.com, you can bid the price you want to pay for a rental.

On top of standard prices, optional charges apply to most car rentals. Most rental companies require that you pay for *theft protection insurance,* because car theft is unfortunately common in Italy. (International gangs operate in Italy and ship stolen cars to Eastern Europe.) Many credit cards cover you for damage to a rental car, so that you don't have to take the rental company's collision insurance. However, check with your company to see if your card's benefit extends outside the United States. If your card covers you, you can avoid paying this hefty fee (as much as $10 per day).

Car rental companies also offer additional *liability insurance* (if you harm others in an accident), *personal accident insurance* (if you harm yourself or your passengers), and *personal effects insurance* (if your luggage is stolen from your car). If you have insurance on your car at home, you're probably covered for most of these unlikelihoods. (However, check to see if your insurance covers overseas rentals). Otherwise, consider the additional coverage. Weigh the likelihood of getting into an accident or losing your luggage against the cost of this extra coverage (as much as $20 per day combined), which can significantly add to the price of your rental.

Some companies also offer *refueling packages,* in which you pay for an entire tank of gas up front. The price is usually fairly competitive with local gas prices, but you don't get credit for any gas remaining in the tank. If you reject this option, you pay only for the gas you use, but you have to return the car with a full tank or face expensive fuel charges. If a stop at a gas station on the way to the airport will make you miss your plane, take advantage of the fuel purchase option. Otherwise, skip it.

Here's a list of car-rental companies operating in Italy:

- ✔ **Avis.** ☎ **06-41-999** in Italy, or 800-331-1212 in the U.S. Internet: www.avis.com.

- ✔ **Hertz.** ☎ **199-112-211** in Italy, or 800-654-3001 in the U.S. Internet: www.hertz.com.

- ✔ **National/Maggiore.** ☎ **1478-67-067** toll free in Italy, or 800-227-7368 in the U.S. Internet: www.maggiore.it.

- ✔ **AutoEurope.** ☎ **800-334-440** toll free in Italy, or 800-223-5555 in the U.S. Internet: www.autoeurope.com or www.sbe.it.

- ✔ **Kemwel.** ☎ **800-678-0678** in the U.S. Internet: www.kemwel.com.

- ✔ **Europe by Car.** ☎ **800-223-1516** in the U.S. Internet: www.europebycar.com.

- ✔ **Europcar.** ☎ **800-014-410** toll free in Italy, or 06-6501-0879. Internet: www.europcar.it.

Chapter 8

Booking Your Accommodations

● ●

In This Chapter

▶ Choosing among Italy's hotels

▶ Booking a room

▶ Avoiding getting stuck without a place to sleep

● ●

*D*espite globalization, hotels aren't the same all over the world. International chains are moving toward a certain standardization of services, but you can still find a lot of individuality out there, especially when you visit countries where hostelry is a long-standing tradition.

Italy is certainly one of those countries. Travelers have journeyed to Italy since before the Romans, and there are inns there that claim several centuries of service. This history creates an enormous variety in Italy's hotels, from romantic fifteenth-century hostels and seventeenth-century *palazzi* with frescoes to simple nineteenth-century farmhouses and modern five-star luxury hotels. In this chapter, we give you all the important tips you need to make your accommodation choices.

Choosing Accommodations in Italy: The Basic or the Best?

Hotels in Italy may not resemble hotels in the United States. American hotels often offer air-conditioned rooms boasting lots of space and huge bathrooms with tub/shower combos, especially hotels that have been recently built or aren't located in one of the older cities, such as New York and Boston. Likewise, the beds come in a variety of sizes from which you can choose, and there are a number of amenities you expect to find in even the most basic room.

Italy, however, is different. Because the buildings that house guest accommodations are sometimes many centuries old, there often isn't room to fit all the modern amenities. If you must have every amenity, you will have to opt for a super-deluxe hotel. Italy offers several types of hotels. *A hotel* is often a bigger building operated by a chain. An *albergo* is also a hotel (often a family business), but one that's usually not humongous. A *pensione* is below an albergo — more modest — and is usually family run and less expensive. (You won't find mints on your pillow or other such amenities.)

Getting amenities: What can you expect?

Not long ago, a friend asked us to help her choose a hotel in Florence and complained of the high prices. "We only need a private bathroom," she said. She then added with surprise, "Does this mean some hotels don't have private baths?" Well, the sooner you know the bad news, the better: In Italy, a private bathroom is an option and not a basic amenity. If you don't like having your bath outside your room (not necessarily shared) or sharing it with another room or two, you have to pay extra. We hasten to add that this rule is rapidly changing, however. Hotels are adding private baths wherever they can, but in some historic buildings, room isn't available to put in a big bathroom or even a tub. Therefore, it's not at all unusual for the shower to be a wall fixture over part of the tiled floor, with a curtain around it (not a door) and the drain below it. (Prepare yourself for wet floors.) Renovating buildings that are protected as historic sites is difficult.

If you absolutely must have a big comfortable room or a bathroom with all the amenities, prepare to fork over extra lire for a bigger, newer, more expensive hotel. Economizing is hard without compromise. Try to be as flexible as possible and you'll enjoy your trip more.

Throughout this guide we include recently built hotels that provide modern amenities (including bathrooms) at good prices. Sometimes the accommodations are a little outside the city center or not in fashionable neighborhoods, but you may not want old-world charm every night; sometimes reading in a decent-sized tub or crashing early and comfortably is more important.

Another difference in accommodations between the U.S. and Italy is beds. The majority of hotels in Italy have only one kind of bed — a large twin. In a double room, you usually find two separate twin beds. If you ask for a double bed, the host or hostess puts together the two twins into a *matrimoniale* (large bed), making the bed up tight together with sheets. You may think this practice is unusual, but you'll discover that it's not uncomfortable. On the good side, most hotels in Italy, and certainly all the ones in our listings, are proud of the quality of their bedding, providing good mattresses with a medium degree of firmness.

Besides the differences between beds and bathrooms, other hotel features in Italy also differ from U.S. hotel standards. For example, despite often sweltering summers, air-conditioning isn't common in Italy, and its installation is still in the early stages. Usually, only the more expensive hotels are air-conditioned, and some have air-conditioning only in specific rooms, for which you must pay more, of course. Regular TVs are standard, but these simple TVs don't offer English-language programs. For English-language programming, you need satellite TVs, which are available only in the higher-category hotels. All rooms usually have telephones. In fact, only in smaller villages or very simple accommodations will you not have a phone in your room.

Checking out rooms online

To look at Italian hotels online and even make reservations, try the following sites:

```
www.giroscopio.com
www.initaly.com
www.italyguide.com
www.italyhotel.com
www.italyhotelink.com
www.italyincoming.com
www.itwg.com
www.venere.it
www.wel.it
```

More and more, hotels are offering their own Web sites, and we note these sites in the hotel listings.

Revealing the Price of Comfort

Getting a room and paying the least possible for it is the name of the game. In the following section we go over the variety of prices, the price scale used in this book, and what you can expect in each category. We also tell you how to make a reservation and get the most for your money.

The **rack rate** is the maximum rate a hotel charges for a room. The rack rate is the rate you get if you walked in off the street and asked for a room for the night (which, a lot of the time in Italy, is exactly what you do). You sometimes see this rate printed on the fire/emergency exit diagrams posted on the back of guest room doors. We quote the rack rate for each of our hotel listings throughout this book.

Hotels are happy to charge you the rack rate, but you don't always have to pay it. Perhaps the best way to avoid paying the rack rate is surprisingly simple: Ask for a cheaper or discounted rate. You may be pleasantly surprised.

On the other hand, in Italy, the price offered for a room is probably close to the price that you have to pay. Italy is mobbed with tourists, and if you don't take the room at the price offered, there's a line of people behind you who will. You have a better chance of getting a deal or a discount in the off-season, which generally means winter, with the exception of Christmas, New Year's, and Carnevale (see Chapter 2 for a calendar of events). Starting with Easter, the travel season gets busy again. In Venice, an off-season doesn't exist anymore.

Knowing the price categories

In this book, we list the best hotels, offering cleanliness, comfort, and the most amenities at the best prices. Each listing includes a key indicating the cost of the hotel with a number of dollar signs that correspond to the following amounts:

$	Up to 150,000L ($80)
$$	150,000–250,000L ($80–$135)
$$$	250,000–350,000L ($135–$190)
$$$$	350,000–450,000L ($190–$245)
$$$$$	Above 450,000L ($245 and up)

A typical hotel with a $ is basic and cheap, with no private baths or air-conditioning. A $$ hotel likely has some rooms with private baths and some without; some may have air-conditioning as well. Consider that to have a more spacious bathroom with a modern-style shower, as well as the general certainty of air-conditioning, you need a $$$ hotel. Hotels in the $$$$ and $$$$$ ranges are luxury places, sometimes hotels of international chains; they offer basic amenities plus specials, ranging from antique furniture and minibars to luxurious bathrooms with deluxe toiletries and pools and gyms.

Room prices are subject to change without notice, so the rates that we quote in this book may differ from the actual rates that you receive when you make your reservations. And remember that the exchange rate varies from day to day, so the U.S. dollar amounts that we quote may be slightly different when you get to Italy.

Making reservations: How and how far ahead?

If you're traveling during high season (Easter to the end of summer, though August is slightly less crowded because of the heat), it's best to reserve your hotel rooms as soon as you've finalized your itinerary and know definitely where you're going. The longer you wait, the less choice you have. In the city and regional chapters in this book, we note any hotels that are so sought-after, you have to make reservations months in advance. Reserving your rooms as far as possible in advance for Venice and Florence is an especially good idea; Rome is much larger and thus offers more rooms, but if you have your eye on a particular place, jump on it as soon as you can.

However, making reservations can get complicated when you buy an e-fare or other last-minute bargain ticket. This cost-effective approach leaves you with relatively little time to get organized and make reservations, so you may end up booking into a large chain hotel that offers lots of rooms or a more expensive hotel with vacancies. (In our opinion, the higher cost for accommodations is worth it. If the money evens out, we'd rather spend more on the place we stay than on our plane ticket.)

In all but the smallest accommodations, the rate you pay for a room depends on many factors, not the least of which is how you make your reservation. With certain hotels, travel agents may be able to negotiate better prices than you can get on your own. (Hotels give the agents discounts in exchange for steering business their way.) And if you reserve your hotel rooms as part of a package, you can save a bundle (see "Acquiring accommodations as part of a package or tour," later in this chapter).

Room rates also change depending on occupancy rates. Obviously, you stand a better chance of receiving a discount if the hotel is almost empty than if it's booked solid. Resorts are most crowded on weekends, so they usually offer discounts for midweek stays. However, the reverse is true for business hotels in downtown locations. Make sure that you mention your membership in AAA, AARP, frequent-flyer programs, and any other corporate rewards programs when making your reservation. You never know when doing so may mean getting a few lire off your room rate.

However, to get these kinds of discount deals in Italy, you have to book a room at a large hotel or at chain hotels, such as Sofitel or Jolly, which are more expensive than cozy family-run places. But in the off-season, you may find a deal anywhere. The magic words at many hotels are, "Is that your best rate?" You can also ask if the hotel offers a smaller room or a room with a shared bath (if you're willing to go that route).

After you've reserved your rooms in whichever cities you plan to visit, remember to request faxed confirmations from the hotels, and then make sure that you bring these with you to Italy. If you check into a hotel that suddenly says they have no record of your reservation, you can produce your faxed confirmation and hopefully avoid an unpleasant scene.

If you don't reserve your accommodations before leaving home, remember that in the train station(s) of each major city you can find a hotel desk whose staff will call around town and find you a room if one is available. (In the high season, there's always the risk that rooms aren't available.) Sometimes this service is free and sometimes you have to pay a small fee. Getting a room at the last minute, however, ensures that you'll pay the full rack rate, because you're standing in the train station with your bags in dire need of a room.

But what if you find yourself stuck in a town with no vacant rooms and it's getting late? Don't panic. Italy isn't that big. Ask the hotel desk in the train station if there are good hotels outside of town or in the town next door. For example, some people stay in Padua because it's cheaper and close to Venice by train. If you have a car, you can alternatively stay at a hotel in the countryside between towns. But don't wait until dark before you start thinking about where you're spending the night.

Getting the best room

To increase your chances of getting a good room, ask for a *corner room*. They're usually larger, quieter, and closer to the elevator and have more windows and light than standard rooms. And they don't always cost more. Note that this applies only to chain and larger hotels; Italian hotels that occupy buildings 500 or more years old often have a weird assortment of rooms in all sorts of sizes. The prevalence of old buildings raises another issue: When you make your reservation, ask if the hotel is renovating. If it is, request a room away from the renovation work, and while you're at it, request a room that's already been renovated. If the hotel is on a busy street, you may want to request a room away from the street (you may even ask if there is a room that overlooks a garden or courtyard). Likewise, inquire about the location of restaurants, bars, and discos in the hotel, which can be noisy. In Italy, don't count on receiving a no-smoking room. If you aren't happy with your room when you arrive, talk to the front desk about moving to another one.

Acquiring accommodations as part of a package or tour

Joining a group tour or purchasing a package tour (see Chapter 6) almost ensures that you'll be staying in a fairly modern large hotel at a reasonable rate. That's because packagers don't make deals for five rooms here and three rooms there; they tend to use large hotels, who give them good deals for bringing in so many customers. However, always price out the offers to see if the deal that you're getting is really as good as it seems. The packager ought to provide you with some pretty detailed information about the hotel options that the package offers, and if the hotel is online, you may be able to see pictures of your room choices.

Even if you don't sign up with a tour or a package, you may want to investigate their offerings to see which hotels they feature. If you think a certain tour operator or packager is reputable, you can use its hotel selection as sort of a recommendation.

Picking Alternative Housing: From Roughing It in a Camp to Luxuriating at a Spa

Italy offers several other accommodation options, ranging from camping to staying at a luxurious spa. If you plan to stay in one place for a week or more, you can also rent an apartment. Another option is to stay at one of the many convents and other religious houses that rent out rooms (they allow couples — the rooms aren't monastic cells).

However, in this book we don't list religious houses that accept guests because they usually have curfews (10 to 11 p.m., sometimes even earlier), and we don't think that you want to deal with a curfew, especially if your trip is relatively short.

Likewise, campsites are usually located outside the cities and aren't convenient. If you have a car and camping gear, contact the **Federazione Italiana Campeggiatori,** Via Vittorio Emanuele 11, 50041 Calenzano (☎ **055-882-391;** Fax: 055-882-5918; Internet: www. federcampeggio.it), or ask at the accommodations desk in the city train stations for prices and directions to nearby campsites.

If you want to rent an apartment, consult an organization that specializes in such arrangements. Here are a few:

✔ **Hideaways International,** 767 Islington St., Portsmouth, NH 03801 (☎ **800-843-4433** or 603-430-4433; Internet: www.hideaways.com).

✔ **At Home Abroad,** 405 E. 56th St., Suite 6H, New York, NY 10022 (☎ **212-421-9165;** Fax: 212-752-1591; Internet: http://hometown. aol.com/athomabrod).

✔ **Rentals in Italy,** 1742 Calle Corva, Camarillo, CA 93010 (☎ **800-726-6702** or 805-987-5278; Fax: 805-482-7976; Internet: www. rentvillas.com).

To rent something really ritzy, like a palazzo or a castle, try **Abitare la Storia,** Località L'Amorosa, 53048 Sinalunga, Siena (☎ **0577-632-256;** Fax: 0577-632-160; Internet: www.arbitarelastoria.it).

Another option — a favorite with Italians — is *agriturismo:* staying on a working farm or former farm somewhere in the countryside. Agriturismo (agricultural tourism) is particularly popular in Tuscany. Contact **Italy Farm Holidays,** 547 Martling Ave., Tarrytown, NY 10591 (☎ **914- 631-7880;** Fax: 914-631-8831; Internet: www. italyfarmholidays. com), for information on some of the farms that offer this type of accommodation. You usually eat some or all of your meals on the farm, and *agriturismo* has a reputation for great food.

Chapter 9

Money Matters

In This Chapter

▶ Saying goodbye to the lira and hello to the euro

▶ Using cash, credit, or check

▶ Knowing what to do in case of loss or theft

*M*oney, money, money makes the world go 'round and makes the vacation machine run. Money is also cultural, and the more you know about Italian finances the better off you'll be — especially when you see that an ice cream cone costs 3,500L and a pair of shoes 179,000L! Get used to the Italian system and decide on which form of money you're going to rely.

Making Sense of the Lira and the Euro

Italy's currency is the *lira* (plural *lire* and abbreviated as "L" in this guide — as in 15,000L) — that is, until early 2002. That's when the new single European currency, the *euro* (€), will fully replace the lira and the currencies of the ten other European Union nations.

Making its last stand : The lira

Even though the lira will soon cease to exist, you need to know something about it if you travel to Italy before 2002. First of all, although the exchange rates vary daily, in this guide we use a *conversion rate* of 1,850L = $1 U.S., and we round off all dollar values above $5.

Paper bills come in 1,000L, 2,000L, 5,000L, 10,000L, 50,000L, and 100,000L denominations (at least, these are the ones you're likely to see). The higher the value, the larger the physical size of the bill. A 100,000L bill is bigger than a dollar bill, and if you have a bunch, you'll find it hard stuffing them in your wallet. In fact, you may want to make an Italian wallet one of your first purchases — a handsome and eminently useful gift to yourself. Remember that shops are always short of change, and breaking those large bills to buy a soft drink is sometimes difficult. Think ahead and try to have enough 10,000L bills with you as you travel in Italy.

Over the years, Italy has introduced some new coins, all still in circulation. The variety is a bit bewildering. The old 100L coin was steel colored and about as big as a quarter, while the new 100L coin is silvery and slightly smaller (alas, pay phones don't know how to digest the new coin yet). You can also find a tiny 100L coin that's a miniature of the steel kind (same engraving). Likewise, there's a new 1,000L coin that you'll frequently receive in your change — a large gaudy silver-and-brass affair worth half a dollar. Be careful with the 1,000L coin, however, because it's similar to the 500L coin but worth twice as much. The other coin values are 50L and 200L. There are three kinds of 50L coins — one steel colored, one more silvery and slightly smaller, and one about the size of a dime (a miniature of the steel type). The 200L coin is thin and brass colored.

One of the most useful coins is the 500L. Hoard them! This coin is very important — you need it to operate the automated light boxes in many churches (you put in the coins and a light illuminates a painting or other artwork for a few minutes) and to use rest rooms that charge. And because a local phone call costs 200L, having a few 200L coins in your pocket or purse is a good idea, too.

Before you get into a hassle with a cashier who you think has short-changed you, know that because the 10L and 5L coins are now almost out of circulation, prices like 2,560L and 10,390L get rounded off. No one has the necessary coins to make change that small, so 2,560L becomes 2,550L. Considering that the rounding up and rounding down equals out (eventually), the discrepancies are no big deal.

You can exchange money at the airport, at banks, and at exchange bureaus, which usually display multilingual signs ("Change/Cambio/Wechsel"). Rates may vary to some degree. For example, some bureaus advertise "no fee," but then give you a lower rate so you come out the same anyway. Arriving with a small supply of lire, at least enough to pay for a cab to your hotel and have a coffee, is a good idea. (Change about $100 — about 185,000L — in the United States before your trip for these kinds of small expenses.)

Once in Italy, the best way to exchange money is at an ATM. (Make sure your debit card bears Cirrus; the only two that work in Europe are Plus and Cirrus, but Plus is much more rare.) If you prefer to exchange cash or traveler's checks, the bureaux de change at airports usually offer the best rates; the bureaux de change outside the airport offer very variable rates.

Given that 1 lira is equal to a fraction of 1 cent, it's easy to think of lire as Monopoly money. Don't get into this mentality, and make sure you keep track of your money. After all, 1 cent is only 20 lire or so, but as you know, cents add up fast.

Introducing the euro

Since January 1, 1999, the exchange rates among the currencies of the 11 European Union countries participating in the changeover to the euro were fixed. This means the exchange rate between the lira and the euro is now set. Therefore, all bills and bank transactions already report the amount both in lire and in euros. Starting January 1, 2002, the actual euro coins and bills will be introduced. The old currencies will continue in use for about 6 months after January 1, 2002, depending on national policies. On July 1, 2002 at the latest, national currencies — including the lire — will be withdrawn. However, old bills will still be exchangeable for a certain time (probably six months) at national banks.

The transformation to euros will make things much easier for Americans, because 1 euro exchanges at about $1 (the exchange rate at press time is about $1 for 1.09 euros). Therefore, in 2002 you can say goodbye to complicated calculations of exchange rates!

For more information and pictures of the new currency, check online at the official site of the European Union: europa.eu.int/euro/.

Choosing Traveler's Checks, Credit Cards, ATMs, or Cash

In what form should you bring your money? Now that ATMs are international, this question is a matter of choice. Some people prefer the security of traveler's checks, though it means standing in line to get the checks at your bank and then standing in line while you're traveling in order to redeem them (and remember that you must show your passport every time you cash one). But, on the other hand, if you get your money out of ATMs in Italy you have to deal with nagging questions like these: What if my card is eaten by the machine? What if I lose my card? What if my card gets demagnetized? What if the network is down and I have 10 minutes to buy my ticket and get on the train?

Using ATMs

In major cities, ATMs are never far away, so you can walk around with 200,000L in your wallet (about $108) and you're set to eat and pay your museum admissions (but not your hotel bill). However, before going off on a driving tour of the countryside, such as in Sicily or Chianti, make sure that you have a good stock of cash in your wallet.

How much cash you carry around daily also depends on how much of your trip you've prepaid and whether the hotels and restaurants you choose accept credit cards. You should know most of this information by the time you reach Italy, so you can plan accordingly.

ATMs are linked to a network that most likely includes your bank at home — but not always. **Cirrus** (☎ **800-424-7787;** Internet: www. mastercard.com/atm/) is the most common international network in Italy. The **Plus** network (☎ **800-843-7587;** Internet: www.visa.com/ atms) also exists but is rarer. The **Banca Nazionale del Lavoro (BNL)** is one of the few banks that offers Plus in its ATMs. **NYCE** is completely unknown. Check the back of your ATM card to see which network your bank belongs to and ask your bank for a list of overseas ATMs.

Before departing for Italy, make sure that you check the daily withdrawal limit for your ATM card and ask whether you need a new PIN. (You need a four-digit PIN for Europe, so if you currently have a six-digit PIN, you must get a new one.)

Not all ATM keypads in Italy display letters as well as numbers. Some have only numbers. Therefore, if your PIN is "SPOT," you need to know how it translates into numbers (better if you do it in advance).

If you have linked checking and savings accounts and you're in the habit of moving relatively small amounts of money from savings to checking as you need it, beware. Italian ATMs won't show you the *transfer between accounts option,* and they won't allow you to withdraw money directly from your savings account. If your checking account runs dry, you must call or write your bank to move money from savings to checking. (We did so, and our bank charged us $30!) Lesson: Before leaving home, fill up your checking account with more money than you think you'll withdraw in Italy.

Remember: Many banks now charge a fee ranging from 50¢ to $3 whenever a non-account-holder uses their ATMs. Your own bank may also assess a fee for using an ATM that's not one of their branch locations. Therefore, in some cases you're charged twice for using your bankcard while you're on vacation. And although an ATM card can be an amazing convenience when traveling in another country, banks are also likely to slap you with a *foreign currency transaction fee* for making them do the lire-to-dollars conversion math. Again, check with your bank.

With many banks these extra fees don't apply, however, and you also get a better rate with your ATM card than what you'd get changing currency or traveler's checks. However, you need to check in advance with your own bank to avoid surprises. In any case, the convenience outweighs the cost.

Paying with plastic

Credit cards are invaluable when traveling. They provide a safe way to carry money as well as a convenient record of all of your travel expenses when you arrive home. You can also receive cash advances from your credit cards at any bank (though you begin paying interest on the advance the moment you receive the cash, you pay a huge interest rate, and you won't receive frequent-flyer miles on an airline credit card).

At most banks, you don't need to go to a teller; you can get a cash advance at an ATM if you know your PIN. (Make sure that it's four digits long, not six digits, or it won't work with European ATMs.) If you've forgotten your PIN or didn't know that you had one, call the phone number on the back of your credit card and ask the bank to send it to you. Receiving your PIN usually takes five to seven business days, though some banks will give you the number over the phone if you tell them your mother's maiden name or some other security clearance. Better yet, just call your bank before you go and set up a PIN for cash advances.

The two most commonly accepted credit cards in Italy are MasterCard and Visa, though American Express and Diners Club availability also pop up.

Taking traveler's checks

Traveler's checks are something of a relic from the days when people used to write personal checks all the time instead of going to ATMs. In those days, travelers weren't sure of finding a place that would cash a check for them on vacation. Because you can replace them if lost or stolen, traveler's checks were a sound alternative to stuffing your wallet with cash at the beginning of a trip.

These days, however, traveler's checks are less necessary because most cities have 24-hour ATMs. You can withdraw only as much cash as you need every couple of days, so you don't feel insecure carrying around a huge wad of cash.

If you prefer the security of traveler's checks, you can find them at almost any bank. **American Express** offers checks in denominations of $20, $50, $100, $500, and $1,000. You pay a service charge ranging from 1 to 4 percent, though AAA members can obtain checks without a fee at most AAA offices. You can also call ☎ **800-221-7282** to get American Express traveler's checks over the phone.

Visa (☎ **800-227-6811**) also offers traveler's checks, available at Citibank locations across the country and at several other banks. The service charge ranges between 1.5 and 2 percent; checks come in denominations of $50, $100, $500, and $1,000.

Likewise, **MasterCard** offers traveler's checks; call ☎ **800-223-9920** for a location near you.

What to Do if Your Wallet or Purse Gets Stolen

Being on vacation is a blissful time of distraction; unfortunately, this makes the day for those whose profession is pickpocketing. This is as true in Italy as in the United States or anywhere else. In this section we deal with the unpleasant occurrence of being robbed. Note, though, that in Italy violent crime is rare; most of the wallets are lost to pickpockets, not muggers.

To minimize the risk of having your wallet or purse stolen, follow these four basic rules:

- ✔ Keep your wallet or purse out of sight, but not in your back pocket or in your backpack.

- ✔ Don't leave your purse, briefcase, backpack, or coat unattended in any public place.

- ✔ Don't flash around your money or credit cards.

- ✔ When walking on the streets, keep your purse on the side away from traffic so a thief on a motorscooter can't speed by and grab it from you.

In the unlikely event that your wallet or purse is stolen, you need to cancel all your credit cards. It's probably wise to do this even before you call the police. (We provide telephone numbers for all the major credit cards later in this chapter.)

Almost every credit card company has an emergency toll-free number that you can call if your card is stolen. The issuing bank's toll-free number is usually on the back of the credit card, but that doesn't help much if your card is stolen. Therefore, write down the number before you leave home and keep it in a safe place, just in case. The company will cancel your card number immediately so someone else can't use it. Likewise, the company may wire you a cash advance off your credit card immediately so you have some money. And, in many places, credit card companies can get you an emergency replacement card in a day or two.

Here are the numbers to call if your credit card gets lost or stolen while you're in Italy:

- ✔ **MasterCard:** ☎ **800-870-866** in Italy or 800-307-7309 in the U.S.

- ✔ **Visa:** ☎ **800-819-014** in Italy or 800-847-2911 in the U.S.

- ✔ **American Express:** ☎ **06-72-282** in Italy (301-214-8228 collect from Italy) or 800-554-AMEX in the U.S.

- ✔ **Diners Club:** ☎ **702-797-5532** in Italy or 800-525-7376 in the U.S.

If you opt to carry traveler's checks, make sure that you keep a record of all their serial numbers (keep the record separate from the checks, of course), and write down the numbers of the checks as you cash them. If your checks are stolen, you must report exactly which checks are gone in order to get them replaced. The check issuer will tell you where to pick up the new checks.

Odds are that if your purse or wallet is gone, you've seen the last of it, and the police aren't likely to recover it for you. However, after you cancel your credit cards, you should call to inform the police. You may need the police report number for credit card or insurance purposes later.

A taxing matter: The IVA

The *value-added tax* in Italy is called the *IVA* and is a whopping 19 percent. However, the tax is always already included in prices, so you don't need to calculate it. What you can do at the airport, though, is get reimbursed for taxes paid on items that you're bringing out of the country that cost over 300,000L ($160). See the Appendix for the details.

Chapter 10

Tying Up Loose Ends: Last-Minute Details to Keep in Mind

• •

In This Chapter

▶ Getting your documents in order

▶ Purchasing insurance — or not

▶ Making reservations in advance

▶ Knowing what to pack

• •

*E*ven after you have a destination, an itinerary, and a ticket, you'll find that every trip has a lot of little last-minute details. Forgetting about some of them — like getting a passport — could put a real crimp in your plans to visit Italy. In this chapter we tell you what documents you'll need, whether or not to get traveler's insurance, how to make reservations, and even what to pack (and what not to pack).

Getting a Passport

Your passport, even more than your money, is the thing that you never want to lose, because it shows (and proves to authorities) that you're you. Safeguard your passport in an inconspicuous, inaccessible place like a money belt. If you don't already have a valid passport, you can download an application from the Internet sites that we list later in the chapter.

If you lose your passport, visit the nearest consulate of your native country as soon as possible for a replacement. Always carry a photocopy of your passport with you and keep it in a separate pocket or purse.

For residents of the United States

If you're applying for a first-time passport, you need to do so in person at one of the 13 passport offices throughout the United States; at a federal, state, or probate court; or at a major post office. You need to present a certified birth certificate as proof of citizenship, and bringing along your driver's license, state, or military ID, and social security card is wise. You also need two identical passport-sized photos (2 x 2 inches), which you can have taken at any photo shop. (You can't, however, use strip photos from a photo-vending machine.)

When you get your passport photos taken, ask for six to eight total. You need them to apply for an International Driving Permit and international student or teacher IDs which may entitle you to discounts at museums. Take the rest with you. You may need one for random reasons on the road and — heaven forbid — if you ever lose your passport, you can use them for a replacement request.

For people over age 15, a passport is valid for 10 years and costs $60 ($45 plus a $15 handling fee); for those 15 and under, it's valid for 5 years and costs $40. If you're over 15 and have a valid passport that was issued within the past 12 years, you can renew it by mail and bypass the $15 handling fee. Allow plenty of time before your trip to apply, however; processing normally takes three weeks but can take longer during busy periods (especially spring). You can take advantage of expedited service by paying an extra fee and presenting yourself in person to the passport office (usually only in major cities). For general information, call the **National Passport Agency** at ☎ **202-647-0518.** To find your regional passport office, call the **National Passport Information Center** at ☎ **900-225-5674** or check the Web at http://travel.state.gov.

For residents of Canada

You can pick up a passport application at one of the 28 regional passport offices or most travel agencies. The passport is valid for five years and costs $60. You may include children under 16 on a parent's passport, but children need their own to travel unaccompanied by a parent. You can pick up applications, which must be accompanied by two identical passport-sized photos (2 x 2 inches) and proof of Canadian citizenship, at travel agencies throughout Canada or from the central **Passport Office,** Department of Foreign Affairs and International Trade, Ottawa, Ontario K1A 0G3 (☎ **800-567-6868**). You can also find applications on the Web at www.dfait-maeci.gc.ca/passport. Processing takes five to ten days if you apply in person or about three weeks by mail.

For residents of the United Kingdom

Though members of the European Union, U.K. residents need a passport to visit Italy. To pick up an application for a regular 10-year passport (the

Visitor's Passport has been abolished), visit your nearest passport office, major post office, or travel agency. You can also contact the **London Passport Office** at ☎ **020-7271-3000** or search its Web site at www.open.gov.uk/ukpass/ukpass.htm. Passports are £28 for adults and £14.80 for children under 16.

For residents of Ireland

You can apply for a 10-year passport, which costs £45, at the **Passport Office,** Setanta Centre, Molesworth Street, Dublin 2 (☎ **01-671-1633**) or on the Web at www.irlgov.ie/iveagh/services/passports/ passportfacilities.htm. If you're under 18 or over 65, you must apply for a three-year passport that costs £10. You can also apply at 1A South Mall, Cork (☎ **021-272-525**), or over the counter at most main post offices.

For residents of Australia and New Zealand

In Australia, apply at your local post office or passport office or check out the government Web site at www.dfat.gov.au/passports/. Passports for adults are A$128 and A$64 for those under 18.

In New Zealand, you can pick up a passport application at any travel agency or Link Centre. For more info, contact the **Passport Office,** P.O. Box 805, Wellington (☎ **0800-225-050**). Passports for adults are NZ$80 and NZ$40 for people under 16.

Buying Travel and Medical Insurance

There are three kinds of travel insurance: **trip-cancellation insurance, medical insurance,** and **lost luggage insurance.** Trip-cancellation insurance is a good idea if you've signed up for an escorted tour and paid a large portion of your vacation expenses up front. (For information on escorted tours, see Chapter 6.) But medical insurance and lost-luggage insurance don't make sense for most travelers. Your existing health insurance should cover you if you get sick while on vacation (though if you belong to an HMO, check to see whether you're fully covered while in Italy), and your homeowner's or renter's insurance should cover stolen luggage if you have off-premises theft coverage.

Check your existing insurance policies before you buy any additional coverage. If they lose your luggage, airlines are responsible for reimbursement in the amount of $1,250 on domestic flights and $635 per bag (maximum of two bags) on international flights. If you plan to carry anything more valuable than that, keep it in your carry-on bag.

Some credit cards (American Express and some gold and platinum Visa and MasterCards, for example) offer automatic flight insurance against death or dismemberment in case of an airplane crash. If you feel that you need more insurance, try one of the following companies:

✔ **Access America,** 6600 W. Broad St., Richmond, VA 23230 (☎ 800-284-8300).

✔ **Mutual of Omaha,** Mutual of Omaha Plaza, Omaha, NE 68175 (☎ 800-228-9792).

✔ **Travel Guard International,** 1145 Clark St., Stevens Point, WI 54481 (☎ 800-826-1300; Internet: www.travel-guard.com).

✔ **Travel Insured International, Inc.,** P.O. Box 280568, East Hartford, CT 06128 (☎ 800-243-3174; Internet: www.travelinsured.com).

Don't pay for more insurance than you need, however. For example, if you need only trip-cancellation insurance, don't buy coverage for lost or stolen property. Trip-cancellation insurance costs about 6 to 8 percent of the total value of your vacation.

Getting Sick Away from Home: What to Do

Getting sick on vacation is no fun, and finding a doctor and obtaining medication can be difficult. But there are precautions that you can take.

A good idea is to bring all of your medications with you, as well as prescriptions for more (in generic — not brand name — form) if you worry that you'll run out. If you have health insurance, make sure that you carry your ID card in your wallet.

If you have a chronic illness, talk to your doctor before taking your trip. For conditions such as epilepsy, diabetes, or a heart condition, wear a Medic Alert Identification Tag, which immediately alerts any doctor to your condition and gives him or her access to your medical records through Medic Alert's 24-hour hot line. A worldwide toll-free emergency response number is on the tag, so if you become ill in Italy, you know exactly whom to call. Membership is $35, plus a $15 annual fee. Contact the **Medic Alert Foundation,** P.O. Box 1009, Turlock, CA 95381-1009 (☎ 800-825-3785; Internet: www.medicalert.org). If getting sick away from home worries you, buy medical insurance (see the section on travel insurance, earlier in this chapter).

If you do get sick, ask the concierge at your hotel to recommend a local doctor — even his or her own doctor if necessary. If you can't locate a doctor, try contacting your embassy or consulate or dial ☎ 113 for the police or 112 for the *carabinieri* (other police corps). If your situation is life-threatening, go to the emergency or accident department at the local hospital.

Under the Italian national health care system, you're eligible only for free *emergency* care. If you're admitted to a hospital as an in patient, even from an accident and an emergency department, you're required to pay (unless you're a resident of the European Economic Area). You're also required to pay for follow-up care. For the names, addresses, and phone numbers of hospitals offering 24-hour emergency care, see the "Fast Facts" section at the end of each destination chapter.

If you do end up paying for health care, especially if you're admitted to a hospital for any reason, most health insurance plans and HMOs will cover at least part of the out-of-country hospital visits and procedures. Be prepared to pay the bills up front at the time of care, however. You'll get a refund after you've returned to your country and filed all the paperwork.

Making Reservations and Getting Tickets in Advance for Events and Sightseeing

To make your trip go a bit smoother, there are a few museums that you'll want to reserve tickets for in advance — as far in advance as possible. If you call ☎ **055-294-883,** you can reserve tickets for several attractions in Florence. The primary sight for which you'll want to reserve is the **Galleria degli Uffizi** (if you don't reserve tickets you could have at least a three-hour wait in line), followed by the **Galleria dell'Accademia,** which houses Michaelangelo's *David.* (You can't reserve your tickets online.) Rome's **Galleria Borghese** accepts a restricted number of visitors at a time, so we advise you to call ☎ **06-32810** to make reservations there as well. When you reserve tickets at these museums, you're given a date and a time for your visit, so you have to arrange your sightseeing schedule around those reservations.

Musical and theatrical events for which we advise you to get advance tickets include the following:

- ✔ **Umbria Jazz Festival.** ☎ **075-573-2432;** Fax: 075-572-2656; Internet: www.umbriajazz.com.

- ✔ **Spoleto Festival.** ☎ **06-321-0288** or 0743-44-325; Fax: 06-320-0747 or 0743-40-696; Internet: www.spoletofestival.net.

- ✔ **Operas performed in Verona's Anfiteatro Romano.** ☎ **045-800-5151;** Internet: www.arena.it. In the U.S., contact the Global Tickets agency, ☎ **800-223-6108** or 914-328-2150.

- ✔ **The alternating performances of Greek tragedies at Selinunte and Syracuse in Sicily.** Instituto Nazionale per il Dramma Antico, ☎ **0931-67-415** or toll-free within Italy 1478-82211.

- ✔ **The performances at Taormina.** Taormina Arte, ☎ **0942-21142**.
- ✔ **The Maggio Musicale concert and dance series in Florence.** ☎ **055-211-158**.

In order to get more information about happenings during the time of your visit, check the Web sites that we list in the Calendar of Events (see Chapter 2) and in the Appendix. Individual municipalities also maintain their own sites. Here are a few sites to check out:

- ✔ www.comune.palermo.it
- ✔ www.comune.venezia.it
- ✔ www.comune.firenze.it
- ✔ www.comune.roma.it

Other useful online sources are the Italian Tourist Web Guide (www. itwg.com), Welcome to Italy (www.wel.it), and ABC's of Italy (www. italiaabc.com). Good sites for Florence include www.tiac.net/ users/pendini/index.html and www.arca.net/florence.htm; for information on Venice, check out www.doge.it and www.iuave. it/~juli/ventoday.htm.

Packing It Up and Taking It on the Road

Usually when packing, you lay out a big pile of stuff on your bed, start to put everything in your bag, and find out that half the items don't fit. You can either get a bigger bag, take two bags, or leave half the stuff at home. We think that the last option is by far the best. We don't say this because the airlines won't let you take all those bags — they will, for a price — but because you don't want to get a hernia from lugging around all that stuff.

Italy is a crowded country where space is always at a premium. Buses and trains are crowded — lots of people will be competing for the luggage bins — so you won't be very popular with your four duffle bags. And if you rent a car, it'll probably be quite compact — gas is horrendously expensive, so cars are light, small, and efficient. (You won't have much room for luggage in a car either.)

Taking what you need

Here are some key items that are essential for your trip to Italy:

- ✔ Comfortable walking shoes
- ✔ Versatile sweater and/or jacket
- ✔ Hat or sun visor

✔ Sunscreen (The Italian sun is cruel.)

✔ Sunglasses (Or you can treat yourself to an Italian pair when you arrive.)

✔ All daily prescription medications (Pack these in your carry-on bag so you have them if the airline loses your luggage.)

✔ Over-the-counter medications and supplements (Vitamins and health preparations are often more expensive in Italy.)

✔ Small binoculars or opera glasses (Use these to get a closer look at faraway frescoes, particularly important in the Sistine Chapel.)

✔ Pocket knife with corkscrew and bottle opener (These come in handy for those great picnics among Roman ruins.)

When packing, make sure that you consider your shopping goals: If you're planning to buy a lot of souvenirs and some clothes, you may want to bring with you only the bare essentials and leave your bag half empty so you can fill it up along the way. (See "Choosing what not to bring," later in this chapter.)

Bringing the right luggage

Bringing the right kind of luggage is as important as what you pack. When choosing your suitcase, think about the kind of traveling you'll do. Here are some points to keep in mind:

✔ **Bags with wheels:** If you'll be walking a lot with luggage over hard floors or level ground, this type of luggage can save you from a lot of heavy lifting.

✔ **Garment bags:** Because much of Italy consists of uneven roads and many stairs, a foldover garment bag may work well for you. They're usually fairly light, you can carry them over your shoulder, and they keep dressy clothes wrinkle-free.

✔ **Hard-sided luggage:** This type of luggage protects breakable items but can weigh a lot. Leave this type of luggage at home and place any breakable items in a carry-on bag.

✔ **Soft-sided luggage:** These bags are a lot lighter to carry than their hard-sided counterparts and you can easily pack them into the small trunks of Italian cars.

When using public transportation, remember that overhead racks won't accommodate huge luggage (in trains there's limited room near the doors for oversized bags). Lock your suitcase with a small padlock (available at most luggage stores if your bag doesn't already have one) and put an ID tag on the outside.

Heeding airline regulations

You're allowed two pieces of carry-on luggage on an airplane, both of which must fit in the overhead compartment or the seat in front of you.

Your carry-on luggage can contain things such as a book, any break-able items that you don't want in your suitcase, all prescription med-ications, a personal headphone stereo, a snack in case you don't like the airline food, any vital documents you don't want to lose in your lug-gage (like your return tickets, passport, wallet, and so on), and some empty space for the sweater or jacket that you wouldn't want to wear while you're waiting for your luggage in an overheated terminal.

Airlines have started cracking down on abuse of carry-on limitations (it was about time!). How many times have you been stuck getting to your seat by someone dragging something they can't handle or lift? (We've heard of someone trying to carry on a surfboard.) Wrestling with your carry-on luggage makes planes late leaving the gate. Your carry-on luggage is now checked for size *and* weight — if it's too heavy, you have to check it as luggage. The limit varies among the airlines, but it hovers around 5 kilos (12 pounds).

Choosing what not to bring

Because Italy is famous for fashion, an obvious tip is not to bring any-thing you intend to buy while you're on your trip, such as a new pair of shoes, an Armani jacket, or even sunglasses. Alternatively, you can bring your worst accessories and discard them after you make your purchase.

You probably won't need heavy clothing unless you're going to Northern Italy in winter. (In the warm months, the south is gloriously sunny most of the time.) Being too hot is more of a concern than get-ting too cold, and unless you're attending a board meeting or wedding or dining at one of the city's finest restaurants, you probably won't need a suit or a fancy dress.

Likewise, we recommend that you leave all of your electronic gadgetry at home. But if you really, really need to bring those appliances, read "Converting Electricity: Don't Get Shocked," later in this chapter.

Dressing Like the Locals

Italians dress more formally than Americans. No matter what your age, you'll stand out if you spend your vacation wearing a sweat suit. (We know one Italian man who puts on a sports coat to go for a walk around the block.) Leave the active wear at home. You can get more use out of a pair of jeans or khakis, a shirt with a collar, and a comfort-able cotton sweater.

Italians don't wear sneakers very much either; sneakers can get very hot. An option that we like for summer is a pair of comfortable walking sandals — they keep your feet cooler, you don't need socks, and (per-haps best of all) they pack flat. At the other end is your headgear. In the United States, people accept Oscar awards wearing baseball caps, but that goofy-cool look in Italy is just goofy. So you may want to bring something a bit more upscale to keep the sun off your head — or buy a hat in Italy, home of the famous Borsalino hats and beautiful straw hats.

Are your kids in the habit of wearing enormously baggy hip-hop clothes? If so, encourage them to keep such attire at home. Some young Italians have adopted this look, but it isn't popular. Italians of all ages like to look trim and not sloppy, and Italian kids ride *motorinis* (motorbikes) — which voluminous hip-hop clothes could make impossible or even dangerous.

Churches in Italy have a strict dress code — no bare shoulders and no bare legs (this goes for men as well as women, by the way). This fact annoys some people, but when was the last time you saw someone wearing a tank top in your church, synagogue, or mosque? Therefore, if you're visiting St. Peter's or St. Mark's or other churches, bring along something to throw over your shoulders (it's also pretty cold inside some of the churches, which have walls several feet thick).

Cultural variances among regions can also dictate an appropriate dress code. The farther south you go, the more traditional people are, especially out in the country. You'll see that women and men tend to cover themselves more. You can either try to look like a local or just do whatever you want; however, if you're a woman, you may risk being annoyed by young men (see Chapter 5 for tips for women travelers).

Converting Electricity: Don't Get Shocked

American current runs 110V, 60 cycles. The standard voltage throughout Italy is 220V AC, from 42 to 50 cycles. Translation: You can't plug an American appliance into an Italian outlet without frying your appliance and/or blowing a fuse. You need a current converter or transformer to bring the voltage down and the cycles up. In Italy, the prongs of plugs are round, so you also need a plug adapter. Plug adapters and converters are available at most travel, luggage, electronics, and hardware stores. (You may find a plug adapter that also doubles as a current converter.)

Travel-sized versions of hair dryers, irons, shavers, and so on are dual voltage, which means that they have built-in converters (usually you have to turn a switch to go back and forth). Likewise, most contemporary laptop computers automatically sense the current and adapt accordingly. (Check the manual, bottom of the machine, or manufacturer first to make sure that you don't burn out your computer.)

Sizing Things Up: Size Conversions

Face it — you're probably going to be tempted to buy some clothes while in Italy. Shopping for clothes in Italy is a bit easier, now that S, M, and L are used in some cases. Hats and shirt collars, however, are measured in centimeters. To find your correct size, multiply the number of inches you require by 1.34.

Consider that Italians are often smaller — and thinner — than Americans. Many women's clothes come in a maximum size of 48 (see Table 10-1), so you have to go to specialty stores to find a larger size, with a very marked change in style. For men, the advantage is that pants are sold without a hem, so you can have them custom tailored for your height.

Here's a size conversion chart to help you with your purchases. However, remember that sizes aren't necessarily standardized among different makers, and that trying clothes on before you buy is always best, especially shoes.

Table 10-1	Size Conversion Chart							
Women's Clothes								
Italy	38	40	42	44	46	48	50	52
U.S.	2	4	6	8	10	12	14	16
Men's Clothes								
Italy	46	48	50	52	54	56	58	60
U.S.	36	38	40	42	44	46	48	50
Women's Shoes								
Italy	35	36	37	38	39	40	41	
U.S.	4	5	6	7	8	9	10	
Men's Shoes								
Italy	39	40	41	42	43	44	45	
U.S.	8½	9	9½	10	10½	11	11½	

Customs Regulations: What Can You Bring Home?

Another part of packing is packing to return home. Buying something in Italy, bringing it back on the plane, and then having it confiscated would really be a drag. Therefore, you need to know as much as you can about customs regulations.

The "no agricultural products" policy is strictly enforced in the United States. That means *absolutely no meat*: Don't buy prosciutto, sausage, or any other meat product that you don't plan to eat before you return. In addition, the threat from agricultural pests means that vegetables and plants — including dried flowers — aren't allowed into the States. You can, however, bring back some products in vacuum-packed sealed plastic bags or in cans and jars — like parmesan cheese (*parmigiano reggiano*). In general, whatever you can buy in a duty-free shop at the airport is legal and anything else is iffy.

For residents of the United States

Returning U.S. citizens who've been away for 48 hours or more are allowed to bring back, once every 30 days, $400 worth of merchandise duty-free, including all gifts. If you expect to go over this limit, think about mailing some of your goodies back. You can send yourself $200 worth of stuff per day and $100 worth of gifts to others — alcohol and tobacco excluded. On the plane, you can bring with you 1 liter of alcohol and 200 cigarettes or 100 cigars. The $400 ceiling doesn't apply to artwork or antiques (antiques must be 100 years old or more), for which you have to pay duty. You're charged a flat rate of 10 percent duty on the next $1,000 worth of purchases. Make sure that you have your receipts handy. On gifts, the duty-free limit is $100. For more information, contact the **U.S. Customs Service,** 1301 Constitution Ave. (P.O. Box 7407), Washington, DC 20044 (☎ **202-927-6724**) and request the free pamphlet "Know Before You Go." You can also find the pamphlet on the Web at www.customs.ustreas.gov/travel/kbygo.htm.

For residents of Canada

If you're a Canadian citizen, write for the booklet "I Declare," issued by **Revenue Canada,** 2265 St. Laurent Blvd., Ottawa K1G 4KE (☎ **613-993-0534**). Canada allows its citizens a $500 exemption, and you can bring back duty-free 200 cigarettes, 2.2 pounds of tobacco, 40 imperial ounces of liquor, and 50 cigars. In addition, you can also mail gifts to Canada from abroad at the rate of Can$60 per day, provided they're unsolicited and don't contain alcohol or tobacco (write on the package "Unsolicited Gift, Under $60 Value"). Declare all valuables on the Y-38 form before departure from Canada, including the serial numbers of valuables that you already own, such as expensive foreign cameras. *Note:* You can use the $500 exemption only once a year and only after an absence of seven days.

For residents of the United Kingdom

U.K. citizens returning from a European Union country go through a separate Customs Exit (called the "Blue Exit"). In essence, there's no limit on what you can bring back from an EU country, as long as the items are for personal use (this includes gifts) and you've already paid the necessary duty and tax. However, customs law sets guidance levels. If you bring in more than these levels, you may be asked to prove that the goods you're bringing back are for your own use. Guidance levels on goods bought in the EU for your own use are 800 cigarettes, 200 cigars, 1kg of smoking tobacco, 10 liters of spirits, 90 liters of wine (of this not more than 60 liters can be sparkling wine), and 110 liters of beer. For more information, contact **HM Customs & Excise,** Passenger Enquiry Point, 2nd Floor Wayfarer House, Great

South West Road, Feltham, Middlesex, TW14 8NP (☎ **0181-910-3744;** from outside the U.K., call 44-181-910-3744), or visit the Web at www. open.gov.uk.

For residents of Australia

The duty-free allowance for Australian citizens is A$400 or, for those under 18, A$200. Mark personal property that you mail back home "Australian Goods Returned" to avoid payment of duty. Upon returning to Australia, citizens can bring in 250 cigarettes or 250 grams of loose tobacco, and 1,125 ml of alcohol. If you're returning with valuable goods that you already own, such as foreign-made cameras, file form B263. A helpful brochure, available from Australian consulates or Customs offices, is "Know Before You Go." For more information, contact **Australian Customs Services,** GPO Box 8, Sydney NSW 2001 (☎ **02- 9213-2000**).

For residents of New Zealand

The duty-free allowance for New Zealand citizens is NZ$700. Citizens over 17 can bring in 200 cigarettes or 50 cigars or 250 grams of tobacco (or a mix of all three if their combined weight doesn't exceed 250 grams), plus 4.5 liters of wine and beer, or 1.125 liters of liquor. New Zealand currency doesn't carry import or export restrictions. Fill out a certificate of export, listing the valuables you're taking out of the country; that way, you can bring them back without paying duty. Most questions are answered in a free pamphlet available at New Zealand consulates and Customs offices: "New Zealand Customs Guide for Travellers," Notice no. 4. For more information, contact **New Zealand Customs,** 50 Anzac Ave., P.O. Box 29, Auckland (☎ **09-359-6655**).

Part III
The Eternal City: Rome

The 5th Wave   By Rich Tennant

"It says, children are forbidden from running, touching objects, or appearing bored during the tour."

In this part . . .

Yes, we've devoted a whole part to Rome. Rome is not only Italy's largest city but also the hub from which you'll probably do most of your traveling. The treasures of Roma (Rome) stretch from pre-Republic ruins to Bernini's baroque marvels to the stylish, convulsive Rome depicted by Fellini in his famous movies. Though modern, today's sprawling city still breathes at the rythm of its history and is set in a beautiful countryside, where affluent Romans have been building palaces and villas since . . . well, the Romans.

Chapter 11 provides everything you need to know to get to Rome, get oriented in the city, find a comfortable place to stay, and order a delicious Italian meal. Included are rundowns of the best hotels and the best restaurants, plus some runner-up choices. In Chapter 12, we describe the major sites and activities (not only how to see the Colosseum and the Vatican Museums but also where to shop and where to go for fun after dark). Chapter 13 takes you into Rome's outskirts, the renowned Castelli Romani — the towns that dot the hills surrounding the city — where Romans go for a meal, a walk, and magnificent views.

Chapter 11

Settling into Rome

The seven hills of **Roma (Rome)** and the surrounding area have been continuously inhabited for the past 3,000 years or so. The Roman Empire, centered in the Eternal City, was not the world's first great empire but it was the longest lasting, and by borrowing liberally from its subject states — particularly Greece — it created the foundation for a cosmopolitan European culture.

What does this history mean for you? It means that nowhere else will you find such a density of amazing things to see. Rome has 913 churches, many packed with great art. In fact, if you visited all the museums and monuments, you'd return pale as a ghost despite the glorious sunshine. You have to budget your time well if you don't want to be trapped indoors and miss a great deal of the city's true life (not to mention the many sights in the environs of Rome). The renovations and refurbishings for Papal Jubilee 2000 made Rome even more special, which means you'll have to compete with many fellow visitors. But don't despair: If you can get a room, a place to eat, and space on the sidewalk, you can have the time of your life — but watch out for that traffic!

Getting There

Although Italy is steeped in history, it's also a contemporary country, boasting all the conveniences of modern transportation. Getting to Rome isn't difficult, and you can make your way there in numerous ways.

By air

Italy has two international ports of entry by air: Rome and Milan. Rome has two airports: Fiumicino and the smaller Ciampino.

Arriving at Fiumicino/Leonardo da Vinci

Rome's international airport is officially called **Leonardo da Vinci** (☎ **06-659-51** or 06-6595-3640), though it's better known as **Fiumicino,** after the nearby town. This airport is also the point of departure for most flights to other Italian cities. Alitalia, Italy's national airline, offers daily flights from Rome to all major Italian towns as well as to major European and world cities. You can reach Alitalia at ☎ **1478-65-643** or 06-65643; Internet: www.alitalia.com.

Despite being Italy's main airport, Fiumicino is relatively small and well organized. Like many major airports, however, it's experiencing a growth spurt, with a new terminal serviced by a monorail. The construction should make it more convenient and less overcrowded than in the past. While at the airport, you may also note the high level of security: Don't be concerned if you see police officers with submachine guns walking around — it's routine.

The heightened security at Fiumicino hasn't yet been able to completely eradicate theft. Therefore, watch over your belongings like a hawk and don't leave anything precious in your check-in luggage.

Navigating your way through passport control and customs

After your plane lands, you arrive at passport control. As in other European cities, there are two passport control lines — one for European Union citizens and one for non-EU citizens. After the passport check, you proceed to the baggage claim area and then through customs. Items for personal use enter duty-free. When you leave customs, you're in the main concourse, where information booths and rental-car desks are located. Taxis are right outside, and there's also van service and the train (the least expensive option).

It's rare not to find a long waiting line in front of the only two ATMs located inside the airport. The only currency-exchange desk also gets very crowded. If you don't like standing in line after a long trip, you may want to arrive with some Italian lire in your pockets to get you to your hotel; you can change more money later in the city. If you aren't planning to use your credit/debit cards, though, you may want to stand patiently in line for the exchange office — its rates are usually the best in town.

On your way out to ground transportation, you'll also find a very good **tourist information desk** (☎ **06-6595-4471** or 06-6595-6074), with one end that answers questions about Rome and the other that answers questions about all of Italy. The tourist desk is also a good place to pick up maps and other details. Nearby is a **help desk** for last-minute hotel reservations — the service, however, doesn't cover all the hotels in town.

At the desk of the well-organized **Opera Romana Pellegrinaggi,** the association for the reception of religious pilgrims, you can purchase the 65,000L ($35) **Carta del Pellegrino,** a special card for religious pilgrims. It entitles you to free rides on public transport for three days, as well as a discount on phone calls worth 20,000L ($11) and other benefits. For more information, check out www.sac.jubil2000.org, the site of the Servizio Accoglienza Centrale (SAC, Piazza San Marcello 4, Roma 00187; ☎ **06-696-221;** Fax: 06-6962-2388), the pilgrim's reception organization for Papal Jubilee 2000. After the Jubilee, pilgrims can receive assistance from **Peregrinatio Ad Petri Sedem** (Piazza Pio XII, 4 Vaticano; ☎ **06-6988-4896;** Fax: 06-6988-5617; E-mail: `peregrinatio@jubilee-2000.va`).

Getting from the airport to your hotel

Fiumicino lies about 30 km (18 miles) from Rome and is well connected by highway, train, shuttle train, and bus.

The easiest way to get to your hotel, of course, is taking a **taxi.** Remember, though, that taxis are expensive in Rome and the airport is quite far from the center of town — expect to pay about 80,000L ($43) for a ride. Be aware of the traffic situation in Rome as well: Your taxi ride will take about an hour at good times, and at rush hour, you risk being in the car for up to two hours (paying all the while), compared with half an hour if you take the train. Also note that taxis charge a per-bag luggage fee of about 2,000L (about $1.10) for everything that goes in the trunk, so keep your purse or any small bags with you inside the car.

A couple of companies offer minivan service to and from most hotels. From the airport to town, you don't need a reservation; just walk to the desk near the tourist information area. The **CON.CO.RA. Autonoleggio** (☎ **06-6595-3934;** Fax: 06-6595-3932) will take you from the airport to your hotel for a flat rate of about 20,000L (about $11) per person, plus a surcharge for luggage. The company offers discounts on return trips.

Taking the local **commuter train,** which leaves every half hour from the train terminal on the second floor of the air terminal, is the fastest and cheapest way to get into Rome. A one-way ticket costs 8,000L ($4.30); you can also buy the 8,500L ($4.60) *BIRG* ticket, which includes unlimited rides on the metro (subway) and bus once you get in Rome and is valid for 24 hours from the time of purchase. Your choice depends on whether you're going to crash at your hotel and recover from jet lag or get right out and hit the sights. You can buy both types of tickets in the train terminal at the ticket booth or at the tobacconist's shop. The train stops at four stations in Rome: Roma Trastevere, Roma Tuscolana, Roma Ostiense, and Roma Tiburtina, in that order.

Roma Ostiense — the train station on the south side of Rome near the Aventino and not far from the Colosseum — is probably the best station to get off if your hotel is near San Pietro (St. Peter's), Cola di Rienzo, or Campo de' Fiori and the Pantheon. The train then continues to Roma Tiburtina, the train station to the northeast of Rome. This station is a good idea if your hotel is in the Porta Pia or Villa Borghese area.

From each of these train stations, you can take a taxi to your hotel (the best idea). You can also get on the metro at Ostiense and Tiburtina— but only if you don't have too much luggage, because you have to go up and down stairs and do some walking to reach the subway station. The bus is another, though unlikely, option (you don't want to make your first bus trip with a lot of baggage).

Your last option is taking the **shuttle train** from Fiumicino's train terminal heading for Rome's central rail station, *Stazione Termini* (see "By
train," later in this chapter). The shuttle costs more (15,000L/$8 at the
ticket booth) than the local train, because it doesn't make intermediate
stops, though it takes the same amount of time. And, there are fewer
shuttles than there are regular trains. The advantage of arriving at
Termini — you're in the center of town in a well-equipped modern
terminal — is tempered by the fact that the station is always crowded
and traffic is always swirling around it. From Termini, you can take the
metro or a bus or catch a taxi.

Arriving at Ciampino

A number of international charter flights arrive at **Ciampino** (☎ **06-
794-941**), a small airport 16 km (10 miles) southeast of Rome. This airport is far from being a large air terminal, and the reception structures
in Ciampino are very limited. It's almost like an American civil aviation
airport.

The easiest way to get to town from Ciampino is taking a **taxi.** Expect to
pay about 60,000L ($32), and be aware that traffic to the center of town
can be quite horrible: Your ride will take 45 minutes to over an hour. You
can also take the **bus** (a Cotral blue bus) to *Ciampino Stazione* (train station of Ciampino), and from there you take a 10-minute train ride to
Stazione Termini (see "By train," later in this chapter). The bus costs
about 2,000L ($1.10) and so does the train. This method is definitely the
fastest. From Termini, you can then take a taxi to your final destination.

Another option is continuing on the bus to the Anagnina stop, where you
can take the metro. Anagnina is the last stop on subway line A, or metro
A. The trip is a little longer, but you may prefer this route if you want to
stop along subway line A and you don't have much luggage.

By car

All roads lead to Rome, said the Romans, and that statement is still
true. However, there are now many more roads, and getting confused
is easy. Rome is the central hub for most of the highways in Italy. The
major highway is the **Autostrada del Sole (A1)** from Milan to Naples,
passing through Florence and Rome. This straight shot, however,
shouldn't encourage you to enter Rome by car.

Rome is large, with an extremely complicated layout. Many Italians
dread using their cars in town: the constant traffic, the aggressive driving style (for Romans it's survival, because they'd never get home otherwise), the impossibility of parking even when you've figured out how
to get where you want to go, and so on. Our warmest recommendation
is this: Don't drive in Rome. If you're arriving in Rome by car, dump it
in a parking lot for the length of your stay (this option is expensive,
however — parking costs a minimum of 2,000L/about $1.08 per hour).
Another option is arranging your trip so you rent your car at the end of
your visit to Rome or return it at the beginning when you arrive.

If you insist on driving, know that Rome is surrounded by a highway
ring called the **Gran Raccordo Anulare,** also known as just the

Raccordo or the **G.R.A.** All the highways empty onto the G.R.A., while the many *consular roads* (state roads built atop ancient Roman roads) cross over it and lead into town. If you arrive by highway, you must get onto the G.R.A. and then exit at the consular road that you need to arrive at your destination (for example, exit at the Aurelia if you're going to San Pietro or the Nomentana if you're going to Via Veneto). The signs on the G.R.A. don't mention all the exits but just the few upcoming exits. Therefore, you have to know which exit comes next when you enter the G.R.A. in order to enter the G.R.A. going the right direction. Heading out of town is much easier, however, so it's a good idea to rent a car from one of the many rental points in Rome at the end of your visit and drive away as directly as you can.

By train

If you're coming from another Italian or European destination, your train will likely arrive at Rome's central rail station: **Stazione Termini** (call ☎ **06-4730-6559** or 1478-880-881 for train info). The large square in front of the station is Piazza dei Cinquecento, Rome's largest city bus hub. Termini is the crossing point of the two Roman subway lines (see "Getting Around Roma," later in this chapter). Italy's train service is excellent, cheap, and reliable. Trains arrive and depart from Rome for every destination every few minutes. Termini is a very large and busy station and is spanking new after a renovation that lasted several years.

Arriving from the tracks at the Stazione Termini, you find that the main exit is right in front of you, after the merchant gallery; there are also exits on the right and left at either end of the merchant gallery, but they're of use only if you're going to the side streets around the station. All ground transportation is on Piazza dei Cinquecento.

The head of the taxi line is outside the station near the metro sign on the right. For some mysterious reason, the line forms at the end farthest from the exit of the train station, so you have to walk a bit. Take your cab from the line of taxis (taxis are white, with a checkered line on the side in yellow and black).

 Although they've basically disappeared, a few pirate cabbies hang around the station and will approach you on your walk from the train to the taxi line. Reject their offers, be firm, and get in line for a regulation ride.

Orienting Yourself in Roma

Rome spreads out like a starfish. From the central body — made up of the ancient Roman center, the medieval town, and Renaissance expansion — spring arms of newer urban development, which have logically formed along the consular roads (the roads built by the ancient Roman Consuls). The central body corresponds to Rome's medieval perimeter — marked by the city walls — and is still the heart of Rome. Consider that Rome didn't spread beyond its walls until the end of the nineteenth century. The central body is the part that you'll visit most.

Rome Orientation

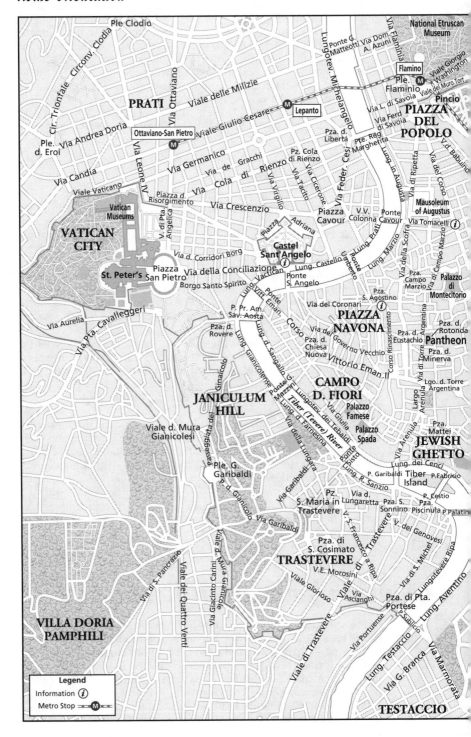

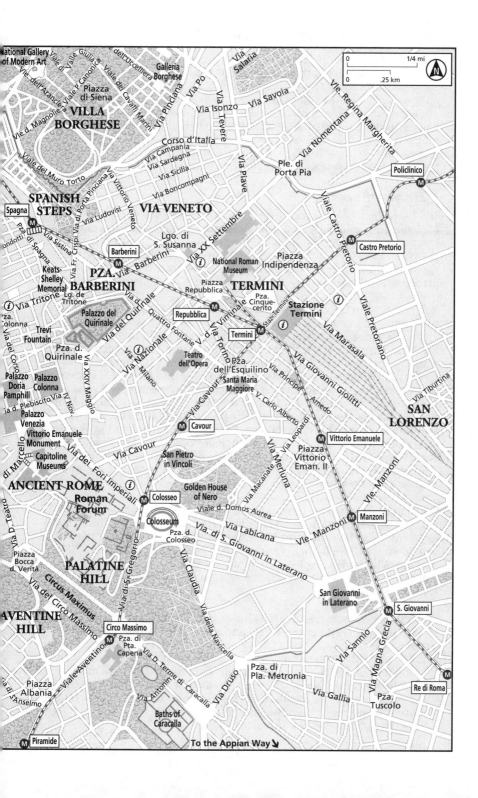

Roma by neighborhood

Rome is divided by the **river Tevere (Tiber)** that runs — or rather meanders — north-south, leaving about a third of the city on its western bank and the rest on its eastern bank. The largest part of Rome is on the eastern bank of the Tevere. Rome's neighborhoods are named after the original seven hills on which Rome was built, with some other names added afterward. Note that Roman neighborhoods are rarely referred to by their proper administrative name, but rather by the name of their core attraction. Therefore, Rome is divided in almost as many neighborhoods as there are attractions.

Il centro (the center)

On the eastern bank of the Tevere, is where Rome started and thrived for over three millennia. Until the beginning of the twentieth century, there was very little development beyond the city walls on this side of the river. The consecutive layers of urban development over the past three millennia have created a confused layout of streets, with tiny medieval roads crossed by larger — and more recent — avenues.

You can picture the *centro* as half of a pie with its western side cut off by the Tevere and its round outer edge defined by the city walls. Along the city walls proceeding from north to south you'll find **Piazza del Popolo,** the **Villa Borghese** park, the **Porta Pia, Stazione Termini (central rail station),** the **Basilica di San Giovanni in Laterano,** the **Terme di Caracalla (Baths of Caracalla),** the **Circo Massimo (Circus Maximus),** and **Testaccio.** Along the eastern bank of the Tevere are the **Aventino (Aventine Hill),** the **Ghetto, Campo de' Fiori, Piazza Navona,** and then back to **Piazza del Popolo.** Inside the pie are the **Pantheon,** the **Fontana di Trevi (Trevi Fountain), Piazza di Spagna,** and **Via Veneto** toward the north, and the heart of ancient Rome, with the **Capitolino (Capitoline Hill),** the **Palatino (Palatine Hill),** the **Foro Romano (Roman Forum)** and **Fori Imperiali (Imperial Forums),** and the **Colosseo (Colosseum)** toward the south.

Two main axes quarter the centro: **Il Corso** (actually Via del Corso), from **Piazza del Popolo** to **Piazza Venezia** and continuing down to **Via del Teatro di Marcello;** and **Via XX Settembre,** running from the **Porta Pia** down to where it changes names to **Via del Quirinale, Via XXIV Maggio, Via del Plebiscito,** and finally **Corso Vittorio Emanuele II.** The two main axes cross at Piazza Venezia, at the location of the Capitolino.

Il centro is certainly the most desirable part of town to stay in, with lively nightlife, restaurants, cafes, and most of the attractions. The drawback is that everybody shows up here, so you have to contend for your space with all the Romans as well as the whole cohort of tourists and Italians. **Testaccio,** the **Ghetto,** and **Campo de' Fiori** are more authentic neighborhoods, while the **Spanish Steps** and **Via Veneto** are the most touristy. The **Pantheon** is in the center of it all. You won't find a more romantic area than the center of Rome, and if crowds and high prices don't scare you, it's the place to be.

The western bank

The western bank makes up the other half of the Roman pie (see *"Il centro,"* earlier in this section). Up to the beginning of the twentieth century, it was occupied only by the walled city of the Vatican (seat of the Holy See), the small residential neighborhood around it, and the popular (in the sense of plebian) neighborhood of Trastevere — the traditional residence of poorer artisans and workers since the Roman times.

These historic neighborhoods have much developed since the beginning of the twentieth century, but they still exist. Starting from the north and just across the Tevere from Piazza del Popolo is the residential neighborhood of **Via Cola di Rienzo,** just north of the Vatican. The San Pietro (St. Peter) area obviously includes the **Basilica di San Pietro (St. Peter's Basilica)** but also **Castel Sant'Angelo,** the **Vatican** with the **Musei Vaticani (Vatican Museums),** and the **Gianicolo (Janiculum Hill).** At the southern edge of what we call the western bank is **Trastevere,** which is just across the Tevere from the Jewish Ghetto and Testaccio.

More residential than the other side of the river, the neighborhoods of the western bank are also quieter. Trastevere gets busy at night, when its many restaurants and bars attract hundreds of locals as well as visitors, while the Gianicolo gets pretty deserted after its moment of glory at sunset. The neighborhood of San Pietro is elegant and quiet, getting more commercial toward the north. Around Via Cola di Rienzo you can find the most action, both during the day — it's a prime shopping area — and at night, with its many restaurants and clubs (though it's more subdued than the *centro*). Hotel prices are also lower in the area around Cola di Rienzo, however.

Street smarts: Where to get information after you arrive

The main office of the **Azienda di Promozione Turistica di Roma (Rome tourist office)** is at Via Parigi 5 (☎ 06-4889-9255; Fax: 06-4889-9228; Internet: www.informaroma.it), a couple of blocks north of Stazione Termini, off of Piazza della Repubblica. Open daily 9 a.m. to 7 p.m., the office offers a choice of material on Rome and a few things on side trips from the city, plus a free map and a calendar of events, published monthly. There's also an info point inside Stazione Termini (☎ 06-4890-6300), which is open daily 8 a.m. to 9 p.m.

The **Comune di Roma** (the city government) maintains eight information kiosks around the city, near major attractions; the staffs at these kiosks are usually less overwhelmed and more available than the staff in the main tourist office. Open daily 9 a.m. to 6 p.m., the kiosks are at the following addresses:

- ✔ **Largo Goldoni,** off Via del Corso (☎ 06-6813-6061; Metro: Piazza di Spagna).

- ✔ **Piazza San Giovanni in Laterano** (☎ 06-7720-3535; Metro: San Giovanni).

✔ **Via Nazionale,** across from the Palazzo delle Esposizioni (☎ 06- 4782-4525; Bus: 64).

✔ **Piazza delle Cinque Lune**, just north of Piazza Navona (☎ 06- 6880-9240; Minibus: 116).

✔ **Lungotevere Castel Sant'Angelo**, to the left of the Castel Sant'Angelo (☎ 06-6880-9707; Metro: Ottaviano – San Pietro).

✔ **Piazza del Tempio della Pace**, off Via dei Fori Imperiali, just across from the entrance (☎ 06-6992-4307; Metro: Colosseo).

✔ **Piazza Sonnino in Trastevere** (☎ 06-5833-3457; Tram: 8).

✔ **Santa Maria Maggiore,** on the south side of the church (☎ 06- 4788-0294; Metro: Termini).

The **Vatican Tourist Office** is in Piazza San Pietro (☎ 06-6988-4466), just left of the entrance to the Basilica di San Pietro. The office is open Monday to Saturday 8:30 a.m. to 7 p.m. Naturally, it contains much information about the Vatican and its collections. For example, you can get a plan of the basilica and make reservations for a visit to the Vatican gardens or get the form to participate in a papal audience. (However, contacting the tourist office and making reservations to participate in a papal audience before leaving home is better than waiting until you're in Rome.)

Another source of information is the friendly staff at **Enjoy Rome** (Via Varese 39, three blocks north off the side of Stazione Termini; ☎ 06- 445-1834; Internet: www.enjoyrome.com), which also offers a free room-finding service and walking tours of the city (see Chapter 12). Enjoy Rome is open Monday to Friday 8:30 a.m. to 2 p.m. and 3:30 to 6:30 p.m. and Saturday 8:30 a.m. to 2 p.m.

Getting Around Roma

There are several modes of transportation, public and private, to help you get around Rome. Our favorite is to go by foot because you see the most. The city is over 2,000 years old, so much of it isn't designed for any other mode of conveyance other than the human foot. Streets curve, combine, change names, and meander among beautiful old buildings.

To enjoy this delightful labyrinth, you need a map. Making your way around Rome without a map is very difficult; the layout of the city is quite complicated. The free tourist office map is pretty good and gives you information on the main bus and metro stops. The free bus map you can get at the bus information stand at the Termini station is also good. However, if you want to get more serious about your exploration, you may want to buy one of the detailed city maps available at any newsstand and many bookstores around town.

On foot

Probably the best way to visit any Italian city is on foot, and Rome is no exception. The center of town is relatively small, and you can visit many attractions in one long stroll. However, Rome has many centers, and to get from one to the other — unless you're reasonably fit — you may want to catch some form of public transport (see the following sections).

Rome is generally safe, especially its most central areas, and you can get around following the same precautions that you'd use in any large city. The only common form of crime is pickpocketing, practiced extensively at crowded locations — such as on buses and at markets — by a variety of characters. Watch out for thieving kids, who surround you with their little hands and beg for a coin. Hold tight to your wallet and purse and brush your way through with a stern "No." In addition, try to stay away from the curbs when walking — thieves on motorscooters sometimes speed by and yank bags or purses from people's shoulders.

By Metropolitana (subway)

There are only two subway lines in Rome, A and B, connecting and crossing each other at Stazione Termini, which is also the head of many bus lines. **Line A** travels near San Pietro, passing Piazza di Spagna and the Palazzo Barberini (Via Veneto) on one side and San Giovanni on the other. **Line B** is the one you take to the Colosseo. Metros and buses (see "By bus," later in this chapter) belong to the same system (ATAC, the city transport system), so your ticket is valid for both. The metro runs Sunday to Friday 5:30 a.m. to 11:30 p.m. and Saturday 5:30 a.m. to 12:30 p.m. Note that the stops Colosseo, Circo Massimo, and Cavour on line B don't offer full elevator/lift service and aren't disabled-accessible. (For tips for travelers with disabilities, see Chapter 5.)

See the Cheat Sheet at the beginning of this book for a map of the Rome Metropolitana (subway).

A regular **biglietto (ticket)** for the bus/metro is valid 75 minutes and costs 1,500L (80¢). As elsewhere in Italy, you need to buy tickets before boarding the metro, tram, or bus, and you can buy them at most bars, tobacconist shops (signed *tabacchi* or by a white "T" on a black background), and newsstands. Tickets and passes are also sold at the ticket booths in the metro, at the ATAC bus information booth in front of Stazione Termini (near Platform C), and from machines at many locations. Within the 75 minutes of validity, you can take as many buses and trams as you wish, but you can take only one metro ride. Remember that you need to stamp the ticket at your first ride using the machine inside the bus or tram and always before your ride in the subway; without the stamp, the ticket isn't valid. If you're still on the bus when you approach the expiration of the 75 minutes of validity — let's say after 65 minutes — stamp your ticket again at its other end; it will show that you boarded the bus during the period of validity of your ticket and not after it expired. Also available are the **daily pass** costing 6,000L ($3.25) and the **weekly pass** costing 24,000L ($13).

By bus

The ATAC bus system is large and under continuous improvement. However, Rome's ancient layout resists any real modernization, and things don't always go smoothly: Buses are very crowded at rush hours, and traffic jams are common. However, buses remain an excellent resource because they go absolutely everywhere in Rome. The buses you're more likely to use are the **64** to San Pietro and the two small electric buses that go around the area of limited circulation in the heart of *il centro* (full of tiny narrow streets) and surroundings, the **116** and **117.**

With the complete overhaul Rome went through to prepare for Papal Jubilee 2000, the bus system was modified several times in the last few years: Lines were discontinued, added, and modified. The city promised that the system would reach its final form for the Jubilee, and it has, but Romans expect that more change will take place in the near future. Therefore, some of the bus numbers we give you in this chapter and the next might've changed by the time you get to town, so make sure you double check which bus you need to take with the tourist information office or the ATAC information office in front of the Termini train station.

When you arrive in Rome, one of the first things you should do is pick up an updated map from the bus information booth outside the main train station in Piazza dei Cinquecento or from the tourist information office inside the station. See the Cheat Sheet at the beginning of this guide for a simplified map of the major bus and tram routes.

Most buses run daily 5:30 a.m. to 12:30 a.m., but some stop at 8.30 p.m. The nighttime lines are very few and marked with an "N" for *notturno* (night). For all information about tickets, see "By Metropolitana (subway)," previously in this chapter.

By tram

Rome's few tram lines belong to the same system as the buses and are very fun to ride. Trams have a separate lane, so they're more rarely stopped by traffic; however, the routes are long, and you may have an extended though scenic ride. A line we like a lot is the **30,** which passes by the Basilica di San Giovanni and the Colosseo. For tickets, see "By Metropolitana (subway)," earlier in this chapter. Trams are indicated on the bus map.

By taxi

Taxis are expensive in Rome, especially because the traffic is terrible. However, they're a great resource for getting to your hotel from the train station, traveling around at night after the buses and metro stop, and reaching some areas that are badly served by public transport, such as the Gianicolo. The taxi is always the best option if you have a lot of luggage, but if you don't and it's not rush hour, the bus is great. It depends on your wallet.

Taxi fare starts at 4,500L ($2.45), and then the meter adds 200L (11¢) for every kilometer or minute, whichever comes first. Another 6,000L ($3.25) is added after 10 p.m. and before 6 a.m. Other supplements are 2,000L ($1.10) for Sunday travel and 2,000L ($1.10) for each piece of luggage put in the trunk.

Hailing a taxi on the street is possible but not too easy, particularly at night. Taxis don't cruise as they commonly do in major U.S. cities but return to taxi stands and wait for a call. Luckily, there are many taxi stands around Rome, especially in the center of town. Look for them near major monuments: Piazza Barberini (at the foot of Via Veneto), Piazza San Silvestro and Piazza SS. Apostoli (both not far from the Fontana di Trevi), and so on. You can identify taxi stands by a smallish telephone on a pole marked *taxi;* usually a few cabs are lined up and waiting. Always go to the first taxi in the line. If you're starting from a place with a phone — a hotel, restaurant, and so on — asking a staff member to call the nearest station or one of the radio taxis for you is a good idea. For a 24-hour **radio taxi,** call ☎ **06-88-177,** 06-66-45, or 06-49-94.

By motor scooter

Yes, most Romans travel around via moped, or so it seems when you're on a street corner waiting for the signal to turn green. If you want to do as the Romans do, you can find a number of places to rent a *motorino.* The best spot is **Treno e Scooter (TeS)** just outside Stazione Termini by the taxi stand and Metropolitana entrance (☎ **06-4890-5823**). TeS gives you a 10 percent discount if you've traveled by train that day. The scooters are very good quality and the prices (from 100,000L/$54 for the weekend) include insurance, taxes, and a free map. To get there, take the metro to Stazione Termini.

Here are a few other scooter rental places: **Rent a Scooter Borgo,** Via delle Grazie 2, just off Via di Porta Angelica, on the right side of the Vatican (☎ **06-687-7239;** Metro: Ottaviano); **Roma Solutions,** Corso Vittorio Emanuele II 50, just off Piazza Navona (☎ **06-687-6922;** Minibus: 116); and **New,** Via Quattro Novembre 96/a, just up from Piazza Venezia (☎ **06-679-0300;** Bus: 64).

Remember that riding a scooter is quite dangerous in Rome's horrendous traffic and that you need to be passably fit (to squeeze in between parked cars and other obstacles). Accidents are increasingly common.

Where to Stay in Roma

Rome boasts a variety of accommodation choices, ranging from the very basic to the supremely elegant. Though there are lots of rooms, they're hard to find because of the tourism flood. Papal Jubilee 2000 brought both good and bad things: Many hotels were refurbished for the event and several new ones opened, but hoteliers consequently raised their rates, sometimes steeply (offset somewhat by a better exchange rate). Following is a rundown of the best places to stay, followed by some acceptable alternatives if you have trouble booking a room. Unless otherwise specified, all rooms in the hotels that we list in this section come with private bathrooms.

If you arrive without a room reservation (something we advise against), remember that there's a hotel desk at the airport and that Enjoy Rome (see "Street smarts: Where to get information after you arrive," earlier in the chapter) offers a free room-finding service.

The top hotels

Albergo Abbruzzi

$ Pantheon

This very basic hotel offers commodious and immaculate guest rooms, but the real draw is that you're right at the Pantheon. The prices for this fantastic location are extremely low because you have to share a bath and there's no air-conditioning or elevator. However, the view is unbeatable. The Abbruzzi is much in demand — reserve well in advance to get a room with a view. Rooms in the back without the view are quieter, though.

Piazza della Rotonda 69 (just across from the Pantheon). ☎ *06-679-2021. Bus: 116 to Pantheon or 64 or 70 to Largo Argentina, and then walk north. Rack rates: 120,000–150,000L ($65–$80) double, including breakfast. No credit cards.*

Albergo del Sole al Pantheon

$$$$$ Pantheon

Claiming to be Rome's oldest hotel — there are accounts of it being a hostelry as far back as 1467 — the Albergo del Sole al Pantheon didn't steal its name: It sits just in front of the famous monument. The original coffered ceilings are hand painted, and the confusing layout is typical of medieval Rome, with a few steps to climb up and down to the slightly different levels. The guest rooms are individually decorated and air-conditioned. The suites offer baths with hydromassage.

Piazza della Rotonda 63 (across from the Pantheon). ☎ *06-678-0441. Fax: 06-6994-0689. E-mail:* solealpantheon@italyhotel.com. *Bus: 116 to Pantheon or 64 or 70 to Largo Argentina, then walk north. Rack rates: 450,000–560,000L ($245–$303) double, including breakfast. AE, DC, MC, V.*

The big splurge

In this chapter we supply entries for several deluxe $$$$$ hotels, among them the Albergo del Sol al Pantheon, the Aldrovandi Palace Hotel, and the Hotel Scalinata di Spagna. If you're looking for the plushest of the plush, here are a few more suggestions:

✔ **Excelsior.** Via Vittorio Veneto 125; ☎ **800-325-3589** in the U.S. or 06-47-081; Fax: 06-482-6205; Internet: www.luxurycollection.com; Metro: Line A to Barberini.

✔ **Hassler.** Piazza Trinità dei Monti 6; ☎ **800-223-6800** in the U.S.or 06-699-340; Fax: 06-678-9991; Internet: www.hotelhasslerroma.com; E-mail: hasslerroma@inclink.it; Metro: Line A to Spagna.

✔ **Hotel de la Ville Inter-Continental Roma.** Via Sistina 67–69; ☎ **800-327-0200** in the U.S. and Canada or 06-67-331; Fax: 06-678-4213; Internet: www.interconti.com; E-mail: rome@interconti.com; Metro: Line A to Spagna or Barberini.

✔ **Hotel de Russie.** Via del Babuino 9; ☎ **06-32-8881**; Fax: 06-32-8888; Internet: http://hotelderussie.it; E-mail: reservations@hotelderussie.it; Metro: Line A to Flaminio.

✔ **Hotel Eden.** Via Ludovisi 49; ☎ **800-225-5843** in the U.S. or 06-478-121; Fax: 06-482-1584, Internet; www.hotel-eden.it; E-mail: reservations@hotel-eden.it; Bus: 119.

Albergo Santa Chiara

$$$ Pantheon

This is one of Rome's oldest hotels, run since 1838 by the Corteggiani family. Just behind the Pantheon and a few steps from Piazza della Minerva, it's functional and comfortable. From the beautiful entry hall, with its statuary and porphyry columns, to the breakfast room with its skylights, the Santa Chiara offers a feeling of elegance. All the guest rooms are air-conditioned and have small safes.

Via Santa Chiara 21. ☎ *06-687-2979. Fax: 06-687-3144. E-mail:* santa.chiara@italyhotel.com. *Bus: 116 to Pantheon or 64 or 70 to Largo Argentina, then walk north. Rack rates: 270,000–395,000L ($146–$214) double, including breakfast. AE, DC, MC, V.*

Aldrovandi Palace Hotel

$$$$$ Villa Borghese

Opened in 1981, the Aldrovandi Palace is housed in an elegant villa, facing Villa Borghese park. Although pricey, the hotel offers many extras you wouldn't expect to find in Rome: a large free parking area, pool, private park, gym and health club, and restaurant with park views. Above all, it's extremely quiet at night — a rare advantage in Rome. All the guest rooms are air-conditioned and have satellite TVs.

Via Ulisse Aldrovandi 15 (behind the Villa Borghese). ☎ *06-322-3993. Fax: 06-322-1435. Internet:* www.aldrovandi.com. *E-mail:* hotel@aldrovandi. com. *Tram: 19 or 30 to Via Ulisse Aldrovandi. Parking: Free. Rack rates: 580,000–680,000L ($314–$368) double, including breakfast. AE, DC, JCB, MC, V.*

Casa Kolbe

$ Teatro di Marcello

Near the Jewish Ghetto, steps from the major classical sites — the Capitolino, Palatino, Foro Romano, and Colosseo — this is an old-fashioned hotel in a former convent. The guest rooms are clean but sometimes a little worn and the furnishings simple. For the price, however, you can't beat it. This is a peaceful area, and the quietest rooms overlook the small inner garden. Many tour groups book here, so reserve in advance.

Via San Teodoro 44. ☎ *06-679-4974. Fax: 06-6994-1550. Bus: 60 or 81 to Bocca della Verità, and then walk east to Via San Teodoro. Rack rates: 130,000–150,000L ($70–$80) double. AE, DC, MC, V.*

Cesari Hotel

$$$ Pantheon

In a building from the first half of the eighteenth century that was renovated in 1999, this hotel is between the Pantheon and the Corso; the Fontana di Trevi is only steps away. Most of the guest rooms are soundproof, and they all offer air-conditioning and satellite TVs. If you're a large party, inquire about the triple and quad rooms.

Via di Pietra 89a. ☎ *06-679-2386. Fax: 06-679-0882. E-mail:* cesari@venere.it. *Bus: 60 or 116 to Via di Pietra, just south of Piazza Colonna on the Corso. Parking: Free nearby. Rack rates: 300,000–340,000L ($160–$185) double, including breakfast. AE, DC, MC, V.*

Duca di Alba

$$ Colosseo

Restored in 1994, the Duca di Alba is near the Colosseo and the Foro Romano. All the guest rooms are soundproof, have air-conditioning, and come with safes. They're decorated with classic accents, and a few have private balconies.

Via Leonina 12. ☎ *06-484-471. Fax: 06-488-4840. Internet:* www.venere.it. *E-mail:* duca.d'alba@venere.it. *Metro: Line B to Cavour, and then walk a block north; Via Leonina is on your left. Parking: Nearby garage 40,000–50,000L ($21.60–$27) per day. Rack rates: 190,000–310,000L ($103–$165) double, including breakfast. AE, DC, MC, V.*

Hotel Alexandra

$$$$ Via Veneto

The Alexandra is a good value, considering it's on famous Via Veneto — you couldn't wish for a more glamorous location. The hotel is very well kept and has recently completed a renovation and expansion. All the guest rooms are air-conditioned and nicely furnished. The pleasant breakfast room was designed by famous Italian architect Paolo Portoghesi.

Via Vittorio Veneto 18. ☎ *06-488-1943. Fax: 06-487-1804. Internet:* www. venere.it. *E-mail:* alexandra@venere.it. *Metro: Line A to Barberini, then walk up Via Veneto. Parking: Nearby garage 50,000L ($27) per day. Rack rates: 390,000L ($211) double, including breakfast. AE, DC, MC, V.*

Hotel Barocco

$$$$ Via Veneto

Right off Piazza Barberini, this charming small hotel has a fantastic location on one of the quieter streets behind Via Veneto, both a little removed from its noise and yet still close by and near major attractions. Its guest rooms are tastefully furnished in cherrywood and have marble baths and stuccoed ceilings. The refined ambiance is pleasant without being stuffy.

Via della Purificazione 4. ☎ *06-487-2001. Fax: 06-485-994. Internet:* www. hotelbarocco.it. *E-mail:* hotelbarocco@hotelbarocco.it. *Metro: Line A to Barberini, and then walk up Via della Purificazione, on the west side of the piazza. Rack rates: 350,000–500,000L ($190–$270) double, including breakfast. AE, MC, V.*

Hotel Columbia

$$ Piazza della Repubblica

Renovated in 1997, this hotel dates back to 1900. The Murano chandeliers are nice touches in otherwise simple modern guest rooms (with air-conditioning). The service is good, and there's a nice rooftop garden with a bar. The Hotel Venezia (later in this section) is under the same management.

Via del Viminale 15. ☎ *06-474-4289. Fax: 06-474-0209. Metro: Line A to Repubblica, and then walk toward Stazione Termini. Rack rates: 215,000–260,000L ($116–$140) double, including breakfast. AE, DC, MC, V.*

Hotel Columbus

$$$$$ San Pietro

Only steps from the Basilica di San Pietro, this wonderful hotel is in the Palazzo della Rovere, built in the late 1400s by Cardinal Domenico della Rovere and surrounding a garden courtyard. Among those who've occupied it is Charles VIII during his visit to Rome. Both the public spaces and the air-conditioned guest rooms are beautifully furnished and feel like those in an aristocrat's palace; some of the frescoes were done by Pinturicchio. La Veranda restaurant offers refined Roman and Italian cuisine and tables in the garden in summer.

Via della Conciliazione 33. ☎ *06-686-5435. Fax: 06-686-4874. Internet:* www.hotelcolumbus.net. *E-mail:* hotel.columbus@alfanet.it. *Bus: 64 to last stop, and then walk south to Via della Conciliazione and turn left. Parking: Free. Rack rates: 570,000L ($308) double, including breakfast. AE, DC, MC, V.*

Hotel Farnese

$$$$$ Cola di Rienzo

Between the Castel Sant'Angelo and Piazza del Popolo in a quiet neighborhood, this hospitable hotel occupies a nineteenth-century patrician palace and was recently completely renovated. The Farnese is steps from one of Rome's best shopping streets — Via Cola di Rienzo — and walking distance from the Vatican and the medieval center. The air-conditioned guest rooms are furnished with subdued elegance. The hotel also offers a roof garden.

Via A. Farnese 30. ☎ *06-321-2553 or 06-321-2554. Fax: 06-321-5129. Metro: Line A to Lepanto, and then walk northeast on Via degli Scipioni to Via A. Farnese. Parking: Free in private garage. Rack rates: 500,000L ($270) double, including breakfast. AE, MC, V.*

Hotel Margutta

$$ Piazza di Spagna

On one of the charming old streets between Piazza del Popolo and Piazza di Spagna, in perhaps the most chic area of the *centro,* the Margutta is a very good value. If you can put up with the lack of air-conditioning and not having a phone in your room, you're compensated by having most of the main attractions only a walk from your doorstep. A couple of guest rooms have terraces (they're more expensive).

Via Laurina 34. ☎ *06-322-3674. Fax: 06-320-0395. Metro: Line A to Spagna; if walking from Piazza del Popolo, Via Laurina is the second street on your left. Rack rates: 190,000L ($103) double, including breakfast. AE, DC, MC, V.*

Hotel Nerva

$$$ Colosseo

Renovated in 1997, this hotel occupies a building from the sixteenth and seventeenth centuries situated above the archaeological area of the Foro Romano. The guest rooms are comfortable and pleasantly decorated in a modern style, all with air-conditioning and other amenities.

Via Tor de' Conti 3–5. ☎ **06-679-3764** *or 678-1835. Fax: 06-699-2204. Bus: 75 to Via Tor de' Conti, which runs between Via Nazionale and Via dei Fori Imperiali. Rack rates: 240,000–540,000L ($130–$292) double, including breakfast. AE, DC, MC, V.*

Hotel Piazza di Spagna

$$$$ Piazza di Spagna

This hotel is only a stone's throw from Piazza di Spagna, and its new managers have renovated and redecorated the place and are undertaking further modernizations. The guest rooms are spartan but comfortable and have air-conditioning and minibars; a few have Jacuzzis. Because the hotel is small and in a prime location, make your reservations well in advance.

Via Mario de' Fiori 61. ☎ **06-679-6412.** *Fax: 06-679-0654. Internet:* www. hotelpiazzadispagna.it. *E-mail:* info@hotelpiazzadispagna.it. *Metro: Line A to Spagna, and then walk a block southeast to Via Mario de' Fiori. Rack rates: 350,000–380,000L ($190–$203) double, including breakfast. AE, MC, V.*

Hotel Scalinata di Spagna

$$$$$ Piazza di Spagna

This clean and pleasant hotel is just above the Spanish Steps and loaded with character; your guest room may have exposed ceiling beams and quaint old furniture. It feels more like a country inn on a hill — the view from the terrace is spectacular — than a hotel smack-dab in the middle of Rome. It's a perfect spot from which to explore the *centro*.

Piazza Trinità dei Monti 17. ☎ **06-679-3006.** *Fax 06-6994-0598. Metro: Line A to Spagna, and then walk up the Spanish Steps. Rack rates: 450,000L ($245) double, including breakfast. AE, MC, V.*

Hotel Villa del Parco

$$$ Porta Pia

This family-run hotel is housed in one of the elegant villas along Via Nomentana and surrounded by a garden. Though outside the historic center, the area boasts beautiful nineteenth-century villas, parks, and quiet tree-lined streets and is well connected by public transportation. The Bernardini family treat their customers as personal guests, so you feel as if you're staying in a refined home. A recent renovation included the installation of an elevator. The guest rooms are decorated in muted tones, with comfortable furnishings.

Via Nomentana 110. ☎ **06-442-7773.** *Fax: 06-4423-7572. Internet:* www.venere. it. *E-mail:* villaparco@mclink.it. *Bus: 60 or 62 to third stop after Porta Pia on Via Nomentana. Rack rates: 250,000L ($135) weekends and 275,000L ($149) weekdays, including breakfast. AE, DC, MC, V.*

Rome Accommodations and Dining

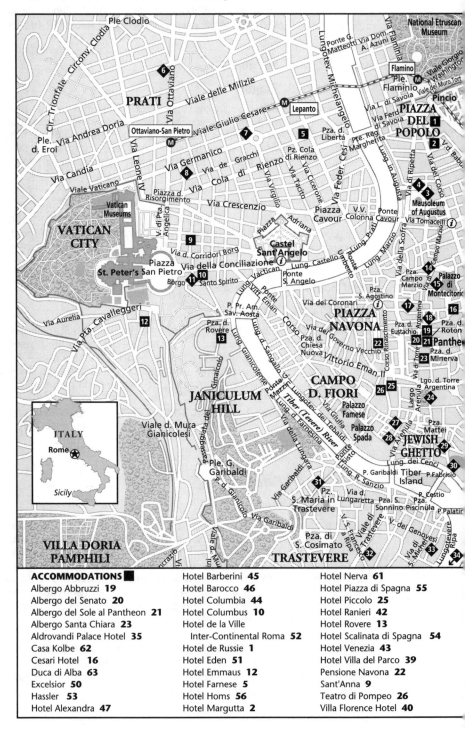

ACCOMMODATIONS ■

Albergo Abbruzzi **19**
Albergo del Senato **20**
Albergo del Sole al Pantheon **21**
Albergo Santa Chiara **23**
Aldrovandi Palace Hotel **35**
Casa Kolbe **62**
Cesari Hotel **16**
Duca di Alba **63**
Excelsior **50**
Hassler **53**
Hotel Alexandra **47**

Hotel Barberini **45**
Hotel Barocco **46**
Hotel Columbia **44**
Hotel Columbus **10**
Hotel de la Ville
  Inter-Continental Roma **52**
Hotel de Russie **1**
Hotel Eden **51**
Hotel Emmaus **12**
Hotel Farnese **5**
Hotel Homs **56**
Hotel Margutta **2**

Hotel Nerva **61**
Hotel Piazza di Spagna **55**
Hotel Piccolo **25**
Hotel Ranieri **42**
Hotel Rovere **13**
Hotel Scalinata di Spagna **54**
Hotel Venezia **43**
Hotel Villa del Parco **39**
Pensione Navona **22**
Sant'Anna **9**
Teatro di Pompeo **26**
Villa Florence Hotel **40**

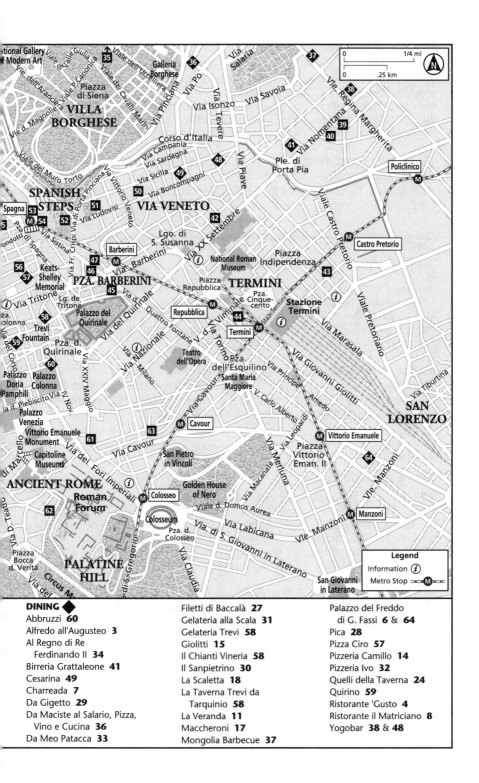

DINING ◆

Abbruzzi **60**
Alfredo all'Augusteo **3**
Al Regno di Re
  Ferdinando II **34**
Birreria Grattaleone **41**
Cesarina **49**
Charreada **7**
Da Gigetto **29**
Da Maciste al Salario, Pizza,
  Vino e Cucina **36**
Da Meo Patacca **33**

Filetti di Baccalà **27**
Gelateria alla Scala **31**
Gelateria Trevi **58**
Giolitti **15**
Il Chianti Vineria **58**
Il Sanpietrino **30**
La Scaletta **18**
La Taverna Trevi da
  Tarquinio **58**
La Veranda **11**
Maccheroni **17**
Mongolia Barbecue **37**

Palazzo del Freddo
  di G. Fassi **6** & **64**
Pica **28**
Pizza Ciro **57**
Pizzeria Camillo **14**
Pizzeria Ivo **32**
Quelli della Taverna **24**
Quirino **59**
Ristorante 'Gusto **4**
Ristorante il Matriciano **8**
Yogobar **38** & **48**

Pensione Navona

$$ Piazza Navona

This family-run pensione is just off Piazza Navona, and the location is its great plus. Otherwise, the guest rooms are simple, with functional modern furniture — this is a pensione, not a hotel. About two-thirds of the rooms offer private baths. air-conditioning is available on request for 40,000L ($22), but the high ceilings keep the house quite cool even on the hottest days.

Via dei Sediari 8. ☎ *06-686-4203. Fax: 06-6880-3802. Bus: 70, 81, or 116 to Via dei Sediari, which is east of the southern tip of Piazza Navona, just off Corso Rinascimento. Rack rates: 150,000–170,000L ($80–$92) double, including breakfast. No credit cards.*

Sant'Anna

$$$$ San Pietro

In one of the most authentic and charming Roman neighborhoods, this hotel is in a sixteenth-century building surrounding a courtyard. Tasteful and elegant, the spacious guest rooms are air-conditioned and include marble baths. The Sant'Anna has a brightly decorated breakfast room, offers wheelchair access, and allows pets.

Via Borgo Pio 134. ☎ *06-6880-1602. Fax: 06-6830-8717. Internet:* www.travel.it. *E-mail:* santanna@travel.it. *Bus: 64 to the next-to-the-last stop, and then walk north to Borgo Pio. Parking: in a nearby lot at 40,000L ($22) per day. Rack rates: 350,000L ($190) double, including breakfast. AE, MC, V.*

Teatro di Pompeo

$$$ Campo de' Fiori

The name of this hotel indicates that the building sits on top of the remains of a 55 B.C. Roman theater, some of which you can still see in the breakfast room. The rest of the building is from the fifteenth century, as revealed by the beamed ceilings in the rooms, which are matched by tasteful furnishings in the old style. All the guest rooms are air-conditioned. The hotel is small, so reserve your room early.

Largo del Pallaro 8. ☎ *06-6830-0170. Fax: 06-6880-5531. E-mail:* genti&paesi@uni.net. *Bus: 64 to Sant'Andrea della Valle, then walk east on Via dei Chiavari and turn right. Rack rates: 290,000–320,000L ($157–$173) double, including breakfast. AE, DC, MC, V.*

Villa Florence Hotel

$$$ Porta Pia

This hotel occupies an 1860 patrician villa with its own garden. Just outside the walls at Porta Pia on Via Nomentana in an area of elegant villas and embassies, the hotel is well connected by public transportation and is a 20-minute walk from Via Veneto. The guest rooms vary in configuration and size (there are some triples and quads), and all come with trouser presses and baths with Jacuzzis. The continental breakfast is served in the garden or in your room.

Via Nomentana 28. ☎ **06-440-3036** *or 06-440-2966. Fax: 06-440-2709. Internet:* www.venere.it. *Bus: 60 or 62 to the first stop after Porta Pia on Via Nomentana. Parking: Free. Rack rates: 250,000–320,000L ($135–$173) double, including breakfast. AE, DC, MC, V.*

Runner-up accommodations

Albergo del Senato

$$$ Pantheon   A good-value hotel near the Pantheon. All the guest rooms are air-conditioned. Piazza della Rotonda 73. ☎ **06-678-4343**. Fax: 06-699-40297. Internet: www.italyhotel.com. E-mail: delsenato@italyhotel.com.

Hotel Barberini

$$$$$ Via Veneto   This hotel is expensive but beautiful, with elegant reproduction furniture and sumptuous baths. It's located just off Via Veneto near the Fontana di Trevi. Via Rasella 3. ☎ **06-481-4993**. Fax: 06-481-5211. Internet: www.hotelbarberini.com. E-mail: info@ hotelbarberini.com.

Hotel Emmaus

$$$ San Pietro   This recently renovated hotel is only a hundred yards from the Basilica di San Pietro. All the guest rooms have modern but tasteful furnishings, and some enjoy views over St. Peter's dome. Via delle Fornaci 23. ☎ **06-638-0370**. Fax: 06-635-658.

Hotel Homs

$$$$ Spanish Steps   Only a short walk from Piazza di Spagna, the Hotel Homs offers nice amenities and reasonably large guest rooms with contemporary furniture, as well as a roof terrace with a view where you can have breakfast. Via della Vite 7–72. ☎ **06-679-2976**. Fax: 06-678-0482.

Hotel Piccolo

$ Campo de' Fiori   The Piccolo lives up to its name — a small hotel squeezed into the narrow streets not far from Campo de' Fiori. Price is the attraction in this popular area; but the guest rooms are nice but quite basic. Via dei Chiavari 32. ☎ **06-6880-2560** or 06-689-2330.

Hotel Ranieri

$$ Termini   This hotel is within walking distance of Via Veneto and was renovated in the 1990s. The guest rooms offer modern baths and air-conditioning. Via XX Settembre 43. ☎ **06-481-4467.** Fax: 06-481-8834. Internet: www.italyhotel.com. E-mail: hotel.ranieri@venere.it.

Hotel Rovere

$$$ San Pietro   Set on the lower slope of the Gianicolo on a quaint side street, the Rovere is close to Trastevere and the Vatican. It's a clean and quiet place, with pleasant modest rooms of comfortable size. A buffet breakfast is also included. Vicolo Sant'Onofrio 4–5. ☎ **06-6880-6739.** Fax: 06-6880-7062.

Hotel Venezia

$$ Termini   In a residential district near the University, this hotel boasts relatively large guest rooms decorated with Murano chandeliers and a very helpful staff. Via Varese 18. ☎ **06-445-7101.** Fax: 06-495-7687. Internet: www.hotelvenezia.com. E-mail: info@hotelvenezia.com.

Where to Dine in Roma

Italian gourmets maintain that there isn't a really good restaurant in Rome. And they're right — sort of. However, you can find hundreds of excellent *trattorie, osterie,* and *pizzerie* — small joints, simple in decor (often even basic), offering delectable preparations of typical Roman cuisine. Other than a few exceptions, truly good food is served only in mom-and-pop places with real homemade cuisine.

Roman cuisine is rich in regional specialties. *Primi* (first courses) include *pasta all'amatriciana* (a tomato-and-bacon sauce with pecorino cheese), *pasta all'arrabbiata* (tomato and lots of hot red pepper), the famous Thursday specialty *gnocchi* (potato dumplings usually in a tomato-based sauce), *spaghetti alle vongole* (spaghetti with clams), and *cannelloni* (pasta tubes filled with meat or fish and baked). *Secondi* (second courses) are dominated by the delicious *abbacchio* (young lamb), prepared *alla cacciatora* ("hunter's style" — sautéed with herbs and wine) or *scottadito* (literally "finger burning" — small grilled cutlets served crispy and hot to eat with your hands); the traditional **contorno** (vegetable side dish) is succulent roasted potatoes. Another justly famous *secondo* is *saltimbocca alla romana* (literally "jump in your mouth" — veal or beef stuffed with ham and sage and sautéed in a marsala sauce). If you're adventurous, try *trippa alla romana* (tripe Roman style) and *coda alla vaccinara* (oxtail stew). Other favorites include a variety of dishes such as roast pork, fried fish and calamari, and *baccalà* (codfish).

The most common food that Romans head out to eat, though, is pizza. Pizza in a pizzeria is strictly an individual-size round pizza (not by the slice; for that, see "Tip," later in the chapter) with a variety of toppings. Traditional toppings include *margherita* (tomato and mozzarella), *Napoletana* (margherita, plus anchovies), *capricciosa* (tomato, mozzarella, and mushrooms with artichoke hearts, olives, ham, and an egg), *rugola e parmigiano* (fresh arugula — called "rocket" on many menus — and thin slices of Parmesan cheese), *funghi* (mushrooms, tomato, and mozzarella), and many others. In addition, *pizzerie* typically serve the following appetizers: *supplì* (rice balls stuffed with a small piece of mozzarella and deep fried), *filetti di baccalà* (deep-fried codfish), *bruschetta* (toasted peasant-style bread topped with oil and garlic and, on request, tomatoes, olive caviar, ham, and so on), *olive ascolane* (large green olives stuffed and deep fried), and *fiori di zucca* (zucchini flowers stuffed with a small piece of anchovy and mozzarella and then deep fried). If you don't want pizza, you can order a *crostino* (different from the Tuscan one, discussed in Chapter 14, or see the Appendix); in Rome, a *crostino* is several slices of bread with mozzarella and a variety of toppings, toasted in the oven.

Typical **dolci** (desserts) in Rome are *torta della nonna* (a pie filled with custard and pine nuts), *torta di crema e visciole* (pie with custardy ricotta and sour cherries), *tiramisù* (layered espresso-soaked lady fingers and marscapone cheese), and of course *gelato* (ice cream — see the sidebar "Looking for a gelato break"). Wines are from the nearby Castelli Romani (hill towns to the east of Rome). You can find whites, such as the Frascati and Marino, as well as a few reds.

Of one thing you can be sure in Rome: You won't starve! You can always get good food while you're on the go and don't have time to stop and sit down.

You can have lunch or a quick snack for little money if you go to a take-out pizzeria. The sign usually says *pizza a taglio* (by the slice) or *rustica* (rustic). On the display counter you can see a number of large square pans containing a variety of pizzas: *rossa* (tomato and mozzarella), *bianca* (oil, salt, and rosemary), *funghi* (tomato and mushrooms), as well as the chef's own inventions. The person serving will cut out a hunk for you (you can indicate if you want it larger or smaller) and sell it by weight. They sometimes also have *calzone* (filled with ham and cheese) and *supplì*.

Rome offers many excellent *trattorie,* and if you want to find your own preferred spot, the best areas to search are *il centro* (the center) between the Corso and the river Tiber and Trastevere. Another option is to make a sandwich and have a picnic in Villa Borghese or on the Gianicolo (see Chapter 12). An excellent place to buy farm-fresh food for your picnic is the **Fattoria la Parrina** (Largo Toniolo 3, between Piazza Navona and the Pantheon; ☎ **06-6830-0111**), with excellent cheese, wine, and veggies. If you're in the mood for a sweet snack, try **Limentani** (Via Portico d'Ottavia 1; ☎ **06-686-0011**), in the Jewish Ghetto, where you can stop for some of the best traditional Roman treats at the pastry shop. Another place to grab a pastry or treat to fill your stomach is **Valzani** (Via del Moro 37a in Trastevere; ☎ **06-580-3792**).

The top restaurants

Alfredo all'Augusteo

$$$$ Piazza del Popolo   Roman/Italian

Alfredo sauce, anyone? Just behind the Mausoleum of Augustus between Via del Corso and the river, this restaurant is where the original Alfredo sauce was invented. The fettuccine Alfredo costs 21,000L ($11.35). Besides excellent fresh pasta, the menu includes a number of Italian specialties, with *secondi* like lamb, beef, pork, and fish (though the pasta is the real attraction). The dining room is more upscale than most in Rome and the service very professional.

Piazza Augusto Imperatore 30. ☎ 06-687-8734. Reservations recommended on weekends. Metro: Line A to Piazza di Spagna. Secondi: 23,500-40,000L ($13–$22). AE, MC, V. Open: Lunch Tues.–Sat.; dinner Mon–Sat.

Al Regno di Re Ferdinando II

$$$$ Testaccio   Neapolitan

In one of the historic cellars of Monte Testaccio — the hill formed by discarded pottery shards under Nero — this restaurant offers excellent Neapolitan food. The choice of fresh pasta is superb and the *Sfizietto del Re* (a huge portion of linguine with a mountain of shellfish from the nearby Tirrenian Sea) delights any palate and leaves an everlasting memory after you finish — if you can finish. All the appetizers are delicious and the *secondi* (particularly the fish) excellent. This restaurant also makes pizza, but the pasta is much better. If you visit in summer, bring a jacket — the place isn't air-conditioned, but the pottery shards maintain an icy temperature inside.

Via di Monte Testaccio 39. ☎ 06-578-3725. Reservations recommended. Metro: Line B to Piramide, but taking a cab is best. Secondi: 20,000–35,000L ($11–$19). AE, DC, MC, V. Open: Lunch Tues–Sat; dinner Mon–Sat.

Birreria Grattaleone

$$$ Porta Pia   Italian/Pizza/Birreria

A lot of care and money made this spacious *birreria* (like a Bavarian beer hall, but with a wood-fired pizza oven and typical Italian specialties) stylish and welcoming. The American-trained chef presents the food — from traditional fried fish to *bistecca alla fiorentina,* the enormous and tender Florentine steak — with a flair learned in New York and Miami. The restaurant features live music on Thursday, Friday, and Saturday.

Via Messina 42. ☎ 06-4424-2379. Reservations recommended on weekends. Bus: 60 or 62 to Porta Pia and Via Nomentana; then turn left on Via Ancona, and then right on Via Messina. Secondi: 12,000–25,000L ($7–$14). AE, DC, MC, V. Open: Lunch and dinner daily.

Cesarina

$$$$ Via Veneto   Roman/Bolognese

Offering a nice selection of specialties from Rome and Bologna, this restaurant is an excellent choice in the residential area north of Via Veneto, away from the crowds. The food is wonderful and perfectly prepared. Go for the many homemade pastas and/or the choice of meat dishes. The *bollito misto* (variety of boiled meats) is delicious.

Via Piemonte 109. ☎ 06-488-0828. Reservations recommended. Metro: Line A to Barberini. Bus: 56 or 58 to Via Piemonte (the fourth street off Via Boncompagni coming from Via Veneto). Secondi: 17,000–45,000L ($9–$25). AE, DC, MC, V. Open: Lunch and dinner Mon–Sat.

Charreada

$$$$ Cola di Rienzo   Mexican

Mexican food in Rome? Sure! But check your wallet before going because this restaurant is trendy and therefore expensive. Charreada is located in one of Rome's prettiest squares and is a popular place — especially late at night — to have guacamole or a nice steak.

Piazza dei Quiriti 4. ☎ 06-3600-0009. Reservations recommended. Metro: Line A to Lepanto, and then walk up Viale Giulo Cesare and take the second left on Via Duileo to the piazza. Secondi: 23,000–40,000L ($12–$22). AE, MC, V. Open: Dinner daily.

Da Gigetto

$$$$ Teatro Marcello   Jewish Roman

This famous restaurant has for decades been the destination of Romans who want to taste some of the specialties of Jewish Roman cuisine. Some Romans say Gigetto is a little past its prime, but we think it's still a good place to sample such typical specialties as *carciofi alla giudia* (crispy fried artichokes), as well as Roman dishes like *fettuccine all'Amatriciana* and *saltimbocca*.

Via del Portico d'Ottavia 21–22. ☎ 06-686-1105. Reservations recommended. Bus: 60 to last stop, and then walk north behind the synagogue. Secondi: 18,000–24,000L ($10–$13). AE, DC, MC, V. Open: Lunch Tues–Sun; dinner Tues–Sat; closed two weeks in Aug.

Da Maciste al Salario, Pizza, Vino e Cucina

$$ Villa Borghese   Roman/Pizza

A great place to go for lunch before or after your visit to the Galleria Borghese, this large basement eatery gets really busy with locals from nearby offices and shops. The food is simple but excellent and the pizza one of the best Roman-style pizzas around — thin and crispy and seasoned to perfection. At lunch, it's cafeteria style — you walk up to the

Looking for a gelato break?

Italian ice cream is among the best in the world. It's called *gelato* and comes in a variety of flavors, divided between fruits and creams. In addition to *limone* (lemon), *arancio* (orange), and other fruits, you can choose from specialties such as *mora* (blackberry) and *frutti di bosco* (mixed berries). The best cream flavors are *zabaglione* (a rum-and-egg combo, like eggnog), *bacio* (hazelnut chocolate), and *stracciatella* (vanilla with chocolate chips).

The oldest ice-cream parlor in Rome is **Giolitti,** Via Uffici del Vicario 40 (☎ 06-699-1243; Minibus: 116), which offers a huge selection of flavors — the fruit and chocolate flavors are usually excellent. The second oldest is the **Palazzo del Freddo di G. Fassi**, with two locations: one on Viale Angelico off San Pietro (Metro: Line A to Ottaviano), and the main store on Via Principe Eugenio 65–67 (☎ 06-446-4740; Metro: Line A to Piazza Vittorio). (We think that the main store is much better.) In Trastevere, try the **Gelateria alla Scala,** Via della Scala 5 (☎ 06-581-3174; Tram: 8), for excellent homemade ice cream. Off Campo de' Fiori, go to **Pica**, Via della Seggiola 12 (☎ 06-6880-3275; Tram: 8) , which prepares one of the best ice creams in Rome. Near the Fontana di Trevi, don't miss the **Gelateria Trevi**, Via del Lavatore 84–85 (☎ 06-679-2060; Bus: 52, 53, 61, 62, 63, 116, or 492).

A new passion in Rome is frozen yogurt, made with real fresh yogurt and fruit. You can find some of Rome's best at **Yogobar,** with several locations, including Viale Regina Margherita 83b, just north of Via Nomentana (☎ 06-855-1374; Bus: 61 or 63; Tram: 19 or 30), and Via Lucania 23–27, off Via Boncompagni, east of Via Veneto (☎ 06-4288-3001; Minibus: 116).

counter and choose from the buffet. Get there early because the best choices disappear fast, and definitely take the side bread dish with a few pieces of *pizza bianca* (focaccia). At dinner they offer a large choice of great *antipasto*, hearty *primi*, and pizza.

Via Salaria 179/a. ☎ *06-884-8267. Reservations only necessary for dinner. Bus: 52 or 53 to Via Salaria; or exit Galleria Borghese in the rear and take Via Pinciana, bearing right on Via Giovannelli to reach Via Salaria. Secondi: 8,000–15,000L ($4.30–$8). AE, DC, MC, V. Open: Lunch Mon–Sat; dinner Tues–Sun.*

Da Meo Patacca

$$$ **Trastevere** **Roman**

Probably Rome's most famous restaurant among locals, Meo Patacca was an ancient inn and stagecoach stop. Romans visit there today for special occasions and enjoy the traditional music and clowning around. The restaurant attracts loads of visitors as well, but the place is huge, with two terraces and a labyrinth of tavern rooms. Food choices include a large selection of grilled meats — the pork is excellent — homemade pastas and staples like *frittata* (Roman omelet), *saltimbocca alla romana*, *lepre in salmì con la polenta* (hare with polenta), and *melanzane alla parmigiana* (eggplant parmigiana).

Piazza dei Mercanti 30. ☎ *06-581-6198. Internet:* www.dameopatacca.com. *Reservations not necessary. Tram/Bus: Tram 8 or bus 23 to Trastevere; from Piazza Sonnino, turn left on Via dei Genovesi and then right on Via de' Vascellari. Secondi: 10,000–28,000L ($5–$15). AE, DC, MC, V. Open: Dinner daily.*

Filetti di Baccalà

$ Campo de' Fiori   Roman

Hidden in a courtyard (or overgrown side street), this restaurant has been famous for decades for one specialty: *filetti di baccalà,* delicious slabs of deep-fried salt cod. The *filetti* are so good, it's almost all they serve, but the menu also includes salad, beans, *puntarelle* (one of the typical fresh greens of Rome) when in season and some reasonably good choices of wine. The desserts are few but homemade. Go early, because lines begin even before darkness falls in the warm months.

Largo dei Librari 88. ☎ *06-686-4018. Reservations not accepted. Bus: 116 to Campo de' Fiori; Largo dei Librari is just off Via dei Giubbonari, down from Campo de' Fiori. Secondi: 5,000L ($2.70) per filetto. No credit cards. Open: Dinner Mon–Sat.*

Il Chianti Vineria

$$$ Fontana di Trevi   Tuscan

Sharing an outdoor terrace with La Taverna Trevi (see the restaurant's listing, later in this chapter) and located in a *largo* (widening of a street, like a small square) behind the Fontana di Trevi, Il Chianti is a wine bar with a buffet that specializes in Tuscan cuisine and offers a variety of light choices. The typical cheese and cold cuts are excellent. Savor the tasty menu choices with a glass from the excellent wine list.

Via del Lavatore 81. ☎ *06-678-7550. Reservations recommended. Bus: 85, 60, 116, or 117 to Via del Tritone, and then turn right on Via Poli, pass in front of the Fontana di Trevi, and turn right on Via del Lavatore. Secondi: 12,000–20,000L ($7–$11). MC, V. Open: Lunch and dinner Mon–Sat.*

Il Sanpietrino

$$$$ Teatro Marcello   Roman

This restaurant, in the Jewish Ghetto, is located steps from all the sites of ancient Rome. In its stylish dining rooms you can taste innovative interpretations of Roman cuisine with a lot of seafood. An ample choice of seafood appetizers (such as fresh anchovies baked between slices of eggplant), seafood ravioli, and other delicacies surprises and satisfies the most demanding palates.

Piazza Costaguti 15. ☎ *06-6880-6471. Reservations recommended. Bus: 60 to last stop, and then walk up Via del Portico d'Ottavia and turn right on Via Progresso to* the piazza. Secondi: 22,000–34,000L ($12–$19). AE, DC, MC, V. Open: Lunch Mon–Fri; dinner Mon–Sat.

La Taverna Trevi da Tarquinio

$$$ Fontana di Trevi   Abbruzzese/Roman

Opening into a courtyard-sized square shared with Il Chianti, the Taverna is a great spot to dine outdoors in good weather. Given its location, you'd expect one of those touristy prix-fixe places, but Romans love the center as much as visitors and this restaurant has so far maintained its quality standards. The food is good traditional Abbruzzese and Roman, with a variety of delicious homemade pastas, *abbacchio,* and a choice of grilled meats.

Via del Lavatore 82. ☎ *06-679-2470. Reservations recommended. Bus: 85, 60, 116, or 117 to Via del Tritone, and then turn right on Via Poli, pass in front of the Fontana di Trevi, and turn right on Via del Lavatore. Secondi: 15,000–28,000L ($8–$15). MC, V. Open: Lunch and dinner Mon–Sat.*

La Veranda

$$$$ San Pietro   Contemporary Italian

This restaurant is in the Palazzo della Rovere, which also houses the Hotel Columbus (see "Where to Stay in Roma"). During fine weather, you can eat in one of Rome's nicest garden courtyards. The changing menu offers seasonal specialties and regional dishes, mainly Roman and Tuscan. Of particular interest are the *piatti della storia,* dishes made from recipes of Renaissance Rome. Of these, try the soup of porcini mushrooms and pears or the rabbit with pistachio sauce. For an appetizer, try the crêpes with chestnuts and radicchio.

Borgo Santo Spirito 73. ☎ *06-687-2973. Reservations recommended on weekends. Bus: 62 to San Pietro, and then turn right on Borgo Santo Spirito. Secondi: 26,000–40,000L ($14–$22), including contorno. AE, MC, V. Open: Lunch and dinner Fri–Wed; closed Aug.*

Mongolia Barbecue

$ Porta Pia   Mongolian

Mongolians in Rome? Well, they're much nicer since the days of Attila the Hun! Even Italians get sick of Italian food sometimes, and an increasing number of ethnic restaurants are opening. The first Mongolian restaurant in Rome, this popular and informal place offers Mongolian barbecue *a volontà* (all you can eat) after a sampling of a dozen appetizers. You select from raw pork, veal, beef, and lamb, complementing it with vegetables and a selection of sauces. Everything is cooked up for you by the chef on an enormous griddle.

Viale Regina Margherita 19–21. ☎ *06-854-7388. Reservations not necessary. Tram: 19 or 30 to Piazza Buenos Aires (two stops from Nomentana). Prix-fixe dinner: 23,000L ($12). AE, MC, V. Open: Dinner daily until after midnight.*

Pizzeria Camillo

$ Pantheon   Pizza a Taglio/Spaghetti

This tavern with simple wooden tables and benches serves some of the best pizza in Italy. The pizza is sold by weight, and going to the counter, ordering, and then bringing it to your table is best. The restaurant also prepares a variety of pasta dishes served at the table and a choice of *rosticceria* (roastery) specialties. One of the most delicious pizzas offers sausages and mushrooms, or you can try the pizza with peppers when it's available.

Via Campo Marzio 45a. ☎ *06-687-1161. Reservations not accepted. Bus: 116 to Pantheon, and then walk north on Via della Maddalena to Via Campo Marzio. Pizza: 4,000–9,000L ($2.15–$4.85) per pound. MC, V. Open: Lunch and dinner Mon–Sat.*

Pizzeria Ivo

$ Trastevere   Pizza

One of Rome's most established pizzerias, Ivo is as popular with locals as it is with visitors. Luckily, the place is big! Here you can enjoy an entire range of pizzeria appetizers, pizzas, crostini, and calzones. All the pizzas are good, but we love the one with *fiori di zucca* (zucchini flowers) when in season and the *capricciosa* (prosciutto, carciofini, and olives).

Via di San Francesco a Ripa 158. ☎ *06-581-7082. Reservations not necessary. Tram: 8 to Via di San Francesco a Ripa (on the right off Viale Trastevere). Secondi: 9,500–15,000L ($5–$8). DC, MC, V. Open: Lunch and dinner Wed–Mon.*

Quelli della Taverna

$ Campo de' Fiori   Roman

In a quiet street in the middle of a very busy area, the Taverna is a quality restaurant in a touristy sector of town where it's sometimes difficult to choose a place to eat. The very moderate prices and hearty portions are the draw, and the well-prepared Roman specialties are served in a country-style ambiance. The *antipasto misto* is a must, with a choice of savory vegetables, cheese, and cold cuts from the nearby hills. The primi are superb; go for the *amatriciana,* the *carbonara,* or any of the fresh pasta specials. For a secondo, the *saltimbocca* is very good and the *involtini di melanzane* (stuffed rolled eggplant) delicious. There's also a selection of homemade desserts.

Via dei Barbieri 25. ☎ *06-686-9660. Reservations recommended. Bus: 58, 60, or 62 to Largo Argentina; Via dei Barbieri is just off Largo Argentina behind the theater. Secondi: 10,000–18,000L ($5–$10). MC, V. Open: Lunch and dinner Mon–Sat.*

Ristorante 'Gusto

$$$ Piazza del Popolo   Italian/International

This restaurant is a very welcome addition to the Roman scene. If an establishment can be all things to all people, this is it: a restaurant, an *enoteca* (a kind of wine shop and bar), a pizzeria, a wine bar, and a cigar club. It even has a store that sells cookbooks and kitchenware. The restaurant offers several prix-fixe options, and you can order the self-service lunch buffet for 14,000L ($8). The pastas are good choices, but the pizzas (like *chicoria* and *funghi*) are nice too. There are even dishes like couscous, wok-prepared Asian dishes, and continental choices. The restaurant is popular with workers during the day and young people at night — especially on weekends, when you can get pizza until 1:30 a.m. The wine bar in back offers a large choice of drinks, whiskies, and *grappas* (Italian brandy).

Via della Frezza 23. ☎ *06-322-6273. Reservations recommended for dinner. Bus: 117 or 119 from Piazza del Popolo to Via della Frezza/Piazza Augusto Imperatore. Secondi: 18,000-32,000L ($10–$17). AE, MC, DC, V. Open: Lunch and dinner daily.*

Ristorante il Matriciano

$$$$ San Pietro   Roman

This family-run restaurant is a wonderful place to eat outside in summer, but you must have a reservation because it's well known and popular. The name reflects one of the specialties, *bucatini all'Amatriciana.* You can also find excellent versions of other typical specialties of Roman cuisine, such as *abbacchio al forno.*

Via dei Gracchi 55 ☎ *06-321-2327. Reservations required. Metro: Line A to Ottaviano/San Pietro, and then walk on Via Ottaviano south toward San Pietro and turn left on Via dei Gracchi. Secondi: 22,000–30,000L ($12–$16). AE, CD, MC, V. Open: Winter, lunch and dinner Thurs–Tues; Summer, lunch and dinner Sun–Fri. Closed three weeks in Aug.*

Runner-up restaurants

Abbruzzi

$$ Fontana di Trevi   At this moderately priced and popular Roman/Abbruzzese trattoria off the Fontana di Trevi, the big attraction is the large selection of cold appetizers. Via del Vaccaro 1. ☎ **06-679-3897.** Bus: 62 or minibus 116 or 119.

La Scaletta

$ Pantheon   A rustic *birreria* and *vineria,* it offers a huge selection of vino (wine), and you can find something to eat for as little as 7,000L ($3.80). Try the polenta with mushrooms for 15,000L ($8). The restaurant stays open until 2 a.m., and it's only a stone's throw from the Pantheon. Via della Maddalena 46–49. ☎ **06-679-2149.** Bus: 116.

Maccheroni

$$ Pantheon This clean, bright, nouveau trattoria has great food, including excellent pastas and wines, just north of the Pantheon. Piazza delle Coppelle. ☎ **06-6830-7895.** Internet: http://italmarket.com/rm/maccheroni. E-mail: maccheroni@italmarket.com. Bus: 116.

Pizza Ciro

$ Piazza di Spagna This pure Neapolitan pizzeria opened in Rome in 1996, after 100 years of service in Naples; it offers an unbeatable 10,000L ($5.40) lunch special including a margherita pizza and a beer. Via della Mercede 43–45. ☎ **06-678-6015.** Bus: 62.

Quirino

$$$ Piazza di Spagna A traditional Roman restaurant with some Sicilian influence, Quirino's focus is on seafood, from fritto di paranza (mixed deep-fried small fish and calamari) to grilled fish. Via delle Muratte 84. ☎ **06-679-4108.** Bus: 62.

Chapter 12

Exploring Rome

• •

In This Chapter

▶ Experiencing Rome's great attractions

▶ Finding Rome's hot shopping spots

▶ Discovering where Rome comes to life at night

• •

The Eternal City awaits you, as it has for millions of others for thousands of years. At its low point in the Dark Ages, only a few hundred people lived in the city among the ruins. Not anymore! Today, a couple million modern people try to live and work in a place designed for chariots instead of cabs and pedestrians instead of hordes of kids on motorbikes. Rome also contains a state — the Vatican, the world's second-smallest sovereign state. Whether you love it or not, one complaint you can't make about Rome (as some do about Florence and Venice) is that it's a lifeless museum of the past.

During your trip, remember that Rome wasn't built in a day. Likewise, you had better give yourself more than one day if you want to sample all of its colors and flavors.

There's No Place like Rome, There's No Place like Rome: The Top Sights

The ticket booths at the sights that we mention in this section usually stop selling tickets about an hour before closing. Similarly, many outdoor sights regulate their closing time by daylight (closing an hour before sunset), which means that attraction hours of operation vary according to the seasons. And, in line with the effort to make all sights more available to the ever-increasing tourist hordes, city cultural officials decided that some major attractions will stay open later in summer. Therefore, when you arrive in Rome, check the information points around town for the latest set of museum and attraction hours.

 To appreciate fully the Roman Forum, Colosseum, and other ruins, buy a copy of the small book entitled *Rome Past and Present* (Vision Publications), sold in bookstores or on stands near the Forum. Its plastic overleafs show you how Rome looked 2,000 years ago.

Rome Attractions

Basilica di San Giovanni in Laterano **41**
Basilica di San Paolo Fuori Le Mura **45**
Basilica di San Pietro **5**
Basilica di Santa Maria Maggiore **24**
Campo de' Fiori **11**
Capitolino **43**
Castel Sant'Angelo **6**
Catacombe di San Callisto **43**
Chiesa dell'Immacolata Concezione **19**

Circo Massimo **36**
Colosseo **38**
Domus Aurea **39**
Fontana di Trevi **26**
Fori Imperiali **30**
Foro Romano **31**
Galleria Borghese **15**
Galleria Doria Pamphili **28**
Gianicolo **13**
Giardini Vaticani **4**
Keats-Shelley House **18**
Mercati Traianei **29**
Musei Capitolini **33**
Musei Vaticani **3**
Museo della Civiltá Romana **42**
Museo Etrusco di Villa Giulia **1**
Museo Nazionale Romano **22**
Palatino **37**
Palazzo Altemps **7**
Palazzo Barberini/Galleria
   Nazionale d'Arte Antica **20**
Palazzo dei Conservatori **34**
Palazzo Farnese **12**
Palazzo Massimo **23**
Pantheon **9**
Piazza Colonna **27**
Piazza del Popolo **2**
Piazza del Quirinale/
   Palazzo del Quirinale **25**
Piazza di Spagna/
   Scalinata di Spagna **17**
Piazza Navona **8**
Santa Maria d'Aracoeli **32**
Santa Maria in Cosmedin/
   Bocca della Verità **35**

Santa Maria sopra Minerva **10**
Santuario della Scala Santa **40**
Terme di Caracalla **44**
Terme di Diocleziano **21**
Testaccio **14**
Tomba di Cecilia Metella **43**
Via Appia Antica **43**
Villa Borghese **16**

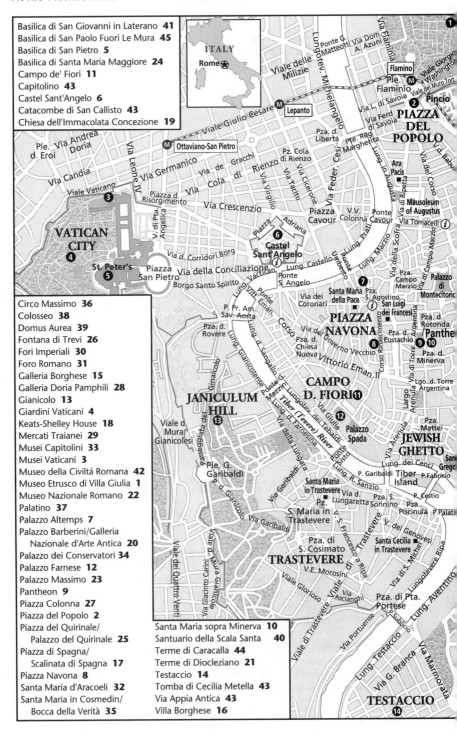

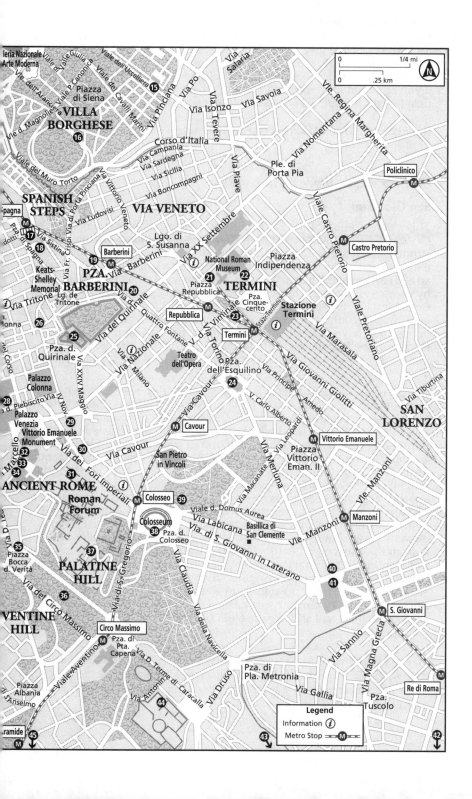

leria Nazionale
Arte Moderna

Viale Giulia

Viale dell'Uccelliera

Via Salaria

Via Po

Via Isonzo

Via Savoia

Vle. Regina Margherita

0   1/4 mi

0   .25 km

N

Viale P. Canonica

Piazza
di Siena **15**

Via Pinciana

Via Tevere

Via Nomentana

Viale del Cavalli Marini

Viale dell'Arancio

Viale P. Canonica

**VILLA
BORGHESE 16**

Via d. Magnolie

Corso d'Italia

Via Campania

Via Sardegna

Via Sicilia

Via Piave

Ple. di
Porta Pia

Policlinico
M

Viale del Muro Torto

Via di Porta Pinciana

Via Vittorio Veneto

Via Boncompagni

Viale Castro Pretorio

**SPANISH
STEPS**

pagna

Via Ludovisi

VIA VENETO

Via di Porta Pinciana

Via XX Settembre

Castro Pretorio
M

dotti

M **17**

Via Sistina

18

Via Fr. Crispi

Lgo. di
S. Susanna

Lgo. di
S. Susanna

Barberini

i

**National Roman
Museum 22**

Piazza
Indipendenza

Via Salaria

Spagna

Via Barberini

M **19**

Piazza
Repubblica

TERMINI

Viale Pretoriano

Keats-
Shelley
Memorial

**PZA.
BARBERINI 20**

Via del Quirinale

Pza.
Cinque-
cento

**Stazione
Termini**

i

i

Via Tritone

Lg. de
Tritone

Quattro Fontane

V. d. Viminale

23
M

Stazione Termini

Via Marasala

Via Giovanni Giolitti

onna

26

Via Nazionale

Repubblica

Termini
M

Via del Corso

25

Pza. d.
Quirinale

Via Milano

Via XXIV Maggio

Teatro
dell'Opera

Pza.
dell'Esquilino
24

V. Carlo Alberto

Via Principe
Amedo

Via Tiburtina

**SAN
LORENZO**

**Palazzo
Colonna**

Via IV Nov.

d. Plebiscito

28

**Palazzo
Venezia**

29

Via Cavour

Cavour
M

Vittorio Emanuele
M

Vittorio Emanuele Monument

30

Via dei Fori Imperiali

Via Cavour

San Pietro
in Vincoli

Piazza
Vittorio
Eman. II

Via Merulana

Via Leopardi

Vle. Manzoni

32

33

31

ANCIENT ROME

i

Via Macanate

34

**Roman
Forum**

Colosseo
M **39**

Viale d. Domus Aurea

Via Labicana

Basilica di
San Clemente

Manzoni
M

Vle. Manzoni

**Colosseum
38**

Pza. d.
Colosseo

Via di S. Giovanni in Laterano

Via D. di S. Gregorio

35

Piazza
Bocca
d. Verità

37

**PALATINE
HILL**

Via Claudia

40

41

36

Via del Circo Massimo

**VENTINE
HILL**

Circo Massimo
M

Pza. di
Pta.
Capena

Via della Navicella

S. Giovanni
M

Viale Aventino

Via D. Terme di Caracalla

Via Druso

Pza. di
Pla. Metronia

Via Sannio

Via Magna Grecia

Piazza
Albania

d. S'Anselmo

Via Antonin di Caracalla

44

Via Gallia

Pza.
Tuscolo

Re di Roma
M

ramide

45
M

43

Legend

Information **i**

Metro Stop M

42

Note that the cumulative ticket for ancient Rome can save you a little money if you want to visit all the included attractions. The pass is valid for three days and gives you access to the Colosseo, Palatino, Terme di Caracalla, and Museo Nazionale Romano (including the Palazzo Massimo, Terme di Diocleziano, and Palazzo Altemps). It's a good idea if you're planning an extensive visit to all ancient Roman sites. The ticket costs 30,000L ($16) and is sold at each of the participating sights.

Here is a rundown of Rome's top attractions (see Chapter 11 for neighborhood locations):

Basilica di San Giovanni in Laterano

San Giovanni

This church, and not the Basilica di San Pietro, is the cathedral of the diocese of Rome. Built in A.D.13 by Constantine, it underwent many vicissitudes, including being sacked by the Vandals (a barbarian tribe whose name has given us the word *vandalism*), burned, and then damaged in an 896 earthquake. The basilica was restored and rebuilt at various times by various architects. The facade, designed and executed by Alessandro Galilei in 1735, is crowned by 15 giant statues (7 m/22 ft. tall) representing Christ, St. John the Baptist, John the Evangelist, and other Doctors of the Church; you can see them from many parts of Rome. Outside is an **Egyptian obelisk,** the tallest in Rome (32 m/105 ft.), consecrated in the fourth century as a symbol of Christianity's victory over pagan cults.

The interior of the basilica as you see it today was redesigned by Borromini in the seventeenth century. The **papal altar** — under a beautiful fourteenth-century *baldacchino* (canopy) — conserves an important relic: the wooden altar on which Peter and the other paleo-Christian popes after him are said to have celebrated mass in ancient Rome's catacombs. In the left transept is the altar of the **Santissimo Sacramento,** decorated with four giant gilded bronze columns that are the only remains of the original basilica. Under the *baldacchino* of this altar is another important relic: It is said to be the table of Christ's last supper. The apse was redone during the nineteenth century, and its mosaics are copies of the original medieval mosaics. However, the fresco fragment depicting Pope Boniface VIII, who declared the first Papal Jubilee in 1300, is from the thirteenth century. The **Battistero (Baptistry)** was built by Constantine in the fourth century, making it the first of the Western world. (The walls are still original, though the interior was restored several times and the present form was designed by Borromini.) The thirteenth-century **cloister** was designed by Vassalletto and is a showcase for remains and art from the older basilica, including paleo-Christian inscriptions.

Piazza di San Giovanni in Laterano. ☎ *06-6988-6433. Metro: Line A to San Giovanni. Bus: 81, 85, 850, or minibus 117. Tram: 3. Open: Basilica and cloister daily 7 a.m.–6 p.m. (in summer to 6:45 p.m.); Baptistry daily 9 a.m.–1 p.m. Admission: Basilica free; cloister 4,000L ($2.20).*

Basilica di San Paolo Fuori Le Mura
(St. Paul Outside the Walls)

Ostiense/San Paolo

According to tradition, the body of St. Paul was buried after his martyrdom on this road (Via Ostiense) leading out of Rome. As early as the time of Emperor Constantine in the fourth century, a church was built around St. Paul's tomb (below the high altar). Consecrated in A.D. 324 but later vastly enlarged, this magnificent church, second in size only to St. Peter's, was almost totally destroyed by fire in 1823 and rebuilt using marble from the original structure. (The apse and triumphal arch are the most ancient parts.) The mosaic in the apse is a faithful copy of the thirteenth-century one, reconstructed using parts of the original damaged by the fire. The **baldacchino (canopy)** — a masterpiece by Arnolfo di Cambio from 1285 — miraculously escaped the fire. Under the altar is the **sepulchre of St. Paul,** the tomb containing the saint's remains; it's accessible via a staircase. The interior is vast and impressive (divided by 80 granite columns), regardless of its age; the windows may look like stained glass but are actually made of translucent alabaster. The **cloisters** are original, and you'd have to go to Sicily to find such distinctively carved and decorated columns of so many diverse patterns.

Via Ostiense 184. ☎ *06-541-0341. Metro: Line B to Basilica di San Paolo. Bus: 23. Open: Church daily 7 a.m.–6:30 p.m.; cloister daily 9 a.m.–1 p.m. and 3–6 p.m. Admission: Free.*

Basilica di Santa Maria Maggiore

Termini

This church's history stretches back 1,600 years, and though it's undergone many changes over the centuries, Santa Maria Maggiore remains one of the city's four great basilicas. Ordered constructed by Pope Sisto III, it was built as a sanctuary for Mary (mother of Jesus) and was originally referred to as Santa Maria della Neve (St. Mary of the Snow) because its outline was drawn in the snow that had miraculously fallen in the summer of A.D. 352. The facade of Santa Maria Maggiore looks like your typical baroque church (Rome is full of them); the current facade was designed by Ferdinando Fuga, who sandwiched it between two palaces that had been built in the meantime (one in the seventeenth and the other in the eighteenth century). The walls, though, are original, as are the mosaics of the apse and side walls. Although restored, the floors are the original twelfth-century Cosmatesco-style, and the fifteenth-century coffered wooden ceiling is richly decorated with gold (said to be the first gold brought back from the New World and donated by the Spanish queen). One of the church's main attractions is in the loggia: the **thirteenth-century mosaics** preserved from the old facade. Look carefully to the right side of the altar for the **tomb of Gian Lorenzo Bernini,** Italy's most important baroque sculptor/architect. In the **crypt** are relics of what many people say are pieces of Jesus' crib.

Piazza di Santa Maria Maggiore. ☎ *06-488-1094. Metro: Line A or B to Termini, and then walk south on Via Cavour. Bus: 70. Open: Daily 7 a.m.–7 p.m. Admission: Free.*

Campo de' Fiori

Centro

Surrounded by cafes, restaurants, and bars, the lovely square of Campo de' Fiori boasts many attractions. Its **fruit-and-vegetable market** is one of the city's best and certainly one of the liveliest. Though popular with working people as a lunch spot, the campo is even more popular with young people (both Romans and foreigners) at night. The central statue of the hooded Giordano Bruno hints at the more sinister parts of the campo's history — it was the site of executions in the Middle Ages and Renaissance, and Bruno was burned at the stake here in 1600. Bruno was a philosopher who championed the ideas of early scientists like Copernicus and maintained such heretical ideas as that the earth revolved around the sun. Nearby on Piazza Farnese is the **Palazzo Farnese** (currently the seat of the French Embassy), surely one of Rome's most dramatic buildings, designed by Sangallo and Michelangelo. The cleaning completed in 1999 turned its somber gray color into a startling pale yellow (you can't visit the interior, however).

Off Largo Argentina, roughly between Via Arenula and Corso Vittorio Emanuele II. Bus: 62 or 64 to Corso Vittorio Emanuele at Largo san Pantaleo or minibus 116 to Campo de' Fiori.

Castel Sant'Angelo

San Pietro/Vatican

This "castle" began as a mausoleum to house the remains of Emperor Hadrian and other important Romans. However, it may have been incorporated into the city's defenses as early as 403 and was attacked by the Goths (one of the barbarian tribes who pillaged Rome in its decline) in 537. Later, the popes used it as a fortress and hideout and connected it to the Vatican palace with an elevated corridor, which you can still see near Borgo Pio stretching between St. Peter's and the castle. Castel Sant'Angelo now houses a museum of arms and armor; you can also visit the papal apartments from the Renaissance as well as the horrible cells in which prisoners were kept (among them sculptor Benvenuto Cellini).

Lungotevere Castello 50. ☎ 06-687-5036. Bus: 23, 62, or 64 to Lungotevere Vaticano, and then walk north along the river. Open: Daily 9 a.m.–7 p.m.; closed Mon and last Tues of each month. Admission: 8,000L ($4.30) adults, children 17 and under and adults 60 and over free.

Catacombe di San Callisto

Via Appia

There are several places to visit the catacombs in Rome (including the catacombs of St. Sebastian and those of Domitilla farther along Via Appia Antica), but this one is among the most impressive, with 20 km (12½ miles) of tunnels and galleries underground and organized on several levels. (It's cold down there at 60 feet, so bring a sweater.) The catacombs began as quarries outside ancient Rome where travertine marble and the dirt used in cement were dug. Early Christians, however, hid out, held mass, and buried their dead in the catacombs. The Catacombs of St. Callixtus (Callixtus III was an early pope, elected in 217) have four levels, including a crypt of several early popes and the tomb where St. Cecilia's remains were found. Some of the original paintings and decoration are still intact and show that Christian symbolism — doves, anchors, and fish — was already developed.

Via Appia Antica 110. ☎ 06-513-6725. Metro/Bus: Line A to Colli Albani (on Sun to Arco di Travertino), and then bus 660 to Via Appia Antica. Open: Thurs–Tues 8:30 a.m. to noon and 2:30–5 p.m. (in summer to 5:30 p.m.). Admission: 8,000L ($4.30) adults, 4,000L ($2.15) children 16 and under.

Colosseo

Centro

The Colosseum, along with St. Peter's Basilica, is Rome's most recognizable monument. However, the Colosseum isn't its official name. Begun under the Flavian emperor Vespasian, it was named the Amphiteatrum Flavium and finished in A.D. 80. The nickname "Colosseo" came from the colossal statue of Nero that once stood nearby — it was part of the 200-plus-acre grounds of Nero's **Domus Aurea (Golden House),** the remains of which you can tour nearby (☎ **06-3974-9907;** admission 10,000L/$5, plus 2,000L/$1.10 for advance reservation; open daily 9 a.m. to 7 p.m.). Estimates show that the Colosseo could accommodate as many as 50,000 spectators. The entertainment included fights between gladiators, battles with wild animals, and naval battles when the arena was flooded (these gory details appeal to kids). In the labyrinth of chambers beneath the original wooden floor of the Colosseum, deadly weapons, vicious beasts, and unfortunate human participants were prepared for the mortal combats. (Historians now believe, however, that Christians were never fed to lions here.) The Colosseo was damaged by fires and earthquakes and eventually abandoned, and then used as a marble quarry for the monuments of Christian Rome, until Pope Benedict XV consecrated it in the eighteenth century. Next to the Colosseo is the **Arch of Constantine,** built in 315 to commemorate the emperor's victory over the pagan Maxentius in 312. Pieces from other monuments were reused, so Constantine's monument includes carvings honoring Marcus Aurelius, Trajan, and Hadrian.

In the summer of 2000, for the first time in centuries, the Colosseo was brought to life again with performances under the aegis of the Estate Romana (see "Calendar of Events" in Chapter 2 and "Nightlife" later in this chapter).

Via dei Fori Imperiali. ☎ 06-700-4261. Metro: Line B to Colosseo. Bus: 81, 85, 850, or minibus 117; Tram: 3. Open: Daily 9 a.m.–6 p.m. (in summer to 7 p.m.). Admission: 10,000L ($5).

Fontana di Trevi

Centro

The massive Trevi Fountain in its little piazza became one of *the* sights of Rome following the opening of the film *Three Coins in the Fountain,* though today it seems that many of the thousands who clog the space in front of it don't take the time to really look at it — instead, they throw coins in it, have their pictures taken in front of it, and go away. You'll be lucky if you have a tranquil moment to actually appreciate the artwork. The fountain was begun by Bernini and Pietro da Cortona, but there was a 100-year lapse in the works and the fountain wasn't completed until 1751 by Nicola Salvi. The central figure is Neptune, who guides a chariot pulled by plunging sea horses. Tritons (mythological figures that live in the ocean) guide the horses, and the surrounding scene is one of wild nature and bare stone.

Of course, you *have* to toss a coin in the Trevi. To do things properly, hold a lira coin in your right hand, turn your back to the fountain, and toss the coin over your shoulder (being careful not to bean anyone behind you). Then the spirit of the fountain will see to it you return to Rome one day — or that's the tradition, at least.

Piazza di Trevi. Bus: 62 or minibus 116 or 119 to Via del Tritone, then walk right on Via Poli.

Foro Romano, Fori Imperiali, and Palatino

Centro

Rome has many forums. The original forum, the **Foro Romano,** lies in the valley between the Palatino and Capitolino (Palatine and Capitoline hills). The **Via Sacra** ("sacred way") runs through it. This area was the heart of Rome for more than a thousand years, and a stone discovered under the Forum in 1899 bears an inscription from the time of the Roman kings (sixth century B.C.). The Forum boasts many ruins (some, like the sanctuary of the sewer goddess Venus Cloaca, are just a mark on the ground) as well as a few standing buildings. The most important (but only a "restored" structure from 1937) is the square **Curia,** on the spot where the Senate once met. (Pop inside to see the third-century marble inlay floor.) The **Temple of Antoninus and Faustina** (Antoninus Pius succeeded Hadrian in 138) was later turned into a church and given a baroque facade (Chiesa di San Lorenzo in Miranda). Near the Curia is the **Arch of Septimius Severus,** built in 203 to commemorate his victories. The arch mentioned his two sons, Caracalla and Geta, but after Caracalla murdered Geta, Geta's name was removed. At the other end of the Forum is the **Arch of Titus.** Titus reigned as emperor from 79 to 81. If you buy a map of the Forum when you enter, you can identify the sometimes faint traces of a host of other structures (also, see our map "The Roman Forum and Imperial Forums").

If you find the ruins in the Foro Romano confusing, you'll find those on the **Palatino** behind it sometimes incomprehensible. Huge blocks of brick surrounded by trees and greenery testify mutely to what was once an

The Roman Forum and Imperial Forums

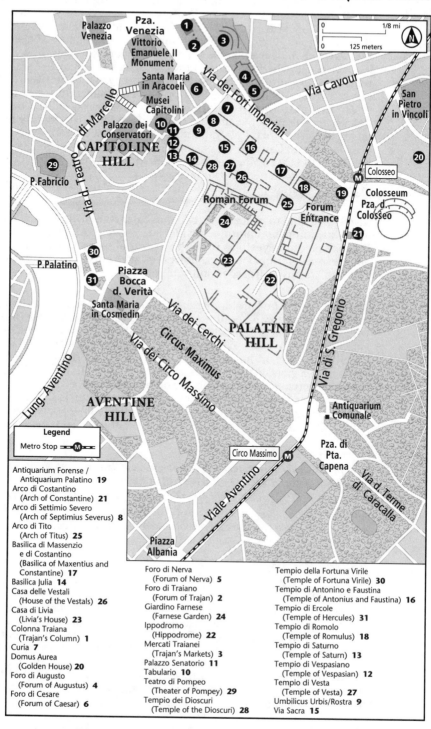

0 ——— 1/8 mi
0 ——— 125 meters

Palazzo Venezia
Pza. Venezia
Vittorio Emanuele II Monument
Santa Maria in Aracoeli
Via dei Fori Imperiali
Via Cavour
San Pietro in Vincoli
Musei Capitolini
Palazzo dei Conservatori
Via di Marcello
CAPITOLINE HILL
P.Fabricio
Via d. Teatro
Colosseo
Colosseum
Pza. d. Colosseo
Roman Forum
Forum Entrance
P.Palatino
Piazza Bocca d. Verità
Santa Maria in Cosmedin
Via dei Cerchi
PALATINE HILL
Via di S. Gregorio
Circus Maximus
Via dei Circo Massimo
Lung. Aventino
AVENTINE HILL
Antiquarium Comunale
Pza. di Pta. Capena
Via d. Terme di Caracalla
Legend
Metro Stop ===M===
Circo Massimo M
Viale Aventino
Piazza Albania

enormous residential complex of patrician houses and imperial palaces, built under the grandiose ambitions of the emperors. The throne room of the **Domus Flavia** was approximately 100 feet wide by 131 feet long. Although Augustus began the development of the Palatine residences, they were vastly expanded under Domitian. The Palatino is also where the first Roman developments started and where Romulus drew the original square for the foundation of Rome. Excavations in the area found remains that date back to the eighth century B.C. The **Casa di Livia (Livia's House)** is one of the best preserved homes. During the Middle Ages, the site was transformed into a fortress, and during the Renaissance it again became the residence of the aristocracy, who built large villas (the **Horti Palatini** built by the Farnese on top of the palaces of Tiberius and Caligula, for example). From the hill, you can look down behind to the **Circo Massimo (Circus Maximus),** where a quarter million Romans once watched chariot races. Unfortunately, the structures flanking the arena were plundered for their stone, like many Roman buildings.

Also interesting to visit are the two museums, the **Antiquarium Forense** and **Antiquarium Palatino,** inside an ex-convent. The Antiquarium Forense contains vestiges from the necropolis underneath the Forum, and the Antiquarium Palatino showcases art from the excavations of the Palatino, including frescoes and sculptures.

After you leave the Foro Romano, walk along the **Via dei Fori Imperiali,** from which you can see the remains of the **Fori Imperiali (Imperial Forums)** built by Caesar, Augustus, and Trajan, which are still being excavated. They were covered in modern times (under Mussolini in the 1920s) to build Via dei Fori Imperiali, a major artery of modern Rome. If you'd like a better view of them, you can visit the **Mercati Traianei (Trajan's Markets),** a two-story construction behind and above Trajan's Forum; it housed stalls and small boutiques, like an ancient mall. Entrance to the Mercati Traianei is on Via 4 Novembre (☎ **06-679-0048;** open Tuesday to Saturday 9 a.m. to 4 p.m. and Sunday 9 a.m. to 1:30 p.m.; admission 3,750L/$2).

Foro Romano: Via dei Fori Imperiali; Palatino: Via di San Gregorio 30; Antiquariums: Piazza Santa Maria Nova 53. ☎ *06-699-0110. Metro: Line B to Colosseo, cross the street to the entrance to the right of the Colosseo. Bus: 85, 850, or minibus 117. Open: Summer daily 9 a.m.–6 p.m. (Sun. to 1 p.m.); winter daily 9 a.m.–3 p.m. (Sun. to 1 p.m.). Admission: Forum free; Palatino and Antiquariums 12,000L ($7).*

Galleria Borghese

Villa Borghese

Reopened in 1997 after 13 years of restoration, the Galleria Borghese is housed in the building that Cardinal Scipione Borghese created for his art collection inside the Villa Borghese (now a large public park; see "More Cool Things to See and Do"). Only a limited number of visitors is allowed inside at one time, so making reservations is essential (see the phone number at the end of this listing). Your visit is limited to two hours, but the large number of truly amazing works makes you wish for more time (or a second visit). The ground floor focuses on sculpture, including Canova's sensual reclining *figure of Paulina Borghese* (Napoleon's sister) and dramatic works by the young Gian Lorenzo Bernini showing breathtaking stone carvings. His *David* is in the middle of a slingshot wind-up and full of charmingly boyish concentration; his *Apollo and Daphne* captures the moment when Daphne turns into a laurel tree, her fingers bursting into leaves and bark climbing her legs. In the *Rape of Proserpine,* a sculpture he executed in collaboration with his father, the god's fingers seem actually to press into her marble flesh. The extensive painting collection contains countless masterpieces: Caravaggio's haunting *self-portrait as Bacchus* and his *St. Jerome Writing,* Antonello da Messina's subtle and mysterious *Portrait of a Man,* a young Raphael's *Deposition,* and Tiziano's *Sacred and Profane Love.* Andrea del Sarto, Coreggio, Lucas Cranach, Bronzino, Lorenzo Lotto, and many other artists are also represented.

After your visit, you can walk in the extensive park; one highlight is the **Piazza di Siena** (see "More cool things to see and do").

Piazzale Scipione Borghese 5. ☎ *06-8424-1607 or 06-32810 for reservations; otherwise, 06-854-8577 or 06-841-6542. Bus: 52, 53, or 910 to Via Pinciana behind the villa, 490 to Viale San Paolo del Brasile inside the park or minibus 116 to the Galleria Borghese. Metro: Line A to Spagna; take the Villa Borghese exit and walk up Viale del Museo Borghese. Internet:* www.ticketeria.it. *Open: Summer Tues–Sat 9 a.m.–7 p.m., Sun 9 a.m.–1 p.m.; Winter Tues–Sat 9 a.m.–5 p.m., Sun 9 a.m.–1 p.m. Admission: 12,000L ($7).*

Musei Capitolini (Museo Capitolino, Palazzo dei Conservatori, and Tabularium)

Centro/Campidoglio

On the Capitolino (Capitoline Hill), the Musei Capitolini open onto the beautiful **Piazza del Campidoglio,** designed by Michelangelo. The oldest public collections in the world, the museums hold a treasury of ancient sculpture and an important collection of European paintings from the seventeenth and eighteenth centuries. The first masterpiece you see stands in the middle of the square, the famous **equestrian statue of Marcus Aurelius** (this is a copy; the original second-century bronze is inside for protection). The statue was saved only because early Christians thought it was the first Christian emperor Constantine. In the **Museo Capitolino** (housed in the Palazzo Nuovo), the other famous sculptures are the *Dying Gaul,* a Roman copy of a Greek original, and two statues of female warriors known as *The Amazons* (under restoration at press time) that were originally in Hadrian's Villa.

Across from the Palazzo Nuovo (Museo Capitolino) is the **Palazzo dei Conservatori.** You may have already seen photos of the huge head, hands, foot, kneecap, and other dismembered pieces of an ancient 40-foot **statue of Constantine II** that stand in the courtyard and of the famous *Lupa Capitolina,* the wolf suckling Romulus and Remus, a fifth-century B.C. bronze. Another famous work is the bronze of a **boy removing a thorn from his foot.** These artworks are ones that will likely appeal to children (especially in the fresh air of the courtyard). On the top floor is the **Pinacoteca Capitolina (Capitoline Picture Gallery):** The paintings in the Pinacoteca are amazing, including Caravaggio's *Fortune Teller* and *John the Baptist,* Titian's *Baptism of Christ,* and works by Veronese, Rubens, and others.

Between the Palazzo Nuovo and the Palazzo dei Conservatori, closing Piazza del Campidoglio to the south, is the **Palazzo Senatorio (Senatorial Palace).** This palace was used for administrative purposes until recently, when it was included in the Musei Capitolini to provide additional expository space and show the results of the recent excavations under it. It was built in the Middle Ages over the Tabularium, an imposing Roman building that housed the public archives of the Republic in Roman times. The Tabularium was built of massive stone blocks with Doric columns in the facade. You can clearly see its remains from the Forum (three of the original eleven arcades remain). It's now part of the Musei Capitolini and its admission is included in the ticket.

The Palazzo Nuovo (Museo Capitolino) was recently restored, and some Roman art was permanently moved to a new site, the **Centrale Acea Montemartini.** The first electrical plant built in Rome in 1912, it was transformed into a multimedia center in 1990 and is a beautiful setting for the art collection. Among the most important pieces are a beautiful giant mosaic with hunting scenes (20 × 40 feet) from an imperial Roman residence and some of the best examples of Roman **sculpture.**

Piazza del Campidoglio. ☎ *06-6710-2071. Bus: 60, 81, or minibus 117 to Campidoglio (on the right around the monument to Vittorio Emmanuele II). Open: Tues.–Sun. 10 a.m.–9 p.m. Admission: 12,000L ($7) for both museums and Tabularium, free last Sun. of the month.*

Extension of Museo Capitolino at the Centrale Acea Montemartini. Via Ostiense 106. ☎ *06-699-1191. Metro: Line B to Pyramide; walk down Via Ostiense. Bus: 23 to Via Ostiense. Tram: 3 to Piazza di Porta San Paolo (Stazione Ostiense, Piramide). Open: Tues–Fri 10 a.m.–6 p.m., Sat–Sun 10 p.m. Admission: 12,000L ($7) adults, 8,000L ($4.30) students and seniors.*

Museo Etrusco di Villa Giulia

Flaminio/Villa Borghese

This museum, housed in a papal villa built by the most prominent architects of the sixteenth century, boasts the world's best Etruscan collection. Originally from Asia Minor, the Etruscans were a mysterious people who preceded and ruled over the Romans up to the fifth century B.C. Many of the objects in this museum came from Cerveteri, an important Etruscan site northwest of Rome. One of the most spectacular objects is the **bride and bridegroom sarcophagus** from the sixth century B.C., upon which two enigmatic figures recline. You can also see a fairly well-preserved **chariot** and some impressive **sculptures.** Some of the most amazing works are the tiniest: The Etruscans made intricate **decorative**

objects from woven gold. (How they managed to create some of these intricate objects is still not known today.) In summer, the garden is the site of musical events (see "Nightlife").

Piazzale di Villa Giulia 9. ☎ 06-322-6571. Tram: 3 or 19 to last stop, and then walk down Viale delle Belle Arti to Piazzale di Villa Giulia or 225 to Via di Villa Giulia. Open: Tues–Sat 9 a.m.–7 p.m., Sun 9 a.m.–2 p.m. Admission: 8,000L ($4.30) adults, children 17 and under and adults 60 and over free.

Museo Nazionale Romano

Termini

The National Roman Museum is actually housed in three separate locations, one of which is the Palazzo Altemps (see the next listing). The two other locations are the **Terme di Diocleziano (Baths of Diocletian)** and the nearby **Palazzo Massimo.** Many of the objects in the National Roman Museum originally came from the Terme, parts of which were later used to build **Santa Maria degli Angeli** on Piazza della Repubblica (☎ 06-488-0812). Other pieces of ancient art and sculpture have been added from excavations in Rome's environs. The museum was founded in 1889, and its heart is the **Ludovisi Collection** — much of which is now housed in the reopened Palazzo Altemps (going here first is a good idea).

Among the pieces in the Museo Nazionale are a **satyr pouring wine,** a Roman copy of the original by Greek sculptor Praxiteles; the *Daughter of Niobe* from the Gardens of Sallust; and an *Apollo* copied from a sculpture by Phidias, one of the greatest Greek sculptors. These few examples are only highlights — the museum's collection includes literally hundreds of statues.

Terme di Diocleziano: Via G. Romita 8. ☎ 06-488-0530. Metro: Line A to Repubblica; Bus: 60, 62, or minibus 116T to Piazza della Repubblica. Palazzo Massimo: Largo di Villa Peretti 1. ☎ 06-4890-3500. Metro: Line A and B to Termini; Bus: 64 or 70. Open (both museums): Tues–Sat 9 a.m.–2 p.m., Sun 9 a.m.–1 p.m. Admission: Terme free; Palazzo Massimo 12,000L ($7) — includes same-day admission to the Palazzo Altemps (see the following listing).

Palazzo Altemps

Centro/Piazza Navona

Behind Piazza Navona, the Palazzo Altemps was begun sometime before 1477; continued by the cardinal of Volterra, Francesco Soderini, from 1511 to 1523; and finished by Marco Sittico Altemps, who enlarged it at the end of the 1500s. The palace was restored in such a way that you can see the layers of medieval, Renaissance, and later decoration. Inside is the **Ludovisi Collection,** one of the world's most famous private art collections, particularly strong in Greek and Roman sculpture, as well as Egyptian works from the collection of the Museo Nazionale Romano (see earlier listing).

The most important piece from the Ludovisi Collection is the **Trono Ludovisi,** a throne thought to be the work of a fifth-century B.C. Greek sculptor brought to Rome from Calabria. One side depicts Aphrodite Urania rising from the waves, another shows a female figure offering incense, and another side features a naked female playing a flute. The remarkable **statue of a soldier** apparently committing suicide with a sword was commissioned by Julius Caesar and placed in his gardens to commemorate his victories in Gaul. The *Ares Ludovisi,* a statue restored by Bernini in 1622, is believed by art historians to be a Roman copy of an earlier Greek work and shows a warrior at rest (possibly Achilles). The colossal head of *Hera* (also known as *Juno*) is one of the best known Greek sculptures; Goethe wrote of it as his "first love" in Rome and said it was like "a canto of Homer." Ithas been identified as an idealized portrait of Antonia Augusta, mother of Emperor Claudius.

Piazza Sant'Apollinare 44. ☎ *06-683-3759. Bus: 70, 81, or minibus 116 to Via dei Coronari, walk northeast away from Piazza Navona. Open: Tues.–Sat. 9 a.m.–2 p.m., Sun. 9 a.m.–1 p.m. Admission: 12,000L ($7); includes admission to the Museo Nazionale Romano (see the preceding listing).*

Palazzo Barberini and Galleria Nazionale d'Arte Antica

Centro/Via Veneto

Finished in 1633, the Palazzo Barberini is a magnificent example of a baroque Roman palace. Bernini decorated the rococo apartments in which the gallery is now housed, and they're certainly luxurious. Also preserved in the Palazzo Barberini is the **wedding chamber** of Princess Cornelia Costanza Barberini and Prince Giulio Cesare Colonna di Sciarra, exactly as it was centuries ago. While the structure itself is an attraction, the collection of paintings that make up the Galleria Nazionale d'Arte Antica is most impressive, including Caravaggio's *Narcissus,* Tiziano's *Venus and Adonis,* and Raphael's *La Fornarina,* a loving informal portrait of the bakery girl who was his mistress (and the model for his Madonnas). The galleria's decorative arts collection contains not only Italian pieces but also fine imported objects, including some from Japan. In addition to the regular collections, the gallery frequently houses special exhibits of great interest.

Via delle Quattro Fontane 13. ☎ *06-481-4430. Metro: Line A to Barberini. Bus: 62 or minibus 116 to Quattro Fontane. Open: Mon–Fri 10 a.m.–2 p.m., Sat 9 a.m.–7 p.m., Sun 9 a.m.–1 p.m. Admission: 12,000L ($7), children 17 and under free.*

Pantheon

Centro

Rome's best preserved monument of antiquity, the imposing Pantheon was built by Marcus Agrippa in 27 B.C. (though later rebuilt by Hadrian) as a temple for all the gods (from the ancient Greek "pan-theon," meaning all Gods). It was eventually saved from destruction by being transformed into a Christian church. The adjective that all descriptions of the Pantheon should contain is *perfect:* The building is exactly 142 feet wide and 142 feet tall. The portico is supported by huge granite columns, all but three of which are original, and the bronze doors weigh 20 tons each. Inside, the empty niches surrounding the space once contained marble statues of Roman gods. Animals were once sacrificed beneath the beautiful **coffered dome** with an 18-foot hole (oculus) in the middle through which light (and sometimes rain) streams. An architectural marvel, this dome inspired Michelangelo when he was designing the dome of St. Peter's, though he made the basilica's dome 2 feet smaller. Buried here are the painter Raphael and two kings of Italy. Crowds always congregate in the square in front, **Piazza della Rotonda** (Piazza del Pantheon for Romans). The square contains a Giacomo della Porta fountain and many cafes — though the eyesore of a McDonald's and the attendant greasy smell make the place less attractive.

Piazza della Rotonda. ☎ *06-6830-0230. Bus: 62, 64, or 70 to Largo Argentina or minibus 116 to Piazza della Rotonda. Open: Mon–Sat 9 a.m.–6:30 p.m., Sun 9 a.m.– 1 p.m. Admission: Free.*

Piazza Colonna

Centro

The focus of Piazza Colonna is the imposing **Colonna di Marco Aurelio,** 83 feet tall and decorated with bas-reliefs. The column was erected in honor of Marcus Aurelius, who ruled from 161 to 180, and the reliefs recount his exploits in battles against the German tribes. A statue of the emperor once adorned the top, but in the sixteenth century, Pope Sixtus V replaced it with the statue of St. Paul that you see today. The **Palazzo Chigi** on one side of the piazza is the residence of the Italian prime minister, so don't be surprised if you see intense guys standing around with submachine guns.

At the intersection of Via Tritone and Via del Corso. Bus: 62, 85, or minibus 116, 117, or 119 to Piazza Colonna.

Piazza del Popolo

Centro

The "piazza of the people" really lives up to its name: Romans like to meet here to talk, have a drink, hang out, and people watch. You can do the same, though be warned that the two cafes fronting the piazza gouge you unmercifully if you sit at an outdoor table (or even an indoor one) instead of taking your coffee at the counter like a Roman. **Santa Maria del Popolo** stands by the gate leading out to busy **Piazzale Flaminio** (where you can catch lots of buses). Founded in 1099, the church contains magnificent Caravaggios as well as a Pinturicchio. The brace of baroque churches directly across the square are the work of Carlo Rainaldi, Bernini, and Carlo Fontana. In the center is an **Egyptian obelisk,** one of Rome's most ancient objects, dating from 1200 B.C. It came from Heliopolis, where Ramses II set it up, and was brought during Augustus's reign (it stood in the Circo Massimo until one of the popes, in their nearly endless reshuffling and meddling with monuments, moved it here). When you leave the piazza, head up the steps into the trees on the east side. This path leads to the **Pincio,** the park overlooking the square, which is one of the best places to see the sun set over Rome.

Intersection of Via del Babuino, Via del Corso, and Via de Ripetta. Metro: Line A to Flaminio. Bus: 490 to Piazzale Flaminio; Minibus 117 or 119 to Piazza del Popolo; Tram: 225 to Piazzale Flaminio.

Piazza del Quirinale and Palazzo del Quirinale

Centro

Now the home of Italy's president, the **Palazzo del Quirinale** was the residence of the king up until the end of World War II, and earlier in history, the pope lived here — or rather hid, in the case of Pius VII, who locked himself in after excommunicating Napoleon (soldiers broke in and carted him off to Fontainebleau for the duration of the Napoleonic era). The fountain (the **Fontana di Monte Cavallo**) has two giant statues of Castor and Pollux, the founders of Rome. The **Egyptian obelisk** adorning the square was taken from the Mausoleum of Augustus by Pius VI in 1793. For this attraction, you need to bring your passport so you can prove who you are. You may also get to see the changing of the guard.

End of Via XX Settembre. Metro: Line A to Barberini. Bus: minibus 116 or 117 to Via del Quirinale. No telephone. Open: Sun 9 a.m.–1 p.m.

Piazza di Spagna and the Scalinata di Spagna

Centro

The **Piazza di Spagna** and the **Scalinata di Spagna (Spanish Steps)** rising from the piazza are *the* meeting place of Rome. In spring, the steps are decorated with colorful azaleas, but in any season the square is a wonderful place to hang out — if you can find space between the wall-to-wall tourists, lovers, backpackers, Roman youth, and so on. The atmosphere is festive and convivial, though. The piazza's name comes from the sixteenth century, when the Spanish ambassador made his residence here. In those days, the piazza was far less hospitable. (People passing through the piazza at night sometimes disappeared. Because it was technically Spanish territory, the unwary could be impressed into the Spanish army.) The area's most famous resident was English poet John Keats, who lived and died in the house to the right of the steps, which is now the **Keats–Shelley Memorial** (☎ 06-678-4235; open daily 9 a.m. to 1 p.m. and 2 to 5:30 p.m.; admission 10,000L/$5). The real name of the steps isn't the Spanish Steps but the *Scalinata della Trinità del Monte,* because they lead to the **Trinità del Monte** church, whose towers loom above; the steps were funded almost entirely by the French as a preface to their church. At the foot of the steps, the **boat-shaped fountain** is by Pietro Bernini, father of Gian Lorenzo.

Via del Babuino and Via dei Condotti. Metro: Line A to Spagna. Bus: minibus 117 or 119 to Piazza di Spagna.

Piazza Navona

Centro

One of Rome's most beautiful *piazze* and also one of its most popular hangouts, Piazza Navona was built on the ruins of the **Stadium of Diocletian,** where chariot races were held (note the oval track form). In medieval times, the popes flooded the square for mock naval battles. Beside the twin-towered facade of the seventeenth-century **Santa Agnes,** the piazza boasts several baroque masterpieces, the greatest being Bernini's **Fontana dei Quattro Fiumi (Fountain of the Four Rivers),** with massive figures representing the Nile, Danube, della Plata, and Ganges — the figure with the shrouded head is the Nile, because its source was unknown at the time. The **obelisk** is Roman, from Domitian's time. At the piazza's south end is the **Fontana del Moro (Fountain of the Moor),** also by Bernini; the **Fontana di Neptuno (Fountain of Neptune),** which balances that of the Moor, is a nineteenth-century addition.

Just off Corso Rinascimento. Bus: 70 or 116 to Piazza Navona.

Santa Maria d'Aracoeli

Centro/Campidoglio

Next to Piazza del Campidoglio (see the listing for the Musei Capitolini), Santa Maria d'Aracoeli dates from 1250 and is reached by an impressive high flight of steps. It stands on the site of an ancient Roman temple. The exterior of the church is austere yet boasts two rose windows, and inside are a number of interesting works of art. The floor is an excellent example of **Cosmati marblework** (the Cosmati were Roman stone workers of the Middle Ages). The **Cappella Bufalini** is decorated with Pinturicchio masterpieces, frescoes depicting scenes from the life of St. Bernardino of Siena and St. Francis receiving the stigmata.

Piazza d'Aracoeli. ☎ *06-679-8155. Bus: 60, 81, or minibus 117 to Campidoglio; then walk to the right around the Vittorio Emanuele II Monument. Open: Daily 7 a.m. to noon and 4–7 p.m. Admission: Free.*

Santa Maria in Cosmedin and Bocca della Verità

Centro/Circo Massimo

Although this orthodox church is very pretty inside and outside — it's one of the few Roman churches to have escaped baroque restoration — the real attraction is the famous **Bocca della Verità (Mouth of Truth),** a Roman marble relief of a head with an open mouth that sits against the wall under the porch outside the church. The round marble piece used to be a manhole cover, but legend has it that if you put your hand inside the mouth while lying, it will bite off your hand. (Do you remember the scene with Gregory Peck and Audrey Hepburn from *Roman Holiday*?) Kids get a kick out of putting their hands in the mouth. The church opens on **Piazza Bocca della Verità,** one of the nicest squares in town — at its best during off hours — with two small Roman temples still standing, believed to be a temple of Vesta and a temple of Castor and Pollux.

Piazza Bocca della Verità. ☎ *06-678-1419. Bus: 81. Open: Daily 7 a.m.–6:30 p.m. Admission: Free.*

Santa Maria sopra Minerva

Centro/Pantheon

The construction of this church started in the eighth century on the foundation of an ancient temple to Minerva (goddess of wisdom), but the present structure dates from 1280. This is the only Gothic church in Rome (though you wouldn't know it from the facade, due to a seventeenth-century revision — one of many). The treasures inside include Michelangelo's *Cristo Portacroce (Redeemer)* in the sanctuary, as well as frescoes by Filippino Lippi. Under the altar are the **relics of St. Catherine of Siena.** The church also houses the tomb of the painter Fra Angelico. On the square in front of the church is the much-photographed Bernini **elephant sculpture** that serves as the base for a sixth-century B.C. Egyptian obelisk.

Piazza della Minerva. ☎ *06-679-3926. Bus: 62, 64, 70, or 81 to Largo Argentina, or minibus 116 to Piazza della Minerva. Open: Daily 7 a.m. to noon and 4–7 p.m. Admission: Free.*

The Vatican, Basilica di San Pietro, and Musei Vaticani

San Pietro/Vatican

In 1929, the Lateran Treaty between Pope Pius XI and the Italian government recognized the independent state of the Holy See, with physical seat in Vatican City (St. Peter's Basilica and adjacent buildings). Politically independent from Italy, the Vatican is the world's second-smallest sovereign state, with its own administration, post office, and tourist office. Making the **tourist office** (☎ **06-6988-4466;** open Monday to Saturday 8.30 a.m. to 7 p.m.) the first stop on your visit is a good idea — it's just to the left of the Basilica di San Pietro's entrance. In the tourist office, you can get a plan of the basilica — very useful given the sheer size of the thing — and make a reservation for a tour of the Vatican Gardens. You can also find the **Vatican Post Office** — nice stamps and faster service than the Italian one — and public rest rooms.

Hot pants may be back in style, but not at the Vatican. Here even the men wear ankle-length gowns. Bare shoulders, halter tops, tank tops, shorts, and skirts above the knee will lead to you being turned away from the basilica— *no kidding.* This is, after all, the heart and brain of the Catholic church and not just a tourist extravaganza.

Piazza San Pietro: The entrance to the Vatican is through one of the world's greatest public spaces — Bernini's Piazza San Pietro (St. Peter's Square). As you stand in the huge piazza (no cars allowed), you're in the arms of an ellipse partly enclosed by a majestic Doric-pillared colonnade, atop which stand statues of some 140 saints. Straight ahead is the facade

Attending a papal audience

An interesting event to attend is a papal audience where the pope addresses a crowd of people gathered in the Vatican. To attend a papal audience on Wednesdays (entrance between 10 and 10:30 a.m.), you must get free tickets from the Prefecture of the Papal Household (☎ 06-6988-3017) at the bronze door under Piazza di San Pietro's right-hand colonnade on Monday to Saturday 9 a.m. to 1 p.m. To get tickets in advance, write to the Prefecture of the Papal Household, 00120 Città del Vaticano, indicating your language, the dates of your visit, the number of people in your party, and (if possible) the hotel in Rome to which the office should send your tickets the afternoon before the audience.

of the Basilica di San Pietro (the statues represent Sts. Peter and Paul, Peter carrying the Keys to the Kingdom), and to the right, above the colonnade, are the dark brown buildings of the papal apartments and the Musei Vaticani. In the center of the square is an **Egyptian obelisk,** brought from the ancient city of Heliopolis on the Nile delta. Flanking it are two seventeenth-century **fountains** — the one on the right by Carlo Maderno, who designed the facade of St. Peter's, was placed here by Bernini himself; the other is by Carlo Fontana. The piazza is particularly magical at night in the Christmas season, when a *presepio* (Nativity scene) and a large tree take center stage.

Basilica di San Pietro: In 324, Emperor Constantine commissioned a sanctuary to be built on the site of St. Peter's tomb. The first Apostle was thought to have been buried here under a simple stone, and excavation and studies commissioned by the Vatican have produced additional proof that the tomb is indeed St. Peter's. You can find the tomb in the present basilica's central nave, under the magnificent altar by Bernini.

The original basilica stood for about 1,000 years — undergoing remodeling, pillaging, sacking, and rebuilding — until it was on the verge of collapse. The basilica you see today, mostly High Renaissance and baroque, was born with the renovation begun in 1503 following designs by Sangallo and Bramante. Michelangelo was appointed to finish the magnificent dome in 1547 but wasn't able to do so; he died in 1564, and his disciple Giacomo della Porta completed it.

The inside of the basilica is almost too huge to take in; walking from one end to the other is a workout, and the opulence will overpower you. On the right as you enter is Michelangelo's exquisite *Pietà,* created when the master was in his early 20s. (Because of an act of vandalism in the 1970s, the statue is kept behind reinforced glass.) Dominating the nave is Bernini's 96-foot-tall *baldacchino* (canopy), supported by richly decorated twisting columns. Completed in 1633, it was criticized for being excessive and because the bronze was supposedly taken from the Pantheon. It stands over the papal altar, which in turn stands over the **tomb of St. Peter.** A bronze statue of St. Peter (probably by Arnolfo di Cambio — thirteenth century) marks the tomb, and its right foot has been worn away by the thousands of pilgrims kissing it in the traditional

The Vatican

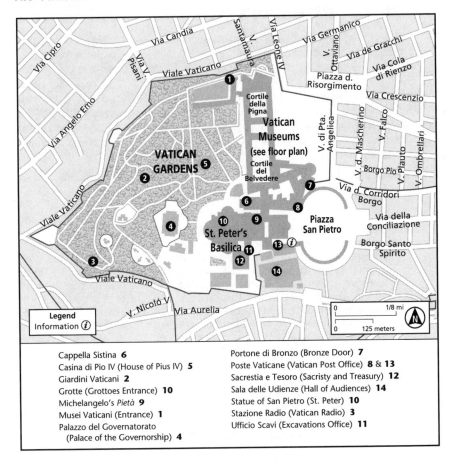

Legend	
Information ⓘ	

Cappella Sistina **6**
Casina di Pio IV (House of Pius IV) **5**
Giardini Vaticani **2**
Grotte (Grottoes Entrance) **10**
Michelangelo's *Pietà* **9**
Musei Vaticani (Entrance) **1**
Palazzo del Governatorato
  (Palace of the Governorship) **4**

Portone di Bronzo (Bronze Door) **7**
Poste Vaticane (Vatican Post Office) **8** & **13**
Sacrestia e Tesoro (Sacristy and Treasury) **12**
Sala delle Udienze (Hall of Audiences) **14**
Statue of San Pietro (St. Peter) **10**
Stazione Radio (Vatican Radio) **3**
Ufficio Scavi (Excavations Office) **11**

devotional gesture to salute the pope. By the apse, above an altar, is the bronze throne sculpted by Bernini to house the remains of what is, according to legend, the chair of St. Peter.

Beneath the basilica are **grottoes,** extending under the central nave of the church, that have been the site of archaeological excavations. You can visit them and wander among the tombs of popes. In addition to the papal tombs, paleo-Christian tombs and architectural fragments of the original basilica have been found here.

To visit Michelangelo's dome and marvel at the astounding view, you have to climb some 491 steps. Make sure that you're ready and willing to climb, however, because once you've started up you're not allowed to turn around and go back down. If you want to take the elevator as far as it goes, it'll save you 171 steps. You have to make a reservation when you buy your ticket to go up in the dome (you'll pay an additional 1,000L/54¢). On busy days, you have to wait in line because the elevator can't accommodate all the people who want to use it.

Musei Vaticani: This enormous complex of museums could swallow up your entire vacation — with tons of Egyptian, Etruscan, Greek, Roman, paleo-Christian, and Renaissance art. After admittance, you must choose which of the **four color-coded itineraries** (A, B, C, or D) you want to follow — they range from 1½ to 5 hours. Don't worry: All the itineraries end at the Sistine Chapel.

Along the way you'll come across highlights such as these: the **Appartamento Borgia (Borgia Apartments),** designed for Pope Alexander VI (the infamous Borgia pope), and the **Cappella di Nicholas V (Chapel of Nicholas V),** with floor-to-ceiling frescoes by Fra Angelico; the **Pinacoteca (Picture Gallery),** with treasures like Raphael's *Transfiguration,* Leonardo da Vinci's *St. Jerome* (which had to be pieced back together — one piece had ended up in a shoemaker's shop, the other in an antiques shop), and Giotto's *Stefaneschi Triptych;* and the **Stanze di Raffaello (Raphael Rooms),** the private apartments of Pope Julius II frescoed wonderfully by the artist.

But what most people can't wait to see is the **Cappella Sistina (Sistine Chapel),** the masterpiece of Michelangelo. Restoring and cleaning Michelangelo's frescoes took a dozen years, and the brilliant colors that were uncovered have amazed some and horrified others who believe that too much paint was removed, flattening the figures. Michelangelo's modeling of the human form is incredible whether you like the colors of the drapery or not. The *Creation of Adam* and the temptation and fall of Adam and Eve are the most famous scenes. Michelangelo also painted a terrifying and powerful *Last Judgment* on the end wall.

Binoculars or even a hand mirror will help you appreciate the ceiling better; your neck tires long before you can take it all in. Just think how poor Michelangelo must've felt while painting it flat on his back atop a tower of scaffolding.

Giardini Vaticani (Vatican Gardens): People often think that the Vatican is made up of only the basilica and the neighboring buildings, but the grounds behind the main structures are actually quite large. Although you can't visit most of the Vatican (you need a special permit to enter the Vatican grounds), guided tours take small numbers of visitors to admire the beautiful Vatican Gardens. If you enjoy touring gardens, you can sign up for a tour at the ticket office of the Vatican Museums.

Basilica: Piazza San Pietro, ☎ 06-6988-4466; Musei Vaticani: Viale Vaticano, walk around the walls of the Vatican to the right of the basilica. ☎ 06-6988-3333. Internet: www.vatican.va or www.christusrex.org. Bus: 23, 62, or 64 to Via della Conciliazione. Metro: Line A to Ottaviano/San Pietro; then walk down Viale Angelico to the Vatican wall. Open: Basilica winter daily 7 a.m.–6 p.m., summer daily 7 a.m.– 7 p.m.; Grottoes daily 8 a.m.–5 p.m.; Dome winter daily 8 a.m.–4:45 p.m., summer daily 8 a.m.–5:45 p.m.; Museums winter Mon–Sat 8:45 a.m.– 1:45 p.m., summer Mon–Fri 8:45 a.m.–4:45 p.m., Sat 8:45 a.m.–1:45 p.m., closed all Catholic religious holy days. Admission: Basilica free; Dome 5,000L ($2.70) adults (with elevator 6,000L/$3.25), 4,000L ($2.15) students; Museums 18,000L ($10) adults, 12,000L ($7) children (last ticket to the museums sell an hour before closing — though an hour is hardly enough time to scratch the surface).

The Vatican Museums

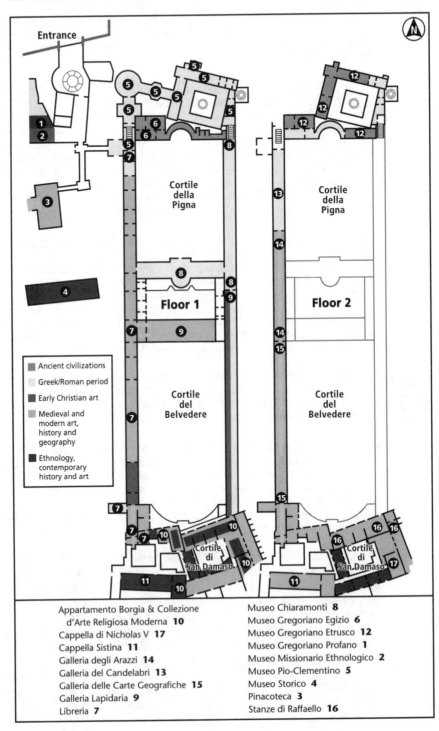

Entrance

Cortile della Pigna

Floor 1

Cortile del Belvedere

Cortile della Pigna

Floor 2

Cortile del Belvedere

Cortile di San Damaso

Cortile di San Damaso

Ancient civilizations
Greek/Roman period
Early Christian art
Medieval and modern art, history and geography
Ethnology, contemporary history and art

Appartamento Borgia & Collezione d'Arte Religiosa Moderna **10**
Cappella di Nicholas V **17**
Cappella Sistina **11**
Galleria degli Arazzi **14**
Galleria del Candelabri **13**
Galleria delle Carte Geografiche **15**
Galleria Lapidaria **9**
Libreria **7**

Museo Chiaramonti **8**
Museo Gregoriano Egizio **6**
Museo Gregoriano Etrusco **12**
Museo Gregoriano Profano **1**
Museo Missionario Ethnologico **2**
Museo Pio-Clementino **5**
Museo Storico **4**
Pinacoteca **3**
Stanze di Raffaello **16**

More Cool Things to See and Do

There's a lot more to see in Rome than the sights we mention in "There's No Place Like Rome, There's No Place Like Rome: The Top Sights," earlier in this chapter, though they're the major ones that most people come to see. If you're traveling with children, you know that they won't stand for seeing museum after museum, particularly those like the Etruscan Museum, full of many cases of small objects. Fortunately, there are plenty of other activities in Rome for whatever your interests are, whether you're a family or a solitary art lover.

✔ The **Chiesa dell'Immacolata Concezione** (Via Veneto 27, not far from the U.S. Embassy; ☎ 06-487-1185; Metro: Line A to Barberini; Bus: 62 or minibus 116 or 119 to Largo Tritone) holds one of the most chilling sights you'll ever see. A Capuchin monk used the bones of 4,000 of his brothers to create a monument to death. There are corpses dressed in monk's robes, and the ceilings and walls are decorated with pieces of skeletons (for example, rows of spinal vertebrae trace the vaults). In an age that confronted death more head-on than ours does, this monument may have been somehow comforting, and it's definitely a sight you won't soon forget. Admission is free but a donation is expected (5,000L/$2.70 per person is nice). The monument is open daily 9 a.m. to noon and 3 to 6 p.m.

✔ The **Galleria Doria Pamphili** (Piazza del Collegio Romano 1/A; ☎ 06-679-7323; Bus: 62, 85, 850, or minibus 117 or 119 to Piazza San Marcello on the Corso or 116 to Piazza del Collegio Romano) is the place to come if you want to know what it was like to live in an eighteenth-century Roman palace. The Doria Pamphili family traces its history back to Admiral Andrea Doria. The palazzo's richly decorated apartments are filled with tapestries, beautiful furnishings, and works by some of the most important Renaissance artists. The gallery hosts works by Filippo Lippi, Raphael, Caravaggio, Tiziano, and others. Velázquez's portrait of Pope Innocent X is a true masterpiece. The gallery is open Friday to Wednesday 10 a.m. to 5 p.m. Admission is 13,000L ($7) adults and 10,000L ($5) students and seniors, plus an extra 5,000L ($2.70) to see the private apartments.

✔ The tall **Gianicolo (Janiculum Hill)**, behind Trastevere, is one of the two best places to see the panorama of Rome, the other being the **Pincio** (see the entry for Piazza del Popolo under "There's No Place like Rome, There's No Place like Rome: The Top Sights"). You can take the no. 870 bus to the top of the hill (though the best idea is taking a cab up and walking down, rather than waiting for the bus and possibly missing the sunset). On the hill is a monument to Giuseppe Garibaldi, and a little farther down is a unique equestrian statue of his wife, Anita, pistol in hand (she fought alongside him and was killed in battle). Perhaps the most beloved figure of the ninteenth-century Italian struggle for self-determination, Garibaldi invaded Sicily in 1860 with 1,000 men, his famous "Red Shirts," opening the way to the unification of Italy. On his statue is his slogan, *Roma o morte* (Rome or death). For some reason,

there's also a lighthouse atop the Gianicolo, but we can't find
anyone who knows why it's there (it photographs nicely, though).

✔ The **Museo della Civiltá Romana** (Piazza Giovanni Agnelli 10;
☎ 06-592-6141;. Metro: Line B to EUR Fermi) houses an excellent
miniature reconstruction of ancient Rome showing the great buildings intact, which helps you make sense of all the broken columns
and holes in the ground. Other models display facets of daily life
in antiquity. Admission is 5,000L ($2.70) adults and free for chil-
dren under 18. The museum is open Tuesday to Saturday 9 a.m. to
7 p.m. and Sunday 9 a.m. to 1:30 p.m.

✔ Just above Piazza del Popolo and extending north beyond the city
walls is the **Villa Borghese,** one of Rome's most beautiful parks.
It's famous for the Galleria Borghese (see "There's No Place like
Rome, There's No Place like Rome: The Top Sights") and the
Pincio, the terrace above Piazza del Popolo offering a beautiful
view over Rome, which is particularly striking at sunset. Inside the
park is also the **Piazza di Siena,** a picturesque oval track surrounded by tall pines, used for horse races and particularly for
the **Concorso Ippico Internazionale di Roma** (Rome's international horse-jumping event), held in May (see the "Calendar of
Events" in Chapter 2). This park is perfect for a family picnic,
especially in summer, when its beautiful Roman pines offer relief
from the heat.

✔ **Testaccio** (Metro: Line B to Piramide; Bus: 23 or tram 3 to Via
Marmorata) is a neighborhood named for Monte Testaccio, a hill
made out of broken pots collected in A.D. 55. The Romans stacked
the shards (*testae*) 200 feet high after Nero whimsically ordered
that they be collected here. Though the top of this dangerous
shifting mountain is closed to visitors, dwellings that were dug
into its lower slopes over the centuries still exist, and some of
them house restaurants and jazz clubs. Testaccio is a real Roman
neighborhood, with a reputation for being less safe after dark.
However, in summer there are big crowds of young people around
and we doubt that you'll have any problems. Other landmarks
here are the **pyramid of Caius Cestius,** a Roman praetor and tribune who died in 12 B.C., and the **Protestant Cemetery** next door
(☎ 06-574-1141), a kind of pilgrimage site for appreciators of
poets John Keats and Percy Bysshe Shelley, who are buried here,
along with the murdered anti-Fascist Antonio Gramsci. Admission
to the cemetery is free; hours of operation are Tuesday to Sunday
9 a.m. to 5 p.m.

✔ On **Via Appia Antica (Appian Way),** you can walk over what was
the first and most important Roman consular road — called the
Regina Viarum (Queen of Roads). Started in 312 B.C., the road
was a main link to Capua but eventually was extended all the way
to Brindisi. It was on this road that St. Peter, in flight from Rome,
had his vision of Jesus (a church stands where Peter asked
"*Domine quo vadis?*" or "Lord, where are you going?") and turned
back toward his martyrdom. The street was paved with large, flat
basalt stones and lined with villas, tombs, and monuments, of
which some ruins remain. One of the most important is the
Tomba di Cecilia Metella, a first-century B.C. mausoleum of a

patrician gentlewoman (☎ 06-780-2465). It's open Monday to Saturday 9 a.m. to 6 p.m. (to 3 p.m. in winter) and Sunday 9 a.m. to 1 p.m., and admission is free. Grab a map from the main tourist office and rent a bike! To get there by public transportation, take metro line A to Colli Albani (on Sunday to Arco di Travertino) and then bus 660 to Via Appia Antica.

And on Your Left, the Colosseo: Seeing Roma by Guided Tour

The French writer Stendhal once wrote, "As soon as you enter Rome, get in a carriage and ask to be brought to the Coliseum or to St. Peter's. If you try to get there on foot, you will never arrive: too many marvelous things will stop you along the way."

Taking a bus tour of this complicated city when you first arrive is an excellent idea. Doing so helps you get the general feeling of the place and gives you an idea of what you'd really like to see more in depth. After you decide what you want to see in more detail, you can take a walking tour of the area or areas that interest you most and do the rest by yourself.

Tons of organized tours in Rome cater to most every interest. Many are organized by cultural associations, and you can find them listed in various magazines like *Roma c'e* (coming out on Thursdays at all newsstands, with a section in English at the end), *Metropolitan,* and *Wanted in Rome* (also available at most newsstands).

Bus tours

The city bus company **ATAC** gives the best bus tours of Rome. The no. 110 bus leaves from Piazza dei Cinquecento in front of Stazione Termini daily at 10:30 a.m. and 2, 3, 5, and 6 p.m. for a 2½-hour tour costing 15,000L ($8) per person; the buses are new and very modern and the tour guides are professionals. The price includes an illustrated guidebook describing the more than 80 sites included in the tour. From this same piazza (Piazza dei Cinquecento) and for the same price, ATAC runs another bus (labeled "linea Basiliche" or "lBs") that takes you to the four basilicas of Rome — San Pietro, San Paolo, San Giovanni, and Santa Maria Maggiore. The linea Basiliche leaves daily at 10 a.m. and 2:30 p.m. To reserve, call ☎ 06-4695-2252 or 06-4695-2256 daily 9 a.m. to 7 p.m. You can buy tickets at the ATAC bus info booth on platform C in front of Stazione Termini.

Stop 'n Go/C.S.R. (Via Ezio 12; ☎ 06-321-7054; E-mail: csr@gisec.it) organizes a self-tailored bus tour with nine departures daily, 9:30 a.m. to 4:30 p.m. in winter and 9:30 a.m. to 5:30 p.m. in summer. At 20,000L ($11) per person, the tour starts in Piazza dei Cinquecento (in front of Stazione Termini) at the corner of Via Massimo d'Azeglio and makes 14 stops; you can get on or off at your leisure. (You can buy the ticket directly on the bus.) A two-day ticket is 30,000L ($16) and a three-day ticket 40,000L ($22), giving you more time to see things than a one-day ticket. The company also organizes an afternoon tour of the Castelli Romani (hill towns around Rome), which leaves at 2:30 p.m., and a morning tour of Tivoli and Hadrian's Villa, which leaves at 9:30 a.m. (see Chapter 13).

Another bus-tour possibility is **American Express** (Piazza di Spagna 38; ☎ **06-67-641;** Metro: Line A to Spagna), which organizes tours of Rome and the Vatican as well as excursions to nearby sites like Tivoli (see Chapter 13). Tours start at 53,000L ($29) per person and leave daily at 9:30 a.m. and 2:30 p.m. American Express also offers day tours to farther-afield destinations like Florence and Pompeii. The American Express office is open Monday to Friday 9 a.m. to 5:30 p.m. and Saturday 9 a.m. to 12:30 p.m.

But if you're interested in Pompeii, a better choice is the day tour organized by **Enjoy Rome** (see "Walking tours," later in this chapter) with a departure at 8:30 a.m. in an air-conditioned minivan fitting eight passengers. The driver speaks English, and you're given material and maps to prepare you for your visit — all for 60,000L ($32).

Walking tours

Enjoy Rome (Via Varese 39, three blocks north off the side of Stazione Termini; ☎ **06-445-1834;** Internet: www.enjoyrome.com; Metro: Termini) offers a variety of three-hour walking tours, including a night tour that takes you through the *centro* and its sights, and a tour of Trastevere and the Jewish Ghetto. All tours cost 30,000L ($16) adults and 25,000L ($14) for those under 26, including the cost of the tour and admission to sights. The office is open Monday to Friday 8:30 a.m. to 2 p.m. and 3:30 to 6:30 p.m. and Saturday 8:30 a.m. to 2 p.m. Enjoy Rome also organizes a bike tour, with English-speaking guides.

For **Scala Reale** (Via Varese 52; ☎ **888-467-1986** or 06-4470-0898; Metro: Termini), American architect Tom Rankin organizes small-group walking tours with an architectural twist for 60,000L ($32). He takes visitors through ancient and baroque Rome and discusses the city's most important buildings. Discounts are available for groups of four, and children under 12 are free. The tour includes a visit to neighborhood *trattoria.*

Boat tours

For a completely different point of view of Rome, take a tour on the motorboat *Tiber.* It leaves Tuesday to Sunday at 10:30 a.m. and 12:45 p.m. from Ponte Umberto I (Bus: 70, 81, or minibus 116), the bridge at the end of Via Zanardelli, off the north tip of Piazza Navona. The tour lasts 1½ hours and costs 20,000L ($11). You can buy tickets directly on the boat. The boat takes you downriver on the Tiber through the heart of Rome, offering a beautiful view of Castel Sant'Angelo with San Pietro in the distance, Trastevere, and the Isola Tiberina.

Air tours

At 95,000L ($51) per person for 20 minutes, **Umbria Fly** (☎ **06-8864-1441**) offers airborne tours of Rome for a minimum of two passengers. It's an unforgettable experience, giving you a panoramic view of Rome from the air; the only drawback is that the tour leaves from the Aeroporto dell'Urbe, on Via Salaria 825, just north of Rome (40 minutes or more from the center of the city by taxi or if you have a car).

Suggested 1-, 2-, and 3-Day Sightseeing Itineraries

Someone once said that you'd need a lifetime to really understand Rome, and we agree. Well, assuming you don't have quite that much time, here are some suggestions for how you can use one, two, or three days to get a strong sense of the flavors and history of this city. However, our itineraries aren't the squeeze-everything-in-so-you-can-say-you've-seen-it-all kind. Your trip will be far more memorable if you enjoy yourself and don't try to cram in too much.

If you have 1 day in Rome

Assuming that you have the whole day at your disposal (you arrived the night before) begin with the 10:30 a.m. ATAC bus tour (see "Bus tours," earlier in this chapter). This tour shows you more of the city in a couple hours than you can cover on foot in a day. On the tour, you'll have a few moments to linger at **San Pietro** and the **Colosseo**. By the time your tour is over, it's time for lunch, so eat at one of the choices that we given you in the *centro* (see Chapter 11), and then walk through the **Villa Borghese,** visiting the **Galleria Borghese** (you have to reserve your tickets in advance). You can walk back through the park after your visit and see the sunset from the **Pincio.** Alternatively, skip the visit to the Galleria Borghese and take the no. 116 bus to the **Pantheon.** Since you're in the *centro* — the best area for shopping — you can take in some of the sights (see earlier in this chapter) there while browsing. Afterward, treat yourself to a super dinner in **Testaccio** or **Trastevere** (see recommendations in Chapter 11), where the nightlife is as good as it gets in Rome — you've earned it!

Of course, because you have only a day, you may want to replace one of the sights that we suggest with a sight that you absolutely want to see in Rome. But, remember to check admission hours beforehand (see "There's No Place like Rome, There's No Place like Rome: The Top Sights" for detailed information on each sight).

If you have 2 days in Rome

If you have two days, first orient yourself with the bus tour as we mention in the itinerary for one day. After lunch, you can go to the **Villa Borghese** and the **Galleria Borghese** (remember to make a reservation ahead of time) or to the **Foro Romano.** In the evening, you can have dinner in the *centro* and see the **Fontana di Trevi** and **Spanish Steps** lit by night. The next morning, arrive at the **Musei Vaticani** very early to avoid wasting time in lines. You can see the **Cappella Sistina** and however much else of the museum's great art you can handle. Afterward, walk around to **San Pietro** and spend a few moments taking in the basilica's grandeur. You can also squeeze in some shopping on nearby Via Cola di Rienzo (see "The best shopping areas") for clothing and shoes. After lunch, see whichever sight you didn't see the previous afternoon (the **Galleria Borghese** or the **Forum**). Spend your last night in Rome sharing the kind of nightlife Romans prefer: having a good dinner, strolling, and having ice cream in summer or a warm drink in winter. The best neighborhoods are the *centro,* **Testaccio,** and **Trastevere.** Alternatively, you could spend this last night in the outlying areas of the city: If you're leaving Rome the next day by car and have already picked it up, you can drive out to the **Castelli Romani** for a rustic dinner.

If you have 3 days in Rome

Having three days to explore Rome gives you a little breathing room, but your choices also multiply. You can use your first two days as we mention earlier in the two-day itinerary to see the things that everyone wants to see: the **Musei Vaticani** and **San Pietro,** the **Pantheon,** the **Fontana di Trevi,** and the **Spanish Steps.** On your third day, you can either see a couple of the more specialized museums, like the **Museo Etrusco di Villa Giulia, Palazzo Massimo, Terme di Diocleziano, Palazzo Altemps,** and **Musei Capitolini.** Alternatively, you can make a day trip to **Tivoli,** the ancient ruins at **Ostia Antica,** or the **Castelli Romani** (see Chapter 13).

Shopping

In terms of crafts, Rome isn't as rich as it was in ages past. Alas, very few workshops still practice traditional arts. On the other hand, Rome is a large city and the capital of the country, so you can find basically everything. Therefore, you can find specialties here from places that you may not have time to visit.

Shopping hours are generally 9 or 9:30 a.m. (later for boutiques) to about 1 to 1:30 p.m., and then from 3:30 or 4 to 7:30 p.m. Many shops close Monday mornings, and most are closed all day Sunday. In the centro, however, many shops now stay open at lunchtime and on Sunday.

Italy's value-added tax (called the IVA) is 19 percent, but you can get reimbursed for taxes paid on the items that you're bringing out of the country that cost over 300,000L ($162) at the airport. See the Appendix for details.

The best shopping areas

The best shopping area is the *centro,* the streets of medieval and Renaissance Rome between Piazza del Popolo and Piazza Venezia. Now with restricted car circulation, **Via del Corso** (also known as just the Corso) is the area's heart, lined with shops selling everything from clothing to shoes to CDs. On the east side of Piazza di Spagna lie the most elegant streets — like **Via Frattina** and **Via dei Condotti** — with designer boutiques and all the big names of Italian fashion (Bulgari, Ferragamo, Valentino, Armani, and so on). You also find interesting small shops, including stylish Italian housewares and antiques. On the west side of the Corso are intricate medieval streets hiding a variety of elegant and original boutiques and some of the oldest establishments in Rome. Here you can find even more variety, from old prints to exclusive fashions, from books to antique furniture.

Another good shopping area is **Via Cola di Rienzo** and **Via Ottaviano** on the San Pietro side of the Tevere. It doesn't boast the luxury shops of Via dei Condotti, but you can find the big names of Italian fashion. This area is also excellent for shoes, with many shops of every level of price and style, and for a variety of other items.

Via Nazionale off Piazza della Repubblica near Stazione Termini and running almost to Piazza Venezia is another major shopping street. Less elegant than the others for general fashion and frequented more by Italians than tourists, it's developed a specialty in leather goods. This may be the best place to find that jacket you want.

What to look for and where to find it

In Rome, you can hardly turn around without knocking over a display of eyewear, but one of the best places to buy eyewear is **Ottica Alessandro Spieza** (Via del Babuino 199; ☎ **06-361-0593;** Bus: minibus 117 or 119 to Piazza del Popolo), right off Piazza del Popolo. The shop is small but the quality very high and includes Spieza's own designs. Likewise, there's an entire store devoted to **Swatch** watches (Via Belsiana 64; ☎ **06-6992-0173;** Metro: Line A to Spagna) in the central shopping district. Here you may find styles that you can't find in the United States.

For leather accessories, the two best areas are **Via dei Condotti** in the *centro* and **Via Cola di Rienzo** in the Vatican area. For leather bags and wallets (if money isn't an issue), go either to **Bottega Veneta** (Piazza San Lorenzo in Lucina 9; ☎ **06-6821-0024;** Bus: 81 or minibus 116 to Piazza San Lorenzo), famous for its beautiful woven designs, or to

Prada (Via dei Condotti 15; ☎ **06-679-4876**; Metro: Line A to Spagna), both off the Corso.

If antiques interest you, the *centro* is the place to go. **Via dei Coronari** literally offers one shop after another on both sides of the street. Likewise, you can find some more refined dealers on **Via Giulia, Via del Babuino,** and **Via Margutta** nearby. For more casual shopping, try **Via del Pellegrino.**

If you forgot to bring a book to read and don't understand Italian, go to the **English Bookshop** (Via di Ripetta 248; ☎ **06-320-3301;** Bus: minibus 117 or 119 to Piazza del Popolo). This store stocks books in English on a wide range of subjects. **Remainders** (Piazza San Silvestro 27–28; ☎ **06-679-2824;** Bus: 85 or 850 to Piazza San Silvestro) also offers a large selection of books in English at discount prices. The **Libreria Babele** (Via dei Banchi Vecchi 116; ☎ **06-687-6628;** Bus: 62, 64, or minibus 116 to Via dei Banchi) is Rome's most central gay/lesbian bookstore. In addition, many of the larger newsstands in the *centro* have English-language newspapers and magazines as well as bestsellers in fiction and perhaps some classics.

For clothing, the best strategy is to shop in the *centro* or in the area of **Via Ottaviano** and **Via Cola di Rienzo** (Vatican/San Pietro). Prices are quite competitive, and there's a good variety. For women's fashion, the hot area is around **Piazza di Spagna** (logically — this area includes the highest concentration of tourists). You can find **Fendi** (Via Borgognona 39; ☎ **06-679-4824**), **Valentino** (Via dei Condotti 13; ☎ **06-67-391**), **Gucci** (Via Condotti 8; ☎ **06-678-9340**), **Armani Boutique** (Via dei Condotti 77; ☎ **06-6991460**), and **Emporio Armani** (Via del Babuino 140; ☎ **06-3600-2197**) nearby. For men's clothes, the specialists are **Battistoni** (Via dei Condotti 57 and 61/a; ☎ **06-678-6241**) and **Testa** (Via Borgognona 13; ☎ **06-679-6174**/Via Frattina 104; ☎ **06-679-0660**). You can find all the shops that we mention in this paragraph a short walk away from the Spanish Steps (Metro: Line A to Spagna). An elegant men's store, **Davide Cenci** (Via Campo Marzio 1–7; ☎ **06-699-0681;** Bus: minibus 116 to Pantheon) is popular with locals.

Although Florence is more the place for leather clothes, you can find some nice stores in Rome, especially on **Via Nazionale.** In Rome, though you can certainly find excellent leather gloves, the best shops are around **Piazza di Spagna.**

One typical product that you find in Rome and nowhere else in such a large variety is religious apparel. Of course, the interest for the public at large is a little limited. However, if you're looking for religious objects, Rome is the place. Stroll around the neighborhood of **Piazza della Minerva** and **Corso Rinascimento** to find a variety of curious artifacts.

For shoes, the two best areas are **Via dei Condotti** in the *centro* and **Via Cola di Rienzo** in the Vatican area. Among the top names are **Dominici** (Via del Corso 14; ☎ **06-361-0591**), **Ferragamo** (Via dei Condotti 73–74; ☎ **06-679-1565**), and **Ferragamo Uomo** (Via dei Condotti 75; ☎ **06-678-1130**). However, if you really want to make your friends green with envy, have a pair of shoes custom-made by **Listo** (Via della Croce 76; ☎ **06-678-4567**). These shops are all a short walk from the Spanish Steps (Metro: Line A to Spagna).

If you insist on finding some typical craft, go to the medieval area of Rome around **Piazza Navona.** There you can find *vimini* (basketry) on **Via dei Sediari,** iron work on **Via degli Orsini,** and reproductions of Roman and Pompeian mosaics in the **Opificio Romano** (Via dei Gigli d'Oro 9–10; ☎ **06-6880-2762;** Bus: 70, 81 or minibus 116 to Via Zanardelli). Another excellent neighborhood is **Trastevere:** Try the **Bottega Artigiana Ceramica Sarti** (Via Santa Dorotea 21; ☎ **06-588-2079;** Bus: 23 to Piazza Trilussa on the Lungotevere; Tram: 8 to Piazza G. Belli on Viale Trastevere), a long-established ceramic workshop, or the **Officina della Carta** (Via Santa Dorotea 26b; ☎ **06-589-5557**) for paper and leather handicrafts.

Italians have been making good blades since the Renaissance, and at **La Mia Coltelleria** (Piazza della Rotonda 64; ☎ **06-679-5221;** Bus: minibus 116 to Pantheon), you can find everything from handmade and handforged pocket knives to fine table cutlery.

Artists have been coming to Rome to paint and draw for centuries, and you've no doubt seen many views of the city's ancient and baroque monuments. For prints, two well-known shops are **Nardecchia** (Piazza Navona 25; ☎ **06-686-9318;** Bus: 70, 81 or minibus 116) and **Alinari** (Via Alibert 16/a; ☎ **06-679-2923;** Metro: Line A to Spagna). **Antiquarius** (Corso Rinascimento 63; ☎ **06-688-02941;** Bus: 70, 81, or minibus 116) is a nice shop across from the Palazzo Madama. At these shops you find higher-quality — and somewhat more reliable — articles than at the nearby antiquarian book and print market on Piazza Fontanella Borghese (Bus: 81 or minibus 117 or 119 to the Corso at Via Tomacelli). The market, however, is a great place to browse if you know your prints, and it offers good deals on dated art books as well as Roman prints.

For refined stationery and paper, go to **Pineider,** founded in 1774 (Via Fontanella Borghese 22; ☎ **06-687-8369;** Bus: 81 or minibus 117 or 119 to the Corso at Via Tomacelli/Via dei Due Macelli 68; ☎ **06-679-5884;** Bus: minibus 116, 117, or 119 to Via Due Macelli). Italians are also crazy for accessories like fountain pens. At **Campo Marzio Penne** (Via Campo Marzio 41; ☎ **06-6880-7877;** Bus: 81 or minibus 116 to Piazza San Lorenzo in Lucina on the Corso), you can find every kind of writing implement, from steel nibs to antique fountain pens — the shop even does repairs.

Rome has many a fine *enoteca* (wine shop). If you want to buy wine to take home, go to the granddaddy of Rome wine stores, **Trimani** (Via Goito 20; ☎ **06-446-8351;** Bus: 60 or 62), a family business since 1821 with literally thousands of bottles in the old residential neighborhood behind the Terme di Diocleziano. Rome's most special source of intoxicants is **Ai Monasteri** (Corso Rinascimento 72; ☎ **06-6880-2783;** Bus: 70, 81, or minibus 116), off the east side of Piazza Navona. Here you can find the liqueurs, elixirs, and other alcoholic concoctions that monks in Italy have traditionally made since the early Middle Ages.

Nightlife

Romans love to stroll about their beloved city by night on what they call a *passeggiata*. All the major monuments are illuminated and the ancient Roman ruins join the Renaissance and baroque buildings to create a fairy-tale atmosphere. Don't miss a tour of the Roman *piazze* by night. Sample Rome's wonderful ice cream (*gelato* — see the sidebar in Chapter 11) or sit on the outdoor terrace of a famous cafe and watch the people parade as you sip an espresso or a glass of Chianti to enhance the experience.

The performing arts

From June to September, Roman nights come alive with the **Estate Romana (Roman Summer),** a series of musical, theatrical, and other cultural events. You can find details on the Web at www.comune. roma.it or call ☎ **06-6880-9505** Monday to Saturday 10 a.m. to 5 p.m. Events include important concerts with appearances by the **Accademia Nazionale di Santa Cecilia** (see the information, later in this section) at the Villa Giulia (☎ **06-322-6571**) and the summer edition of the opera at the monumental **Stadio Olimpico (Olympic Stadium),** across the Tevere from Piazza Mazzini.

Among the most picturesque initiatives is the opening of some of the major ancient Roman sights by night for special guided visits (call the Villa Cecilia to make a reservation) or performances. During the summer of 2000, the **Colosseum** opened its doors to the public again after 15 centuries with a performance of Sophocles' *Oedipus.* If you're lucky, the program may include a performance in the dramatic setting of the **Terme di Caracalla (Baths of Caracalla).** You can also check out a summer season of theater in the **Teatro Romano** at Ostia Antica (see Chapter 13).

One of Italy's premier musical associations is the **Accademia Nazionale di Santa Cecilia** (Via della Conciliazione 4, just off San Pietro; ☎ toll free **800-085-085** or 06-6880-1044; Internet: www.santacecilia.it; Bus: 23, 62, or 64). Its season runs October to May, with symphonic concerts Saturdays through Tuesdays and soloist and ensemble chamber music on Fridays. In summer, the association holds outdoor concerts at the Villa Giulia (☎ **06-322-6571**). The organization **Amici della Musica Sacra** (☎ **06-6880-5816**) sponsors free choral and other religious music concerts by mostly foreign traveling groups in the theatrical setting of Sant'Ignazio church, between the Corso and the Pantheon (Bus: 62, 85, 850, or minibus 117 or 119 to the Corso at Via Caravita or minibus 116).

Rome is famous for theater — but,of course, if you don't understand Italiano you won't get much out of it. Opera, however, is an exception, because you may already know the story and the same operas are performed everywhere. At the newly restored **Teatro dell'Opera** (Piazza Beniamino Gigli 1, just off Via Nazionale; ☎ **06-481-601;**

Internet: www.themix.it; Metro: Line A to Repubblica; Bus 60, 64, 70, or minibus 116 to Via A. Depretis), opera performances run from January to June, with a special July/August season that changes venues every year. (There's a rumor they may even start putting on *Aïda* at the Baths of Caracalla again.) The Rome Opera Ballet performs classical and modern ballet at this venue as well. Likewise, the **Teatro Olimpico** (Piazza Gentile da Fabriano; ☎ 06-323-4890; Tram: 225 from Piazzale Flaminio) hosts musical performances of all kinds.

Caffès

Rome boasts many famous old cafes that have never lost their glamour. Very pleasant, if a little expensive, the **Antico Caffè della Pace** (Via della Pace 3–7; ☎ 06-686-1216; Bus: minibus 116 to Piazza Navona) is one of the most popular cafes in the last few decades. Another is the beautifully furnished **Caffè Greco** (Via Condotti 84; ☎ 06-679-1700; Metro: Line A to Spagna), which saw among its customers famous writers Stendhal, Goethe, and Keats. The **Caffè Sant'Eustachio** (Piazza Sant'Eustachio 82; ☎ 06-686-1309; Bus: minibus 116) is a traditional Italian bar serving Rome's best espresso since 1938, made with water carried into the city on an ancient aqueduct.

Also famous is the **Caffè Rosati** (Piazza del Popolo 4–5; ☎ 06-322-5859; Bus: minibus 117 or 119), which retains its 1920s art nouveau decor. **Tre Scalini** (Piazza Navona 30; ☎ 06-687-9148; Bus: 70 or 81 to Corso Rinascimento, minibus 116) is a perfect spot for a drink or an ice cream (they're famous for *tartufo* — ice cream coated with bittersweet chocolate, cherries, and whipped cream). Less famous but trendy and enjoyable is the **Bar del Fico** (Vicolo del Fico; ☎ 06-686-5205; Bus: minibus 116 to Piazza Navona).

Jazz and other live music

Romans love jazz and Rome offers many jazz clubs and other venues where you can hear live jazz. The most famous are the **Alexanderplatz** (Via Ostia 9, just off the Musei Vaticani; ☎ 06-3974-2171; Metro: Line A to Ottaviano/San Pietro; Bus: 23 to Via Leone IV), where reservations are recommended and the cover is 12,000L ($7), and the **Big Mama** (Vicolo S. Francesco a Ripa 18 in Trastevere; ☎ 06-581-2551; Tram: 8), with a 10,000L ($5) cover. If you like understated modernist surroundings for cocktails and jazz, head to trendy **Chiavari** (Via dei Chiavari 4–5, near Campo de' Fiori; ☎ 06-683-2378; Bus: 62, 64, 70, or 81 to Corso Vittorio Emanuele at Largo dei Chiavari).

The **Aldebaran** (Via Galvani 54 in Testaccio; ☎ 06-574-6013; Bus: 23; Tram: 3 to Via Marmorata) is a quieter lounge with music and an ample choice of drinks; there's no cover. The **Caffè Latino** (Via Monte Testaccio 96; ☎ 06-5728-8384; Bus: 23; Tram: 3 to Via Marmorata, and then walk down Via Galbani — it's best to take a taxi) is a trendy spot for a mix of live music, including funk and acid jazz. The 15,000L to 20,000L ($8 to $11) cover includes one drink.

Bars and pubs

On Campo de' Fiori you can find a full range of alcohol-oriented nightspots. The exceedingly popular but old-fashioned wine bar called **Vineria** at building no. 15 (no phone) still holds its own amid the nightly crowds of this trendy piazza. There's a crowded **Taverna del Campo** snack stop with crostini, panini, and beer next door at no. 16 (☎ 06-687-4402), and a few more doors down you can groove to the live DJ-spun music (and air-conditioning) of the American-style bar **The Drunken Ship** at nos. 20–21 (☎ 06-6830-0535). To get to these hot spots, take bus 62 or 64 to Corso Vittorio Emanuele at Largo San Pantaleo or minibus 116 to Campo de' Fiori.

The Italian craze for Irish pubs hit Rome very hard. These are among the nicest ones: **Mad Jack** (Via Arenula 20, off Largo Argentina; ☎ 06-6880-8223; Tram: 8) is the place for Guinness and a choice of light food. It also features live music on Wednesday and Thursday. The **Abbey Theatre Irish Pub** (Via del Governo Vecchio 51–53, near Piazza Navona; ☎ 06-686-1341; Bus: 62 or 64 to Corso Vittorio Emanuele II) is in the oldest part of town and features an authentic decor and souvenirs from the famous theater. **The Albert** (Via del Traforo 132, off Via del Tritone, before the tunnel; ☎ 06-481-8795; Bus: 62 or minibus 116, 117, or 119 to Largo del Tritone) provides a real English atmosphere and beer, with everything from the furnishings to the drinks imported from England.

Dance clubs

The **Alpheus** (Via del Commercio 36 near Via Ostiense; ☎ 06-574-7826; Bus: 23; best to take a cab) is a very popular spot with several rooms offering different music — from Latin to rock — for dancing and bars for sitting. The cover is 15,000L ($8) on Friday and Saturday. The **Fonclea** (Via Crescenzio 82/a behind Castel Sant'Angelo; ☎ 06-689-6302; Bus: 23 to Via Crescenzio) offers live music every evening, including jazz, soul, funk, and rock; the cover on Saturday is 10,000L ($5). The trendy **Goa** (Via Libetta 13, off Via Ostiense near the Basilica di San Paolo; ☎ 06-574-8277; Bus: 23; best to take a cab) is a dance club mixing ethnic elements and multimedia into a unique blend that keeps people coming back. Cover charge is 15,000L to 30,000L ($8 to $16).

Rome's attempt at a major Manhattan- or London-style disco is **Alien** (Via Velletri 13–19; ☎ 06-841-2212; Bus: 490 to Piazza Fiume). Alien features a funky sci-fi decor with underground, garage, and house music pumping and mainly 20-somethings dancing. The cover charge is 35,000L ($19). More glitzy is the perennially packed **Gilda** (Via Mario de Fiori 97; ☎ 06-679-7396; Metro: Line A to Spagna), a disco with a pizzeria/restaurant where the beautiful — and older — people congregate. The cover charge is 40,000L ($22).

Gay and lesbian bars

The hottest gay club in Rome is **Alibi** (Via di Monte Testaccio 40–44; ☎ 06-574-3448; Bus: 23 or tram 3 to Via Marmorata, and then walk down Via Galbani — taking a cab is best), with a rotating schedule of DJs and a great summer roof garden. The cover is 10,000L to 20,000L ($5 to $11). **The Hangar** (Via in Selci 69; ☎ 06-488-1397; Metro: Cavour) is Rome's oldest gay club, frequented by the under-30 crowd and American visitors; admission is free. At the gay disco **Angelo Azzurro** (Via Cardinale Merry del Val 13 in Trastevere; ☎ 06-580-0472; Tram: 8 to Viale Trastevere at Piazza Mastai), guys of all ages groove to the mix of dance, house, and pop. Admission is free, and Friday night is ladies only.

Lesbians get a few women-only nights at some clubs across town: **New Joli Coeur** (Via Sirte 5; ☎ 06-8621-5827; Bus: 38, 80, or 88 to Piazza Sant'Emerenziana) on Saturdays, and **L'Angelo della Notte** (Via dei Sabelli 10; no phone; Tram: 3) on Fridays with live music.

Fast Facts: Roma

American Express

The office is at Piazza di Spagna 38 (☎ 06- 676-41; Metro: Line A to Spagna), open Monday to Friday 9 a.m. to 5:30 p.m. and Saturday 9 a.m. to 12:30 p.m.

ATMs

They're available everywhere in the center and near hotels. Most banks are linked to the Cirrus network, so if you need the Plus network, look for a BNL (Banca Nazionale del Lavoro) ATM.

Country Code and City Code

The **country code** for Italy is **39.** The **city code** for Rome is **06;** use this code when calling from anywhere outside or inside Italy. As of 1998, you must add it even within Rome itself (and you must include the zero every time, even when calling from abroad).

Currency Exchange

There's a very good exchange bureau at the airport and another inside Stazione Termini (the main train station). Otherwise, you can find *change* offices scattered all around town and concentrated in the *centro.*

Doctors and Dentists

Contact your embassy or consulate to get a list of English-speaking doctors or dentists.

Embassies and Consulates

Rome is the capital of Italy and therefore the seat of all the embassies and consulates. **United States:** Via Vittorio Veneto 119a (☎ 06-46-741; Metro: Line A to Barberini; Bus: minibus 116); Canada: Via Zara 30 (☎ 06-445-981; Bus: 60 or 62 to Via Nomentana); **United Kingdom:** Via XX Settembre 80a (☎ 06-482-5441; Bus: 60, 62, or 490 to Porta Pia); **Ireland:** Piazza Campitelli 3 (☎ 06-697-9121; Bus: 81 to Via del Teatro di Marcello); **Australia:** Via Alessandria 215 (☎ 06-852-721; Tram: 19 or 3 to Viale Regina Margherita); **New Zealand:** Via Zara 28 (☎ 06-440-2928; Bus: 60 or 62 to Via Nomentana).

Emergencies

Ambulance, ☎ 118; Police, ☎ 113; Carabinieri (other police force), ☎ 112; Fire, ☎ 115; Polizia Stradale (Road Police), ☎ 06-67-691.

Hospital

All large hospitals in Rome have a 24-hour *Pronto Soccorso* (first aid) service. Two examples are the **Santo Spirito** on Lungotevere in Sassia 1 (Bus: 23, 62, or 64) and the **Fatebenefratelli** on the Isola Tiberina (Bus: 23; Tram: 8), both in the centro.

Information

The main office of the **Azienda di Promozione Turistica di Roma** (Agency for the Promotion of Tourism) is on Via Parigi 5 (☎ **06-4889-9255;** www.informaroma.it), just a couple of blocks from Stazione Termini, off Piazza della Repubblica. It's open daily 9 a.m. to 7 p.m. There's also an info point inside Stazione Termini (☎ **06-4890-6300**), open daily 8 a.m. to 9 p.m., and others scattered around the city near major attractions (see Chapter 11). The tourist information hotline is ☎ **06-3600-4399.**

Internet Access

Thenetgate has opened several locations around Rome and more are on the way (Piazza Firenze 25; ☎ **06-689-3445;** Bus: 81 or minibus 117 or 119 to Via Tomacelli/Via in Arcione 103; ☎ **06-6992-2320;** Bus: 62 or minibus 116 or 119 to Via del Tritone). You can get an updated listing of locations at www.thenetgate.it. Near Termini, behind the Terme di Diocleziano, you can go to **Freedom Traveller** (Via Gaeta 25; ☎ **06-4782-3862;** www.freedom-traveller.it; Metro: Line B to Castro Pretorio).

Mail

Rome has many post offices. The **central post office** is in Piazza San Silvestro 19 (off Via del Tritone and the Corso; Bus: 62, 81, 85, 850, or minibus 116, 117, or 119), open Monday to Friday 9 a.m. to 6 p.m. and Saturday 9 a.m. to 2 p.m. Another possibility is the Vatican Post Office in Piazza San Pietro (Metro: Ottaviano; Bus: 23, 62, or 64).

Maps

You can find free maps at the **Azienda di Promozione Turistica di Roma** (see the Information listing). If you want something more detailed, you can buy maps at newsstands and kiosks around Rome. One of the best maps is **Tutto Città,** which costs about 12,000L ($7).

Newspapers and Magazines

All the newspaper kiosks in the center offer the *International Herald Tribune,* European issues of *Time,* and usually *The Economist,* and the *Financial Times.* Another good place for English-language periodicals is the kiosk on Via Veneto across from the U.S. Embassy (Via Veneto 119a; Metro: Line A to Barberini; Bus: minibus 116).

Pharmacies

Call ☎ **06-110** or 06-5820-1030 to get a list of pharmacies open at night.

Police

Call ☎ **113.**

Rest Rooms

Some public toilets are scattered around town, but not many. You can find one outside the Colosseum across the road toward Via Labicana, and a convenient one is halfway up the steps from Piazza del Popolo to the Pincio, on the left side. Facing San Pietro, you can find toilets under the colonnade on the right. The best bet for a rest room is often to go to a nice-looking cafe (though you have to buy something, like a cup of coffee).

Safety

Rome is a very safe city except for pickpockets. Pickpockets concentrate in tourist areas, on public transportation, and around crowded open-air markets like the Porta Portese. One area that gets somewhat seedy at night is behind the main rail station Termini.

Smoking

Smoking is allowed in cafes and restaurants and is very common. Unfortunately for non-smokers, finding a restaurant with a no-smoking area is virtually impossible, although some are beginning to appear.

Taxes

Rome doesn't have a local tax. Other taxes are always included in the prices quoted. You can get a refund of the 19 percent **IVA** (value-added tax) for purchases costing more than 300,000L ($162). See "Keeping a Lid on Hidden Expenses" in Chapter 4.

Taxis

If you need a taxi, call ☎ **06-88-177, 06-66-45, 06-49-94, 06-55-51,** or **06-65-45.**

Transit/Tourist Assistance

Call ☎ **147-888-088** daily 7 a.m. to 9 p.m. for FS, the state railroad. The number for Leonardo da Vinci Airport is ☎ **06-65951.** However, operators often only speak Italian. Instead, call the tourist information **hotline** at ☎ **06-3600-4399.**

Weather Updates

For forecasts, your best bet is to look at the news on TV (there's no phone number to get weather forecasts). On the Web, check out meteo.tiscalinet.it.

Web Sites

At the city's own Web site, www.comune. roma.it, under *Cultura,* you can find all the galleries and museums in Rome and lists of hotels and restaurants. They're mostly in Italian, but you can get phone and fax numbers and addresses. Written delightfully in "English as a second language," www. informaroma.it directs you to everything you may need to feel at home in Rome. Time Out's site www.timeout.co.uk lists the latest in everything from sightseeing to nighclubbing in the Eternal City.

At www.tourome.com/tourrome.htm you can find day tours of Rome's sights and attractions, led by local tour leaders who pick you up and drop you off at your hotel. The Vatican features a multilingual site at www.vatican.va — the official site of the Holy See — while at www. christusrex. org you can find tourist information as well as a tour of the Vatican Museums. A private site where you can see a reconstruction of ancient Rome is www.ancientsites. com/users/COCCIEIUSCAESAR. Other good sites are www.virtualrome.com and www.romaonline.it.

Chapter 13

Side Trips from Rome

• •

In This Chapter

▶ Visiting the fountains of Tivoli

▶ Dining with the Romans in the Castelli

▶ Traveling back in time to Ostia Antica

• •

*L*azio, the region surrounding Rome, is rich in beautiful and interesting sites you can easily reach from the capital. If you have the
leisure, you can stay a couple extra days in Rome and branch out from
there for some enjoyable day trips.

Tivoli and Its Trio of Villas

Try not to miss the splendor of **Tivoli**, northeast of Rome. Like Rome,
it's situated on a hill — actually on the pre-Apennines — and is the
seat of three famous villas, one ancient Roman, one baroque, and one
romantic. Here you can see Rome's architectural history as it developed over almost 2,000 years.

The ancient "Tibur" (Tivoli) of the Romans was the destination of
choice for the wealthy and famous. Many constables and even emperors had their villas here to escape from the stress of daily life in
ancient Rome — not such a joke if you remember that at the height
of the Empire, Rome-the-city counted two million inhabitants. The
tradition continued during the Renaissance, and even nowadays Tivoli
remains a favorite retreat for Romans in search of a cool breeze, good
food, and beautiful vistas.

Getting there

A short drive from the capital — only 31 km (20 miles) northeast —
Tivoli lies on Via Tiburtina, one of the consular roads, running northeast of Rome and just southeast of the Via Nomentana. Given the traffic
and Italian driving habits, though, you'd be better off going by public
transportation. Tivoli is like a "suburb" of Rome, and many people commute to and from the city daily, so traffic at peak hours can be horrible.

Rome's Environs

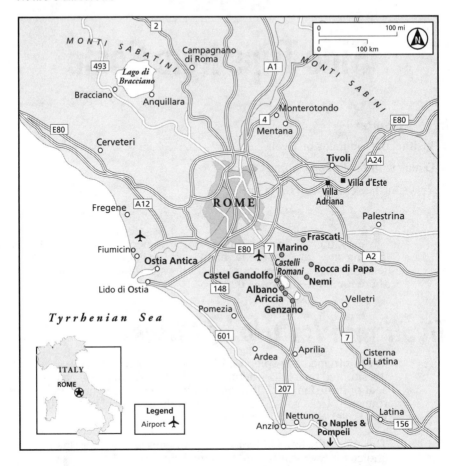

The best idea is taking **Metro Line B** to the last stop, Rebibbia (a 15-minute trip), and then switching to a **COTRAL** bus for Tivoli (☎ **0774-720-096** in Tivoli) at the terminal outside the Metro station (a 30-minute trip). Buses depart about every 20 minutes and tickets cost 10,000L ($5). Beware: Buses are less frequent on Saturdays and quite infrequent on Sundays. If you wish to use the bus on a Sunday, check the schedule in advance to ensure that you'll have a bus at a convenient time for your way out.

Alternatively, you could take the **train:** One train departs from Rome's Stazione Termini for Tivoli about every hour on the hour. The ticket costs about 4,000L ($2.15) for the half-hour trip. Note, however, that the Tivoli train station is a little outside the town center and a bit of a walk. Of course, you can always take a taxi at the train station.

Taking a tour and getting information

If you sign up with a tour, you can avoid the hassle of driving and the trouble of dealing with transportation in a foreign language. A reliable agency that organizes excursions to Tivoli is **American Express** (Piazza di Spagna 38; ☎ **06-67-641**). Another is **Stop'n Go/C.S.R.** (Via Ezio 12; ☎ **06-321-7054;** E-mail: csr@gisec.it), which offers half-day tours (morning only). Both charge about 20,000L ($11) for the tour.

The **tourist office** in Tivoli is in the central square of Largo Garibaldi (☎ **0774-334-522**); summer hours are Monday to Saturday 9 a.m. to 6 p.m. and Sunday 9 a.m. to 2 p.m. (in winter it closes an hour earlier).

Seeing the sights

The two main villas are within walking distance of the center of town and from each other. The Villa Adriana is about 5 km (3½ miles) from the center of Tivoli and can be reached by the local **C.A.T.** city bus no. 4 (☎ **0774-334-229**) from Largo Garibaldi, a few minutes' ride costing 1,500L (80¢). A more expensive option is taking a **taxi** from the main square in town or having one called for you by the restaurant where you had lunch; the five-minute trip will cost about 5,000L ($2.70).

The visit to the three villas shouldn't make you forget to have a look at the town of Tivoli itself. The highlights are the second-century B.C. **Tempio della Sibilla**, on the Roman Acropolis (on the other side of the Aniene River); the twelfth-century churches of **San Silvestro** (southwest of the Villa d'Este) and **Santa Maria Maggiore;** and the 1461 **Rocca Pia,** Pope Pius II's castle, which was turned into a prison after 1870.

Villa Adriana

5 km (3 ½ miles) from the center of Tivoli

Hadrian, one of Rome's "good" emperors, had this villa built between A.D. 118 and 138 as his holiday home. He spent the last three years of his life here. The villa, placed on the site of a Roman villa from Republican times, is magnificent, though it has lost its marbles, so to speak — many of its sculptures are now conserved in Roman museums. Much of the marble once covering the structures has gone, for the estate was used as a "quarry" during the Renaissance, as were many other Roman buildings, like the Colosseo. Here Hadrian wanted to be surrounded by the architectural marvels he'd seen during his trips across the Empire: On the 300 acres of this self-contained world for his vast royal entourage, he constructed replicas of famous buildings of antiquity, such as the **Canopus** (the Egyptian round canal ringed with statues) and the **Lyceum** (the school of Aristotle), as well as temples and theaters, monumental thermal baths, fountains and gardens, and a library. Although most of the monuments are today in ruins, the effect is still impressive. For a glimpse of what the villa looked like in its heyday, see the reconstruction at the entrance. Like any ruin in Italy, the villa gets very hot at midday during summer, so the best time to visit is early in the morning or late in the afternoon.

Via di Villa Adriana ☎ *0774-530-203. Bus: 4 to Villa Adriana. Admission: 8,000L ($4.30) adults; children free. Open: Daily 9 a.m. – 1½ hours before sunset.*

Villa d'Este

Center of Tivoli

Built in 1550 by Cardinal Ippolito d'Este of Ferrara — the son of notorious Lucrezia Borgia and Alfonso I d'Este — this villa is relatively banal. The real attractions are the magnificent gardens surrounding it, where architect Pirro Ligorio, using an underground spring and the natural slope of the land, designed a masterpiece of linked fountains and hidden rivulets. The work is really magnificent and isn't diminished by the other master-pieces in the garden: the **Fontana dell'Organo (Fountain of the Organ)** by Claude Veanard, the **Fontana del'Ovato (Ovato Fountain)** by Ligorio, and the **Fontana del Bicchierone (Fountain of the Big Glass)** by Bernini. The gardens are incredibly refreshing in summer and a perfect spot to be at midday on your visit to Tivoli.

Piazza Trento. ☎ *0774-312-070. Bus: COTRAL bus from Rome has a stop in Largo Garibaldi, just east of Piazza Trento. Admission: 8,000L ($4.30) adults; children free. Open: Daily 9 a.m. – 1½ hours before sunset.*

Villa Gregoriana

Center of Tivoli

The latest of the three famous villas of Tivoli, the Villa Gregoriana was built in the nineteenth century and isn't a villa at all. It's in reality a beau-tiful garden built to enhance the natural beauty of the gorges of the Aniene — the river that meets the Tiber in Rome. Pope Gregory XVI had carved a path all the way down to the bottom of the ravine to allow him to admire the 300-foot waterfall, grottoes, and ponds. The deep slopes are covered with vegetation and mighty trees, making it a magic spot, especially in summer.

Via di Villa Adriana. ☎ *0774-530-203. Bus: 4. Admission: 8,000L ($4.30) adults; chil-dren free. Open: Daily 9 a.m. – 1½ hours before sunset.*

Where to dine

Tivoli has a number of *trattorie* and restaurants that are Sunday favorites for Romans on outings. The food is typically Roman, with such specialties as *cannelloni, saltimbocca, abbacchio,* and *trippa alla Romana* (see Chapter 11 for descriptions).

Albergo Ristorante Adriano

$$$$ Villa Adriana Roman

Countryside elegance describes this tree-surrounded villa offering a variety of Roman specialties. Everything is homemade, from the delicious pastas to the desserts. And if you decide to stay overnight, you can rent one of the few guest rooms at 200,000L ($108) per double.

Via di Villa Adriana 194, near the ticket booth to Villa Adriana. ☎ *0774-535-028. Reservation not necessary. Bus: 4 to Villa Adriana. Secondi: 15,000–32,000L ($8–$17). Prix-fixe menu: 75,000L ($41). AE, DC, MC, V. Open: Lunch daily; dinner Mon–Sat.*

Le Cinque Statue

$$$ Villa Gregoriana Roman

Decorated with marble statues — the five statues in the restaurant's name — this reliable family-run restaurant offers a number of typical Roman dishes you can enjoy with a choice of local wines, mostly from the nearby Castelli (see "The Castelli Romani and Their Wines" in this chapter).

Via Quintilio Varo 8, just off the entrance to the Villa Gregoriana. ☎ *0774-335-366. Reservations recommended on weekends. Bus: Near the last stop of the COTRAL bus from Rome. Secondi: 12,000–25,000L ($6–$14). AE, DC, MC, V. Open: Lunch and dinner Sat–Thurs; closed the second 2 weeks in Aug.*

The Castelli Romani and Their Wines

The **Castelli Romani,** the hill towns surrounding Rome to the southeast, are a preferred destination where locals (including the pope) go to cool off and relax in summer. These towns are famous for their history and the production of excellent wine and foodstuffs. Each town is dominated by its own castle — the smallest called a *rocca* — and surrounded by fertile countryside, the produce of which is masterly prepared and served in the many *trattorie*.

The Castelli towns are Albano, Ariccia, Castel Gandolfo, Frascati, Genzano, Marino, Nemi, and Rocca di Papa. Frascati is probably familiar from the white wine produced there.

Getting there

The best way to visit the Castelli is by **car,** because that'll allow you to visit more than one of these attractive small towns. If you decide to rent a car, take the Tuscolana out of Rome and follow it to Frascati, then continue with the local road — almost a loop — to Marino on one side and Rocca di Papa on the other. It'll take you through all the other Castelli. You can also reach Marino from the Appia Nuova, taking a

4½-mile detour to the north. From the Appia, you can take another side road for Castel Gandolfo. The Appia then continues to Albano, Ariccia, and Genzano.

If you don't care for driving, a good alternative is taking an **organized tour** (see "Taking a tour and getting information" a little later in this chapter). Another possibility is using one of the several public transportation options. The public company **COTRAL** (☎ **800-431-784** for schedules) offers buses for each of the Castelli every 20 minutes or so. They leave from the Subaugusta and Anagnina (last) stops on metro Line A. There's also some service among the Castelli; Albano is the hub for this service, and you can catch COTRAL buses from Albano to Nemi, Ariccia, and Genzano. Of course, the length of the trip will vary depending on your destination, but all of them are under an hour. The price of the ride ranges from 6,000L to 10,000L ($3.25 to $5).

Some of the Castelli are also connected by train. A train leaves from Rome's Stazione Termini and heads to Albano, also stopping at Marino and Castel Gandolfo, and there's a separate train to Frascati. The ride will be about half an hour and cost 4,000L ($2.15).

Taking a tour and getting information

Stop 'n Go/C.S.R. (Via Ezio 12; ☎ **06-321-7054**; E-mail: csr@gisec.it) organizes a tour of the Castelli Romani leaving at 2:30 p.m. from Rome's Piazza dei Cinquecento (at the corner of Via Massimo d'Azeglio) for 20,000L ($11). The bus will bring you back to its point of departure in Rome by around 6:30 p.m.

The **central tourist office** for the Castelli Romani is in Albano, Viale Risorgimento 1 (☎ **06-932-4081**; Fax: 06-932-0040). Another large office is in Frascati (Piazza Marconi 1; ☎ **06-942-0331**). They're open Monday to Friday 8 a.m. to 2 p.m. and 3:30 to 6:30 p.m. and Saturday 8 a.m. to 2 p.m.

Seeing the sights

The Castelli towns and their surrounding countryside are all attractive. Each of the towns could justify at least a day-long stay, but few visitors nowadays have the leisure to do this. We indicate below the highlights of each town. Don't forget that they each have some food specialties well worth sampling during your visit.

Albano

Though the most built-up of the Castelli, **Albano** still maintains its unique charm. It's the center of the area producing the table wine Colli Albani, a pleasant white you often find in *trattorie* around Rome. Albano was the site of an ancient Roman town; later, Emperor Septimius Severus housed Roman legions here; and still later, Renaissance Italians built villas here. Albano, because of its beautiful views, was a regular stop of tourists on the Grand Tour (though the 1829 earthquake and the 1867 cholera epidemic put a damper on tourism).

Ariccia

On Ariccia's main square is the seventeenth-century **Palazzo Chigi,** a villa still belonging to the Chigi family and surrounded by a splendid garden. Across from the palazzo is the church of the **Assunta,** designed by Bernini. Unfortunately, modern and quite ugly buildings have been built around the historic center. The main reason to come here are the *fraschette* (small taverns), often with outdoor dining areas, where you can sample local wine and the town's specialty: *porchetta*. If you aren't vegetarian or aren't otherwise limited by a no-pork rule, *porchetta* is something not to be missed — it's a whole (deboned) pig carefully roasted with herbs, then sliced and served with peasant bread. A *porchetta* sandwich is one of the best "fast foods" you'll ever have.

Castel Gandolfo

On the slopes of the beautiful Lago Albano, **Castel Gandolfo** has a great beach — you can even swim — and a very pleasant promenade along the lake. It's the summer residence of the pope, whose seventeenth-century villa, surrounded by an enormous garden, was built atop the villa of the Roman emperor Domitian. Obviously, you can't visit the papal villa, but you can enjoy the rest of the town — including Bernini's **San Tommaso di Villanova** church and his fountain on the main square, **Piazza della Libertà.**

Frascati

Frascati is probably the best known of the Castelli because of the wine of the same name, produced in the surrounding countryside. Romans come here to visit the various *cantine* (cellars), where you can sample the wine and eat simple fare — a sandwich made with local bread and salami or *porchetta* and *pecorino* (sheep's-milk cheese). The town is dominated by the imposing sixteenth-century **Villa Aldobrandini,** atop a steep slope above the main square. Daily 9 a.m. to 1 p.m., you can visit its gardens by getting a free ticket from the **tourist office** on Piazza Marconi 1 (see "Taking a tour and getting information" earlier in this chapter).

Genzano

Picturesquely situated above the Lago di Nemi, which is actually the crater of an extinct volcano, **Genzano** is a charming small town surrounded by beautiful countryside. Among the highlights are the seventeenth-century **Palazzo Sforza-Cesarini** and the nearby cathedral. Genzano's main event is the **Infiorata** (flowering) — one Sunday in spring, the main street is covered with a carpet of flowers. The wine is good here, and you'll find a few nice *trattorie*.

Marino

The closest of the Castelli to Rome (only 15 miles), **Marino** is a pleasant small town — though the surroundings are modern and bland. The town is most famous for its wine, particularly enjoyable when it's fresh. On the occasion of the **harvest celebration** in October, the main fountains in town pour wine instead of water, to the great delight of all those present. The rest of the time, you can sample it in the various *osterie* and *cantine* in town — just look for the sign "Vino"!

Nemi

Nemi is a jewel of a small town. It has its own lake, the **Lago di Nemi,** on the slopes of which are cultivated some of the best strawberries of the world and certainly the best in Italy. Nemi also specializes in the production of salami, sausages, *pancetta* (Italian bacon), and other mouthwatering items. Alas, you can't bring meat products back into the States, but that's only one more reason to sample them here. They keep quite well and you can include them in a future picnic during your trip.

Rocca di Papa

The town of **Rocca di Papa,** named after its castle, dominates the Lago di Albano and enjoys breathtaking views of the surrounding hills. It's worth climbing the hill above the town to see the great view; it's now a park, and all that's left here is the ruin of an old *albergo* where people once came to eat and enjoy the pure air. The town below is quite picturesque. The **Chiesa dell'Assunta** is a baroque church that was reconstructed after an 1806 earthquake.

Where to dine

The Castelli are a procession of small and big *trattorie* and *ristoranti.* They're all quite reliable; but keep in mind the rule of "trust the locals" (if it's dinnertime and nobody is eating in a place, there must be a reason). We've given you some safe bets, but you can follow your nose and find many other great places on your own.

The food is typically Roman in the Castelli, including fresh pasta and grilled meats. People come to sample the variety of local salami and cheeses, usually served as antipasto. *Porchetta* is a specialty of Ariccia (see the previous section) but is prepared to some extent everywhere in the Castelli. The wine of the Castelli is probably the best in Lazio; particularly famous are the white Frascati and the Marino (white and red).

Antico Ristorante Paganelli

$$$$ Castel Gandolfo Roman/Seafood

The Roman menu here includes a variety of traditional specialties as well as more common Italian dishes. The prix-fixe menus change in price according to what's included. As is usually the case in Italy, fish is the most expensive.

Via Gramsci 4. ☎ *06-936-0004. Reservation recommended on weekends. Secondi: 18,000–40,000L ($10–$22). AE, DC, MC, V. Open: Lunch and dinner Wed–Mon.*

Cacciani

$$$ Frascati Roman

The renowned Cacciani is family run and serves some of the best food and wine in the area — and that's high praise. The restaurant is modern inside and has a terrace from which you can enjoy the beautiful view over the hills. The typical Roman specialties are wonderfully prepared; go for the homemade pasta and the other pasta specialties. The meat dishes are also excellent — for example, the *abbacchio alla cacciatora* (lamb cooked with white wine and rosemary).

Via Armando Diaz 13. ☎ *06-942-0378. Reservations required on weekends. Secondi: 19,000–32,000L ($10–$17). AE, DC, MC, V Open: Lunch and dinner Tues–Sun; closed 10 days in Jan and 10 days in Aug.*

Cantina Comandini

$ **Frascati   Wine Tavern**

Not a restaurant but a "cellar," this family-run business is the outlet of one of Frascati's vineyards. Here you'll be able to sample the famous Frascati wine and accompany it with a sandwich or a choice of local cold cuts and cheese. You can also buy wine to bring away, but you'll probably want to drink it before you go home (wine that has traveled by air has to sit for at least two months and sometimes never fully recovers).

Via E. Filiberto 1 ☎ *06-942-0915. Reservation recommended. Secondi: 5,000–12,000L ($2.70–$7). MC, V. Open: Dinner Mon–Sat.*

Ostia Antica: Rome's Ancient Seaport

Southwest of Rome, toward the sea, is **Ostia Antica,** the commercial harbor of ancient Rome. Its ruins are particularly attractive early in the morning or at sunset, when many Romans like to come for an evening *passeggiata* (stroll). It's popular also on weekends for picnics, but most popular are the shows — music and theater — held in the Roman theater, the **Teatro Romano,** in July.

The ancient city of Ostia served as a shipyard, a gathering place for the fleet, and a distribution center for ancient Rome. Founded in the fourth century B.C. as a military colony for the defense of the river Tevere, Ostia flourished for about eight centuries before being progressively abandoned due to the silting up of the river and the spread of malaria in the region (no longer a concern, thankfully).

Getting there

Ostia Antica is at about 28 km (16 miles) from Rome. It's linked by **train** from Stazione Ostiense (take metro Line B to the Piramide stop and follow the signs for Ostia), with trains departing every half hour and costing about 2,000L ($1.10) for the 25-minute trip. You can easily reach the site on foot from the train station, which is across the street.

You can also get to Ostia by **car** on Via Ostiense or Via del Mare (they run parallel to each other). You can take Via Ostiense from Piramide and Via del Mare from Eur. Note, however, that this is also the route to the beaches, so if you set off on a beautiful weekend you may find heavy traffic heading out of Rome.

Keep in mind that the ruins are incredibly hot in summer. They're spread across a flat plane, and shade is hard to come by. If you don't like heat, it's a good idea to come early, end your visit just before lunch, and head elsewhere to eat.

Seeing the sight

Ostia Antica includes a small village, quite cute but really small, and the major site of the archaeological area, which is what people come here to visit. Note that there's nowhere to eat inside or by the archaeological area. Bring a picnic lunch or plan to eat elsewhere. There are a couple of small restaurants and a bar in the village of Ostia Antica.

Area Archeologica di Ostia Antica

The archaeological site covers the impressive excavations of the ancient town of Ostia. The main streets of the town have been unearthed, as well as some of the principal monuments. After entering the site, on the right you'll find **Via delle Corporazioni,** leading to the **Teatro Romano (Roman Theater).** It's interesting to note the mosaics indicating the nature of each of the businesses once housed along this street. The theater is still in use today for performances of works by modern and ancient authors during July as part of the **Estate Romana** (details on the Web at www.comune.roma.it or call ☎ **06-6880-9505** Monday to Saturday 10 a.m. to 5 p.m.).

Returning to the main street and continuing ahead, you'll find on your left the **Foro (Forum)** and behind it the **Terme (thermal baths).** There are two temples on the left, and the **Capitolinum** on the right. The site also includes many interesting houses and buildings. The tourist office in Rome has a relatively good map of the park. Remember to bring a picnic; it's great to eat under a tree among the ruins (there's little to eat close by). Allow a minimum of three hours for the visit, more if you visit the museum. The **Museo (Museum)** — conserving all the material found during the excavations of the site — just opened its doors after a restoration that lasted several years. The entrance to the museum is within the excavations and the admission is included; it observes the same hours as the site as a whole.

Via Ostiense ☎ *06-5635-8099. Admission: 8,000L ($4.30). Open: Summer Tues–Sun 9 a.m.–6:30 p.m.; winter Tues–Sun 9 a.m.–5 p.m.*

To take a guided tour of the sights, check out **Stop 'n Go/C.S.R.** (Via Ezio 12; ☎ **06-321-7054;** E-mail: csr@gisec.it). It organizes morning and afternoon tours of Ostia Antica for 20,000L ($11).

Part IV

Florence and the Best of Tuscany and Umbria

The 5th Wave   By Rich Tennant

I know how to ask for directions to a McDonald's in Italian, I'm just afraid to.

CUCINA

In this part . . .

*T*oscana (Tuscany) is *the* most visited region in Italy
and for a great reason: The concentration of attractions here — sights, scenery, food, and wine — is beyond
imagination. Practically every hill town offers something
interesting to visit. (This is true of all Italy, but Tuscany
boasts so many more hills!) Tuscany has a proud tradition
and a unique character and flavor, including the regional
delicacies that each part of Italy seems to offer. Umbria is
a less touristed region, but it's also famous for its cuisine
and the art of its towns. Perugia, a city on a hill (of course)
with a rich artistic patrimony, is Umbria's capital.

In the following chapters, we give you the top of the top,
the not-to-be-missed things to see and do in this region.
Chapter 14 is dedicated to the beautiful city of Florence.
Chapter 15 covers the northern Tuscan towns of Lucca
and Pisa and detours to the Italian Riviera for a glimpse
of the Cinque Terre (five fishing villages). In Chapter 16
we take you to southern Tuscany and explore the Chianti
region and the towns of Siena and San Gimignano. Chapter 17 covers the highlights of Umbria, including the cities
of Assisi, Perugia, and Spoleto.

Chapter 14

Florence

• •

In This Chapter

▶ Finding your way to and around Florence

▶ Discovering the best neighborhoods, hotels, and restaurants

▶ Exploring the magnificent sights of Florence

▶ Sampling the best of Italian food

▶ Getting the scoop on the best shopping areas and nightlife attractions

• •

Along with Venice, **Firenze (Florence)** is the top destination for Americans in Italy. So why does everyone go to Florence? Well, Venice seems a bit unreal, a beautiful but almost dead city, and Rome is a crazy mix of ancient and modern — but Florence, despite its incredible wealth of art and architecture, still maintains its medieval scale and feels like a *real* place. The Botticellis and Leonardos in the Galleria degli Uffizi, Michelangelo's *David* in the Galleria dell'Accademia, Brunelleschi's dome crowning the Duomo, Giotto's Campanile, Ghiberti's "Gates of Paradise" on the Battistero, the Ponte Vecchio . . . the list of Florence's treasures is long.

Florence thrived from its ninth-century B.C. beginnings, but in medieval times — when it grew to be a great banking center, dominating the European credit market — the city truly reached its apogee. Florence's riches enabled the flourishing of the arts: Dante was born here in 1265, and so was painter Cimabue (Giotto's teacher), around the same time. The Renaissance blossomed in the 1300s, despite a flood, the Black Plague, and political upheaval. The fifteenth century brought the rule of Lorenzo the Magnificent, head of the powerful Medici clan, and then a brief restoration of the Republic. In this, Florence's greatest period, Leonardo, Michelangelo, and Raphael were producing amazing works. In 1537, the Medici family returned to power in the person of Cosimo I.

Florence has remained a center of intellectual life and advanced ideas into the modern period; in fact, it was the capital of Italy from 1865 to 1870. By that time, it had become one of the paramount stops on the Grand Tour, and its past had been transformed into its most important asset. Tourism has exploded in recent years — though really a small town, Florence is crammed with *6 million* visitors annually (that's why you feel that elbow digging into the small of your back).

Getting There

Located in the region of Tuscany, Florence is easy to reach by air, train, or car.

By air

There are no direct flights from the United States to Florence. If you're leaving from the States, you have to fly first to Rome or Milan — the only two international airports in Italy — and then get a connecting flight. The situation is different if you're flying from one of the European Union countries: There are direct flights between a number of European cities and Florence.

Florence is served by two airports — in addition to its own airport, the Aeroporto Amerigo Vespucci, the city is accessible from Pisa's nearby Aeroporto Galileo Galilei (for Pisa information, see Chapter 15). Both airports are easy to get around, though the Florence airport is smaller.

Arriving at Aeroporto Amerigo Vespucci/Peretola

The **Aeroporto Amerigo Vespucci** (☎ **055-373-498;** Internet: www. safnet.it), is generally called the **Aeroporto di Peretola,** which is the name of the small town where it's located (like the Leonardo da Vinci/Fiumicino confusion for Rome's airport). The airport is only 4 km (2½ miles) outside of Florence.

The easiest method to get from the airport to your hotel is taking a **taxi,** which will take about 10 to 15 minutes and cost about 40,000L ($22). You can also get into Florence by regular city **bus no. 62,** which takes about half an hour and arrives at the central train station, Santa Maria Novella, for 1,500L (81¢).

The **SITA bus** (☎ **055-214-721**) is slightly more expensive at 6,000L ($3.25) but is also faster (10 to 15 minutes) because it's nonstop; about one bus leaves per hour, arriving at the Florence's SITA bus terminal, just behind the rail station of Santa Maria Novella.

Landing at Aeroporto Galileo Galilei

Pisa's well-organized **Aeroporto Galileo Galilei** (☎ **050-500-707**) is just outside the city and 80 km (50 miles) from Florence. From the airport, you can take a special **shuttle train** to Florence's Santa Maria Novella rail station, costing about 8,000L ($4.30) and taking about an hour. Leaving Florence, you can even check your bags for your flight at the rail station of Santa Maria Novella (look for the sign "Air Terminal") and avoid lugging them to the airport yourself.

By train

This is by far the best way to get to Florence from other destinations in Italy — there are fast connections from all major Italian cities, such as Rome, Milan, and Venice. One train about every hour arrives from both

Rome and Venice. The trip takes about two hours from Rome and three from Venice, depending on the kind of train (intercity or the faster Eurostar). You'll arrive at Florence's **Stazione Santa Maria Novella,** often abbreviated SMN Firenze (☎ **055-288-765**), from which you can get to almost anywhere in the city via a cab, a bus, or your feet. Some trains stop at other stations on Florence's outskirts, but don't get off there.

At Santa Maria Novella, you can leave luggage at the office at the head of Track 16. The station's tourist office (see "Street smarts: Where to get information after you arrive" in this chapter) mainly arranges hotel rooms but also gives out some information, such as the free city map; this is where you can pick up your reserved tickets for the Uffizi or the Accademia (see the tip under "Exploring Florence").

By car

Florence is at the intersection of several major highways, so it's easy to get there from the north, south, east, and west. Once you're inside the city, however, your car will become a big pain in the neck. The city center is closed to autos except those of the residents; and the historic center — the part you're interested in — is closed to all vehicles except city buses. If you already have a hotel reservation, you're allowed to drive in to your hotel and unload, but then you have to find a place to stow your car, and city parking lots are expensive (your hotel may have one; check when you book). Rates near the center are about 2,000L to 6,000L ($1.10 to $3.25) per hour. You might get a daily rate, but you're still renting a space for a vehicle you can't use.

For these reasons, if you're doing a driving tour of smaller towns in Tuscany, it makes sense to schedule it before or after your stay in Florence. That way, you can either dump the car off at the agency when you arrive or can pick it up when you're ready to leave. You'll spare yourself a lot of headaches.

Orienting Yourself in Firenze

Unlike Rome and Venice, Florence has a relatively simple layout, bisected by the river Arno. The city has much expanded in recent times, but the new areas have little of historic interest. Like other Italian cities, Firenze developed beyond its medieval perimeter only toward the end of the nineteenth century. The historic center is quite small and easy to get around.

Firenze by neighborhood

Here we give you the layout of the historic districts of Florence, the part that interests you as a tourist. Most of the historic part lies on the north side of the Arno. This area is packed with monuments and museums. We don't want you to neglect the other bank of the river, however, so we describe the major attractions in that neighborhood as well.

Florence Orientation

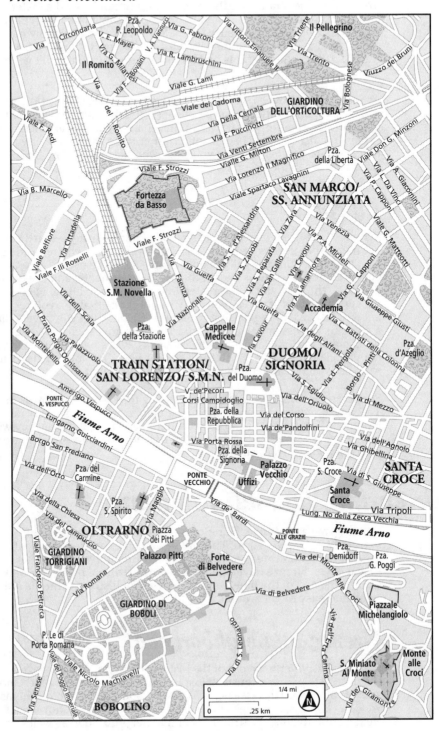

Il Pellegrino

Pza. Circondaria
P. Leopoldo
V. E. Mayer
Via V. E. Mayer
Via G. Fabroni
Via Bovaini
Via G. Milani
V. A. Vannucci
Via R. Lambruschini
Via Vittorio Emanuele II
Via Trieste
Via Trento
Viuzzo de' Bruni

Il Romito
Via
Via F.
Viale G. Lami
Via del Romito
Via Bolognese

Viale F. Redi
Viale dei Cadorna
GIARDINO DELL'ORTICOLTURA

Via B. Marcello
Viale F. Strozzi
Viale Della Cernaia
Via F. Puccinotti
Via Venti Settembre
Viale G. Milton
Via Lorenzo Il Magnifico
Pza. della Libertà
Viale Don G. Minzoni
Via A. Giacomini
Via I. Da Vinci
Via P. Capponi
Viale G. Matteotti

Fortezza da Basso
Viale Spartaco Lavagnini
SAN MARCO/ SS. ANNUNZIATA

Viale Belfiore
Via Cittadella
Via F.lli Rosselli
Viale F.lli Rosselli
Viale F. Strozzi
Via Faenza
Via S. C. d'Alessandra
Via S. Zanobi
Via S. Reparata
Via S. Gallo
Via Zara
Via P. A. Micheli
Via Cavour
Via Venezia
Via Capponi
Via G. Giuseppe Giusti

Via della Scala
Stazione S.M. Novella
Via Guelfa
Via Nazionale
Via Guelfa
Via A. Lamarmora
Via degli Alfani
Accademia
Via C. Battisti della Colonna
Pza. d'Azeglio

Il Prato
Via Palazzuolo
Borgo Ognissanti
Via Montebello
Pza. della Stazione
Cappelle Medicee
Via Cavour
DUOMO/ SIGNORIA
Via S. Egidio
Borgo
Via d. Pergola
Via di Mezzo

PONTE A. VESPUCCI
Amerigo Vespucci
TRAIN STATION/ SAN LORENZO/ S.M.N.
Pza. del Duomo
V. de' Pecori
Corsi Campidoglio
Via dell'Oriuolo
Via dell'Agnolo
Via Ghibellina

Lungarno Guicciardini
Fiume Arno
Pza. della Repubblica
Via del Corso
Via de' Pandolfini

Borgo San Frediano
Via dell'Orto
Pza. del Carmine
Via Porta Rossa
Pza. della Signoria
Palazzo Vecchio
Pza. S. Croce
Via di S. Giuseppe
SANTA CROCE

Via della Chiesa
Pza. S. Spirito
Via Maggio
PONTE VECCHIO
Uffizi
Santa Croce
Via Tripoli

Via del Campuccio
OLTRARNO
Piazza dei Pitti
Via de' Bardi
Lung. No della Zecca Vecchia
Fiume Arno

GIARDINO TORRIGIANI
Palazzo Pitti
Forte di Belvedere
PONTE ALLE GRAZIE
Pza. Demidoff
Via del Monte Alle Croci
Pza. G. Poggi

Viale Francesco Petrarca
Via Romana
GIARDINO DI BOBOLI
Via di Belvedere
Piazzale Michelangiolo

P. Le di Porta Romana
Via del Poggio Imperiale
Viale Niccolo Machiavelli
Via di S. Leonardo
Via dell'Erta Canina
S. Miniato Al Monte
Monte alle Croci

Via Sensese
BOBOLINO
Via del Giramonte

0   1/4 mi
0   .25 km

The centro storico (historic district)

Florence began here in a square area defined by the Stazione Santa Maria Novella, Piazza SS. Annunziata, and the Arno. Most of the tourist draws are in this neighborhood, as well as the major shopping areas.

From SMN to the river is the elegant **commercial district** along Via dei Tornabuoni and eastward on Piazza della Repubblica and Via Roma. From Piazza SS. Annunziata — where you'll find the **Galleria dell'Accademia (Accademia Gallery)** with Michelangelo's *David* — to the Arno is the "**monumental**" **district**. Within the monumental district, Via dei Calzaiuoli leads from the **Duomo (Santa Maria del Fiore)**, whose striped marblework and red-tiled dome symbolize Florence, to **Piazza della Signoria**, right in front of the **Palazzo Vecchio** and **Loggia dell'Orcagna** (the massive structure and soaring tower that have dominated political life since the thirteenth century). Next to the Duomo and also banded in pink, white, and green marble are the octagonal **Battistero di San Giovanni (Baptistry),** with its famous bronze doors and thirteenth-century mosaics, and the **Campanile di Giotto (Giotto's bell tower),** a masterpiece from late in the painter's life.

Just behind the Palazzo Vecchio and overlooking the river is the **Galleria degli Uffizi (Uffizi Gallery),** containing one of the most important painting collections in the world and showcasing the great Florentine painters of the Renaissance. If you turned right and walked along the riverbank, you'd come to the **Ponte Vecchio (New Bridge)**, one of the symbols of the city, dating from 1345.

Oltrarno (across the Arno)

Included within the walls of Florence only in 1173, the south side of the Arno is a quieter and more elegant residential area. The number of attractions there is limited, yet the magic of the medieval city is still present (and with reduced crowds). Crossing the Ponte Vecchio, you arrive on Via Guicciardini, which leads to the **Palazzo Pitti,** the largest Florentine palace, built by banker Luca Pitti in the fifteenth century and then transformed into the grand Medici residence. It now houses seven museums, including a *pinacoteca* (picture gallery) with works by Raphael, Andrea del Sarto, and others. Behind the palazzo is a beautiful garden, the **Giardino di Boboli.** Also on this side of the Arno is the **Chiesa di Santa Maria del Carmine,** a thirteenth-century church famous for frescoes by Masaccio and Masolino da Panicale.

Fiesole

The one other "neighborhood" you might want to visit outside the center is actually a separate town 4.5 km (3 miles) away, **Fiesole** (see "Exploring Florence"), from which there are marvelous views of Florence and the surrounding hills. It's particularly pleasant in summer, when it offers cooler air and a welcome break from the stuffy city. Fiesole is a preferred outing for Florentines on summer nights and is an excellent place to stay if you want to be away from the crowds (see the hotel and restaurant listings later in this chapter).

Street smarts: Where to get information after you arrive

Florence has several tourist offices. One is inside the SMN train station (☎ 055-212-245), open daily 8 a.m. to 7 p.m. Another is at Via Cavour 1R (☎ 055-290-832 or 055-290-833; Fax: 055-276-0383; Bus: 14, 23, or 71 to Duomo), about 3 blocks north of the Duomo; it's open Monday to Saturday 8 a.m. to 7 p.m. in summer (to 2 p.m. in winter). Yet another is at Borgo Santa Croce 29R (☎ 055-234-0444; Bus: A or 14 to Piazza Santa Croce), just behind Piazza Santa Croce; it's open the same hours as the Via Cavour branch. You can get information on the Web at www.firenze.turismo.toscana.it.

Getting Around Firenze

Florence's city center has long been closed to automobiles except those of the residents and the historic center free from all traffic except city buses — no cars, no taxis, and no mopeds (the ubiquitous and very noisy *motorinis*). Although some still protest — taxi drivers in particular — we think it was a great decision, because it made the city much more pleasant for visitors (for everybody, in fact) and easier to visit.

The free tourist office map is completely adequate for most visitors. If you're an ambitious explorer and don't feel satisfied with that map, you can pick up the yellow **Studio FMB Bologna map** of the city at a newsstand for about 8,000L ($4.30).

Florence has its own peculiar way of marking street addresses: Restaurants, agencies, and shops have numbers of their own, separate from the residential and hotel building numbers, even if the shop, restaurant, or agency is located within that building. Business numbers have the letter R appended to the number (for *rosso* or "red") and are painted in red, while residential numbers are painted in black or blue. For example, the address of one branch of the tourist office, Via Cavour 1R, refers to shop no. 1 on Via Cavour, whereas the address Via Cavour 1 is the private building with the entrance no. 1. Such seemingly similar addresses can be many doors away from each other.

On foot

The best way to get around Florence is on foot. The full walk from the Duomo at one end of the major historic district to the Palazzo Pitti at the other takes only about 30 minutes at a leisurely pace; you'd also pass most of the major sights in town. As compact as any medieval city, Florence has a dense concentration of attractions, so you can basically walk from one sight to another.

By bus

The only sight that's far away from the center and absolutely requires a bus ride is the town of Fiesole. However, buses come as a welcome rest to the tired visitor — especially after a long day at the Uffizi — and the view on the way up to Fiesole is exquisite. Also, we found the bus particularly useful to move back and forth between the Palazzo Pitti/Giardino di Boboli and the center of town on the other side of the river Arno.

Florence's bus system is well organized and easy to use. You can get a bus map at the main ticket booth outside the SMN train station — in fact, that's the only place where you can get one. Each bus stop has a name that's neatly written on the post at the stop and is reported on the map and also has a number when there's more than one stop by the same name (for example, on the same street). This helps you figure out where you are and check your progress on the map as you ride.

A regular *biglietto* (ticket) is valid for an hour and costs 1,500L (80¢). As elsewhere in Italy, you need to buy tickets before boarding the bus and can buy them at most bars, tobacconist shops (signed *tabacchi* or by a white "T" on a black background), and newsstands. Tickets are also sold at the bus information booth outside the Santa Maria Novella rail station. Within the hour of validity, you can take as many buses as you wish. Remember that you need to stamp the ticket at your first ride using the machine inside the bus; without the stamp, the ticket isn't valid. After hours (9 p.m. to 6 a.m.), you can buy a ticket on the bus, but the charge is double. Also available are the *multiplo* ticket, which is good for four one-hour rides and costs 5,800L ($3.15), a slight savings; the **3-hour pass,** which costs 2,500L ($1.35); the **24-hour pass** for 6,000L ($3.25), and the **3-day pass** for 11,000L ($6).

Always have a ticket when boarding the bus and be sure to properly stamp it; some people may tell you that "no one ever checks," but they're wrong! Within five minutes of boarding our first bus, someone was nabbed by the ticket inspector, a scene we saw repeated several times. And, come on, why try to wriggle out of a bargain 70¢ ride?

Where to Stay in Firenze

Florence boasts hundreds of hotels, but because it's a medieval city filled with old buildings, they can be rather cramped and their amenities limited. Another thing to consider is that Florence is dominated by tourism and therefore relatively expensive. Hotels also often have complicated rate structures of high season, low season, and middle season (note that all of August is often considered low season, because it's so hot and Italians are on vacation). We offer a rundown of the best places to stay, followed by some acceptable alternatives if you have trouble booking a room. Unless otherwise specified, all rooms in the hotels listed come with private bathrooms.

If you arrive without a room reservation (something we advise against), remember that the tourist office in Stazione Santa Maria Novella offers a room-finding service. If you arrive by car, stop at the office in the Area di Servizio AGIP Peretola (rest area) on Hwy. A11 (☎ **055-421-1800**) or in the office at the Area di Servizio Chianti Est on Hwy. A1 (☎ **055-621-349**). They maintain hotel databases and can tell you if rooms are available in town and can even make reservations if you like.

The top hotels

Hotel Bellettini

$$ Centro storico

Just west of the Duomo, this fourteenth-century palazzo has been a guest house for the past 300 years. The old-fashioned Bellettini offers simple and clean guest rooms — some with fantastic views — and one of the best breakfasts in town, with the buffet including ham and fresh fruit. The owners, two sisters, are very friendly and helpful — many of their guests keep coming back, so you'll have to reserve in advance. Some of the rooms share a bath, so be sure to ask when you reserve.

Via de' Conti 7. ☎ *055-213-561. Fax: 055-283-551. E-mail:* hotel. bellettini0da.it. *Internet:* www.firenze.net/hotelbellettini. *Bus: 1, 6, 11, or 17 to Martelli; walk south to the Baptistry, turn right on Via de' Cerretani, and right again on Via de' Conti. Parking: 30,000L ($16). Rack rates: 160,000–200,000L ($87–$108) double, including breakfast. AE, DC, MC, V.*

Hotel Boboli

$$ Oltrarno

Just south of the Palazzo Pitti and a short walk from the Ponte Vecchio, this simple modern hotel is a good value in a residential part of town that's full of much pricier choices. The Boboli is a good choice if you want to be in a quiet area, yet near the major sights; it's convenient for families as well, since it has some triple rooms and a couple of quads. The bathrooms are really tiny but still very clean and sufficient for most people.

Via Romana 63. ☎ *055-229-8645 or 055-233-6518. Fax: 055-233-7169. Bus: 11, 36, or 37 to Serragli 05; walk south on Via dei Serragli, turn left on Via Serumido, and left again on Via Romana. Parking: 15,000–20,000L ($8–$11). Rack rates: 150,000–220,000L ($81–$119) double, including breakfast. MC, V.*

Hotel Chiari-Bigallo

$$ Centro storico

Just by the Duomo, this hotel has a great central location for very moderate prices, but because of that location it'll be a little noisy at night, especially in summer. The view from the windows, though, will more than compensate. The recently renovated guest rooms have parquet floors and new bathrooms (some with Jacuzzis). The hotel has the same owners as the Hotel de' Lanzi.

Vicolo degli Adimari 2. ☎ *055-216-086. Fax: 055-216-086. Bus: 1, 6, 11, or 17 to Martelli; walk south between the Baptistry and the Duomo at the corner with Via Calzaiuoli to Vicolo degli Adimari. Parking: 27,000L ($15). Rack rates: 170,000–180,000L ($92–$97) double, including breakfast. AE, MC, V.*

Hotel de' Lanzi

$$$ Centro storico

This hotel a block from the Duomo has been recently renovated and offers carpeted guest rooms and new bathrooms. Owned by the same people as the Chiari Bigallo, it has the advantage of being less noisy, but fewer of the rooms have the breathtaking vista over the Duomo. The breakfast is nice too, including ham and fruit.

Via delle Oche 11. ☎ *055-288-043. Fax: 055-288-043. Bus: 1, 6, 11, or 17 to Martelli; walk south between the Baptistry and the Duomo to Via Calzaiuoli and turn left onto Via delle Oche. Parking: 27,000L ($15). Rack rates: 280,000L ($191) double, including breakfast. AE, MC, V.*

The big splurge

In this chapter we supply entries for several deluxe $$$$$ hotels, among them the Helvetia & Bristol, the Hotel Monna Lisa, and the Plaza Lucchesi. If you're looking for the plushest of the plush, here are a few more suggestions:

✔ **Grand Hotel** (Piazza Ognissanti 1; ☎ **800-325-3589** in the U.S. and Canada, or 055-288781; Fax: 055-217400; Bus: 6 or 17)

✔ **Grand Hotel Villa Medici** (Via il Prato 42; ☎ **055-238-1331**; Fax: 055-238-1336; E-mail: sina@italyhotel.com; Internet: www.venere.it/firenze/villa_medici.html; Bus: 9, 13, 16, 17, or 26)

✔ **Hotel Excelsior** (Piazza Ognissanti 3; ☎ **800-325-3535** in the U.S. and Canada, or 055-264201; Fax: 055-210278; Internet: www.deluxurycollection.firenze.net; Bus: 6 or 17)

✔ **Savoy Hotel** (Piazza della Repubblica 7; ☎ **055-283-313**; Fax: 055-284-840; E-mail: savoyhtl@firenzealbergo.it; Internet: www.firenzealbergo.it; Bus: A)

✔ **Villa La Massa** (Via della Massa 24; ☎ **055-626-11**; Fax: 055-633-102; E-mail: villamssa@galactica.it; free shuttle bus to/from villa and Ponte Vecchio in Florence during the day)

Florence Accommodations and Dining

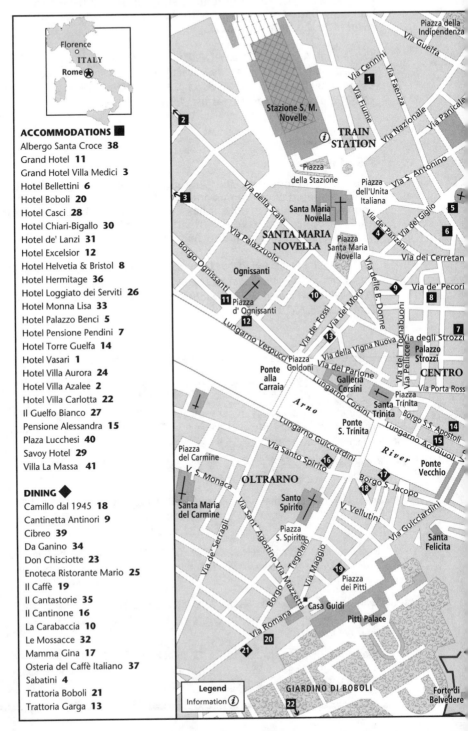

ACCOMMODATIONS ■
Albergo Santa Croce **38**
Grand Hotel **11**
Grand Hotel Villa Medici **3**
Hotel Bellettini **6**
Hotel Boboli **20**
Hotel Casci **28**
Hotel Chiari-Bigallo **30**
Hotel de' Lanzi **31**
Hotel Excelsior **12**
Hotel Helvetia & Bristol **8**
Hotel Hermitage **36**
Hotel Loggiato dei Serviti **26**
Hotel Monna Lisa **33**
Hotel Palazzo Benci **5**
Hotel Pensione Pendini **7**
Hotel Torre Guelfa **14**
Hotel Vasari **1**
Hotel Villa Aurora **24**
Hotel Villa Azalee **2**
Hotel Villa Carlotta **22**
Il Guelfo Bianco **27**
Pensione Alessandra **15**
Plaza Lucchesi **40**
Savoy Hotel **29**
Villa La Massa **41**

DINING ◆
Camillo dal 1945 **18**
Cantinetta Antinori **9**
Cibreo **39**
Da Ganino **34**
Don Chisciotte **23**
Enoteca Ristorante Mario **25**
Il Caffè **19**
Il Cantastorie **35**
Il Cantinone **16**
La Carabaccia **10**
Le Mossacce **32**
Mamma Gina **17**
Osteria del Caffè Italiano **37**
Sabatini **4**
Trattoria Boboli **21**
Trattoria Garga **13**

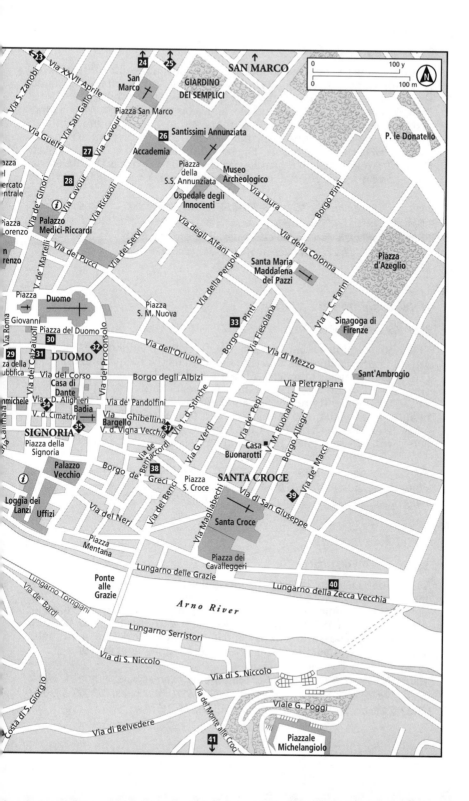

Hotel Helvetia & Bristol

$$$$$ Centro storico

A block east of Via dei Tornabuoni, this upscale nineteenth-century hotel is within walking distance of Via dei Calzaiuoli and the major sights. It was the elegant choice of belle époque Florence, visited by Eleonora Duse, Enrico Fermi, Luigi Pirandello, and Giorgio De Chirico. After a long restoration, the Helvetia & Bristol reopened in 1989, with modernized marble baths and antique furnishings. There's much original art on the walls, even in the guest rooms. The beautiful Giardino d'Inverno (Winter Garden), a renowned meeting place in the 1920s, serves as the breakfast room and later as a cocktail bar (the buffet breakfast is 36,000L/$19).

Via dei Pescioni 2. ☎ *055-287-814. Fax: 055-288-353. E-mail:* hbf@ charminghotels.it. *Internet:* www.charminghotels.it. *Bus: 6, 11, 36, or 37 to Antinori; walk east on Via del Campidoglio and turn left on Via dei Pescioni. Parking: 40,000L ($22). Rack rates: 540,000-750,000L ($292-$405) double. AE, DC, MC, V.*

Hotel Loggiato dei Serviti

$$$ Centro storico

This hotel occupies a landmark sixteenth-century building designed by Antonio da Sangallo il Vecchio (the Elder) to match the twin buildings of the Ospedale degli Innocenti (Hospital of the Innocents) across the square — by the way, the square is the beautiful one just by the Accademia. Recently renovated and restored to its simple Renaissance beauty (it was built as a monastery and transformed into a hotel only early in the twentieth century), the Loggiato dei Serviti is a hotel of character, with pleasant guest rooms and furnishings.

Piazza SS. Annunziata 3. ☎ *055-289-593. Fax: 055-289-594. Internet:* www.venere.it. *Bus: 6, 31, or 32 to SS. Annunziata. Parking: 35,000-45,000L ($19-$25). Rack rates: 320,000L ($173) double, including breakfast. AE, DC, MC, V.*

Hotel Monna Lisa

$$$$$ Centro storico

The Monna Lisa (no, that's not a misspelling) yearns to be a private collector's home. The guest rooms of this beautiful fourteenth-century palazzo, once home to the Neri family, vary in style and size. The antique furnishings, original coffered ceilings, inner garden and patio, modern bathrooms (some with Jacuzzis), and important artworks make this hotel very desirable. Alas, the prices are a little steep in most seasons.

Borgo Pinti 27. ☎ *055-247-9751. Fax: 055-247-9755. Internet:* www.monnalisa.it. *Bus: A, 14, or 23 to Salvemini. Parking: 20,000L ($11). Rack rates: 300,000-570,000L ($162-$308) double, including breakfast. AE, DC, MC, V.*

Hotel Palazzo Benci

$$$ Centro storico

Recently opened west of the Duomo, this hotel occupies a lovingly restored sixteenth-century palazzo, the residence of the Renaissance Benc family. The guest rooms are simple but tasteful, and comfort in summer is ensured by air conditioning; other amenities include safes and minibars. Many rooms open onto the delightful inner garden courtyard. The common spaces are absolutely gorgeous, with richly stuccoed walls, and the breakfast room boasts coffered wooden ceilings.

*Piazza Madonna degli Aldobrandini 3. ☎ **055-213-848** or 055-238-2821. Fax: 055-288-308. Bus: 1, 6, 11, or 17 to Martelli; walk west on Via dei Gori, then across Piazza San Lorenzo and around the church on Corso Tonelli into Piazza Madonna degli Aldobrandini. Rack rates: 250,000–300,000L ($135–$162) double, including breakfast. AE, MC, V.*

Hotel Pensione Pendini

$$$ Centro storico

Minutes from Via dei Calzaiuoli and the top sights, the old-fashioned Pendini is just off busy Piazza della Repubblica. This family-style pensione dates from the nineteenth century, when Florence was briefly the capital of Italy. It has undergone renovations during the 1990s and offers insulated guest rooms with double-paned windows (so you won't be bothered by the nearby traffic) and new bathrooms.

*Via Strozzi 2. ☎ **055-211-170**. Fax: 055-281-807. E-mail:* pendini@dada.it. *Internet:* www.tiac.net/users/pendini. *Bus: A to Strozzi stop or 6, 11, 36, or 37 to Antinori; walk south on Via dei Tornabuoni and turn left on Via Strozzi. Parking: 35,000–40,000L ($19–$22). Rack rates: 250,000L ($135) double, including breakfast. AE, DC, MC, V.*

Hotel Vasari

$$ Centro storico

On the east side of the SMN train station, the Vasari is a good value for a location within walking distance of the main sights and the historic district. Once home to French poet Alphonse de Lamartine, this nineteenth-century building offers simple but comfortable guest rooms with recently renovated bathrooms.

*Via B. Cennini 9–11. ☎ **055-212-753**. Fax: 055-294-246. Bus: 7, 14, 23, 36, or 37 to FS S. Maria Novella; walk left across Piazza Adua and turn right onto Via B. Cennini. Parking: 15,000L ($8). Rack rates: 230,000–250,000L ($124–$135) double, including breakfast. AE, DC, MC, V.*

Hotel Villa Aurora

$$$ Fiesole

In Fiesole's central square, just by the terminus of the city bus from Florence, this hotel is elegant and comfortable if a bit pretentious. The guest rooms in back enjoy the gorgeous view over Florence, while the ones on the side overlook the garden. Some rooms have balconies, and there are Jacuzzis in some bathrooms. Although the old-world feeling doesn't extend to the rooms, the fixtures and furniture are modern.

Piazza Mino 39. ☎ *055-59100. Fax: 055-59587. Internet:* www.logicad. net/aurora. *Bus: 7 to last stop. Rack rates: 290,000–350,000L ($157–$190) double, including breakfast. AE, DC, MC, V.*

Hotel Villa Azalee

$$$ Centro storico

Just beyond the historic district to the west, the Azalee is minutes from the SMN train station though a bit removed from the top sights. This villa offers a welcome break from the crowds and is surrounded by a flower garden; the soundproofed guest rooms are furnished in cozy English style, with flowery fabrics and wooden floors. The stables have been converted into rooms and are among the best in the hotel. Bikes are rented at a very low 5,000L ($2.70) per day.

Viale Fratelli Rosselli 44. ☎ *055-214-242. Fax: 055-268-264. E-mail:* villaazalee@ fi.flashnet.it. *Bus: 9, 13, 16, or 17 to Porta Prato. Parking: 35,000L ($19). Rack rates: 270,000–300,000L ($146–$162) double, including breakfast. AE, DC, MC, V.*

Hotel Villa Carlotta

$$$ Oltrarno

This beautiful early-1900s villa, surrounded by an attractive garden, is in a residential area a short walk from the Ponte Vecchio. The guest rooms are very nicely decorated, and the hotel maintains the air of a private home. The Carlotta is an excellent choice if you came by car — it offers that rare luxury of free parking. This hotel offers a very enjoyable way to escape the crowds in the center and yet still be close by.

Via Michele di Lando 3. ☎ *055-220-530. Fax: 055-233-6147. E-mail:* villacarlotta@ flashnet.it. *Internet:* www.venere.it. *Bus: 38 to Bobolino. Parking free. Rack rates: 290,000–435,000L ($157–$235) double, including breakfast. AE, DC, MC, V.*

Il Guelfo Bianco

$$$ Centro storico

North of the Duomo and a few steps from the Accademia, this recently renovated hotel occupies a fifteenth-century palazzo and a neighboring seventeenth-century palazzo. The guest rooms in the former are pleasantly furnished and come with beautiful bathrooms; many overlook the inner garden and courtyard. Don't worry about noise, though, even in rooms overlooking the street — the new windows are *triple*-paned! The rooms in the neighboring building boast ceiling frescoes, and some have painted wood and antique furniture.

Via Cavour 29. ☎ *055-288-330. Fax: 055-295-203. Bus: 1, 6, or 17 to Cavour 02 or 1, 6, 7, 10, 11, 17, 25, 31, or 32 to San Marco 01; walk south on Via Cavour, the hotel is near the corner with Via Guelfa. Parking: 25,000–40,000L ($14–$22). Rack rates: 240,000–360,000L ($130–$195) double, including breakfast. AE, MC, V.*

Pensione Alessandra

$$ Centro storico

Steps from the Ponte Vecchio and the Uffizi, this pensione offers simple guest rooms — many quite large — at moderate prices. The private bathrooms have been recently renovated; the shared ones are oldish though large and spotless. This all adds up to a very good value. Only some rooms are air-conditioned, so reserve in advance if you absolutely want one (and if it's August, you want one).

Borgo SS. Apostoli 17. ☎ *055-283-438. Fax: 055-210-619. Internet:* www. hotelalessandra.com. *Bus: B to SS. Apostoli or 6, 11, 36, or 37 to Tornabuoni; walk right on Borgo SS. Apostoli. Parking: 30,000–35,000L ($16–$19). Rack rates: 150,000–200,000L ($81–$108) double, including breakfast. AE, MC, V.*

Plaza Lucchesi

$$$$$ Centro storico

Near Santa Croce, the Plaza Lucchesi opened in 1860 at the eastern edge of the historic district. It's tastefully decorated and modernized, and you'll be pampered by the spacious guest rooms, modern baths, and comfortable furniture; 20 rooms have balconies. In addition to the normal amenities for a hotel of this caliber, it offers Internet access for guests.

Lungarno della Zecca Vecchia 38. ☎ *055-26-236. Fax: 055-248-092. E-mail:* plazalucchesi@italyhotel.com. *Internet:* www.plazalucchesi.it. *Bus: B or 13 Zecca Vecchia. Parking free. Rack rates: 550,000L ($297) double, including breakfast. AE, DC, MC, V.*

Runner-up accommodations

Albergo Santa Croce

$$ Centro storico   This is a simple family-run hotel charging modest prices in an expensive town; just renovated, it's behind Piazza della Signoria and the Uffizi Via de' Bentaccordi 3; ☎ **055-217-000**; Fax: 055-217-000; Bus: 23.

Hotel Casci

$$ Centro storico Occupying a fifteenth-century palazzo, it offers comfortable guest rooms and an excellent location just north of the Duomo. The breakfast room is decorated with original frescoes. Via Cavour 13; ☎ **055-211-686**; Fax: 055-239-6461; E-mail: casci@pn.itnet.it; Internet: www.hotelcasci.com; Bus: 14 or 23.

Hotel Hermitage

$$$ Centro storico This hotel is right off the Ponte Vecchio toward the Uffizi and has been recently renovated; many of the guest rooms have beautiful views over the river and all have antique furniture and premium bathrooms. Vicolo Marzio 1; ☎ **055-287-216**; Fax: 055-212-208; E-mail: hermitage@italyhotel.com; Internet: www.hermitagehotel.com; Bus: 23.

Hotel Torre Guelfa

$$ Centro storico Near the Ponte Vecchio and the Uffizi, the Torre Guelfa offers pleasant guest rooms (many air-conditioned), good service, and a breathtaking view from the thirteenth-century tower. The owners of this landmark also own the **Villa Rosa** in Panzano, in the heart of the Chianti region (see Chapter 16). Borgo SS. Apostoli 8; ☎ **055-239-6338**; Fax: 055-239-8577; Bus: 23.

Where to Dine in Firenze

Tuscan cuisine is considered — by Tuscans obviously, but also by other Italians — the best in Italy. It's known for being flavorful yet light — Tuscany is poised between the north, where the food is heavier and uses butter and animal fats, and the south, where the flavors (dominated by tomato sauces) tend to be sharper. Many of the traditional dishes are simple farmland recipes (lots of vegetables and game), though others were refined for the Florentine sovereigns and are fit for more modest modern stomachs.

Italians love to remind people that French cuisine is derivative, largely descended from Tuscan specialties imported to France by the gourmet queen Caterina de' Medici in the sixteenth century — she brought her cooks with her when she married Henri II of France (not trusting northern barbarians to cook food, apparently). For example, French *crêpes* are derived from Florentine *crespelle*, a delightful preparation of layered dough and ham, cheese and tomato sauce, and often spinach as well.

The thing to order if you love meat is *bistecca alla fiorentina* (and if you like meat only once in a while, make this one of those whiles). This specialty is a two-plus-pound steak for two — you can have it all by yourself if you feel up to it. The real *fiorentina* comes from the Chianina cow, a breed raised only in the Tuscan countryside and blessed with espe-cially delectable meat. Most restaurants in Tuscany will have the *fiorentina* on their menus, but watch out for imitations. The real thing isn't cheap, is always a T-bone steak for two, and is from Chianina cows.

Other Tuscan specialties are *crostini* (toasted bread with savory top-pings), *affettati* (traditional cold cuts), *ribollita* (cabbage, bread, and vegetables in a thick soup) and *pappardelle al sugo di lepre* (large fettuccine with hare sauce). All of these are **primi,** or first courses. *Coniglio* (rabbit), *cinghiale* (wild boar), and a variety of meats grilled or fried are common for **secondi,** or main courses, and *fagioli all'uccelletto* (white Tuscan beans in a light tomato sauce) are a traditional **contorno,** or side dish. For **dolce** (dessert), the typical thing to have is *cantucci col vin santo* (hazelnut biscotti with a strong sweet wine) or *zuccotto* (a dome-shaped sponge cake filled with chocolate mousse, cream, dried fruits, and nuts).

To go with all of this, there's Chianti wine. In Tuscany, it's served as table wine (even on tap, from huge casks) in most restaurants — just ask for *vino della casa.* For those who want to splurge, special Vino Nobile di Montepulciano or — even better — Brunello di Montalcino are among Italy's greatest wines. For a white wine, try Vernaccia di San Gimignano, and for a dessert wine, the famous *vin santo. Buono appetito!*

For a cheap but delicious meal that'll give your wallet a rest and let you do as the locals do, drop by an *alimentari* (grocery shop) for the fixings of a picnic. You can buy some delicious Tuscan bread, country ham and cheese, fruit, mineral water, or wine. If you like this idea, remember the **Consorzio Agrario Pane & Co.,** Piazza S. Firenze 5R, at the corner of Via Condotta (☎ **055-213-063;** Bus: A to Condotta), where you'll find excellent cinghiale salami and a choice of local cheeses and cured pork delicacies, plus water, wine, and all the rest. The best place to have a picnic is in Fiesole or the Giardino di Boboli (see "The top sights" in this chapter).

The top restaurants

Camillo dal 1945

$$$ Oltrarno   Tuscan

This popular restaurant is housed in a palazzo that once belonged to the Medici family. The food is more upscale than that of the nearby Mamma Gina (listed in this section) and offers hearty and traditional dishes like fried boneless pigeon with artichokes, chicken with truffles and Parmesan cheese, and a choice of homemade fresh pastas with simple yet refined sauces.

Borgo San Jacopo 57R–61R. ☎ *055-212-427. Reservations required. Bus: D to San Jacopo. Secondi: 25,000–40,000L ($14–$22). AE, DC, MC, V. Open: Lunch and dinner Thurs–Tues; closed most of Aug and last two weeks in Dec.*

Cantinetta Antinori

$$$$ Centro storico Tuscan

Antinori is the family name of the oldest and one of the largest producers of wine in Italy. The *cantinetta* (small wine cellar) occupies the fifteenth-century palazzo of this noble family and serves as their winery in town. Typical Tuscan dishes and many specialties from the Antinori farms are served in the restaurant to accompany the wine. Wine tasting, though, remains the top activity here, and you can stay at the counter and sample the various vintages.

Piazza Antinori 3R. ☎ 055-292-234. Reservations recommended. Bus: 6, 11, 36, or 37 to Antinori; Piazza Antinori is at the north end of Via de' Tornabuoni. Secondi: 25,000–35,000L ($14–$19). MC, V. Open: Lunch and dinner Mon–Fri.

Cibreo

$$ (tavern), $$$$ (restaurant) Centro storico Tuscan

This is a renowned chef's restaurant, where the menu depends on the daily market finds and the kitchen's imagination. The backbone is historical Tuscan, with some recipes that go back to the Renaissance, but the interpretation is more modern. You won't find pasta or grilled meat, but there are soufflés, roasted and stuffed birds, and other oven-cooked specialties. On one side of the kitchen is a formal dining room and on the other a small tavern serving a smaller selection of dishes at lower prices.

Via de'Macci 118R. ☎ 055-234-1100. Reservations recommended. Bus: A to Borgo la Croce or Agnolo 04 stop; walk south on Via de' Macci from Piazza S. Ambrogio (outdoor vegetable market). Secondi: 20,000L ($11) at trattoria and 45,000L ($25) at restaurant. AE, DC, MC, V. Open: Lunch and dinner Tues–Sat; closed mid-July to early Sept.

Da Ganino

$$$ Centro storico Tuscan

At this centrally located cozy restaurant, you'll find ubiquitous Florentine specialties like *bistecca alla fiorentina* and *tagliatelle con tartufi* (home-made pasta with truffle sauce). In addition to the traditional menu there's a wide selection of daily specials. The food is deliciously prepared and served by an attentive staff.

Piazza dei Cimatori 4R. ☎ 055-214-125. Reservations recommended. Bus: A to Condotta or Cimatori; Via dei Cimatori is 2 short blocks north of Piazza della Signoria. Secondi: 16,000–30,000L ($9–$16). AE, DC, MC, V. Open: Lunch and dinner Mon–Sat.

Don Chisciotte

$$$ Centro storico Tuscan/Seafood

This restaurant is especially known for its fish dishes, like risotto with broccoli and baby squid and black squid-ink ravioli stuffed with shrimp and crayfish. The dining room is on the second floor of a typical palazzo and gets quite busy, especially on weekends. The food here is more creative and experimental than in other Florentine restaurants.

Via Ridolfi 4R. ☎ 055-475-430. Reservations recommended. Bus: 10, 14, or 23 to Strozzi 01 stop; northeast of the train station, walk on Via Filippo Strozzi and turn right on Via Ridolfi. Secondi: 28,000–35,000L ($15–$19). AE, DC, MC, V. Open: Lunch Tues–Sat; dinner Mon–Sat.

Enoteca Ristorante Mario

$$$$ Fiesole Tuscan

On Fiesole's main square, this restaurant offers a choice of excellent wines to accompany the nicely prepared Tuscan specialties. You'll find dishes that are typical of various parts of Tuscany, and the service is very good. You can start with *crostini* or *affettati misti* and follow with *pappardelle al sugo di lepre* and a wild boar stew or some delicious grilled vegetables. The restaurant occupies two floors, and the decor is stylish tavern style, with wooden ceiling beams and a small art gallery on the walls.

Piazza Mino 9R. ☎ 055-59-143. Reservations recommended on Sat. Bus: 7 to last stop in Fiesole; walk up toward the northwest side of the square, the restaurant is on the left. Secondi: 20,000–32,000L ($11–$17). AE, MC, V. Open: Lunch and dinner Tues–Sun.

Il Caffè

$$ Oltrarno Tuscan

Across from the Palazzo Pitti, this is a good spot for a quick bite during your touristic marathon. It's a *snack bar* that offers a basic choice of dishes all day long, with two prix-fixe menus at lunch and dinner. It's frequented by young crowds — especially at night, since it stays open to 2 a.m.

Piazza Pitti 9R. ☎ 055-239-6241. Reservations recommended on Sat. Bus: D to Pitti or 11, 36, or 37 to Serragli 03 or San Felice. Secondi: 13,000–17,000L ($7–$9). Prix-fixe menus: Lunch 12,000L ($6) with appetizer and primo or 18,000L ($10) with secondo as well; dinner 30,000L ($16) or 40,000L ($22), respectively. AE, MC, V. Open: Lunch and dinner daily.

Il Cantastorie

$$$ Centro storico Tuscan

Near the top sights, this pleasant country-style ristorante boasts wooden tables, high ceilings, and ironwork chandeliers and serves excellent wine and hearty food. It defines itself as a pinch of Tuscan countryside in the heart of Florence, and you'll find all the typical specialties and some of the best Chianti you've ever had. *Ribollita, salsiccia e bietola* (sausages and green chard), *crostoni* (larger version of *crostini*), *filetto di maiale al finocchio* (pork filet in fennel sauce), Tuscan cold cuts and *sottoli* (vegetables preserved in herbs and olive oil), and homemade desserts are some of the choices you may find on a menu that changes daily. The same management runs Il Cantinone (also listed in this section).

Via della Condotta 7–9R. ☎ *055-239-6804. Reservations recommended on Sat. Bus: 14 or A to Ghibellina 01; walk west toward the Palazzo Vecchio to Via della Condotta. Secondi: 14,000–22,000L ($8–$12). MC, V. Open: Lunch and dinner Wed–Mon.*

Il Cantinone

$$$ Oltrarno Tuscan

Twin restaurant to Il Cantastorie, this has an even more convivial atmosphere, with low arched ceilings and long wooden tables. The food choice is similar, with all the best of traditional cuisine: soups, pasta, *cinghiale*, *coniglio*, *crostoni*, and delicious *affettati* and cheese, all accompanied by excellent wine. A particularly interesting offering is the prix-fixe *menu degustazione*, a meal for two including a different wine with each serving.

Via Santo Spirito 6R. ☎ *055-218-898. Reservations recommended on Sat. Bus: 11, 36, or 37 to Sauro or Frescobaldi; walk south to Via Santo Spirito, a block south of the river, off Ponte Santa Trinita and Ponte alla Carraia. Secondi: 14,000–22,000L ($8–$12). Menu degustazione: 40,000L ($22) per person. MC, V. Open: Lunch and dinner Tues–Sun.*

La Carabaccia

$$$ Centro storico Tuscan

The name of this restaurant refers both to a traditional working boat that once plied the Arno and to *zuppa carabaccia*, a hearty onion soup favored by the Medicis during the Renaissance. The menu features daily choices of pasta, fresh vegetables, and fish according to what caught the chef's eye in the market, plus a variety of delicious homemade breads.

Via Palazzuolo 190R. ☎ *055-214-782. Reservations recommended on Sat. Bus: A to Moro; turn left from Via del Moro into Via Palazzuolo, west of Via de' Tornabuoni. Secondi: 15,000–30,000L ($8–$16). AE, MC, V. Open: Lunch Tues–Sat; dinner daily; closed two weeks in Aug.*

Looking for a gelato break?

Ice cream is certainly one of the best treats in Italy, and Florence is famous for its gelato. Of a different school from the Venetian, the Roman, or the Sicilian gelati, Florentine ice cream was invented — as were many of the other Tuscan gastronomic specialties — to gratify the palates of the Medicis. Alas — for our taste — the Medicis had a very big sweet tooth, judging from the result. Florentine ice cream is extremely sweet. The flavors are basically the same that you'll find all over Italy, with all kind of nuts—such as *pistacchio* (pistachio) and *nocciola* (filbert), fruit such as *limone* (lemon) and *pera* (pear), and creams such as chocolate and vanilla based. If you try it all over, you can practice being Italian by developing a strong opinion and defending it vociferously (we feel the best gelato is in Venice or Rome).

Try the celebrated **Gelateria Vivoli** (Via Isola delle Stinche 7R, between the Bargello and Santa Croce; ☎ **055-292-334**; Bus: A or 14 to Piazza Santa Croce), which is truly a marvel for its zillions of flavors. There are many other gelaterie in town, such as **Coronas Café** (Via Calzaiuoli 72R; ☎ **055-239-6139**; Bus: A to Orsanmichele) for good *produzione propria* (homemade) ice cream, and **Perchè No** (Via dei Tavolini 19R, just off Via Calzaiuoli; ☎ **055-239-8969**; Bus: A to Orsanmichele), one of the oldest Florentine gelateria. And if you can't go to Sicily on this trip, try the **Gelateria Carabè** (Via Ricasoli 60R, near the Accademia; ☎ **055-289-476**; Bus: 6, 31, or 32 to S.S. Annunziata) for a typical Sicilian gelato or granita; the owner has the ingredients — lemons, almonds, pistachios — shipped from Sicily, and his ice cream has been rated one of the best in Italy.

Le Mossacce

$$ Centro storico   Tuscan

Between the Duomo and the Museo Nazionale del Bargello, this small *osteria* offers a choice of Tuscan specialties like *crespelle* and *ribollita* as well as *spaghetti alle vongole* (spaghetti with clams) and lasagna. Opened for a hundred years, it serves food that's excellent and moderately priced.

Via del Proconsolo 55R. ☎ 055-294-361. Reservations recommended. Bus: 14 or 23 to Proconsolo. Secondi: 12,000–25,000L ($6–$14). AE, MC, V. Open: Lunch and dinner Mon–Fri.

Osteria del Caffè Italiano

$$ (tavern), $$$ (restaurant)   Centro storico   Tuscan

With a restaurant in one room and a tavern in the other, this place allows you to choose between a complete meal or light fare. It serves the usual specialties with a fantastic choice of some of the best Tuscan wines. No wonder — thanks to the imaginative owners, this *osteria* is the urban antenna of Tuscany's ten best vineyards, which send here a choice of their finest products. *Ribollita, farinata al cavolo nero* (thick black cabbage soup), *bollito misto* (mixed boiled meats), *cinghiale in salmì* (wild boar stew), *bistecca alla fiorentina,* and a great choice of *affettati misti* (Tuscan cold cuts) will satisfy you. The **Caffè Italiano** (Via Condotta 56R, near Via Calzaiuoli; ☎ 055-291-082) and **Alle Murate** (Via Ghibellina 52R; ☎ 055-240-618) are two other restaurants by the same owners, offering the same quality food but at higher prices.

Via Isola delle Stinche 11–13R. ☎ 055-239-6241. Reservations recommended on Sat. Bus: A or 14 to Piazza Santa Croce. Secondi: 12,000–25,000L ($6–$14). MC, V. Open: Lunch and dinner daily.

Sabatini

$$$$ Centro storico Tuscan

One of Florence's most famous restaurants and almost an institution, Sabatini is located practically in front of the rail station. The food is strictly Tuscan, and you'll be able to taste a *fiorentina* as well as a large choice of typical meat and pasta dishes, such as *bollito in salsa verde* (boiled meat with an herb sauce) and *scaloppine ai carciofi* (sautéed veal with artichokes). Typical desserts are served as well.

Via dei Panzani 9/aR. ☎ 055-211-559. Reservations recommended. Bus: A, 6, 11, 36, or 37 to FS Santa Maria Novella 01; walk toward the church and turn right on Via dei Panzani on the east side of the church. Secondi: 35,000–45,000L ($19–$25). AE, DC, MC, V. Open: Lunch and dinner Tues–Sun.

Runner-up restaurants

Mamma Gina

$$$ Centro storico Just across the Ponte Vecchio, it's part of a chain of restaurants in Tuscany but none the worse for it. Borgo San Jacopo 37R; ☎ 055-239-6009.

Trattoria Boboli

$$ Centro storico Near the Palazzo Pitti, this is a real mom-and-pop operation (it keeps weird hours because the chef also teaches school a few days a week in winter) where you'll find all the specialties of Tuscan cuisine and a lot of warmth. Via Romana 45R; ☎ 055-233-6401.

Trattoria Garga

$$$$$ Centro storico An elegant restaurant on the centro's western edge, it offers contemporary interpretations of Tuscan fundamentals; the

imaginative chef has become famous for his *taglierini alla Magnifico,* fresh angel-hair pasta with a mint-cream sauce flavored with lemon and orange rind and Parmesan cheese. The *secondi* include game and seafood prepared with a variety of herb sauces and vegetables. Via del Moro 48R; ☎ 055-239-8898.

Exploring Firenze

Florence is known as the birthplace of the Renaissance, as well as its heart. This city is the hometown of many of the greatest artists who ever lived. At every turn, there are beautiful paintings, legendary statues, and magnificent buildings. Take a look at the top sights we recommend and be sure to give yourself enough time to admire the ones that interest you the most.

Remember that to visit Florence, particularly in the high season, you have to contend with millions of fellow visitors. The line for the Uffizi can easily be over 3 hours, and the one for the Accademia is no joke either.

If you care about seeing the top museums and saving yourself hours of waiting in line, don't forget to make reservations by calling ☎ 055-294-883 (Internet: www.firenzemusei.it) before leaving home. You can reserve for each of the Florentine State museums — Galleria degli Uffizi, Galleria dell'Accademia, Palazzo Pitti, Cappelle Medicee, Museo San Marco, Museo Nazionale del Bargello, Museo Archeologico, and Museo delle Pietre Dure. But you probably need to reserve tickets only for the Uffizi and Accademia. How does it work? You make an appointment for a certain day and time, pay by credit card (or international bank draft if you don't have a credit card), and pick up your tickets at the Florence train station tourist office or at the Uffizi sales booth. Schedule your visit at the Uffizi first and you can pick up all your tickets there.

Another good idea is to pick up at an information booth the photocopied sheet giving the most recent opening and closing times of museums and monuments. Florence has the most mind-boggling system of opening hours, with certain sites open on certain Saturdays, Sundays, and Mondays but not on others.

For some second tier and minor museums you can buy a *carnet* ticket for 10,000L ($5). You get a guidebook at any participating sight and you'll receive a 50 percent reduction on all the civic museums (*musei comunali*): Palazzo Vecchio, Museo di Santa Maria Novella, Cappella Brancacci, Museo di Firenze Com'Era, Cenacolo di Santo Spirito, Raccolta della Ragione, Museo Stibbert, and Museo Marino Marini. It's good for a year but is worth it only if you have time to visit these minor sights.

The top sights

Basilica di San Lorenzo and Cappelle Medicee

Centro storico

San Lorenzo, founded in the fourth century, was the parish church of the powerful Medici family, some of whom are buried in the **Cappelle Medicee (Medici Chapels).** The church in its present form was designed by Brunelleschi (the inside of the facade was done by Michelangelo). The **Sagrestia Vecchia (Old Sacristy)** is a masterpiece of Renaissance architecture, designed by Brunelleschi and then decorated by Donatello, who executed the cherubs all around the cupola; also note the bronze pulpits from 1460 and his terra-cotta bust of St. Lawrence.

Leaving the church, you enter the Medici Chapels from Piazza Madonna. The octagonal **Cappella dei Principi (Chapel of the Princes)** is a gaudy baroque affair, decorated with marble and semiprecious stones and containing monumental sarcophagi of Medici grand dukes. By contrast, the **Sagrestia Nuova (New Sacristy),** begun by Michelangelo and finished by the artist/author Vasari, is somber and impressive. The design reflects some of the elements of the Old Sacristy, but with bold innovations (it became one of the founding works of the Mannerist style). Michelangelo's funerary sculptures are brilliant. The **Monumento a Lorenzo Duca d'Urbino** represents the seated duke flanked by *Aurora* (Dawn) and *Crepuscolo* (Dusk). The **Monumento a Giuliano Duca di Nemours** (the son of Lorenzo the Magnificent) is shown rising, with the figures of *Giorno* (Day) and *Notte* (Night) at his sides. In front of the sacristy's altar is Michelangelo's ***Madonna col Bambino (Madonna and Child).*** Lorenzo the Magnificent is buried under this sculpture; because Michelangelo didn't live to complete his plan (he died in 1564), Lorenzo got a far less magnificent tomb than some of the lesser Medicis.

To the left of the altar is a small subterranean chamber containing some drawings attributed to Michelangelo, and you can see them by making an appointment when you enter. The place is more a tribute to Michelangelo than to the people who bankrolled the Renaissance. He also designed the 1524 **Biblioteca Laurenziana (Laurentian Library),** where a few of the Medicis' fabulous manuscripts are displayed and which you can reach via an elaborate stone staircase from the cloister on the left of the basilica facade.

Cappelle Medicee: Piazza Madonna; and Basilica: Piazza San Lorenzo (just off from the Baptistry). Basilica ☎ 055-218-534; Cappelle Medicee ☎ 055-238-8602. Bus: 1, 6, or 17 to Martelli 02 or 36 or 37 to Olio. Open: Basilica daily 7 a.m.–noon and 3:30–6:30 p.m.; Cappelle Medicee Tues–Sun 8:30 a.m.–5 p.m., holidays 8:30 a.m.– 1:50 p.m., closed second and fourth Sun of each month and open second and fourth Mon of each month 8:30 a.m.–1:50 p.m.; Biblioteca Laurenziana Mon–Sat 9 a.m.– 1 p.m. Admission: Basilica and Biblioteca Laurenziana free; Cappelle Medicee 11,000L ($6).

Basilica di Santa Croce and Cappella Pazzi

Centro storico

Santa Croce, the world's largest Franciscan church, is significant both for its architecture and for what (and whom) it contains. The basilica was begun in 1294 by Arnolfo di Cambio, the first architect of the Duomo, and boasts some Giotto frescoes (not the most well preserved of his works); its fifteenth-century **Cappella Pazzi,** a wonderful example of early Renaissance architecture by Brunelleschi, is a museum containing Cimabue's famous *Crucifixion* among other works. You'll also find the final resting places of many notable Renaissance figures — over 270 tomb-stones pave the floor, and monumental tombs house luminaries like Michelangelo, Galileo, Rossini, and Machiavelli. Note that Dante's tomb is really just a cenotaph: He died in exile in Ravenna and was buried there.

Piazza Santa Croce, just off Via de' Benci. ☎ *055-244-619. Bus: 23 or 71 to Santa Croce. Open: Summer Tues–Sat 8 a.m.–6:30 p.m., Sun 3–6 p.m.; winter Tues–Sat 8 a.m.–12:30 p.m. and 3–6:30 p.m., Sun 3–6 p.m. Admission: Free.*

Basilica di Santa Maria Novella and Museo di Santa Maria Novella

Centro storico

This Dominican church, built in the Gothic style from 1246 to 1360, is dec-orated with frescoes by Domenico Ghirlandaio, Filippino Lippi, and others. Adjoining the church is the entry to the museum, which occupies what was originally the cloisters annexed to the church. From here, you can access the **Chiostro Verde (Green Cloister),** named for the beautiful coloration of its frescoes, some by Paolo Uccello, and the **Cappellone degli Spagnoli,** named for Cosimo de' Medici's wife, Eleonora of Toledo (who permitted her fellow Spaniards to be buried here), and frescoed by Andrea di Buonaito between 1367 and 1369. The frescoes depict scenes from the lives of Christ and St. Peter, but the *Trionfo di San Tommaso* and the *Trionfo dei Domenicani* (the triumphs of St. Thomas and the Dominicans, respectively) are especially beautiful.

Piazza Santa Maria Novella. ☎ *055-23885. Bus: 6, 11, 36, 37, or A to S.M. Novella 01 or 1, 17, and 23 to S.M. Novella 02. Open: Basilica Mon–Fri 7 a.m.–noon and 3–6 p.m., Sat 7 a.m.–noon and 3–5 p.m., Sun 3–5 p.m.; Museum Mon–Thurs and Sat 9 a.m.–2 p.m., Sun 8 a.m.–1 p.m. Admission: Basilica free; Cappellone degli Spagnoli 5,000L ($2.70).*

Battistero di San Giovanni

Centro storico

Part of the tricolored marble trio on Piazza del Duomo (see also the Duomo and the Campanile di Giotto, in this section), the octagonal Baptistry is a beautiful example of the Florentine Romanesque style from

Florence Attractions

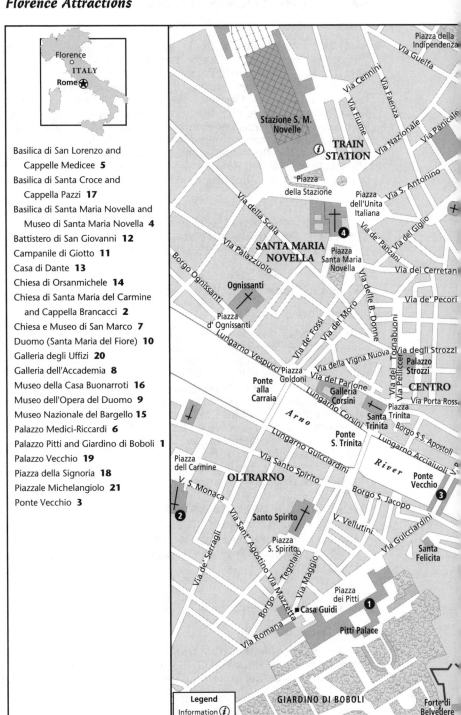

Basilica di San Lorenzo and
   Cappelle Medicee **5**
Basilica di Santa Croce and
   Cappella Pazzi **17**
Basilica di Santa Maria Novella and
   Museo di Santa Maria Novella **4**
Battistero di San Giovanni **12**
Campanile di Giotto **11**
Casa di Dante **13**
Chiesa di Orsanmichele **14**
Chiesa di Santa Maria del Carmine
   and Cappella Brancacci **2**
Chiesa e Museo di San Marco **7**
Duomo (Santa Maria del Fiore) **10**
Galleria degli Uffizi **20**
Galleria dell'Accademia **8**
Museo della Casa Buonarroti **16**
Museo dell'Opera del Duomo **9**
Museo Nazionale del Bargello **15**
Palazzo Medici-Riccardi **6**
Palazzo Pitti and Giardino di Boboli **1**
Palazzo Vecchio **19**
Piazza della Signoria **18**
Piazzale Michelangiolo **21**
Ponte Vecchio **3**

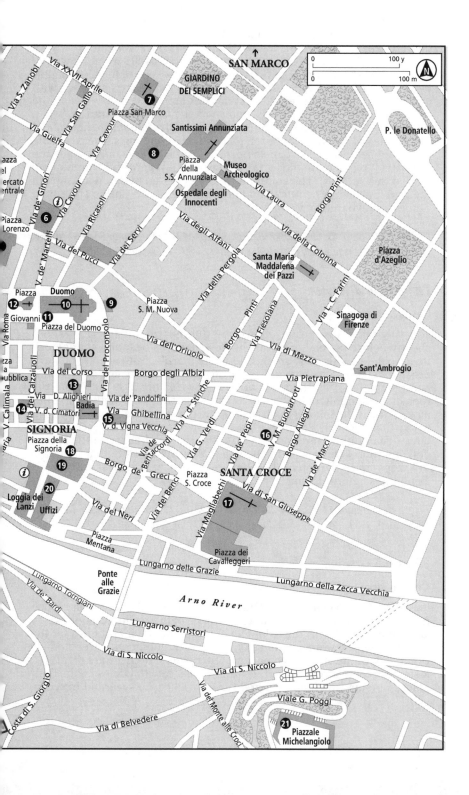

the eleventh and twelfth centuries. It was likely built on the site of a Roman palace. The Baptistry's marvels are the exterior doors: The beautiful bronze reliefs adorning the north and east doors were the life's work of Lorenzo Ghiberti. He began the north doors in 1401 when he was 20 and finished them more than two decades later — one of the most important pieces of Renaissance sculpture, they depict Issac's sacrifice with marvelous detail. However, the east doors, completed shortly before the artist's death, are the real stars, known as the **Gates of Paradise** (when he saw them, Michelangelo supposedly said, "These doors are fit to stand at the gates of Paradise"); the ten panels show stunning scenes from the Old Testament. Alas, the panels presently in place are copies, since the originals have been moved to the **Museo dell'Opera del Duomo** (see later in this section). The south doors were created by Andrea Pisano in the mid-fourteenth century and show a more static Gothic style than Ghiberti's revolutionary work.

Piazza del Duomo. ☎ *055-230-2885. Bus: 14, 23, or 71 to Duomo or 36 or 37 to Olio. Open: Mon–Sat noon–6:30 p.m., Sun 8:30 a.m.–1:30 p.m. Admission: 5,000L ($2.70).*

Campanile di Giotto

Centro storico

You may ask, "Wasn't Giotto a painter and not an architect?" Yes, but shortly before the end of his life he designed this beautiful soaring bell tower banded with pink, green, and white marble, from which you have excellent views of the city and especially of the Duomo next door. Giotto had completed only the first two levels by his death in 1337, and the replacement architect had to correct the mistakes he'd made — like not making the walls thick enough to support the structure. Some of the artworks that originally graced the tower — by Donatello, Francesco Talenti, Luca della Robbia, and Andrea Pisano — are now housed in the **Museo dell'Opera del Duomo** and copies take their place. Note that there are 414 steps up to the top of this 84-meter tower, and the last entrance is 20 minutes before closing.

Piazza del Duomo. ☎ *055-230-2885. Bus: 14, 23, or 71 to Duomo. Open: Mar–Oct daily 9 a.m.–6:50 p.m.; Nov–Feb daily 9 a.m.–4:20 p.m. Admission: 10,000L ($5).*

Chiesa di Orsanmichele

Centro storico

In the fourteenth century, the Orsanmichele was just a warehouse when it was the site of a miracle — after an image of the Madonna supposedly appeared there, it was turned into a church. The original statues for the external niches were commissioned by city guilds and executed by Donatello, Ghiberti, Verrocchio, and others; most of these are displayed inside, protected from further weather damage, with copies taking their places outside. You'll find vaulted Gothic arches, 500-year-old frescoes, and an encrusted fourteenth-century tabernacle by Andrea Orcagna protecting a 1348 *Madonna and Child* by Bernardo Daddi. The church is connected by a second-floor walkway to the palazzo of the powerful wool merchants guild, built in 1308.

Via dei Calzaiuoli, between the Duomo and Piazza della Signoria. ☎ *055-284-944. Bus: A to Orsanmichele. Open: Daily 9 a.m.–noon and 4–6 p.m.; closed the first and last Mon of each month. Admission: Free.*

Chiesa di Santa Maria del Carmine and Cappella Brancacci

Centro storico

Luckily, the 1771 fire that devastated Santa Maria del Carmine didn't ruin the **Cappella Brancacci,** one of the masterpieces of Renaissance art. Here you'll find Masaccio's greatest works: Although he died at 27, the frescoes he executed here between 1424 and 1428 are remarkable not only for their perspective but also for their intense emotion, seen most clearly in the *Expulsion from the Garden.* Other frescoes by Masaccio are *St. Peter Healing the Sick with his Shadow* and the *Baptism of the Neophytes.* Near the end of the fifteenth century, the fresco cycle was completed by Filippino Lippi, son of the libertine monk and great painter Filippo Lippi.

Piazza del Carmine. ☎ *055-238-2195. Bus: 11, 36, or 37 to Serragli 01 or D to Carmine. Admission: Chiesa free; Cappella Brancacci 5,000L ($2.70). Open: Mon and Wed–Sat 10 a.m.–5 p.m., Sun 1–5 p.m.*

Chiesa e Museo di San Marco

Centro storico

This Dominican monastery is a stop on the Grand Tour of Florence's art treasures because of one Fra Beato Angelico, whose vividly painted, exceptionally human works are early Renaissance masterpieces. The dormitory contains his famous *Annunciation,* and the part of the structure that's now a museum contains panel paintings and altar pieces, including the *Crucifixion.* Another notable work is Ghirlandaio's *Last Supper.* The church itself is decorated with works by Fra Bartolomeo and other artists. Another former resident — actually the prior — of the monastery was the passionate reformer Girolamo Savonarola. His sermons against worldly corruption brought him into conflict with Pope Alexander VI (who had four illegitimate children, including Cesare and Lucrezia Borgia); excommunicated and betrayed by the Florentines who at one time supported him, he was executed on Piazza della Signoria in 1498.

Piazza San Marco. ☎ *055-238-8608. Bus: 1, 6, 7, 10, 11, 17, 20, 25, or 33 to San Marco 01. Open: Tues–Fri 8:30 a.m.–1:50 p.m., Sat 8:30 a.m.–6:50 p.m.; open second and fourth Sun 8:30 a.m.–7 p.m. and first, third, and fifth Mon 8:30 a.m.–1:50 p.m. Admission: Chiesa free; museum 8,000L ($4.30).*

Duomo (Santa Maria del Fiore)

Centro storico

The Duomo, surmounted by Filippo Brunelleschi's famous red-tiled dome, is the symbol of Florence. The largest in the world at the time it was built, the dome is 150 feet wide and 300 feet high from the drum — where previous builders had left off, unsure how to complete the building until Brunelleschi showed them how — to the distinctive lantern at the top of the cupola. Brunelleschi's ingenious solution was constructing the dome of two layers with a space inside and having each layer become progressively thinner toward the top, thus reducing the weight. You can climb 463 spiraling steps to the top inside the space between the layers (the last ascent is 40 minutes before closing). The dome was finished in 1436, but other architects fiddled with it through the ages, and the facade was redone in neo-Gothic style hundreds of years later. As a whole, the Duomo is more impressive on the outside than on the inside, its alternating bands of white, green, and pink marble echoing the patterns on the Battistero and Campanile. Inside are Paolo Uccello frescoes from the 1430s and 1440s, including his memorial to Sir John Hawkwood, an English mercenary hired by the Florentines (they promised him a statue but gave him a fresco of a statue instead). Restored in 1996, the frescoes inside the dome were begun by Giorgio Vasari and finished by Frederico Zuccari in 1579. The New Sacristy is where Lorenzo de' Medici hid out after he and his brother (who was murdered) were ambushed during mass by some of their rivals in one of Florence's endless power struggles; its bronze doors are the work of Luca della Robbia.

Under the Duomo are the remains of **Santa Reparata,** the former Duomo, torn down in 1375 to build the new cathedral. Excavations, begun in 1966, uncovered a rich trove of material dating back over centuries, including walls of Roman houses and Roman ceramic, glass, and metalwork, as well as paleo-Christian and medieval objects (Brunelleschi's tombstone was also discovered here).

Piazza del Duomo. ☎ 055-213-229. Bus: 14, 23, or 71 to Duomo. Open: Summer Mon–Fri 9 a.m.–6 p.m., Sat 8:30 a.m.–5 p.m., Sun 1–5 p.m. (morning for services only); Sun cupola and excavations closed. Winter Mon–Fri 10 a.m.–7 p.m.; Sat 10 a.m.–3:30 p.m., Sun 1–5 p.m. (morning for services only); Sun cupola and excavations closed. Admission: Cathedral free; cupola 10,000L ($5); excavations 5,000L ($2.70).

Galleria degli Uffizi

Centro storico

The Uffizi is mind-blowing, occupying a Renaissance palazzo built by Vasari to house the administrative offices (*uffizi* means "offices") of the Granducato di Toscana (Tuscan Duchy). Here you pictorially experience the birth of the Renaissance, seeing how the changing ideas about the nature of humanity (the new humanism) were translated into visual form.

(The medieval artists weren't bad painters — their work reflected a holistically Christian viewpoint, with no concept of "nature" as something separate from the divine.) Start with Cimabue's great *Crucifixion,* still inspired by the flat forms and ritualized expressions of Byzantine art. With the work of his student Giotto, the human figure began to take on greater and greater realism.

The rooms devoted to Sandro Botticelli — with his *Birth of Venus* (the goddess emerging from the waves on a shell) and *Primavera* (an ambiguous allegory of spring) — show how the revival of classical (pagan) myth opened a new range of expression and subject. Don't miss, across from Botticelli's *Venus*, the spectacular **triptych** of Hugo van der Goes, whose humanism emerges in the intensity of expression and powerful realism of his poor peasants (also look for the fanciful monster lurking in the right panel). Piero della Francesca's **diptych** with full-profile portraits of Federico da Montefeltro and his wife is a justly famous work painted in the third quarter of the fifteenth century. Francesca's luminosity is matched by incredible detail — he brings his subjects to life, warts and all. Masaccio's *Madonna and Child with St. Anne,* Leonardo's *Adoration of the Magi* and *Annunciation,* several Raphaels, Michelangelo's *Holy Family,* Caravaggio's *Bacchus* . . . there's so much at the Uffizi you should really come twice if you can.

Piazza degli Uffizi 6, just off Piazza della Signoria (Palazzo Vecchio). ☎ *055-23-885 or 055-294-883 for reservations. Bus: 23 or 71 to Galleria Uffizi. Open: Summer Tues–Fri 8:30 a.m.–9 p.m., Sat 8:30 a.m.–midnight, Sun 8:30 a.m.–8 p.m.; winter Tues–Sun 8:30 a.m.–6:50 p.m. Admission: 12,000L ($6).*

Remember to reserve your tickets for the Uffizi and the Accademia (for details, see the beginning of this section).

Galleria dell'Accademia

Centro storico

The Accademia's undisputed star is Michelangelo's *David* (there's often a line to go in to see him, so make a reservation or try getting to the museum just as it opens or an hour or two before closing). Michelangelo was just 29 when he took a 17-foot column of white Carrara marble abandoned by another sculptor and produced the masculine perfection of *Il Gigante* (The Giant), as *David* is nicknamed. The statue stands beneath a rotunda built expressly for it in 1873, when it was moved here from Piazza della Signoria (a copy stands in its place on the square). In 1991, *David* was attacked by a lunatic with a hammer, so you have to view him through a reinforced-glass shield (like the *Pietà* in Rome).

Many people don't realize that the gallery offers many other remarkable Florentine works as well. Among the paintings are Perugino's *Assumption* and *Descent from the Cross* (the latter done in collaboration with Filippino Lippi); *The Virgin of the Sea*, thought to have been painted by Botticelli; and Pontormo's *Venus and Cupid. David* isn't the only

The Uffizi

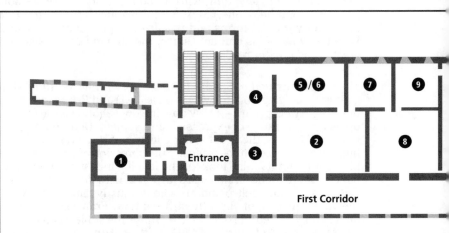

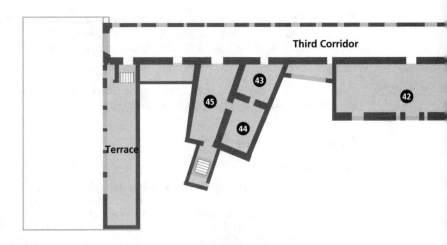

1 Archaeological Room	**15** Leonardo da Vinci
2 Giotto & 13th-Century Paintings	**16** Geographic Maps
3 Sienese Paintings (14th Century)	**17** Ermafrodito
4 Florentine Paintings (14th Century)	**18** The Tribune
5/6 International Gothic	**19** Perugino & Signorelli
7 Early Renaissance	**20** Dürer & German Artists
8 Filippo Lippi	**21** Giovanni Bellini & Giorgione
9 Antonio del Pollaiolo	**22** Flemish & German Paintings
10/14 Botticelli	**23** Mantegna & Correggio

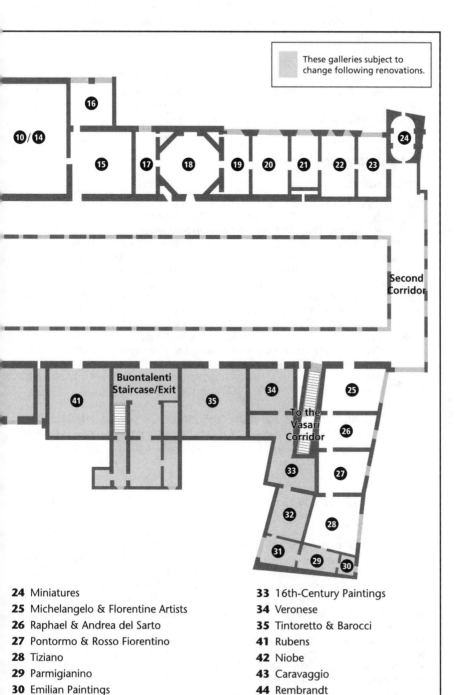

These galleries subject to change following renovations.

16

10 / 14

15 **17** **18** **19** **20** **21** **22** **23** **24**

Second Corridor

Buontalenti Staircase/Exit

41 **35** **34** **25**

To the Vasari Corridor **26**

33 **27**

32 **28**

31 **29** **30**

24 Miniatures
25 Michelangelo & Florentine Artists
26 Raphael & Andrea del Sarto
27 Pontormo & Rosso Fiorentino
28 Tiziano
29 Parmigianino
30 Emilian Paintings
31 Dosso Dossi
32 Sebastiano del Piombo & Lorenzo Lotto

33 16th-Century Paintings
34 Veronese
35 Tintoretto & Barocci
41 Rubens
42 Niobe
43 Caravaggio
44 Rembrandt
45 18th-Century Paintings

Michelangelo sculpture here — his *St. Matthew* and interesting series of *Slaves* (which are either unfinished or were poetically left partly escaped from the original hunks of stone) also illustrate the master's remarkable skills.

Via Ricasoli 60 between the Duomo and Piazza San Marco. ☎ *055-238-8609 or 055-294-883 for reservations. Bus: 6, 31, or 32 to S.S. Annunziata. Open: Summer Tues–Fri 8:30 a.m.–9 p.m., Sat 8:30 a.m.–midnight, Sun 8:30 a.m.–8 p.m.; winter Tues–Sun 8:30 a.m.–6:50 p.m. Admission: 12,000L ($6).*

Museo Nazionale del Bargello

Centro storico

The Bargello, built in 1255, shows you what a medieval/early Renaissance government office building looked like. The word *bargello* means "cop," and it was used to refer to the chief of police, a post created in 1574; this was his headquarters; it also housed an armory. Now the Bargello is a treasury of Renaissance sculpture, including two Donatello *Davids* (one in marble, the other in bronze) and several works by Michelangelo, including another *David* (it might also be *Apollo*), a bust of *Brutus,* and a *Bacchus* he executed when he was only 22. You'll also find works by Benvenuto Cellini, whose *Autobiography* offers a fascinating look at Florence during the Renaissance and is well worth reading. You can also compare two bronze panels of the *Sacrifice of Isaac,* one by Brunelleschi and one by Ghiberti, which were submitted in the famous contest to see who'd get to do the Baptistry doors (see "Battistero di San Giovanni" in this section). The Bargello also has impressive collections of Islamic art, majolica, and terra-cotta works by the della Robbia family.

Via del Proconsolo 4. ☎ *055-238-8606 or 055-294-883 for reservations. Bus: 23 to Galleria Uffizi or B to Loggia del Grano. Open: Tues–Sat 8:30 a.m.–1:50 p.m.; also open second and fourth Sun and first, third, and fifth Mon each month. Admission: 8,000L ($4.30).*

Museo dell'Opera del Duomo

Centro storico

This museum is where you'll need to go to see the original Renaissance works, such as Ghiberti's breathtaking bronze **Gates of Paradise** panels for the Baptistry (see "Battistero di San Giovanni" in this section), that were removed from their settings to avoid damage from pollution or maniacs with hammers. The museum also contains works that once graced Giotto's Campanile, like Donatello's highly realistic sculpture of **Habbakuk;** his *Maddalena* (Mary Magdalen), in polychromed wood, is perhaps equally striking for its tortured expression. Michelangelo is represented with a *Pietà;* Luca della Robbia's **cantoria** (choir loft) faces a similar work by Donatello, offering an example of the diversity of Renaissance styles. At press time, the museum was temporarily closed; ask at the tourist office when you arrive.

Piazza Duomo 9, behind the Duomo. ☎ *055-230-2885. Bus: 14, 23, or 71 to Duomo. Open: Daily 8 a.m.–2 p.m. Admission: 10,000L ($5).*

Palazzo Pitti and Giardino di Boboli

Oltrarno

Begun in 1458 by the textile merchant/banker Luca Pitti, this golden palazzo was finished by the Medicis in 1549 (they tripled its size and added the Boboli Garden). It houses an important painting collection in the **Galleria Palatina (Palatine Gallery).** Some of the greatest works are a collection of Raphaels, including his *Madonna of the Chair* and *La Fornarina* (The Baker's Daughter, modeled on the features of his Roman mistress); perhaps the largest single collection of works by moody psychological painter Andrea del Sarto (see Robert Browning's poem on him); and several Titians.

The palazzo also houses seven other museums. On the mezzanine from the left of the courtyard, the **Museo degli Argenti (Silver Museum)** houses collections of objects in precious metals, ivory, and crystal. Notable are the semi-precious stone vases of Lorenzo de' Medici and the cameos and carved precious stones of the Medici collection. On the third-floor is the **Galleria d'Arte Moderna (Modern Art Gallery),** with a collection of Italian paintings from the 1800s and early 1900s, including some famous paintings of the movement of the *Macchiaioli* (the Italian counterpart to the French Impressionists; notably the paintings of Giovanni Fattori and Telemaco Signorini). By appointment you can visit the second-floor **Appartamenti Reali (Royal Apartments),** with furnishings from various Medici villas; the **Museo delle Porcellane (Porcelain Museum),** a collection of precious porcelain by great European makers, including Sèvres, Chantilly, and Meissen; and the **Donazione Contini-Bonacossi (Contini-Bonacossi Collection),** temporarily housed in the **Palazzina della Meridiana,** an eighteenth-century neoclassical pavilion, and including paintings by important artists like Cimabue, Veronese, and Bellini and sculpture like the famous *Martirio di San Lorenzo* (Martyrdom of St. Lawrence) by Bernini. You can make the appointment for your visit to the museum that interests you (or for all of them) at the information booth inside the Uffizi, where you can also buy your ticket (access will depend on availability of personnel, while the admission should be included in your ticket to the Uffizi).

Of lesser interest are the **Museo delle Carrozze (Carriage Museum),** with a collection of historic carriages; and the **Galleria del Costume (Costume Gallery),** exhibiting clothing from 1700 to the early 1900s; both were closed at press time.

The palace is backed by the famous **Giardino di Boboli,** 45,000 square meters (11.1 acres) of gardens, designed in the sixteenth century and added to in the eighteenth and nineteenth centuries. It's one of the most grandiose examples of an Italian garden. Among the highlights are several fountains and sculptures, such as the seventeenth-century **Fontana del Carciofo (Artichoke Fountain)** and the **Piazzale dell'Isolotto (Islet Square)** off the Viottolone (large lane) lined with laurels, cypresses, and pines and punctuated by statues. On the piazzale is the beautiful **Fontana dell'Oceano (Ocean Fountain).**

Piazza de' Pitti, just on the other side of the Ponte Vecchio. ☎ *055-238-8614 or 055-294-883 for reservations. Bus: D to Pitti. Open: Galleria Palatina summer Tues–Fri 8:30 a.m.–9 p.m., Sat 8:30 a.m.–midnight, Sun 8:30 a.m.–8 p.m.; winter Tues–Sun 8:30 a.m.–6:50 p.m. Giardino di Boboli summer daily 9 a.m.–8 p.m.; winter daily 9 a.m. to an hour before sunset; closed first and last Mon of each month. Museo degli Argenti Tues–Sun 8.30 a.m.–1:50 p.m.; closed second and fourth Sun and open second and fourth Mon of each month; Galleria d'Arte Moderna Tues–Sat 8:30 a.m.– 2 p.m; open on the first, third, and fifth Sun. of each month at the same hours. Admission: Galleria Palatina 14,000L ($8); Giardino di Boboli 4,000L ($2.15); Museo degli Argenti 4,000L ($2.15); Galleria d'Arte Moderna 8,000L ($4.30).*

Palazzo Vecchio

Centro storico

The Palazzo Vecchio (Old Palace) looks either like a fortress disguised as a palace or a palace trying to be a fort. It's actually a little bit of both, built as the town hall from 1299 to 1302. Cosimo de' Medici (that's Giambologna's equestrian statue of him in the middle of the piazza; see "Piazza della Signoria" in this section) and his family made changes to the palazzo in the mid-sixteenth century. The highlight of the interior is the **Sala dei Cinquecento (Hall of the 500),** where the 500-man council met when Florence was still a republic and before the Medicis' despotic rule. The frescoes by Vasari and others are nothing to write home about, yet those planned by Michelangelo but never painted would've been; note Michelangelo's *Genius of Victory* statue. Bronzino's paintings in the private chapel of Eleanora di Toledo (wife of Cosimo), Donatello's *Judith and Holofernes,* and Ghirlandaio's fresco of *St. Zenobius Enthroned* are other notable works. Some of the collections are open only at certain times (mainly in summer), such as the collection of musical instruments. In summer, you can view the city from the balustrade and hope for a breath of wind.

Piazza della Signoria. ☎ *055-276-8465. Bus: 23 or 71 to Galleria Uffizi or B to Loggia del Grano. Open: Tues, Wed, and Sat 9 a.m.–7 p.m.; Mon and Fri 9 a.m.–11 p.m.; Thurs and Sun 9 a.m.–2 p.m. Admission: 10,000L ($5).*

Piazza della Signoria

Centro storico

Florence's most famous square was built in the thirteenth and fourteenth centuries. *Signoria* is the name of the political system that governed the city at the time — the Medicis were the *signori* (lords) — and this was the political heart of Florence. A beautiful example of medieval architecture, the L-shaped square is flanked by the **Palazzo Vecchio** (see listing in this section) on the east side and the famous **Loggia della Signoria** on the south. The loggia is also called the Loggia dei Lanzi (after the *Lanzichenecchi*, soldiers who camped there in the sixteenth century) or the Loggia dell'Orcagna (after a belief it was built by Andrea di Cione, who was known as Orcagna). In fact, this Gothic structure was built from 1376 to 1382 by Benci Cione and Simone Talenti for political ceremonies. Later it was used as a sculpture workshop and is still used as a show-place for statues. The most famous piece here is Giambologna's *Ratto delle Sabine (Rape of the Sabines),* an essay in three-dimensional Mannerism; also by Giambologna are the bronze of **Duke Cosimo de' Medici** on horseback and *Hercules with Nessus the Centaur.* Also here is Benvenuto Cellini's famous *Perseus* holding up the severed head of Medusa (the original was moved to the Uffizi in 1996 and replaced with a copy, but the original was replaced here in late 2000).

The **Fontana del Nettuno (Fountain of Neptune),** at the corner of the Palazzo Vecchio, was built by the architect Ammannati in 1575 and crit-icized by many, including Michelangelo; Florentines used to mock it as *Il Biancone* ("big whitey"). The **small disk** in the ground near the foun-tain marks the spot where the famous Dominican monk Savonarola was executed. His efforts to purify the Florentines and clean the church from corruption (he directed the burning of jewels, books, riches, and art pieces judged too "pagan" on pires erected in Piazza della Signoria) gave him increased political power but also led to his excommunication from the church. He was condemned as an heretic and burned on the square in 1498.

The *David* that you can see in the square is a copy of the original statue by Michelangelo, which was moved to the Accademia in the nineteenth century. The statue flanking it is *Ercole (Heracles)* by Baccio Bandinelli.

Off Via dei Calzaiuoli. Bus: 23 or 71 to Galleria Uffizi or B to Loggia del Grano.

Ponte Vecchio

Centro storico

The Ponte Vecchio (Old Bridge) is the only remaining original of Florence's many lovely medieval bridges spanning the Arno — the Germans blew the rest of them up during their retreat from Italy near the end of the World War II (they've since been rebuilt). This symbol of Florence offers beautiful views and thrives with shops selling leather goods, jewelry, and other commodities. If you look up, you'll see the famous **Corridoio Vasariano (Vasari Corridor):** The bridge was built in 1345, but after the completion of the Palazzo Pitti in the sixteenth cen-tury, Cosimo de' Medici commissioned Vasari to build an aboveground "tunnel" running along the Ponte Vecchio rooftops linking the Uffizi with the Pitti. The corridor was richly decorated with art, and you can visit it from the Uffizi at certain times (ask at the gallery).

At the end of Via Por Santa Maria. Bus: B to Ponte Vecchio.

More cool things to see and do

Florence's major sites are so extensive they could easily soak up all your time, so you probably won't get to the minor ones. On the other hand, you could get sick of being inside, and museum fatigue is always a risk (especially for kids). Here are some further and lighter ways to see Florence:

✔ The **Casa di Dante** (Via Dante Alighieri; ☎ 055-219-516; Bus: A to Condotta) may be called Dante's House but isn't really. It's in the neighborhood where he lived but is actually a 1910 reconstruction and contains a museum of Dante's life and work. If you're especially interested in the man many consider the greatest European poet of any age, it contains memorabilia and objects you may find curious. The house is open Wednesday to Monday 10 a.m. to 4 p.m. (Sunday to 2 p.m.), and admission is 4,000L ($2.15).

✔ **Fiesole** makes a wonderful day trip, 8 km (5 miles) north of Florence. Probably one of the nicest bus rides you'll ever take is the one through the green fields and past the villas lining the route to this hill town (take the no. 7 from SMN train station or Piazza San Marco and get off at the last stop). Fiesole existed before Florence — it started as an Etruscan settlement in the sixth century B.C. and retains the character of a small town and its independence as a municipality. In summer, the town hosts music, theater, and other cultural events, making it a great place to escape the heat and congestion below. Be sure to visit the 1028 **Duomo (Cattedrale di San Romolo)** on the main square, Piazza Mino da Fiesole. Also definitely worth a visit are the **Teatro Romano e Museo Civico (Roman Theater and Civic Museum,** Via Partigiani 1; ☎ 055-59-477). The theater, built in the first century B.C., is where outdoor concerts are held in summer. Surrounding this picturesque ruin are the remains of baths and even some Etruscan walls from the fourth century B.C., as well as a Roman temple. They're open daily: winter 9 a.m. to 5 p.m. and summer 9 a.m. to 7 p.m. (closed the first Tuesday of each month). The 10,000L ($5) admission includes entrance to the Museo Bandini near the Duomo with its thirteenth- to fifteenth-century Tuscan art.

✔ The **Museo della Casa Buonarroti** (Via Ghibellina 70; ☎ 055-241-752; Bus: 14 or A to Ghibellina 01) may never have had Michelangelo as a tenant, but he and his heirs did own it. His grand nephew got the homage going early by turning the house into a museum. Some of the holdings are very interesting: The display of original drawings is changed regularly, and there are some of the master's earliest works, including the *Madonna of the Steps* he did when only in his mid-teens. The museum is open Thursday to Tuesday 9.30 a.m. to 7 p.m., and admission is 15,000L ($8).

✔ The **Palazzo Medici-Riccardi** (Via Cavour 1; ☎ 055-276-0340; Bus: 14, 23, or 71 to Duomo) is where Cosimo de' Medici and his family lived before they took over the Palazzo Vecchio. It was built by Michelozzo in 1444 and has a less heavy feeling than later palazzi, such as the Pitti. Benozzo Gozzoli, a student of Fra

Angelico's, decorated the chapel with marvelous frescoes. The palazzo gives a good idea of what upper-class Florentine life was like during the Renaissance. It's open Thursday to Tuesday 9 a.m. to 1 p.m. and 3 to 6 p.m. (Sunday to noon), and admission is 6,000L ($3.25).

And on your left, the Uffizi: Seeing Firenze by guided tour

To get the ins and outs of Florence's sights, a guided tour may be just the ticket. Some tour companies are better than others. We've listed a few that we feel will give you a comprehensive tour that you'll enjoy. Be sure to ask about the length of tours, lunch breaks, and the maximum number of participants allowed per tour — that way you can pick the tour that's right for you.

If you want to participate in a bus tour, call **American Express** (☎ 055-50-981) or **SitaSightseeing** (☎ 055-214-721), both offering the same kinds of tours of Florence and of the major attractions in Tuscany. We feel, though, that Florence is best seen on foot since the historic center is closed to traffic. If you contact the **Ufficio Guide Turistiche** (Viale Gramsci 9a; ☎ 055-247-8188) you'll be able to organize a guided tour more tailored to your needs. You could even have a private tour, if you decided.

Suggested 1-, 2-, and 3-Day Sightseeing Itineraries

Considering that you could easily spend a full day in the Uffizi (you're allowed only two hours, however) or the Pitti, it can take a lot of time to see Florence — even though it's nowhere near as large as Rome. Here are some suggestions for how to budget your time if you have one, two, or three days.

If you have 1 day in Florence

Arrive by train the night before your big day and get up early to head directly to the **Uffizi,** where you've reserved your time slot (see "Exploring Firenze" in this chapter). By the time you come out two hours later, the **Duomo** and **Giotto's Campanile** will be open; see the outside of the Duomo and do a quick tour inside (forego the long climbs in the bell tower and the dome unless you desperately want to see the view). Walk around the **Battistero** and head for the **Museo dell'Opera del Duomo,** where you can see Ghiberti's original **Gates of Paradise.** Now treat yourself to a hearty late lunch (see our recommendations in this chapter). Fortified, walk through the heart of the city toward the river, passing the **Palazzo Vecchio** and strolling across the **Ponte Vecchio.** Here you can either continue on foot on this side of the river to the **Palazzo Pitti** or catch a bus to the **Accademia** and see Michelangelo's *David* (you'll need a reservation here too). Afterward, take a leisurely stroll to one of Florence's fine restaurants for dinner (or you can take the bus to **Fiesole** and round out your day with a meal and a beautiful sunset). Obviously, if you have only one day in Florence, you'd better make your reservations for the museums far in advance.

If you have 2 days in Florence

The one-day Florence tour will tax your stamina, mind, and feet. However, we think arriving the night before and seeing the **Uffizi,** the **Duomo** and **Giotto's Campanile,** and the **Museo dell'Opera del Duomo** in the morning when you're freshest is still a good idea. But if you have two days, you can relax a bit on the afternoon of the first day, having a nice lunch and then wandering the back streets of the old town and possibly shopping. During this break, you'll pass the **Palazzo Vecchio** and the **Ponte Vecchio.** You can dine at one of the restaurants we recommend in the center. On the second day, get to the **Accademia** when it opens (you'll have made a reservation for that time). Afterward, you can visit the **Medici Chapels** or the church of **San Marco** and its art treasures, depending on your taste. Then have lunch and make a leisurely visit to the **Palazzo Pitti** and the refreshing **Boboli Garden.** End your day with an evening in **Fiesole.**

If you have 3 days in Florence

Follow the two-day itinerary given earlier. On the third day, begin by seeing whichever of the **Medici Chapels** or the church of **San Marco** you didn't see the day before. Afterward, you can spend more time wandering the center; after lunch, make the trek across the river to **Santa Maria del Carmine** to see the great works of Masaccio. If it happens to be a Saturday in summer, we have a radical suggestion: Since the **Uffizi** is open until midnight, go back for a second look. If you've overdosed on art, however, you might enjoy seeing the charming **Orsanmichele** before you eat and call it a day.

Shopping

Remember that shops are usually open daily 10 a.m. to 1:30 p.m. and 4 to 8 p.m. and closed on Monday mornings, whereas open-air markets are usually open during lunchtime but close earlier in the evening.

Florence offers some very nice specialty products, many available at the outdoor markets, where you can make some great buys if you keep in mind a few simple shopping rules. First, don't expect things to be cheap — a good leather jacket will cost a few hundred dollars, but you should be able to get a level of quality that would be difficult to find back home, especially at that price. And remember that light bargaining is allowed in outdoor markets. The important thing is to try to have a fair idea in your mind of what things are worth (if you aren't an expert on the items you want to buy, shop around and learn as much as you can before making your decision). The bottom line? Buy an item if you really like it for what sounds to you a fair price, without worrying too much about getting the best bargain in the world — being happy with what you bought matters more than saving $20.

Remember that all crowded areas are the preferred hunting ground for pickpockets and purse snatchers. Therefore, don't display your money too liberally and keep an eye on your pockets and purse — otherwise your shopping spree will be very short indeed.

The best shopping areas

For elegant shopping, the place to go is the area of town along **Via de' Tornabuoni** and left on **Via della Vigna Nuova;** you'll find all the big names of Italian fashion and a choice of reliable but expensive boutiques. Less luxurious is the parallel area of **Via Roma, Piazza della Repubblica,** and **Via Calimala** toward the Ponte Vecchio.

What to look for and where to find it

Florence is famous for its leather and woven straw, embroidered linen and lace, paper goods, and gold jewelry. It's also a great place to buy Italian fashions and designs, in both garments and housewares. Go to **Via Tornabuoni** for fashion while for housewares follow our suggestions later in this section.

Starting by the church of San Lorenzo, just northwest of the Duomo, the **Mercato San Lorenzo** (Bus: 1, 6, or 17 to Martelli 02 or 36 or 37 to Olio) is a famous open-air leather market, but the average quality of its goods has much declined over the years. Finding a really wonderful item is difficult and requires a lot of looking. On the other hand, the market is an attraction in itself, and many consider that a visit to Florence isn't complete without it.

If you prefer the reliability and service of a boutique, head for Via de' Tornabuoni and the side street Via del Parione. Among the dependable leather shops here are the famous **Beltrami** (Via de' Tornabuoni 48R; ☎ **055-287-779;** Bus 6, 11, 36, or 37 to Tornabuoni/Via de' Panzani 1, near the church of Santa Maria Novella; ☎ **055-212-661;** Bus: 6, 11, 36, 37, or A to S.M. Novella 01 or 1, 17, or 23 to S.M. Novella 02) — the first address is the main shop and the second is where to go for last season's discounted items. For gloves, cross the Ponte Vecchio and go to **Madova Gloves** (Via Guicciardini 1R; ☎ **055-239-6526;** Bus: D to Pitti). If you want to learn about the ancient art of leather embossing, head for **Santa Croce's** leather school (Piazza Santa Croce, enter from the church's right transept; ☎ **055-244-533;** Bus: A or 14 to Piazza Santa Croce).

Stretching from Piazza della Repubblica to the Ponte Vecchio is the **Mercato Nuovo** (or della Paglia, "of straw"), where all kinds of straw products are sold (Bus: B to Ponte Vecchio). The items range from hats to bags to baskets to things you didn't know could be made out of straw.

Florentine embroideries are renowned around the world but don't come cheap. Try **Cirri** (Via Por Santa Maria; ☎ **055-239-6593;** Bus: B to Ponte Vecchio). Exquisite papers, especially the marbelized kind, are another Florentine specialty. The most famous paper shop is **Pineider** (Piazza della Signoria 13R; ☎ **055-284-655;** Bus: 23 or 71 to Galleria degli Uffizi or B to Loggia del Grano/Via Tornabuoni 76; ☎ **055-211-605;** Bus: 6, 11, 36, or 37 to Tornabuoni). Opened in 1774, it has been a purveyor of paper to many crowned heads. Another top store, this one dating back to the nineteenth century, is **Giulio Giannini & Figlio** (Piazza Pitti 37R; ☎ **055-212-621;** Bus: D to Pitti), where you'll find an excellent choice of stationery and marbleized paper.

The **Ponte Vecchio** is the place to go for the gold: It's one shop after another, all with pretty much the same merchandise. The prices are far from as good as tradition holds — maybe after 500 years and a trillion tourists, the street has gotten a tad stale — and it's difficult to find something original. One of the best jewelry stores in town is **C.O.I.** (Via Por Santa Maria 8R, second floor; ☎ **055-283-970;** Bus: B to Ponte Vecchio), with a very large selection organized by type — bunches of bracelets, drawers of earrings, and so on. Go with a precise idea in mind; it isn't the place for browsing, the staff is overworked and the shop always crowded.

For browsing and also for some great gift ideas, try **Viceversa** (Via Ricasoli 53R; ☎ **055-239-8281;** Bus: 6, 31, or 32 to S.S. Annunziata) for housewares, and **Emporium** (Via Guicciardini 122R; ☎ **055-212-646;** Bus: D to Pitti) for a variety of stylish accessories. **Controluce** (Via della Vigna Nuova 89R; ☎ **055-239-8871;** Bus: 6, 11, 36, or 37 to Tornabuoni) has a beautiful assortment of designer lamps and accessories.

Nightlife

As is true in the rest of Italy, the most common version of nightlife in Florence usually is hanging out in a pub with a group of friends, going for a drink in a trendy bar, or taking a stroll and enjoying some gelato in the historic center. The other preferred activity is listening to some music in a club or (mainly for the young) dancing in one of the popular discos out of town.

The performing arts

During the month of May, Florence blossoms with music. It's the month of the **Maggio Musicale Fiorentino,** Italy's oldest music festival. Continuing on into June, this concert and dance series includes famous performers and world premiers. It's mainly held in the **Teatro Comunale** (Corso Italia 16; ☎ **055-211-158**), which also has a regular program of ballet and opera at other times of the year.

Many churches during the season present evening concerts. The easiest way to find out about these performances is to check the posters on the walls for announcements and pick up a free copy of the listing of events at the Via Cavour tourist office (see "Street smarts: Where to get information after you arrive" in this chapter). The most sought after are the concerts of the **Florentine Chamber Orchestra** in the Chiesa di Orsanmichele during fall; tickets are available at the city's box office in Via Faenza 139R (☎ 055-210-084; Bus: A to Orsanmichele).

The **Teatro Verdi** (Via Ghibellina 99; ☎ 055-212-320) is a smaller theater that offers mainly dance and classical music performances.

Bars and pubs

The oldest caffè in town is **Gilli** (Piazza della Repubblica 39R/Via Roma 1R; ☎ 055-213-896; Bus: A to Orsanmichele), dating back to the eighteenth century. Not only is it in a great location but it has an elegant decor. **Giacosa** (Via de' Tornabuoni 83R; ☎ 055-239-6226; Bus: 6, 11, 36, or 37 to Tornabuoni) is known for its drinks, particularly the Negroni (the ancestor of Italian *aperitivo*, the bittersweet pre-lunch or pre-dinner drink), which apparently was invented here.

The upscale **Caffè degli Artisti/Art Bar** (Via del Moro 4R; ☎ 055-28-76-61; Bus: 6, 11, 36, or 37 to Antinori), is a longtime expatriate favorite. An interesting crowd comes to mingle and talk (though the music can get loud) and sample the long list of cocktails and mixed drinks that are uncommon in this wine-imbibing society.

Florence has been invaded by the passion for Irish pubs. The beer is original but the atmosphere a little less. Try the **Fiddler's Elbow** (Piazza Santa Maria Novella 7R; ☎ 055-215-056; Bus: 6, 11, 36, 37, or A to S.M. Novella 01 or 1, 17, or 23 to S.M. Novella 02), a very successful branch of the Italian chain, or the **Dublin Pub** (Via Faenza 27R; ☎ 055-293-049; Bus: A to Orsanmichele).

Dance clubs

Inside the Cascine Park, the **Meccanò** (Viale degli Olmi 1; ☎ 055-331-371; best to take a taxi) is a large disco/music club with several dance floors and bars, including an outdoor space. It's open to 4 a.m., excluding Sunday, Monday, and Wednesday. Keep your eyes open when outside in the park as it's not one of Florence's safest areas.

A popular place for live rock is a garage on the road to the airport, **Tenax** (Via Pratese 46a; ☎ 055-308-160; best to take a taxi), where bands come from all over Europe (it's closed on Mondays). A more laid-back club is **Full Up** (Via della Vigna Nuova; ☎ 055-293-006; Bus: 6, 11, 36, or 37 to Tornabuoni), where nicely dressed Italians come to dance on the small floor or linger at the piano bar. It's open to 4 a.m. and closed Sundays.

Gay and lesbian bars

Tabasco (Piazza Santa Cecilia 3; ☎ 055-213-000; Bus: 23 or 71 to Galleria degli Uffizi or B to Loggia del Grano) is Florence's (and Italy's) oldest gay dance club, near Piazza della Signoria. The crowd is mostly men in their 20s and 30s. The dance floor is downstairs, while a small video room and piano bar are up top. There are occasional cabaret shows and karaoke. The club is open Thursday to Tuesday 10 p.m. to 3 a.m., with a 15,000L to 30,000L ($8 to $16) cover.

In summer at **Flamingo Bar** (Via del Pandolfini 26; ☎ 055-243-356; Bus: A or 14 to Piazza Santa Croce), near Piazza Santa Croce, the crowd is international. Thursday to Saturday its a mixed gay/lesbian party; the rest of the week, men only. It's open Sunday to Thursday 10 p.m. to 4 a.m. and Friday and Saturday 10 p.m. to 6 a.m. The bar is open year-round; the disco only September to June. Cover, including the first drink, is 12,000L ($6) Sunday to Thursday and 15,000L to 20,000L ($8 to $11) Friday and Saturday.

Fast Facts: Firenze

American Express

The main office is at Via Dante Alighieri 22R (☎ 055-50-981; Bus: A to Condotta), open Monday to Friday 9 a.m. to 5:30 p.m. and Saturday 9 a.m. to 12:30 p.m.

Country Code and City Code

The **country code** for Italy is 39. The **city code** for Florence is 055; use this code when calling from anywhere outside or inside Italy, even within Florence itself (include the zero every time, even when calling from abroad).

Currency Exchange

There are a ton of banks and exchange offices along Via dei Calzaiuoli, between the Duomo and the Palazzo Vecchio.

Doctors and Dentists

Call your consulate or the American Express office for a list of English-speaking doctors and dentists.

Embassies and Consulates

United States: Lungarno Amerigo Vespucci, 38 (☎ 055-239-8279 or 055-7283-780; Bus: 12 to Palestro), near the intersection with Via

Palestro. **United Kingdom:** Lungarno Corsini, 2 (☎ 055-284-123 or 055-289-556; Bus: 11, 36, or 37 to Lungarno Corsini). For citizens of **Canada, Ireland, Australia,** and **New Zealand,** see Chapter 12 for the addresses of embassies and consulates in the capital.

Emergencies

Ambulance, ☎ 118 or 055-212-222; Fire, ☎ 115; Pronto Soccorso (first aid) Careggi, Viale Morgagni 85, ☎ 055-427-7235.

Hospitals

The **Tourist Medical Service** (Via Lorenzo il Magnifico 59; ☎ 055-475-411) is open 24 hours and can be reached by bus nos. 8 and 80 (stop Lavagnini) or 12 (stop Poliziano). The **Ospedale di Santa Maria Nuova** (Piazza Santa Maria Nuova; ☎ 055-27-581; Bus: 14 or 23 to Piazza Santa Maria Nuova) is just a block northeast from the Duomo.

Information

For tourist info and assistance, call ☎ 055-276-0382 or 055-290-832. The best of the tourist offices is at Via Cavour 1R (☎ 055-290-832 or 055-290-833; Fax: 055-276-0383;

Bus: 14, 23, or 71 to Duomo), about three blocks north of the Duomo; it's open Monday to Saturday 8 a.m. to 7 p.m. in summer (to 2 p.m. in winter). See "Street smarts: Where to get information after you arrive," earlier in this chapter, for the other addresses of Florence's tourist offices.

Internet Access

The **Internet Train** chain has five locations, the most convenient being Via Guelfa 24a (☎ 055-214-794; Bus: 7, 14, 23, 36, or 37 to FS Santa Maria Novella) near the train station; Via dell'Oriuolo 40R (☎ **055-263-8968**; Bus: 14, 23, or 71 to Duomo) near the Duomo; and Borgo S. Jacopo 30R (☎ **055-265-7935**; Bus: B to Ponte Vecchio) near the Ponte Vecchio.

Mail

The main post office is the **Ufficio Postale** (Via Pellicceria 3, just off Piazza della Repubblica; Bus: A to Orsan-michele), open Monday to Friday 9 a.m. to 6 p.m. and Saturday 9 a.m. to 2 p.m.

Maps

The city bus and street maps available at the tourist office are adequate.

Pharmacies

There are many pharmacies in Florence, but the **Farmacia Molteni** (Via Calzaiuoli 7R; ☎ 055-212-472; Bus: A to Orsanmichele) is open 24 hours.

Police

Call ☎ **113**; for the Carabinieri (other Police force), call ☎ **112**.

Rest Rooms

As elsewhere in Italy, public rest rooms aren't plentiful and are often closed. Your best bet is to go to a cafe; better yet, since Florence is chock-full of museums, remember to use one while you're inside.

Safety

Florence is quite safe; your only major worries are pickpockets and purse snatchers because of the huge concentration of tourists. Avoid deserted areas after dark (such as behind the train station and Casine Park) and exercise normal urban caution.

Smoking

Smoking is allowed in caffès and restaurants and is very common. Unfortunately for non-smokers, it's virtually impossible to find a restaurant with a separate no-smoking area.

Taxes

There's no local tax in Florence. Other taxes are always included in the prices quoted. You can get a refund of the 19 percent **IVA** (value-added tax) for purchases above 300,000L ($160) — see Chapter 4 for detailed information.

Taxi

If you need a taxi, call ☎ **055-4390,** 055-4798, or 055-4242.

Transit/Tourist Assistance

The airports are **Aeroporto Amerigo Vespucci** (☎ 055-373-498), known as Peretola, and the Pisa airport, **Aeroporto Galileo Galilei** (☎ 050-500-707). For buses, call **SITA** (☎ 055-214-721); for trains, **Stazione Santa Maria Novella,** sometimes abbreviated SMN Firenze (☎ **055-288-765**). The tourist office is ☎ **055-212-245.**

Weather Updates

For forecasts, the best bet is to look at the news on TV (there's no phone number to get weather forecasts). On the Web, you can check meteo.tiscalinet.it.

Web Sites

The city maintains a useful site at www.
comune.firenze.it. Much of it, however,
is in Italian. At www.florence.ala.it,
most of the places listed are ranked — hotels
by luxury, restaurants by price, and museums
by importance. You'll also find links to
Florence's concert listings, weather reports,
business information, and Internet facilities.
If you're going to Florence to see its magnificent works of art, first take a peek at
www.arca.net/florence.htm for a
combined tour guide and Florence art history
lesson that includes a glossary of art terms.
The site provides hotel reviews and city
news as well.

Chapter 15

Northern Tuscany and the Cinque Terre

• •

• •

*N*orthern Tuscany is an area rich in history and natural beauty. Of its many fascinating destinations, we chose to cover the two very best: Pisa and Lucca. We also cover the nearby Cinque Terre, a group of five picturesque villages along the coast. For each of these destinations, Pisa makes an excellent base. Pisa is not only central but also a pleasant city, with a choice of moderately priced hotels. Alternatively, you can easily visit each of the destinations in this area as a day trip from Florence.

What's Where?: Northern Tuscany and Its Major Attractions

If you travel west from Florence along the Arno River on its route toward the sea, you pass through **Lucca,** an unspoiled medieval walled town, often bypassed by tourists. (Their great loss and your advantage!) Lucca's architecture speaks of its past glory, and its ancient ramparts, **Duomo (cathedral),** and local olive oil will impress you.

Continuing on your route and shortly before you run out of land, you arrive at beautiful **Pisa.** Famous for its Leaning Tower, Pisa was one of the powerful Italian Maritime Republics from the eleventh to the thirteenth century. These rival ports developed far-flung mercantile empires (see Chapter 1 for a brief history of Italy). Centuries later, the city lost its water access (the river silted up) and its power (it was defeated by Genoa's navy). You can still see evidence of Pisa's great period, however, and the medieval buildings overlooking the curving Arno offer some of Italy's nicest riverside views. The city's highlights are the **Leaning Tower, Duomo, Battistero,** and **Camposanto.**

Tuscany and Umbria

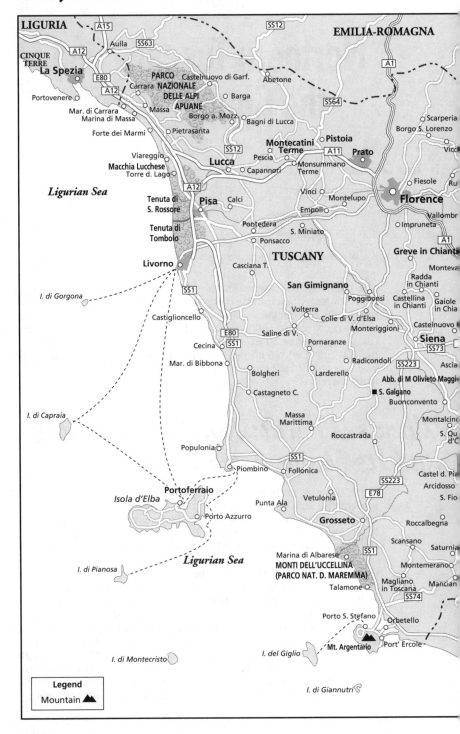

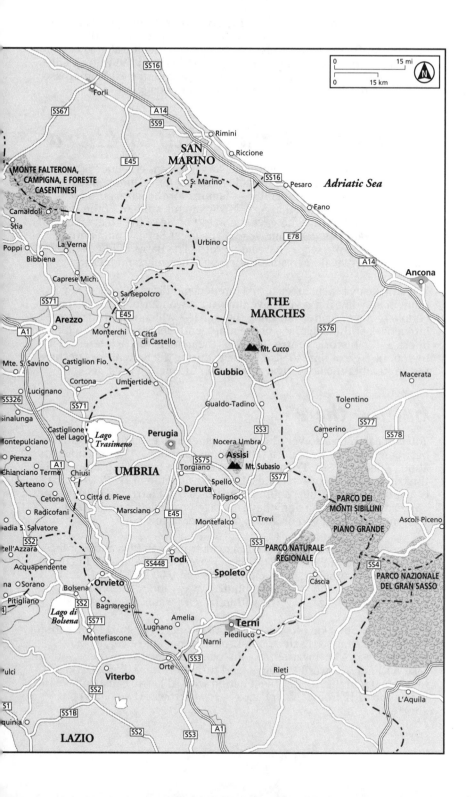

SS16

Forlì

SS67

A14

SS9

Rimini

SAN
MARINO

E45

Riccione

MONTE FALTERONA,
CAMPIGNA, E FORESTE
CASENTINESI

S. Marino

SS16

Pesaro

Adriatic Sea

Camaldoli

Fano

Stia

Poppi

La Verna

Urbino

E78

Bibbiena

A14

Caprese Mich.

Ancona

SS71

Sansepolcro

THE
MARCHES

Arezzo

E45

A1

Monterchi

Città
di Castello

SS76

Mte. S. Savino

Castiglion Fio.

Mt. Cucco

Macerata

Cortona

Umbertide

Gubbio

Lucignano

SS326

Gualdo-Tadino

Tolentino

SS71

inalunga

Castiglione
del Lago

*Lago
Trasimeno*

Perugia

SS3

Camerino

SS77

SS78

ontepulciano

Nocera Umbra

Pienza

A1

Chiusi

Assisi

Chianciano Terme

UMBRIA

Torgiano

SS75

Mt. Subasio

SS77

Sarteano

Spello

Cetona

Città d. Pieve

Deruta

Foligno

PARCO DEI
MONTI SIBILLINI

Radicofani

Marsciano

E45

Montefalco

Trevi

PIANO GRANDE

Ascoli Piceno

adia S. Salvatore

SS2

SS3

tell'Azzara

PARCO NATURALE
REGIONALE

SS4

Acquapendente

SS448

Todi

PARCO NAZIONALE
DEL GRAN SASSO

na Sorano

Bolsena

Orvieto

Spoleto

Cáscia

Pitigliano

SS2

Bagnoregio

*Lago di
Bolsena*

SS71

Amelia

Lugnano

Terni

Montefiascone

Narni

Piediluco

4

ulci

Orte

SS3

Rieti

Viterbo

SS2

SS1B

L'Aquila

S1

quinia

LAZIO

SS2

SS3

A1

0 ____ 15 mi
0 ____ 15 km
N

If you push on a bit farther along the coast, into neighboring Liguria and the Riviera di Levante (part of the Italian Riviera), you discover the **Cinque Terre (Five Lands)**, a fishing and agricultural area of great natural beauty. Five small towns are perched here at the water's edge and insulated from the inland by towering promontories: Monterosso al Mare, Vernazza, Corniglia, Manarola, and Riomaggiore.

Uncovering the Walled City of Lucca

Located west of Florence, Lucca was an important city under the Romans and later became a republic, fighting for its independence against Pisa. It was — and still is — famous for the works produced in its music school, founded in A.D. 787. A famous student of the school was Giacomo Puccini, who gave the world some of the greatest operas, such as *Madame Butterfly* and *Tosca*. The great English poet Percy Bysshe Shelley passed by here and wrote "The Baths of Lucca" about this small medieval town surrounded by powerful red ramparts.

You can easily reach Lucca from Florence and Pisa and can see everything in one day. But if you have time, it's a wonderful place to spend a couple of days leisurely strolling the walls — which were transformed into a park at the beginning of the nineteenth century — or catching an opera at the historic **Teatro Il Giglio** (theater). If you're interested in the opera, a great time to visit Lucca is during the **Settembre Lucchese,** the September music festival celebrating the memory of Puccini.

Getting there

You can catch trains every hour and sometimes even more frequently between Florence and Lucca. The trip takes about 1¼ hours and costs about 7,000L ($3.80). Trains from Pisa to Lucca travel as frequently, but the trip is only 20 to 30 minutes. Lucca's rail station (☎ **0583-467-013**) is just outside the walls, south of the Porta San Pietro (St. Peter's Gate). You can walk — if you don't have luggage or you left it at the train station — or take a taxi or bus to the center of town.

The company **Lazzi** runs buses to Lucca from both Pisa and Florence (☎ **050-46-288** in Pisa, 055-215-155 in Florence, 0583-584-877 in Lucca). The trip lasts about an hour and costs about 9,000L ($4.90) from Florence. Pisa is only about 30 minutes away (about 4,000L/$2.15). Buses arrive in Piazzale Verdi, within Lucca's walls, on the west side.

Lucca is about 64 km (40 miles) west of Florence (22 km/14 miles from Pisa) and is easy to reach by *autostrada*. If you have a **car,** from Florence take **A11** toward Prato, Pistoia, and Lucca. From Pisa, you can take **A12** north toward Viareggio and turn off toward Florence on A11; Lucca is the first exit after the junction with A11. You can also take the local road SS12 from Pisa to Lucca — it's narrower (two lanes) but shorter.

Lucca

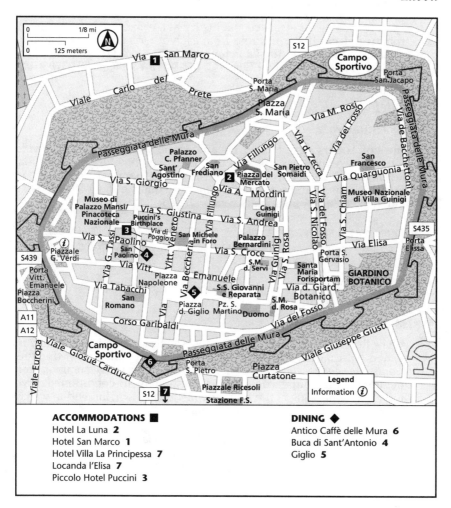

ACCOMMODATIONS ■	**DINING** ◆
Hotel La Luna **2**	Antico Caffè delle Mura **6**
Hotel San Marco **1**	Buca di Sant'Antonio **4**
Hotel Villa La Principessa **7**	Giglio **5**
Locanda l'Elisa **7**	
Piccolo Hotel Puccini **3**	

Getting around

Although residents' cars are allowed within the city walls, Luccans
seem to prefer biking. You see a lot of them — especially the older
ones — pedaling around the city and atop the walls. You can rent a
bike at the city stand (☎ **0583-44-22**), near the walls by the tourist
office in Piazzale Verdi (see "Fast Facts: Lucca"). Otherwise, the
best way to visit the city is on foot. Should you get tired, though, the
public transport system is well organized, with small buses running on
schedule.

Where to stay

If you're looking for elegance and luxury at a price, you can choose from two places that are across from each other 3 km (2 miles) south of the city: the **Hotel Villa La Principessa** (☎ **0583-370-037**; Fax 0583-379-136) and the **Locanda l'Elisa** (☎ **0583-379-737**; Fax 0583-379-019).

Hotel La Luna

$ Anfiteatro

This hotel offers a great value. Located in the historic center, it's divided between two buildings; some of the ceilings in the older building boast seventeenth-century frescoes. All the guest rooms are spacious and nicely furnished, and some of the suites are quite grand, with large beds and high ceilings. The hotel is very well kept.

Corte Compagnoni 12, off Via Fillungo. ☎ *0583-493-634. Fax: 0583-490-021. E-mail:* LaLuna@onenet.it. *Parking: Free. Rack rates: 130,000L ($70) double. AE, DC, MC, V.*

Hotel San Marco

$$ Residential Lucca

A new hotel just outside the city walls, the San Marco is beautifully furnished with modern Italian furniture. Because it's so new, the guest rooms offer good-sized modern baths. The hotel has large common areas, including a pleasant garden, and is completely air-conditioned. If you don't mind not being in the romantic medieval town, but within walking distance, this hotel is a very good value.

Via San Marco 368. ☎ *0583-495-010. Fax: 0583-490-513. Internet:* www.hotelsanmarcolucca.com. *E-mail:* hotelsanmarcoLU@onenet.it. *Parking: Free. Rack rates: 175,000L ($95) double. AE, DC, MC, V.*

Piccolo Hotel Puccini

$ Piazza San Michele

In the heart of the historic center, this hotel is housed in a small fifteenth-century palazzo; it's just across from the house where Puccini was born, hence its name. The guest rooms are small and so are the new bathrooms, but they're nicely furnished and very romantic.

Via di Poggio 9. ☎ *0583-55-421. Fax: 0583-53-487. Internet:* www.hotelpuccini.com. *E- mail:* hotelpucciniLU@onenet.it. *Parking: Free parking available nearby the hotel in a parking lot that does not belong to the hotel. Rack rates: 125,000L ($68) double. AE, DC, MC, V.*

Where to dine

Lucca's specialty is its *olio di oliva delle Colline Lucchesi* (extra-virgin olive oil), one of the best olive oils in the world. The already good Tuscan dishes become absolutely delectable when prepared with it. You can taste the difference when you eat in Lucca's restaurants.

Antico Caffè delle Mura

$$$ City Ramparts   Luccan

With its fantastic location atop the city walls, this elegant restaurant is a good competitor for the Buca di Sant'Antonio (see following listing), although its food doesn't quite reach the same heights. The food is very good, however. Try the homemade fresh pasta and some of the delectable *secondi* (main courses), including such specialties as rabbit, duck, and lamb.

Piazza Vittorio Emanuele 2. ☎ 0583-47-962. Reservations necessary. Secondi: 20,000–30,000L ($11–$16). AE, DC, MC, V. Open: Lunch and dinner Wed–Mon; closed three weeks in Jan.

Buca di Sant'Antonio

$$$$ Piazza San Michele   Luccan

Lucca's best restaurant, the Buca di Sant'Antonio boasts excellent food (try the *capretto allo spiedo*, spit-roasted baby goat) and an interesting history (the restaurant has existed since the eighteenth century). The remarkable atmosphere is characterized by a labyrinthine succession of small rooms decorated with musical instruments and copper pots.

Via della Cervia 3. ☎ 0583-55-881. Reservations necessary. Secondi: 20,000–35,000L ($11–$19). AE, DC, MC, V. Open: Lunch Tues–Sun; dinner Tues–Sat; closed three weeks in July.

Giglio

$$ Piazza del Giglio   Luccan

Less elegant and refined than the other restaurants that we mention in this section, Giglio offers excellent traditional Luccan specialties and a friendly atmosphere. Try the famed *zuppa di farro* (thick spelt soup) or the homemade tortellini. The *secondi* are also very tasty, and you can never go wrong with the *coniglio alla cacciatora* (rabbit) or the roasted lamb.

Piazza del Giglio 2. ☎ 0583-494-058. Reservations recommended. Secondi: 18,000–25,000L ($10–$14). AE, DC, MC, V. Open: Lunch Thurs–Tues; dinner Thurs–Mon; closed two weeks in Feb.

Exploring Lucca

Take advantage of the city tourist office's **Cityphone Guided Tour.** For 15,000L ($8) — 10,000L ($5) for the second person — you can rent a recorded guided tour in your own language that offers explanations and historic facts on all of Lucca's sights. Together with the free city map, it's all you need to explore the city in as much depth as you like. See "Fast Facts: Lucca," later in this chapter, for the location of the tourist office. However, if you prefer exploring the city without the aid of a recorded tour, we provide the highlights in the following section.

The top sights

Duomo (Cattedrale di San Martino)

Sitting on a medieval square, this cathedral is a perfect example of Luccan-Pisan Romanesque architecture. Made of striped green and white marble, the facade is decorated with three tiers of polychromed small columns. Take some time to walk behind the church and admire the imposing apse, surrounded by a small park. The interior is Gothic, divided into three naves, and contains several fine pieces, the most important in the **Sacristy:** Ghirlandaio's *Madonna with Saints* and Ilaria del Carretto Guinigi's **funeral monument,** a Jacopo della Quercia master-piece that's one of the finest examples of fifteenth-century Italian sculpture. Ilaria was the first wife of Paolo Guinigi, ruler of Lucca, and he had the monument built to commemorate her death (she died at 26 after only 2 years of marriage) and beauty. Other interesting works are the Tintoretto *Ultima Cena (Last Supper)* on the third altar of the right nave and several sculptures by fifteenth-century Luccan artist Matteo Civitali (among which are the two angels in the Cappella del Sacramento/Chapel of the Sacrament and the altar dedicated to San Regolo in the adjacent chapel). Also by Matteo Civitali is the marble housing for the Duomo's relic: the *Volto Santo,* a wooden crucifix showing the real face of Christ, said to have been miraculously carved.

Piazza San Martino. ☎ *0583-494-726. Admission: Duomo free; Sacristy 3,000L ($1.60). Open: Daily 7 a.m.–5:30 p.m.*

Passeggiata delle Mura

Erected between the sixteenth and seventeenth century, this is the third and last set of city walls built by the independent Republic of Lucca. In fact, they're Europe's only practically undamaged set of defense ram-parts from the Renaissance, measuring 115 feet at the base and soaring 40 feet high. The tops of the walls were transformed into a tree-lined 4.2-km-long (2½-mile-long) public promenade in the early nineteenth century and today is a wonderful attraction overlooking the whole city, which visitors and Luccans both enjoy. Do as the Luccans do and rent a bike in Piazzale Verdi (see "Getting around Lucca"), entering the prome-nade at the nearby entrance.

Surrounds the historic center, with 11 bastions and several points of access. Admission: Free. Open: 24 hours.

San Frediano

Built in the early twelfth century, this church has a simple facade decorated with a beautiful Byzantine-style mosaic depicting the ascension of Christ, as well as a soaring bell tower. Among the works inside the church are noteworthy Jacopo della Quercia **carvings** in the left nave's last chapel, the twelfth- and thirteenth-century **mosaic floor** around the main altar, and the beautifully carved **Romanesque font** at the right nave's entrance.

Piazza San Frediano. ☎ 0583-493-627. Admission: Free. Open: Mon–Sat 9 a.m.–noon and 3–6 p.m., Sun 9 a.m.–1 p.m. and 3–5 p.m.

San Michele in Foro

Probably one of the greatest examples of Luccan-Pisan Romanesque architecture, the church of San Michele was built between the twelfth and fourteenth centuries. The church derives its name from the fact that it was built over the ancient Roman city's Foro (Forum). The facade is graced by four tiers of small columns and luxuriously decorated with different colors of marble, while the apse powerfully illustrates the Pisan influence. Inside is a beautiful **Filippino Lippi painting** on wood representing four saints — Sebastian, Jerome, Helen, and Roch. Piazza San Michele, which surrounds this wonderful church is itself lovely.

Piazza San Michele. ☎ 0583-48-459. Admission: Free. Open: Daily 7:30 a.m.–12:30 p.m. and 3–6 p.m.

More cool things to see and do

Here are some more sights to check out in and around Lucca:

- ✔ The **Museo di Palazzo Mansi** (Via Galli Tassi 43; ☎ 0583-55-570) houses the **Pinacoteca Nazionale (National Picture Gallery),** and the structure itself is interesting in its own right; many of its rooms are still decorated with part of the original furnishings and frescoes. Of special note are the Salone della Musica (Music Room) and Camera degli Sposi (Nuptial Room). The collection of paintings includes Italian and foreign artists from the Renaissance to the eighteenth century; highlights are a portrait by Pontormo of a youth and works by a few big names, such as Andrea del Sarto, Veronese, and Domenichino. The museum is open Tuesday to Saturday 9 a.m. to 7 p.m. and Sunday 9 a.m. to 2 p.m. and charges 6,000L ($3.25) for admission.

- ✔ The twelfth-century church of **SS. Giovanni e Reparata** (Piazza San Giovanni; ☎ 0583-490-530) was partly rebuilt in the seventeenth century, and it and its adjacent baptistry (with a Gothic dome) are handsome. However, the real attraction here are the excavations under the church that take you back in time through layers of history. Beneath the later constructions, you see the remains of a previous basilica, a paleo-Christian church, a Roman temple, and a more ancient Roman house. (Excavations are accessible to the public.) The church is open daily 8 a.m. to 1 p.m. and 3 to 6 p.m. Admission is free.

✔ **Via Guinigi** is one of Lucca's most evocative streets, flanked by the houses of the Guinigi, Lucca's ruling family. The houses are a compact block of fourteenth-century towers and brick palaces, perfect examples of monumental Luccan Romanesque-Gothic. Note the large palace at the corner of Via Sant'Andrea; you can visit its tower, the **Casa Guinigi** (☎ **0583-48-524**), topped by a garden with trees (entrance on Via Sant'Andrea). The tower is open daily in summer 9 a.m. to 7:30 p.m. and in winter 10 a.m. to 4:30 p.m., with a 4,500L ($2.45) admission.

✔ **Via Fillungo** is the main street of the historic center, where the shops now housed in the buildings don't dilute the strong med-ieval character. Via Fillungo connects to the famous **Piazza del Mercato:** a ring of medieval houses built atop a Roman theater, the remains of which you can see in the lobbies of the buildings.

Other Northern Tuscan favorites

If you have extra time and are looking for a few more interesting places to visit in the area, try the following:

Prato: Among the draws of this city — 17 km (10 miles) northwest of Florence — is a green-and-white Romanesque Duomo (cathedral) containing wonderful Filippo Lippi frescoes in the apse and the beautifully carved Pergamo del Sacro Cingolo (pulpit) to the right of the main entrance. The cherub bas-reliefs are copies of the originals, which are conserved in the attached Museo dell'Opera del Duomo. The highlights of the museum's collection are Filippo Lippi's painting the *Morte di San Gerolamo* (Death of St. Jerome), and Donatello's famous bas-reliefs *Danza dei putti* (Dance of Cherubs).

Pistoia: This town, 35 km (21 miles) northwest of Florence, lies halfway between Pisa and Florence and has kept much of its fourteenth-century walls. The twelfth-century Duomo (cathedral), a beautiful example of the Pisan style, contains the famous Dossale di San Jacopo, a richly decorated covering for the front of the altar. The octagonal Battistero (Baptistry) was designed by Andrea Pisano, and, like the Duomo, is in white and green marble.

Montecatini Terme: This is one of Italy's most fashionable spas, 31 km (19 miles) north of Florence, drawing visitors who want to test its fine mineral water and try out its thermal centers and perhaps take a mud bath.

Fast Facts: Lucca

Country Code and City Code

The **country code** for Italy is 39. The **city code** for Lucca is **0538**; use this code when calling from anywhere outside or inside Italy and even within Lucca (including the zero, even when calling from abroad).

Currency Exchange

There's a *cambio* (exchange office) in the rail station and one near the tourist office on Piazzale Verdi, as well as others around town. You can also find a number of ATMs throughout the city.

Embassies and Consulates

The nearest location is in Florence. **United States:** Lungarno Amerigo Vespucci, 38 (☎ **055-239-8279** or 055-7283-780; Bus: 12 to Palestro), near the intersection with Via Palestro. **United Kingdom:** Lungarno Corsini, 2 (☎ **055-284-123** or 055-289-556; Bus: 11, 36, or 37 to Lungarno Corsini). For citizens of **Canada, Ireland, Australia,** and **New Zealand,** see Chapter 12 for the addresses of embassies and consulates in the capital.

Emergencies

Ambulance, ☎ **118**; Fire, ☎ **115**; road assistance ☎ **116**.

Hospital

The **Ospedale Campo di Marte** is on Via dell'Ospedale (☎ **0583-9701**).

Information

The **tourist office** is on Piazzale Verdi at the west side of the city walls (☎ **0583-419-689**; Fax: 0583-442-505; E-mail: luccadgt@tin.it). Here you can pick up the Cityphone guide and a free map that's useful. The office is open daily 9:30 a.m. to 6:30 p.m. (to 3:30 p.m. in winter).

Mail

The **Ufficio Postale** (Post Office) is at Via Vallisneri 2 (☎ **0583-43-352**).

Police

Call ☎ **113**; for the Carabinieri (other police force) call ☎ **112**.

Pisa: Home of the Leaning Tower

The origins of Pisa stretch back to Roman times, when the Italic settlement that had existed since 1000 B.C. was transformed into a commercial harbor (in the second century B.C.). The city's maritime power increased over the centuries, and by the eleventh century, Pisa was one of the four powerful Italian Maritime Republics, along with Venice, Amalfi, and Genoa. Pisa controlled Corsica, Sardinia, and the Balearic Islands, competing with Genoa for commerce with the Arabs. In 1284, Genoa finally won its struggle against Pisa, whose fleet was destroyed. Genoa became the dominant power in the Tyrrhenian (the sea to the west of the Italian peninsula) while Pisa shrank to a possession of Florence. During the three centuries of its splendor, however, the wealth coming from far-flung commerce funded the construction of the monumental town that you can still admire today.

You can see most of Pisa's attractions on a day trip from Florence. However, Pisa makes a perfect base for exploring most other destinations in northern Tuscany and, like Lucca, has a good selection of moderately priced hotels and restaurants.

Getting there

Only 3 km (2 miles) south of town, Pisa's **Aeroporto Galileo Galilei** (☎ **050-500-707**) is Tuscany's main airport, with daily flights from other major towns in Italy and Europe. You can take a 2,000L ($1.10) train to Pisa Centrale (Pisa's rail station), departing about every half an hour, or take a 1,500L (80¢) ride on city bus no. 7, departing every 40 minutes. The trip takes about 5 minutes by train and a little longer by bus. You can also take a taxi for about 15,000L ($8) if you're dying to see the tower right away and want to get the center of town as fast as possible.

The train is also an excellent way to get into Pisa, especially if you're coming from the south. It allows you to avoid the traffic along the coast road (SS1), which is terrible in summer. The junction of the two major rail lines from Rome and Florence to Genoa is at Pisa. So you can catch a train about every hour from Rome and one every half hour from Florence. (The trip is about 3½ hours from Rome and a little over an hour from Florence.) Likewise, the trip costs about 10,000L ($5) from Florence and 40,000L ($22) from Rome. The rail station is **Pisa Centrale** (☎ **050-41-385**), toward the south end of the historic center and on the opposite side from the Duomo and its tower. Bus no. 1 brings you across town to the Duomo.

Pisa is about 96 km (60 miles) west of Florence, and if you have a car, count on making the drive in about an hour or less. You can easily get to Pisa by the *autostrada* (turnpike). From Florence, take **A11** to Lucca and follow the signs for **A12** toward Livorno; watch for the exit for Pisa shortly after the junction with A12 South. From Florence, you can also follow the directions for Empoli-Livorno to reach Pisa by the more direct but slower *superstrada* (super-road); the turnoff for Pisa is after the exit for Pontedera. From Rome and Venice, take the *autostrada* to Florence and then follow the directions that we provide earlier in this paragraph.

Getting around

Pisa is a relatively small town, and you can easily visit everything on foot, which allows you to discover the little streets and beautiful views over the Arno River and its bridges. However, the town has a system of city buses, and you can get tickets and a map at the train station. Chances are, though, that the only bus you may need is the no. 1 that runs between Pisa Centrale (the train station) and the Duomo for 1,500L (80¢).

Pisa

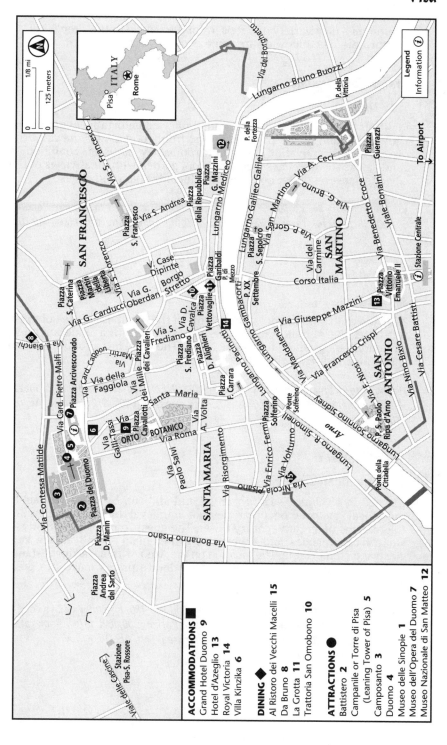

ACCOMMODATIONS ■
Grand Hotel Duomo **9**
Hotel d'Azeglio **13**
Royal Victoria **14**
Villa Kinzika **6**

DINING ◆
Al Ristoro dei Vecchi Macelli **15**
Da Bruno **8**
La Grotta **11**
Trattoria San Omobono **10**

ATTRACTIONS ●
Battistero **2**
Campanile or Torre di Pisa
 (Leaning Tower of Pisa) **5**
Camposanto **3**
Duomo **4**
Museo delle Sinopie **1**
Museo dell'Opera del Duomo **7**
Museo Nazionale di San Matteo **12**

Where to stay

Pisa offers a nice variety of hotels, from the deluxe to the simple but comfortable. The following are some of our favorites.

Grand Hotel Duomo

$$$ Duomo

Right off Piazza del Duomo, this hotel offers comfortable guest rooms with high ceilings and parquet floors; front rooms offer views of the piazza. A 1997 renovation gave all the rooms new baths, air-conditioning , and safes. The hotel has a covered roof garden with great views of the city and serves a buffet breakfast that includes ham and cheese.

Via Santa Maria 94. ☎ *050-561-894. Fax: 050-560-418. Bus: 1 to Duomo. Parking: 30,000L ($16). Rack rates: 290,000L ($157) double, including breakfast. AE, DC, MC, V.*

Hotel d'Azeglio

$$ Stazione

Near the train station and in the middle of the commercial area of town, this hotel offers comfortable modern guest rooms for a moderate price, air-conditioning and minibars included. The hotel has a rooftop garden with a nice view over the town.

Piazza Vittorio Emanuele II 18B. ☎ *050-500-310. Fax: 050-28-017. Bus: 1 to Piazza Vittorio Emanuele. Parking: 15,000L ($8). Rack rates: 230,000L ($124) double. AE, DC, MC, V.*

Royal Victoria

$ Ponte di Mezzo

Opened in 1839 as Pisa's first hotel and still run by the same family, the Royal Victoria occupies several medieval buildings, including the remains of a tenth-century tower. The guest rooms differ greatly — some have frescoes and others are rather plain — but all are kept clean and comfortable. The location on the Arno, within walking distance from all the major attractions, and moderate prices make it a great value.

Lungarno Pacinotti 12. ☎ *050-940-111. Fax: 050-940-180. E- mail:* rvh¢info.it. *Bus: 1, 2, 3, 4, 5, 7, or 13 to Ponte di Mezzo. Parking: 30,000L ($16). Rack rates: 105,000–165,000L ($57–$89) double, including breakfast. AE, DC, MC, V.*

Villa Kinzika

$ Duomo

Across from the famous tower, this hotel offers great views of the tower from many of its air-conditioned guest rooms (some are rather small). Otherwise, the place is quite simple, with an average level of comfort but nothing exceptional.

Piazza Arcivescovado 2. ☎ 050-560-419. Fax: 050-551-204. Bus: 1 to Duomo. Parking: Free. Rack rates: 145,000L ($78) double, including breakfast. AE, DC, MC, V.

Where to dine

Food in Pisa includes typical Tuscan fare, such as *ribollita* (here called *zuppa pisana*, or Pisan soup — old rivalries die hard), *fiorentina* steak, and excellent *coniglio* (rabbit), plus a variety of local specialties. Because the sea is nearby, you can also find lots of seafood: Typical is the *baccala* (codfish), prepared in various ways but often with chickpeas, and many other fish *secondi* (main courses). For *antipasto*, you can choose between the inland specialities (typical cheeses and cold cuts) and a variety of fish and seafood.

An excellent place to eat around town is the **food market** on Piazza delle Vettovaglie, just north of Piazza Garibaldi and the Ponte di Mezzo, and off Via D. Cavalca on the west side of the market. Daily 7 a.m. to 1:30 p.m., food producers from the countryside offer their specialties for sale, and you may want to save a few bucks and have a great picnic — perhaps along the riverbanks — with fresh produce and Tuscan specialties. You can buy bread, salami, fruit, and everything else you will need for a picnic. However, if you prefer to dine out, check out the following restaurants.

Al Ristoro dei Vecchi Macelli

$$$$ Piazza Solferino   Pisan/Seafood

A little outside the historic district, this is Pisa's best restaurant, frequented by locals. The traditional Pisan and Tuscan recipes are reinterpreted with genius and elegance. The homemade ravioli are stuffed with fish and served with shrimp sauce or stuffed with pork and served with broccoli sauce. Other inventions are gnocchi with pesto and shrimp, stuffed rabbit with truffle sauce, sea bass with onion sauce, and oysters au gratin. If you're looking for a formal dining experience and not just something to eat, this is the place to go.

Via Volturno 49. ☎ 050-20-424. Reservations necessary. Bus: 1 to Via Nicola Pisano; then turn right on Via Volturno, southwest of the Duomo. Secondi: 20,000–36,000L ($11–$19). AE, DC. Open: Lunch and dinner Mon–Tues and Thurs–Sat; closed two weeks in Aug.

Da Bruno

$$$ Duomo   Pisan

Just outside the city walls northeast of the Duomo, this trattoria offers real homemade food in a warm atmosphere. The dishes are chosen from the traditional local cuisine and include homemade fresh pasta like the *pappardelle al sugo di lepre* (with hare sauce), *baccala coi porri* (codfish with fresh tomatoes and leeks), *coniglio* (rabbit), and lamb.

Via Luigi Bianchi 12. ☎ 050-560-818. Reservations recommended. Bus: 2, 3, or 4 to Porta Lucca. Secondi: 20,000–30,000L ($11–$16). AE, DC, MC, V. Open: Lunch daily; dinner Wed–Sun.

La Grotta

$$$ Ponte di Mezzo   Tuscan

A favorite among locals and visitors alike, this friendly trattoria has an interesting decor — a papier-mâché grotto — and a lively atmosphere. The traditional food is nicely prepared and includes such specialties as *tortelli* (a special kind of stuffed pasta), *pappardelle alla lepre* (in hare sauce), *gnocchi di ricotta e spinaci* (gnocchi with ricotta cheese and spinach), and a variety of *secondi* like stuffed rabbit and roasted meats.

Via Luigi Bianchi 12. ☎ 050-560-818. Reservations recommended. Bus: 2, 3, or 4 to Porta Lucca. Secondi: 15,000–25,000L ($8–$14). AE, DC, MC, V. Open: Lunch Mon–Sun; dinner Wed–Sun.

Trattoria San Omobono

$$ Ponte di Mezzo   Pisan

Near the food market, this trattoria offers traditional Pisan fare at very moderate prices. Try the homemade pasta specialties or one of the tasty *secondi*, which include *baccala alla livornese* (codfish with onion and fresh tomatoes) and pork roast.

Piazza San Omobono 6. ☎ 050-540-847. Reservations recommended. Bus: 1, 2, 3, 4, 5, 7, or 13 to Ponte di Mezzo Secondi: 14,000L ($8). No credit cards accepted. Open: Lunch and dinner Mon–Sat; closed two weeks in Aug.

Exploring Pisa

The monumental **Piazza del Duomo,** also known as the **Campo dei Miracoli (Field of Miracles),** is where Pisa's top attractions are concentrated. The square was built in medieval times abutting the city walls — a quite unusual location for the city's cathedral, as far as cities in Italy go. Another unusual feature is that the piazza is covered with shining green grass — a perfect background for the carved marble masterpieces in the monumental compound.

If you want to visit several or all of the sights on Campo dei Miracoli, you may want to buy the **cumulative ticket** (sold at all the monuments). It's available for 18,000L ($10) for all five monuments or 10,000L ($5) for your choice of two.

The top sights

Battistero

In front of the Duomo (see "Duomo," later in this section) on Campo dei Miracoli stands the Baptistry. It was built between the twelfth and the fourteenth century, and its architecture reflects the passage from the Romanesque to the Gothic style during those years. This Baptistry is the largest in Italy and is actually taller — counting the statue on top — than the famous Campanile (the Leaning Tower). The exterior was once richly decorated with Giovanni Pisano statues, but many have been removed to the Museo dell'Opera del Duomo (see the listing, later in this chapter) and only a few were replaced with plaster casts. Inside is a hexagonal pulpit carved by Nicola Pisano (father of Giovanni) between 1255 and 1260 and a baptismal font carved and inlaid by Guido Bigarelli da Como.

Piazza del Duomo. ☎ 050-560-547. Admission: 5,000L ($2.70). Bus: 1 to Piazza del Duomo. Open: Summer daily 8 a.m.–8 p.m.; winter daily 9 a.m.–5 p.m.

Campanile or Torre di Pisa (Leaning Tower of Pisa)

Behind the Duomo is the famous Leaning Tower, the Duomo's Campanile (bell tower). Started in 1173 by the architect Bonnano, this beautiful eight-story carved masterpiece, with open-air arches matching those on the Duomo, was finally finished in 1360. It took so long to build because it started leaning almost from the beginning, so the Pisans stopped construction in 1185. In 1275, they started again and built up to the belfry, cleverly curving the structure as they went to compensate for the lean. The construction was then halted again until 1360, when the belfry was added. During the following centuries, architects and engineers studied the problem — the shifting alluvial subsoil, saturated with water — but couldn't devise a solution (one attempt to fix it made it lean more). In 1990, the lean became so bad — 15 feet out of plumb — the tower was closed to the public, so you can no longer climb its 294 steps. Two years later, a belt of steel cables was placed around the base, and in 1993, it was decided to stop ringing the bells to prevent vibrations from shaking the tower. Engineers also tried to compensate for the lean with heavy lead weights. The maneuver was successful and the tower is slowly — less than an inch a year — realigning itself. The idea is to move the tower back to a safe angle and open it again to the public. Stay tuned.

Piazza del Duomo. ☎ 050-560-547. Bus:1 to Piazza del Duomo.

Camposanto

On the edge of the piazza stands the beautiful wall of the Camposanto (Cemetery). Designed by Giovanni di Simone and built in 1278, this monumental cemetery has been the burial ground for Pisa's constables, and you can find sarcophagi, statues, and marble bas-reliefs. The dirt used in the cemetery isn't common dirt but holy dirt from Golgotha in Palestine — where Christ was crucified — brought back by ship after a crusade. During the 1944 U.S. bombing of Pisa to dislodge the Nazis, the cemetery's loggia roof caught fire and most of the magnificent frescoes were destroyed. Parts of the frescoes that were salvaged — particularly interesting are the *Triumph of Death* and the *Last Judgment* — are exhibited inside, along with photographs showing the Camposanto before the destruction.

Piazza del Duomo. ☎ *050-560-547. Bus: 1 to Piazza del Duomo. Admission: 5,000L ($2.70). Open: Summer daily 8 a.m.–8 p.m.; winter daily 9 a.m.–5 p.m.*

Duomo

The center of Campo dei Miracoli is occupied by the magnificent Duomo, built by Buschetto in the eleventh century. However, its current facade, with four layers of open-air arches diminishing in size as they ascend, is from the thirteenth century. In 1595, the cathedral was heavily damaged by a fire that destroyed the three bronze exterior doors and much of the art inside. It was restored during the sixteenth century, integrating some baroque elements. Still original are the monumental bronze door at the south entrance (the Porta San Ranieri) cast by Bonanno Pisano in 1180, the Andrea del Sarto painting of *Sant'Agnese* at the choir entrance, the thirteenth-century mosaic of *Christ Pantocrator,* and the Cimabue *San Giovanni Evangelista* in the apse. The polygonal pulpit carved by Giovanni Pisano was restored in 1926 when the original pieces were found — they had been put in storage after the fire in the sixteenth century.

Piazza del Duomo. ☎ *050-560-547. Bus: 1 to Piazza del Duomo. Admission: Duomo 3,000L ($1.62). Open: Summer daily 8 a.m.–8 p.m.; winter Mon–Sat 7:45 a.m.–1 p.m. and 3–5 p.m., Sun 9 a.m.–1 p.m. and 3–6 p.m.*

Museo dell'Opera del Duomo

On the south side of the Leaning Tower is the Museo dell'Opera del Duomo, which houses plans for the Duomo, ancient artifacts found on the site at the time the Duomo was constructed, illuminated books and religious paraphernalia, and original artworks that were removed from the Duomo and the other monuments for preservation. Particularly notable are the **griffin** that decorated the Duomo's cupola before being replaced by a copy (an eleventh-century Islamic bronze, it was booty from a crusade) and Giovanni Pisano's **Madonna col Bambino,** carved from an ivory tusk in 1299. Also interesting are the Carlo Lasinio **etchings,** which were prepared for the nineteenth-century restoration of the Camposanto's frescoes. Colored by Lasinio's son, they're the best record of the frescoes that were made before their destruction in World War II.

Piazza del Duomo. ☎ 050-561-820. Bus: 1 to Piazza del Duomo. Admission: 5,000L ($2.70). Open: Summer daily 8 a.m.–8 p.m.; winter daily 9 a.m.–5 p.m.

Museo delle Sinopie

On the other side of the piazza, across from the Camposanto, is the Museo delle Sinopie. This museum houses the *sinopie* — the preparatory sketches for frescoes — found under the charred remains of the frescoes in the Camposanto. Each *sinopia* faces an engraving that shows what the Camposanto frescoes looked like before their destruction.

Piazza del Duomo. ☎ 050-560-547. Bus: 1 to Piazza del Duomo. Admission: 5,000L ($2.70). Open: Summer daily 8 a.m.–8 p.m.; winter daily 9 a.m.–5 p.m.

More cool things to see and do

If you have more time to spend in Pisa, check out these sights:

- The **Museo Nazionale di San Matteo** (Piazzetta San Matteo 1, near Piazza Mazzini; ☎ 050-541-865) has a collection of paintings and sculptures from the twelfth to the fifteenth century. Some of the works come from nearby churches, particularly from Santa Maria della Spina. Important masterpieces include the 1426 painting *San Paolo* by Masaccio, the two paintings of the *Madonna con i Santi* by Ghirlandaio, and the sculpture of the *Madonna del Latte* by Nino Pisano. The admission is 8,000L ($4.30), and the museum is open Tuesday to Saturday 9 a.m. to 7 p.m. and Sunday 9 a.m. to 2 p.m.

- A traditional fun event is the **Gioco del Ponte,** held on the last Sunday in June, when teams from the north and south sides of the Arno fight each other. Wearing Renaissance costumes, the teams use a decorated 7-ton cart to push each other off the Ponte di Mezzo — the Roman bridge at the center of town. Contact the tourist office for more information (see "Fast Facts: Lucca").

- Another town celebration is the **Festa di San Ranieri,** on June 16 and 17, for Pisa's patron saint. The Arno is lit with torches all along its length, which makes a very beautiful sight. Contact the tourist office for more information (see "Fast Facts: Lucca").

- If you prefer to see Pisa via guided tour, you can contact **American Express** (☎ 055-50-981) or **SitaSightseeing** (☎ 055-214-721) in Florence. Both offer a tour of Pisa from Florence for about 50,000L ($27).

Fast Facts: Pisa

Country Code and City Code

The **country code** for Italy is **39**. The **city code** for Pisa is **050**; use this code when calling from anywhere outside or inside Italy, even within Pisa (include the zero every time, even when calling from abroad).

Currency Exchange

There's a *cambio* (exchange office) at the airport and several in town, including one on Piazza del Duomo.

Embassies and Consulates

The nearest location is in Florence. **United States:** Lungarno Amerigo Vespucci, 38 (☎ **055-239-8279** or 055-7283-780; Bus: 12 to Palestro), near the intersection with Via Palestro. **United Kingdom:** Lungarno Corsini, 2 (☎ **055-284-123** or 055-289-556; Bus: 11, 36, or 37 to Lungarno Corsini). For citizens of **Canada, Ireland, Australia,** and **New Zealand,** see Chapter 12 for the addresses of embassies and consulates in the capital.

Emergencies

Ambulance ☎ **118**; Fire ☎ **115**; road assistance ☎ **116**.

Hospital

The **Ospedale Santa Chiara** is at Via Roma 67 (☎ **050-992-111** or 050-923-111).

Information

The **main tourist office** is at Via B. Croce 26 (☎ **050-40-096**; Fax: 050-40-903). It maintains two **info booths,** one outside Pisa Centrale, just to the left when you exit (☎ **050-42-291**), and one near the Duomo, inside the entrance to the Museo dell'Opera del Duomo (☎ **050-560-464**). Hours are daily 9 a.m. to 7 p.m. in summer (to 5:30 p.m. in winter).

Mail

The **Poste Centrali** (Central Post Office) is at Piazza Vittorio Emanuele 9 (☎ **050-519-411**).

Police

Call ☎ **113**; for the Carabinieri (other police force), call ☎ **112**.

Farther Afield: The Cinque Terre

Although not in Tuscany, but in the neighboring region of Liguria, the five villages on this portion of rocky coast are just beyond the regional border with Tuscany and easy to reach from either Pisa or Lucca. Because of its unique character, merging land and sea in a most spectacular way, the **Cinque Terre (Five Lands)** enjoy a protected status and are almost like a national park.

A day trip is certainly enough time to take in the sights of the Cinque Terre, unless you have time to spare and want to take a break from the noise and fast pace of modern life. The area's main attractions are beaches and scenery, not art or architecture.

The Cinque Terre

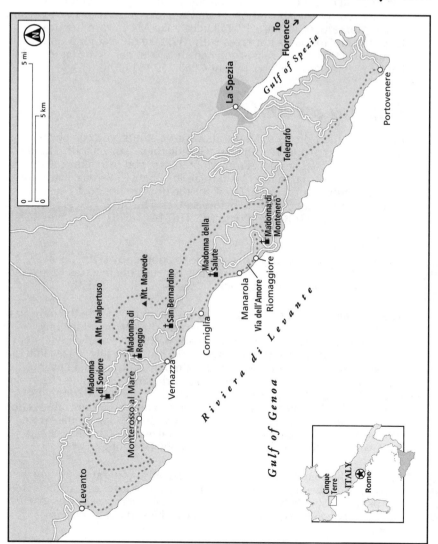

Getting there

From Florence, Lucca, or Pisa, take a train to **La Spezia,** where
you change to the local train line running between La Spezia and
Monterosso al Mare, making stops at each of the other four villages of
the Cinque Terre in between. The trains run frequently and the entire
ride costs only about 5,000L ($2.70).

Because of their protected status, you can't access the Cinque Terre by car, but you can get as far as Monterosso, where you can change to another type of transportation. From Pisa, take A12 toward Genova and exit at Monterosso al Mare. From Lucca, take A11 toward Genova–La Spezia and follow as it merges with A12; take the exit for Monterosso al Mare. Once in Monterosso, you can stow your car in the large parking lot provided for visitors (about 4,000L/$2.15 per hour).

Getting around

Because of their protected natural preserve status, you can access the Cinque Terre only by rail (see "Getting there") or on foot. There's also a limited boat service: From Monterosso, you can take boats to Riomaggiore, Vernazza, and Manarola. The boats to Vernazza are run by the **Motobarca Vernazza** (look for the boat on the dock) every hour, with the last run a little before sunset. The other two are run by the **Navigazione Golfo del Porto** (☎ 01871-967-676) about five times a day.

If you intend to travel from one village to another by train, be aware that most of the run is through tunnels because the line was excavated along the cliff. Don't expect scenic views — you'll see mostly solid rock!

The best way to visit the Cinque Terre is on foot, which is the only way to fully enjoy the beauty of the villages and the surrounding cliffs, because some of the "roads" are actually paths over many stone steps cut into the earth. Two **trails** marked with red-and-white blazes link the five villages: The more difficult one is a mountain trail from Levanto to Portofino (difficulty level: medium), requiring a 12-hour hike; the easier one is the coastal route from Monterosso to Riomaggiore (difficulty level: easy), which requires 5 hours. You can also walk only one section of a trail and travel the rest of the way by train or boat. To hike from Riomaggiore to Manarola, for example, it takes only 30 minutes, but from Vernazza to Monterosso it takes about 1½ hours.

Although the easy trail requires you to be only moderately fit, you need to go with at least one companion, bring at least a quart of water per person (especially in summer, when it gets very hot), and wear sturdy walking shoes. The trail is along a cliff and landslides are common.

Where to stay in the Cinque Terre

When visiting the Cinque Terre, the best place to stay is in the small town of **Monterosso.** The largest of the villages and Cinque Terre's door to the outside world, this is the busiest and some say the least authentic of the towns, but those attributes are good when it comes to finding a place to stay and eat. Of course, staying in one of the smaller villages is more romantic. The following includes a list of hotels.

Pasquale

$$ **Monterosso**

This small modern hotel sits right next to the beach. It was recently revamped with the addition of satellite TVs, hair dryers, and air-conditioning in every guest room (the decor remains old-fashioned, however). Although small, the rooms offer beautiful views over the ocean and coastline. The common areas include a real bar (with seating area, not one of those skimpy affairs) that doubles as a restaurant.

Via Fegina 4. ☎ *0187-817-477. Fax: 0187-817-056. Internet:* www.pasini.com. *E-mail:* pasquale@pasini.com. *Rack rates: 170,000–250,000L ($92–$135) double, including breakfast. MC, V.*

Porto Roca

$$$ **Monterosso**

The Porto Roca offers everything you'd find in a luxury hotel in a larger town, plus spectacular views from its high cliff location. The air-conditioned guest rooms are very spacious, bright, and comfortable, and most have large balconies. The hotel's amenities include a bar, a restaurant with an extensive cellar of Italian wines, and a private beach. The hotel accepts pets for a charge and provides a free car service to the train station.

Via Corone 1. ☎ *0187-817-502. Fax: 0187-817-692. Internet:* www.portoroca. it. *E-mail:* portoroca@cinqueterre.it. *Parking: Free. Rack rates: 280,000–430,000L ($151–$232) double, including buffet breakfast and beach umbrella and chairs for the day. AE, DC, MC, V.*

Villa Adriana

$$ **Monterosso**

This hotel is a real bargain for the area. Although it doesn't include some modern amenities (no air-conditioning), it compensates with a private beach, a garden, a good restaurant, and moderate prices. The guest rooms are modest in size though not cramped, and your pets are welcome.

Via IV Novembre 23. ☎ *0187-818-109. Fax: 0187-818-128. Rack rates: 145,000–160,000L ($78–$87) double, including breakfast. AE, MC, V.*

Villa Steno

$$ **Monterosso**

This is the hotel we prefer most in the Cinque Terre. Unpretentious, it offers comfortably appointed guest rooms with a minimalist look and bright white walls. In addition, each room has a private terrace or small garden. However, there are limited extras: It doesn't have air-conditioning or a restaurant.

Via Roma 109. ☎ *0187-817-028. Fax: 0187-817-354. E-mail:* steno@pasini.com. *Parking: Free. Rack rates: 170,000–250,000L ($92–$135).*

Where to dine

The cuisine of the Cinque Terre is typical Ligurian, with a lot of fish and simple produce from the surrounding almost vertical fields, sloping steeply toward the sea. Pesto sauce, now famous around the world, originated in the Cinque Terre and tastes best with *linguine* pasta. Another Ligurian specialty is *zuppa di pesce,* a savory, brothy fish stew. You can complete your meal with your choice of local grilled fish. For tasty treats while visiting Cinque Terre, try the following restaurants.

Al Carugio

$$ Monterosso Ligurian

The restaurant of this small pensione serves excellent food at moderate prices. You can find all the typical dishes of Ligurian cuisine proudly prepared and served in a friendly atmosphere. Go for the classic *linguine al pesto* and the *zuppa di pesce*, both delicious.

Via Roma 100. ☎ *0187-817-453. Reservations recommended. Secondi: 16,000–25,000L ($9–$14). AE, MC, V. Open: Lunch and dinner Wed–Mon.*

Marina Piccola

$$$ Riomaggiore Ligurian

An unpretentious restaurant, Marina Piccola is the trattoria of a nearby hotel. Liked by locals, it's known for its grilled fish — try the *spigola alla griglia* or the *San Pietro.*

Via Discovolo 192. ☎ *0187-920-103. Reservations recommended. Secondi: 18,000–35,000L ($10–$19). AE, DC, MC, V. Open: Lunch and dinner Wed–Mon.*

Ristorante l'Alta Marea

$$$ Monterosso Ligurian

In the center of town, this lively restaurant offers a casual atmosphere that appeals to younger crowds. Although trendy, the food is as good as in more old-fashioned and traditional restaurants. The delicious *linguine al pesto* is tangy and fresh.

Via Roma 54. ☎ *0187-817-170. Reservations recommended. Secondi: 18,000–35,000L ($10–19). AE, MC, V. Open: Summer lunch and dinner daily; winter lunch and dinner Thurs–Tues.*

Trattoria Gianni Franzi

$$ Vernazza Ligurian

Tradition is the key word at Gianni's, where the recipes of Ligurian cuisine are prepared with care and attention to detail and include local fish, herbs, and vegetables. You can find all the classics — including *zuppa di pesce* and delicious octopus — and a pleasant setting.

Piazza Marconi 5. ☎ *0187-821-003. Reservations recommended. Secondi: 16,000– 28,000L ($9–19). MC, V. Open: Lunch and dinner Thurs–Tues.*

Exploring the Cinque Terre

The Cinque Terre region is a great place to spend some time with your kids. The breathtaking views, the sea, the swimming, and the hiking provide a great respite from all the usual cultural attractions.

If you intend to walk, take an early train from Monterosso to the last of the villages, Riomaggiore. From there you can easily walk the first three sections of the easy trail (30 minutes for the first stretch and 45 each for the two others) to have a taste of it, and then catch the boat in Vernazza back to Monterosso. If you don't want to walk, you can take a mix of boat and train, but make sure that you check the train schedule so you make it back to Monterosso (or La Spezia if you went only for the day) at a decent hour.

If you're traveling in the hot season and you don't start your trip by 9 a.m. at the latest, you may have to walk in broiling-hot air. Doing so isn't a good idea.

The real attraction of the Cinque Terre are the splendid views over the sea and the tiny villages poking out among the rocky cliffs of the coast. It's amazing to see that the cliffs are cultivated — using terraces — and planted with luscious fruit and olive groves and grapevines. If you're lucky, during your walk you may see a local farmer standing where you'd think only goats can stand, tending lovingly to one of his plants. During the harvest, farmers secure themselves with ropes to prevent falling. Progress has come to the area, however, so here and there you may notice small lifts that look almost like monorails.

The five villages are all unique and offer a gorgeous sight from a distance, either by sea or by land. The entry to the area, **Monterosso al Mare,** is the largest of the Cinque Terre and the only town where cars are allowed. However, it maintains the feeling of an unspoiled seaside resort. It's also the only one of the villages to have a nice sandy beach (wonderful for swimming, even though most of it is divided into private swaths for the hotels lining the beachfront). Art isn't a big draw here, but in the **Chiesa dei Cappuccini (Church of the Capuchins),** in Luccan-Pisan green-and-white-striped marble, you can find a fine crucifixion attributed to Van Dyck.

Vernazza, on the other hand, is a very tiny fishing village with a strong medieval flavor. Overlooking the village is the Gothic church of **Santa Margherita di Antiochia.** The fishing harbor offers a fine view over the rest of the bay. The cobblestone streets of **Corniglia** wind from door to door and to its church, **San Pietro;** the whole town is like a step back in time. The only inland village of the Cinque Terre — though you can reach the sea by way of an old flight of steps — Corniglia is the most agricultural of the last three villages. Its agricultural tradition goes back millennia: it was already exporting wine to Pompeii during the Roman period.

In contrast, **Manarola,** a lovely sight from a distance with its gaily colored houses, and **Riomaggiore,** the last of the Cinque Terre, are real fishermen's villages still dependent upon and closely related to the sea. In addition to its colorful houses, Manarola contains the fourteenth-century church of **San Lorenzo,** highlighted by a splendid rose window, while in Riomaggiore you can find the church of **San Giovanni Battista,** also from the fourteenth century.

The most famous section of the coastal path is the **Via dell'Amore,** the romantic path between Manarola and Riomaggiore, which was excavated in the cliff and offers fabulous views. It was closed for more than five years due to a landslide and has only recently reopened.

Fast Facts: The Cinque Terre

Country Code and City Code

The **country code** for Italy is **39.** The **city code** for the Cinque Terre is **0187;** use this code when calling from anywhere outside or inside Italy, even within the Cinque Terre (include the zero every time, even when calling from abroad).

Embassies and Consulates

The nearest location is in Florence. **United States:** Lungarno Amerigo Vespucci, 38 (☎ **055-239-8279** or 055-7283-780; Bus: 12 to Palestro), near the intersection with Via Palestro. **United Kingdom:** Lungarno Corsini, 2 (☎ **055-284-123** or 055-289-556; Bus: 11, 36, or 37 to Lungarno Corsini). For citizens of **Canada, Ireland, Australia,** and **New Zealand,** see Chapter 12 for the addresses of embassies and consulates in the capital.

Currency Exchange

You can exchange money at the *Pro loco office* (tourist information) in Monterosso (see "Information" in this listing) and in banks in both Monterosso and Vernazza.

Emergencies

Ambulance ☎ **118;** Fire ☎ **115;** road assistance ☎ **116.**

Hospital

The nearest hospital is in the town of Levanto, just west of Monterosso al Mare (☎ **0187-808-125).**

Information

In Monterosso al Mare, the **Pro loco office** (tourist office) is at Via Figena 38 (☎ **0187-817-506;** Fax: 0187-817-825), open

Monday to Saturday 10 a.m. to noon and 5 to 7:30 p.m. and Sunday 10 a.m. to noon. From June to September, there's an **additional office** on Via del Molo (☎ **0187-817-204**), which is open the same hours.

Mail

The main post office for the area is in Monterosso al Mare, on Piazza Garibaldi, in the center of town.

Police

Call ☎ **113**; for the Carabinieri (other police force), call ☎ **112**.

Chapter 16

Southern Tuscany

● ●

In This Chapter

▶ Discovering hills and wine

▶ Exploring medieval towers and towns

● ●

*W*e could spend hundreds of pages describing and you could spend many weeks exploring the rich chain of cities and hills surrounding Florence. This region's incomparable beauty — a cultivated rather than wild beauty, whether you're passing through the vineyards of Chianti or the olive groves of southern Tuscany — matches the richness of its artistic heritage. A castle, walled city, or church-cum-fortress (called a *pieve*) seem to surmount each hill.

If you have the time, spend a few rewarding days exploring southern Tuscany. However, if your time is limited, you can visit each destination in this chapter as a day trip from Florence.

What's Where?: Southern Tuscany and Its Major Attractions

Lying between Florence and Siena is the **Chianti region,** famous for its wine. This region is an agricultural area of uncommon beauty, the soft slopes of its hills boasting magnificent colors in every season, and the tallest hills topped by medieval walled towns and *pieve* (fortified churches in the countryside). The food is also superb.

South of the Chianti is **San Gimignano,** famous for its medieval towers. During the thirteenth century, the city experienced an economic boom. As was the custom in that time, the rich merchants marked their increasing wealth and pride by building palaces, each with its own tower. This started a competition, and towers became so high that the city's government had to intervene and forbid that no tower could be higher than the tower of the municipal palace. Of the original 72 or so towers, only 15 remain, but the view is still quite impressive. Continuing southeast, you arrive at **Siena,** Italy's most beautiful medieval town, in our opinion. Famous for the Palio delle Contrade (the dangerous horse competition held since medieval times), which occurs in July and August, Siena is a jewel of a town, giving unending pleasure to those who stroll its streets and visit its monuments.

Sampling the Fruit of the Vine: A Tour of the Chianti

Break our rule about driving in Italy and take a ride in the Chianti region (or at least take a bus tour). This marvelous region between Florence and Siena has it all: velvety hills, tiny medieval walled towns, imposing *pieve,* and acres of vineyards and olive groves. You can visit the area as a day trip from Florence, but there are enough churches, villages, vineyards, inns, and restaurants to keep you busy for longer. The region's tourist office is in Greve in Chianti (see "Fast Facts: The Chianti").

Getting there

The *strada statale* (state road) **SS222** — called the **Chiantigiana** — crosses the Chianti region, linking Siena to Florence. Although only 66 km (41.3 miles), this winding road (winding because it was established as the route to collect wine from each vineyard in the region and bring it to Florence) is the best way to explore the Chianti. It passes through each of the major points of interest of the area.

The bus company **SITA** (☎ **055-294-955**) runs lines that connect Florence with most small towns in the Chianti. A good destination is Greve, the main town in Chianti, at the center of the region; the trip takes about an hour and 15 minutes and costs 5,000L ($2.70). There are also a number of busses departing from Siena with the bus company **TRA-IN** (☎ **0577-204-221** or 0577-204-245) for many of the small towns in the Chianti.

Getting around

Although driving is the best way to discover most of the Chianti's beauties, you can also move around by bus. You still get a good view of the countryside, and you can stop for some excellent meals. If you decide to move by bus, the best is to go to Greve (see the previous section for information on bus companies serving the Chianti). If you feel up to it, in Greve you can rent bikes or mopeds to visit the outlying region.

Alternatively, you can take a guided bus tour from Florence, a solution that requires less organization on your part and might allow you to see more in less time (see the section on bus tours later in this chapter). It is a particularly good solution if you're pressed for time.

If you drive, get a good map of the region from the tourist office in Florence or from newspaper stands, souvenir shops, and bookstores in Florence or Siena. And remember that many of the roads are unpaved and have poor signage.

The Chianti Region

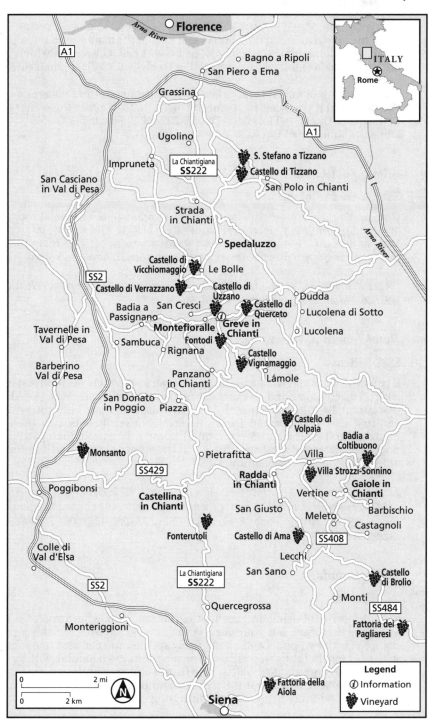

Florence

Arno River

A1

o Bagno a Ripoli
o San Piero a Ema

Grassina o

ITALY

Rome

A1

Ugolino o

La Chiantigiana
SS222

S. Stefano a Tizzano

Impruneta o

Castello di Tizzano

San Casciano
in Val di Pesa

San Polo in Chianti

Strada
in Chianti

Arno River

Spedaluzzo o

Castello di
Vicchiomaggio   o Le Bolle

SS2

Castello di Verrazzano

Castello di
Uzzano

o Dudda

Badia a   San Cresci o
Passignano o

Castello di
Querceto   o Lucolena di Sotto

Montefioralle   **Greve in
Chianti**

o Lucolena

Tavernelle in
Val di Pesa   o Sambuca   Fontodi
o Rignana

Barberino
Val di Pesa

Castello
Vignamaggio

Panzano
in Chianti   o

Lámole

San Donato
in Poggio   Piazza

Castello di
Volpaia

Badia a
Coltibuono

Monsanto   o Pietrafitta   Villa o

Villa Strozzi-Sonnino

SS429

**Radda
in Chianti**

**Gaiole in
Chianti**

Poggibonsi o

**Castellina
in Chianti**

Vertine o

San Giusto

Barbischio

Meleto o

Castagnoli

Colle di
Val d'Elsa

Fonterutoli   Castello di Ama

SS408

Lecchi o

San Sano o

Castello
di Brolio

SS2

La Chiantigiana
SS222

San Sano o

Monti

SS484

o Quercegrossa

Fattoria dei
Pagliaresi

Monteriggioni

0   2 mi
0   2 km

Legend
(i) Information
Vineyard

Fattoria della
Aiola

Siena

Where to stay

In this section, we give you a small selection of proven places to stay. The Chianti is rich in not only hotels and inns in the main towns but also rural accommodations (*agriturismo,* as Italians call it), some of which are luxurious farming villas more similar to elegant castles than farms.

Just over 5 km (3 miles) from Greve is the little agricultural village of Panzano, and if you want to spend the night there, contact the owners of the Torre Guelfa in Florence (☎ **055-239-6338;** Fax: 055-239-8577) and ask about their **Villa Rosa** (see Chapter 14).

Albergo del Chianti

$$ Greve in Chianti

On Greve's main square, this hotel offers a great value. The guest rooms are comfortable, very clean, and moderately priced. The service is excellent, and you can enjoy the hotel's garden and pool. The restaurant serves all the specialties of the region and a superb *fiorentina* steak.

Piazza Matteotti 86. ☎ *and fax* ***055-853-673.*** *Parking: Free. Rack rates: 170,000L ($92) double, including breakfast. AE, DC, MC, V.*

Hotel Tenuta di Ricavo

$$$$ Ricavo

If you have a car and want to splurge, you can stay on this beautiful estate with all its comforts and an excellent restaurant, La Pecora Nera (see the restaurant listings for Chianti, later in this chapter). This fifteenth-century villa transformed from medieval houses boasts two tennis courts, a golf course, an 8-km (5-mile) horse-riding path, bike paths, a pool, a terrace, and a garden. The guest rooms are elegant and comfortable, with country-style antiques.

Ricavo (3.2 km/2 miles north of Castellina in Chianti). ☎ ***0577-740-221.*** *Fax: 0577-741-014. E-mail:* ricavo@ricavo.com *or* ricavo@chiantinet.it. *Internet:* www.ricavo.com. *Parking: Free. Rack rates: 330,000–425,000L ($178–$230) double. AE, DC, MC, V.*

Villa Miranda

$$ Radda

The old inn — housing an excellent restaurant — is where you sign in and have breakfast, but your guest room may be anywhere in this large complex with two pools and open grassy spaces. You can stay in a room in the old inn, but they're, well, old. The new units are beautiful, with very large rooms and modern baths. The furnishings are antiques, and the baths are a little small, but the fixtures and bright decoration create a feeling of modernity in a countryside setting.

Neighborhood of Villa (1.1 km/0.7 miles east of Radda in Chianti) ☎ *0577-738-021.*
Fax: 0577-738-668. Parking: Free. Rack rates: 150,000–210,000L ($80–$114) double.
MC, V.

Where to dine

The products of this magnificent fertile land include not only milk
and honey but also some of the best wine in the world — the famous
Chianti Classico. The region is justly famous for the many wineries,
where you can stop to sample the wine, which is accompanied by tasty
local specialties.

If you're into food, the milk of this region comes from a special variety
of cow, the Chianina. Cheese makers turn the milk into a delicious
caciotta cheese, while the cow itself, poor beast, is made into some of
the best steak you'll ever eat, the *bistecca alla fiorentina*. A bona fide
fiorentina is a minimum of one-inch thick (that's more than two pounds
of meat) — a problem if you're alone but perfect if you're a couple fam-
ished after a day of sightseeing and walking.

The Chianti also offers all the specialties of typical Tuscan cuisine, prepared as well or better than what you can find in Florence and closer to
the source. (See Chapter 14 for a more detailed description of
Tuscany's cuisine.)

Bottega del Moro

$$$ Greve   Tuscan

In Greve's center, this restaurant is a perfect place for a not-too-heavy
lunch. The cooks prepare Tuscan specialties with an eye to tradition
but also to modern health standards (less fatty). This restaurant is a
favorite with locals, who come for the grilled or stewed meats and fresh
pastas — including scrumptious ravioli.

Piazza Trieste 14R ☎ *055-853-753. Reservations necessary. Secondi: 19,000–30,000L*
($10–$16). AE, MC, V. Open: Lunch and dinner Thurs–Tues; closed Nov and one
week in June.

La Cantinetta

$$ Spedaluzzo   Tuscan

In this two-centuries-old farmhouse that's surrounded by a garden, you
can taste real Tuscan countryside food. You can find all the regional specialties here, including some that are more difficult to locate, such as
involtini (veal rolls) and stuffed pigeon. The *tagliata* (Tuscan equivalent
of prime rib) and *salsicce* (sausages) are excellent.

Via Mugnano 93, in Spedaluzzo (2.25 km/1.4 miles north of Greve). ☎ *055-857-2000.*
Reservations necessary. Secondi: 12,000–25,000L ($6–$14). AE, DC, MC, V. Open:
Lunch and dinner Tues–Sun.

La Pecora Nera

$$$$ Ricavo Tuscan

The dining room of this luxurious farm-villa measures up to what you'd expect of a fine country inn in this region: a fireplace, white walls and red bricks, arched passageways, and wooden beams. The excellent food includes all the traditional Tuscan specialties prepared in the classic manner.

At the Hotel Tenuta di Ricavo, in Ricavo (3.2 km/2 miles north of Castellina in Chianti), ☎ *0577-740-221. Reservations recommended on weekends. Secondi: 20,000–35,000L ($11–$19). AE, DC. Open: Lunch and dinner Mon–Tues and Thurs–Sat; closed two weeks in August.*

Villa Miranda

$$$ Radda Tuscan

Inside an old roadside inn (see "Where to stay"), this restaurant is intensely atmospheric and decorated with country-style furniture. The food is well-prepared traditional Florentine. You can't go wrong with the grilled meat (like the *fiorentina*) or the delicious homemade pastas. As an appetizer, the *crostini* are a must if you want to get the full experience of southern Tuscany. If you're in the mood for typical vegetable soup, the *ribollita* is wonderful.

Villa (1.12 km /.7 miles east of Radda in Chianti). ☎ *0577-738-021. Reservations recommended. Secondi: 15,000–35,000L ($8–$19). MC, V. Open: Lunch and dinner Tues–Sun.*

Exploring the Chianti

A rural farming area dotted with small towns, the Chianti is a perfect place to do some exploring. It'll give you a different feeling for Italy than you'd ever get in the cities, as well as show you more of the country's natural beauty.

The top sights

If you ask anybody who's been there, the Chianti's major attractions are its food and wine. In fact, after visiting the Chianti, you'll have fantastic memories of the high-quality basic ingredients joined with a centuries-old tradition and the delicious local vintage. Hundreds of Italians and foreigners come each year to explore the area's dusty roads in search of the ultimate *trattoria*. Wine tasting at vineyards has also become a popular attraction.

However, the Chianti is also a region to visit for natural beauty and art. It's not the home of massive collections such as those in Florence, Rome, and Venice, but you can visit the abbeys and *pieve* (fortified churches surrounded by farms) that were the fabric of society during the Middle Ages. (Many *pieve* hide interesting works of art.)

The three main towns in Chianti — Greve, Radda, and Castellina — are all worth visiting. On the river Greve, **Greve in Chianti** (on SS222, 30 km/19 miles from Florence, about halfway to Siena) is a medieval town that began developing during the thirteenth and fourteenth centuries and today is the capital of the Chianti. Thanks to its central location, it hosts the annual **Rassegna del Chianti** (☎ 055-854-243), a market-fair of producers and sellers of Chianti Classico — the highest in the hierarchy of Chianti wines — during the second week of September. The center of town is picturesque, with a unique triangular main square, Piazza Matteotti, surrounded by arcades full of shops, restaurants, and hotels. The church of Santa Croce, in a small square farther west, is another focus of life.

Just 1.28 km (0.8 miles) east of Greve is a detour well worth making: **Montefioralle,** a tiny hamlet that's one of the few remaining perfectly preserved medieval fortified villages. Built on a steep hill and surrounded by walls, Montefioralle's houses and diminutive cobblestone squares are decorated with bright red geraniums, making walking around the circular main road during the good weather months a real delight. Just northeast of Greve (on a side road from the SS222; about 5 km/3 miles or an hour on foot) is the **Castello di Uzzano** (☎ 055-854-032;** Fax: 055-854-375), an eleventh-century castle transformed into an imposing villa in the sixteenth century. The surrounding estate produces both wine and olive oil. In addition to visiting the cellars (8,000L/$4.30), you can tour the famous Italianate Renaissance gardens (10,000L/$5). From Easter to October, the gardens are open daily 8:30 a.m. to 6 p.m. (by reservation only in winter).

Built on a steep hill about 20 km (12.5 miles) from Greve, **Radda in Chianti** is much smaller than Greve, with parts of its defense walls still standing. The town conserves a more definite medieval character. The Palazzo Comunale (city hall) boasts an interesting fifteenth-century fresco under its portico. However, it's in **Castellina in Chianti** 10 km (6.25 miles) from Radda, that the medieval flavor is the most intact. Still surrounded by most of its walls and dominated by the *Rocca* (a fortress with crenellated walls), Castellina has a typical vaulted street — Via delle Volte — once used by the soldiers for defense purposes during the wars between Florence and Siena.

No visit to the Chianti is complete without a stop at the **Castello di Brolio** (☎ 0577-7301 or 0577-749-066), about 11.2 km (7 miles) southeast of Radda. Owned by the Baron Ricasoli, this is one of the region's oldest wine-producing estates (the vineyards trace back to at least the eleventh century) and the inventor of the Chianti Classico as its known today, a masterly mix of grapes finalized in the mid–nineteenth century. You can visit part of the grounds and gardens (5,000L/$2.70) Monday to Saturday 9 a.m. to noon and 2:30 to 5:30 p.m. or take a wine-tasting tour of the cellars on Mondays at 3 p.m. (March to September only). The on-site store (open year-round) sells their award-winning wines.

And on your left, the Castello di Brolio: Seeing the Chianti by guided tour

If you don't have a car, you can take a guided tour of the Chianti organized by **SITA Sightseeing** (☎ 055-214-721) or **American Express** (☎ 055-50-981). Tours leave from Florence for about 60,000L ($32).

Other Southern Tuscan favorites

✔ **Volterra:** Known since Etruscan times for the translucent calcium sulfate deposits found around the mountain on which it perches, this "City of Alabaster" (50 km/31 miles west of Siena) offers several interesting sights, including an Etruscan Museum where you can see 600 gorgeous funerary urns, most carved from alabaster.

✔ **Massa Marittima:** This overlooked gem, sitting atop a mount with a sweeping view 65 km (40 miles) southwest of Siena, boasts a wonderful Pisan-Romanesque/Gothic Duomo and a museum containing the town of Massa's art treasure, Ambrogio Lorenzetti's *Maestà*.

✔ **Montalcino:** Dominating the skyline of this walled town 42 km (25 miles) south of Siena is a fourteenth-century Sienese fortress. However, Montalcino's claim to fame is its Brunello di Montalcino, one of Italy's mightiest red wines.

✔ **Pienza:** Pienza isn't called an ideal Renaissance city for nothing. And apparently filmmakers agree, because Franco Zefferelli chose Pienza, 55 km (33 miles) southeast of Siena, to stand in for Verona in his *Romeo and Juliet*. Scenes from *The English Patient* and *A Midsummer Night's Dream* were also filmed here.

✔ **Montepulciano:** The biggest of southern Tuscany's hill towns, Montepulciano, 67 km (40 miles) southeast of Siena, boasts many Renaissance palaces and churches but is best known for its Vino Nobile di Montepulciano, an orange-speckled red wine.

✔ **Arezzo:** In Arezzo, 81 km (50 miles) southeast of Florence, life is beautiful (Roberto Benigni filmed parts of his Oscar-winning *La Vita è Bella* here), and you can marvel at superb Piero della Francesca frescoes and Guillaume de Marcillat stained glass.

These trips allow you to get a good taste of the region without having to drive (and get lost on) the snaking backroads. On the downside, you have fewer opportunities for discovery and adventure off the beaten track.

Fast Facts: The Chianti

Country Code and City Code

The **country code** for Italy is **39**. The **city code** for towns within the province of Florence is **055,** and the city code for towns within the province of Siena is 0577; use these codes when calling from anywhere outside or inside

Italy, even within the same town (include zero, even when you call from abroad).

Embassies and Consulates

See "Fast Facts: Florence," in Chapter 14.

Currency Exchange

Although we recommend that you get your cash before coming to the Chianti (it's a farming area with few services), you can exchange currency at banks in the major urban centers. Note, however, that you'll probably receive a better rate using ATMs — try Greve, Castellina, and Radda.

Emergencies

Ambulance ☎ **118**; Fire ☎ **115**; road assistance, ACI ☎ **116.**

Hospital

The **Ospedale Castellina** is on Via Ferruccio (☎ **0577-740-897**) in Castellina in Chianti.

Information

The tourist office for the region is in Greve in Chianti (Via Luca Cino 1; ☎ **055-854-5243**). It's open daily 8 a.m. to 1 p.m. and 3 to 6 p.m. in summer and 8 a.m. to 2 p.m. in winter.

Mail

An *Ufficio Postale* (Post Office) is at Via Chiantigiana (☎ **0577-741-000**) in Castellina in Chianti.

Police

Call ☎ **113**; for the Carabinieri (other police force), call ☎ **112.**

Stunning Siena: City of the Palio delle Contrade

Siena is a magnificent medieval city surrounded by the hilly country-side that makes Tuscany famous. The particularity of Siena is that it's well preserved and yet still alive as a town. The traditional Palio horse race (see "More cool things to see and do") is far from just a tourist attraction and is instead a deeply felt and hotly contested competition among the city's 17 *contrade* (districts) — the Super Bowl doesn't incite as much passion as this race.

The same kind of passion pervades Sienese life, and if you have the time, spend some extra hours or days here. Siena developed a unique artistic style during the Rennaisance — as in all things, in opposition to its archrival, Florence. Some consider its Duomo the most beautiful in Italy. For information on Siena's tourist office, see "Fast Facts: Siena," later in this chapter.

Getting there

Siena is 62 km (37 miles) south of Florence, so you can easily reach it via car on the Florence/Siena highway or on one of the older and more scenic roads. From Rome, take the A1 (the coast road) north toward Florence and exit at Val di Chiana for SS326, or alternatively take the Via Cassia from Rome (one of Italy's old consular roads). Once in Siena, park for the duration of your stay, because traffic in the historic district is heavily restricted (it's also a shame to drive around a medieval town). You can find pay parking lots at the various gates of town, particularly around the north entrance. You can park for free outside the

Siena

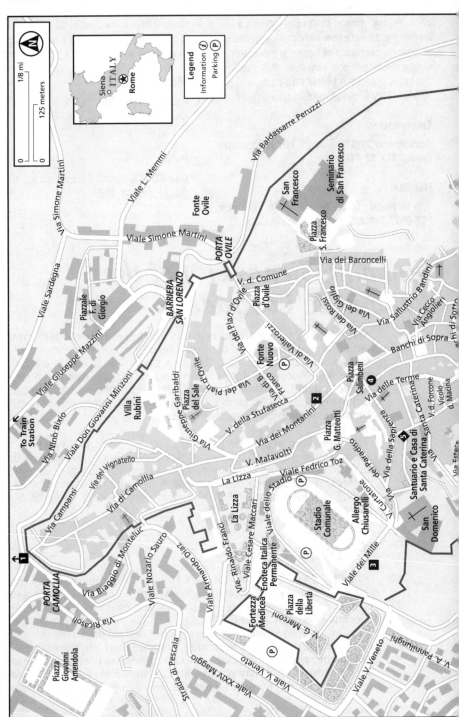

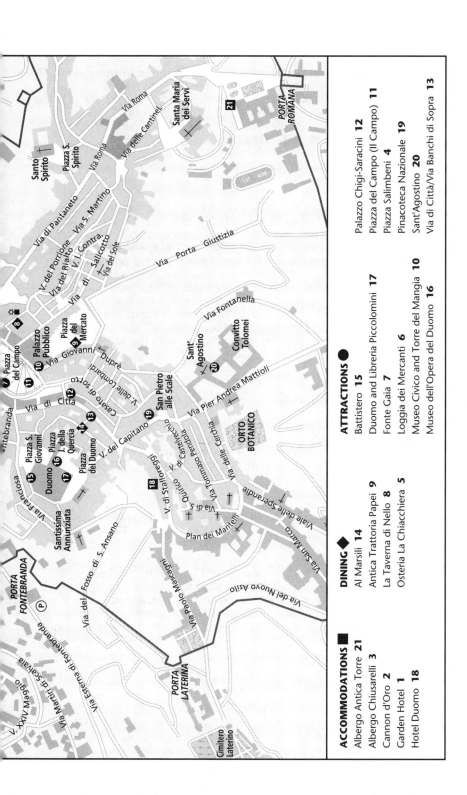

ACCOMMODATIONS ■

Albergo Antica Torre **21**
Albergo Chiusarelli **3**
Cannon d'Oro **2**
Garden Hotel **1**
Hotel Duomo **18**

DINING ◆

Al Marsili **14**
Antica Trattoria Papei **9**
La Taverna di Nello **8**
Osteria La Chiacchiera **5**

ATTRACTIONS ●

Battistero **15**
Duomo and Libreria Piccolomini **17**
Fonte Gaia **7**
Loggia dei Mercanti **6**
Museo Civico and Torre del Mangia **10**
Museo dell'Opera del Duomo **16**

Palazzo Chigi-Saracini **12**
Piazza del Campo (Il Campo) **11**
Piazza Salimbeni **4**
Pinacoteca Nazionale **19**
Sant'Agostino **20**
Via di Città/Via Banchi di Sopra **13**

town walls, but remember that you can't leave cars alone for too long in Italy — they tend to get broken into or disappear.

Siena is on a secondary rail line, so if you take the train, you have to change in Empoli (from Florence and Venice) or Chiusi (from Rome). The trip from Rome takes about three hours and costs 32,000L ($17), the trip from Florence takes about 1¾ hours and costs 29,000L ($16), and the trip from Venice takes about five hours and costs 55,000L ($30). Siena's rail station (☎ 0577-280-115) is on Piazza Fratelli Rosselli, about 2.5 km (1½ miles) from the town center. Minibus C takes you from the train station to Piazza Gramsci, the northern tip of the historic district, a pedestrian-only area.

The **TRA-IN company** (Piazza San Domenico 1, northwest of the historic district; ☎ 0577-204-221 or 0577-204-245) offers bus runs to many other Tuscan cities and, in particular, to Florence about every hour. The ride lasts about 1¼ hours (less than the train) and costs 8,000L ($4.30). The **SENA company** (Via Montanini 92, ticket booth at Piazza San Domenico; ☎ 0577-247-934) runs seven daily rides to Rome's Stazione Tiburtina (five on Sunday) for 25,000L ($14). Reservations are obligatory from Rome to Siena, but not from Siena to Rome. You can make a reservation and buy a ticket by phone at **Eurolines** (☎ 06-4425-2461), which will deliver your ticket by messenger service to your hotel. (In Siena, the SENA company provides the same delivery service.)

Getting around

Built on three hills, Siena is divided in *terza* (districts that cover a third of town). North, along Via Banchi di Sopra, is the **Terza di Camollia;** southwest, along Via di Città, is the **Terza di Città** (with the Duomo); and southeast, along Via del Porrione, is the **Terza di San Martino.** The three *terza* meet at Piazza del Campo.

You can best visit Siena on foot, especially since motorized traffic has been restricted in the historic district (most of it is reserved for pedestrians only). And most of Siena's attractions are very close to one another.

Siena runs a system of minibuses (☎ 0577-204-246; fare 1,500L/80¢) daily 6 a.m. to 9 p.m., including the C from the train station to Piazza Gramsci at the northern tip of the historic district, a good starting point for exploring the town. Note that the buses are color-coded; hence the funny names in the hotel listings that we give you later in this chapter.

Where to stay in Siena

Siena has a number of hotels in town, but they're all full during the Palio delle Contrade (see "More cool things to see and do," later in this chapter). If you're planning to visit during the Palio, remember that hotels accept reservations for the Palio period as far as a year in advance. Think ahead!

Albergo Antica Torre

$$ Porta Romana

You can't find a much more romantic room than in this hotel's sixteenth-century tower (*torre* — hence the name). This family-run hotel is elegant, from the marble staircase and floors to the attractive old furniture. A few of the guest rooms offer views of Siena and the countryside. Because it's a tower, however, don't expect huge rooms.

Via di Fieravacchia 7. ☎ **0577-222-255.** *Fax: 0577-222-255. Bus: A, B, or N to the Porta Romana. Rack rates: 160,000L ($87) double. AE, MC, V.*

Albergo Chiusarelli

$$ Piazza San Domenico

This nineteenth-century building, a five-minute walk from Piazza del Campo, has been renovated and features plain but modern guest rooms. The facade displays Ionic columns and a second-floor loggia and is shaded by palm trees, but you may want to get a room toward the back to avoid street noise. Note that a few rooms may remain unrenovated.

Viale Curtatone 9. ☎ **0577-280-562.** *Fax: 0577-271-177. Bus: C to Piazza San Domenico. Parking: Free. Rack rates: 160,000–220,000L ($87–$119) double, including breakfast. AE, MC, V.*

Cannon d'Oro

$ Piazza Salimbeni

Just north of Piazza del Campo, this fifteenth-century palazzo is on a commercial street. Its guest rooms are simple but large, furnished with old pieces that make you feel like you've gone back in time. On the other hand, the bathrooms have modern fixtures (but are quite small). This hotel is a nice mix of the once grand and the now economical.

Via Montanini 28. ☎ **0577-44-321.** *Fax: 0577-280-868. Bus: C to Piazza Salimbeni. Rack rates: 80,000–110,000L ($43–$59) double. AE, MC, V.*

Garden Hotel

$$$ North of Siena

Just north of the city, this elegant 1700 villa is 1.5 km (1 mile) up a hill among vineyards, olive groves, and a park full of oaks. (The walk is very pleasant if you feel up to it, but take a taxi when you arrive with your luggage.) Some of the guest rooms are in the villa but most are in the modern annex; there are even some four-star rooms with additional amenities. Guests have access to a tennis court and an outdoor pool (nice on really hot days). The terrace affords panoramic views over Siena and the countryside.

Via Custoza 2. ☎ *0577-47-056. Fax: 0577-46-050. E-mail:* garden@venere.it. *Parking: Free. Rack rates: 150,000–290,000L ($80–$157) double, including breakfast. AE, MC, V.*

Hotel Duomo

$$ Duomo

You can't beat this hotel's location halfway between Piazza del Campo and the Duomo. As in many other hotels occupying ancient palazzi — this one from the twelfth century — you get charm outside but sparse amenities inside. In the basement is an atmospheric breakfast room. The guest rooms are fairly good sized and have been redone with modern furnishings, but the baths are very small. When you make your reservations, ask for one of the rooms with a Duomo view.

Via Stalloreggi 38. ☎ *0577-289-088. Fax: 0577-43-043. Bus: A to Duomo. Parking: 16,000L ($9). Rack rates: 180,000–240,000L ($97–$130) double. AE, DC, MC, V.*

Where to dine

Sienese cuisine shares many of the specialties of Florentine cooking (see Chapter 14). The cuisine typical of inland Tuscany has few fish dishes but a lot of game and prepared meats. The *primi* include *pici* (handrolled spaghetti), usually prepared with breadcrumbs and tomato sauce, and *pappa col pomodoro* (a soup of tomatoes and bread). Among the cold cuts are *finocchiona,* a fennel-flavored salami famous all over Italy.

Al Marsili

$$$ Duomo Sienese

If you've come to Siena for a getaway with your significant other or you just feel like splurging on a great dinner, Al Marsili is a superb romantic choice. The service is formal, the atmosphere is elegant, and the food lives up to its reputation. Here you can find staples of Sienese cuisine, such as the ubiquitous *pici,* but also specialties like *faraona alla Medici* (guinea hen with pine nuts, almonds, and prunes), and an excellent selection of wines.

Via del Castoro 3. ☎ *0577-47-154. Reservations recommended. Bus: A to Duomo; then walk past the Museo dell'Opera Metropolitana toward Via di Città. Secondi: 18,000–30,000L ($10–$16). AE, DC, MC, V. Open: Lunch and dinner Tues–Sun.*

Antica Trattoria Papei

$ Piazza del Mercato Sienese

This trattoria, very close to Piazza del Campo, is a favorite with the Sienese. The place itself is charming and the food good and sometimes remarkable (like the *anatra alla Tolomei* — duck stewed with tomatoes).

You can also try the Tuscan favorite _pasta al sugo di cinghiale_ (pasta with wild boar sauce) and wash it down with local wine.

Piazza del Mercato 6. ☎ _0577-280-894. Reservations suggested. Bus: A to Piazza del Campo; then walk behind the Palazzo Pubblico. Secondi: 8,000–15,000L ($4.30–$8). DC, MC, V. Open: Lunch and dinner Tues–Sun._

La Taverna di Nello

$$ Duomo   Sienese

In this rustic tavern off Piazza del Campo, you can find a real country atmosphere and excellently prepared food using fresh vegetables from the countryside, as well as homemade pasta. Try the green lasagna (the pasta is made with spinach) and the fine _secondi._ This restaurant also offers a very nice local wine.

Via del Porrione 28–30. ☎ _0577-289-043. Reservations necessary. Bus: A, B, and N to Via del Porrione. Secondi: 16,000–28,000L ($9–$15). AE, DC, MC, V. Open: Summer: lunch and dinner daily; closed Sun–Mon in Dec and Feb; closed in Jan._

Osteria La Chiacchiera

$ San Domenico   Sienese

This osteria is cheap, with a minimum of decor and really good peasant food, for example _pici_ and _salsicce e fagioli_ (sausages cooked with beans). Anything on the daily menu is good.

Costa di Sant'Antonio 4. ☎ _0577-280-631. Reservations recommended. Bus: A to San Domenico; then walk up Via di Sapienza and turn right. Secondi: 9,000–12,000L ($4.85–$6). No credit cards accepted. Open: Lunch and dinner daily._

Exploring Siena

Siena's main sight isn't a site but an event. The famous **Palio delle Contrade** (see "More cool things to see and do," later in this chapter) is a medieval-style derby in which riders representing the city's neighborhoods compete on horseback for top honors. Siena is a small town; however, and during the Palio it's literally crammed with excited and noisy crowds. If you're visiting Siena primarily to see its art, try to avoid the Palio delle Contrade season.

Siena, with its rich orange tones and myriads of tiled roofs baking in the strong sun, is a sculpture in its own right. The city has some fierce supporters, including art historian Bernard Berenson, who called it the "sorceress and queen among Italian cities." Although strolling the narrow medieval streets is one of Siena's great pleasures, there's plenty to see indoors, from the Duomo to the collections of Siena's unique Renaissance school of art.

Buy the cumulative ticket for the Museo dell'Opera del Duomo, Libreria Piccolomini, and Battistero for 8000L ($4.30) to save some money on the price of admission for these sights.

The top sights

The heart of Siena is the shell-shaped **Piazza del Campo (Il Campo),** described by Montaigne as "the finest of any city in the world." Pause to enjoy the **Fonte Gaia,** which locals call the Fountain of Joy, because it was inaugurated to great jubilation throughout the city, with embellishments by Jacopo della Quercia. (The present sculptured works are reproductions. You can find the badly beaten originals in the Museo Civico, which we describe later in this chapter.)

Battistero

Built in the fourteenth century, the Baptistry's unfinished Gothic facade is by Domenico di Agostino. But you won't care about the facade when you're inside admiring the lavish frescoes, most of which depict the lives of Christ and St. Anthony. In addition, the Baptistry boasts a splendid masterpiece: a baptismal font made of several panels, each cast by one of the best artists of the time. Particularly noteworthy panels are the *Annunciation to Zacharias* by Sienese master Jacopo della Quercia, the *Baptism of Christ* by Lorenzo Ghiberti, and the *Feast of Herod* by Donatello.

Piazza San Giovanni, behind the Duomo. ☎ *0577-283-048. Bus: A red or A green to Piazza del Duomo. Admission: 3,000L ($1.60). Open: Summer daily 9 a.m.–7:30 p.m.; winter daily 10 a.m.–1 p.m. and 2:30–5 p.m.*

Duomo and Libreria Piccolomini

Decorated with contrasting colored marble both inside and out, the Duomo was built during the first half of the thirteenth century in Romanesque and Gothic styles. It contains many artworks, including a superb thirteenth-century **pulpit** carved by Nicola Pisano — the artist who crafted the magnificent pulpit in Pisa's Baptistry and father of Giovanni Pisano (who carved the pulpit in Pisa's Duomo). Another masterpiece inside the Duomo is the **Libreria Piccolomini (Piccolomini Library),** founded by Cardinal Francesco Piccolomini (later Pius III) to honor his uncle, Pope Pius II; the library was completely decorated by Pinturicchio in the early sixteenth century with frescoes illustrating the life of Pius II. Inside the library is the *Three Graces,* an exquisite Roman sculpture designed after a Greek model of the third century B.C.

Piazza del Duomo. ☎ *0577-283-048. Bus: A red or A green to Piazza del Duomo. Admission: Duomo free; Library 2,000L ($1.10). Open: Duomo summer daily 7:30 a.m.–1:30 p.m. and 2:30–7:30 p.m.; winter daily 7:30 a.m.–1:30 p.m. and 2:30–5 p.m.; Library summer daily 9 a.m.–1:30 p.m. and 2:30–7 p.m.; winter daily 10 a.m.–1 p.m. and 2:30–5 p.m.*

Museo Civico and Torre del Mangia

The **Museo Civico** is housed in the beautiful thirteenth-century Palazzo Pubblico, the seat of the government in Siena's republican period. Its richly frescoed rooms host some of Siena's important artworks. On the second floor, the loggia is the showcase for the eroded panels from the masterpiece fountain that decorated Piazza del Campo — the fourteenth-century *Fonte Gaia* (Gaia Fountain) was carved by Jacopo della Quercia and replaced by a replica in the nineteenth century. In the **Sala del Mappamondo (Globe Room),** just off the chapel, are two important pieces by fourteenth-century Sienese painter Simone Martini: the *Maestà* and the magnificent fresco of *Guidoriccio da Fogliano,* captain of the Sienese army (though there's been debate about the attribution of the latter work to Martini). In the **Sala della Pace (Peace Room),** the meeting room of the Council of Nine (Siena's government), is a famous series of frescoes by another fourteenth-century Sienese painter, Ambrogio Lorenzetti: the secular medieval *Allegory of the Good and Bad Government and Its Effects on the City and the Countryside.* From the palazzo's fourteenth-century **Torre del Mangia** — accessible from the courtyard — is a breathtaking view of the town and the surrounding hills (if you're up to climbing the 503 steps). At 335 feet, the Torre del Mangia is the second tallest medieval tower in Italy (the tower in Cremona is taller).

Piazza del Campo. ☎ *0577-292-226. Bus: A pink, B, or N to Piazza del Campo. Admission: Museo 8,000L ($4.30); Tower 4,000L ($2.15). Open: Summer daily 10 a.m.– 7 p.m.; winter Mon–Sat 10 a.m.–6 p.m., Sun 10:30 a.m.–1:30 p.m.*

Museo dell'Opera del Duomo

This museum occupies a part of the originally projected Duomo, which was never built; the current Duomo would've been just the transept (this ambitious plan was reworked because of engineering problems and the plague of 1348). The gallery contains artworks that were removed from the Duomo for safekeeping and to prevent further decay. The main works are the statues that Giovanni Pisano carved for the facade; Duccio di Buoninsegna's painting of the Virgin, the *Maestà* (Duccio was a forerunner of Martini); and sculpture by Jacopo della Quercia.

Piazza del Duomo. ☎ *0577-283-048. Bus: A red or A green to Piazza del Duomo. Admission: 5,000L ($2.70). Open: Summer daily 9:30 a.m.–7:30 p.m.; winter daily 9:30 a.m.–1:30 p.m.*

Pinacoteca Nazionale

This picture gallery is housed in the fifteenth-century Palazzo Buonsignori and contains an expansive collection of art showing the unique Sienese style, which retained Greek and Byzantine influences long after realism came into play elsewhere (notably Florence), and emphasized rich coloration. Guido da Siena, an early developer of the Sienese school, is well represented, along with the more famous Duccio, the real founder of the style; his painting of the Virgin is a marvel of delicacy and pathos. Also represented are the moody Sodoma, the brothers Lorenzetti (in particular, Pietro's *Pala del Carmine* altarpiece), and Giovanni di Paolo (don't miss his beautiful little painting of the Virgin).

Via San Pietro. ☎ 0577-286-143. Bus: A red or A green to Piazza del Duomo. Admission: 8,000L ($4.30). Open: Summer Mon–Sat 9 a.m.–7 p.m. and Sun 8 a.m.– 1 p.m.; winter 8:30 a.m.–1:30 p.m., Sun 8 a.m.–1 p.m.

More cool things to see and do

Here are some more things to experience in Siena:

✔ The best thing to do in Siena, besides visiting its monuments, is watching the **Palio delle Contrade** on July 2 and August 16. This frantic horse race has been going on since the Middle Ages and is still a Sienese passion. The town's 17 *contrade* (neighborhoods) fight dearly to win the race around Piazza del Campo, which is temporarily filled with dirt for the event. Perhaps not surprisingly, this is the world's most difficult horse race and to some the most brutal — injuries aren't uncommon. It's sort of like a circus act held outdoors but performed in dead earnest. A number of colorful parades in medieval costumes — each *contrada* has its own colors — accompany the race; particularly famous is the flag juggling.

If you want to attend the Palio, don't bother buying expensive tickets for the day of the race. Standing in the middle is free — and a lot more fun. Get to Piazza del Campo very early and bring lots of refreshments (and a hat if it's sunny and hot). The square quickly fills to capacity.

✔ Not far from the **Pinacoteca Nazionale** (see "The top sights"), the church of **Sant'Agostino** (Via Mattioli 6) was built in the thirteenth century and renovated in the seventeenth, and it features a baroque interior. It houses several art treasures, such as Perugino's *Adorazione di Cristo in Croce (Adoration of the Crucifix)*, as well as works by Lorenzetti, Sodoma, and other Sienese masters. The church is open daily 8:30 a.m. to noon and 3 to 6 p.m., and admission is free.

✔ Running like a main artery through the heart of Siena, **Via di Città**, and its continuation **Via Banchi di Sopra**, are lined with medieval and Renaissance palaces. To truly experience Siena, stroll along these streets, which still have their original flagstone pavement. The buildings along these streets continue to serve important functions, like the beautiful Gothic **Palazzo Chigi-Saracini**, today the academy of music, and the **Loggia dei Mercanti**, now a court building. The palazzi that line the **Piazza Salimbeni** illustrate the city's architectural development over several hundred years and make a fine end for your walk.

And on your left, the Campo: Seeing Siena by guided tour

If you want to participate in a bus tour, call **American Express** (☎ 055-50-981) or **SitaSightseeing** (☎ 055-214-721) in Florence. Both offer similar tours of the major attractions in Tuscany, visiting the most important places and monuments, and give a tour of Siena for 90,000L ($49).

Shopping

Siena offers a variety of elegant and interesting shops. Besides the usual Italian shops, where you find clothing, shoes, leather goods, and personal and home accessories, Siena has a few shops that sell specialized Sienese crafts. Included among the city's specialties is the wine of the surrounding hills, which you can find at *enoteche* (wine stores). Note that like all spirits, *grappa* (clear Italian brandy) travels better than wine, which "bruises" and has to be left to sit for months after being carried on a plane. Try the **Enoteca San Domenico** (Via del Paradiso 56; ☎ **0577-271-181**), which offers a good selection of local wines as well as an assortment of the region's food specialties.

Local products include embroidery, and you can find a variety of hand-embroidered goods at **Siena Ricama** (Via di Città 61; ☎ **0577-288-339**), where you can also place an order for custom-made items fashioned after Renaissance patterns. Another interesting shop is **Ceramiche Santa Caterina** (Via di Città 51; ☎ **0577-280-098**), the showcase of an important producer of Sienese ceramics. This shop will even make something for you if you don't find what you're looking for among their selection of artistic ceramics.

If you're in town on a Wednesday, check out the **outdoor city market** in the streets around the Fortezza Medicea and the park of La Lizza at the north end of the historic district. It's a colorful and lively affair. Merchants set up stands selling everything from food and cooking utensils to rugs and clothes. You may not need a new screwdriver on your vacation, but it's a good place to see the hubbub of Siena. The market begins early in the morning and packs up around 2 p.m.

Fast facts: Siena

Country Code and City Code

The **country code** for Italy is **39**. The **city code** for Siena is **0577**; use this code when calling from anywhere outside or inside Italy, as well as within Siena. Include the zero every time, even when calling from abroad.

Embassies and Consulates

See "Fast Facts: Florence" in Chapter 14.

Currency Exchange

There are many exchange offices in town, near major attractions. You can also change money at banks or get cash from ATMs.

Emergencies

Ambulance ☎ **118**; Fire ☎ **115**; road assistance ACI ☎ **116**.

Hospital

The Policlinico Le Scotte is at Viale Bracci 16 (☎ **0577-585-111**).

Information

Before your trip, write to Siena's **main tourist office** at Via di Città 43 (☎ **0577-42-209**; Fax 0577-281-041). Once in town, you can pick up brochures and ask questions at the **tourist booth** at Piazza del Campo 56 (☎ **0577-280-551**). Summer hours are Monday to Saturday 8:30 a.m. to 7:30 p.m. Winter hours are Monday to Friday 8:30 a.m. to 1 p.m. and 3:30 to 6:30 p.m. and Saturday 8:30 a.m. to 1 p.m.

Internet Access

The **Internet Train** chain of shops has a branch at Via Pantaneto 54, near the Campo (☎ 0577-247-460).

Mail

The **main post office** is at Piazza Matteotti 37 (☎ 0577-42-178).

Police

Call ☎ 113; for the Carabinieri (other police force), call ☎ 112.

San Gimignano: The Manhattan of Tuscany

A perfectly preserved medieval town, **San Gimignano** is one of southern Tuscany's most famous destinations and is known as the "Manhattan of Tuscany" because of its skyscraper-like towers. Try to visit this town in the off-season so you won't be overwhelmed by tourists from all over the world.

Though it's an easy day trip from Siena or even Florence, San Gimignano is a great place to spend the night — if only so you can enjoy the pleasurable experience of seeing it (mostly) devoid of tourists.

Getting there

With a **car,** you can reach San Gimignano (which is on a secondary route southwest of Florence and northwest of Siena) using the *autostrada* Florence-Pisa and exiting at Poggibonsi. From this exit, follow the directions for San Gimignano on S324. The trip takes about 1½ hours from Florence and slightly less from Siena.

The companies **TRA-IN** (☎ 0577-204-111 or 0577-204-245) in Siena and **SITA** (☎ 055-294-955) in Florence offer regular bus service to San Gimignano, with a transfer at Poggibonsi. The bus ride from Siena takes about 50 minutes and costs 7,000L ($3.80); the trip from Florence takes half an hour longer and costs approximately 8,000L ($4.30).

You can also utilize the regular **train** service from Siena to Poggibonsi. The ride takes only about 30 minutes and costs 8,000L ($4.30). From Florence to Poggibonsi, the trip is a little longer because you must change trains in Empoli (the whole trip takes about an hour and a half and cost 8,000L/$4.30). If you're traveling from Venice or Rome, you must go to Florence first. From Poggibonsi, a regular bus service starts from outside the train station and arrives in the center of San Gimignano in about 20 minutes— but be aware that there's little service on Sundays (only two runs — one in the early morning and one around noon).

San Gimignano

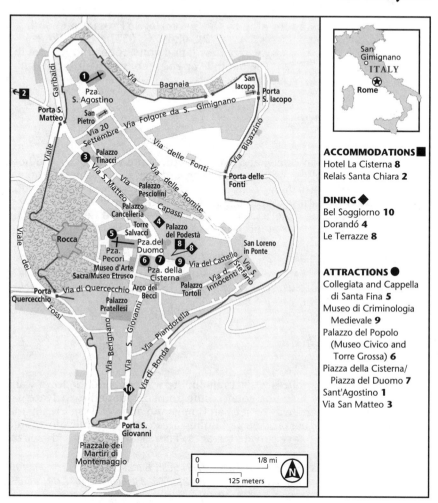

ACCOMMODATIONS■
Hotel La Cisterna **8**
Relais Santa Chiara **2**

DINING◆
Bel Soggiorno **10**
Dorandó **4**
Le Terrazze **8**

ATTRACTIONS●
Collegiata and Cappella
  di Santa Fina **5**
Museo di Criminologia
  Medievale **9**
Palazzo del Popolo
  (Museo Civico and
  Torre Grossa) **6**
Piazza della Cisterna/
  Piazza del Duomo **7**
Sant'Agostino **1**
Via San Matteo **3**

Getting around

San Gimignano is closed to private traffic. Only public buses and taxis are allowed in the center of town. The only exception is for tourists who are allowed to use their cars to reach their hotels and deposit their luggage, but they need to have the authorization arranged by the hotel (ask when you make your reservation and allow enough time for the paperwork to go through). The town is quite small, and you can easily explore it on foot.

Where to stay

For help finding a room, stop by the **Siena Hotels Promotion** booth on Piazza San Domenico (☎ **0577-288-084**; Fax: 0577-280-290; E-mail: shpnet@novamedia.it), where they'll find you a room and reserve it for a 3,000L ($1.70) fee. The booth is open Monday to Saturday 9 a.m. to 7 p.m. (open to 8 p.m. in summer).

Hotel La Cisterna

$$ Duomo

Opening onto San Gimignano's most picturesque square, this old hotel was once the only game in town. The ivy-covered medieval walls, though, hide modern-furnished guest rooms. The best — and also the most expensive — feature charming balconies with super views of the city or countryside. The hotel's restaurant is the renowned Le Terrazze (see "Where to dine," later in this chapter).

Piazza della Cisterna 24. ☎ 0577-940-328. Fax: 0577-942-080. E-mail: lacisterna@iol.it. Internet: www.sangimiano.com. Parking: 25,000L ($14) outside the walls of town. Rack rates: 160,000–190,000L ($87–$103) double, including breakfast. AE, DC, MC, V.

Relais Santa Chiara

$$$ Duomo

This beautiful hotel/resort is a ten-minute walk outside the town walls. Overlooking the luscious countryside and surrounded by private gardens, it's the grand way to see San Gimignano and yet it isn't really that expensive. The guest rooms and public areas are beautifully decorated, and some rooms have private terraces. There's also a pool and Jacuzzi.

Via Matteotti 15. ☎ 0577-940-701. Fax: 0577-942-096. E-mail: rsc@rsc.it. Internet: www.rsc.it. Parking: Free. Rack rates: 210,000–390,000L ($114–$211) double, including buffet breakfast. AE, DC, MC, V.

Where to dine

You can have an excellent meal at several places in San Gimignano. The cuisine is classic Tuscan, often of the Sienese variety, and always with a heavy accent on game. For example, you can find roasted wild boar and hare, both of which are also used to season the *pappardelle* (homemade ribbon-like flat pasta). The very famous local wine is the white Vernaccia di San Gimignano.

Dorandó

$$$ Duomo Sienese

On a tiny street just off the Collegiata, this excellent restaurant is a popular destination for locals and Italian tourists. The food is classic Tuscan, and you can find all the local specialites, including an excellent Vernaccia wine.

Vicolo dell'Oro 2; off Piazza del Duomo, turn right at the beginning of Via San Matteo. ☎ *0577-941-862. Reservations recommended. Secondi: 18,000–32,000L ($10–$17). MC, V. Open: Lunch and dinner Tues–Sun; closed two weeks in Jan.*

Bel Soggiorno

$$$ South of Duomo Tuscan

Inside the hotel of the same name, this is one of the nicest restaurants in San Gimignano. The dining room overlooks the countryside, and you can enjoy lovely views while splurging on the delectable food. You can find all the classic Tuscan specialties, plus a few unique creations of the chef. The chef is proud to use the local saffron — a rare herb that brought wealth to San Gimignano during medieval times — to flavor some of the dishes. Your choice of wines is also excellent.

Via San Giovanni 91. ☎ *0577-940-375. Reservations recommended. Secondi: 20,000–30,000L ($11–$16). AE, DC, MC, V. Open: Lunch and dinner Thurs–Tues; closed two weeks in Jan.*

Le Terrazze

$$$ Duomo Tuscan

Located in Hotel La Cisterna (see "Where to stay," earlier in this section), this restaurant is one of the classiest places to dine in San Gimignano. It features two dining rooms, one of which is original from the thirteenth century and has a classic Tuscan countryside feeling, with medieval beamed ceilings and wooden furniture. Both rooms have large windows giving you a breathtaking view of the surrounding valley. Try the *crostini*, grilled meat, or game *ragù*.

Piazza della Cisterna 24. ☎ *0577-940-328. Reservations recommended. Secondi: 22,000–34,000L ($12–19). AE, DC, MC, V. Lunch and dinner daily.*

Exploring San Gimignano

San Gimignano's **combination ticket** costs 16,000L ($9) and includes admission to the Museo Civico, Torre Grossa, Cappella di Santa Fina, and Museo di Arte Sacra–Museo Etrusco (this museum contains sculptures from the thirteenth to fifteenth century — none of great note — and also a small collection of Etruscan and Roman artifacts).

The top sights

The medieval towers attached to the local palazzi have become the symbol of the town and the source of its nickname, San Gimignano delle Belle Torri (San Gimignano of the beautiful towers). Once the symbol of palace-owners' wealth, the towers flourished in San Gimignano during its period of great economic success in the thirteenth century. So much competition existed in tower-building — always taller and taller — that the government made a law forbidding any tower taller than the tower on the Palazzo del Popolo — the seat of the government.

The town's economic success was suddenly wiped out by the plague (which hit San Gimignano several times between the fourteenth and the seventeenth centuries), a disaster that preserved the town, allowing it to remain basically intact as a typical walled medieval town, with no modern additions. Obviously, time has taken its toll and some of the buildings have collapsed. Of the original 72 or so towers, only 15 remain today, including the tower on the Palazzo del Popolo (177 feet, 3 inches).

The triangular **Piazza della Cisterna,** together with the attached **Piazza del Duomo,** constitutes the heart of the town. Piazza della Cisterna, an elegant example of medieval architecture, is one of the most attractive sights in San Gimignano. At the center of the square (beautifully paved with bricks) is the well that gives access to the underlying cistern. Surrounding the square are some of the town's important palaces, such as the **Palazzo Tortoli-Treccani** at no. 22, with its elegant double row of *bifora* ("bifold;" divided by a stone arch) windows.

Collegiata and Cappella di Santa Fin

Still called the Duomo by locals — long ago, the town lost its bishop and the cathedral was downgraded to a Collegiata — the basilica opens onto a beautiful square connected to Piazza della Cisterna. Built in the twelfth century, the Collegiata has a very plain unfinished facade but a gorgeously decorated Romanesque interior with tiger-striped arches and a galaxy of gold stars. Among the treasures inside are the wooden statues of *Gabriele* and *Annunziata* by Jacopo della Quercia and the fourteenth-century frescoes decorating the naves. The right nave's last chapel is the **Cappella di Santa Fina (Chapel of St. Fina),** one of the most beautiful of the Tuscan Renaissance. Designed by Giuliano and Benedetto da Maiano — Benedetto also carved the panel of the altar — it boasts a beautiful cycle of frescoes by Domenico Ghirlandaio describing the life of a local girl named Fina, who became the town's patron saint.

Piazza del Duomo. ☎ *0577-940-316. Admission: Church free; Cappella di Santa Fina 6,000L ($3.25) adults, 3,000L ($1.60) children 6–18. Open: Summer Mon–Fri 9:30 a.m.–7:30 p.m., Sat 9:30 a.m.–5 p.m., and Sun 1–5 p.m.; winter Mon–Sat 9:30 a.m.–5 p.m., Sun 1–5 p.m.*

Palazzo del Popolo (Museo Civico and Torre Grossa)

The Palazzo del Popolo (the government's palace) was built between 1288 and 1323 — the crenels were added in the nineteenth century. Its tower, the **Torre Grossa (Big Tower)** — the tallest in town — was added in 1311. Visiting the Torre Grossa awards you with a superb view over the town. The interior of the palace is decorated with great frescoes and furnishings from the fourteenth and fifteenth centuries. Particularly worth visiting in the **Museu Civico** inside the palace is the *Sala di Dante (Dante's Room)*, which you reach via an external staircase from the courtyard. (This external staircase is decorated with splendid frescoes by Lippo Memmi — his *Maestà* is considered a masterpiece.) The museum also houses a *pinacoteca* (picture gallery), which includes works by the early Sienese painter Guido da Siena, Filippino Lippi's *Annunciation,* and Pinturicchio's *Madonna in Glory with Saints.*

Piazza del Duomo 1. ☎ **0577-990-312.** *Admission: 7,000L ($3.80) adults, 5,000L ($2.70) youth under 18; Torre Grossa 8,000L ($4.30). Open: Summer daily 9:30 a.m.–7 p.m.; Winter Tues–Sun 9:30 a.m.–12:30 p.m. and 2:30–4:30 p.m.*

More cool things to see and do

San Gimignano is a small town but rich in sights. If you have more time, you may want to explore more of the medieval delights of this once very important artistic and commercial center. Here are a few more choices:

- ✔ **Sant'Agostino** (Piazza Sant'Agostino; ☎ **0577-940-383**) is a beautiful thirteenth-century Romanesque-Gothic church. Its plain facade hides a superb cycle of frescoes by Benozzo Gozzoli on the life of St. Augustine; also interesting is his fresco of St. Sebastian on the third altar to the left. The church is open daily 7 a.m. to noon and 3 to 6 p.m. (open to 7 p.m. in summer), and admission is free.

- ✔ **Via San Matteo** is a section of the Via Francigena, the medieval highway to France. Besides its historic interest — it was the most important communication path between northern and southern Europe — it's a beautiful section of medieval San Gimignano, lined with palaces and towers.

- ✔ The **Museo di Criminologia Medievale (Medieval Criminology Museum)** is housed in the Torre del Diavolo (Devil's Tower) and contains an ample choice of torture instruments as well as a collection of drawings and etchings concerning their use, complete with descriptions in English. These displays are creepy but soberingly relevant, especially considering that modern versions of these instruments are still used today. To visit the museum, go to Via del Castello 1, off Piazza della Cisterna. Call ☎ **0577-942-243** for more information.

And on your left, another tower: Seeing San Gimignano by guided tour

If you want to participate in a bus tour, call **American Express** (☎ **055-50-981**) or **SitaSightseeing** (☎ **055-214-721**) in Florence. Both companies offer tours of the major attractions in Tuscany, including San Gimignano, for about 90,000L ($49).

Fast Facts: San Gimignano

Country Code and City Code

The **country code** for Italy is **39**. The **city code** for San Gimignano is **0577**; use this city code when calling from anywhere outside or inside Italy, even within San Gimignano, and always include the zero whether you are calling from Italy or from abroad.

Embassies and Consulates

The nearest are in Florence; See "Fast Facts: Florence" in Chapter 14.

Currency exchange

You can exchange money at the tourist office (see the tourist office information, later in this chapter) and in banks in San Gimignano that have ATMs.

Emergencies

Ambulance and *Pronto Soccorso* (first aid) ☎ **118**; Fire ☎ **115**; road assistance, ACI ☎ **116**.

Hospital

The nearest hospital is the **Ospedale Poggibonsi** (Via Pisana 2; ☎ **0577-915-555**).

Information

The **Pro Loco office (tourist office)** is at Piazza Duomo 1 (☎ **0577-940-008**; fax 0577-940-903). Summer hours are daily 9 a.m. to 1 p.m. and 3 to 7 p.m. Winter hours are 9 a.m. to 1 p.m. and 2 to 6 p.m. daily.

Mail

The **Ufficio Postale** (post office) is at Piazza delle Erbe 8 (☎ **0577-941-983**).

Police

Call ☎ **113**; for the Carabinieri (other police force), call ☎ **112**.

Chapter 17

Umbria

. . . .

In This Chapter

▶ Taking in beautiful medieval Perugia and sweet Baci

▶ Visiting saints and monasteries in Assisi

▶ Enjoying the music festivals in Spoleto

. . . .

*U*mbria is a small region tucked away between Lazio (the region in which Rome is located); Toscana (Tuscany), where Florence is located; and the Marches, with no access to the sea. Famous for its deep green hills and natural beauty, it's also a region of art and religious accomplishments. It is the land of San Francesco (St. Francis) and Santa Chiara (St. Clare), as well as of painter Pietro Vannucci, who brought fame to himself and his town under the name "Il Perugino." Like other parts of Italy, Umbria has its own food specialties, including *tartufi* (truffles) and *porcini* mushrooms.

Perugia and Spoleto make excellent starting points from which to visit the rest of this region. Keep in mind, though, that you can reach all destinations in Umbria as day trips from Florence or Rome.

What's Where?: Umbria and Its Major Attractions

Umbria is traversed north-to-south by the river Tevere, the river of Rome that ends at the sea near Ostia Antica (see Chapter 13). In its early segment, the river goes through ravines and steep valleys, which explains why **Perugia,** the region's capital, wasn't built along the river. At the heart of Umbria, this delightful city is rich in art and historic sights as well as being a lively university town. The city's highlights are the Palazzo dei Priori and its magnificent art and the famous Fontana Maggiore — and nowhere else will you find a Perugina chocolate as big as your rental car!

Not far away to the east is **Assisi,** hometown of San Francesco, Italy's patron saint. The 1997 earthquakes and aftershocks luckily didn't destroy the town's monuments entirely and spared most of the masterpieces by the major artists of the Renaissance. The highpoints of Assisi are the Basilica di San Francesco and its frescoes, the Basilica di Santa Chiara, and the Eremo delle Carceri.

Spoleto is famous for its music and art festivals — the Festival di Spoleto and the Stagione Lirica — but it's also a delightful small medieval town offering beautiful vistas, a majestic Duomo, and the Ponte delle Torri.

Enticing Perugia: Home of Perugina

Etruscan in origin, **Perugia** developed as an important urban center during the Middle Ages and the Renaissance. It was infamous during the Renaissance for its fierce battles and was finally subjugated by the popes, who imposed a few hundred years of steady rule. The city is renowned today for its universities and art — and for its chocolate, as it's the home of the famous chocolate house of Perugina.

Getting there

Because Perugia lies on a secondary line, only a few direct **trains** connect it to Florence or Rome. From Rome, the ride takes about 2¾ hours and costs 20,600L ($11); from Florence, it's 2½ hours and 14,500L ($8), and you have to change in Terontola. From Venice, you have to go to Florence first; the whole trip takes around six hours and costs 62,000L ($34). Trains arrive at the **Stazione FS Perugia** (☎ 075-500-7467) on Piazza Vittorio Veneto. From there you can catch one of many buses to Piazza Italia in the town center (a trip of about 15 minutes). Perugia is also on a privately run line connecting Sansepolcro to Terni with a frequent schedule. These trains arrive and depart from the **Stazione Sant'Anna** (☎ 075-572-9121) in the center of town.

The company **SULGA** (☎ 075-500-9641) has three daily **bus** runs from Rome and one from Florence; the trip from Rome takes 2½ hours and costs about 22,000L ($12); the trip from Florence is 45 minutes shorter and costs about 19,000L ($10). The company **SITA** (☎ 055-214-721) also makes one daily run to and from Florence for about the same price. The company **ASP** (☎ 075-573-1707) connects Perugia with Assisi on a daily basis for 5,000L ($2.70) and with other cities in Umbria. Buses arrive in Perugia in Piazza Partigiani, an escalator ride from Piazza Italia at the center of town.

Perugia is 180 km (115 miles) from Rome and 150 km (94 miles) from Florence. If you're **driving** from Florence, take A1 to the Val di Chiana Bettolle-Sinalunga exit and switch to SS75bis to Perugia. From Rome, take A1 to Orte and then SS204 to SS36 to Perugia. The center of the historic town is at the top of a steep hill; because the center has restricted traffic, you have to leave your car in one of the numerous parking lots — a convenient one is Piazza Partigiani's underground parking lot, just south of the historic center, but they're all linked to the center by elevators or escalators.

Perugia

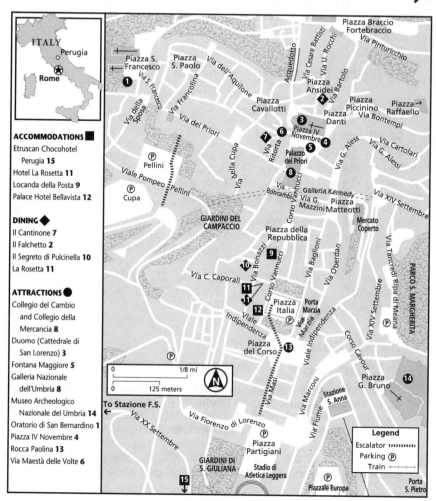

ITALY
Perugia
Rome

ACCOMMODATIONS ■
Etruscan Chocohotel
  Perugia **15**
Hotel La Rosetta **11**
Locanda della Posta **9**
Palace Hotel Bellavista **12**

DINING ◆
Il Cantinone **7**
Il Falchetto **2**
Il Segreto di Pulcinella **10**
La Rosetta **11**

ATTRACTIONS ●
Collegio del Cambio
  and Collegio della
  Mercancia **8**
Duomo (Cattedrale di
  San Lorenzo) **3**
Fontana Maggiore **5**
Galleria Nazionale
  dell'Umbria **8**
Museo Archeologico
  Nazionale del Umbria **14**
Oratorio di San Bernardino **1**
Piazza IV Novembre **4**
Rocca Paolina **13**
Via Maestà delle Volte **6**

Legend
Escalator ▪▪▪▪▪▪▪▪▪
Parking Ⓟ
Train ├──┼──┤

You're allowed to drive up into town to bring your luggage to your
hotel before parking — but keep an eye on it (someone broke the
window of our rental car in the few minutes we left it unattended).
Maybe because of its bloody past, Perugia has a reputation for having a
slightly violent edge (though, as elsewhere in Italy, physical violence
isn't as much a concern as theft).

Getting around

The historic center has a relatively simple layout along Corso Vannucci,
with the bus and train arrivals at one end (at the bottom of a public
escalator) in Piazza Italia and the major sites on Piazza IV Novembre

at the other end. As often in small medieval Italian towns, Perugia is easily visited on foot; however, the city maintains a system of buses with the central hub in Piazza Italia. If you want a **taxi,** call ☎ 075-500-4888.

Where to stay

Etruscan Chocohotel Perugia

$$ Piazza dei Partigiani

This almost glitzy (for Italy) hotel offers style at a moderate price. All the air-conditioned guest rooms have modern Italian-style furniture and large baths. The real draw, though, is staying in a "chocohotel": Each floor is dedicated to a type of chocolate (milk, dark, gianduia) and each room has a "chocodesk" . . . we'll leave you to discover that surprise. The restaurant features a cocoa-based menu, and in the chocostore you can sample many concoctions. Nonchocolate amenities include a large roof deck with a panoramic view and a good-sized pool.

Via Campo di Marte 134. ☎ *075-583-7314. Fax: 075-583-7314. E-mail:* etruscan@ chocohotel.it. *Internet:* www.chocohotel.it. *Parking: Free. Rack rates: 140,000–200,000L ($76–$108). AE, DC, MC, V.*

Hotel La Rosetta

$$ Piazza Italia

Considered one of the best hotels in town, La Rosetta is very convenient and boasts a national historic landmark in one of its guest rooms (suite 55, which is richly decorated with frescoes). The rooms vary widely in furnishings but are uniformly comfortable, airy, and well kept.

Piazza Italia 19. ☎ *075-572-0841. Fax: 075-572-0841. Parking: 30,000L ($16). Rack rates: 199,000–245,000L ($108–$132) double, including breakfast. AE, DC.*

Locanda della Posta

$$$ Corso Vannucci

The first hotel to open in Perugia — it counts Goethe among its past guests — the Locanda is an old-fashioned place. Although the atmosphere is very classic, the hotel was revamped with modern amenities, and the commodious guest rooms have up-to-date baths and air-conditioning. The management is friendly and available.

Corso Vannucci 97. ☎ *075-572-8925. Fax: 075-572-2413. E-mail:* locanda@ assind.perugia.it. *Bus: 1 to Piazza Vittorio Emanuele. Parking: 20,000L ($11) Rack rates: 220,000–320,000L ($119–$173) double, including buffet breakfast. AE, DC, MC, V.*

Palace Hotel Bellavista

$$ Piazza Italia

Once part of Perugia's most expensive hotel — still existing next door — the Bellavista has a curious but charming layout. The public areas are grand and bestow a feeling of timeless elegance, but the rest of the hotel is modern. The spacious guest rooms have contemporary furnishings and functional baths, and the service is excellent.

Piazza Italia 12. ☎ *075-572-0741. Fax: 075-572-9092. Parking: 25,000L ($14). Rack rates: 200,000–240,000L ($108–$130) double, including breakfast. AE, DC, MC, V.*

Where to dine

Landlocked Umbria developed a cuisine relying heavily on regional produce. Particularly famous for its truffles, both black and white, it uses them lavishly in its cuisine, usually under the label *alla Norcina* (in the manner of Norcia). Another specialty of Umbria — and Norcia — is wild boar, so *alla Norcina* might also refer to a sauce prepared with the wild boar sausages that make Norcia famous (if you're lucky, you may even get both).

A university town, Perugia has a lot of *pizzerie* and cheap *trattorie* where you can have a bite in a lively casual atmosphere; you'll often see crowds of young people waiting to get into these places.

Il Cantinone

$$$ Piazza Italia   Umbrian

Just off Piazza IV Novembre, in the medieval district, this restaurant has vaulted ceilings and a simple decor. The food is traditional and excellent; try the grilled meats or the *torello alla Perugina* (veal with chicken livers), one of Perugia's specialties.

Via Ritorta 6. ☎ *075-573-4130. Reservations recommended. Secondi: 12,000–28,000L ($7–$19). AE, DC, MC, V. Open: Lunch and dinner Wed–Mon.*

Il Falchetto

$$$$$ Duomo   Umbrian

With a real medieval atmosphere (one dining room is from the fourteenth century) and a traditional menu, Falchetto is an excellent place for discovering Umbrian cuisine — especially if you're in the mood for a splurge. Try the *lepre alle olive* (hare with olives). The terrace is particularly in demand during the summer Umbria Jazz concerts (see "More cool things to see and do" later in this chapter).

Via Bartolo 20. ☎ *075-573-1775. Reservations recommended. Secondi: 30,000–60,000L ($16–$32). AE, DC, MC, V. Open: Lunch and dinner Tues–Sun.*

Il Segreto di Pulcinella

$$ Piazza Italia   Pizza

To give your wallet a break, you may want to sample the tasty pizza prepared in this popular hangout. It's located just a couple of blocks off the most crowded street of the historic center.

Via Larga 8. ☎ 075-573-6284. Reservations recommended on weekends. Pizza: 10,000–16,000L ($5–$9). No credit cards accepted. Open: Lunch and dinner Wed–Mon.

La Rosetta

$$$ Piazza Italia   Umbrian

In the hotel by the same name, La Rosetta is a famous restaurant in Perugia, offering a large choice of dishes prepared according to the best Umbrian tradition. Try the *spaghetti alla Norcina* (with truffles) or the *scaloppine alla Perugina* (veal sautéed with wine and chicken livers).

Piazza Italia 19. ☎ 075-572-0841. Reservations recommended. Secondi: 15,000–40,000L ($8–$22). AE, DC, MC, V. Open: Lunch and dinner daily.

Exploring Perugia

Although it would be best to have a couple of days to really savor the treasures of the capital of Umbria — both the visual and the edible arts — Perugia is a small town you can easily visit as a day trip from Rome or Florence. For the location of the tourist office, see "Fast Facts: Perugia."

The top sights

Once a Roman reservoir, **Piazza IV Novembre** is the heart of Perugia. On one side is the fifteenth-century facade of the **Duomo (Cattedrale di San Lorenzo)** — a beautiful face on an otherwise dull baroque church. On the other side is the magnificent thirteenth-century **Palazzo dei Priori,** created as the seat of the government and one of the finest examples of Gothic architecture in Italy. Built between 1298 and 1353, the palazzo is a striking travertine building with white and red marble inlays. The main portal — accessible by a wide semicircular staircase — is off-center in the facade; it leads to the spacious Sala dei Notari (Hall of the Notables). There are two bronzes over the door, of the griffin and the lion, symbols of the city. You can visit the palazzo's many frescoed rooms (summer daily 9 a.m. to 1 p.m. and 3 to 7 p.m.; winter Tuesday to Sunday 9 a.m. to 1 p.m. and 3 to 7 p.m.). It also houses the Collegio del Cambio and the Galleria Nazionale dell'Umbria (see descriptions in the following paragraphs). In front of the palace, the **Fontana Maggiore (Grand Fountain),** a Gothic masterpiece carved by the famous Pisan sculptors Nicola and Giovanni Pisano, was under restoration for many years and was finished in 2000. Departing from the piazza is **Via Maestà delle Volte,** a typical medieval street with covered passages.

Collegio del Cambio and Collegio della Mercancia

On the Palazzo dei Priori's ground floor, the **Collegio del Cambio** was the goods exchange in Renaissance times. This section of the palace is very interesting for its architecture and also for its magnificent frescoed ceilings, in particular those of the **Sala dell'Udienza (Hall of the Audience)** by Perugino and his assistants, one of whom was a young Raphael. These frescoes illustrate the life of Christ; there's also a self-portrait of Perugino himself. Also of interest is the **Cappella di S. J. Batista (Chapel of S. J. Batista),** with frescoes by Giannicola di Paolo. If you enter at Corso Vannucci 15, you'll find the **Collegio della Mercancia (Merchant's Guild),** decorated with intricately carved wood paneling and beautiful vaulted ceilings.

Palazzo dei Priori, Corso Vannucci 25. ☎ *075-572-8599. Collegio della Mercancia, Corso Vannucci 15.* ☎ *075-573-0366. Admission: Collegio del Cambio 5,000L ($2.70); Collegio della Mercancia 2,000L ($1.10); combined ticket to both 6,000L ($3.25). Open: Collegio del Cambio, summer Mon–Sat 9 a.m.–12:30 p.m. and 2–5:30 p.m., Sun 9 a.m.–12:30 p.m.; winter Tues–Sat 8 a.m.–2 p.m., Sun 9 a.m.–12:30 p.m. Collegio della Mercancia Mon–Sat 9 a.m.–1 p.m. and 2:30–5:30 p.m., Sun 9 a.m.–1 p.m.*

Galleria Nazionale dell'Umbria

On the Palazzo dei Priori's third floor, this gallery is remarkably well organized, with explanatory material for each work. The collection of Umbrian art from the thirteenth to the nineteenth century is indeed rich, including a number of marvelous Peruginos, a Gentile da Fabriano *Madonna and Child*, and a famous (and stunning) Piero della Francesco polyptych. An interactive computer display provides a guide to the latter piece. This museum is strong in the late medieval/early Renaissance period, documenting the important phase during which Giotto and Cimabue revolutionized painting techniques. It's probably the most enjoyable Italian museum outside the famous ones in the larger cities.

Palazzo dei Priori, Corso Vannucci 19. ☎ *075-574-1257. Admission: 8,000L ($4.30). Open: Mon–Sat 9 a.m.–7 p.m., Sun 9 a.m.–1 p.m.; closed the first Mon of every month.*

Museo Archeologico Nazionale del Umbria

Founded at the end of the eighteenth century, this museum occupies a former convent and is divided into a prehistoric section and an Etruscan-Roman section. The latter includes jewelry, funerary urns, statues, and other objects. Of particular interest are the sets of objects that, according to Etruscan custom, were entombed with the dead; these come from the necropoli of Frontone and Monte Luce. You can also see the Cippo **Perugino,** the stone that marked the boundary of Perugia in Etruscan times — it's important for its long inscription in Etruscan (a language still not fully understood).

Piazza G. Bruno 10. ☎ *075-572-7141. Admission: 4,000L ($2.15). Open: Mon–Sat 9 a.m.–1 p.m. and 2:30–7 p.m., Sun 9 a.m.–1 p.m.*

Oratorio di San Bernardino

Built in 1461 and designed by Agostino di Duccio, this oratory is a particularly attractive example of northern Italian Renaissance architecture. Constructed of multicolored marble, the church has a facade decorated with intricate reliefs illustrating the life of the saint. A paleo-Christian sarcophagus (fourth century) is now the main altar.

Piazza San Francesco, at the end of Via dei Priori. Admission: Free. Open: Daily 9 a.m.–12:30 p.m. and 3–6 p.m.

More cool things to see and do

If you have some extra time to spend in Perugia, check out some of these other sights:

✔ The **Rocca Paolina,** built in 1540 by Pope Paul III (hence the name) and designed by the famous architect Antonio da Sangallo the Younger, is a fortress that was constructed on top of medieval buildings and even earlier structures (you can still see an arch from the original Etruscan city walls). The upper part of the Rocca was demolished in 1860, but the lower sections were preserved, and the archaeological site has now been excavated. By a series of escalators, you can see the inside, viewing the fortification's huge walls, parts of dwellings and ancient streets, and even fragments of the ancient stadium where a forerunner of soccer was played. There are three main entrances: Piazza Italia, Via Marzia, and Via Masi. The Rocca is open daily 9 a.m. to 1 p.m. and 4 to 7 p.m., and admission is free.

✔ Perugia owes its fame to the world-famous chocolate manufacturer Perugina, and Perugina's claim to fame is its brilliant creation of Baci ("kisses"). You might've seen these bonbons — wrapped in silver paper speckled with purple-blue stars — in your country. They're delicious balls of soft chocolate mixed with finely chopped hazelnuts, each topped by a whole toasted hazelnut and dipped in dark chocolate. Call ☎ 075-52-761 in advance to schedule a free tour of the **Perugina chocolate factory,** in the neighborhood of San Sisto, 6 km (3 miles) west of the city center (take a cab). A delicious experience! Inside the factory is a **Museo Storico,** the historic museum of the Perugina factory (☎ 075-527-6796); it's open Monday to Friday 9 a.m. to 1 p.m. and 2:30 to 5 p.m. (Saturday and Sunday by appointment only), and admission is free.

✔ Because of its role in the chocolate world, Perugia is the seat of many an event involving the dark delicacy. The most important is the international **Eurochocolate** (☎ 075-572-3327; Internet: www.chocolate.perugia.it), showcasing the latest developments in the centuries-old art of making chocolate (held in October). You can buy chocolate by weight in huge pieces in Perugia — and at Easter they make a giant Bacio weighing hundreds of kilos and let children and chocolate-mad adults hack away at it!

✔ Come in September for the **Sagra Musicale Umbra,** a festival of sacred music (Associazione Sagra Musical Umbra, Via Podianai 11; ☎ **075-572-1374;** Fax: 075-572-7614), or the **Perugia Classico**, a festival of classical music (Comitato Promotore Perugia Classico, c/o Comune di Perugia, Via Eburnea 9; ☎ **075-577-2253;** Fax: 075-577-2255).

✔ The **Umbria Jazz Festival,** one of Europe's major jazz festivals, attracts big names from all over the world. It takes place in the second half of July and has a mini winter version over the New Year's holiday. Contact the **Associazione Umbria Jazz** (Piazza Danti 28, Casella Postale 228; ☎ **075-573-2432;** Fax: 075-572-2656; Internet: www.umbriajazz.com).

Nightlife

As a university town, Perugia enjoys a lively nightlife. Things happen Italian style, and so one of the main things to do is stroll along Corso Vannucci showing off your smart clothing and sampling a gelato or visiting one or more of the cafes and then continuing with a visit to one of the many pubs.

Other Umbrian favorites

Gubbio: Known as the "Town of Festivals," Gubbio, 39 km (24 miles) northeast of Perugia, rests on the side of a mountain offering lovely vistas of the surrounding countryside. The town is known for its medieval palaces, interesting churches, and Roman ruins.

Todi: Another hill town, 40 km (24 miles) south of Perugia, Todi preserves its medieval flavor. It attracts art pilgrims with its masterpiece, the High Renaissance Templo di Santa Maria della Consolazione, a domed structure on a Greek cross plan.

Orvieto: Orvieto, 86 km (52 miles) from Perugia, is famous for its Duomo, whose facade features beautiful mosaics and Gothic stone work. Inside is another treasure, a marvelous fresco cycle begun by Fra Angelico. The town also boasts some interesting Etruscan ruins; Orvieto also gave its name to the delicious white wine known generally as Orvieto Classico.

Deruta: Deruta has been one of Italy's great centers for artists of ceramics since the fourteenth century. Lying 25 km (16 miles) south of Perugia, Deruta now has large modern factories that turn out plates, bowls, and vases in traditional colors that you can buy in the various factory showrooms on the new town's main shopping strip. If you get away from the touristic center, you can find true artisans maintaining their age-old art, and you may pick up a handsome handpainted piece.

Among the many cafes where Perugians congregate, we recommend a couple of particularly nice places: **Caffè del Cambio** (Corso Van-nucci 29; ☎ 075-572-4165) is a real temple of sweets, with a long counter where you can sample ice cream and pastries. **Pasticceria Sandri** (Corso Vannucci 32; ☎ 075-572-4112) serves not only pastries and sweets but also sandwiches and even regular meals. Of course, the two jazz festivals, the major summer event and the winter version, add a whole other dimension to social life in Perugia.

Fast Facts: Perugia

Country Code and City Code

The **country code** for Italy is **39**. The **city code** for Perugia is **075**; use this code when calling from anywhere outside or inside Italy, even within Perugia itself (include the zero every time, even when calling from abroad).

Embassies and Consulates

See "Fast Facts: Florence" in Chapter 14 and "Fast Facts: Rome" in Chapter 12.

Currency Exchange

You can change money at the **F.S. Piazza Vittorio Veneto** rail station and **Genefin** at Via Pinturicchio 14–16 and also at the numerous banks that have ATMs.

Emergencies

Ambulance and *Pronto Soccorso (first aid)*, ☎ 118; Fire, ☎ 115; road assistance, ☎ 116.

Hospital

The **Ospedale Monteluce** is on Piazza Monteluce (☎ 075-57-81).

Information

You can write for information to Perugia's main tourist office: **APT** (Via Mazzini 21; ☎ 075-572-3327; Fax: 075-573-6828). Once in town, visit its **tourist booth** just off the stairs of the Palazzo dei Priori at Piazza IV November 3 (☎ 075-573-6458), open daily 9 a.m. to 1 p.m. and 4 to 6 p.m.

Mail

The **Ufficio Postale** is on Piazza Matteotti.

Police

Call ☎ 113; for the Carabinieri (other police force), call ☎ 112.

Visiting Assisi: An Artistic and Religious Pilgrimage

The hometown of Italy's patron saint, St. Francis (San Francesco), **Assisi** is famous around the world for its art and religious monuments. Many of its visitors aren't tourists but pilgrims who come to honor the humble man who was said to speak with animals and who created the Franciscan order. San Francesco was born in 1182 to a wealthy merchant family and died in 1226 in a simple hut. How he traversed the social scale and caused a revolution in Christianity is a remarkable story.

In 1209, after a reckless youth and even imprisonment, Francis experienced visions that led him to sell his father's cloth and give away the proceeds. He tried to follow the Bible literally and live the life of Christ, publicly renouncing his inheritance and rejecting wealth absolutely (this didn't endear him to the rich medieval church hierarchy). Two years before his death, he received the stigmata on a mountaintop — this and other scenes from his life were popular subjects for painters of the late medieval period and the Renaissance.

Assisi is only a small town of about 3,000 souls, though millions flock to it every year. You can easily visit it on a day trip from Florence or Rome but can also stay overnight. For the location of the tourist office, see "Fast Facts: Assisi," later in this chapter.

Getting there

Assisi isn't on a main **train** line but a spur. If you're coming from Perugia or Rome, you'll have to change at Foligno; from Florence, you'll have to change in Terontola. Trains for Assisi are frequent from each of these stations. A ticket from Rome and Florence costs about 25,000L ($14) and from Perugia (a half hour away) about 3,000L ($1.60). Figure on 3½ hours from Rome and 3 hours from Florence, depending on connections. Trains arrive at the rail station of **Santa Maria degli Angeli,** a small town 6 km (3¾ miles) from Assisi. The station is well connected to the historic center of Assisi by a shuttle bus departing every half hour and stopping in Piazza Matteotti, within Assisi's walls; the price is 2,500L ($1.35). There also are taxis available at the station, but they cost much more.

The bus company **ASP** (☎ **075-573-1707**) connects Perugia with Assisi on a frequent schedule — about every half hour. Buses leave Perugia from Piazza Partigiani and arrive at Piazza Matteotti behind the Duomo for 5,000L ($2.70). There are also daily runs from Florence and Rome — one a day from Rome (a 3-hour trip costing 30,000L/$16) and two from Florence (a 2½-hour trip costing 25,000L/$14).

Assisi is 27 km (16.9 miles) from Perugia. If you're driving, take SS3 in the direction of Foligno, then look for the exit for Assisi. The town is almost totally closed to traffic, so you have to park outside. You can park under Piazza Matteotti where there's a large lot — but "large" doesn't mean much when the place is packed with thousands of tourists and pilgrims. If you're going in summer, get there early or use public transportation. All parking lots outside the walls are connected with the town center by **public minibuses** costing 1,200L (65¢); you can buy tickets at bars, tobacconists, and newsstands.

Getting around

Assisi is small and can be seen on foot since the town's attractions are concentrated around the main square. However, outside Assisi are some interesting sights you could walk to — but it's far easier to get

Assisi

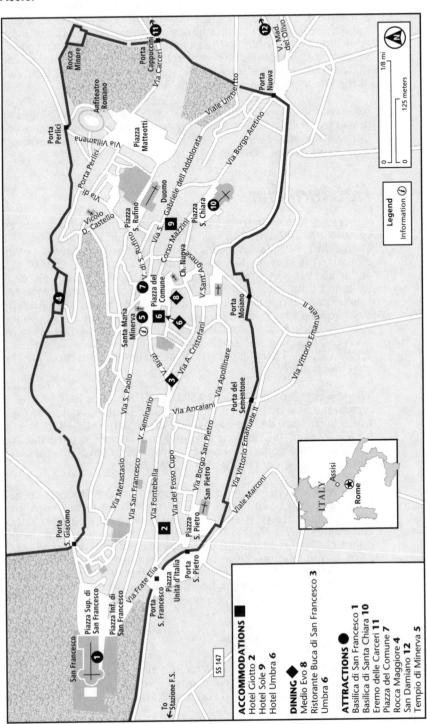

Legend
Information ⓘ

ACCOMMODATIONS ■
Hotel Giotto **2**
Hotel Sole **9**
Hotel Umbra **6**

DINING ◆
Medio Evo **8**
Ristorante Buca di San Francesco **3**
Umbra **6**

ATTRACTIONS ●
Basilica di San Francesco **1**
Basilica di Santa Chiara **10**
Eremo delle Carceri **11**
Piazza del Comune **7**
Rocca Maggiore **4**
San Damiano **12**
Tempio di Minerva **5**

there by public transportation or taxi. The public minibus service links all major sites (see "Getting there"). You can also buy tickets on the bus at a surcharge. If you prefer to take a **taxi,** look for the several stations in town where taxis wait for their fares or call ☎ **075-813-193.**

Where to stay

If you want to come to Assisi for religious holidays like Easter, the Feast of St. Francis (October 3–4), and the Calendimaggio in May, you'll have to *reserve as much as half a year or more in advance.* Otherwise, the only choices left may be big, ugly hotels in Santa Maria degli Angeli, the nearby little town.

At the tourist office (see "Fast Facts: Assisi" later in the chapter) you can get help with accommodations — but don't count on finding a room in the high season without a reservation.

Hotel Giotto

$$ Porta San Francesco

This big hotel caters to groups but is still a good choice, and you may have a chance of finding a room here if you didn't plan ahead. The guest rooms are modern, even though the building isn't (a work of the centuries). Built on the side of a hill, it offers sweeping vistas, terraces, and a garden.

Via Fontebella 41. ☎ *075-812-209. Fax: 075-816-479. Parking: Free. Rack rates: 210,000L ($114) double, including breakfast. AE, DC, MC, V.*

Hotel Sole

$ Piazza del Comune

In the center of town and only a few steps from Santa Chiara, this hotel probably won't be the greatest place you ever stayed in, but it's convenient; though the guest rooms are a little worn, the accoutrements are serviceable (there are baths in all but 2 of the 37 rooms). The hotel's excellent restaurant is in the ancient palazzo; across the street is the annex, the more modern half.

Corso Mazzini 35, just off Piazza del Comune (east side). ☎ *075-812-373 or 075-812-922. Fax: 075-813-706. E-mail: sole@techonet.it. Rack rates: 100,000L ($54) double. AE, DC, MC, V.*

Hotel Umbra

$$ Piazza del Comune

Like many other hotels in Umbria and Tuscany, this one is housed in an old palazzo, but the Umbra has more of the touches one looks for — old or even antique furniture, views of the surrounding hills and valleys, renovated bathrooms, and balconies. The Umbra's restaurant (see "Where to dine") is particularly good and popular with locals as well as guests. The walled garden is an especially nice place to take a meal if you're in town in summer.

Via degli Archi 6, just off Piazza del Comune (west side). ☎ 075-812-240. Fax: 075-813-653. E-mail: humbra@mail.caribusiness.it. *Parking: 15,000L ($8). Rack rates: 180,000–230,000L ($97–124) double. Closed mid-Jan to mid-Mar. AE, DC, MC, V.*

Where to dine

Assisi's food is basically the same as that of Perugia. There are lots of restaurants in town — some very touristy, others more authentic. Prices in general are above average.

Medio Evo

$$$ Piazza del Comune   Umbrian/Italian

A little south of Piazza del Comune, this family-run restaurant may be the town's most interesting place to eat, combining traditional Umbrian cuisine with accents from other cultures. The building itself rests on 1,000-year-old foundations (note the name, which means "Middle Ages") and has vaulted medieval ceilings. For a *primo,* try the *tortelloni* (large ravioli) or pasta with truffles; for a *secondo,* try one of the variety of grilled and roasted meats.

Via dell' Arco dei Priori 4/b. ☎ 075-813-068. Reservations recommended. Secondi: 18,000–28,000L ($10–$19). AE, DC, MC, V. Open: Lunch and dinner Thurs–Tues; closed a month in Jan/Feb and three weeks in July.

Ristorante Buca di San Francesco

$$$$ Piazza del Comune   Umbrian

In the center of town, this restaurant is housed in a medieval building and serves traditional, if pricey, food. The menu is excellent and changes with the seasons and what's available at the market. One dish we particularly like is the *cannelloni* (homemade pasta tubes filled with cheese or meat and served with tomato sauce). The garden provides a view of Assisi's historic center.

Via Brizzi 1. ☎ 075-812-204. Reservations recommended. Secondi: 25,000–40,000L ($14–$22). AE, DC, MC, V. Open: Lunch and dinner Tues–Sun; closed two weeks in July.

Umbra

$$$ Piazza del Comune   Umbrian

In the hotel of the same name, this popular restaurant opened nearly 80 years ago and is an institution. Don't miss the garden if the weather is fine. Umbra serves traditional dishes from the countryside, including *primi* with truffles (like the coveted white ones, when in season) and well-prepared *secondi*.

Via degli Archi 6. ☎ *075-812-240. Reservations recommended. Second: 17,000–30,000L ($9–$16). AE, DC, MC, V. Open: Lunch and dinner Mon–Sun; closed mid-Jan to mid-Mar.*

Exploring Assisi

The 1997 earthquakes and multiple aftershocks that rocked Umbria had tragic consequences for Assisi. The main quake did severe damage to the Basilica di San Francesco, and the beautifully decorated church and the monastery were greatly endangered. Tragically, two Franciscan friars and two surveyors examining the damage right after the first quake were killed when pieces of the ceiling fell on them. Further tremors did more damage.

Restoration was immediately started with an ambitious (breakneck) schedule of repairs, calling for restoration of the damage to be finished by 2000, in time for the Papal Jubilee. This was accomplished, thanks to the great support received from donors all over the world — the total cost of repairing the destruction in the region was estimated at more than $1 billion — and the many experts who volunteered their time. The difficulties, though, were enormous. The upper basilica had severe structural damage; in addition to the loss of the art inside, it was in danger of collapse, therefore imperiling the lower basilica. Frescoes that fell from a great height were completely pulverized and beyond repair: All that was left were small chips of colored dust. Other frescoes crumbled into pieces the size of a dime, which had to be painstakingly catalogued and reassembled over full-size copies of the frescoes or scanned and input into a computer and then positioned. After three years of steady work, the basilica's structural damage has been repaired — its ceiling and walls reinforced and its columns braced with steel.

The top sights

Piazza del Comune is in the heart of Assisi, at the end of Via San Francesco, and at the junction with Corso Mazzini. With so much religious art to see in Assisi, many people forget it was actually a Roman town. Graced with Renaissance fountains, this medieval piazza was built over the Roman Forum and the **Tempio di Minerva (Temple of Minerva)** from the first century B.C., which is still standing with its portico of six Corinthian columns. Later Christians converted the temple into a church (and even later, gave it a baroque overhaul), which saved it from the destruction of time and accounts for why it's one of the best preserved Roman temples in Italy. Adjoining the temple is the thirteenth-century **Torre (Tower),** built by the Ghibellines. The site is open daily 7 a.m. to noon and 2:30 p.m. to dusk.

Basilica di San Francesco

Begun in 1228 to house the bones of St. Francis, the basilica is not one church but two churches — an upper basilica and a lower basilica. The scaffolding that covered the church has been removed, and although the quake destroyed some frescoes beyond repair, some have been reassembled — immense puzzles of thousands of pieces. The **Upper Basilica** contains Cimabue's *Crucifixion* and Giotto's celebrated cycle of frescoes on the life of the saint, including *St. Francis Preaching to the Birds.* The **Lower Basilica** is a somber Gothic monument to Francis's life, from which stairs descend to the crypt where his coffin was hidden (rediscovered in the nineteenth century). The **Cappella della Maddalena (Magdalen Chapel)** was frescoed by Giotto and his followers. Pietro Lorenzetti's beautiful *Deposition* is in the left transept; on the right is Cimabue's *Madonna Enthroned with Four Angels and St. Francis.* The **Treasury** contains various religious objects, and the **Perkins Collection,** donated by a U.S. philanthropist, has paintings by Lorenzetti, Fra Angelico, and others. Friars assist visitors and even give church tours, some of them in English (though the tour is free, it's customary to make a donation because the order exists only on alms).

Piazza Superiorie di San Francesco/Piazza Inferiore di San Francesco. ☎ *075-819-001. Admission: Basilica free; Treasury and Perkins Collection 3,000L ($1.60). Open: Basilica summer daily 8:30 a.m.–7 p.m. (winter to 6 p.m.); Treasury and Perkins Collecton summer Mon–Sat 9:30 a.m.–noon and 2–6 p.m.*

Basilica di Santa Chiara

Pilgrims come to this cavernous 1260 church to see the **tomb of Santa Chiara (St. Clare).** Canonized in 1255, she was the founder of the order of the Poor Clares. Chiara left her family to follow St. Francis, abandoning wealth and worldly pretensions as he did and cutting off her hair to symbolize her renunciation of the world. A number of miracles are attributed to her, one of which, a vision, led to her being proclaimed the patron saint of TV (saints don't get asked whether they want these honors). The other object attracting pilgrims is in the **Oratorio** — the crucifix that miraculously spoke to St. Francis and led him to start on his difficult path in the face of family, church, and society. Only some of the church's original frescoes remain. Note that Santa Chiara was closed at press time but should be open by the time you arrive.

Piazza di Santa Chiara. ☎ *075-812-282. Admission: Free. Open: Summer daily 6:30 a.m.–noon and 2–7 p.m.; winter daily 6:30 a.m.–noon and 2–6 p.m.*

Eremo delle Carceri

Eremo means "hermitage," and this is the site where St. Francis retired to meditate and pray, on the peaceful slopes of Mt. Subasio. The name of the site comes from the fact that Francis and his followers withdrew here as though to a prison (*carcere*). Several of his miracles occurred here, and you can still see the sites — such as the ancient tree believed to be the one where he preached his sermon to the birds (see Giotto's fresco of this scene in the Basilica di San Francesco). Also here are the unforgiving stone bed where he slept and the dried-out stream he quieted because its noise was interrupting his prayers. If you want to partake of the silence of Mt. Subasio yourself, there are marked trails through the park (the mountain is a protected site).

4 km (2½ miles) east of Assisi, out the Porta Cappuccini. ☎ *075-812-301. Bus: A minibus links the major sights (see "Getting Around"). Admission: Voluntary by donation. Open: Daily 6:30 a.m.–7:30 p.m.*

More cool things to see and do

If you still haven't gotten your fill of the sights of Assisi, here are some more you can visit:

✔ At the end of Via della Rocca is the **Rocca Maggiore** (☎ 075-815-292), a monument to a spirit opposite that of St. Francis's. With foundations going back to ancient times, this fourteenth-century fort was built by the papacy when it subdued Assisi and brought the area under Roman rule. It's somber and dark inside, but from the top you have a fabulous view of the walls and the town. In the spring of 2000, a bolt of lightning struck the Rocca and a tower partially collapsed, so the site is closed until further notice.

✔ The convent of **San Damiano** (☎ 075-812-273), 2.5 km (1.6 miles) from Assisi out the Porta Nuova, was built around the place of worship where St. Francis, praying before a wooden crucifix (today in the Basilica di Santa Chiara), had his first vision. The original seat of the order of the Poor Clares, this simple convent and its oratory, refectory, and cloister are beautifully decorated with frescoes from the fourteenth to the sixteenth century. You can also visit the dormitory where St. Clare died. It's open daily 10 a.m. to 12:30 p.m. and 2 to 6 p.m., and admission is free.

And on your left, the Basilica di San Francesco: Seeing Assisi by guided tour

Free tours of Assisi are given by the Franciscan order in town, starting from the office just outside the entrance to the lower basilica on the left in Piazza Inferiore di San Francesco (☎ 075-819-0084; Fax: 075-819-0035; E-mail: chiu@krenet.it). Tours last about an hour and take place Monday to Saturday 9 a.m. to noon and Monday to Sunday 2 to 5:30 p.m (winter to 4:30 p.m.).

Fast Facts: Assisi

Country Code and City Code

The **country code** for Italy is **39**. The **city code** for Assisi is **075**; use this code when calling from anywhere outside or inside Italy, even within Assisi itself (include the zero every time, even when calling from abroad).

Embassies and Consulates

See "Fast Facts: Florence" in Chapter 14 and "Fast Facts: Rome" in Chapter 12.

Currency Exchange

You can change money in the ticket office at the rail station in Santa Maria degli Angeli.

Emergencies

Ambulance and *Pronto Soccorso,* ☎ **118**; Fire, ☎ **115**; road assistance ACI, ☎ **116**.

Hospital

The **Ospedale di Assisi** is just outside town in the direction of San Damiano (☎ **075-81-391**).

Information

The main tourist office is **APT** at Piazza del Comune 27 (☎ **075-812-450**; fax: 075-813-727). It's open Monday to Friday 8 a.m. to 2 p.m. and 3:30 to 6:30 p.m., Saturday 9 a.m. to 1 p.m. and 3:30 to 6:30 p.m., and Sunday 9 a.m. to 1 p.m. It also maintains a seasonal **tourist booth** outdoors at Largo Properzio, just off Piazza del Comune (☎ **075-812-534**), where you can get brochures and maps; April to October, it's open daily 9 a.m. to 6 p.m.

Mail

The **Ufficio Postale** is at Largo Properzio 4 (☎ **075-812-355**).

Police

Call ☎ **113**; for the Carabinieri (other police force), call ☎ **112.**

Enjoying Spoleto and the Spoleto Festival

A small medieval city overlooked by a powerful fortress, **Spoleto** is surrounded by the countryside that has made Umbria famous: olive groves, green hills, and beautiful mountains. The city bears the traces of its development, going back to pre-Roman times, when the Umbri people founded the town.

Small enough to be visited as a day trip from Rome or Florence, it's also a wonderful place to spend some days of leisure, especially during one of its art and music festivals. For the location of the tourist office, see "Fast Facts: Spoleto."

Getting there

Spoleto is well connected by **rail** to all major destinations. There's direct service from Rome (the trip takes 1½ hours and costs about 23,000L/$12); you need to change in Foligno if traveling to and from Perugia (a trip of less than an hour, costing about 12,000L/$6). Trains arrive at Spoleto's **Stazione FS** on Piazza Polvani (☎ **0743-48-516**), across the river Tessino to the north of the city's center. The station is well connected with the town by bus (*circolare* A, B, C, or D).

The bus company **SSIT** (☎ **0743-212-211**) has two daily runs to Perugia (a 90-minute trip for about 11,000L/$6) and many daily runs to Terni, where you can switch to one of the two daily trips to Rome (the whole thing takes about 2½ hours).

Spoleto lies about 130 km (80 miles) from Rome on the Flaminia (SS3), the scenic but narrow consular road heading north from Rome. If you're **driving**, a faster possibility is A1; you exit at Orte and take the *superstrada* for Terni (follow the directions for Terni). The *superstrada* merges back into SS3 right after Terni; then just follow the directions for Spoleto.

Getting around

Spoleto is a small town on the slope of a mountain. Although the city develops on two levels (a lower one around the river Tessino and a upper one toward the Rocca), the *centro storico* with most of Spoleto's attractions is on the upper level, and you can easily visit it on foot. However, you can make use of the well-organized bus service; tickets cost 1,200L (65¢) and are sold at the usual places (tobacconists and bars).

Where to stay

Because of its festivals, Spoleto sports a large range of accommodations; in case of need, the local tourist office can arrange a room for you. Consider, though, that reservations for the Spoleto Festival are made *as much as a year in advance,* and that it's very unlikely you'll find accommodations around that season if you just breeze into town without a reservation.

Hotel Charleston

$$ Centro

A reliable choice in the historic center (*centro storico*), the Charleston occupies a seventeenth-century building. The recently renovated hotel offers comfortable, large guest rooms with wooden-beamed ceilings and

Spoleto

wooden floors, as well as public areas with terra-cotta floors and open fireplaces.

Piazza Collicola 10. ☎ *0743-220-052. Fax: 0743-221-244. E-mail:* hotelcharleston@ krenet.it. *Internet:* www.qsa.it/hotelcharleston. *Parking: 15,000L ($8). Rack rates: 140,000–180,000L ($76–$97) double, including breakfast. AE, DC, MC, V.*

Hotel Clarici

$$ Piazza Garibaldi

In the lower part of town, the Clarici offers modern comforts. The pleasantly furnished guest rooms come with air-conditioning, satellite TVs, and VCRs; most also boast private balconies.

Piazza della Vittoria 32. ☎ *0743-223-311. Fax: 0743-222-020. E-mail:* clarici@ tiscalinet.it. *Internet:* www.qsa.it/hotelclarici. *Parking: Free. Rack rates: 150,000L ($80) double, including breakfast. AE, DC, MC, V.*

Hotel Gattapone

$$$ Rocca

Named after the architect who built the Rocca Albornoz (see "More cool things to see and do" later in this section), this hotel is the nicest in Spoleto. The two seventeenth-century buildings forming the hotel dominate the town from a splendid location on the side of the Rocca. The guest rooms — furnished with antiques — are spacious and offer all the comforts, including good beds and modern baths.

Via del Ponte 6. ☎ *0743-223-447. Fax: 0743-223-448. E-mail:* gattapone@ mail.caribusiness.it. *Internet:* www.caribusiness.it/gattapone. *Parking: Free. Rack rates: 250,000–370,000L ($135–$146) double, including breakfast. AE, DC, MC, V.*

Where to dine

More famous for its art than for its food, Spoleto nonetheless offers a number of good places to sample Umbrian cuisine, including the famous *tartufo* (truffle) — which you owe it to yourself to try. Truffles exist in white and black varieties, the former the most coveted but with a milder flavor. By a quirk of the palate, some people find the flavor very strong while for others it's hardly noticeable.

Apollinare

$$$ Teatro Romano   Umbrian

Probably the best restaurant in town, the Apollinare is underneath the hotel Aurora, across the square from the Sant'Agata monastery. The food is excellent and includes traditional Umbrian dishes as well as imaginative — and delicious — interpretations of the classics. Be prepared for the crowds, especially if you're coming on a weekend.

Via S. Agata 14. ☎ *0743-223-256. Reservations necessary. Secondi: 16,000–24,000L ($9–$13). AE, DC, MC, V. Open: Lunch and dinner Wed–Mon; closed two weeks in Jan or Feb and in Aug.*

Il Tartufo

$$$ Piazza Garibaldi   Umbrian

Among the best restaurants in town, Il Tartufo — as its name suggests — specializes in dishes based on truffles. Its other specialties are mushrooms — especially *porcini,* a specialty of the region. You can taste them in various preparations, including as a sauce for fresh pasta or grilled meat.

Piazza Garibaldi 24. ☎ *0743-40-236. Reservations necessary. Secondi: 18,000–26,000L ($10–$14). AE, DC, MC, V. Open: Lunch and dinner Tues–Sun; closed two weeks in July and Aug.*

Pentagramma

$$ Teatro Romano   Umbrian

You'll find here all the specialties of Umbrian cuisine, but the area of expertise of this restaurant is pasta, homemade or not. You have a choice of sauces and — of course — truffles and *porcini* mushrooms when in season.

Via Martani 4. ☎ 0743-223-141. Reservations recommended. Secondi: 15,000–28,000L ($8–$15). MC, V. Open: Lunch and dinner Thurs–Tues; closed 2 weeks in Jan or Feb and in Aug.

Exploring Spoleto

Created by Gian Carlo Menotti, the **Festival di Spoleto** (also known as the Festival dei Due Mondi/Festival of Two Worlds) opened in 1958 as a way to bring together the best of "two worlds," Europe and America. Definitely a resounding success, the festival today, held two weeks from the end of June to the beginning of July, attracts major performing-arts figures from around the world and is famous for its great performances. This international event includes theater, dance, music, and even cinema (in the branch Spoletocinema); there are some quality art exhibits as well. Performances are held all around town, including in the **Teatro Romano** (Piazza della Libertà; ☎ 0743-223-419), the Rocca and the scenic Piazza del Duomo, but mainly in the **Teatro Nuovo** (Via Filetteria 1; ☎ 0743-223-419) and the **Teatro Caio Melisso** (Piazza del Duomo; ☎ 0743-222-209). Tickets run 10,000L to 60,000L ($5–$32), depending on the event, and the **ticket office** is at Piazza del Duomo 8 (☎ 0743-220-320; Fax: 0743-220-321; E-mail: info@oletofestival.it or tickets@oletofestival.it); Internet: www.spoletofestival.net or www.spoletofestival.it). Once in Spoleto, you can get tickets at the Teatro Nuovo.

The top sights

Duomo (Santa Maria Assunta)

This twelfth-century Romanesque cathedral boasts a majestic facade, graced by one major rose window embellished with rich marble carvings and mosaics. Around and above it are several minor rose windows and a famous 1207 mosaic by Salsternus. The **campanile (bell tower)** was pieced together using stone looted from Roman temples. The church's interior, refurbished in the seventeenth century, still has the original mosaic floor in the central nave. In a niche at the entrance is the bronze bust of Urban VIII by Gian Lorenzo Bernini. Among all the treasures inside, the most important are in the **apse**, which was decorated in the fifteenth century with great Filippo Lippi frescoes. The painter died in Spoleto in 1469 and was buried in the Duomo under a stone monument in the **right nave** — though his bones were stolen from the tomb a few centuries later. Also in the right nave, in the first chapel, is a Pinturicchio fresco representing the Madonna and Saints. The final concert of the Spoleto Festival is held every year in the piazza in front of the Duomo.

Piazza del Duomo. Admission: Free. Open: Summer daily 8 a.m.–1 p.m. and 3–6:30 p.m.; winter daily 8 a.m.–1 p.m. and 3–5:30 p.m.

Teatro Romano

This theater dates back to the first years of the Roman Empire and is one of numerous vestiges of ancient Spoleto that are still visible. It was uncovered by a local archaeologist under Piazza della Libertà at the end of the nineteenth century and excavated in the 1950s, revealing some well-preserved structures. A little farther east is the first-century **Arco di Druso** (Via Arco di Druso), once the monumental arched entry to the Forum (now Piazza del Mercato). The monumental baroque **fountain** in the piazza was built on the site of the facade of a Romanesque church, of which a few pieces survive. Nearby are the remains of a **temple** with six marble columns. Up a narrow lane is the church of **Sant'Ansano,** which was built on the site of a Roman temple (first century A.D.) and contains the crypt of Sant'Isacco, which has some interesting early frescoes.

Piazza della Libertà. ☎ 0743-223-277. Admission: 4,000L ($2.15). Open: Daily 9 a.m.–1:30 p.m., Mon–Sat 2:30 p.m.–sunset.

More cool things to see and do

Haven't gotten enough of Spoleto? Check out these other sights:

- ✔ Overlooking the city to the east, the **Rocca Albornoz** was built in the fourteenth century by master architect Gattapone to establish the power of the popes over the city and was used as a prison in recent times (up until 1982, in fact). From Piazza Campello at the east end of town, you can take Via del Ponte, which goes around the southern side of the fortress and brings you to the famous **Ponte delle Torri,** a bridge/aqueduct over the rivet Tessino. The ten arches of this gigantic bridge — 264 feet tall and 760 long, built in the twelfth century to bring water to the Rocca — offer a majestic view. The bridge was refurbished by Gattapone during the construction of the Rocca. On the other side of the bridge is a beautiful wood (considered sacred in Etruscan and Roman times; an inscription of the third century B.C. has been found outlawing the cutting of its trees).

- ✔ In lower Spoleto just off Piazza Garibaldi, you'll find the **Ponte Sanguinario,** a Roman bridge from the Augustan era that became disused because of a change in the course of the Tessino. It once opened the way to the grandiose second-century **Anfiteatro Romano (Roman Amphitheater)**, of which only some fragments are still visible on Via Anfiteatro (in the courtyard of the Caserma Minervio, a military barracks); most of its stone was used by the popes to build the Rocca (see the first bullet).

✔ In the eleventh-century **Sant'Eufemia** (Via Saffi, between Piazza del Duomo and Piazza del Mercanto; ☎ **0743-23101**), note the gallery above the nave, where women were required to sit, a holdover from the Eastern Church; it's one of the few such galleries in Italy. In the courtyard, double stairs lead to the **Museo Diocesano (Diocese Museum)**, noted for its Madonna paintings, one from 1315. One room contains Filippino Lippi's 1485 *Madonna and Child with Sts. Montano and Bartolomeo.* Admission to both is 5,000L ($2.70) and by reservation only, daily 10 a.m. to 12:30 p.m. and 3:30 to 7 p.m. (to 6 p.m. November to February).

✔ If you have a car or are a good walker, you can admire beautiful **San Pietro** and **San Salvatore**, churches east of the Flaminia (SS3) at the two extremes of town. San Salvatore — 1.2 km (.7 miles) northeast of Piazza Garibaldi — is a paleo-Christian basilica of the fourth and fifth century, the oldest in Italy. Though it has been refurbished several times, the original apse still survives; don't miss the ninth-century painted cross in the apse. San Pietro, at the southeast of town, is an interesting church built over preexisting Roman buildings; the twelfth-century Romanesque facade is decorated with refined marble carvings, while the interior is of less interest, having been rebuilt in the eighteenth century.

Fast Facts: Spoleto

Country Code and City Code

The **country code** for Italy is **39**. The **city code** for Spoleto is **0743**; use this code when calling from anywhere outside or inside Italy — you must add the codes even within Spoleto itself (and you must include the zero every time, even when calling from abroad).

Embassies and Consulates

See "Fast Facts: Florence" in Chapter 14 and "Fast Facts: Rome" in Chapter 12.

Currency Exchange

You can exchange money at banks and ATMs in town.

Emergencies

Ambulance and *Pronto Soccorso (first aid),* ☎ **118**; Fire, ☎ **115**; road assistance ACI, ☎ **116**.

Hospital

There's an **Ospedale** on Via San Matteo (☎ **0743-21-01**).

Information

The **tourist office** is on Piazza della Libertà (☎ **0743-220-311**). Summer hours are Monday to Saturday 9 a.m. to 1 p.m. and Monday to Sunday 4 to 7 p.m.; winter hours are Monday to Saturday 9 a.m. to 1 p.m. and 3:30 to 6:30 p.m. and Sunday 10 a.m. to 1 p.m.

Mail

The **Posta Centrale** is on Piazza della Libertà (☎ **0743-40-231**).

Police

Call ☎ **113**; for the Carabinieri (other police force), call ☎ **112**.

Part V
Venice and the Best of the Veneto

In this part . . .

American poet Mark Rudman once wrote, "Venice is anti-simile; it isn't *like* any other place." It may be one of the few cities where you'll never hear an automobile (though the growling diesel motors of boats are never very far). Venice, arguably the world's most romantic city, has grown up over thousands of years on marshy ground where people once hid in the reeds from barbarian hordes. From those humble beginnings, Venice became one of the greatest maritime empires history has ever seen and gave birth to great art, great institutions, and a unique architecture. And still, when you think of Venice, you first think of water — beguiling, mesmerizing, relaxing. The artistic and cultural influence of Venice spread to the surrounding region of the Veneto, whose towns offer many splendid sights.

In Chapter 18, we take you through the watery roads and alleys of Venice and the most interesting of the nearby lagoon islands. In Chapter 19, we introduce you to the Veneto's other two important cities — Padua and Verona, with their own beauties and treasures.

Chapter 18

Venice

In This Chapter

▶ Getting around without getting your feet wet

▶ Beating the competition — lodging and food

▶ Experiencing the sites, smells, and tastes of Venice

*V*enezia (Venice) feels important — its massive public structures and elegant private palazzi lining the canals show a city of tremendous wealth, power, and culture. It's a magnificent human achievement. On the other hand, tourists have been calling Venice a dead city for a century and a half. Henry James once wrote, "She exists only as a battered peep-show and bazaar." Only 70,000 people actually live in Venice, but if you're ever alone anywhere in the city for more than five minutes, consider yourself lucky. The crowds are unbelievable: Everywhere you go, someone is already there.

And yet . . . the Canal Grande at sunset, Piazza San Marco and the Basilica di San Marco, the Gallerie dell'Accademia, the lagoon, the Lido, the Canaletto skies, and the stillness beneath the hubbub are sights you just *have* to experience. And Venice's famous serenity (the republic was called *La Serenissima*, the "serene one") is as seductive as ever. Cranky Henry James and many other famous travelers have succumbed to Venice before you: "The only way to care for Venice as she deserves it is to give her a chance to touch you often — to linger and remain and return."

Venice became independent from Bisance (Constantinople, the capital of the Eastern Roman Empire) in the eighth century A.D. with its first *doge* (the head of the government). The word *doge* is the Venetian mutation of the Latin word *dux* ("leader"). Venice was established as a great harbor of international importance in the tenth century, when the Republic started regulating the commerce between Europe and the Orient. The city we know today started developing around the Basilica di San Marco (St. Mark's Basilica), constructed to house the relics of the saint. The group of islands in the lagoon was built up, the canals drained and their edges reinforced. The city had begun its metamorphosis.

The Venetian Republic was a great experiment in government. Over the centuries, a complicated network of institutions and checks and balances was built to limit the power of the *doge* and all the other political institutions that governed the city-state and preserve the republican form of government. At the heart was the Maggior Consiglio (Great Council) who elected the *doge*. Originally elective, membership to the Maggior Consiglio became hereditary in 1297. The smaller Council of Ten was established in 1310 to judge conspirators in a failed plot, but it became permanent (the *doge* and his counselors were also members). It got so powerful that the Maggior Consiglio passed legislation to limit its powers in 1582, 1628, and 1762. Most powerful of all, perhaps, was the Grand Chancellor, who as the head of the secret police knew all the dark secrets of the nobility, but other institutions where established to limit his power.

The experiment was successful: Venice remained a republic until May 12, 1797, when Napoleon invaded northern Italy and established a new European order. That represents over a thousand years of democracy. It left behind one of the most beautiful and extraordinary cities ever built. In constant danger of collapse, Venice has been the subject of study of experts from the entire world. In spite of the cement injections and continuous work of restoration and solidification of the canals, the city is sinking. The increase in the sea levels registered all over the planet in recent years has had dramatic consequences for Venice.

Getting There

Regardless of Venice's unique location, it is easily accessible by plane, train, ship, or car.

By air

Small but not too small, Venice's **Aeroporto Marco Polo** (☎ 041-260-9260), is situated in a mainland locality called Tessera, about 10 km (6¼ miles) from the city. **Alitalia** (☎ 041-258-1333) has several flights a day to Venice from other Italian cities. The hour-long flight from Rome is about 270,000L ($146) round-trip.

Note that you can't fly directly to Venice from outside Italy — first you must go through Rome or Milan.

From the airport, you can reach the city by bus or water. The *moto-scafo* **(shuttle boat)** to Piazza San Marco run by **Cooperativa San Marco** (☎ 041-522-2303) takes about 50 minutes and costs 17,000L ($9) per person. Though romantic, a **water taxi** (☎ 041-541-5084) costs a whopping 130,000L ($70); perhaps this is for honeymooners only. A less expensive option is to take the **shuttle bus** to Piazzale Roma (Venice's car terminal on the mainland) operated by **ATVO** (☎ 041-520-5530). It runs every hour and costs 5,000L ($2.70) per person. The trip takes about half an hour. You can also take the regular **city bus no. 5**; it runs every half hour and brings you to Piazzale Roma for 1,500L (80¢). Once at Piazzale Roma, you have to switch to another form of transportation.

By train

Venice's rail station is the **Stazione Ferroviaria Santa Lucia.** Many trains head directly to **Santa Lucia,** but sometimes you have to change in **Mestre,** Venice's inland rail hub. The trip from Mestre to Santa Lucia takes about 10 minutes, with connections every few minutes. The fastest train to Venice is the Eurostar, getting you to Venice in about 5 hours from Rome and 3½ from Milan; the Intercity takes just a little longer (both will take you directly to Santa Lucia). Try to avoid the slower regular train that makes many stops. A one-way ticket from Rome costs about 65,000L ($35), depending on the category of train you choose. In Santa Lucia, you can find a branch of the tourist office, the hotel association (in case you don't have a reservation), and, just in front of the exit, the ticket booth for the *vaporetto* (see "By vaporetto"), as well as water taxis.

By ship

Traditionally, Venice was accessible only by water — the bridge to the mainland was built only in 1846. It's still possible to get to Venice by ship, but pleasant as it is, it's also rare. Several international cruising companies offer cruises to Venice; ask your travel agent if you have an interest in this kind of trip. Remember that it's a long way to Venice from most international ports of call, usually a minimum of a month (most travelers don't have that kind of time). Your ship arrives at the **Stazione Marittima (Marine Terminal)** in **Santa Croce,** in the heart of Venice. From there, the regular city transportation is at your disposal.

By car

If you drive to Venice from Rome, take A1 to Bologna, then A13 to Padua and A4 to Venice. The distance is 530 km (327 miles). The A1 passes through Florence, so you also follow these directions if you're starting from there (though Florence is 287 km/179 miles closer to Venice than Rome).

No cars are allowed to enter Venice. The closest you can get is the car terminal in Piazzale Roma, where you have to say goodbye to your mechanical pet. Expect to pay $25 or more per day for a garage, depending on the size of your car. (Don't even think about leaving your car on the street for a day or two.) The **Garage Comunale** (Piazzale Roma 496; ☎ 041-522-2308 or 041-523-7763) and the **Garage San Marco** (Piazzale Roma 467/f; ☎ 041-523-5101 or 041-523-2213; fax 041-528-9969) are convenient to boat stops. A cheaper alternative is on the island of **Tronchetto,** where the **Parcheggio del Tronchetto** (☎ 041-520-7555) costs about 20,000L ($11).

But all these parking places are hard to get to in summer and on week-ends because of humongous traffic jams. It's a better (and cheaper) idea to leave your car on the mainland, in Mestre, where there are park-ing lots at the train station or on Via Stazione. There are two garages in the city of Mestre: **Garage Serenissima (☎ 041-938-021)** and **Crivellari (☎ 041-929-225)**. You can also find parking in Merghera. From Mestre or Marghera you have to take a train (see "By train") or a bus. For the bus, you have to buy a ticket in advance at a tobacconist or a bar; ask the parking officer for directions. Note, however, that the bus can get stuck in the same traffic jams we mentioned earlier.

Orienting Yourself in Venezia

Venice grew haphazardly over a period of centuries, one of the reasons why it's a wonderful maze of canals and tiny streets, with small squares scattered all around. Larger groupings did form, however, and these determine the main neighborhoods. Each has a character of its own, which we describe in this section.

Venezia by neighborhood

Venice is composed of three major areas: the *centro storico* (historic district), the mainland development on the coast (where a large part of the city's population actually lives), and the islands of the *laguna* (lagoon). The parts you may be most interested in are the historic district and the lagoon.

The centro storico (historic center)

The group of islands forming the heart of Venice is divided into *sestieri* (meaning a sixth of the city, they're in effect boroughs or districts; singular is *sestiere*), three on each side of the **Canal Grande (Grand Canal)**. The Canal Grande is the central canal, S-shaped (but reversed) and crossed by only three bridges: the Accademia, the famous Rialto, and the Ponte degli Scalzi at the rail station. The canal divides the historic district in two; *de citra* ("this side" of the canal) and *de ultra* (across the Canal Grande), as the locals say.

San Marco is the central tourist destination, with the **Basilica di San Marco (St. Mark's Basilica), Palazzo Ducale** and **Ponte dei Sospiri (Doge's Palace and Bridge of Sighs), Museo Correr (Correr Museum)**, **Teatro La Fenice** (the opera house not yet rebuilt after a 1996 fire), and **Palazzo Gritti**. San Marco is a neighborhood with lots of hotels — including some of the most expensive ones — and a number of city offices. The many restaurants tend to be "touristy" and the *calli* (streets, singular is *calle*) overcrowded. To appreciate its picturesque side, explore the area at night, when the crowds have receded. San Marco is connected to other *sestieri* by two of the three bridges crossing the **Canal Grande:** the Rialto, connecting San Marco to **San Polo,** and the Accademia, connecting San Marco to **Dorsoduro.**

Castello begins behind the **Basilica di San Marco.** Inland from the **Riva degli Schiavoni** — the grandiose promenade overlooking the bay of San Marco with some expensive hotels and restaurants — is a much more popular district, in the original sense. "Real" Venetians still live

Venice Orientation

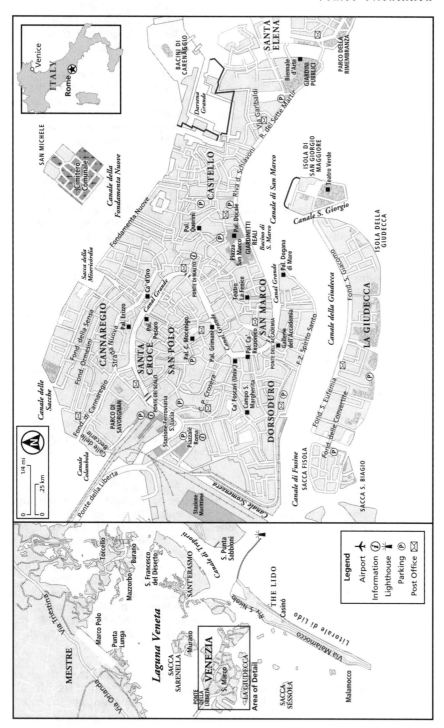

and work there, particularly between the **Arsenale** and the **Giardini Pubblici (Public Gardens).** Running through the heart of Castello is **Via Garibaldi,** with its many shops, outdoor market, and *osteria* offering typical Venetian fare. More inland is the grandiose **Basilica dei Santi Giovanni e Paolo (Basilica of Sts. John and Paul).**

Cannaregio is also a popular neighborhood. The painter Tintoretto was born here, near the Madonna dell'Orto church, not far from the Ghetto. On the Canal Grande end are the **Ca' d'Oro,** and, farther up, the **Stazione Ferroviaria Santa Lucia.** It's from this borough, on the lagoon side, that you find the Fondamenta Nuove station, from which you can take the *vaporetto* (ferry) to the islands of **Murano, Burano,** and **Torcello.**

San Polo, just across from the rail station and over the Rialto Bridge from San Marco, is a less touristy neighborhood. Traditionally, San Polo was the main market in Venice at the time when Rialto was the marine terminal of the medieval city, and is still a commercial neighborhood with many shops. You can also find the **Scuola Grande di San Rocco** and the **Basilica dei Frari** there.

Dorsoduro is where the university is located. It's a more artsy and trendy neighborhood, where you can find the **Gallerie dell'Accademia (Accademia Galleries), Ca' Rezzonico,** and **Collezione Peggy Guggenheim (Peggy Guggenheim Collection);** you can stroll along the beautiful promenade of the **Zattere** — famous for its outdoor ice-cream cafes — to the majestic church of **Santa Maria della Salute.** This area also includes the **Isola della Giudecca (Island of the Giudecca),** across from the promenade of the Zattere, separated by the Canale della Giudecca, the second in importance after the Canal Grande and the main water route to the maritime terminal.

Santa Croce is the borough where you arrive when you come by car. It has the marine and automobile terminal but also some very interesting churches and a beautiful promenade. It's the least visited part of Venice.

The laguna (lagoon)

The lagoon stretches from the Adriatic Sea to the mainland, enclosing Venice proper and many other islands. Among those not to be missed are **Murano, Burano,** and **Torcello**. Smaller than Venice, they keep exactly the same spirit in a quieter way. Murano is the island of the glassmakers, famous for centuries. It has the **Museo Vetrario di Murano (Glass Museum),** and you can find a few glassworks that still produce artistic glass. Burano is the island of lace and fishermen and still a major producer of lace and embroidered linen. Torcello was actually the urban center of the lagoon before Venice, but the population decamped to the present site of Venice after Torcello had begun to get too swampy. The only remains of Torcello's past glory is the magnificent cathedral, Santa Maria Assunta.

The **Lido** is the long barrier island protecting the lagoon from the open sea. Inhabited since ancient times, it bloomed at the end of the nineteenth century with the development of an elegant art nouveau resort that includes the Excelsior Palace, the Hotel des Bains, and the Casino. It's here that Venetians come to swim and tan on the long beaches. Many tourists come to stay here, because it's only a short *vaporetto* ride from San Marco and you get much better hotels for your money.

Venezia by address

You'll find that the names of things are different in Venice— even from those in other parts of Italy. That's because Venice developed its own unique dialect and words to deal with its unique geography. A *calle* (pronounced with a hard *l*) is a narrow street, a paved road a *salizzada* or a *calle larga*, a *rio terà* a canal that was filled in to make a street, a *fondamenta* a long street running alongside a canal, and a *sottoportico* a passage under a building. Note that there's only one piazza in Venice and that's Piazza San Marco — all the others are either a *campo* or a *campiello* (a smaller square).

As if that weren't enough, buildings are numbered differently from the way you're probably used to seeing them: You may need to find addresses like "2534 San Marco" and "2536 San Marco," and they may be on two different streets — oops, *calli!* So, if you're looking for a particular street number, don't expect sequential numbers. Just use the building numbers as boy-scout marks on a forest path and always ask directions according to street names and recognizable sites. That's why all hotels and restaurants have small maps printed on the back of their business cards and why even Venetians call for directions before going to an address they haven't been to before.

This applies to postal addresses. However, since Venetians understand the difficulty, when asked, they give you the name of the street or square, as we're used to (no number, though). So, for example, the address "Hotel Bernardi-Semenzato, Calle dell'Oca, 4366 Cannaregio" means this hotel is in building no. 4366 on Calle dell'Oca in the borough of Cannaregio. Always make sure you have also the name of the *sestiere* (borough): There are many streets of the same name!

As you wander, look for the ubiquitous signs (sometimes a little old, but still readable) whose destinations and arrows direct you toward major landmarks: Ferrovia (the train station), Piazzale Roma, vapoetto, the Rialto (Bridge), (Piazza) San Marco, and the Accademia (Bridge), and so on. If you decide to ask someone for directions, be aware that people are more likely to know the name of the actual place you're looking for than the name of a small street, often unmarked.

Street smarts: Where to get information after you arrive

The tourist board operates several offices around town and is planning to open a few small booths at the main tourist spots. The best thing is to get your information at the arrival points: the **Stazione Ferroviaria**

Santa Lucia (☎ and fax **041-719-078**), open in summer daily 8 a.m. to 8 p.m. and in winter Monday to Saturday 8 a.m. to 7 p.m.; and the **Aeroporto Marco Polo** (☎ **041-541-5887**), open daily 8 a.m. to 7 p.m. If you arrive by car, you can find an information point in Marghera at the Nuova rotatoria autostradale (new highway traffic circle), where the highway ends.

The tourist offices are worth a visit if only to get the latest opening hours of churches and museums — they change all the time, as in the rest of Italy. If you need wheelchair access, you can pick up a special map. The office at the train station (☎ and fax **041-719-078)** is the most logical place to get this material.

Getting Around Venezia

Made up of over 100 islands linked by 354 bridges over 177 canals, Venice can be quite confusing to the visitor, either Italian or foreign. These waterways have always been the main means of access to houses, which is why the facades of buildings are on the canals. Crossing these canals are small bridges with steps up and down — a major difficulty for anything on wheels. You can just imagine how it is loading and unloading for shops and catering places.

On foot

Walking is the best way to visit Venice, and you'll be doing *a lot* of it. The only things you need are a good map (try the smartly folded Falk map, available at many bookstores and newsstands), very comfortable shoes, and perhaps good foot balm (an end-of-the-day treat for your faithful "wheels"). We've seen many a tourist, unprepared for the rigors of walking, slumped in dismay in front of the steps of yet another bridge.

 The famous *acqua alta* (high water) should't be a concern. From November to March, in periods of high tides, many streets of the historic district are inundated with water. To facilitate walking, wooden platforms are placed around, so you don't have to pack your waders, unless you want to wander in the smallest and out-of-the-way streets. Many hotels ($$$ and above) provide plastic boots in an ample choice of sizes for you to borrow (ask when you reserve if you're planning your visit for the *acqua alta* season).

When walking around Venice, remember two things: First, Venice isn't dangerous. No matter how narrow a calle may be or how poor a place may look, there's no "bad neighborhood" in the historic district, even at night. That shouldn't induce you, though, to do foolish things such as display large quantities of money or leave your expensive camera unattended. Plenty of pickpockets are still around, and some bag snatchers, too.

Second, don't let people scare you with "It's impossible not to get lost there" or "Venice is like a maze and you'll never find your way." The city is, indeed, like a maze, but you really can't get lost — at worst, you may arrive at a canal and have to backtrack and then try the next turn. Big deal — you'll have discovered yet another fantastic view of the city you came to visit.

Although the city has made big efforts, Venice still isn't easy for wheelchair-bound visitors. The only real problem, but a major one, are the bridges over the canals, all with steps up and down. Any longish route passes over a canal, hence the steps; otherwise you're condemned to go around in circles on the same tiny island. Still, the main attractions are all accessible by water (boats are boarded by gangway), you can take strolls without crossing a bridge, and a few bridges have been equipped with motorized lifts (alas, we saw a number that were inoperable).

The tourist board has prepared a city map with yellow-highlighted wheelchair-accessible itineraries. The lifts on the few bridges equipped with them require a key to work, and the key is available free at the tourist office (see "Street smarts: Where to get information after you arrive"). Keep in mind that the lifts are sometimes out of order, so ask the tourist office for the latest details.

By vaporetto

The bus system of the historic district is the *vaporetto* (water bus). Riding these strange motorboats — something between a small barge and a ferry — is great fun: *Vaporetti* are relatively slow, but what a view you get! One *must-do* is the ride down the Canal Grande, both by day and by night (see "Exploring Venice").

See the Cheat Sheet at the front of this guide for a map of Venice's *vaporetto* lines.

The cost is quite high for a *vaporetto* (6,000L/$3.25) for the minimal ride, more for special rides to the far islands, so it's a good idea — if you stay more than a day — to go for one of the long-term tickets: a **giornaliero** (daily pass) at 18,000L ($10), a *biglietto tre giorni* (three-day pass) at 35,000L ($19), and a *settimanale* (weekly pass) at 60,000L ($32). The pass gives you access to the whole public transportation system, including the beautiful islands of Torcello, Murano, and Burano (see "More cool things to see and do") and the Lido.

A cost-effective way to tote the family around town is by purchasing a **family pass.** The daily pass for a family of three is 45,000L ($24), for a family of four 60,000L ($32), and for a family of five 75,000L ($41).

By gondola

Yes, we know, *gondolas* are for tourists . . . but what can be more romantic than being rowed in a *gondola* along the Canal Grande? Alas, a *gondola* ride is also very expensive: The official rates are 120,000L ($65) for 50 minutes for a maximum of six people during the day and

150,000L ($80) during the night. Discuss the price in advance, though, since many *gondolieri* (the guys who row) contend that they'd be underpaid if they respected those rates and that these prices have been raised little in the past years. You may be able to settle for a somewhat higher price or a shorter ride. Your chances of getting a good deal at any of the many *gondola* stations along the Canal Grande are about equal. What will really make a difference is how busy the *gondolieri* are.

Many people don't know that a traditional type of boat is still used as public transport: the *traghetto*, very similar to the *gondola*, only it's moved by two rowers instead of one and is much less fancy in decoration. Because only three bridges span the Canal Grande, *traghetti* take you across at various points for a mere 800L (43¢) per person. You just walk down to the small wooden dock, indicated by a sign saying "*traghetto*" (often the street leading to the dock is called Calle del Traghetto) and wait for the boat to come if there isn't one waiting. Note that Venetians ride them standing, proudly displaying their sea legs. The only drawbacks are that the *traghetti* operate for limited hours (most only mornings, a few also in the afternoon) and that the ride won't last more than 5 minutes.

By water taxi

Though a little expensive, *taxi acquei* (water taxis) are a great way to get to and from your hotel with your luggage or to have a taste of luxury. They cost 27,000L ($15) for the first seven minutes and then 500L (27¢) for each 15 seconds; and a ride from Piazzale Roma to Piazza San Marco is about 80,000L ($43) for up to four passengers. Remember that certain locations — and hotels — even water taxis can't reach, in which cases you have to walk the rest of the way. There are several companies in town, among them the **Cooperativa San Marco** (☎ 041-522-2303), **Cooperativa Veneziana** (☎ 041-766-124), and **Cooperativa Serenissima** (☎ 041-522-1265).

Where to Stay in Venezia

Because Venice is such a major tourist attraction, there are a wide variety of hotels to choose from. The ones we've chosen to list offer nice amenities in a good location and will serve you well as a home base. Most of our choices are accessible by water or by a short walk without crossing bridges.

Remember that luggage is your enemy in Venice. Pack as light as you can. No vehicles are allowed in the city, so whatever you bring with you you have to carry. Beware also that the bridges over the canals have steps. Not many of them, but enough to transform that luggage with wheels into an unbearable load.

The big splurge

Venice is the lap of luxury, with palatial hotels at every turn. In this chapter we supply entries for the deluxe hotels **Londra Palace** and **Hotel des Bains**. If you're looking for the plushest of the plush, here are a few more suggestions (even if you can't afford to stay at these places, you can always stop by to admire their opulent public rooms and rest your weary feet):

- ✔ **Danieli Royal Excelsior** (Riva degli Schiavoni, Castello 4196; ☎ **800-325-3535** in the U.S. and Canada, or 041-522-6480; fax 041-520-0208; Internet: www. ittsheraton.com; Vaporetto: San Zaccaria).

- ✔ **Excelsior Palace** (Lungomare Marconi 41; ☎ **800-325-3535** in the U.S. and Canada, or 041-526-0201; fax 041-526-7276; Internet: www.ittsheraton.com; Vaporetto: Lido, then bus A, B, or C).

- ✔ **Gritti Palace** (Campo Santa Maria del Giglio, San Marco 2467; ☎ **800-325-3535** in the U.S. and Canada, or 041-794-611; fax 041-520-0942; Internet: www. ittsheraton.com or www.italyhotel.com/hotelm/653.html; Vaporetto: Santa Maria del Giglio).

- ✔ **Hotel Bauer/Bauer Palace** (Campo San Moisè, San Marco 1459; ☎ **041-520-7022**; fax 041-520-7557; Internet: www.bauervenezia.it; E-mail: bauer@bauervenezia.it; Vaporetto: San Marco).

- ✔ **Hotel Cipriani** (Isola della Giudecca 10; ☎ **800-223-6800** in the U.S., or 041-520-7744; fax 041-520-7745; Internet: www.orient-expresshotels.com; E-mail: cipriani@gipnet.it; Vaporetto: Zitelle).

If you want to see Venice during Carnevale, reserve your hotel room way in advance.

If you don't have a reservation when you get to Venice, stop at one of the three locations of the **Hotel Association of Venice**, AVA (Associazione Veneziana Albergatori): at the Aeroporto Marco Polo (☎ **041-541-5133**), the Stazione Ferrovia Santa Lucia (☎ **041-715-016** or **041-715-288**), or the Garage San Marco on Piazzale Roma (☎ **041-520-6335**).

A helpful small publication to pick up in all major hotels is *Un Ospite a Venezia,* a guide on everything useful, from public transportation to the program of special events and to addresses of all kinds.

You can get special discounts for youth (under 30) if you have the **Rolling Venice** card (see "Exploring Venice," in this chapter).

The top hotels

Albergo La Meridiana

$$$ Lido di Venezia

Here's a way to factor out many of Venice's special difficulties. Staying on the Lido in the hot weather gets you near the beach and away from the smelly canals. There's a ferry to the Lido from Tronchetto (where the parking lots are) every hour, and you can bring your car. La Meridiana is a member of the Logis hotel association, a guarantee of quality and excellent service. All the guest rooms have air-conditioning, minibars, and safes; they're generally spacious, and most are decorated with simple but comfortable furniture. The nicest are those that have rows of casement windows and look out over the garden. The hotel also has a private beach.

Via Lepanto 45, Lido di Venezia. ☎ *041-526-0343. Fax: 041-526-9240. Internet:* www. lameridiana.com. *E-mail:* info@lameridiana.com. *Parking: Free. Vaporetto: 62 to Casino; walk left on Via Dardanelli, turn left on Via Lorenzo Marcello, and right on Via Lepanto. Rack rates: 240,000–360,000L ($130–$195) double, including breakfast. AE, DC, MC, V. Closed Nov 15–Jan 31.*

Al Sole Palace

$$ Santa Croce

Away from the tourist crowds near the university and Ca' Foscari (see "More cool things to see and do"), this hotel occupies a delightful fifteenth-century palazzo and offers pleasant air-conditioned guest rooms with old Venetian furniture and beamed ceilings. Ask for one of the rooms with a view over the canal. There's a restaurant on the premises.

Fondamenta Minotta, 136 Santa Croce. ☎ *041-710-844. Fax: 041-714-398. Internet:* www.alsolepalace.com. *E-mail:* info@alsolepalace.com. *Vaporetto: 1, 82, 41, 42, 51, or 52 to Piazzale Roma; follow the Fondamenta Croce to your left, turn right on Fondamenta dei Tolentin along the Canali, and continue to Fondamenta Minotta on your left. Rack rates: 200,000–380,000L ($108–$205) double, including buffet breakfast. AE, DC, MC, V.*

Hotel Bernardi-Semenzato

$ Cannaregio

Renovated in 1995, this hotel a few minutes from the Ponte di Rialto combines an antique look with modern amenities and includes an annex 3 blocks away. The air-conditioned guest rooms are of a good size and the baths mostly new; you can get a really cheap room if you're willing to do without a private bath. Nearby Strada Nuova is a busy shopping street where Venetians actually outnumber tourists and linger for a chat, a coffee, or an ice cream. The hotel has a 40-percent-off deal with a parking lot in Tronchetto.

Calle dell'Oca, 4366 Cannaregio. ☎ ***041-522-7257****. Fax: 041-522-2424. Vaporetto: 1 to Ca' d'Oro; walk up to Strada Nuova, turn right, then turn left on Calle del Duca and right on Calle dell'Oca. Rack rates: 120,000–200,000L ($65–$108) double. MC, V.*

Hotel Campiello

$$$ Castello

This pink fifteenth-century building is easy to find — just off posh Riva degli Schiavoni — and is a bargain for its area. It's somewhat quieter than the nearby Riva, and the location is just about perfect. The recently renovated guest rooms are decorated either in Venetian Liberty (art nouveau) style or in a mod Italian look. The staff of this family-run hotel is friendly as well as expert. The buffet breakfast is more substantial than many and served in a rather glitzy hall.

Campiello del Vin, 4647 Castello, ☎ ***041-520-5764****. Fax: 041-520-5798. Internet:* www. hotelcampiello.com. *Vaporetto: 1, 14, 41, 42, 51, 52, 71, 72, or 82 to San Zaccaria; walk up Calle del Vin. Rack rates: 240,000–290,000L ($130–$157) double. AE, MC, V.*

Hotel Casanova

$$$$ San Marco

Only 20 yards from Piazza San Marco, this hotel puts you right in the touristic heart of the city. If you reserve in advance and are lucky, you may be able to get the *mansarda* (attic room) with a private terrace and a view over Venice's rooftops. The furnishings are adequate and modern, though the guest rooms vary in size; some have exposed brick walls and beamed ceilings.

Frezzeria, 1284 San Marco. ☎ ***041-520-6855****. Internet:* www.saidsette.it/ casanova. *E-mail:* hotel.casanova.ve@iol.it. *Vaporetto: 1 or 82 to San Marco–Vallaresso; walk up Calle Vallaresso, turn left on Salizzada San Moisè, then right on the Frezzeria. Rack rates: 360,000L ($195) double, including breakfast. MC, V.*

Hotel des Bains

$$$$$ Lido

Now owned by Sheraton, this grand art nouveau hotel is one of Venice's most famous. Everybody who was anybody in the early 1900s stayed here (Thomas Mann's *Death in Venice* was set here). The guest rooms boast handsome furnishings as well as modern conveniences too numerous to list. The amenities include baby-sitting, laundry service, and a motorboat shuttle between the Lido and Venice, plus tennis courts and a pool in the surrounding park, horseback riding, and so on.

Lungomare Marconi 17, Lido di Venezia. ☎ **800-325-3535** *in the U.S. or 041-526-5921. Fax: 041-526-0113. Internet:* www.sheraton.com. *Vaporetto: 1, 6, 14, 51, 52, 61, 62, or 82 to the Lido; walk up Gran Viale Santa Maria Elizabetta and turn right (the hotel is in the park) or take bus A, B, or C. Rack rates: 475,000–1,000,000L ($257–$541). AE, DC, MC, V. Closed Nov–Mar.*

Hotel Flora

$$$ San Marco

Friendly and handicapped accessible, this hotel is between Piazza San Marco and the still-unrepaired Teatro La Fenice. All the guest rooms are furnished Venetian style; many have views of the beautiful private garden (a rare treasure in Venice) and rooms 3 and 47 have views of the dome of La Salute — try to get one of these as they're the most beautiful.

Calle dei Bergamaschi, 2283/A San Marco. ☎ **041-520-5844**. *Fax: 041-522-8217. Vaporetto: 1 to Giglio; walk up Calle Gritti, turn right on Calle delle Ostriche, cross the bridge and continue onto Calle Larga XXII Marzo, then turn right on Calle dei Bergamaschi. Rack rates: 290,000L ($157) double, including breakfast. MC, V.*

Hotel Locanda Remedio

$$$ Castello

In the calm residential borough of Castello, this quiet hotel is actually just behind the Basilica di San Marco. The building dates from the early sixteenth century and the atmosphere is old world; you can even see some remnants of ceiling frescoes. On the other hand, the air-conditioned guest rooms have been upgraded with modern amenities and new baths.

Calle de Remedio, 4412 Castello. ☎ **041-520-6232**. *Fax: 041-521-0485. Vaporetto: 1, 14, 41, 42, 51, 52, 71, 72, or 82 to San Zaccaria; walk up Calle del Vin, continue toward the left along the canal on Fondamenta del Vin and then turn left, crossing the bridge onto Salizzada San Provolo, and turn right on Calle della Chiesa, go left around the side of the church, bear right along the canal, and turn left on Calle de Remedio. Rack rates: 230,000–280,000L ($124–$151) double, including breakfast. MC, V.*

Hotel Marconi

$$ San Polo

At the foot of the Ponte di Rialto and overlooking the Canal Grande, the Marconi has an understated elegance. Refurbished in 1999, the building dates from the 1500s and is in a beautiful — particularly at night — part of Venice with many cafes and restaurants. All the guest rooms have air-conditioning, safes, and Venetian-style furniture; only four open onto the canal, so reserve early. Whichever room you get, you can eat breakfast in fair weather at the tables outside by the canal.

Riva del Vin, 729 San Polo.☎ ***041-522-2068***. *Fax: 041-522-9700. Internet:* www. hotelmarconi.it. *E-mail:* info@hotelmarconi.it. *Vaporetto: 1 and 82 to Rialto; walk to the Rialto Bridge and cross over and turn left along the canal on Riva del Vin. Rack rates: 120,000–450,000L ($65–$245) double, including breakfast. AE, MC, V.*

Hotel Pantalon

$$ Dorsoduro

In the nice neighborhood between San Polo, the Accademia, and Santa Maria de' Frari, this hotel has been renovated with care and is a good alternative to the more pricey ones around San Marco. All the moderate-sized guest rooms have air-conditioning, minibars, and safes; one has a handicapped-accessible bathroom, and a few have terraces. They're decorated with tasteful reproductions. The decor in the common areas has a French feel (the place is popular with French tourists).

Crosera San Pantalon, 3942 Dorsoduro. ☎ ***041-710-896***. *Fax: 041-718-683. Internet:* www.venere.it. *Vaporetto: 1 or 82 to San Tomà; walk up to Campo San Tomà, turn left on Calle Campanièl, cross a bridge onto Calle Balbi, turn right on Fondamenta del Fornèr, then left onto the bridge and Calle Larga Foscari and right on Crosera. Rack rates: 150,000–360,000L ($80–$195) double, including breakfast. MC, V.*

Hotel San Cassiano Ca' Favretto

$$$$ Santa Croce

This comparatively moderately priced hotel occupies a fourteenth-century palazzo on the Canal Grande — what more can you ask for? It's just across from the Ca' d'Oro and left of the Ca' Corner della Regina. The building has been completely renovated (explaining why the prices shot up), and all the guest rooms have massive, dark wood furniture, relieved by the light-colored papers on the walls and the large windows. Many have views of the Ca' d'Oro or the smaller canal on the side.

Calle della Rosa, 2232 Santa Croce. ☎ ***041-524-1768***. *Fax: 041-721-033. E-mail:* cassiano@cassiano.it. *Vaporetto: 1 to San Stae; walk to the left of Campo San Stae, cross the canal and turn right on Fondamenta Rimpetto Mocenigo, then left on Calle del Forner, cross the bridge, continue on Calle del Ravano, cross the bridge, and turn left on Calle della Rosa. Rack rates: 300,000–450,000L ($162–$245) double, including breakfast. AE, V.*

Hotel Tivoli

$$ Dorsoduro

This simple family-run hotel is between the Frari and the Scuola Grande di San Rocco and the Accademia. Some of the guest rooms overlook the sunny garden courtyard where breakfast is served in warm weather. The

Venice Accommodations and Dining

ACCOMMODATIONS ■
Albergo La Meridiana **36**
Al Sole Palace **3**
Boston Hotel **26**
Danieli Royal Excelsior **23**
Excelsior Palace **36**
Gritti Palace **34**
Hotel Bauer/
 Bauer Palace **30**
Hotel Bernardi-
 Semenzato **14**
Hotel Campiello **37**
Hotel Casanova **27**
Hotel Cipriani **35**
Hotel des Bains **36**
Hotel Do Pozzi **32**
Hotel Flora **31**
Hotel Geremia **7**
Hotel Locanda
 Remedio **21**
Hotel Marconi **19**
Hotel Metropole **39**
Hotel Pantalon **5**
Hotel San Cassiano
 Ca' Favretto **15**
Hotel Tivoli **6**
Londra Palace **38**
Pensione Accademia
 Villa Maravegie **8**
Pensione La Calcina **9**
Pensione Seguso **9**

DINING ◆
A La Vecia Cavana **11**
Al Pantalon **4**
Antica Besseta **1**
Antico Gatoleto **12**
Antica Ostaria Ruga
 Rialto **17**
Antico Martini **28**
Bar Pizzeria di Paolo
 Melinato **40**
Da Raffaele **33**
Do Forni **22**
Fiaschetteria
 Toscana **13**
Locanda Cipriani **10**
Ostaria ai Vetrai **10**
Ostaria a la
 Campana **24**
Ostaria à la
 Valigia **25**
Osteria da Fiore **2**
Ostaria da Franz **20**
Ostaria Enoteca
 Vivaldi **16**
Trattoria alla
 Madonna **18**
Trattoria Busa alla
 Torre **10**
Trattoria da
 Romano **10**
Vino Vino **29**

Legend
Church ✝ ■

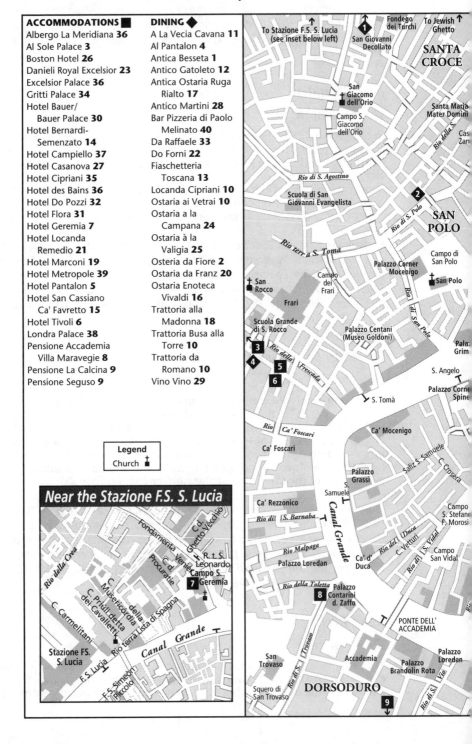

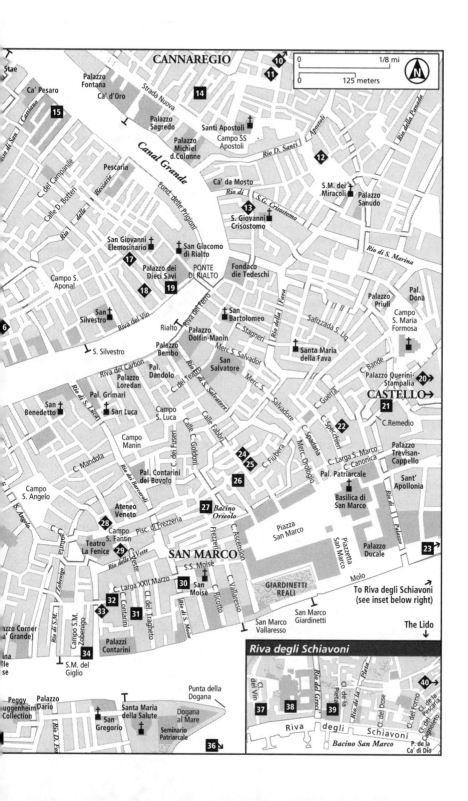

CANNAREGIO

Stae

Palazzo
Fontana

Ca' Pesaro

Ca' d'Oro

15

10

11

0   1/8 mi

0   125 meters

N

14

Strada Nuova

Palazzo
Sagredo

Palazzo
Michiel
d.Colonne

Santi Apostoli

Campo SS
Apostoli

Rio D. Santi

Apostoli

Rio della Pendale

Canal Grande

Pescaria

C. del Campanile

Calle D. Botteri

Barcarie

delle

Rio

6

Campo S.
Aponal

San Giovanni
Elemosinario

17

Palazzo dei
Dieci Savi

18

19

Fond. delle Prigioni

San Giacomo
di Rialto

PONTE
DI RIALTO

Ca' da Mosto

Rio di

S.G. Crisostomo

13

S. Giovanni
Crisostomo

S.M. dei
Miracoli

Palazzo
Sanudo

12

Rio di S. Marina

Fondaco
die Tedeschi

Pal.
Donà

Palazzo
Priuli

Campo
S. Maria
Formosa

San
Silvestro

Riva del Vin

Rialto

S. Silvestro

Palazzo
Dolfin-Manin

Palazzo
Bembo

Rio del Ferro

San
Bartolomeo

C. Stagneri

Rio della Fava

Merc S. Salvador

San
Salvatore

Salizzada S. Liq.

Santa Maria
della Fava

C. Bande

C. Guerra

Palazzo Querini-
Stampalia

20

CASTELLO

21

Riva del Carbon

Pal.
Dandolo

Palazzo
Loredan

Pal. Grimani

San
Benedetto

San Luca

Campo
S. Luca

Rio di S. Luca

Calle C. Goldoni

Calle Fabbri

C. del Teatro

Rio di S. Salvatore

Merc. S. Salvadore

C. dei Fuseri

Campo
Manin

C. Mandola

Rio del Barcaroli

Campo
S. Angelo

Pal. Contarini
del Bovolo

24

25

26

C. Fiubera

Merc. Orologio

C. Spadaria

C. Specchieri

22

C.Remedio

Palazzo
Trevisan-
Cappello

Sant'
Apollonia

C. Larga S. Marco

C. Canonica

Pal. Patriarcale

Basilica di
San Marco

Rio di

Palazzo

23

Ateneo
Veneto

28

Campo
S. Fantin

Teatro
La Fenice

29

Pisc. di Frezzeria

27 *Bacino
Orseolo*

Piazza
San Marco

Piazzetta
San Marco

Palazzo
Ducale

C. Ascension

Frezzeria

SAN MARCO

S.S. Moisè

C. Larga XXII Marzo

30

San
Moisè

32

33

31

Cl. del Traghetto

C. Contarini

Rio di S. Moisè

C. Vallaresso

C. Ricotto

GIARDINETTI
REALI

San Marco
Giardinetti

San Marco
Vallaresso

Molo

To Riva degli Schiavoni
(see inset below right)

The Lido

Palazzi
Contarini

34

S.M. del
Giglio

Rio delle Veste

Campo S.M.
Zobenigo

Rio S. M.

azzo Corner
a' Grande)

Peggy
uggenheim
Collection

Palazzo
Dario

San
Gregorio

Santa Maria
della Salute

Punta della
Dogana

Dogana
al Mare

Seminario
Patriarcale

36

Riva degli Schiavoni

Cl.
del Vin

Rio del Greci

Cl. de la
Pieta

Rio de la
Pieta

Cl. de la

Cl. de Dose

Cl. del Formo

Cl. de la
Pescaria

Cl. de la
Capparello

40

37

38

39

Riva   degli   Schiavoni

Bacino San Marco

P. de la
Ca' di Dio

two ground floor rooms are more accessible. The continental breakfast is a bit more substantial than many — fruit, yogurt, and cheese are available. Though the furnishings may seem a bit dated (Mediterranean style), at this price and in this location the Tivoli is a good deal.

Calle Larga Foscari, 3838 Dorsoduro. ☎ *041-524-2460. Fax: 041-522-2656. Vaporetto: 1 or 82 to San Tomà stop; walk up to Campo San Tomà, turn left on Calle Campanièl, cross a bridge onto Calle Balbi, turn right on Fondamenta del Fornèr, then left onto the bridge and Calle Larga Foscari at the intersection with Crosera. Rack rates: 150,000–310,000L ($80–$168) double, including breakfast. No credit cards.*

Londra Palace

$$$$ **Castello**

You can't miss the Londra Palace — it has a hundred windows facing the lagoon and is only steps from Piazza San Marco. Tchaikovsky stayed here several times and wrote some of his works here during his stays. The hotel is wheelchair accessible. All the guest rooms are gorgeously furnished, and two attic rooms boast beamed ceilings and Regency furniture. The bar is almost like an English pub, and there's a comfortable reading room. The ground-floor restaurant is the famous Do Leoni; like the hotel, it's pricey.

Riva degli Schiavoni, 4171 Castello. ☎ *041-520-0533. Fax: 041-522-5032. Internet: www.hotelondra.it. E-mail: info@hotelondra.it. Vaporetto: 1, 14, 41, 42, 51, 52, 71, 72, or 82 to San Zaccaria; walk right on Riva degli Schiavoni. Rack rates: 409,000–785,000L ($221–$424) double, including buffet breakfast. AE, DC, MC, V.*

Pensione Accademia Villa Maravegie

$$$ **Dorsoduro**

In a beautiful location two steps from the Accademia, this hotel occupies a seventeenth-century villa with a garden. The guest rooms contain nineteenth-century furnishings, and all have private bathrooms. The whole place has a wonderfully old-fashioned feeling. It's very popular, so you have to reserve well in advance to secure a room with a view over the garden.

Fondamenta Bollani, 1058 Dorsoduro. ☎ *041-521-0188. Fax: 041-523-9152. E-mail: pensione.accademia@flashnet.it. Vaporetto: 1 or 82 to Accademia; turn right on Calle Corfù, left on Fondamenta Priuli, right on the first bridge, and then again right on Fondamenta Bollani. Rack rates: 220,000–400,000L ($119–$216) double, including breakfast. AE, DC, MC, V.*

Pensione La Calcina

$$$ **Dorsoduro**

This is where Victorian writer John Ruskin stayed in 1876. The location overlooking the Canale della Giudecca is both beautiful and less hectic than the area around San Marco. Nicely restored, it's an excellent value. All the guest rooms have parquet floors and air-conditioning, and some furnishings are original. In warm weather, the buffet breakfast is served on the large terrace by the water. The hotel also has a solarium (roof terrace). Note that you can't have an extra bed placed in a double and that you need to reserve six months in advance for summer.

Zattere ai Gesuati, 780 Dorsoduro. ☎ *041-520-6466. Fax: 041-522-7045. Vaporetto: 51, 52, 61, 62, or 82 to Zattere; turn right along the Canale della Giudecca to the Rio di SanVio. Rack rates: 200,000–300,000L ($108–$162) double, including breakfast. AE, DC, MC, V.*

Pensione Seguso

$$ Dorsoduro

If you want to stay where Victorian writer John Ruskin stayed, stay at La Calcina; if you want to *feel* like Ruskin, stay here. From the bull's-eye glass front to the antique furnishings, glass chandeliers, and marble floors, this old-fashioned pensione transports you back in time. The corner guest rooms are very large and have balconies, but their bathroom is across the corridor and in some cases is shared by two rooms. Note that in low season you have to take — or at least pay for — half board: breakfast and your choice of dinner or lunch.

Zattere ai Gesuati, 779 Dorsoduro. ☎ *041-528-6858. Fax: 041-522-2340. Vaporetto: 51, 52, 61, 62 or 82 to Zattere; turn right along the Canale della Giudecca to the little campiello at Rio di San Vio. Rack rates: 160,000–300,000L ($87–$162) double, including breakfast. AE, MC, V.*

Runner-up accommodations

Boston Hotel

$$$ San Marco   The Boston Hotel isn't too expensive (for its area) and is a good alternative just off Piazza San Marco. Some of the guest rooms have views of the canal from their balconies (you have to stand, however; they're very small) and about half have air-conditioning. Ponte dei Dai, 848 San Marco; ☎ **041-528-7665.** Fax: 041-522-6628. Vaporetto: 1 or 82 to San Marco–Vallaresso

Hotel Do Pozzi

$$$ San Marco   The Hotel Do Pozzi has a quiet yet central position between Piazza San Marco and the Teatro La Fenice. The guest rooms have been renovated but are still furnished in antique style; guests get a 10 percent discount at the Ristorante Da Raffaele (see "Where to Dine in Venezia"). Corte dei Do Pozzi, 2373 San Marco; ☎ **041-520-7855.** Fax: 041-522-9413. Vaporetto: 1 to Giglio.

Hotel Geremia

$$ Cannaregio   The Hotel Geremia   is within walking distance of the rail station — a nice hotel in an area where many are not. A lot of care has been put into the renovation, especially the baths, and the service is good. Campo San Geremia, 290/A Cannaregio; ☎ **041-716-245.** Fax: 041-524-2342. Vaporetto: 1, 82, 71, 72, 51, 52, 41 or 42 to Ferrovia.

Hotel Metropole

$$$$ Castello   The Metropole is a romantic hotel with an entrance on a canal and baroque furnishings. Riva degli Schiavoni, 4149 Castello; ☎ **041-520-5044.** Fax: 041-522-3679. Internet: www.hotelmetropole.com. E-mail: Venice@hotelmetropole.com. Vaporetto: 1, 82, 41, 42, 51, or 52 to San Zaccaria.

Where to Dine in Venezia

Fish and shellfish from the lagoon and the Adriatic served on rice, pasta, or polenta (corn meal) are the staples of Venetian cuisine. Typical dishes are *risi e bisi* (rice and peas), *risotto* (creamy rice cooked with fish or vegetables), *bigoli in salsa* (whole-wheat spaghetti with anchovy-and-onion sauce), *sarde in saor* (sardines in a sauce of vinegar, onions, and pine nuts), *baccalà mantegato* (creamed cod fish served cold), and the famous *fegato alla veneziana* (liver sautéed with onions and wine). For dessert, visit one of the many pastry shops for one of the local cakes or the famous *Bussolai* and *S e' Buranei* — O- and S-shaped cookies, respectively, originally from the small island of Burano (see "More cool things to see and do"). Or go for a delicious *gelato*, the best in Italy after Rome (see the sidebar "Taking a sweet break").

The best local wines are Amarone and Valpolicella (red) or, if you prefer it white and fizzy, Cartizze or Prosecco. The wine is as important as — more important than, some locals would say — the food in Venice.

The most traditional places to eat are small *osterie* and *bacari*, which look on the inside as if you've just stepped into somebody's house. Although Venice has the reputation of having bad and expensive restaurants, it's possible to eat really well here. In general, simple places with wooden tables and paper atop the tablecloths (or directly on the tables) are the best bet. At the other end of the spectrum, there are a number of well-established reputed restaurants that serve you excellent fare, but at much higher prices. Both of these kinds of restaurants have steady customers (we often think that the more a restaurant advertises, the worse the place is likely to be).

If you want to seek out your own finds, the best places to hunt are along **Via Garibaldi** in Castello, **Strada Nuova** in Cannaregio, and **Rialto** in San Polo.

The top restaurants

A La Vecia Cavana

$$$$ Cannaregio Venetian

This renowned restaurant is housed in a seventeenth-century building where *gondole* (more than one *gondola*) were repaired and stationed. The cuisine is typically Venetian; among the dishes is *granchio al forno* (oven-roasted crab), an excellent antipasto. The prices are high but well worth it, given the quality of the food.

Rio Terrà dei Franceschi, 4624 Cannaregio. ☎ *041-528-7106. Reservations recommended. Vaporetto: 1 to Ca' d'Oro; walk straight ahead to Strada Nuova and turn right, bear left around Campo dei Apóstoli and the church, take Rio Terrà SS Apóstoli, and turn left at Rio Terrà dei Franceschi. Secondi: 40,000–60,000L ($21–$32). AE, DC, MC, V. Open: Lunch and dinner Fri–Wed.*

Al Pantalon

$$ Dorsoduro Venetian

This is a great place for lunch in the busy area near the university, and lots of Venetians know it — it's best to go early if you want to avoid the line. The food is traditional, extremely fresh, and served by a friendly young staff. Try the *antipasto di pesce* (mixed seafood appetizer) or the *baccalà mantegato* as a starter and continue with one of the many *secondi*. You can have a pasta dish, like excellent *spaghetti alle vongole* (with clams), for less than 15,000L ($8).

Campo San Fantin, 3958 Dorsoduro. ☎ *041-710-849. Reservations not accepted. Vaporetto: 1 or 82 to San Tomà; follow the red signs to the Scuola di San Rocco but just before the Scuola turn left on Sottoportego San Rocco and cross the bridge. Secondi: 20,000–40,000L ($11–$22). No credit cards. Open: Lunch and dinner daily.*

Antica Besseta

$$$$ Santa Croce Venetian

This small trattoria from 1700 is very popular with locals — it's best to make a reservation. Try one of the many excellent *risotti*. With the fish *secondi*, you have an opportunity to try delicious versions of the main dishes of Venetian cuisine.

Salizzada de Ca' Zusto, 1395 Santa Croce, ☎ *041-721-687. Reservation recommended. Vaporetto: 1 to Riva de Biasio; walk up Calle Zen, turn left, and make an immediate right on Salizzada de Ca' Zusto. Secondi: 30,000–35,000L ($16–$19). AE, MC, V. Open: Lunch Thurs–Mon; dinner Wed–Mon.*

Antica Ostaria Ruga Rialto

$$ San Polo Venetian

Italians who don't have a lot of money still manage to eat well at places like this, where the decor is minimal, the tablecloth is likely to be a piece of paper, and all the food is local and fresh. Popular with students, this *ostaria* serves an excellent antipasto, specialties like *baccalà mantegato*, and abundant and tasty pastas. There's lots of space, lots of people, and (sometimes) lots of noise, but you never have a bad meal.

Ruga Vecchia San Giovanni, 692 San Polo. ☎ *041-521-1243. Reservations recommended for large parties. Vaporetto: 1 or 82 to Rialto; walk to the Rialto Bridge and cross over, continue straight through the arcades and make your first left on Ruga Vecchia San Giovanni. Secondi: 14,000–20,000L ($8–$11). No credit cards. Open: Lunch and dinner Tues–Sun.*

Antico Gatoleto

$$ Castello Venetian

Although it's in Castello, this restaurant is in the northwest corner and so isn't far from the Ponte di Rialto. It's on a quiet little square and has some tables outside. In addition to Venetian specialties and seafood, you can get inexpensive pasta dishes and even pizza.

Campo Santa Maria Nova, 6055 Castello. ☎ *041-522-1883. Reservations recommended on Sat. Vaporetto: 1 or 82 to Rialto; turn left and pass the bridge, make a right when you can't go any farther, take your first left on Salizzata San Giovanni Crisóstomo, follow it, and immediately after the second bridge take a right on Salizzata San Canciano; when you reach Campo San Canciano, take the dogleg to the right that leads to Campo Santa Maria Nova. Secondi: 12,000–25,000L ($6–$14). DC, MC, V. Open: Lunch and dinner daily.*

Antico Martini

$$$$$ San Marco Venetian

This elegant restaurant on the site of an eighteenth-century cafe is one of the city's best. You can sample Venetian specialties as well as other innovative dishes. A real gourmet spot, it comes with a high price. The Antico Martini is famous for their *involtini di salmone al caviale* (salmon rolled up and stuffed with caviar).

Campo San Fantin, 1983 San Marco. ☎ *041-522-4121. Reservations recommended. Vaporetto: 1 to Giglio; walk up Calle Gritti, turn right on Calle delle Ostreghe, continue into Calle Larga XXII Marzo, turn left on Calle delle Veste and follow it to Campo San Fantin. Secondi: 35,000–50,000L ($19–$27). AE, DC, MC, V. Open: Lunch Thurs–Mon; dinner Wed–Mon.*

Taking a sweet break

Venetians definitely have a sweet tooth! They not only make scrumptious pastries but, together with Rome, Florence, and Sicily, are contenders for the best *gelato* (ice cream) in Italy and maybe in the world. One of the best places for *gelato* is **Algiubagiò** (☎ **041-523-6084;** Internet: www.algiubagio.com), on Fondamenta Nuove right in front of the *vaporetto* stop of that name. It also has a coffee shop and restaurant. (Twenty yards down the *fondamenta,* it has a little storefront selling just ice cream.) You should definitely sample their delicious flavors — try the fantastic crema Veneziana, a cream-flavored ice cream with chunks of chocolate (the recipe is a secret). For typical and delicious pastries, a good address is **Pasticceria Tonolo** (San Pantalon, 3764 Dorsoduro; Vaporetto: San Tomà). Of course, there are many other ice cream and pastry shops in Venice. Don't be afraid to stop and sample, they're usually all good.

 ### *Bar Pizzeria di Paolo Melinato*

$$ Castello   Pizza

Pizza? In Venice? After two or three days of nonstop meat and shellfish consumption, your liver may be asking for a break. This pizzeria, in front of the Arsenale, is simple to find and has really good pizza, especially for the north of Italy. You can get all the classics — margherita, capricciosa, and so on. The small campo with the Arsenale and its canal in the background are especially quiet and picturesque at night.

Campo Arsenale, 2389 Castello. ☎ *041-521-0660. Reservations not necessary. Vaporetto: 1, 41, or 42 to Arsenale; follow Calle dei Forni to its end, turn left on Calle di Pegola, and turn right into Campo Arsenale. Secondi: 12,000–20,000L ($7–$11). No credit cards. Open: Lunch Tues–Sat; dinner Mon–Sat.*

 ### *Da Raffaele*

$$$ San Marco   Venetian

Go to this canal-side restaurant for excellent fresh fish and other specialties. If you're tired of seafood, try the very tasty pastas and grilled meats. Everything on the menu is reliable — which is why this place has been a major tourist magnet for years (make a reservation). A nice plus is the terrace, so you can dine outdoors in summer.

Ponte delle Ostreghe, 2347 San Marco. ☎ *041-523-2317. Reservations recommended on weekends. Vaporetto: 1 or 82 to San Marco–Vallaresso; walk up Calle Vallaresso, turn left on Salizzada San Moisè, and continue into Calle Larga XXII Marzo and Calle delle Ostreghe. Secondi: 25,000–38,000L ($14–$21). AE, DC, MC, V. Open: Lunch and dinner Wed–Mon.*

Do Forni

$$$$ San Marco Venetian

A very popular restaurant especially with younger people, Do Forni is constantly busy. It has made it into many guidebooks, so don't expect to be alone among the locals. The food, however, justifies the wait. The room in back has a casual coziness. The specialties of the house are *risi e bisi* and *bigoli in salsa*.

Calle degli Specchieri, 457–468 San Marco. ☎ 041-523-0663. Reservations recommended. Vaporetto: 1 or 82 to San Marco–Vallaresso; cross Piazza San Marco, turn right in Piazzetta dei Leoni on the left side of the Basilica di San Marco, and turn left on Calle degli Specchieri. Secondi: 30,000–50,000L ($16–$27). AE, DC, MC, V. Open: Lunch and dinner daily.

Fiaschetteria Toscana

$$ Cannaregio Tuscan/Italian

The Venetian-Tuscan merging has given birth here to a refined cuisine, making this one of Venice's best restaurants. You can get steaks in true Tuscan style, as well as seafood in various faultless preparations, all served amid an elegant decor.

Salizzada San Giovanni Crisostomo, 2347 Cannaregio. ☎ 041-528-5281. Reservations required. Vaporetto: 1 or 82 to Rialto; walk past the Rialto Bridge along the Canal Grande, then turn right and left onto Salizzada San Giovanni Crisostomo. Secondi: 18,000–38,000L ($10–$21). AE, DC, MC, V. Open: Lunch and dinner Wed–Mon.

Locanda Cipriani

$$$$ Torcello Venetian

If you have to eat in one of the Cipriani restaurants — there's the Ristorante Cipriani in the luxurious hotel of the same name on the Isola della Giudecca, and Harry's Bar on Calle Vallaresso just off Piazza San Marco — do it here. From its Venetian base, this family has gained world renown (they even took over New York's Rainbow Room), but it's in this traditional venue that you find the best food. The menu is simple yet refined; the only drawback is the high-season crowds. (If you really like it, you can stay overnight in one of the several guest rooms; they've been closed for years but are now renovated and due to reopen in early 2001.)

Piazza Santa Fosca 29, Torcello. ☎ 041-730-150. Reservations recommended. Vaporetto: 12 from Fondamenta Nuove to Torcello; walk right and up the Fondamenta dei Borgognoni along the canal and turn left. Secondi: 30,000–40,000L ($16–$22). AE, DC, MC, V. Open: Lunch Wed–Mon; dinner Fri–Sat; closed winter.

Ostaria ai Vetrai

$$ Murano Venetian

If you're on Murano and looking for lunch, this *ostaria* serves excellent seafood at a more affordable price than many comparable restaurants in Venice. It prepares every type of local fish and also serves pastas with seafood. The huge antipasto for two at 25,000L ($14) contains all the Venetian seafood specialties — virtually a meal in itself — and you can eat it at a canal-side table.

Fondamenta Manin 29, Murano. ☎ *041-739-293. Reservations not necessary. Vaporetto: 41, 42, 71, or 72 to Colonna; walk along the canal to the right until you come to the first bridge, then cross over to Fondamenta Manin and turn left. Secondi: 17,000L–35,000L ($9–$19). DC, MC, V. Open: Lunch Wed–Sun.*

Ostaria a la Campana

$ San Marco Venetian

It's hard to find a place that's dirt cheap without the dirt. This *ostaria* is really small but neat and simple, and you can get a plate of steaming pasta with a delicious sauce for the equivalent of about $5. A half-liter of wine runs another $1.75. This is good hearty food with a complete absence of tourist ambiance. The place is convenient because it's on Calle dei Fabbri, the main drag (very straight, for Venice) between Piazza San Marco and the Ponte di Rialto.

Calle dei Fabbri, 4720 San Marco. ☎ *041-528-5170. Reservations not accepted. Vaporetto: 1 or 82 to Rialto; turn right and walk along the canal, then turn left on Calle Bembo, which turns into Calle dei Fabbri. Secondi: 8,000–15,000L ($4.30–$8). No credit cards. Open: Lunch and dinner Mon–Sat.*

Ostaria Enoteca Vivaldi

$$ San Polo Venetian

This charming *ostaria/enoteca*, with its wood interior and bar, low ceilings, and rustic feeling, is a cozy place for dinner. It offers typical Venetian cuisine and, as the name suggests, excellent wine. It has a faithful following and may be hard to get into as it's not that large; it's best to call ahead.

Calle Madonnetta, 1457 San Polo. ☎ *041-523-8185. Reservations necessary. Vaporetto: 1 to San Silvestro; follow the narrow street behind the Palazzo Barzizza to Campo Aponàl, turn left toward Campo San Polo, and cross the bridge onto Calle Madonnetta. Secondi: 14,000–20,000L ($8–$11). No credit cards. Open: Lunch and dinner Mon–Sat.*

Osteria da Fiore

$$$$ San Polo   Seafood/Venetian

One of the city's most popular restaurants, this *osteria* offers excellent traditional cuisine but at high prices. Among the specialties are risotto with scampi and fried calamari. Though a bit difficult to find and also crowded, the Osteria da Fiore is one of the best places to sample Venetian cuisine.

Calle del Scaleter, 2202/A San Polo. ☎ *041-721-308. Reservations required. Vaporetto: 1 or 82 to San Tomà; walk straight ahead to Campo San Tomà, continue straight on Calle larga Prima toward Santa Maria dei Frari and the Scuola di San Rocco and a block before the scuola and behind the Frari, turn right on Calle del Scalater. Secondi: 45,000–50,000L ($25–$27). AE, DC, MC, V. Open: Lunch and dinner Tues–Sat.*

Trattoria alla Madonna

$$ San Polo   Venetian

Seafood and more seafood! In this local *trattoria,* celebrated by both locals and tourists, you find all the critters the Adriatic can offer, some existing only in the Venetian lagoon, prepared in various traditional ways — grilled, roasted, fried, or served with pasta, risotto, or polenta. The moderate prices attract crowds, so be prepared for a long wait.

Calle della Madonna, 594 San Polo. ☎ *041-522-3824. Reservations accepted only for large parties. Vaporetto: 1 or 82 to Rialto; cross the Rialto Bridge, turn left on Riva del Vin along the Canal Grande, and turn right onto Calle della Madonna. Secondi: 18,000–22,000L ($10–$12). AE, MC, V. Open: Lunch and dinner Thurs–Tues.*

Trattoria da Romano

$$ Burano   Venetian

A very busy address in Burano, this restaurant is renowned for its *risotti.* You may choose among squid risotto, mixed seafood risotto, and other delicious combinations. If you're still hungry after one of these dishes, try the excellent fish *secondi.*

Via Baldassarre Galuppi 221, Burano. ☎ *041-730-030. Reservations recommended. Vaporetto: 12 from Fondamenta Nuove to Burano; walk up and then left onto Via Baldassarre Galuppi. Secondi: 18,000–25,000L ($10–$14). AE, MC, V. Open: Lunch and dinner Wed–Mon.*

Runner-up restaurants

Ostaria à la Valigia

$$ San Marco   Venetian   The Ostaria à la Valigia caters to tourists but the food is good, from the pasta with seafood to the more expensive Venetian secondi. The restaurant has lots of room, making it a good fallback, and there's seating outside on the quieter side street. Calle dei Fabbri, 4696 San Marco; ☎ 041-521-2526. Vaporetto: 1 or 82 to San Marco Vallaresso.

Ostaria da Franz

$$$$ Castello   Venetian   The Ostaria da Franz is way off the beaten track and popular with well-to-do locals. Fondamenta San Giuseppe, 754 Castello; ☎ 041-522-0861. Vaporetto: 1, 82, 41, 42, 51, or 52 to S. Zaccaria.

Trattoria Busa alla Torre

$$$ Murano   Venetian   On a broad piazza, the Trattoria Busa alla Torre is open for lunch only, but it's open every day. You can find the typical range of pastas and Venetian specialties, well prepared and relatively cheap. Campo San Stefano 3, Murano; ☎ 041-739-662. Vaporetto 41, 42, 71, 72, 12, or 13.

Vino Vino

$ San Marco   Venetian   Vino Vino (is a Venetian bacaro (wine bar) just behind the remains of the Teatro La Fenice; the service is simple but the food very good. You can find traditional Venetian fare and a large choice of wines. Calle del Cafetier, 2007/A San Marco; ☎ 041-523-7027. Vaporetto: 1 or 82 to San Marco–Vallaresso.

Exploring Venezia

In Venice, every side street leads to another wonderful view of the city. But the main sights — such as Piazza San Marco — are truly remarkable and you'll be glad you took the time to visit this one-of-a-kind city.

If you're under 30, buy a **Rolling Venice card** to get substantial discounts — from 10 to 40 percent — on hotels, restaurants, museums, public transportation, and shops. Working on the premise that young people are put off by schlepping around the famous sights at the end of a long line of tourists (very uncool), Rolling Venice provides alternative itineraries, places to meet and be seen, and a more lively approach to the "dead" city. To have access to the discounts you need only to register and pay 5,000L ($2.70) at one of the Rolling Venice info points, the easiest being the **Stazione Ferroviaria Santa Lucia** booth (☎ **041-524-2852;** July to October, open daily 8 a.m. to 8 p.m.) and the **Transalpino** booth, also in the station (☎ **041-524-1334;** Fax: 041-716-600; open Monday to Friday 8:30 a.m. to 12:30 p.m. and 3 to 7 p.m. and Saturday 8:30 a.m. to 12:30 p.m.).

Besides the card (it helps if you bring an ID photo for the card or you may have to show another picture ID with the card when you present it), you get a map of Venice charting the location of all the participating hotels, restaurants, clubs, and shops, as well as a small guidebook including facts about Venetian history and culture and smart itineraries. You can also get the ACTV **Rolling Venice Rover** ticket, a three-day pass for all public boats and buses for 25,000L ($14). A booklet — the *agenda* — gives a load of useful info, from cultural listings to locations of supermarkets and emergency numbers (5,000L/$2.70). You can even get a T-shirt (10,000L/$5) with the Rolling Venice logo and a canvas bag (12,000L/$6).

Older travelers can buy a 15,000L ($8) three-day pass to 14 churches in Venice at any of the participating churches. It allows you to visit 6 churches of your choice out of the 14, saving time at the ticket booth (but not necessarily money; it depends on where you go). The sights included are the Treasury of the Basilica di San Marco, the Basilica dei Frari, the Chiesa della Madonna dell'Orto, the Chiesa di San Sebastiano, San Polo, San Stae, San Giacomo dall'Orio, Santa Maria del Giglio, San Stefano, Santa Maria Formosa, San Pietro di Castello, Sant'Alvise, Santa Maria dei Miracoli, and the Chiesa del Redentore. All are rich in paintings and works by famous artists of the fifteenth and sixteenth centuries.

There are two other combo tickets: one for the Ca' d'Oro and the Museo d'Arte Orientale Ca' Pesaro for 8,000L ($4.30) and one for the Ca' d'Oro, Museo d'Arte Orientale Ca' Pesaro, and Gallerie dell'Accademia for 18,000L ($10).

The period before Lent — celebrated as Mardi Gras in New Orleans — is celebrated as **Carnevale** all over Italy, but Venice's celebrations are spectacular, beginning the week before Ash Wednesday (usually in February) and culminating on the last day, *martedi grasso* (Fat Tuesday). In 1797, Napoleon suppressed Carnevale, which had grown into a months-long bacchanal. But this festive holiday was revived in 1980 and has become a big deal in Venice, famous for the elaborateness of its costumes and masks, which are historic and elegant rather than Halloween-ish (no Darth Vader or Mutant Ninja Turtles). Music events take place at all times, and crowds — big crowds — surge all over. Some of the events are reserved only for those who are disguised, such as the Gran Ballo in Piazza San Marco, with prizes given for the best costume. Other events include a Children's Carnevale daily on Piazza San Polo, a cortege of decorated boats on the Canal Grande, and a market of Venetian costumes at Santo Stefano (see "Shopping" for other sources of masks and authentic Venetian getups). You can also rent a costume at **Tragicomica di Gualtiero dell'Osto** (Campiello dei Meloni, 2800 San Polo; ☎ **041-721-101;** vaporetto: 1 to San Staè).

The top sights

The **Canal Grande** (Grand Canal) was and still is the heart of Venice. Whether you're riding in a *vaporetto* packed as tight as a can of tuna or whispering along in a *gondola* with only your significant other, you can find the procession of buildings stunning — nowhere else is the feeling of the past so bittersweet and mesmerizing. One of the most interesting things to do is catch a *vaporetto* and take a ride (catch the no. 1 or the no. 82). It's the best way to admire the city's showcase of the Venitian Gothic — the delicate marble decorations of the *palazzi* opening onto the canal are best seen from the water. These were once the residences of Venice's noble and most opulent families. Many have been transformed into museums or hotels, others are still lived in (lucky tenants!), and a few seem forlorn and abandoned.

Leaving **Stazione Santa Lucia** behind you, be on the lookout for (in this order) the **Palazzo Vendramin-Calergi** (hosting the Casino in winter) on the left, the **Ca' Pesaro** on the right, the famous and delightful **Ca' d'Oro** (a Gothic jewel built at the beginning of the fifteenth century) on the left, the beautiful red-and-white **Ponte di Rialto** as you pass beneath it, the **Ca' Foscari** (one of the best examples of Venetian Gothic, today the seat of the university) farther down on the right, then the **Ponte Accademia.** You know you're coming out to the lagoon when you see the imposing white dome of the **Basilica della Salute** to your right. The best *vaporetto* is no.1: Slower than others (making every stop), it allows a more leisurely perusal and runs at night under the letter N (for *notturno*). For the busy or impatient, the express *vaporetto* is no. 82 (same route, fewer stops).

Basilica dei Frari (Santa Maria Gloriosa dei Frari minori Francescani)

This church is a magnificent example of the Venetian Gothic, built in the first half of the fourteenth century and enlarged in the fifteenth. Beside it is the fourteenth-century **campanile (bell tower).** The Frari contains many significant artworks, none more so than Titian's *Pala Pesaro* **(Pesaro altarpiece)** and *L'Assunta* **(Assumption)** over the main altar, a glorious composition that combines billowing forms with exquisite colors and a feeling of serenity. Also important are Giovanni Bellini's triptych *Vergine con il Bambino e Quattro Santi (Virgin and Child with Four Saints)* and Donatello's *San Giovanni Battista (St. John the Baptist),* a rare sculpture in wood. Be sure to visit the original **wooden choir,** where monks participated in Mass — this is the only extant choir of its kind in Venice. The triangular marble monument dedicated to sculptor Antonio Canova was actually designed by Canova to be a monument to Titian (Canova's followers appropriated the design for their master after he died in 1822). A bit of trivia: If you look carefully at the walls near the monument, you see an **Austrian bomb** that was dropped on the church during World War I but miraculously failed to explode.

Campo dei Frari, San Polo. ☎ *041-522-2637. Vaporetto: 1 or 82 to San Tomà; walk up to Calle Campaniel, turn right, turn left on Campo San Tomà, continue onto Calle*

Venice Attractions

Arsenale **22**
Basilica dei Frari
  (Santa Maria Gloriosa dei Frari
  minori Francescani) **2**
Basilica della Salute
  (Santa Maria della Salute) **21**
Basilica di San Marco **13**
Ca' d'Oro **9**
Ca' Foscari **4**
Campanile di San Marco **16**
Canal Grande **10**
Ca' Pesaro **8**
Ca' Rezzonico **5**
Collezione Peggy Guggenheim **20**
Gallerie dell'Accademia **6**
Jewish Ghetto **1**
Museo Correr **19**
Palazzo Ducale **14**
Palazzo Vendramin-Calergi **7**
Piazza San Marco **18**
Piazzetta San Marco **15**
Ponte dei Sospiri **12**
Ponte di Rialto **11**
Scuola Grande di San Rocco **3**
Torre dell'Orologio **17**

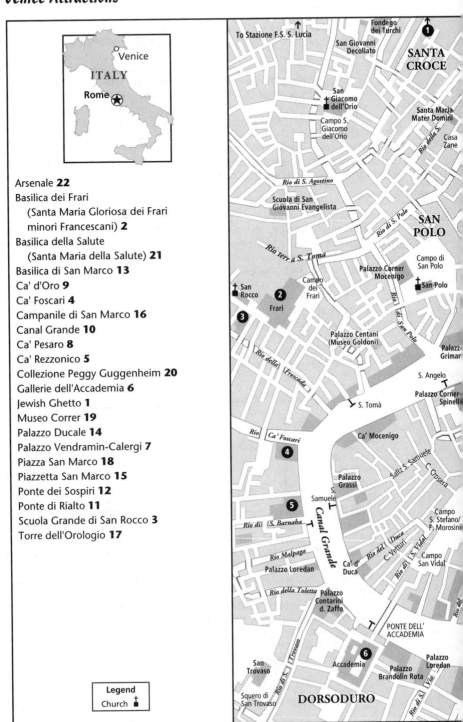

Legend
Church

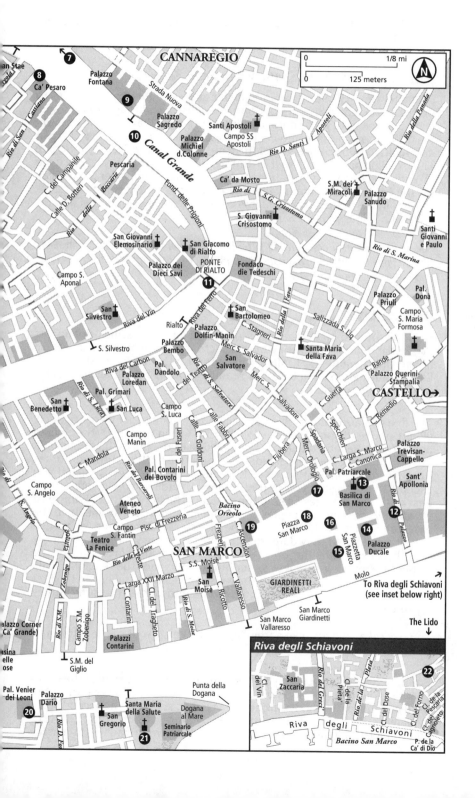

larga Prima, and turn right. Admission: 3,000L ($1.60). Open: Mon–Sat 9 a.m.–6 p.m., Sun 1–6 p.m.

Basilica della Salute (Santa Maria della Salute)

Built after the 1630 black plague epidemic as an ex-voto (thanks offering to God), the octagonal St. Mary of Good Health is an enduring baroque landmark at the end of Dorsoduro, almost across from Piazza San Marco. On the main altar is a thirteenth-century Byzantine icon and Titian's *Discesa dello Spirito Santo* **(Descent of the Holy Spirit)**; in the Sacristy are three Titian ceiling paintings as well as Tintoretto's wonderful *Le Nozze di Cana* (Wedding at Cana). If you happen to be in town on November 21, you can see the **feast of the Madonna della Salute,** a centuries-old commemorative pageant in which a pontoon bridge is constructed across the Canal Grande, linking La Salute with the San Marco side.

Campo della Salute, Dorsoduro. ☎ 041-523-7951. Vaporetto: 1 to Salute. Admission: Church voluntary offering; Sacristy 2,000L ($1.10). Open: Summer daily 9 a.m.–noon and 3–6 p.m. (winter to 5:30 p.m.).

Basilica di San Marco

Dedicated to St. Mark, the city's patron saint, the basilica dominates Piazza San Marco (see listing in this section). It was built in A.D. 829 to house the remains of St. Mark (martyred by the Turks in Alexandria, Egypt), burned down in 932, was rebuilt, and was rebuilt again in 1063, taking its present shape.

The five portals of the basilica are topped by domes that were originally gilded; above the portals is the loggia from which the *doges* (the elected heads of the Venetian Republic) presided over the public functions held in the square, under the shade of the famous gilded bronze horses brought from Constantinople in 1204 after the Fourth Crusade. (If you ascend to the loggia, you find multilingual audio boxes giving a brief description of the sites around the piazza.) The horses (the *Triumphal Quadriga*) outside are copies, but you can admire the originals in the museum within the basilica (see the Museo Marciano later in this listing); it's estimated they date from the fourth century B.C. Also from the Fourth Crusade are the bronze doors of the main portal and of the **Cappella Zen (Zen Chapel,** named for a family, not the religion). Only one of the mosaics above the doorways is original — the one in the first doorway to the left. The others are seventeenth- and eighteenth-century reproductions.

You can take advantage of a free English-language tour of the basilica on Wednesdays, Thursdays, and Fridays at 11 a.m.

Entering the portal, you may be overwhelmed by the luxury of the decorations: gold mosaics and colored inlaid marble. The lower part of the basilica is decorated in Byzantine and Venetian style and the second story in Flamboyant Gothic. The atrium's ceiling mosaics date from 1225–1275 and depict Old Testament scenes. The floors are in geometric marble

Basilica di San Marco

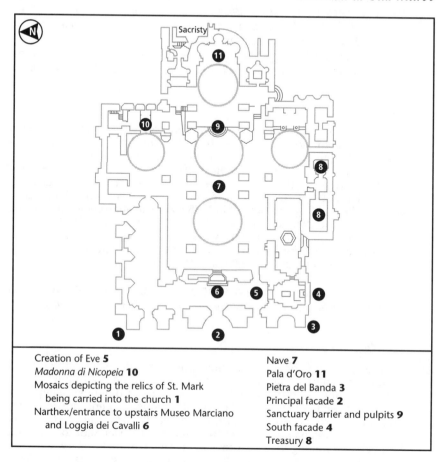

Creation of Eve **5**
Madonna di Nicopeia **10**
Mosaics depicting the relics of St. Mark
  being carried into the church **1**
Narthex/entrance to upstairs Museo Marciano
  and Loggia dei Cavalli **6**

Nave **7**
Pala d'Oro **11**
Pietra del Banda **3**
Principal facade **2**
Sanctuary barrier and pulpits **9**
South facade **4**
Treasury **8**

mosaics of typical Byzantine style from the eleventh and twelfth centuries. The inner basilica mosaics, depicting scenes from the New Testament, were begun in the twelfth century and finished in the thirteenth.

The **Tesoro (Treasury)** holds the basilica's riches, and its masterpiece is the famous **Pala d'Oro,** a magnificent altarpiece in gold, finely chiseled in Byzantine-Venetian style. You have to pay 3,000L ($1.60) in order to see it up close. Inside the basilica is also the small **Museo Marciano** (on the right after you enter, up a long and steep flight of stone steps); the main attraction is the original *Quadriga*, but there are also mosaics, altarpieces, and other works. The **Presbytery** features some beautiful mosaics depicting scenes from the life of Jesus, including the Resurrection.

As in Rome's Basilica di San Pietro, bare shoulders, halter tops, tank tops, shorts, and skirts above the knee all lead to your being turned away from the Basilica di San Marco — no kidding.

Piazza San Marco, San Marco. ☎ *041-522-5205. Vaporetto: 1 or 82 to San Marco–Vallaresso. Admission: Basilica free; Treasury 4,000L (2.15); Museo Marciano 3,000L ($1.60); Presbytery 3,000L ($1.60). Open: Basilica summer Mon–Sat 9:30 a.m.–5:30 p.m., Sun 2–5:30 p.m.; winter Mon–Sat 9:30 a.m.–5 p.m., Sun 2–4:30 p.m. Treasury Mon–Sat 9:45 a.m.–4:30 p.m., Sun 2–4:30 p.m. Museo Marciano summer Mon–Sat 10 a.m.–5:30 p.m., Sun 2–4:30 p.m.; winter Mon–Sat 10 a.m.–4:45 p.m.*

Ca' d'Oro

The Ca' d'Oro (Gold House), as its name suggests, was once richly decorated with gold, now worn away to reveal the pink and white marble beneath. Begun in 1422, it's one of the most beautiful of the palazzi fronting the Canal Grande. Its elegant tracery of carvings, even without the gold, are evocative of the Venetian spirit — ornate without being gaudy, Gothic but without the broodingly morbid feel of north European Gothic. The building was bought in 1895 by musician/art collector Giorgio Franchetti, who donated the Ca' d'Oro and his collections to the public in 1916. The collection's primary works are Mantegna's *San Sebastian,* Titian's *Venus at the Mirror,* works by Carpaccio and Tintoretto, and Venetian ceramics from as far back as the twelfth century.

Calle Ca' d'Oro, Cannaregio. ☎ *041-523-8790. Vaporetto: 1 to Ca' d'Oro. Admission: 6,000L ($3.25) adults; children 16 and under free. Open: Daily 9 a.m.–1:30 p.m.*

Ca' Rezzonico

Despite its name, the Ca' Rezzonico was begun in 1649 for the Bon, an important Venetian family. The Rezzonico acquired it a hundred years later and completed the structure — now one of the most magnificent palazzi on the Canal Grande. The most famous resident, however, was English poet Robert Browning, who died here in 1889. The Ca' Rezzonico contains the **Museo del Settecento Veneziano (Museum of the 1700s in Venice),** and among its elegant rooms is the Throne Room, whose ceilings were painted by Giovanni Battista Tiepolo. It also contains works by Francesco Guardi and other artists. You can step out onto the balcony and gaze down at the Grand Canal like a tortured lover or brooding poet and get a feeling for the life of a Venetian aristocrat.

Fondamenta Rezzonico, Dorsoduro. ☎ *041-241-0100. Vaporetto: 1 to Ca' Rezzonico. Admission: 14,000L ($8) adults; 8,000L ($4.30) children 12–18, 4,000L ($2.15) children under 12. Open: Summer Sat–Thurs 10 a.m.–5 p.m.; winter Sat–Thurs 10 a.m.–4 p.m.*

Collezione Peggy Guggenheim

In the Palazzo Venier dei Leoni on the Canal Grande, this museum holds one of Italy's most important collections of avant-garde art. The reason the building looks so short is that it's the ground floor of a 1749 palazzo that was never completed. American expatriate collector Peggy Guggenheim lived here for 30 years; after her death in 1979, the building and collection became the property of New York's Guggenheim Foundation. Peggy G.'s protégés included Jackson Pollock, represented by 10 paintings, and Max Ernst, whom she married. From dada and surrealism to expressionism and abstract expressionism, the collection is rich and diverse, with works by Klee, Magritte, Mondrian, De Chirico, Dalí, Kandinsky, Picasso, and others. The sculpture garden includes works by Giacometti. Temporary exhibits are also mounted.

Calle San Cristoforo, 701 Dorsoduro. ☎ *041-540-5411. Vaporetto: 1 or 82 to Accademia; walk left past the Accademia, turn right on Rio Terrà A. Foscarini, turn left on Calle Nuova Sant'Agnese, continue on Piscina Former, cross the bridge, continue on Calle della Chiesa and then Fondamenta Venier along the small canal, and turn left on Calle San. Cristoforo. Admission: 12,000L ($6) adults; 8,000L ($4.30) students and children 16 and under. Open: Wed–Mon 10 a.m.–6 p.m. (Sat to 10 p.m.).*

Gallerie dell'Accademia

Rivaling Florence's Galleria degli Uffizi and Rome's Galleria Borghese, Venice's Gallerie dell'Accademia contains great paintings from the thirteenth to the eighteenth century. Its 24 rooms are housed in a former church (deconsecrated in 1807), its monastery, and its **Scuola Grande di Santa Maria della Carità**, one of Venice's religious associations. The complex also houses Venice's **Academy of Fine Arts.** You can follow the development of art from the medieval period to the Renaissance through the galleries, while also walking through the history of Venetian art.

In room 1 you find the luminous, influential works of Veneziano, still very medieval in feeling. Then you pass into the totally different world of the fifteenth century, marked by greater naturalism, fuller figures, and the introduction of perspective. For example, Jacopo Bellini's *Madonna and Child* shows the figures in three-quarter view rather than head-on, giving an intimate feeling. In succeeding rooms are Mantegna's *St. George,* works by Mantegna's brother-in-law Giovanni Bellini, and examples of Tintoretto's revolutionary work (radical postures, greater looseness, and theatricality, as well as an instantly recognizable palette).

There's too much in the Accademia to even give an adequate summary, but don't miss Lorenzo Lotto's striking **portrait of a young man** watched by a small lizard on a table; Giorgione's haunting **portrait of an old woman;** and the Tiepolo **ceiling paintings** rescued from a now destroyed building. One of the most famous works is Veronese's incredible, enormous *Last Supper:* Its frenzied energy and party atmosphere (with wine flowing and dwarf figures in the foreground) brought a charge of heresy (and a hasty change of title to *The Banquet in the House of Levi*). At the end of room 15 is Palladio's gravity-defying staircase. Room 20 contains a fascinating series of paintings by Carpaccio, Bellini, and others, all commissioned to illustrate miracles of the True Cross, a fragment of which was brought to Venice in 1369, but also illustrating Venice as it once was.

Campo della Carità, Dorsoduro, at the foot of the Accademia Bridge. ☎ *041-522-2247. Vaporetto: 1 or 82 to Accademia. Admission: 12,000L ($7) adults; children 16 and under and seniors 60 and over free. Open: Tues–Sat 9 a.m.–9 p.m. (Sun–Mon to 2 p.m.).*

Museo Correr

The Correr, which gets less press than the more famous Venetian museums, offers an interesting and eclectic collection, including not only art but also items that make up a history of daily Venetian life, like games, cards, coins, and weapons. Among the clothing are robes worn by the *doges*. The artwork highlights are Canova **bas-reliefs**; a Cosmé Tura *Pietà* from 1460, a fanciful and in some ways surreal painting with a red Golgotha in the background; the famous Carpaccio *Two Venetian Ladies* (familiarly called *The Courtesans* but now known to be a pair of respectable Venetian ladies, a fragment from a larger painting); and a strange Lucas Cranach, with Christ rising from the tomb and two bearded soldiers looking trollish. Hugo van der Goes's emotional small **Crucifixion** is striking.

Procuratie Nuove in Piazza San Marco, San Marco. ☎ *041-522-5625. Vaporetto: 1 or 82 to San Marco–Vallaresso. Admission: See the Palazzo Ducale entry. Open: Summer daily 9 a.m.–7 p.m. (winter to 5 p.m.).*

Piazza San Marco

The symbol of Venice, its center past and present, this piazza is the site richest in monuments in the whole city. The square itself is majestic. Obviously, the **Basilica di San Marco** represents its main attraction (see earlier listing), but there's much more to see. Outside the basilica is the **Torre dell'Orologio**, a clock tower built in 1496. This is a Venetian masterpiece: The clock indicates the phases of the moon and signs of the zodiac, while above it a complicated mechanism propels statues of the Magi (the three kings bringing offerings to Jesus) guided by an angel to come out at the striking of the hour and pass in front of the Virgin and Child. Above this, yet another mechanism propels two bronze Moors to strike a bell on the hour. A gruesome legend has it that when the clock was completed, it was such a wonder that the workman who designed and built it was blinded so he could never duplicate it anywhere else. The whole tower was completely restored for the new millennium, and the delicate mechanisms were completely taken apart by the renowned watchmaker Piaget. An exhibit in the tower explains how this magnificent timepiece works.

Next to the basilica is the **Palazzo Ducale** (see listing later in this section). Its exterior, though beautifully carved in marble, gives little hint of the vast spaces and many treasures inside (and a few horrors).

Also on the square is the **Campanile di San Marco** (bell tower) from which you can admire a 360-degree panorama of the city — and you can do so without climbing hundreds of steps because there's an elevator. The campanile is only about a century old, for the original fell down in 1902 and had to be rebuilt. On the other end of the square is the **Museo Correr** (see listing earlier in this section). As you approach the museum, on your left you see the famous **Caffè Florian** and on the right the **Caffè Quadri** (see "Nightlife").

Piazza San Marco

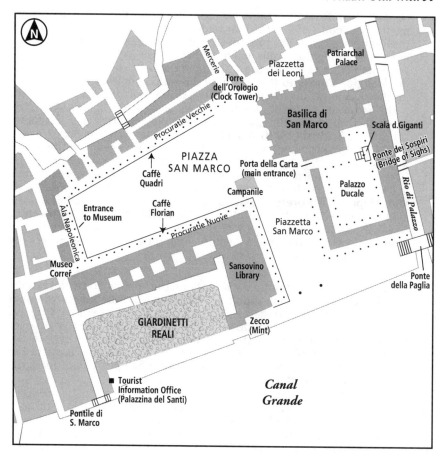

The smaller square between Piazza San Marco and the water is known as the **Piazzetta San Marco**, once a little harbor and later filled in. The piazzetta has been modified in various ways since the ninth century. One of the public functions that went on here was executions, carried out between the two granite columns topped by Venetian-Byzantine capitals. One of the columns supports the famous statue of the lion of St. Mark; next to him is a statue of the patron saint of the city Mark put out of a job, St. Theodore.

Piazza San Marco. ☎ *041-522-4951 (Torre dell'Orologio).* ☎ *041-522-4064 (Campanile). Vaporetto: 1 or 82 to San Marco–Vallaresso. Admission: Torre dell'Orologio free; Campanile 8,000L ($4.30) adults; 3,000L ($1.60) children. Open: Campanile summer daily 9 a.m.–8 p.m.; winter daily 9:45 a.m.–4 p.m. Torre dell'Orologio daily 9:45 a.m.–5:30 p.m.*

Palazzo Ducale and Ponte dei Sospiri

Once the private home of the *doges* (elected for life), the seat of the government, and a court of law, the pink-and-white marble **Palazzo Ducale** was the Republic's heart. The present Gothic-Renaissance building was begun in 1173 and integrated walls and towers of an A.D. 810 castle. The palazzo was enlarged in 1340 with the addition of the new wing housing the **Sala del Maggior Consiglio (Great Council Room)**, a marvel of architecture for the size of the unsupported ceilings. On the left side of the courtyard is the **Scala dei Giganti,** guarded by two giant stone figures. After you reach the top of these steps, you enter the loggia, from which departs the famous **Scala d'Oro (Golden Staircase);** it leads to the doge's apartments and government chambers, where are conserved beautiful paintings by the major artists of the sixteenth century (all the work by fifteenth-century artists decorating the older wing was destroyed by fires at the end of the sixteenth century), such as Titian, Tintoretto, Veronese, and Tiepolo. Tintoretto's ***Paradiso,*** in the Great Council Room, is said to be the largest oil painting in the world (not Tintoretto's best, however). A little-known part of the palace's collection is a group of paintings bequeathed by a bishop, including interesting works by Hieronymous Bosch.

From the palace you continue your visit on the famous **Ponte dei Sospiri (Bridge of Sighs)**, which didn't get its name from the lovers who met under it. The bridge connects the palace to the 16th-century **Prigioni Nuove (New Prisons)**, and those condemned to death had to pass over this bridge (supposedly sighing heavily) both on their way into the prison and eventually on their way out to be executed in Piazzetta San Marco. The two red columns in the facade of the Doge's Palace mark the place where the death sentences were read out.

If you're interested in the dark history of these ages, you'll love the special guided tour, the **Itinerari Segreti** ("Secret Itineraries") offered: It takes you into the doge's hidden apartments and the **Palazzo di Giustizia (Palace of Justice),** where the most important decisions were made. You also visit the famous **Piombi** ("leads"), the prisons under the lead roof of the palace; horribly hot in summer and cold in winter — this is where Casanova was held and from where he made his illustrious escape. You then visit the Prigioni Nuove, built when the palace's limited facilities became insufficient. The guided tour is available in English, and you need to book in advance by calling the number at the end of this listing; the admission includes the guided visit and the regular ticket.

If you want to follow your own guided tour, you can rent an audio guide at the entrance (available in six languages, including English), with headphones (up to two people); it tells you the history and interesting features of the various attractions inside and outside.

Don't be misled by the exterior; the Palazzo Ducale is huge, especially when you count the labyrinthine prison next door, through which you can wander (and shudder at the medieval conditions — the place was used into the 1920s). You can easily spend four hours inside, especially if you take one of the special tours.

When you pay admission to the Palazzo Ducale, you get a **package ticket** including same-day admission to the palazzo as well as the Biblioteca Marciana and Museo Archeologico (Piazzetta San Marco), Museo Correr, Museo Vetrario di Murano, Scuola di Merletti di Burano (on Burano), and Palazzo Mocenigo (on Salizzada di San Stae in San Polo, housing a museum of fabric and costumes).

Piazza San Marco; the entrance to the palace is from the Porta del Frumento on the water side. ☎ *041-522-4951. Fax: 041-528-5028 Advance reservations recommended (with your reservation you go directly to the booth and buy your ticket without standing in line). Vaporetto: 1, 14, 41, 42, 51, 52, 71, 72, or 82 to San Zaccaria. Admission: 18,000L ($10) adults, 10,000L ($5) students 15–29, and 6,000L ($3.25) children under 15; children under 6 free. "Secret Itineraries" tour Thurs–Tues 10:30 a.m. in English (in Italian at 10 a.m. and noon) 24,000L ($13) adults, 14,000L ($8) students, and 8,000L ($4.30) children under 14. Open: Daily summer 9 a.m.–7 p.m. (winter to 5 p.m.); ticket booth closes 1½ hours before.*

Ponte di Rialto

The original wooden bridge here started rotting away, and the citizens of Venice couldn't decide what to do. Finally, in 1588, they decided to replace it with the current stone marvel. The bridge opens onto the Rialto district in San Polo, the merchant area of the past. Ships arrived here after stopping at the Dogana (Customs house) at the tip of Dorsoduro and discharged their merchandise in the large warehouses. Goods were then sold at the market surrounding the warehouses. The fish and vegetable market had survived until 1998, when it was moved to the current merchant and maritime area of Venice, near the Stazione Ferroviaria Santa Lucia.

Across the Canal Grande, between Riva del Vin and Riva del Carbon. Vaporetto: 1 or 82 to Rialto.

Scuola Grande di San Rocco

San Rocco is Jacopo Tintoretto's Sistine Chapel. From 1564 to 1587, Tintoretto, a brother of the school, decorated the **Sala dell'Albergo**, the **sala inferiore** (lower hall), and the **sala superiore** (upper hall) with an incredible series of paintings on biblical and Christian subjects. There are 21 paintings on the upper hall ceiling alone (mirrors are available so you don't have to strain your neck). The most impressive is his *Crucifixion,* a painting of almost overpowering emotion and incredible detail (the tools used to make the cross are strewn in the foreground); the painter shows the moment when one of the two thieves' crosses is raised. The upper hall is also decorated with a fascinating collection of Francesco Pianta wood sculptures from the seventeenth century; some depict artisans and the tools of their trade with an amazing realism. Works by Bellini, Titian, and Tiepolo are also on display.

Campo San Rocco, 3058 San Polo. ☎ *041-523-4864. Vaporetto: 1 or 82 to San Tomà; walk up to Calle Campaniel, turn right, turn left on Campo San Tomà, continue onto Calle Larga Prima and Salizzada San Rocco, and turn left. Admission: 9,000L ($4.85) adults; 6,000L ($3.25) students, 3,000L ($1.60) children. Open: Summer daily 9 a.m.–5:30 p.m.; winter daily 10 a.m.–4 p.m.*

More cool things to see and do

No matter how long you decide to stay in Venice, you'll discover that the length of your visit is always too short. There are so many interesting things to see and do that time is never enough. Here are some more sights you can check out in and around Venice, many of these geared toward children, who can stand only so many hours in a museum:

✔ Built in the thirteenth century, the **Arsenale** (vaporetto: 1, 41, or 42 to Arsenale; follow Calle dei Forni to its end, turn left on Calle di Pegola, and turn right into Campo Arsenale) was the Venetian Republic's shipyard, the largest in the Mediterranean. At its heyday, crews could assemble a vessel from prefab timbers in a single day! Although you can't visit the Arsenale — it's still a restricted military area — the portal is beautiful and so is the view of the canal flowing into the Arsenale's large pond. The lions decorating the entrance were brought back to Venice as spoils of war; the standing lion was taken in the Crusades and once overlooked the harbor of Piraeus in Greece.

✔ The word *ghetto* has been used to name the neighborhood once set apart for Jews in European cities, but the Venetian **Ghetto (Ghetto Novo)** was Europe's first. It was established in 1516 on a small island accessible by only one bridge that was closed at night (you can still see the grooves in the marble sottoportico where the iron bars fitted). In 1541, when groups of Jews from Germany, Poland, Spain, and Portugal fled to Venice, the government allowed the community to expand into the **Ghetto Vecchio (Old Ghetto)**, the area between the Ghetto Novo and the Rio di Cannaregio, which has the two largest places of worship — the **Scola Levantina** and **Scola Spagnola** (the Levantine and Spanish synagogues). To accommodate the growing population, buildings were made taller and taller, so that this area has some of the tallest buildings in Venice. Every hour daily beginning at 10:30 a.m., guided tours of the Ghetto (at 12,000L/$6 adults or 9,000L/$4.90 children, students, and seniors) start at the **Museo Ebraico** (Campo del Ghetto Novo; ☎ **041-715-359**; vaporetto: 1 or 82 to San Marcuola); the museum is open summer daily 10 a.m. to 7 p.m. in summer and Sunday to Friday 10 a.m. to 4:30 p.m. in winter, and admission is 5,000L ($2.70) adults and 3,000L ($1.60) students and seniors.

✔ A visit to Venice isn't complete without a trip to the lagoon. Of the three famous islands nearby Venice, **Murano** is the closest and largest (connected via a navetta direct from rail station and vaporetti nos. 41, 42, 71, 72, 12, and 13). This community of more than 6,000 contains about 70 glass factories, some of which allow you to sit and watch glass being blown. There are many shops selling glass of all kinds and several good seafood restaurants (see "Where to Dine in Venezia"). Glassmaking was moved from Venice to Murano by a 1291 decree because of the danger of fire. One indicator of just how important Murano's wealth has been over the centuries is that aristocrats could marry the daughters of the island's glass masters without compromising their noble titles. Some people think Murano is industrial and not exactly "picturesque"; we like Murano because it has real people doing real things (and eating real good food). At the **Museo Vetrario di Murano** (Fondamenta Giustinian; ☎ **041-739-586**), you can see a wonderful selection of glass. Summer hours are Thursday to Tuesday 10 a.m. to 5 p.m. (winter to 4 p.m.), and admission is 8,000L ($4.30) adults and 5,000L ($2.70) students, with children under 10 free. The Venetian-Byzantine **Chiesa di Santa Maria e Donato** is really one of the wonders of the whole Venetian region. Founded in the seventh century, it was rebuilt in the twelfth. The floor is decorated with a mosaic of birds and animals dating from 1140. In the apse is a dramatic and simple mosaic of the Virgin Mary, from the first half of the thirteenth century; she wears a deep blue gown and is pictured against a shimmering gold background. The church also has a Paolo Veneziano *Madonna and Child with Saints.*

✔ The second island of the trio (vaporetto no. 12 from Fondamenta Nove), **Torcello** is where the civilization of the lagoon began. In 639, the diocese of Altino was moved here because of the barbarian invasions. It grew into a town of 20,000 inhabitants and was the focus of the lagoon — until this area became more and more marshy and the population center shifted to Venice. Torcello today is abandoned, and because Venice used it as a quarry, few buildings are left. The **Cattedrale di Santa Maria Assunta,** however, is magnificent, founded in 639 and added to over the centuries (in 824 and in 1004). The campanile is one of the lagoon's highest, but the real attractions are the thirteenth-century Byzantine mosaics inside — a striking *Madonna and Child* and an almost Boschian *Last Judgment* full of demons and beasts. Open daily 10 a.m. to 12.30 p.m. and 2 to 6:30 p.m., the church sits in the middle of a grassy plain reached by a canal from the dock; you can do the walk in 15 minutes or so, but there may be gondoliers hanging around to convince you to make the trip by boat.

✔ The farthest from Venice — about half an hour by *vaporetto* no. 12 from Fondamenta Nove — **Burano** is a fishing village renowned for its lacemaking. The typical craft is still alive and there are still a few fishermen left too, but a lot of boats seem to be lying unused in people's backyards. The houses are also famous for their bright colors, ranging from purple to mustard to bright yellow. The town itself is almost wholly given up to lace shops, and the **Scuola di Merletti di Burano** (San Martino Destra 183; ☎ **041-730-034**) is right in the middle of town on Piazza Baldassare Galuppi. It has a lace museum where you can study some of the amazing creations of this world-renowned center at leisure (without people pressing you to buy). Summer hours are Wednesday to Monday 10 a.m. to 5 p.m. (winter to 4 p.m.). The **Duomo** is just across the street and features a Tiepolo *Crucifixion;* it's open daily 9 a.m. to 12:30 p.m. and 3 to 6 p.m. You can observe the radical tilt of the campanile from almost anywhere on the island — it's truly frightening from some angles!

✔ The island of **Lido** (take vaporetto no. 1, 6, 14, 41, 42, 61, 62, or 82 to Lido) is the stretch of sand protecting the lagoon from the open sea. It's called Lido (beach) because it's here that Venetians come to enjoy the beaches on the open-water side. On the lagoon side, you have a fantastic view of Venice. The Lido is also the seat of some of the most elegant hotels from the early 1900s, such as the art nouveau Hotel des Bains (see "Where to Stay in Venezia"). The two best things to do here are spending a decadent evening at the elegant casino (in summer) after dinner in a fancy restaurant (see "Where to Dine in Venezia") and biking around this barrier island, which extends for 11 km (6.9 miles). If you choose this second option, you can rent a bike at the shop on Piazzale Santa Maria Elisabetta where the ferry arrives or in the three shops on Gran Viale leading away from the vaporetto station (Gardin Anna Vallè, Piazzale Santa Maria Elisabetta 2/a, ☎ **041-276-0005**; Lazzari Bruno, Gran Viale Santa Maria Elisabetta 21/b, ☎ **041-526-8019**; or Barbieri Giorgio, Via Zara 5, ☎ **041-526-1490**). You can take either of the two parallel roads, the one running on the lagoon side or the one running on the sea side. If you go left from the *vaporetto* station, you soon arrive at the end of the island and can take a ride along the narrow sandbar leading to the lighthouse. It overlooks one of the three entry channels to the lagoon. If you prefer a more urban landscape, go toward the right and the sea; you come to the casino and the art nouveau buildings. If you're in good shape, you can reach **Malamocco** (one of the lagoon's oldest settlements) and, even farther, **Alberoni** (a fishing village protected by dikes).

And on your left, San Marco: Seeing Venice by guided tour

Many travel agencies organize tours of Venice, but the best are offered by **American Express** (Salizzada San Moisè, 1471 San Marco; ☎ **041-520-0844**; vaporetto: 1 or 82 to San Marco–Vallaresso). At about 35,000L ($19) for a half day and 60,000L ($32) for a full day, a guide walks you around the sights and keeps you from getting lost. American Express also has the best prices — half that of other guide services.

Suggested 1-, 2-, and 3-day Sightseeing Itineraries

If you're adventurous, you can easily visit Venice by yourself. As we mention earlier, we think that the difficulty of touring Venice is overrated: Getting lost is quite fun because there are no dangerous neighborhoods and it's easy to get "unlost." Just arm yourself with a good map and go!

If you have only 1 day in Venice

Assuming you arrive very early in the morning, or even better the night before, and have a full day, you may want to aim immediately for **San Marco.** Start at **Stazione Santa Lucia** (*vaporetto* stop Ferrovia) or **Piazzale Roma** (if you arrive by car), and take *vaporetto* no. 1 for a leisurely descent of the **Canal Grande.** Admire the gorgeous architecture of the *palazzi* along the way and stop at **Piazza San Marco.** Visit the **Basilica di San Marco** and — if you have time and you have an advance reservation — the **Palazzo Ducale.** From Piazza San Marco, take an adventurous walk toward the **Ponte di Rialto** and lunch on your way (see "Where to Dine in Venezia"). At the bridge, take *vaporetto* no. 1 or 82 heading south and get off at the Accademia. Spend the afternoon visiting the splendid **Gallerie dell'Accademia.** In the evening, see the colorful neighborhoods of **San Polo** and **Dorsoduro** or have dinner on the island of **Lido** — and maybe, if it's summer, indulge in a game at the **casino.**

If you have 2 days in Venice

An extra day in Venice allows you to visit the city with more leisure. You can follow the same suggestions as in the one-day itinerary above, but instead of skipping (or limiting yourself at) the **Palazzo Ducale,** take your time to visit it, including the prisons, as well as the rest of **Piazza San Marco,** with the **Museo Correr,** the **Torre dell'Orologio,** and the **Campanile.** In the evening of the first day, follow the suggested one-day itinerary. On the second day, get up early and visit the **Gallerie dell'Accademia.** For lunch, head to the *vaporetto* for the islands and go to **Murano,** where you can eat and see the glassmaking (alternatively, visit the **Scuola Grande di San Rocco** and the **Basilica dei Frari** to round out your knowledge of Venetian Renaissance painting). Afterward, you can either come back to town for a romantic dinner and stroll in **San Polo, Dorsoduro,** and/or the **Giudecca** or head for the **Lido,** depending on what you chose to do the evening before.

If you have 3 days in Venice

In this case you can splurge. Use the first two days to visit all the "must sees" as suggested in the itineraries above, but keep **Murano** for later (choose the **Scuola Grande di San Rocco/Basilica dei Frari** option for day two). Use the third day for a cruise of the islands: Get up early in the morning and take *vaporetto* no. 12 to **Torcello,** visit the **Cattedrale di Santa Maria Assunta,** and eat lunch at the Locanda Cipriani (see "Where to Dine in Venezia") or one of the other *trattorie,* then continue on to Murano and **Burano.** If you get going early, you should still have time to stroll around **San Marco** before dinner.

Shopping

Venice is known for blown glass, lace, fabric, antiques, and fine paper. Remember that shopping hours generally are daily 9 a.m. to 1 p.m. and 3.30 to 7.30 p.m. (only local neighborhood shops close on Sunday).

Don't part with your money too quickly. In a place with as many tourists as this, a 10-minute walk away from Piazza San Marco can yield a significant price reduction. Examine whatever you buy with care — there are many cheapo versions of the genuine article that aren't worth a thing. Our philosophy is, "If I like it, and I have X lire to spend on it, then I won't be disappointed." Some people, on the other hand, want not only something they like but something they can feel is valuable to others and would've cost more back home. If you're hoping to find a bargain — like what the Dutch paid for Manhattan — consider that the Venetians have been merchants for over a thousand years and there's not much they don't know about bargaining. 'Nuff said?

The best shopping areas

For glass, the best shops are in Murano and around Piazza San Marco, and for lace you need to go to Burano or to the area between Piazza San Marco and the Ponte di Rialto. For these two specialized items and paper, see the reliable shops we list.

For browsing, the best streets are the **Mercerie** (the zigzag route from the Piazza San Marco clock tower to the Ponte di Rialto) and the path leading from Piazza San Marco to Campo Santo Stefano and includes **Calle Larga XXII Marzo.** Here you can find big-name Italian stores specializing in everything from shoes to housewares to clothing. Of course, these kinds of shops also exist in Florence or Rome.

The **Ponte di Rialto** is famous for its shops, which spill over into the surrounding neighborhood, particularly on the Dorsoduro side. Many of these merchants, however, aren't selling Murano chandeliers and Burano tablecloths, but T-shirts with pictures of Piazza San Marco and plastic Campaniles. Don't count on finding much more than some souvenirs and trinkets for the folks back home.

What to look for and where to find it

In Venice, you feel like a bull in a china shop — there's glass here, there, and everywhere. Some of it is low quality, however, and some isn't even from Venice! If you already know a lot about glass, you're okay. If not, be very careful.

Here are a couple of recommendations of reputable glass shops. **Venini** (Piazzetta dei Leoncini, 314 San Marco; ☎ **041-522-4045**; vaporetto: 1 or 82 to San Marco–Vallaresso) is just to the left of the basilica and near the clock tower. This emporium is world-renowned and has its own furnace, so it's not just a store. Prices are what you'd expect for works of art; one drinking glass could cost up to 2,000,000L ($1,081). **Marco Polo** (Frezzeria, west of Piazza San Marco, 1644 San Marco; ☎ 041-522-9295; vaporetto: 1 or 82 to San Marco–Vallaresso), has some small and therefore more affordable items. Its selection of Murano glass is exceptional. Another option, of course, is to go to Murano itself and shop around; a huge array of glass shops and showrooms lines both sides of the **Rio dei Vetrai,** which means "the small canal of the glassmakers" (see "More cool things to see and do"). Prices will be the same as in town, but the selection will be much larger.

The deal with lace is the same as with glass: You may find something handmade in Venice, not handmade in Venice, or not handmade and actually produced thousands of miles away. You can go to Burano — go there anyway just for the experience (see "More cool things to see and do") — but some of the shops there feel very fake, some subject you to heavy sales pressure, and we hear rumors about some lace coming from other parts of Italy or even the Far East. Again, if you know your linens and laces, you can tell what you're buying. If not, it may be better to go to a reputable shop in Venice. For example, **Jesurum** (Mercerie del Capitello, 4857 San Marco; ☎ 041-520-6177; vaporetto: 1 or 82 to San Marco–Vallaresso) is a reliable lace shop that has been in business since the 1870s. High quality is expensive, though the range of items, from cocktail napkins to bed linens, means you stand a good chance of finding something for your budget.

If you're in town to enjoy Carnevale and didn't pack your eighteenth-century finery, you're going to need a mask at the very least. The **Laboratorio Artigianale Maschere**, just a short way from SS. Giovanni e Paolo (Barbaria delle Tole, 6657 Castello; ☎ 041-522-310; vaporetto: 41, 42, 51, or 52 to Ospedale) has some of the most beautiful costumes. Another good shop is the more affordable **Mondonovo** (Rio Terra Canal, 3063 Dorsoduro; ☎ 041-528-7344; vaporetto: 1 or 82 to Accademia). Still, expect to pay 30,000L ($16) for a basic mask; for the beautiful and artful masks, prices run into the millions of lire.

Handmade marbleized paper is a specialty of Venice. **Piazzesi** (Campiello della Feltrina, just off Santa Maria del Giglio, 2511 San Marco; ☎ 041-522-1202; vaporetto: 1 to Giglio) is said to be one of the oldest in the business — founded in 1900. The marbleizing is produced by blowing the ink onto the paper by hand (or rather by mouth). Some of the molds used here are from the 1700s. Note that Piazzesi's paper is for sale all over Italy.

Nightlife

As often in Italy, nightlife for the locals means visiting pubs, sitting at outdoor terraces in well-placed cafes, going to concerts, and dancing at discos — usually for the youngest. Night ends early in Venice, and it's rare to find things that stay open much past midnight. For the big discos you have to go to the mainland.

The performing arts

Venice is famous for music; it seems there are always a dozen perfor-mances and concerts going on, whether in the major theaters or in a former church. The **Orchestra di Venezia**, which performs in period costumes, is one of the most entertaining ensembles. Performances are held in the **Scuola Grande di San Giovanni Evangelista** (Campo San Giovanni Evangelista, 2454 San Polo; vaporetto: 1 or 82 to San Tomà), near the Frari church. Prices range from 40,000 to 60,000L ($22 to $32). For information, call ☎ **041-522-8125;** Fax: 041-523-5807; or check the Web site at www.orchestra.venezia.it.

The **Teatro Goldoni** (Calle Goldoni, 4650/B San Marco; ☎ **041-520-7583;** vaporetto: 1 or 82 to Rialto) is one of Venice's premier theaters, espe-cially with the sad demise of the La Fenice. Indeed, Venice's largest opera theater, the **Teatro La Fenice** (Campo San Fantin, 1965 San Marco) is still being reconstructed after the fire that gutted it in 1996. The theater has a temporary site at the **Palafenice** (☎ **041-786-501;** Fax: 041-786-580; Internet: www.palafenice.it; E-mail: fenice@ interbusiness.it; vaporetto: 72 or 82 to Tronchetto), an outdoor tent on the Tronchetto island. Tickets are 30,000 to 80,000L ($16 to $43). You can also book online at www.tin.it/fenice.

The best way to find music is to keep your eyes peeled for the poster ads, which are plastered everywhere there's a free wall.

Bars and pubs

Since Hemingway's days in Venice, one of the classic things for visitors to do is head to **Harry's Bar** (Calle Vallaresso, 1323 San Marco; ☎ **041-528-5777;** vaporetto: 1 to San Marco–Vallaresso) for a martini or a Bellini (*prosecco,* a champagne-like white wine, and the juice of white peaches). Harry's also has great food, but the prices are as huge as the reputation — figure on 80,000L ($43) as the base price for a main dish. Even the simplest cocktail costs around $10.

If you're looking for relaxed nightlife, Dorsoduro is the place to go. Among the many pubs, we like **Senso Unico** (Calle della Chiesa, just off Campo S. Vio, 684 Dorsoduro; ☎ **041-241-0770;** vaporetto: 1 or 82 to Accademia), where you can have a drink in a cheerful ambiance and listen to some music; the beer is not bad either. Senso Unico stays open untill 1 a.m. too. Another place where you can hear music and have a drink is **Caffè Blue** (San Pantalon, 3778 Dorsoduro; ☎ **041-523-7227;** vaporetto: 1 or 82 to San Tomá), which stays open until 2 a.m.

In Castello, the American Bar **Lanterna Blu** (Campo San Lorenzo, 5063 Castello; ☎ **041-523-5571;** vaporetto: 1, 14, 41, 42, 51, 52, 71, 72, or 82 to San Zaccaria) offers live music and cabaret. Closer to the heart of things is the **Devil's Forest Pub** (Calle Stagneri, 5185 San Marco;

☎ **041-520-0623**; vaporetto: 1 or 82 to Rialto), which is very popular and often crowded.

You won't find any gay or lesbian bars in Venice, but you can find some in nearby Padua, a lovely old city about 35 minutes from Venice by train (see Chapter 19).

Caffès

Right on Piazza San Marco are two cafes that square off (sorry) against each other with classical music groups. They've been there for centuries: **Caffè Florian** (☎ **041-528-5338**) from 1720 and **Caffè Quadri** (☎ **041-522-2105**) from 1638. You won't find a more central place in Venice (Byron, Wagner, and other famous people used to hang out here), and these cafes are always packed with visitors admiring the basilica, watching the clouds of pigeons take off and land, and sipping expensive drinks.

If you want something a little more authentic, **Le Cafe** (Campo San Stefano, 2797 San Marco; ☎ **041-523-7201**; vaporetto: 1 or 82 to Accademia, then cross the bridge) serves at its outdoor tables a large assortment of drinks, good coffee, and salads (the last, at 23,000L/$12, are a bit expensive but cheap compared to anything you can get on Piazza San Marco). More than just a poor man's St. Mark's experience (here you can enjoy a martini for 10,500L/$6), the campo is a place where you see many Italians stopping on their way to the train station after work. Le Cafe is easy to find because the statue in the campo looks straight at it.

If you happen to be out at Murano, a nice place to have a beer, a coffee, or a light snack is **Ai Pianta Leoni** (Riva Longa 25; ☎ **041-736-794**; Internet: www.datanduo.it; vaporetto: 41, 42, 71, or 72 to Museo), a modern, bright bar and "snack restaurant" where you can rest and relax out of the heat.

Take a gamble

A treat of a different kind is to try your luck at the casino, which is a little more formal than Las Vegas — they won't let you in with tennis shoes, T-shirts, and shorts. During summer, the casino operates at **Casino Municipale** (Lungomare G. Marconi 4, Lido; ☎ **041-529-7111**; vaporetto: 1, 6, 14, 41, 42, 61, 62, or 82 to Lido). In the off-season, the gambling shifts to Venice proper — the fifteenth-century **Palazzo Vendramin-Calergi** (Strada Nuova, 2040 Cannaregio; same phone; vaporetto: 1 or 82 to San Marcuola), where Wagner died in 1883. Admission to the casino is 18,000L ($10).

Fast Facts: Venezia

Country Code and City Code

The **country code** for Italy is **39**. The **city code** for Venice is **041;** use this code when calling from anywhere outside or inside Italy and even within Venice itself (including the zero, even when calling from abroad).

American Express

The office is at Salizzada San Moisè, 1471 San Marco (☎ **041-520-0844;** vaporetto: 1 or 82 to San Marco–Vallaresso). Summer hours are Monday to Saturday 8 a.m. to 8 p.m. (currency exchange) and 8 a.m. to 5:30 p.m. (everything else); winter hours are Monday to Friday 9 a.m. to 5.30 p.m. and Saturday 9 a.m. to 12.30 p.m.

ATMs

You can find banks with ATMs all around town, especially in the commercial areas of Mercerie, Campo Santo Stefano, Calle Larga XXII Marzo, and Strada Nuova.

Currency Exchange

You can change currency at banks or specialized exchange offices, such as the many on the north side of Piazza San Marco. Remember you can get cash from ATMs that have Cirrus or Plus signs.

Doctors and Dentists

See the "Hospital" entry or call the U.K. consulate or the American Express office for a list of English-speaking doctors and dentists.

Embassies and Consulates

The **U.K. Consulate** is at Campo della Carità, 1051 Dorsoduro (☎ **041-522-7207**). All other consulates are in Milan, three hours away by train.

Emergencies

Ambulance, ☎**118;** Fire, ☎**115;** Pronto Soccorso (first aid), ☎ **041-520-3222.**

Gondola Stands (Gondole)

Molo San Marco (☎ 041-520-0685, vaporetto: 1 or 82 to San Marco–Vallaresso); Ponte di Rialto (☎ 041-522-4904; vaporetto: 1 or 82 to Rialto).

Hospital

The 24-hour **Ospedali Civili Riuniti di Venezia** (Campo SS. Giovanni e Paolo; ☎ **041-260-711;** vaporetto: 41, 42, 51, or 52 to Ospedale) has doctors who speak English.

Information

See "Street Smarts: Where to get information after you arrive" in this chapter.

Internet Access

Venetian Navigator (www. venetiannavigator.com) has three locations (all vaporetto: 1, 14, 41, 42, 52, 52, 71, 72, or 82 to San Zaccaria): Casselleria, 5300 Castello (☎ **041-277-1056**); Calle delle Bande, 5269 Castello (☎ **041-522-6084**), and Spadaria, 676 San Marco (☎ **041-241-1293**). You can also try **Omniservice** (Fondamenta dei Tolentini, 220 Santa Croce; ☎ **041-710-470;** vaporetto: 41, 42, 51, 52, 71, 72, or 82 to Piazzale Roma).

Mail

You can find many post offices around town, but the central one is the **Ufficio Postale** (Fontego dei Tedeschi, 5550 San Marco; ☎ **041-271-7111;** vaporetto: 1 or 82 to Rialto).

Maps

One of the best maps is **Falk,** especially because of the smart way it folds, but there are many other maps available at most bookstores and newsstands around town.

Newspapers and Magazines

Most newsstands in town sell English papers. One of the largest is in the Stazione Santa Lucia.

Pharmacies

A centrally located one is the **International Pharmacy** (Calle Larga XXII Marzo, 2067 San Marco; ☎ **041-522-2311;** vaporetto: 1 or 82 to San Marco–Vallaresso). If you need a pharmacy after hours, ask your hotel or call ☎ **192** to have a list of one open near you.

Police

Call ☎ **113;** for the Carabinieri (other police force), call ☎ **112.**

Rest Rooms

There are few public toilets in town. Clean public toilets are at the foot of the Accademia Bridge (you need 500L) and inside the Stazione Santa Lucia. The best bet for a rest room is often to go to a nice-looking cafe (though you have to buy something, like a cup of coffee).

Safety

Venice is very safe, even in the off-the-beaten-path solitary areas. The only real danger are pickpockets, always plentiful in areas with lots of tourists: Watch your bags and cameras and don't display wads of money or jewelry.

Smoking

Smoking is allowed in cafes and restaurants and is very common. Unfortunately for nonsmokers, it's virtually impossible to find a restaurant with a separate no-smoking area.

Taxes

There's no local tax in Venice. Other taxes are always included in the prices quoted. You can get a refund of the 19 percent **IVA (value-added tax)** for purchases above 300,000L ($160) — (see "Keeping a Lid on Hidden Expenses" in Chapter 4).

Weather Updates

For forecasts, the best bet is to look at the news on TV (there's no "weather number" by telephone as in the States). On the Internet, you can check meteo.tiscalinet.it.

Web Sites

The city maintains a useful site at www.comune.venezia.it, and the official tourist board site is at www.provincia.venezia.it/aptve. At www.carnivalofvenice.com/uk, you can find out what's planned for Carnevale each year and get details on transportation and other basics. Two other good general sites are www.meetingvenice.it and www.doge.it.

Chapter 19

Padua and Verona

● ●

In This Chapter

▶ Touring the art cities of the Veneto

▶ Discovering Padua and the famous Giotto frescoes

▶ Visiting Verona, the setting for the legend of Romeo and Juliet

● ●

*T*he region of the **Veneto** is rich in art cities. Though Venice is the capital of the Veneto and towers above all other cities, some of the smaller ones feature unique works and monuments that are well worth your visit. For example, many visitors stop at Padova (Padua) just to see Giotto's famous chapel full of frescoes (note, however, that the frescoes are undergoing a restoration that started in January 2001). Verona attracts both romantics(it was the setting for Shakespeare's *Romeo and Juliet*) and architecture lovers (Palladio, the sixteenth-century architect who revived classical styles, created magic there). If you can tear yourself away from Venice, you'll find plenty of pleasures in the surrounding towns.

Although you can see each of the destinations in the Veneto as a day trip from Venice, basing yourself away from Venice in order to avoid its inflated prices and dense crowds makes more sense. Either Verona or Padua makes an excellent starting point for the region, although Verona is farther away from Venice.

What's Where?: The Veneto and Its Major Attractions

Just south of Venice, along the coast, lies **Padova (Padua),** with its churches and museums. Although only a medium-sized town, it's still an important contemporary center of art and business that retains a laid-back and pleasant feeling. Padua's star sight is the Cappella degli Scrovegni, where you find Giotto's frescoes. In fact, their fame dwarfs the other art of the city, such as the Duomo and its Baptistry, the Basilica di Sant'Antonio, and the Palazzo della Ragione (however, the Scrovegni Chapel closed in 2001 for renovations that are expected to last until the end of the year). Farther inland, to the west, is pleasant **Verona,** an ancient city whose development dates back to the Romans, as the famous theater in the middle of town attests. Famous for its Romanesque churches, beautiful squares, and attractive Renaissance

The Veneto

architecture, Verona also draws visitors from all over the world who want to see the Casa di Giulietta with its balcony, where people like to believe that the tragic Juliet once lived.

Exciting Padua: Home of Giotto's Fabulous Frescoes

Padova (Padua) is a bustling modern town that's the Veneto's economic heart. However, Padua has been around since time immemorial — it began as a fishing village — and became a Roman municipium in 45 B.C. Ever prosperous, Patavium (the ancient Roman name of Padova) was the site of great public buildings and an amphitheater, but much was destroyed by the barbarian Longobards in A.D. 602. Padua rose from the ashes in the late Middle Ages and early Renaissance, and the university was founded in 1222, making it the second in Italy.

Padua is a nice town where everything is on a human scale, and you can enjoy its magnificent attractions in relative calm (most of the time). The presence of the university makes for an active cultural life, open to whomever wants to take advantage of it. Padua is also linked to St. Anthony, who's buried in the basilica bearing his name. For the location of the tourist office, see "Fast Facts: Padua."

Getting there

On the main line from Rome to the northeast, Padua enjoys excellent rail connections. The city is only 30 minutes from Venice, with trains running as frequently as every few minutes at rush hours for about 5,000L ($2.70). The train trip from Rome lasts about five hours and costs about 55,000L ($30). The **Stazione F.S.** is on Piazza Stazione (☎ **049-875-1800**), only minutes north of the historic center. If you don't feel like walking, use the excellent bus service for 1,500L (80¢).

If you're driving, Padua lies at the convergence of the *autostrada* **A4** (east-west) and **A13** (north-south), thus you can easily reach it via car from any direction.

Buses leave for Padua about every half an hour from Venice. The ride lasts less than an hour and costs 5,000L ($2.70). Padua's bus station is on Via Trieste (☎ **049-820-6844**), off Piazza Boschetti, not far from the train station.

Getting around

Padua's center is relatively small, so you can certainly walk among the sights. The train station is slightly outside the center, but nothing is terribly remote. For example, the Giotto chapel is approximately a 10- or 15-minute walk from the train station. (Other attractions are farther, but in the same direction—for example, it'll take another 20-minute walk to reach the Prato della Valle.) However, if you don't feel like walking, the city has a good bus system. Get a bus map from the tourist office in the train station. For a taxi, call ☎ **049-651-333.**

Where to stay

Albergo Leon Bianco

$$ Center

This small nineteenth-century hotel is very romantic. Stay here in warm weather for the rooftop garden or anytime for its convenient central location. The guest rooms are all modernized and renovated: They're quite large and have parquet floors, air-conditioning, and white or pale color washes on the walls.

Padua

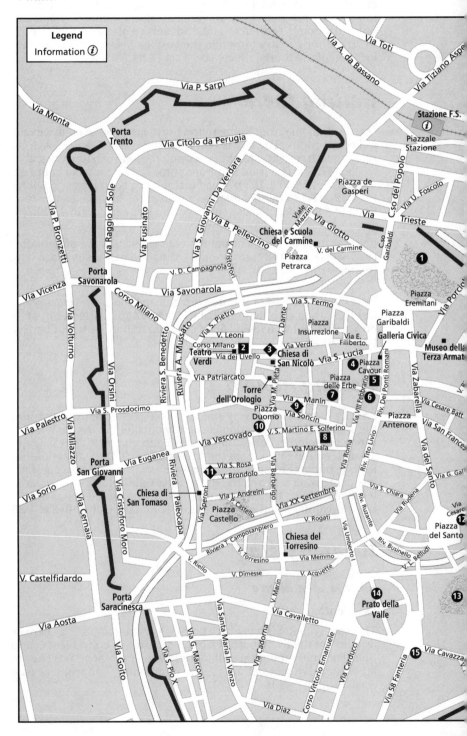

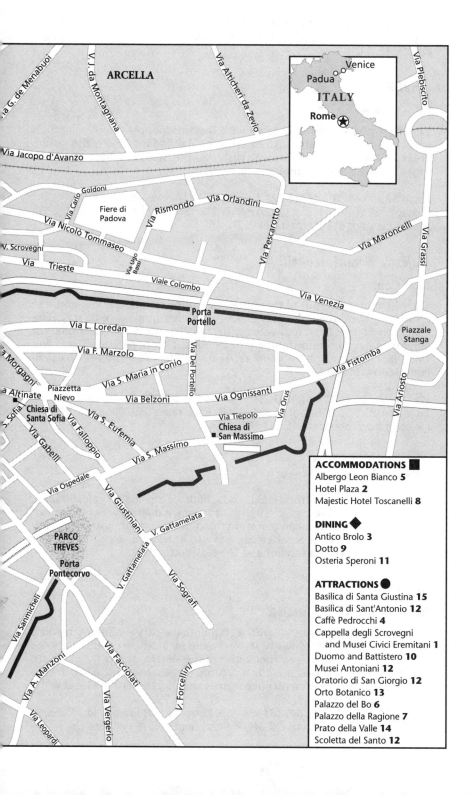

ARCELLA

V.J. da Montagnana

Via Altichieri da Zevio

a G. de Menabuoi

Via Jacopo d'Avanzo

Via Carlo Goldoni

Fiere di
Padova

Via Rismondo   Via Orlandini

Via Nicolò Tommaseo

Via Pescarotto

Via Maroncelli

Via Grassi

V. Scrovegni

Via Ugo Bassi

Via   Trieste

Viale Colombo

Via Venezia

Porta
Portello

Piazzale
Stanga

Via L. Loredan

Via F. Marzolo

Via Del Portello

Via Fistomba

a Morgagni

Via S. Maria in Conio

Via Ognissanti

Via Ariosto

a Altinate

Piazzetta
Nievo

Via Belzoni

Via Orus

S. Sofia

Chiesa di
Santa Sofia

Via S. Eufemia

Via Fallopio

Via Tiepolo

Chiesa di
San Massimo

Via Gabelli

Via S. Massimo

Via Ospedale

Via Giustiniani

PARCO
TREVES

V. Gattamelata

Porta
Pontecorvo

V. Gattamelata

Via Sografi

Via Sanmicheli

Via A. Manzoni

Via Facciolati

V. Forcellini

Via Vergerio

Via Leopardi

Venice

Padua

ITALY

Rome

ACCOMMODATIONS ■
Albergo Leon Bianco **5**
Hotel Plaza **2**
Majestic Hotel Toscanelli **8**

DINING ◆
Antico Brolo **3**
Dotto **9**
Osteria Speroni **11**

ATTRACTIONS ●
Basilica di Santa Giustina **15**
Basilica di Sant'Antonio **12**
Caffè Pedrocchi **4**
Cappella degli Scrovegni
     and Musei Civici Eremitani **1**
Duomo and Battistero **10**
Musei Antoniani **12**
Oratorio di San Giorgio **12**
Orto Botanico **13**
Palazzo del Bo **6**
Palazzo della Ragione **7**
Prato della Valle **14**
Scoletta del Santo **12**

Piazzetta Pedrocchi 12. ☎ *049-657-225. Fax: Same as telephone number. E-mail:* leonbianco@toscanelli.it. *Parking: 25,000L ($14). Rack rates: 162,000L ($88) double. AE, MC, V.*

Hotel Plaza

$$$ Center

The most popular hotel in town with businesspeople, the Plaza offers accommodations in line with international standards. Both the public areas and the guest rooms are stylish and pleasant, and the rooms feature air conditioning and minibars.

Corso Milano 40. ☎ *049-656-822. Fax: 049-661-117. Internet:* www.bcedit.it. *E-mail:* plazapf@gpnet.it. *Parking: 25,000L ($14). Rack rates: 310,000L ($168) double, including buffet breakfast. AE, DC, MC, V.*

Majestic Hotel Toscanelli

$$$ Center

The old square in front of this hotel, the lobby's marble floors and fine furnishings, and the balconies make this a charming place to stay. The guest rooms have been renovated with stylish furniture and offer modern amenities like air-conditioning and satellite TVs. If you stay here, you won't lack for atmosphere, comfort, or something to eat (there's an excellent pizzeria in the hotel).

Via dell'Arco 2. ☎ *049-663-244. Fax: 049-876-0025. E-mail:* majestic@ toscanelli.it. *Parking: 25,000L ($14). Rack rates: 250,000L ($135) double, including buffet breakfast. AE, DC, MC, V.*

Where to dine

Not strong on special traditional foods, Padua's cuisine is typical Italian, with a Venetian influence. As a university town, it offers a variety of cheap lunch spots where you can enjoy anything from pasta and pizza to sandwiches. These cheap eateries are easy to spot all around the center, particularly on Piazza Cavour and Via Matteotti.

Antico Brolo

$$$$ Teatro Verdi Italian

This beautiful restaurant — with a sixteenth-century dining room and a terrace garden — is Padua's best. The menu includes an excellent choice of Italian recipes as well as specialties of the Veneto, such as grilled fish. In the stone-walled basement is a *taverna (tavern)* serving a much simpler but still delicious menu (like pastas and pizzas). Try the local wine.

Corso Milano 22. ☎ *049-664-455. Reservations recommended. Secondi: 25,000–40,000L ($14–$22). AE, DC, MC, V. Open: Lunch and dinner Tues–Sun.*

Dotto

$$ Center   Italian

If you don't want to spend as much as you would at Antico Brolo (see listing) and still get more than a pizza, Dotto is an excellent choice. The menu includes a great selection of pasta dishes, wines of the Veneto, and good *secondi* (all homemade).

Via del Soncin 8. ☎ *049-875-1490. Reservations recommended. Secondi: 14,000–25,000L ($8–$14). MC, V. Open: Lunch Tues–Sun; dinner Tues–Sat.*

Osteria Speroni

$$ Center   Seafood

Just down the street from the Basilica di Sant'Antonio, this restaurant offers an excellent *antipasto* buffet with a variety of fish and vegetable preparations. The regular menu includes regional dishes from coastal Veneto, with an accent on fish. Try the *capitone* (a special kind of eel) when it's in season.

Via Speroni 32–36. ☎ *049-875-3370. Reservations recommended. Secondi: 15,000–25,000L ($8–$14). AE, MC, V. Open: Lunch and dinner Mon–Sat.*

Exploring Padua

Padua is a wonderful place to walk. Many if not most of the buildings have *portici* (porticoes, meaning that they overhang the street and are supported by columns) and the sidewalk runs along beneath them. This gives wonderfully picturesque views, as well as ample space for pedestrians (you won't be worrying about being mowed down by motorscooters, as in some other places). The town also has a few canals and quite a few bridges, giving it a little bit of Venetian feeling.

If you have time for an extensive visit, buy the **biglietto unico Padova Arte** (cumulative ticket) available at the tourist booths and all partici-pating sights. It costs 15,000L ($8) and includes admission to the Musei Civici Eremitani, Cappella degli Scrovegni, Baptistry, Scoletta del Santo, Orto Botanico (Botanical Gardens), and Musei Antoniani.

The top sights

Basilica di Sant'Antonio

Built in the thirteenth century, this basilica houses the remains of St. Anthony of Padua (including his tongue, still amazingly undecayed). Its distinctive Romanesque-Gothic style includes eastern influences, most visible in the eight round domes and the several *campanili* (bell towers) vaguely reminiscent of minarets. Several prominent Renaissance artists worked on the interior: The basilica's treasures include Donatello's **bronze crucifix, reliefs** and **statues** on the high altar (1444–1448) and **frescoes** by fourteenth-century artists Altichiero and Giusto de' Menabuoi. In the square in front of the church is Donatello's **equestrian**

statue of Gattamelata (considered one of his masterpieces). Attached to the basilica is the **Oratorio di San Giorgio (Oratory of St. George)**, which opened for the Jubilee after a period of restoration; here you find a fine cycle of frescoes by Altichiero. Also adjacent to the basilica are the **Scoletta del Santo (School of the Saint),** holding three famous frescoes attributed to Titian, and the **Musei Antoniani,** housing the basilica's rich collection of paintings and precious ceremonial objects.

Piazza del Santo 11. Basilica ☎ *049-878-9722; others 049-875-5235. Admission: Basilica free; Oratorio di San Giorgio 3,000L ($1.60); Scoletta 3,000L ($1.60); Musei Antoniani 5,000L ($2.70). Open: Basilica summer daily 7 a.m.–7:45 p.m., winter daily 6:30 a.m.–7 p.m.; Oratorio and Scoletta summer daily 9 a.m.–12:30 p.m. and 2:30–7 p.m., winter daily 9 a.m.–12:30 p.m. and 2:30–5 p.m.; Musei Antoniani summer Tues–Sun 9 a.m.–1 p.m. and 2:30–6:30 p.m., winter Tues–Sun 10 a.m.–1 p.m. and 2–5 p.m.*

Cappella degli Scrovegni and Musei Civici Eremitani

The **Cappella degli Scrovegni (Scrovegni Chapel)** is surrounded by the archaeological remains of the **Arena Romana (Roman Arena)** — hence its other name, the **Cappella dell'Arena (Arena Chapel)**. You can enter the chapel from the courtyard of the **Musei Civici Eremitani (Civic Museums),** which are well worth a visit themselves. These museums house a large collection of paintings, as well as sculpture and artifacts documenting the history of Padua. The artists showcased here include Giorgione, Titian, Veronese, and other Venetian masters.

The **Scrovegni Chapel** is what makes Padua an artistic pilgrimage site. In 1267, Giotto di Bondone was born in a village not far from Florence and went on to become an apprentice of the great painter Cimabue. The frescoes Giotto executed in the Cappella degli Scrovegni are one of his masterpieces. Construction of the chapel itself began in 1303 by banker Enrico Scrovegni, partly as an act of contrition because of his family's ill-gotten (in Christian terms) wealth. (In his *Inferno,* Dante put Enrico's father, Reginaldo, in the circle of hell reserved for usurers, because usury was considered sinful.) Ironically, the jewel that the chapel became under Giotto's hands led local monks to complain about the excessive luxury of the Scrovegni family. Sometimes you can't win.

The Scrovegni Chapel closed in January 2001 for renovation and is expected to reopen by the end of the year. When it does reopen, you'll need to make a reservation in advance (at the number that we give you at the end of this listing) because of crowds.

The chapel is an early example of a complex project that reflects the vision of a single artist. The unusual design — windows on one side but not the other, no internal architectural decorations — made it a perfect canvas for Giotto's work. The stories that he depicts move from left to right. The top row or band contains scenes from the life of Joachim and Anna, parents of the Virgin Mary. The story isn't very familiar (it comes from the Apocrypha, not the Bible): Joachim is kicked out of the temple and his offering is rejected because he and his wife are childless; while he wanders despondently in the countryside, an angel announces to Anna that she'll give birth to Mary. Meanwhile, Joachim offers a sacrificial animal and then has a dream in which he learns that his wife has conceived; the two are reunited at the gate of Jerusalem in a touchingly human scene that's one of the most celebrated of the chapel's fresco series. The middle and lower levels of the chapel contain scenes from the life of Jesus. Giotto also painted allegorical figures representing six virtues and six vices.

Giotto's frescoes broke with tradition in a number of ways, making them striking and important in art history. His composition is dramatic rather than static as in Byzantine art; he chose scenes that weren't usually depicted; and, above all, he represented human beings with much greater psychological realism, which a glance at these beautiful faces shows. Note that a sign outside says that visits to the chapel are limited to 20 minutes; however, if the crowds aren't large, this rule isn't strictly enforced.

Piazza Eremitani 8, off Corso Garibaldi. ☎ *049-820-4550. Admission: 10,000L ($5) adults, 5,000L ($2.70) children, including both the chapel (by reservation only) and museums. Open: Summer daily 9 a.m.–7 p.m., winter Tues–Sun 9 a.m.–6 p.m.*

Duomo

Built between the sixteenth and eighteenth centuries, the Duomo was partly designed by Michelangelo. Behind the unfinished facade, the two points of interest are the paintings in the **Sagrestia dei Canonici (Sacristy)** and the statues by Florentine artist Giuliano Vangi in the new **Presbiterio (Presbetery).** Attached to the Duomo, the beautiful Romanesque **Battistero (Baptistry)** from 1075 is especially remarkable. The interior is decorated with Giusto de' Menabuoi frescoes, one of the masterpieces of the fourteenth century; they have been recently restored and illustrate scenes from the lives of John the Baptist and Christ. A vision of paradise is gloriously depicted on the domed ceiling. Around the altar, the artist illustrated scenes from the Apocalypse of St. John the Evangelist on 43 panels.

Piazza del Duomo. ☎ *049-662-814. Admission: Duomo free; Battistero 3,000L ($1.60). Open: Duomo Mon–Sat 7:30 a.m. to noon and 3:45–7:30 p.m., Sun 7:45 a.m.–1 p.m. and 3:45–8:30 p.m.; Battistero summer daily 9:30 a.m.–1:30 p.m. and 3–7 p.m., winter daily 9:30 a.m.–1 p.m. and 3–6 p.m.*

Palazzo della Ragione

Known as Il Salone (the Great Hall), this elegantly colonnaded structure was built in 1218 and an upper level added in 1306. It served as the seat of the city's courts of law. On the ground floor, it divides the **Piazza delle Erbe** (green market) from the **Piazza della Frutta** (fruit market). (These markets still occupy the squares today and are a lively affair.) The top floor is the *salone,* one huge open hall (81 × 27 meters). The rich wall frescoes, illustrating religious and astrological themes, date from the thirteenth century. The palazzo's largest conversation piece is a giant fifteenth-century wooden horse for jousting events.

Via VIII Febbraio, between Piazza delle Erbe and Piazza della Frutta. ☎ *049-820-5006. Admission: 12,000L ($6) adults, 10,000L ($5) children. Open: Tues–Sun 9 a.m.–7 p.m.*

More cool things to see and do

If you're able to spend more time in Padua, check out these other sights:

- ✔ **Caffè Pedrocchi** (Piazza Pedrocchi, just off Piazza Cavour; ☎ 049-876-2576) has been the main intellectual gathering place of the city's intelligentsia. The café opened in 1831, when Padua was under Austrian rule, and still had political importance as late as 1948, when it was the scene of a student uprising. There are two porches, one outside and one inside, a bar of travertine marble and elegant nineteenth-century furniture, and a pub. The historic rooms are on the second floor; this is where revolutionary students met informally. The café is undergoing renovation, but it's supposed to be open again by the time you read this. The café's normal hours resemble a museum's — it's closed Monday.

- ✔ The seat of the University of Padua, the **Palazzo del Bo** (Via VIII Febbraio, just off Piazza delle Erbe; ☎ 049-820-9773) was built in the sixteenth century and later enlarged. Founded in 1222, the University of Padua is Italy's second oldest and counted among its scholars Galileo Galilei. It was the first university in the world to have a Teatro Anatomico (Anatomy Theater), an architectural masterpiece by G. Fabrici d'Acquapendente, built in 1594. Here medical students observed dissections of cadavers (sometimes in secret, for it was long forbidden by the church) in order to learn about the human body. Also of interest are the Cortile Antico (Old Courtyard) and the Sala dei Quaranta (Room of the Forty), with the *cattedra* of *Galileo Galilei (Galileo's chair).* You can visit only by free guided tour (Tuesday, Thursday, and Saturday at 9, 10, and 11 a.m.; Monday, Wednesday, and Friday at 3, 4, and 5 p.m.). Call for reservations or show up at one of the listed times.

- ✔ Padua boasts the world's first **Orto Botanico (Botanical Garden;** off Via San Michele, behind the Basilica di Sant'Antonio; ☎ 049-656-614). It was founded in 1545 as the garden for the university's faculty of medicine, where medicinal plants and herbs were grown. Today it houses a very important collection of rare plants. You can also visit the old library and the university's collection of botanical specimens. There's nothing dusty and academic about this garden, however — it's organized as a Renaissance garden and is very pleasurable to stroll through. Summer hours are daily 9 a.m. to 1 p.m. and 3 to 6 p.m. and winter hours Monday to Saturday 9 a.m. to 1 p.m. Admission is 5,000L ($2.70).

- ✔ The **Prato della Valle** (between Via Umberto I and Via Belludi) is a traditional recreational area for Paduans. This monumental park was built in 1775, reclaiming an ancient Roman theater that had degenerated into a swampy pond. Majestic statues line both sides of a large canal that runs around a grassy island. Opening on the Prato is the **Basilica di Santa Giustina** (☎ 049-875-1628), a sixteenth-century church built over ancient temples. Inside the church, over the main altar, is Veronese's painting *Martirio di Santa Giustina (Martyrdom of St. Justine).* The basilica is open daily 8.30 a.m. to noon and 3 to 6 p.m.

Other Veneto favorites

Riviera del Brenta: During the Renaissance, the 17-km (10½-mile) stretch along the Brenta Canal known as the Riviera del Brenta was an elegant resort for noble Venetians, who came here during summer to avoid the heat and smell of Venice and its canals. They built fabulous homes (some designed by the architect Palladio), including the Villa Foscari and the Villa Pisani (where Napoleon once lived), and you can visit many of them.

Vicenza: About 68 km (42 miles) west of Venice, Vicenza was the birthplace of the great High Renaissance architect Andrea di Pietro, known as Palladio, and the city and its environs are filled with palazzi, basilicas, and villas designed by him. Look particularly for his Teatro Olimpico and Villa Rotonda; Goethe said, "You have to see these buildings with your own eyes to realize how good they are."

Treviso: Famous for the cherries grown in the surrounding countryside and for being the birthplace of the famous dessert known as tiramisù, Treviso is 31 km (19 miles) north of Venice. This town draws art lovers because of its many works by Tommaso da Modena.

Marostica: About 7 km (4½ miles) from nearby Bassano del Grappa (after which the Italian brandy, *grappa*, is named), Marostica is famous for the *Game of Life.* During the second week of September in even-numbered years, costumed townspeople use the town square as a chessboard as they become the board's pieces to re-create a medieval contest.

Fast Facts: Padua

Country Code and City Code

The **country code** for Italy is **39.** The **city code** for Padua is **049;** use this code when calling from anywhere outside or inside Italy, even within Padua. Include the zero every time, even when calling from abroad.

Embassies and Consulates

See "Fast Facts: Venice" in Chapter 18.

Currency exchange

You can change money at the train station as well as in the **exchange office at** Via Belludi 15 (☎ **049-660-504**).

Emergencies

Ambulance, ☎**118**; Fire, ☎**115**; road assistance ☎**116**; First Aid (Pronto Soccorso), ☎ **049-821-2856** or 049-821-2857.

Hospital

The **Ospedale Civile** is at Via Giustiniani 1 (☎ **049-821-1111**).

Information

You can write to the main **tourist office** before your trip: APT (Riviera dei Mugnai 8; ☎ **049-875-0655**; Fax: 049-650-794). After you arrive, visit the **tourist booth** inside the train station (☎ 049-875-2077). With a very nice staff and excellent material, the tourist booth can help you find a hotel room if you don't have a reservation. Summer hours are Monday to Saturday 9 a.m. to 7 p.m. and Sunday 9 a.m. to noon. Winter hours are Monday to Saturday 9:15 a.m. to 5:45 p.m. and Sunday 9 a.m. to noon.

Mail

The **Ufficio Postale** (Post Office) is at Corso Garibaldi 33 (☎ 049-820-8511).

Police

Call ☎113; for the Carabinieri (other police force), call ☎112.

Romancing Verona: City of Juliet and Her Romeo

Like Padua, **Verona** was a Roman city that now has a historic center surrounded by a bustling modern urban area (Verona, too, is a major economic hub). After its glory during the reign of Augustus, Verona suffered under barbarian invasions and went into decline. The Scaliger family ruled it in the thirteenth and fourteenth centuries much as the Medici family ruled Florence. Venice absorbed Verona in 1405, and Venetian rule lasted until Napoleon made everybody equal (sort of). Austrian domination followed, and they ruled until 1866 and the unification of Italy.

Today Verona is a popular destination — even though Romeo and Juliet may never have existed, there's plenty to see here — but because of its contemporary vitality, it's not as overwhelmed with tourists as Venice. For the location of the **tourist office,** see "Fast Facts: Verona."

Getting there

The **train** to Verona takes two hours from Venice and six from Rome. The fare is approximately 10,000L ($5) from Venice and 40,000L ($22) from Rome. Trains arrive at the **Stazione Porta Nuova** on Piazza XXV Aprile (☎ 045-590-688).

Verona's **Aeroporto Valerio Catullo,** in Villa Franca, is 16 km (10 miles) from the center. **Meridiana** offers hour-long flights daily from Rome (☎ 06-4780-4222 or 02-864-771) for about 260,000L ($141) round-trip. You can take a taxi from the airport (about 15 minutes), or you can take a regular city bus running from the airport to the town center (1,500L/80¢) in about 20 minutes.

If you're **driving** from Rome, take **A1** to Campogalliano and then Autostrada del Brennero (A22) to the Verona Sud exit (about six hours). The trip is a total distance of 505 km (315 miles). From Venice, take **A4** heading west; the drive requires approximately two hours (it's about 110 km/68 miles).

Verona

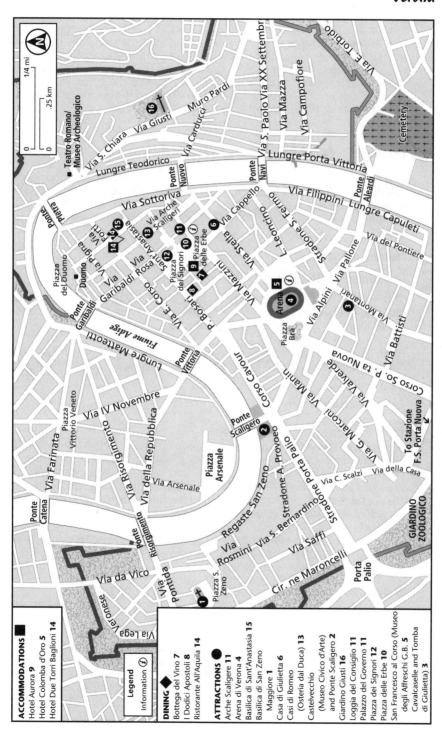

1/4 mi

.25 km

Teatro Romano/
Museo Archeologico

Verona

Cemetery

Via E. Torbido
Via S. Paolo Via XX Settembre
Via Mazza
Via Campofiore
Muro Pardi
Via Carducci
Via Giusti
Via S. Chiara

Lungre Porta Vittoria

Lungre Teodorico

Ponte Navi

Via Filippini Lungre Capuleti

Ponte Aleardi

Via Sottoriva

Via Cappello

Ponte Nuovo

Via del Pontiere

Via Arche
Scaligeri

Via Stella

Via Pallone

Via Sant'Anastasia

Stradone S. Fermo

Via Pigna

L. Leoncino

Piazza
delle Erbe

Via Montanari

Piazza
del Duomo

Duomo

Via E. Corso

Piazza
dei Signori

Via Mazzini

Via Alpini

Ponte
Pietra

Via Garibaldi Rosa

P. Bosari

Arena

Via Battisti

Ponte
Garibaldi

Fiume Adige

Piazza
Brà

Corso So. P.ta Nuova

Lungre Matteotti

Ponte
Vittoria

Corso Cavour

Via G. Marconi

Via Valverde

To Stazione
F.S. Porta Nuova

Via IV Novembre

Piazza
Vittorio Veneto

Via Valverde

Via della Casa

Ponte
Catena

Via Farinata

Via Risorgimento

Via della Repubblica

Ponte
Scaligero

Via C. Scalzi

Via Arsenale

Piazza
Arsenale

Corso Cavour

A. Provoeo

Stradone Porta Pallo

Ponte
Risorgimento

Regaste San Zeno

Via S. Bernardino

Via
Rosmini

Via Saffi

GIARDINO
ZOOLOGICO

Via da Vico

Piazza S.
Zeno

Cir. ne Maroncelli

Porta
Palio

Via Pontida

Via Lega

Veronese

ACCOMMODATIONS ■
Hotel Aurora **9**
Hotel Colomba d'Oro **5**
Hotel Due Torri Baglioni **14**

Legend
ⓘ Information

DINING ◆
Bottega del Vino **7**
I Dodici Apostoli **8**
Ristorante All'Aquila **14**

ATTRACTIONS ●
Arche Scaligere **11**
Arena di Verona **4**
Basilica di Sant'Anastasia **15**
Basilica di San Zeno
  Maggiore **1**
Casa di Giulietta **6**
Casi di Romeo
  (Osteria dal Duca) **13**
Castelvecchio
  (Museo Civico d'Arte)
  and Ponte Scaligero **2**
Giardino Giusti **16**
Loggia del Consiglio **11**
Palazzo del Governo **11**
Piazza dei Signori **12**
Piazza delle Erbe **10**
San Francesco al Corso (Museo
  degli Affreschi G.B. **5**
  Cavalcaselle and Tomba
  di Giulietta) **3**

Getting around

You can easily reach Verona's main attractions on foot, or you can use **city buses.** Tickets cost 1,500L (80¢), and you must purchase them before boarding, either from *tabacchi* (tabacconists) or inside the station. The main bus hubs are the train station (Stazione Ferroviaria) and the Roman Arena (Piazza Brà, see "Exploring Verona"). The winding river Adige flows through Verona much like the Tiber in Rome. Most of the city's attractions are in the river's southern bend.

Where to stay

Verona houses several hotels; if you arrive without a reservation, you can contact the **Cooperativa Albergatori Veronese** (Via Patuzzi 5, parallel to Via Leoncino off the Arena; ☎ **045-800-9844**), which will help you find a room.

Hotel Aurora

$$ Piazza delle Erbe

This good basic hotel, a fifteenth-century structure resting on older foundations, offers views over a piazza. The guest rooms and common areas are functional with modern furnishings.

Piazzetta XIV Novembre 2, off Piazza delle Erbe. ☎ *045-594-717. Fax: 045-801-0860. Rack rates: 150,000–190,000L ($81–$103) double, including breakfast. AE, MC, V.*

Hotel Colomba d'Oro

$$$ Arena

A couple of steps from the Roman Arena (see "Exploring Verona"), this hotel occupies an impressive old building, with fifteenth-century frescoes decorating the hall. It's been an inn since the nineteenth century and in previous incarnations was a villa and a monastery. The guest rooms are comfortable and tasteful. This is a good medium-range choice if you don't want to spring for something really pricey.

Via C. Cattaneo 10. ☎ *045-595-300. Fax: 045-594-974. Parking: 27,000L ($15). Rack rates: 260,000–325,000L ($141–$176) double, including buffet breakfast. AE, MC, V.*

Hotel Due Torri Baglioni

$$$$$ Center

This is *the* elegant place to stay. In the town center, this hotel occupies a building that was the home of the powerful Scaligeri family. In 1990, a major chain took it over and totally restored it. However, the beautiful antique furniture remains, and the public areas are decorated in the grand hotel style. We recommend the hotel's Ristorante All'Aquila, later in this chapter, in "Where to dine."

Piazza Sant'Anastasia 4. ☎ _**045-595-044.** Fax: 045-800-4130. E-mail:_ duetorri. verona@baglionipalacehotel.it. _Parking: 45,000L ($25). Rack rates: 570,000–750,000L ($308–$405) double, including breakfast. AE, DC, MC, V._

Where to dine

Verona offers plenty of cheap places to eat, as well as elegant restaurants that cater to business travelers and well-heeled visitors. You'll find good food as well as good wine: The important wine-growing region of the Veneto supplies Verona with an interesting assortment of fine wines.

Bottega del Vino

$$ Center   Italian

This old _osteria_ is a good place to go for lighter fare; it's more famous as a wine bar, with a large selection of wines from all over Italy and especially the Veneto, but it also serves food with the wine. Accompany your wine samplings with a choice of simple dishes, particularly the _primi._

Via Scudo di Francia 3, near the northern end of Via Mazzini. ☎ **045-800-4535.** _Reservations not necessary. Secondi: 12,000–25,000L ($6–$14). Open: Lunch and dinner Wed–Mon._

I Dodici Apostoli

$$$ Center   Italian

This restaurant has existed for more than two centuries, and its interior is decorated with frescoes. I Dodici Apostoli specializes in regional cuisine, but the chef has added many innovative twists to traditional recipes (marinated salmon stuffed with scallops is one example).

Vicolo Corticella San Marco 3. ☎ **045-596-999.** _Reservations recommended. Secondi: 25,000–32,000L ($14–$17). AE, DC, MC, V. Open: Lunch Tues–Sun; dinner Tues–Sat; closed two weeks in June._

Ristorante All'Aquila

$$$ Center   Italian

Inside the town's most elegant hotel (see Hotel Due Torri Baglioni), this restaurant offers a Liberty-style (art nouveau) decor. The menu changes periodically and includes regional and seasonal specialties. The pastas are prepared with a variety of creamy sauces, and you can order such unusual items as smoked horsemeat. This is a place to go for a real dinner, not just something to eat.

Piazza Sant'Anastasia 4 in the Hotel Due Torri Baglioni. ☎ **045-595-044.** _Reservations recommended. Secondi: 30,000–36,000L ($16–$19). Open: Lunch and dinner daily._

Exploring Verona

A harmonious mix of Roman, medieval, and Renaissance architecture, Verona is one of the preferred destinations of international tourism in northern Italy. Here we selected for you its most famous and worthwhile attractions.

The top sights

Arena di Verona

This famous elliptical Roman arena dates from the reign of Diocletian (it was built around A.D. 290) and remains in surprisingly good condition. The inner ring is basically intact, though a twelfth-century earthquake destroyed most of the outer ring (only four of the arches remain). This was Italy's third largest Roman amphitheater and the second most important to have survived after Rome's Colosseum. The arena's overall length was 152 m (470 feet) and its height 32 m (97.5 feet). Its 44 rows of seats could originally hold as many as 20,000 spectators, who watched gladiators and animals fighting and biting.

These days, however, the arena hosts more civilized entertainments: One of the greatest experiences in Verona is attending an opera or a ballet here during July or August. The setting speaks for itself. Tickets cost 38,000L to 290,000L ($20 to $157); for schedule and ticket information, call ☎ 045-800-5151. To make a reservation in the United States, call the **Global Tickets** agency (☎ 800-223-6108 or 914-328-2150; Fax: 914-328-2752) and the company will mail or fax a voucher to you. You can also make reservations and buy tickets online at www.arena.it.

Piazza Brà. ☎ 045-800-3204. Admission: 6,000L ($3.25) adults, 4,000L ($2.15) children. Open: Tues–Sun 8 a.m.–6:30 p.m.; free first Sun of every month. On performance days, arena closes at 1:30 p.m.

Basilica di San Zeno Maggiore

A wonderful example of the Romanesque style and the most beautiful in northern Italy, this church and campanile were built between the ninth and twelfth centuries above the tomb of Verona's patron saint (the origins of the church go several centuries farther back). Some of its most fascinating artworks are the eleventh- and twelfth-century **bronze door panels** illustrating San Zeno's miracles. Like other works in this part of Italy (notably Venice), they reflect a mix of Byzantine, Gothic, and Turkish influences. The interior has a fourteenth-century timbered roof, and over the entrance is the famous **Ruota della Fortuna (Wheel of Fortune)** rose window from the early twelfth century. Note particularly the Romanesque capitals on the columns and the frescoes (dating from the thirteenth to fifteenth century). On the high altar is a *Madonna and Saints* triptych by Mantegna. Also don't miss the Romanesque **cloister** at the north end of the church.

Piazza San Zeno, just west of the Arena. ☎ 045-800-4325. Admission: 3,000L ($1.60). Open: Summer Mon–Sat 9 a.m.–6 p.m. and Sun. 1–6 p.m.; winter Mon–Sat 10 a.m.–4 p.m. and Sun 1–4 p.m.

Castelvecchio (Museo Civico d'Arte) and Ponte Scaligero

The fourteenth-century **Castelvecchio** perched on the Adige River was the fortress of the Scaligeri family but now houses an art museum containing paintings by artists of the school of the great Renaissance painter Paolo Veronese. Veronese himself is represented, as well as Venetian artists like Tiepolo and Tintoretto. The castle itself is worth a visit, with its labyrinthine passageways and the tower from which you can see sweeping vistas of the city and its environs. The bridge linking the castle with the other side of the river is the famous **Ponte Scaligero** (built between 1355 and 1375), which was destroyed by the Nazis during their retreat at the end of World War II and rebuilt using the pieces that remained in the river.

Corso Castelvecchio 2, at the western end of Corso Cavour. ☎ *045-594-734. Admission: 6,000L ($3.25) adults, 2,000L ($1.10) students. Free the first Sun of each month. Open: Tues–Sun 9 a.m.–6:15 p.m.*

Piazza dei Signori and Arche Scaligere

One of northern Italy's most beautiful *piazze*, surrounded by beautiful palaces, this square was the center of Verona's government during its heyday. The **Palazzo del Governo** is where Cangrande della Scala (one of the first Scaligeri) extended the shelter of his hearth and home to the fleeing Florentine poet Dante Alighieri. A marble statue of Dante stands in the center of the square. The **Palazzo della Ragione,** on the south side of the piazza, was built in 1123 but underwent changes many times in later centuries, including receiving a Renaissance facade in 1524. From its courtyard rises a tower, the majestic **Torre dei Lamberti** (84 m/277 feet), also called the Torre del Comune. An elevator takes you to the top, and the views are magnificent. On the north side of the piazza is the fifteenth-century **Loggia del Consiglio,** which was the town council's meeting place; it's decorated with frescoes and surmounted by five statues of famous Veronese citizens. Five arches lead into Piazza dei Signori.

Just off Piazza dei Signori are the **Arche Scaligere,** outdoor tombs of the Scaligeri princes, enclosed behind wrought-iron gates bearing the representation of ladders, the family's heraldic symbol. The grandest of the monuments is that of Cangrande I (he was certainly top dog — his name means "Big Dog"), which stands apart from the other tombs. Some of the other Scaligeri were Cansignorio (more or less "Sir Dog") and Mastino ("Mastiff"). Adjoining is the twelfth-century **Santa Maria Antica,** through which you can access the Arche. The mausoleum contains many Romanesque features and is crowned by a copy of an equestrian statue of Cangrande (the original is at the Castelvecchio). Tickets for both the Arche and the Torre are sold at the booth by the Torre's entrance.

Off Via Sant'Anastasia and Via P. Bosari. Torre dei Lamberti and Arche Scaligere ☎ *045-803 2726. Admission: Torre 3,000L ($1.60) on foot and 4,000L ($2.15) by elevator; Arche 5,000L ($2.70). Open: Tues–Sun 9 a.m.–7 p.m. (ticket booth to 5:30 p.m.).*

Piazza delle Erbe

The piazza (Square of the Herbs) was built where the Forum stood in Roman times. Today, it's the fruit-and-vegetable market where Veronese shoppers and vendors mill about, surrounded by Renaissance palaces. In the center is the **Berlina,** a canopy supported by four columns where the election of the town's *signore* (elected prince) and the *Podestà* (the governor) took place. On the north side is a fourteenth-century **fountain** and the *Madonna Verona,* which is actually a restored Roman statue. Important buildings on the piazza include the early-fourteenth-century **Casa dei Mercanti (House of the Merchants),** restructured in 1870 to restore its original 1301 form; the baroque **Palazzo Maffei;** the adjacent **Torre del Gardello**, a tower built in 1370; and the **Casa Mazzanti,** another Scaligeri palace, decorated with frescoes.

Intersection of Via Mazzini and Via Cappello.

More cool things to see and do

Verona is a small city, but it offers a number of interesting sights. If you still have time after visiting the city's main attractions, try some of these other points of interest:

✔ The small **Casa di Giulietta (Juliet's House),** at Via Cappello 23 (☎ 045-803-4303), is a thirteenth-century house that the city bought in 1905 and turned into a tourist site (the famous balcony was added in 1935). Shakespeare's Capulets and Montagues (from his famous play *Romeo and Juliet*) were indeed versions of two historic Veronese families, the Cappuletti (or Cappello) and the Montecchi. No proof exists that a family of Capulets ever lived in this house, but that doesn't stop people from flocking here to see the balcony where Juliet would've stood, if she'd been here at all. Tradition calls for you to rub the right breast of the bronze statue of Juliet for good luck. The house is open Tuesday to Sunday 9 a.m. to 7 p.m., and admission is 6,000L ($3.25) adults and 2,000L ($1.10) children. Of course, there can't be a Juliet without a Romeo and there's a so-called **Casa di Romeo (House of Romeo),** at Via Arche Scaligeri 2 (east of Piazza dei Signori), which is said to have been the home of the Montecchi family and now houses a restaurant called the Osteria dal Duca (☎ 045-594-4174).

✔ The **Museo degli Affreschi G. B. Cavalcaselle (Fresco Museum)** and the **Tomba di Giulietta (Juliet's Tomb)** are housed in the twelfth-century complex of **San Francesco al Corso** (Via Shakespeare; ☎ 045-800-0361). It was inaugurated in 1935 with the display of a sarcophagus that, according to legend, holds the bodies of Romeo and Juliet. The museum also displays an interesting collection of frescoes from a number of buildings in Verona, as well as nineteenth-century sculptures. The church of San Francesco houses several paintings from the fifteenth, sixteenth, and seventeenth centuries, and a large collection of Roman amphoras in the vaults. The complex is open Tuesday to Sunday 9 a.m. to 7 p.m., and admission is 5,000L ($2.70).

✔ The **Basilica di Sant'Anastasia** (Piazza Sant'Anastasia; ☎ 045-800-4325) is Verona's largest church. Begun in 1290 and completed almost 200 years later, it boasts a beautiful Gothic facade and an ornate campanile. Although the architecture (rather than the contents of the church) is its noblest feature, it does contain a Pisanello fresco of *San Giorgio* (*St. George and the Dragon*) in the **Cappella Giusti (Giusti Chapel)** and terra cotta works by Michele in the **Cappella Pellegrini (Pellegrini Chapel).** Admission to the church is free, and it's open Monday to Saturday 10 a.m. to 1 p.m. and 1:30 to 4 p.m. (to 5 p.m. on Sunday).

✔ The **Giardino Giusti** (Via Giardino Giusti 2; ☎ 045-803-4029) is a perfect example of an Italian garden. It has survived for many centuries (it was built in the fourteenth century and given its current layout in the sixteenth) more or less intact. Crossed by a main alley lined with secular cypress trees, the garden is embellished with grottoes, statues, and fountains. From a balcony at one end of the garden, known as the "monster balcony," you can enjoy a panoramic view of the city. The garden is open daily 9 a.m. to 8 p.m. in summer (to 7 p.m. in winter), and admission is 8,000L ($4.30).

Fast Facts: Verona

Country Code and City Code

The **country code** for Italy is **39.** The **city code** for Verona is **045;** use this city code when calling from anywhere outside or inside Italy, even within Verona and always include the zero whether you are calling from Italy or from abroad.

Embassies and Consulates

See "Fast Facts: Venice" in Chapter 18.

Currency Exchange

You can change currency inside the rail station or at numerous banks around town (for example, on Corso Cavour, where you can also find ATMs).

Emergencies

Ambulance, ☎ 118; Fire, ☎ 115; road assistance, ☎ 116.

Hospital

The **Ospedale Civile Maggiore Borgo Trento** is at Piazzale Stefani 1 (☎ 045-807-1111).

Information

The main **tourist office** is at Via Leoncino 61, near the Arena (☎ 045-806-8680). Summer hours are Monday to Saturday 8 a.m. to 8 p.m. and Sunday 9 a.m. to noon (open til 7 p.m., Monday to Saturday, in winter). There are two **tourist booths,** one inside the train station Stazione Porta Nuova (☎ 045-800-0861), open Monday to Saturday 8 a.m. to 7:30 p.m. and Sunday 9 a.m. to noon, and the other in Piazza delle Erbe (☎ 045-800-0065), which is open the same hours but closed an hour for lunch.

Mail

The **Ufficio Postale (post office)** is at Piazza Viviani 7 (☎ 045-8051111).

Police

Call ☎ 113; for the Carabinieri (other police force), call ☎ 112.

Part VI
Naples, Pompeii, and the Amalfi Coast

The 5th Wave   By Rich Tennant

©RICHTENNANT

"He had it made after our trip to Italy. I give you the Fontana di Clifford."

In this part . . .

*N*aples is the capital of Campania, a beautiful region south of Rome. Campania is in many ways the heart of Italy — warm, welcoming, and mysterious. Naples, its capital, borrows some of its character from Vesuvio (Mt. Vesuvius), the unpredictable volcano in whose shadow the city lies.

Chapter 20 covers the best of Naples, a city rich in art (often overlooked by visitors) that's undergoing a marked resurgence after years of having a bad reputation. Chapter 21 guides you to nearby excursions, including the Roman ruins of Herculaneum and Pompeii, which are really more than just ruins. In fact, their violent instant destruction by Vesuvius's eruption gives them a poignancy that peaceful ruins, eroded over centuries, don't have. Another day trip is to the beautiful isle of Capri, which has entranced the artistic and well-to-do since the Roman Emperor Tiberius rioted here with his playthings. And Chapter 22 leads you along the most celebrated stretch of Italian coast, the justly renowned Costiera Amalfitana (Amalfi Coast).

Chapter 20

Naples

• •

In This Chapter

▶ Finding your way to and around the city

▶ Choosing where to stay and where to eat

▶ Soaking up the atmosphere: What to see and do

• •

*U*rban **Napoli (Naples),** former capital of the Kingdom of the Two Sicilies, is rich in art, churches, and historic sights and may be daunting or seductive, depending on who you are. Naples is one of the most vital cities anywhere, legendary for its craziness, terrible drivers, thieves, and dirt (a cholera outbreak occurred in the 1970s). The city gets a bad rap from the rest of Italy because of its poverty and grunginess, but major improvements have been made in recent years and Naples has marvelous things to see and do. Above all, Naples's character is incredibly vivid — it has its own dialect that's indecipherable to outsiders, and the place is bursting with life. In a sense, if you haven't seen Napoli, you haven't seen Italy.

For first-time (and even second-time) visitors, however, Naples — the real one, outside the main tourist attractions — is usually a little too intense and is frequently bypassed or used simply as a departure point for Capri and points south. Don't make this mistake, though. The city underwent a real renaissance during the 1990s, with many monuments refurbished and the main squares cleaned up and reclaimed for pedestrians.

Naples is also an excellent starting point for exploring some sites nearby (see Chapters 21 and 22) and is the jumping-off point for Sicily if you go by boat (see Chapter 23).

Getting There

Although Naples may feel like a world apart from Rome or Florence, it is quite convenient to reach in a variety of ways: rail, air, sea, or road.

By train

One or more trains per hour leave Rome for Naples; the trip takes about 2½ hours and costs 25,000L ($14). The trip from Florence is about 4½ hours and costs 60,000L ($32) and the trip from Venice

7½ hours and 85,000L ($46). Naples's **Stazione Centrale** (☎ 081-554-3188), is on Piazza Garibaldi, in the city center. (Napoli's other train station, **Stazione Mergellina** on Piazza Piedigrotta, is convenient to the western part of town.) Piazza Garibaldi is a major hub for city buses and the subway line and also has a taxi station. The city center lies only a few blocks west, but the area around the station is grungy, so you may want to catch some form of public transportation to get to the city center; walking through the station area could spoil your first impression of this otherwise beautiful town.

By plane

About 7 km (4 miles) from the city center, the small **Aeroporto Capodichino** (☎ 081-789-6111) receives daily flights from other cities in Italy. The easiest way to get into town is by taking a taxi directly at your hotel. However, expect to pay up to 50,000L ($27) for the 15-minute trip. Much cheaper is taking the regular **ATAN** city bus no. 14. The trip to the **Stazione Centrale** in Piazza Garibaldi, at the center of town, takes only 15 minutes and costs 3,500L ($1.90).

By ferry

Naples's harbor is the major port of central Italy, with ferries and cruise ships pulling in and out from various destinations. Coming into the **Stazione Marittima** (seaport, just off Via Cristoforo Colombo) is the best way of arriving in Naples, not only because of the legendary beauty of the bay but also because you arrive at the heart of town, where most of its historic attractions lie. One of the most interesting possibilities is taking a ferry to or from Sicily, saving many hours of driving. The company **Tirrenia** (☎ 081-761-3688) leaves from the Stazione Marittima for the overnight trip to Palermo. A faster ferry, the **SNAV** (☎ 081-761-2348), takes about half the time; see Chapter 23 for complete details on rates and schedules.

By car

Driving in Naples is challenging. The best thing to do is put your car in a garage when you get there and continue by foot and bus. By the way, when we say a garage, we mean it; Naples is infamous for prevalent car theft. All roads lead to Rome, and your road to Naples passes by Rome. From Rome, take or continue on *autostrada* **A1**, which ends in Naples. You can find parking lots just off the highway at the exit Corso Malta (behind the Stazione Centrale), on Piazza Garibaldi (in front of the Stazione Centrale), and at the Stazione Marittima by the harbor.

Orienting Yourself in Napoli

Forced by the shape of the surrounding land — high cliffs overlooking the sea — Naples developed like a crescent along the bay. The more fashionable neighborhoods are up on the hill, but the historic part of

Naples

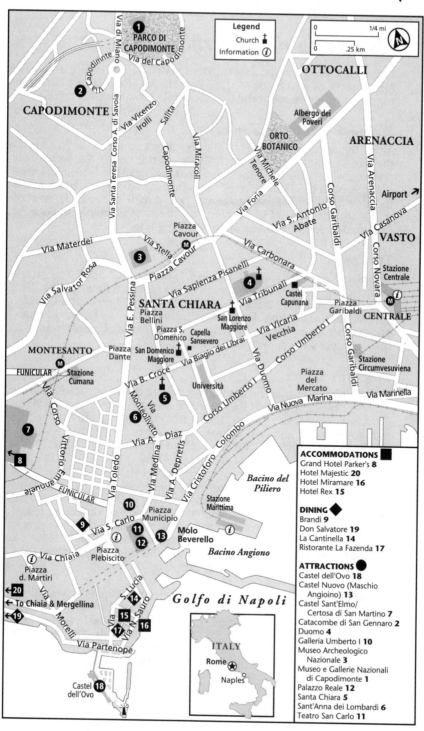

Legend
Church ✝
Information ⓘ

0   1/4 mi
0   .25 km

PARCO DI CAPODIMONTE ❶

OTTOCALLI

Albergo dei Poveri

ORTO BOTANICO

CAPODIMONTE ❷

ARENACCIA

Via Arenaccia

Airport ↗

Via Casanova

VASTO

Via di Miano

Via del Capodimonte

Via Vincenzo Irolli

Salita

Via Miracoli

Capodimonte

Corso A. di Savoia

Via Santa Teresa

Via Michele Tenore

Via Foria

Via S. Antonio Abate

Corso Garibaldi

Corso Novara

Stazione Centrale

Via Materdei

Via Stella

Piazza Cavour

Via Salvator Rosa

Piazza Cavour ⓜ

Via Carbonara ❸

Via Carbonara

Via Sapienza Pisanelli

Via Tribunali ❹

Castel Capuana

SANTA CHIARA

Via E. Pessina

Piazza Bellini

Piazza S. Domenico

San Lorenzo Maggiore

Capella Sansevero

Via Vicaria Vecchia

Piazza Garibaldi

CENTRALE ⓜ ⓘ

MONTESANTO ⓜ

FUNICULAR

Stazione Cumana

Piazza Dante

San Domenico Maggiore

Via Biagio dei Librai

Via B. Croce ❺

Via Montoliveto

Università

Corso Umberto I

Corso Umberto I

Via Duomo

Stazione Circumvesuviana

Piazza del Mercato

Via Marinella

❻

❼

Via Corso Vittorio Emanuele FUNICULAR

Via A. Diaz

Via Toledo

Via Medina

Via A. Depretis

Via Cristoforo Colombo

Via Nuova Marina

Bacino del Piliero

❽

❾

❿

⓫ ⓬ ⓭

Via S. Carlo

Piazza Municipio

Piazza Plebiscito

Stazione Marittima

Molo Beverello ⓘ

Bacino Angiono

Via Chiaia ⓘ

Piazza d. Martiri

⓴

← To Chiaia & Mergellina

⓳

Via Morelli

Via S. Lucia

Via N. Sauro

⓮

⓯ ⓰

⓱

Golfo di Napoli

Via Partenope

Castel dell'Ovo ⓲

ITALY

Rome ✪

Naples

ACCOMMODATIONS ■
Grand Hotel Parker's 8
Hotel Majestic 20
Hotel Miramare 16
Hotel Rex 15

DINING ◆
Brandi 9
Don Salvatore 19
La Cantinella 14
Ristorante La Fazenda 17

ATTRACTIONS ●
Castel dell'Ovo 18
Castel Nuovo (Maschio Angioino) 13
Castel Sant'Elmo/ Certosa di San Martino 7
Catacombe di San Gennaro 2
Duomo 4
Galleria Umberto I 10
Museo Archeologico Nazionale 3
Museo e Gallerie Nazionali di Capodimonte 1
Palazzo Reale 12
Santa Chiara 5
Sant'Anna dei Lombardi 6
Teatro San Carlo 11

town — the original development — is down by the water. The old part of town is where you'll spend most of your time.

Napoli by neighborhood

Developed along a beautiful stretch of coast, Naples is divided into four major parts, of which one — the *centro storico* — is of foremost interest to the tourist because of the richness of its artistic endowment.

Riviera di Chiaia and Santa Lucia

Along the water, this area is famous for its elegant hotels and view over the bay — which, by the way, was much better before the nineteenth century, when they filled the waterfront and advanced the *lungomare* (promenade) of **Via Partenope** to its present position. **Santa Lucia** is the area right behind the **Castel dell'Ovo (Castle of the Egg);** west of that is the **Riviera di Chiaia,** along the pleasant green of the **Villa Comunale** and the gardens of the **Villa Pignatelli**.

The Vomero

The higher part of town, the **Vomero,** is where the *Napoli bene* (the city's middle and upper classes) live. The high cliff houses offer some interesting sights for everybody, however, such as the **Castel Sant'Elmo,** the **Certosa di San Martino,** and the villa **La Floridiana**. Also a hill but technically not part of the Vomero is **Capodimonte,** with its royal palace, park, and museum.

The centro storico

The *centro storico* is the city's heart, where it was born from the two original Greek colonies of Partenope and Neapolis and continued to grow under successive dominations, from the Romans to the Normans to the Angevins (house of Anjou) and finally to the Spanish and the Borbone (the Bourbons). Each group left its mark, making Naples one of the richest art cities in Italy.

The city's central part was historically turned toward the sea. Inland from the Stazione Marittima (seaport) are the major monuments of the Neapolitan political establishment: the **Palazzo San Giacomo,** today the city hall; the **Castel Nuovo (New Castle),** built by the Angevins as the center for their two-century-long kingdom; the **Palazzo Reale (Royal Palace)** on Piazza del Plebiscito, built under the Spanish; and the **Teatro San Carlo,** built by the Borbone.

Beginning in Piazza del Plebiscito, **Via Toledo** is Naples's main street, lined with elegant palaces and fashionable shops. Opening from Via Toledo on the right is the famous glass-and-iron **Galleria Umberto I** shopping mall. On the left are the **Quartieri Spagnoli,** the tight grid of narrow streets built by the Spanish in the sixteenth century, mainly to house their troops; today it's the embodiment of "neapolitanness" — laundry drying at windows, mammas screaming at their kids down in the street, motorscooters rushing past, and so on. Continuing on Via Toledo across Piazza Dante and into Via E. Pessina, you arrive at the important **Museo Archeologico Nazionale.**

Via Benedetto Croce and Via Biagio dei Librai are colloquially referred to by the name **Spacca Napoli** because they seem to divide the center of town in two parts, with **Via dei Tribunali** parallel to the north and **Corso Umberto I** to the south. Along those streets are concentrated some of the most important attractions, as well as the university. In the area are churches and palaces galore, including **Sant'Anna dei Lombardi** (also called the **Chiesa di Monteoliveto**), **Santa Chiara** with its unique beautiful cloister, **San Gregorio Armeno** with its cloister and a bay view, the **Duomo,** and **Castel Capuano.**

Mergellina and Via Posillipo

Mergellina is the pleasure harbor of Naples, where Neapolitans come for a romantic dinner by the sea. West of this is **Via Posillipo,** along the towering promontory, at the tip of which is the very pretty small square of **Marechiaro.**

Street smarts: Where to get information after you arrive

The main **tourist office** is APT (Piazza dei Martiri 58; ☎ 081-405-311; Bus: R3 to Riviera di Chiaia). **Tourist booths** can also be found in the Stazione Centrale on Piazza Garibaldi (☎ 081-268-799; Metro: Piazza Garibaldi) and in the Stazione Mergellina on Piazza Piedigrotta (☎ 081-761-2102; Metro: Mergellina). These booths are open daily 8:30 a.m. to 8:30 p.m.

Getting Around Napoli

Although Naples isn't that large and you can cover substantial parts on foot, it's large enough that you'll welcome public transportation now and then.

On foot

Naples offers beautiful walks, particularly nearby its major sights. All the areas we describe in the preceding sections are safe to walk on foot.

Outside the central district are scattered pockets of poverty, and you may want to avoid walking in these neighborhoods (the only one close to the area of tourist interest, though, is in the vicinity of the Stazione Centrale). Although sociologically interesting, they're potentially dangerous for visitors (don't flash expensive cameras and other accessories), but if you dress unobtrusively and look local, nobody should bother you. These neighborhoods may also be unpleasant for lone young women, who'll get whistled at and approached. Brushing off these attentions isn't too difficult, but sometimes it tends to get a bit too much. If you're a lone woman, stick to the sightseeing areas; if you want to go farther, join forces with another visitor.

By subway

The Metropolitana (subway) line makes a few widely spaced stops but is quite useful for avoiding the city traffic. Surprisingly, little of it is actually underground; it's an urban railroad more than a subway and is, in fact, linked to the rail system. It runs daily 5 a.m. to 11:30 p.m., and you can use the same tickets as on the bus (see the next section).

By bus or tramway

ANM is the city bus system (☎ **081-7000-1000**), which is quite complete and includes a few lines of tramway and the funicular described in the next section. You can get an excellent map at the info booth at Stazione Centrale on Piazza Garibaldi. Tickets cost 1,500L (80¢) and are valid for 90 minutes. You can buy them at bars, tobacconists, and newsstands around town. You can also buy a one-day ticket offering unlimited travel for 4,500L ($2.45) — if you plan to do Naples and see a number of sites, you'll probably break even on this ticket before lunch. Both tickets are labeled **GiraNapoli.**

Due to traffic, regular buses are slow and crowded, but most tourist destinations are served by special fast lines (*linee rosse,* red lines, marked by a letter R) running much more frequently. Each bus and tram line has its own schedule — this is Italy after all! The *linee rosse* run daily roughly 5:30 a.m. to midnight; other buses stop earlier, some as early as 8:30 p.m. A number of *linee notturne* (night lines) usually start around midnight and run with an hourly frequency.

By Funivia

Given the city's development over the cliffs surrounding the bay, Naples enjoys a special kind of transportation: the funicular — the *Funivia* as it is called. Three funiculars connect the lower town to the higher one: **Montesanto** (at the metro station Montesanto, running daily 7 a.m. to 10 p.m.), **Chiaia** (from Piazza Amedeo, running Monday to Thursday 7 a.m. to 9 p.m., Friday to Sunday to 1 a.m.), and **Centrale** (from Via Toledo, off Piazza Trieste e Trento, running daily 6 a.m. to 1 a.m.). Mergellina also has a funicular, from Via Mergellina by the harbor (running daily 7 a.m. to 10 p.m.). The *Funivia* accepts regular bus tickets (see the preceding section).

By taxi

There are a number of taxi stations, where taxis wait in line for customers, near major hubs and attractions. You can also call a radio taxi at ☎ **081-556-4444**. Beware, though, that the driving in Naples is reckless — even if you're in a taxi — and that Neapolitans are reputed for rounding up their fares to make a little extra money (it's a bad town in which to go around looking gullible). If taxi drivers see that you're a visitor, some (but not the majority) might say their meter is broken. If so, take another cab.

Out-of-town destinations have fixed fares and not using the meter is therefore legal. Ask the price before boarding.

Beware of illegal taxis, from which most of the bad reputation of Naples's cabs stems. Always take a taxi from an official taxi stand or make sure you get in only marked vehicles, painted white (or yellow for the older models) and sometimes with a Comune di Napoli (Naples municipality) mark.

Where to Stay in Napoli

As in other large cities, Naples offers a big selection of hotels — the city is a thriving commercial center, so you can find not just glitzy tourist hotels but places for the lonely traveling salesperson as well. This selection gives you plenty of choice; however, we don't give any really cheap suggestions because it's not worth being in a marginal area just to save a little — you can economize in many other areas instead to balance things out.

Grand Hotel Parker's

$$$$ Vomero

Dating from 1870, this hotel sits on the hill above the harbor and offers grand views of the city and the sea. It has preserved its neoclassical interior and ornate plasterwork. The elegant large guest rooms are decorated in period furniture. The roof garden houses a restaurant, where you can enjoy regional specialties and a magnificent view. Parker's also features some less usual amenities, such as a business center.

Corso Vittorio Emanuele 135. ☎ *081-761-2474. Fax: 081-663-527. E-mail:* ghparker@ tin.it. *Internet:* www.bcedit.it/parkershotel.htm. *Metro: Piazza Amedeo. Parking: 20,000L ($11). Rack rates: 410,000L ($222) double, including buffet breakfast. AE, DC, MC, V.*

Hotel Majestic

$$$ Riviera di Chiaia

A modern hotel favored by locals, the Majestic is in a pleasant area of town. The guest rooms are of a fairly good size and look like tasteful modern apartments, with hardwood floors, dark wood furniture, and walls painted in earth tones. They have all the comforts, including air-conditioning. We definitely recommend La Giara, the hotel's restaurant.

Largo Vasto a Chiaia 68. ☎ *081-416-500. Fax: 081-410-145. E-mail:* info@ majestic.it. *Internet:* www.majestic.it. *Metro: Piazza Amedeo. Parking: 30,000L ($16). Rack rates: 300,000L ($162) double, including buffet breakfast. AE, DC, MC, V.*

Hotel Miramare

$$$ Santa Lucia

This charming hotel right on the water was once a villa — built in 1914 — and then became the American consulate before being converted into a hotel. The public areas are still decorated in Liberty style (Italian art nouveau); the renovated guest rooms have beautiful baths, air-conditioning, and minibars. Guests at the hotel get a 10 percent discount at the restaurant La Cantinella (see the description of this restaurant later in this chapter).

Via Nazario Saura 24. ☎ *081-764-7589. Fax: 081-764-8775. E-mail:* info@
hotelmiramare.com. *Internet:* www.hotelmiramare.com. *Bus/Tram: Bus R3 or tram 4 to Via Acton. Parking: 30,000L ($16). Rack rates: 300,000–495,000L ($162–$268) double, including buffet breakfast. AE, DC, MC, V.*

Hotel Rex

$$ Santa Lucia

The Rex is well known as a moderately priced hotel in the waterside neighborhood of Santa Lucia near the Castel dell'Ovo. The guest rooms aren't big but have all the necessary comforts; however, the baths are very small. The location and the price of the hotel (and its lavish exterior, not matched by the rooms) make it always much in demand.

Via Palepoli 12. ☎ *081-764-9389. Fax: 081-764-9227. Bus/Tram: Bus R3 or tram 4 to Via Acton. Parking: 30,000L ($16). Rack rates: 170,000L ($92) double, including breakfast. AE, DC, MC, V.*

Where to Dine in Napoli

Neapolitan food has been made famous by pizza — the Neapolitans invented it, and everyone agrees that theirs is the best (thicker and with better mozzarella than anywhere else). But this city has more to offer than just good pizza, such as its many seafood dishes, including one of our favorites, *pasta alle cozze* (pasta with mussels), and grilled seafood.

If you have a sweet tooth, try Naples's specialty: the *sfogliatella,* a fragrant, crisp, crusty triangular pocket filled with sweet ricotta. We've never had them anywhere else as good as here, and they're the perfect counterpart to a Neapolitan coffee — justly famous as the best in Italy (we know some Romans who drive to Naples for coffee). Another specialty is the *babá,* a soft brioche soaked in rum and sugar syrup and often filled with cream — they're addictive, and it's not the alcohol. You can sample these treats at the **Pasticceria Scaturchio** (Via Porta Medina 22–24; ☎ 081-551-3850; Bus: R1, R2, R3, or R4), one of the oldest pastry shops in town, established in 1903.

Brandi

$$ Centro storico   Pizza

Literally fit for a queen, this pizzeria opened in the nineteenth century and is the place where *pizza Margherita* was invented. It takes its name from Margherita di Savoia, first queen of Italy, who graciously accepted to have a pizza named after her (how many sovereigns can say that?). The pizza is with tomato, basil, and mozzarella — red, green, and white, not coincidentally the colors of the united Italy. Brandi's menu includes many other dishes and kinds of pizza, all well prepared.

Salita Sant'Anna di Palazzo. ☎ *081-416-928. Reservations required. Bus: R1 or R4 to Piazza Trieste e Trento. Secondi: 12,000–25,000L ($6–$14). No credit cards accepted. Open: Lunch and dinner Tues–Sun.*

Don Salvatore

$$$ Mergellina   Neapolitan/Seafood

On the Mergellina waterfront, near the dock where the ferries leave for Capri, Don Salvatore is an excellent example of a Neapolitan seaside trattoria. The grilled fish is fresh, accompanied by local vegetables, and served on pasta or rice. The restaurant features an excellent choice of wine, including a variety of local winners.

Strada Mergellina 4/a. ☎ *081-681-817. Reservations recommended. Metro: Mergellina. Secondi: 12,000–30,000L ($6–$16). AE, DC, MC, V. Open: Lunch and dinner Thurs–Tues; daily in summer.*

La Cantinella

$$$ Santa Lucia   Italian/Neapolitan/Seafood

One of the best restaurants in Naples, this waterfront spot has plenty of style, and not only in the food. It seems like a 1930s nightclub or something out of a movie, but the food is pure Neapolitan, with an excellent *antipasto* and grilled seafood.

Via Cuma 42. ☎ *081-764-8684. Reservations required. Bus/Tram: Bus R3 or tram 4 to Via Acton. Secondi: 20,000–35,000L ($11–$19). AE, DC, MC, V. Open: Lunch and dinner Mon–Sat, daily in summer; closed two weeks in Aug.*

Ristorante La Fazenda

$$$$ Santa Lucia   Neapolitan/Seafood

With a beautiful view over the bay and an informal atmosphere, La Fazenda pleases both locals and visitors. The terrace is popular in summer (so don't go then without a reservation). The place is famous for its fish specialties, including *pasta alle vongole* (pasta with clams) and the fresh grilled seafood.

*Via Mare Chiaro 58/a. ☎ **081-575-7420**. Reservations required. Bus/Tram: Bus R3 or tram 4 to Via Acton. Secondi: 20,000–40,000L ($11–$22). AE, MC, V. Open: Lunch Tues–Sun, dinner Mon–Sat; closed one week in August.*

Exploring Napoli

Visiting Naples's major attractions is the best way to discover the city and understand its spirit. Entering the museums, palaces, and churches will put you in tune with the city's history, which is very much imprinted in the soul of its inhabitants. Here we give you a list of the best that Napoli offers.

The top sights

Castel dell'Ovo

The "Castle of the Egg" sits on a promontory projecting into the harbor. The first Greek colonists landed here in the ninth century B.C. In Roman times, it's believed that Lucullus (the celebrated gourmet) had his villa here. A symbol of the city and an important landmark, the current fortress was built by Frederick II and enlarged by the Angevins. The name originated in the Middle Ages: One explanation has it that Virgil (author of the *Aeneid* and reputed magician) placed a sacred egg under the castle's foundations to protect it; this ploy apparently wasn't too successful, because the castle collapsed and the present one was built over the site. You have a beautiful view of the castle from **Via Partenope,** the promenade overlooking the sea, which merges into the **Riviera di Chiaia** farther west. The castle houses the **Museo Etno-Preistorico (Ethno-Prehistoric Museum),** with a collection of artifacts and objects dating back 700,000 years (call for reservations; see the next paragraph). The castle itself is very interesting — see the **Sala delle Colonne (Hall of the Columns),** for example — and from it you can enjoy a superb view over the city.

*Porto Santo Lucia, off Via Partenope. ☎ **081-764-5688** for castle or 081-764-5343 for museum reservations. Bus/Tram: Bus R3 or tram 4 to Via Acton, Porto Santa Lucia. Admission: Castle and museum free. Open: Mon–Sat 9 a.m.–3 p.m.*

Castel Nuovo (Maschio Angioino)

Built in the thirteenth century by Carlo d'Angió (Angevin dynasty) as the new royal residence — the Castel dell'Ovo and Castel Capuano didn't fit the needs of the new kingdom — this castle was renovated in the fifteenth century. The inland facade is graced by the **Arco di Trionfo di Alfonso (Triumphal Arch of Alfonso),** a splendid example of early Renaissance architecture, the work of Francesco Laurana to commemorate the 1442 expulsion of the Angevins by the forces of Alphonso I. Inside, note the **Sala dei Baroni (Hall of the Barons),** a monumental room with a star-shaped vaulted ceiling (today the seat of the Municipal Council), and the **Museo Civico (Civic Museum),** with a nice collection of sculpture and other art, some from the **Cappella Palatina (Palatine Chapel),** the only original part remaining of the Anjou castle, once frescoed by Giotto.

Piazza del Municipio ☎ ***081-795-2003**. Bus: R1, R2, R3, or R4 to Piazza del Municipio. Admission: 10,000L ($5). Open: Mon–Sat 9 a.m.–7 p.m.*

Duomo

The fourteenth-century Duomo may not be the most interesting church in town, but it houses the **Cappella di San Gennaro (Chapel of St. Gennaro),** named after the patron saint of Naples. The chapel is richly decorated with goldwork, including a gold bust of the saint that contains his relics. Also here is the famous relic of San Gennaro containing vials of his blood — the blood is said to become again liquid in May and September, and it's a sign of great misfortune for the whole town should the miracle not take place. In the left nave is the original paleo-Christian basilica of **Santa Restituta;** it and its adjoining baptistry are decorated with beautiful mosaics and were absorbed into the Duomo and refurbished in the seventeenth century.

Via del Duomo 147. ☎ ***081-449-097**. Metro: Piazza Cavour. Admission: Free. Open: Daily 8 a.m.–12:30 p.m. and 4:30–7:15 p.m.*

Museo Archeologico Nazionale

The National Archaeological Museum contains one of the greatest collections of treasures from antiquity in Europe and probably the world. If you want to visit just one archaeological museum in Italy, make it this one. Among the holdings is a superb collection of **Roman sculptures** copied from Greek originals of the fourth and fifth centuries B.C. and reflecting the Roman incorporation of Hellenism into its art. The most famous works are a pair of statues of **Armodio and Aristogitone.** In addition, this museum is the repository for the findings from many of the archaeological excavations in southern Italy. In particular, various objects that were found at Pompeii and Herculaneum wound up here, including bronzes and gorgeous mosaics.

Piazza Museo Nazionale 18–19. ☎ ***081-440-166**. Metro: Piazza Cavour. Admission: 12,000L ($6). Open: Wed–Mon 9 a.m.–7 p.m., Sun 9 a.m.–8 p.m.*

Museo e Gallerie Nazionali di Capodimonte

This museum holds a first-class painting collection that contains several masterpieces, including Masaccio's *Crucifixion,* Simone Martini's *Coronation,* Perugino's *Madonna and Child,* Luca Signorelli's *Adoration of the Child,* and Filippino Lippi's *Annunciation and Saints,* plus works by Mantegna, Raphael, Titian, Caravaggio, and Botticelli. The building is a masterpiece itself: The Palazzo Capodimonte and its surrounding park were built in the eighteenth century and sited to afford beautiful views over the city and bay. You can also see what the palace was like originally in the **State Apartments,** full of priceless objects, tapestries, and statuary.

Palazzo Capodimonte, Via Milano 2. ☎ 081-744-1307. Bus: R4 to Parco Capodimonte. Admission: 14,000L ($8); 12,000L ($6) after 2 p.m. Open: Tues–Sun 10 a.m.–7 p.m., Sun 9 a.m.–8 p.m.

Palazzo Reale

The imposing neoclassical Royal Palace was designed by Domenico Fontana and built by the Bourbons in the seventeenth century; the eight statues on the facade are of Neapolitan kings. Inside you can visit the **royal apartments,** richly appointed with marble floors, tapestries, frescoes, and baroque furniture. The **library,** established by Charles de Bourbon, is one of the greatest in the south, with over 1,250,000 volumes. The palazzo retains its glamour to this day and was used as the venue for a G7 summit meeting in 1994.

Piazza del Plebiscito 1. ☎ 081-580-8111. Bus: R1 or R4 to Piazza Trieste e Trento. Admission: 8,000L ($4.30). Open: Thurs–Tues 9 a.m.–6 p.m., Sun to 8 p.m.

Sant'Anna dei Lombardi

Built in the fifteenth century and renovated in the seventeenth, Sant'Anna dei Lombardi (also called the Chiesa di Monteoliveto) is famous for its rich collection of Renaissance sculpture. Noteworthy are the **Cappella Piccolomini (Piccolomini Chapel),** with the tomb of Maria d'Aragona by Antonio Rossellino and Benedetto da Maiano; the **Cappella Terranova (Terranova Chapel),** with the *Annunciazione* by Benedetto da Maiano; and the Tuscan-influenced **Cappella Tolosa (Tolosa Chapel),** decorated in the styles of Brunelleschi and della Robbia. In the **oratory** on the right is the fifteenth-century *Compianto,* an outstanding group of eight terracotta figures by Guido Mazzoni. In the **Sacristy** are frescoes by Giorgio Vasari and helpers.

Via Monteoliveto. ☎ 081-552-7826. Metro: Montesanto. Admission: Free. Open: Daily 8:30 a.m.–12:30 p.m. and 4:30–6:30 p.m.

Santa Chiara

Built in the fourteenth century as the burial church for the d'Angió dynasty, Santa Chiara once was the center of a large monastic complex for the order of the Clarisse. The church was severely damaged by World War II bombing and an ensuing fire, but it has been restored somewhat to its original look. Although damaged, the monumental **tomb of Roberto d'Angió** at the end of the nave is still a magnificent example of Tuscan-style Renaissance sculpture. Also interesting is the **Coro delle Clarisse** (choir of the Clarisses), where the nuns can sit protected from the public during mass. The key attraction is the **Chiostro delle Clarisse,** the unique beautiful cloister behind the church (turn around the church to the left). This fourteenth-century cloister was refurbished in the eighteenth century by Domenico Antonio Vaccaro, who used hand-painted majolica tiles to exceptional effect. On the piazza outside the church is one of Naples's several baroque spires, the **Guglia dell'Immacolata,** a tall pile of statues and reliefs from 1750.

Via Santa Chiara, ☎ *081-552-6209. Metro: Montesanto. Admission: Free. Open: Mon–Sat 8:30 a.m.–12:30 p.m. and 3:30–6 p.m., Sun 8:30 a.m.–12:30 p.m.*

More cool things to see and do

Here are some more sights to explore:

✔ Built at the end of the nineteenth century (20 years after its larger Milanese counterpart), the **Galleria Umberto I** (Bus: R1 or R4 to Piazza Trieste e Trento) is a splendid example of the Liberty style (Italian art nouveau). Opening to the right of Via Toledo as you come from Piazza del Plebiscito, the glass-and-iron galleria contains graciously decorated buildings and elegant shops. Come to marvel at the architecture and even to shop (see "Shopping" later in this chapter).

✔ Built by the Borbone at the beginning of the eighteenth century, the **Teatro San Carlo** (Via San Carlo 98/f; ☎ **081-797-2111** or 081-797-2331; Bus: R2 or R3 to Via San Carlo) is among Europe's most beautiful opera houses, and it's said to have even better acoustics than Milan's famous La Scala. You can come during the day to appreciate its architecture and decoration, but of course you can also come for a performance (see "Nightlife") and hear the building in its full glory.

✔ If you want an excuse to visit the Vomero and take the funicular (take the funivia Centrale from Piazza Trento e Trieste to last stop), head to the **Castel Sant'Elmo (St. Elmo Castle)** and **Certosa di San Martino (Carthusian Monastery of St. Martin).** The fourteenth-century castle (restored in the sixteenth century) and the monastery below (also from the fourteenth century but rebuilt in the seventeenth) lie in a beautiful park. From their location on the Vomero, they dominate the city, affording great views from the terraced gardens. The monastery's cloister — the *chiostro grande* — is particularly interesting, with the sculpted busts of the monastery's saints and the sculpted balustrade of the little cemetery. The monastery houses the **Museo Nazionale di San Martino (National Museum of St. Martin),** displaying maps, *presepi* (creches), and other historic relics. The castle is open daily 9 a.m. to 2 p.m. and costs 4,000L ($2.15); the monastery is open Tuesday to Sunday 9 a.m. to 2 p.m. and costs 9,000L ($4.90).

✔ In use between the second and the ninth century, the **Catacombe di San Gennaro (Catacombs of St. Gennaro,** entrance Via di Capodimonte 13, down a small alley running alongside the church Madre del Buon Consiglio; ☎ **081-741-1071;** Bus: R4 to Via Capodimonte) are particularly famous for the well-maintained frescoes covering the whole period of the use of the catacombs, therefore including early Christian paintings. Also buried in these catacombs is San Gennaro, the patron saint of Naples — hence the name — whose remains were moved here in the fifth century. Guided tours take place at 9:30, 10:15, 11, and 11:45 a.m., and admission is 5,000L ($2.70).

And on your left, the Castel dell'Ovo: Seeing Naples by guided tour

The agency **Every Tours** (Piazza del Municipio 5; ☎ **081-551-8564**; Metro: Garibaldi) is the American Express antenna in Naples and organizes tours of the city as well as day excursions to Vesuvio and other sights. It's open Monday to Friday 9 a.m. to 1:30 p.m. and 3:30 to 7 p.m. and Saturday 9 a.m. to 1 p.m.

Suggested 1-, 2-, and 3-day Sightseeing Itineraries

You can visit Naples in three hours, one day, one month, or a lifetime. Each length will give you a different picture of the city. The longer you'll be able to stay, the more layers of culture you'll discover. Here we give you a choice of itineraries that make sure you see the major sights.

If you have only 1 day in Naples

Whether you arrive by land or by sea, the place to start is by the sea, where you can take in the **Castel Nuovo, Palazzo Reale,** and **Castel dell'Ovo.** Then you should head for at least one of the two important museums: the **Museo Archeologico Nazionale** or the **Museo e Gallerie Nazionali di Capodimonte**. You can conclude your day either by tasting the pizza that's the mother of all pizzas at **Brandi** or by having a typical romantic seafood dinner by the sea (see "Where to Dine in Napoli").

If you have 2 days in Naples

Start your day as in the one-day itinerary, but then continue in the afternoon with a visit to the rest of the *centro storico* with its beautiful churches of **Santa Chiara, Sant'Anna dei Lombardi,** and the **Duomo.** In the evening, try the original pizza, as suggested in the one-day itinerary. Use the second day to visit the two major museums and then go either to the **Teatro San Carlo** for an opera performance (if your visit is during the season) or for a seafood dinner by the water.

If you have 3 days in Naples

In this case, your possibilities widen considerably. You can follow the same suggestions in the shorter itineraries for seeing the most important sights, and then you can use the extra time to visit some of the other attractions, such as the **Castel Sant'Elmo** and **Certosa di San Martino** and the **Catacombe di San Gennaro,** and take a stroll along the **Riviera di Chiaia** and maybe even squeeze in some shopping (see the next section). Alternatively, you can use the extra time to visit the nearby attractions, such as **Vesuvio, Herculaneum,** and **Pompeii,** or maybe even to take a day trip to **Capri.**

Shopping

Although not a shopping mecca, Naples does offer some serious possibilities. In the elegant area behind the **Riviera di Chiaia** are all the big names of Italian fashion, such as Valentino, Versace, Ferragamo, and Prada. The best places for this kind of shopping are **Via dei Mille, Piazza dei Martiri,** and **Via Calabritto**.

Another good area for shopping is **Via Roma,** the animated street leading into Via Toledo. From Via Roma you can catch the funicular to the Vomero, where you can find many pedestrian streets and plenty of moderately priced shops, away from the most touristed areas downtown.

Naples is an excellent place to buy antiques, with a major antiques fair and many major stores. But beware that some Neapolitans are reputed to be experts in the difficult art of "antiquing" — making something new look antique. If you know a lot about antiques, try the important antiques market, the **Fiera Antiquaria** in the Villa Comunale di Napoli on Viale Dohrn, held every third Saturday and Sunday of each month 8 a.m. to 2 p.m. (except in August). Nearby is **Via Domenico Morelli,** home of the city's most established antiques dealers, specializing in eighteenth-century furniture and paintings. Two fine choices are **Regency House** (Via D. Morelli 36; ☎ **081-764-3640**) and **Navarra** (Piazza dei Martiri; ☎ **081-764-3595**). For these shops, take bus R3 to Riviera di Chiaia.

Naples used to be famous for its crafts, and you can still find some specialized crafts typical of the region. Among the traditional industries, the most dear to Neapolitans probably is the carving of figurines for the *presepio* (creche). **Via San Gregorio Armeno** is lined with historic workshops still producing the vividly painted figurines — or perhaps figurines is the wrong word, since some are life-sized — for the traditional creche. A small figurine is a beautiful souvenir of Naples and Italy, but these carvings don't come cheap.

Also typical of Naples is porcelain — from the tradition of the royal plant of Capodimonte — and hand-painted majolica. You can find some shops in the **Galleria Umberto I,** off Via Toledo (see "More cool things to see and do" earlier in this chapter).

Nightlife

Seeing an opera at the **Teatro San Carlo** (Via San Carlo 98/f; ☎ **081-797-2111** or 081-797-2331; Bus: R2 or R3 to Via San Carlo) is an unforgettable experience. The acoustics are excellent, and the program always includes some grandiose production. The season opens in December and closes in June, with shows Tuesday to Sunday and tickets at 80,000L to 160,000L ($43 to $87). Call the number given for reservations or contact the tourist office (see the "Fast Facts" section at the end of this chapter).

As a real harbor town, Naples offers a lively nighttime scene with discos and clubs. One of the most popular is **Chez Moi** (Via del Parco Margherita 13; ☎ 081-407-526) in the neighborhood of the Riviera di Chiaia, a small chic hangout. Nearby is **La Mela** (Via dei Mille; ☎ 081-401-0270), where the best night is Thursday. For both of these clubs, take bus R3 or tram 2 or 4 to Riviera di Chiaia or the Metro to Amadeo.

The best local jazz is often heard at **Riot** (Via San Biagio 38; ☎ 081-552-32-31; bus: 42 to Via Duomo), which attracts students from the nearby university.

If you're in a younger mood, Naples's largest disco is **Madison** (Via Sgambati 47; ☎ 081-546-6566), known for its theme evenings; it's located in the Vomero, so take a cab. For a gay atmosphere, go to **Tongue** (Via Manzoni 202; ☎ 081-769-0888; Metro: Mergellina, then take a cab), where you'll find a mixed crowd but with a large proportion of gays and lesbians.

Like other Italians, Neapolitans like to stroll in the evening, maybe having an ice cream or sitting on the terrace of a popular cafe, such as the oldest cafe in Naples, the **Gran Caffè Gambrinus** (Via Chiaia 1; ☎ 081-417-582; bus: R3 to Piazza Trieste e Trento) with its 1860s decor). With their waterfront, they have a lot of beautiful areas from which to watch the sunset, such as the **Riviera di Chiaia,** along the pleasant green of the **Villa Comunale** and the gardens of **Villa Pignatelli.**

Fast Facts: Napoli

American Express

American Express business is handled by **Every Tours** (Piazza del Municipio 5; ☎ 081-551-8564; Bus: R1, R2, R3, or R4 to Piazza del Municipio). It's open Monday to Friday 9 a.m. to 1:30 p.m. and 3:30 to 7 p.m. and Saturday 9 a.m. to 1 p.m.

ATMs

ATMs are available everywhere in the city center and near hotels. Most banks are linked to the Cirrus network; if you have access only to the Plus system with your card, you have to look for a BNL (Banca Nazionale del Lavoro).

Country Code and City Code

The **country code** for Italy is **39.** The **city code** for Naples is **081;** use this code when calling from anywhere outside or inside Italy, even within Naples itself (include the zero every time, even when calling from abroad).

Currency Exchange

There are three **exchange offices** on Piazza Garibaldi (Metro: Piazza Garibaldi) and four on Corso Umberto at nos. 44, 92, 212, and 292 (Bus: R2 to Corso Umberto); **Thomas Cook** is on Piazza del Municipio (Bus: R1, R2, R3, and R4 to Piazza del Municipio).

Doctors

Call the 24-hour **Guardia Medica Specialistica** at ☎ 081-43-1111; you can also contact any embassy or consulate to get a list of English-speaking doctors.

Embassies and Consulates

The **U.S. Consulate** is at Piazza della Repubblica (☎ 081-583-8111); the **U.K. Consulate** is at Via Francesco Crispi 122 (☎ 081-663-511). For other embassies and consulates, See "Fast Facts: Rome" in Chapter 12.

Emergencies

Ambulance ☎ **118**, 081-780-4296, or 081-584-1481; *Eliambulanza* (helicopter ambulance, necessary for Naples's traffic) ☎ **081 780-4296** or 081-780-5841; Fire ☎ **115**; *pronto soccorso* (first aid), ☎ **081-752-0696**.

Hospital

The **Ospedale Fatebenefratelli** is at Via Manzoni 220 (☎ 081-769-7220).

Information

The **tourist office** is APT (Piazza dei Martiri 58; ☎ 081-405-311; Bus: R3 to Riviera di Chiaia). There are also **tourist booths** in the Stazione Centrale at Piazza Garibaldi (☎ 081-268-799; Metro: Piazza Garibaldi) and the Stazione Mergellina (☎ 081-761-2102; Metro: Mergellina). The station booths are open daily 8:30 a.m. to 8:30 p.m.

Internet Access

Try the **ClickNet Internet Café** (Via Toledo 393; ☎ 081-552-9370; E-mail: clicnet@ mbx.clicnet.it; Bus: R1 or R4 to Via Toledo) on one of the main streets in the city center.

Mail

The **Ufficio Postale** is at Piazza Matteotti (☎ 081-551-1456; Bus: R3 to Piazza Matteotti).

Pharmacies

A good one is the large one near the Stazione Centrale, **Farmacia Helvethiam** (Piazza Garibaldi 11; ☎ 081-554-8894; Metro: Piazza Garibaldi).

Police

Call ☎ 113; for the Carabinieri, call ☎ 112.

Rest Rooms

There are very few public toilets in town, so your best bet is to go to a nice-looking cafe (though you'll have to buy something, like a cup of coffee).

Safety

Naples is considered less safe than other cities in Italy, although notable efforts have been made in recent years, with tremendous improvement. Still, pickpocketing and car theft are popular. In dark alleys off the beaten track, getting mugged is also possible, but that's quite rare in the city center or in the areas we describe in this book. Definitely seedy at night is the area around the rail station.

Smoking

Smoking is allowed in cafes and restaurants and very common. Unfortunately for non-smokers, it's virtually impossible to find a restaurant with a separate no-smoking area.

Taxes

Naples has no local tax. Other taxes are always included in the prices quoted.

Transit/Tourist Assistance

You can call ☎ 147-888-088 daily 7 a.m. to 9 p.m. for the FS, the state railroad.

Weather Updates

For forecasts, the best bet is to look at the news on TV (there's no "weather number" by telephone as in the States). On the Internet, you can check meteo.tiscalinet.it.

Web Sites

For a virtual reality tour of Naples, try ww2.webcomp.com/virtuale/us/napoli/movie.htm. The insider's Naples site is www.napolinapoli.it, where you can find details on the city's culture as well as interesting articles.

Chapter 21

Side Trips from Naples

Campania lies just south of Lazio, the region where Rome is. Naples is the capital of Campania, which has mountainous inland areas as well as a beautiful coastline. Its beauty and its nearness to Rome made Campania a favorite resort of the ancient Romans (even though Mt. Vesuvius destroyed Herculaneum and Pompeii). Ancient historians reported that Caligula had a bridge of ships built all the way across the nearby Gulf of Baia— maybe there's always been something a little nutty about this place! Tiberius retreated to the nearby island of Capri to concentrate on his decadent pleasures. Campania today is a wonderful region that offers very different destinations, and some of those places are easily reached as day trips from Naples.

Visiting Mighty Mt. Vesuvius

From Naples, you can visit the famous **Vesuvio (Mt. Vesuvius)**, the volcano that swallowed Herculaneum and Pompeii in its A.D. 79 eruption. There are two major kinds of volcanoes: ones that slowly ooze magma, like the ones on Hawaii, and ones that build and build and *build* the pressure inside and then blow their tops, like Vesuvius. Neapolitans live below a sleeping monster. Although Vesuvius has belched only a few puffs of smoke since the last real eruption in 1944, nobody knows whether the volcano is really losing its punch (it sent out a puff of smoke in 1999, in case anyone thought it was really sleeping). Luckily, one of the best (and the first) observatories for the study of vulcanology is right there on the mountain, taking its pulse.

Getting there

You can reach Vesuvius from Naples via the **Circumvesuviana Railway,** which leaves from the Stazione Circumvesuviana on Corso Garibaldi, off to the right from Piazza Garibaldi (Metro: Garibaldi). After about

15 minutes the train stops at Herculaneum, where you can catch a bus for the crater. The trip costs about 2,500L ($1.35).

By **car,** you can take the *autostrada* Napoli Salerno (Naples-Salerno) and exit at Ercolano (Heraculaneum), where the windy road going up to the crater begins. The road is 13 km (8 miles) long and reaches a height of 1,017 m (3,106 feet).

Taking a tour

You can take a tour of the crater — indeed, you can closely approach the crater only with a guide — for 5,000L ($2.70); sign up at the site's entrance. You can also join a tour group organized from Naples — for example, by the agency that handles American Express business, **Every Tours** (Piazza del Municipio 5; ☎ **081-551-8564**).

Seeing the sight

Crater

Mt. Vesuvius is the only continental volcano still active in Europe. Rising 1,281 m (3,944 feet), the slopes of Vesuvius are green with vineyards — the Lacrima Christi (Tears of Christ) wine made here is very famous — and become more rugged only as you approach the top. Before the top, at 608 m (1,994 feet), you can make a short detour to visit the **Vesuvian Observatory,** which has observed the volcano's activity day by day since around 1850. Closer to the top, the path becomes lava, the typical black-and-purple rough pieces of stone. From the top on a good day, you can enjoy a fantastic view over the Bay of Naples.

Admission: 4,000L ($2.15), guided tour 5,000L ($2.70). Open: Daily 9 a.m.–1 hour before sunset.

Viewing Amazing Ruins and More at Herculaneum and Pompeii

Few archaeological sites are as moving as these towns that shared a similar catastrophic destiny. However, each is still unique: **Pompei (Pompeii)** was buried beneath volcanic ash and pumice stone that fell on those who were taking flight and transformed them into human statues that remain to this day. **Ercolano (Herculaneum)** was buried beneath volcanic mud that preserved its houses to a remarkable extent. In the 1990s, a boat was found near the water at Herculaneum, still filled with the corpses of victims caught in frantic postures. These are unforgettable sights, and the towns have yielded great numbers of artifacts and sculptures as well (however, most of the great finds have been carted off to be displayed in Naples's Museo Archeologico Nazionale).

You can visit either — or both — of these towns as a day trip from Naples. Consider, though, that you'll spend several hours at each, especially if you also visit the worthwhile museum.

Getting there

The **Circumvesuviana** (☎ 081-772-2444) leaves from Naples's Stazione Circumvesuviana on Corso Garibaldi (between Piazza Nolana and Piazza G. Pepe), off to the right of Piazza Garibaldi. For Herculaneum, get off at the Ercolano stop, where you can catch a shuttle bus for the site. For Pompeii, take the *Sorrento* train (not the train going to modern Pompeii, on the Poggiomarino line) and get off at the Pompei Scavi stop, from which you can walk to the site. The one-way fare is about 2,000L ($1.10), and trains leave every half hour. The ride to Herculaneum takes 20 minutes and to Pompeii 45 minutes.

If you have a **car,** take the *autostrada* toward Salerno (which becomes **A3**); Ercolano (Herculaneum) and Pompei Scavi (Pompeii) each have an exit. It's about 8 km (4½ miles) to Herculaneum and 24 km (14½ miles) to Pompeii.

Taking a tour

At each sight, when you get your ticket at the ticket office you can ask for an official guide. Doing so is a good idea, because the guide can show you those houses that are protected by gates. If you're on your own, you can't enter these locked structures and you'll have to squint between the iron frames.

Seeing the sights

Unless you're visiting in the dead of winter, remember to bring a hat, plenty of sunscreen, and water. There are no trees among the ruins, and it can get really hot. Remember to wear comfortable shoes as well, especially if you're visiting larger Pompeii.

Herculaneum

Herculaneum is the smaller of the two ancient towns; much of it still lies under the present-day town and has never been excavated (digging into the solidified volcanic mud is quite a chore). Many of Herculaneum's buildings were more elaborate than Pompeii's because this was a seaside resort for rich Romans. Although all the streets and buildings of Herculaneum hold interest, some ruins merit more attention than others. Among the most interesting are the two sets of *terme* **(thermal baths)** — particularly the smaller but more elegantly decorated **Terme Suburbane (Suburban Baths).** The **Palestra** was a kind of sports arena, where games were staged to satisfy the spectacle-hungry denizens.

The average townhouse was built around an uncovered atrium. In some areas, Herculaneum boasted the forerunner of the modern apartment house. Important private homes to seek out are the **Casa del Bicentenario (House of the Bicentenary)**, the **Casa a Graticcio (House of the Latticework)**, the **Casa del Tramezzo di Legno (House of the Wooden Partition)**, and the **Casa di Nettune (House of Neptune)**, which contains the most striking mosaic found in the ruins. The finest example of how the aristocracy lived is the **Casa dei Cervi (House of the Stags)**, named because of the sculpture found inside. Note that several houses are locked and opened only with permission. For this reason, it's a good idea to take a guided tour. Herculaneum is easier to see because it's smaller, but it's less impressive than Pompeii — though the sites share an eerie feeling of having been abandoned not very long ago.

Ufficio Scavi di Ercolano, Corso Resina, Ercolano ☎ *081-739-0963. Admission: 12,000L ($6). Open: Daily 9 a.m.–1 hour before sunset.*

Herculaneum

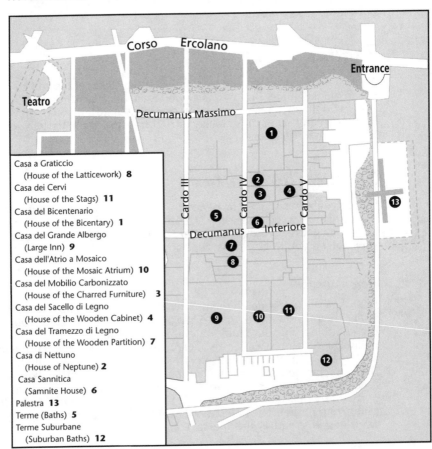

Casa a Graticcio
(House of the Latticework) **8**
Casa dei Cervi
(House of the Stags) **11**
Casa del Bicentenario
(House of the Bicentary) **1**
Casa del Grande Albergo
(Large Inn) **9**
Casa dell'Atrio a Mosaico
(House of the Mosaic Atrium) **10**
Casa del Mobilio Carbonizzato
(House of the Charred Furniture) **3**
Casa del Sacello di Legno
(House of the Wooden Cabinet) **4**
Casa del Tramezzo di Legno
(House of the Wooden Partition) **7**
Casa di Nettuno
(House of Neptune) **2**
Casa Sannitica
(Samnite House) **6**
Palestra **13**
Terme (Baths) **5**
Terme Suburbane
(Suburban Baths) **12**

Pompeii

Pompeii is as much as four times larger than Herculaneum, and visiting the whole thing is somewhat laborious. Count on a minimum of four hours just to get a general idea of the place and have a quick look at most of the attractions. Pompeii was a commercial town as well as a residential resort, and its urban fabric was mixed, with elegant villas, shops, and more modest housing. The town was buried under volcanic ash and pumice stone that then solidified, allowing the residents who had escaped to come back and salvage some of their treasures; of course, this same situation also made it easier for the treasure hunters of later centuries to try their hand at looting the place. But although the site was picked over by scavengers, the city was very well preserved, and the archaeological excavations have uncovered much about the life of the times.

The most elegant of the patrician villas is the **Casa dei Vettii (House of the Vettii),** boasting a courtyard, statuary, paintings, and a black-and-red Pompeiian dining room known for its frescoes. The house was occupied by two brothers named Vettii, both of whom were wealthy merchants. Another treasure is the **Casa dei Misteri (House of the Mysteries),** near the Porto Ercolano outside the walls, decorated with frescoes of mythological scenes related to the cult of Dionysus (Bacchus), one of the cults that flourished in Roman times. The most famous and the largest of the houses is the **Casa del Fauno (House of the Faun),** so called because of the bronze statue of a dancing faun that was found there; the house takes up a city block and has four dining rooms and two spacious gardens.

Also interesting are the public areas of the ancient city. In the center of town is the **Foro (Forum)** — parts were severely damaged in an earthquake 16 years before the eruption of Vesuvius and hadn't been repaired when the final destruction came. Three buildings surrounding the Forum are the **basilica** (the city's largest single structure) and the **Tempio di Apollo (Temple of Apollo)** and **Tempio di Giove (Temple of Jupiter).** The **Terme Stabiane (baths)** are in good condition, among the finest baths to survive from antiquity. Other buildings of interest are the **Teatro Grande,** built in the fifth century B.C.; the **Casa degle Amorini Dorati (House of the Gilded Cupids),** a flamboyant private home; and the **Casa del Poeta Tragico (House of the Tragic Poet),** which gets its name from a mosaic discovered here (later sent to Naples). It depicts a chained watchdog on the doorstep with this warning — *Cave Canem* ("beware of the dog").

Particularly evocative — and disturbing — are the "statues" of the victims: The ash hardened on the dead bodies and became a shell that preserved all the details, including the agonizing facial expressions. The archaeologists were then able to make casts of these bodies by pouring plaster into the cavities.

Ufficio Scavi di Pompei, Piazza Esedra. ☎ *081-861-0744. Admission: 12,000L ($6). Open: Daily 9 a.m.–1 hour before sunset.*

Pompeii

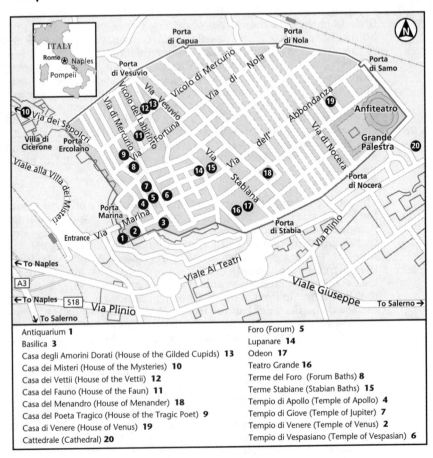

Antiquarium **1**	Foro (Forum) **5**
Basilica **3**	Lupanare **14**
Casa degli Amorini Dorati (House of the Gilded Cupids) **13**	Odeon **17**
Casa dei Misteri (House of the Mysteries) **10**	Teatro Grande **16**
Casa dei Vettii (House of the Vettii) **12**	Terme del Foro (Forum Baths) **8**
Casa del Fauno (House of the Faun) **11**	Terme Stabiane (Stabian Baths) **15**
Casa del Menandro (House of Menander) **18**	Tempio di Apollo (Temple of Apollo) **4**
Casa del Poeta Tragico (House of the Tragic Poet) **9**	Tempio di Giove (Temple of Jupiter) **7**
Casa di Venere (House of Venus) **19**	Tempio di Venere (Temple of Venus) **2**
Cattedrale (Cathedral) **20**	Tempio di Vespasiano (Temple of Vespasian) **6**

Where to dine

There's little to eat at the excavations, so it's a good idea to pack a picnic lunch to bring with you (don't forget plenty of water during summer). If you want to eat in a restaurant, you have to head for the modern town. Herculaneum is relatively poor, but it has a few snack bars near the center; Pompeii offers better chances.

Il Principe

$$$ Pompei città Neapolitan

This is one of the best restaurants in the whole region, and you'll find the height of Neapolitan cuisine, such as grilled fish and pasta with seafood. The decor is quite funny, giving a local interpretation of ancient Pompeian life (including mosaics and frescoes).

Piazza Bartolo Longo, near the basilica in the center of town. ☎ *081-850-5566. Reservations necessary. Bus: From the excavations to the rail station of the town of Pompeii. Secondi: 25,000–35,000L ($14–$19). AE, DC, MC, V. Open: Lunch and dinner Tues–Sun; daily in summer.*

˙loring the Isle of Capri
˙ ˙ Blue Grotto

– now only in the off-season — **Capri** (pronounce it *Cap*-ree), wɪᴛʜ ɪᴛѕ famous Blue Grotto and emerald water, makes a perfect getaway from busy Naples. It's just a ferry ride south of the city off the peninsula of Sorrento, and you can visit it in a day trip, thus avoiding high hotel charges.

Should you want to take a romantic break by the sea, however, Capri is well worth a longer stay. Ever since Emperor Tiberius sought amusement at Villa Jovis here, the island has been a haunt for eccentric characters (such as movie stars hiding out, artists in exile, and the like). Norman Douglas's *South Wind* is a very funny novel about various strange people living on Capri who engage in long philosophical debates and repartee. Douglas also wrote *Siren Land,* about Sorrento and Capri, where he lived for many years.

If you stay for a day or a year, remember to bring very little luggage: The island is very steep and you may have to walk up many steps. At the more exclusive hotels you can find staff to carry your stuff, but otherwise plan on having to lug your suitcases by yourself.

Getting there

Ferries leave Naples frequently for Capri. The **ALILAURO** *aliscafo* (hydrofoil) takes 45 minutes (☎ **081-761-1004**), and the **Tirrenia** *traghetto* (regular ferry) takes twice as long (☎ **081-761-3688**). The fast one costs 18,000L ($10) and the regular one 11,000L ($6). They both leave from Molo Beverello at Naples's Stazione Marittima several times a day.

The ferry and hydrofoil line run by **Alicost** (☎ **089-875-092**) has daily runs to Capri from Positano on the Amalfi Coast (see Chapter 22); a one-way ticket is 18,000L ($10) for the hydrofoil and 12,000L ($6) for the regular ferry. Crossing time is slightly shorter than from Naples. Remember, though, that you need to reserve at least 24 hours in advance.

From the ferry terminal you can also catch a funicular (in summer) or a bus (in winter) that brings you up the steep coast to the town of Capri. From there, you can reach Anacapri — the second town on the island, higher up on the promontory — by taxi, by bus, or on foot. A bus also links Capri to Marina Piccola, a village by the sea (see "Seeing the sights" later in this chapter).

While you're in Capri, you can get information from the **tourist office** at Piazza Umberto I 19 (☎ **081-370-686**). Summer hours are Monday to Saturday 8:30 a.m. to 8:30 p.m. and Sunday 8:30 a.m. to 2:30 p.m.; winter hours are Monday to Saturday 9 a.m. to 1 p.m. and 3:30 to 6:30 p.m.

Taking a tour

Boat tours of the island leave from **Marina Grande** (where the ferry and hydrofoil from Naples arrive). The cost is about 30,000L ($16) per person for the whole tour.

Seeing the sights

This legendary island has been the chief destination for the rich and famous since antiquity. It has two main urban centers: the town of **Capri** (where you can find the most glamorous hotels, cafes, and shops) and the smaller one of **Anacapri** (up a steep climb from Capri through the old **Scala Fenicia** staircases — read on for details — or via a hair-raising bus ride). From Anacapri you can take the chairlift up to **Monte Solaro,** the highest point on the island. On the south shore is the **Marina Piccola,** a tiny harbor with a beach offering views over the famous **Faraglioni,** the tall rocks off the island's southeastern tip. The windy roads climbing up the promontory are picturesque, though less entertaining when clogged with tourists. Capri boasts beautiful cliffs and views of the sea and out over the Bay of Naples and Vesuvius.

If you're moderately fit, you may enjoy exploring the island on foot. Most of the footpaths offer fantastic views. One of the musts is to climb the **Scala Fenicia,** the steep path linking Anacapri to Capri that was begun by Greek colonists thousands of years ago. It's so steep that it is actually a staircase (*scala* means "stairs") with over 500 steps.

If your real reason to come to Capri is to swim, you won't be disappointed: The water is beautiful and marvelously refreshing under the hot sun. Because Capri is very rocky, though, the **beaches** are small. The easy-to-reach beaches are often very crowded, but you can walk to several others for lesser crowds. The best idea, however, is to avail yourself of one of the small boats that take you to a difficult-to-reach beach for about 10,000L ($5).

The **Bagni di Tiberio** is a nice sandy beach on the north side of the island, near the ruins of an ancient villa. For 8,000L ($4.30), you can take a boat there from Marina Grande or walk (it takes about half an hour). The beach is freely accessible.

Grotta Azzurra

Kids will love visiting the Grotta Azzurra (Blue Grotto) — an underwater cave that can be reached only by small boats. It conjures up visions of pirates and at the same time is a natural wonder.

Capri

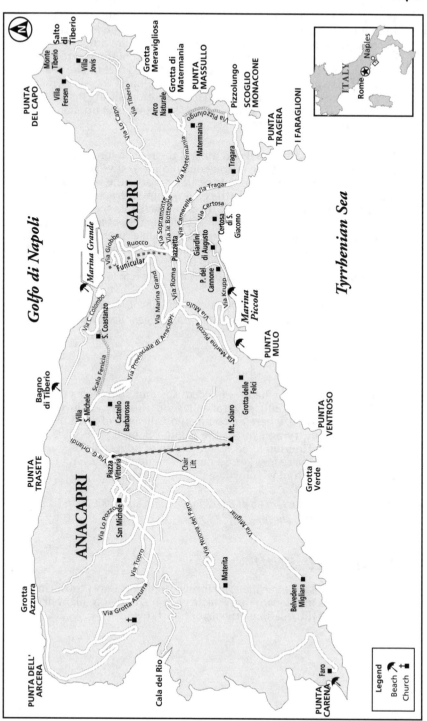

However, the Blue Grotto is also Capri's top attraction, and it has been overexploited by entrepreneurs. When you board that big boat going there, don't think that's how you see the grotto. You have to get off onto a rowboat that takes you into the grotto, which is reached by a narrow passage — so narrow and low that if you're not limber or have claustrophia you won't like it. The slow sinking of the grotto over time has reduced the opening to slightly more than 3 feet above sea level. Another way to see the grotto is the old-fashioned way — swim to it. However, we strongly advise against this option during peak season because of the incessant traffic of boats. If you insist upon swimming, it's best to do it toward evening.

When you get inside, you'll understand the reason for all the commotion and even forget about the outrageous money you've paid to see it. The grotto was known to the ancients but later lost to the world until an artist stumbled on it in 1826. Inside the cavern, light refraction (the sun's rays entering from an opening under the water) creates the incredible colors and a magical atmosphere. Stunning, indeed. Alas, chances are you won't be able to stay as long as you'd like because at the height of tourist season no lingering is allowed. For all these reasons, we think that the grotto, like Capri in general, should be seen in the off season if possible. Then you at least get a feeling for what it was like in the old days.

Near the northwestern tip of the island. Admission: Boat tour 23,000L ($12) plus 15,000L ($8) "tip" to be rowed inside the grotto. Open: Daily 9 a.m.–1 hour before sunset.

Villa Jovis

Capri has long been a haunt of eccentrics and sometimes degenerates: Emperor Tiberius built several villas on the island during his self-imposed exile here, where he could enjoy all sorts of illicit pleasures far away from the prying eyes of the Roman Senate. The Villa Jovis, the palace where Tiberius lived, extended over several levels for an estimated 63,000 square feet (just a modest summer home) but is now only a romantic ruin from which you get beautiful views.

Via Tiberio, at the eastern tip of the island. Admission: 4,000L ($2.15). Open: Daily 9 a.m.–1 hour before sunset.

Where to stay

If you want to stay overnight, be forewarned that Capri town isn't cheap. Hotels in Anacapri are a little cheaper, and you might like to be away from the bustling crowds of Capri town.

Grand Hotel Quisiana Capri

$$$$$ Capri

At the top of the scale, the Grand Hotel Quisiana is *the* chic place to stay on Capri — Georgio Armani has kept a suite here for years. What was a sanatorium in the nineteenth century is today the most popular place in Capri. If you can't afford one of the ritzy guest rooms, lounge in the terrace of the hotel cafe, maybe sipping the blue-colored house cocktail, or take a sauna or swim in the pool. The room furnishings are stylish, and some of the more expensive ones have fine antiques, marble columns, and extravagant baths.

Via Camerelle 2. ☎ *081-837-0788. Fax: 081-837-6080. E-mail:* info@quisi.com. *Internet:* www.quisi.com. *Rack rates: 400,000–800,000L ($216–$432) double, including breakfast. Closed Nov to mid-Mar.*

Hotel Luna

$$$$ Capri

A less pricey choice than the Grand Hotel Quisiana but still upscale, Hotel Luna offers beautiful vistas over the Faraglioni and the bay from its location atop a cliff. Most guest rooms have private terraces overlooking the cliffs or gardens, and all are quite luxurious; you even get a phone in the bathroom.

Viale Matteotti 3. ☎ *081-837-0433. Fax: 081-837-7459. E-mail:* luna@capri.it. *Rack rates: 340,000–490,000L ($185–$265) double, including breakfast. Closed end of Oct–Easter.*

Hotel San Michele

$$ Anacapri

A beautiful pool (the largest on Capri), gardens overlooking the sea, and pleasant guest rooms make Hotel San Michele an excellent moderately priced (for Capri) choice. The atmosphere is more relaxed and the hotel much quieter than one of the more expensive ones in Capri. Every room has some kind of view, whether of the sea, the mountain, or the gardens. The furnishings are contemporary and functional.

Via Orlandi 1–3. ☎ *081-837-1427. Fax 081-837-1420. E-mail:* smichele@ capri.it. *Rack rates: 200,000–250,000L ($108–$135) double, including breakfast. AE, MC, V. Closed Nov–Mar.*

Where to dine

Restaurants on Capri can be excellent although expensive. One of the specialties is *zuppa di cozze* (mussel soup) with beans; another is the *Caprese,* the simple salad of fresh mozzarella, basil leaves, and tomatoes sprinkled with extra-virgin olive oil. Don't be afraid to explore — some very nice small trattorie are tucked away among the rocks of this magnificent island.

Casanova

$$$ Capri Neapolitan/Caprese

Quite central, this restaurant offers a good choice of seafood and pasta dishes to satisfy the hungriest customers. If you're thirsty as well, you'll be pleased that it also has an excellent wine cellar, with a good selection of local wines. The Casanova features two dining rooms: the main one with arched ceilings, trestle tables, and tiled floors, and a smaller tavern room. The antipasto buffet is excellent; for a *secondo,* try the *totanetti affogati* (a type of squid, "drowned" — that is, stewed — in herbs and wine).

Via le Botteghe 46, just off Piazza Umberto. ☎ *081-837-7642. Reservations necessary for dinner. Secondi: 15,000–30,000L ($8–$16). AE, DC, MC, V. Open: Lunch and dinner daily; closed Dec to mid-Mar.*

Grottino

$$$$ Capri Neapolitan

Of historic importance — the preferred spot for the celebrities of the 1950s — Grottino still deserves its popularity. You can taste some true Caprese specialties, such as *zuppa di cozze,* and the old-fashioned Neapolitan everyday delicacy (think of it as old-world junk food) *mozzarella in carrozza* (deep-fried mozzarella), here prepared in four varieties.

Via Longano 27. ☎ *081-837-0584. Reservations necessary for dinner. Secondi: 18,000–30,000L ($10–$16). AE, MC, V. Open: Lunch and dinner daily; closed Nov–Mar.*

Chapter 22

The Amalfi Coast

••

In This Chapter

▶ Living the relaxed life in Positano

▶ Sunning yourself on the beaches of the Amalfi Coast

▶ Taking in the sights in Ravello

••

The **Costiera Amalfitana (Amalfi Coast)** is a stretch of shore famous for its natural beauty; its terraced cliffs overlooking the sea are covered with lemon trees, olive groves, and vineyards interspersed with small villages and historic towns, among which the queen is Amalfi. It was one of the four Italian historic maritime republics, with Siena, Genoa, and Venice.

The Amalfi Coast is only a couple of hours from Naples, so you can choose to visit this famous area as a day trip. However, given the difficult driving — the road is narrow and winding, sometimes without a guardrail — and the beauty of the place, you may be tempted to extend your stay and spend at least one night.

Getting There

There are several ways to get to and to see the Amalfi Coast. Some are more adventurous than others — read on for more about cliffside roads and breathtaking vistas.

By bus

The bus company **SITA** (☎ **089-871-016** or 089-871-009 in Amalfi) makes daily runs from Sorrento to Positano and Amalfi. The fare is 2,200L ($1.25) to Positano and 4,000L ($2.15) to Amalfi. The ride can be hair-raising at moments, but it's certainly panoramic. From Naples, get the 4,000L ($2.15) express train to Sorrento on the **Circumvesuviana** (☎ **081-772-2444**), then switch to the bus. Trains leave Naples from the Stazione Circumvesuviana, on Corso Garibaldi (between Piazza Nolana and Piazza G. Pepe) off to the right of Piazza Garibaldi. The train ride takes about an hour; the bus a little more depending on the traffic. SITA also has frequent runs between Amalfi and Ravello.

The Amalfi Coast

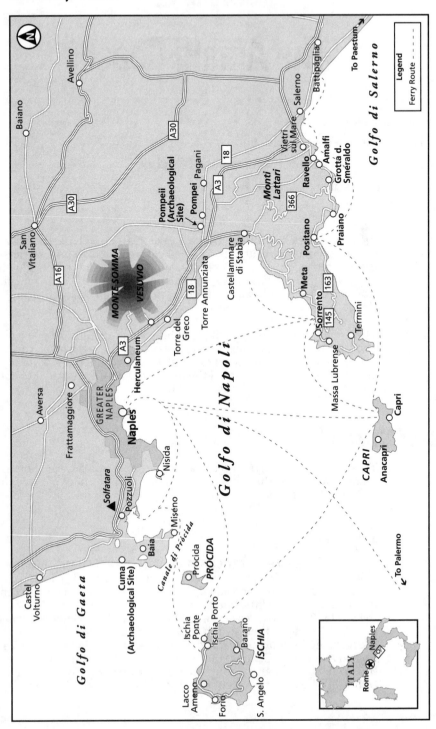

By ferry

The company **Alicost** (☎ **089-875-092**) has daily runs to Capri from Positano, by ferry and hydrofoil. A one-way ticket is 18,000L ($10) for the hydrofoil and 12,000L ($6) for the regular ferry. Crossing time is slightly shorter than from Naples. In order to take the ride, you need to make a reservation at least 24 hours in advance. Using this ferry, you could take ferries from Naples to Capri and then from Capri to Positano, thus avoiding all driving.

By car

If you have a car, take the *autostrada* Napoli-Salerno and exit either at **Vietri** — the southern limit of the Costiera Amalfitana — and follow the windy *strada statale* **SS163** back toward Sorrento, or do it the other way around, taking the exit for **Sorrento** and then following the signs for Positano and Amalfi east on SS163, which actually starts before Sorrento at the village of **Meta.** The road cuts from Meta across the peninsula, avoiding Sorrento, but if you continue on toward Sorrento, you can take an extra piece of windy road around the promontory (SS145), which then merges back with SS163. Farther along, note that Ravello is inland off SS163, posted from Amalfi.

Road maps are flat, of course, and show little topography. On the Amalfi Coast, something that's slightly inland is more up than it is in. And it may be *way* up the cliffs. This lack of correspondence between maps and reality is why sometimes you think you're lost but really you aren't. The other thing to remember is that when driving west to east, you're in the outside lane and thus close to the plunging cliff edge; if the prospect makes you nervous, you can drive the Amalfi Coast east to west, so you're on the inside lane.

Getting Around

Each of the towns along the Amalfi Coast is small and easily visited on foot. Especially in Positano, though, you may prefer to wear comfortable shoes without heels, to climb the steep alleys and many ramps of steps. To move among the attractions, you can use a **SITA** bus (☎ **089-871-016** or 089-871-009 in Amalfi), connecting Positano to Amalfi and Amalfi to Ravello.

Where to Stay

If you're looking for another splurge choice, try the famous **Hotel Le Sirenuse** (Via Cristoforo Colombo 30; ☎ **089-875-066;** Fax 089-811-798; E-mail: sirenuse@macronet.it. Internet: www.sirenuse.it), in a villa a few minutes' walk up from the bay. It's owned by the Marchesi Sersale family and was their residence until 1951. You may have seen the hotel featured in the film *Only You* with Marisa Tomei and Robert Downey, Jr.

Albergo L'Ancora

$$$ **Positano**

Not one of the most elegant choices in Positano, this moderately priced hotel still offers good value. Most guest rooms have air-conditioning, and each boasts comfortable beds, some antiques, and a private terrace. Open only to guests, the hotel's restaurant serves meals on the terrace.

Via Colombo 36. ☎ *089-875-318. Fax: 089-811-784. Parking: Free. Rack rates: 230,000–280,000L ($124–$151) double, including breakfast. AE, DC, MC, V. Closed Nov–Mar.*

Hotel Cappuccini Convento

$$$$ **Amalfi**

One of Amalfi's most beautiful hotels, this twelfth-century landmark is a convent turned into a hotel, and the "cells" are now luxuriously appointed guest rooms with dark wood furniture. Accommodations are now accessed by elevator and a glass-walled corridor with sweeping views. The magnificent hotel's restaurant is only rivaled by the terrace, open in the good season and renowned for its unrivaled view over the cliffs.

Via Annunziatella 46. ☎ *089-871-877. Fax: 089-871-886. E-mail:* cappuccini@ amalfinet.it. *Internet:* www.amafinet.it/cappuccini. *Parking: 30,000L ($16). Rack rates: 260,000–360,000L ($141–$195) double, including breakfast. AE, DC, MC, V.*

Hotel Lidomare

$$ **Amalfi**

This moderately priced hotel near the beach is housed in a thirteenth-century building. The guest rooms are brightly decorated in typical Amalfitan style (tiling, strong colors, lots of sparkling white). Most rooms have air-conditioning; the baths are small but very clean, and the staff is extremely friendly.

Largo Duchi Piccolomini 9. ☎ *089-871-332. Fax: 089-871-394. Parking: 15,000L ($8). Rack rates: 120,000–140,000L ($65–$76) double, including breakfast. AE, MC, V.*

Hotel Poseidon

$$$$ **Positano**

A villa from the 1950s, this hotel offers luxury accommodations at moderate prices. Each guest room has a terrace and unique decor. In addition to a beautiful garden and terrace with a spectacular view, the hotel has a pool and a small spa with a sauna, a Jacuzzi, and a choice of massages. The hotel's restaurant is not only convenient but up to the standards of the area.

Via Pasitea 148. ☎ ***089-811-111****. Fax: 089-875-833. E-mail:* poseidon@starnet. it. *Internet:* www.starnet.it/poseidon. *Parking: 40,000L ($22). Rack rates: 320,000–450,000L ($173–$245) double, including breakfast. AE, DC, MC, V. Closed Jan to mid-Mar.*

Villa Cimbrone

$$$$ Ravello

This villa, home to the Vuillemier family, who are the owners, offers hospitality to a small number of guests (20 maximum) in great luxury and privacy. Each of the rooms is unique and decorated with antiques. From Ravello, call the hotel; they'll send a porter to carry your luggage to the villa. The villa is an attraction in itself (see later in this chapter).

Via Santa Chiara 26. ☎ ***089-857-459****. Fax: 089-857-777. E-mail:* villacimbrone@ amalfinet.it. *Rack rates: 380,000–480,000L ($205–$259) double, including breakfast. AE, DC, MC, V. Closed Dec–Mar.*

Where to Dine

On the Amalfi coast, the sea reigns: It's a paradise for seafood — grilled, fried, or prepared in the local version of *zuppa di pesce* (fish stew). Similar to the Neapolitan cuisine, Amalfitan cuisine is rich in the flavors of the local countryside — ripe tomatoes, fresh herbs, and citrus fruits. The mussel-bound coast is also known for *zuppa di cozze* (mussel soup), and mussels are used in pasta dishes as well. For cheese, the winner is the *mozzarella di bufala* (buffalo mozzarella), the delicious specialty from the nearby Salerno region.

Buca di Bacco

$$$$ Positano Amalfitan

At this popular restaurant right on the beach, you find local cuisine at its best, with a large array of flavorful seafood dishes. The tables are set on the large shaded terrace with a great view over the sea. Try the *zuppa di cozze* or the grilled fish.

Via Rampa Teglia 8. ☎ ***089-875-699*** *Reservations necessary. Secondi: 35,000–55,000L ($19–$30). AE, DC, MC, V. Open: Lunch and dinner daily; closed Nov–Mar.*

Da Adolfo

$$$ Positano Amalfitan

If you're here in the right season, this restaurant provides you with an extra experience: Its motorboat (with a red fish on the side) waits for customers at the dock in Positano and carries them to the small resort. For the price of an excellent lunch — including fish, *zuppa di cozze,* and *pasta con cozze e vongole* (pasta with mussels and small clams) — you get access to the private beach and facilities (you have to pay extra, though, if you want to rent a beach umbrella and chair). July and August, the resort is open daily 10 a.m. to midnight (to about 7:30 p.m. in June and September); the boat leaves the Positano dock every 30 minutes.

Laurito, just off Positano. ☎ 089-875-022. Reservations recommended. Secondi: 12,000–24,000L ($6–$12). No credit cards. Open: Lunch daily, dinner Sat in July and Aug only; closed Oct–May.

Da Gemma

$$$ Amalfi   Amalfitan

One of the best restaurants on this stretch of coast, Da Gemma serves all the typical regional dishes. The *zuppa di pesce per due* (fish stew for two) is definitely a winner; the *fritto misto* is one of the lighter fried mixed seafoods you've ever tasted, and the *polipo* (tender octopus) is great. The homemade *crostata* (a thick crust topped with jam, a typical Italian home-style dessert) also deserves a mention, prepared with local citrus fruit jam.

Via Fra Gerardo Sassi 9. ☎ 089-871-345 Reservations necessary. Secondi: 20,000–50,000L ($11–$27). AE, DC, MC, V. Open: Lunch and dinner Thurs–Tues; closed Jan.

Ristorante Luna Convento

$$$ Amalfi   Amalfitan/Italian

Across from the hotel of the same name (which was once a convent), this is a popular and fashionable rendezvous. It's housed in a sixteenth-century tower and includes both a restaurant and a bar. Just underneath is a pool and the beach. Besides charming surroundings, you get great food. The ample menu includes pasta and seafood but also several meat dishes. The hotel itself also has a dining room with a nice terrace and views over the sea.

Via Pantaleone Comite 33. ☎ 089-871-002. Reservations recommended. Secondi: 26,000–32,000L ($14–$17). AE, DC, MC, V. Open: Lunch and dinner daily.

Cumpà Cosimo

$$ Ravello   Amalfitan

At this great family-run restaurant, you can order all the local specialties prepared home-style but at a lower price than in the more "resorty" restaurants. The pasta is very good, and so are the *secondi* (main dishes of meat or fish), among which you'll find a good *zuppa di pesce* and a fine *fritto misto.*

Via Roma 44. ☎ 089-857-156. Reservations recommended. Secondi: 16,000–45,000L ($9–$25). AE, DC, MC, V. Open: Lunch and dinner daily.

Other Amalfi Coast favorites

Baia: In the days of imperial Rome, Baia, only a few kilometers west of Naples, was a favorite place for the emperors and patricians to disport themselves. Emperor Claudius built an extravagant villa at Baia for his lascivious first wife, Messalina (her adultery led eventually to her execution). Claudius also met his end at Baia — he was poisoned by his last wife, his niece Agrippina (she was Nero's mother, and Nero in turn murdered her, keeping up the family tradition). Archaeological finds include the Temple of Baie and the Thermal Baths.

Cuma: About 19 km (12 miles) west of Naples, Cuma was one of the first areas on the Italian peninsula to be settled by the Greeks. Cuma's great importance in ancient times was that it was the site of the Cave of the Cumaean Sibyl, who supposedly wrote the *Sibylline Oracles,* a book of prophesies. You can visit the cave as well as some evocative temple ruins.

Ischia: This island in the Gulf of Gaeta, 34 km (21 miles) west of Naples, has been nicknamed the "Emerald Island" for its pine groves. Ischia is also famous for its fine beaches, health spas and thermal springs, vineyards, and dead volcano, Monte Epomeo.

Lago d'Averno: The Lake of Averno, occupying an extinct volcanic crater 16 km (10 miles) west of Naples, was known to the ancients as the Gateway to Hades. Facing the lake are the ruins of a first-century Temple of Apollo.

Sorrento: The famous resort of Sorrento, 50 km (31 miles) from Naples, stands on a cliff overlooking the Bay of Naples. The beaches here aren't the best in Campania, but Sorrento has some interesting sights as well as some of the best shopping along the Amalfi Coast.

Paestum: This ancient city, 100 km (62 miles) from Naples, was another Greek settlement and contains the best examples of Greek architecture in Italy outside of Sicily (see Chapters 24 and 25). The three major Greek temples are astoundingly well preserved and sited on an open plain free of any modern buildings — really giving you a feeling of how it was in ancient times. There's also an archaeological museum.

Exploring the Costiera Amalfitana

The attractions of the Amalfi Coast are mainly natural; people come to drive along the spectacular cliffs, play in the sea, and eat delicious seafood. The towns themselves vary — Positano is mainly a resort, while Amalfi itself retains more art and architecture from the area's glory days (about 800 years in the past); Ravello is somewhere in between — it offers some art but is mostly a tranquil, elegant resort.

The top sights

Positano

The westernmost of the three famous towns of the Amalfi Coast,
Positano is also the most dramatic. Built in the narrow gap between
two mountains, the village slopes steeply to the Tyrrhenian Sea. Just
off its coast are the legendary Sirenuse Islands, Homer's siren islands
in the *Odyssey,* which form the privately owned mini-archipelago of
Li Galli (The Cocks). Don't expect white Caribbean beaches here: The
beach is gray and rather pebbly; however, the sea is splendid.

Beside the town itself, the big attraction here — as you see as soon as
you step into town — is the swimsuits. Whether maillot, bikini, or
thong, they all have colorful and unique patterns. Because people here
spend two-thirds of their time in swimsuits, this local industry has
exploded. We know someone who buys her bikinis only in Positano, no
matter how far she has to travel to get them! The town is an exclusive
resort, and its small alleys and ramps are filled with boutiques, restaurants, and hotels.

The topography of the town, you'll soon discover, is impossibly steep.
Wear comfortable walking shoes — no heels!

Amalfi

Having known its moment of glory between the tenth and the twelfth
century — Amalfi was the first of Italy's maritime republics, before
Genoa and Venice — the city of **Amalfi** is rich in monuments and
mementos from the past. The grandiose **Duomo,** Piazza del Duomo
(☎ **089-871-059**) — named in honor of St. Andrew (Sant'Andrea) —
has a black-and-white facade redone in the eighteenth century; inside,
though, is the original tenth-century cathedral integrated into the
Duomo as the **Cappella del Crocifisso (Chapel of the Crucifixion).**
The Duomo is open daily 7:30 a.m. to 8 p.m., and admission is free.
To the left of the Duomo is the **Chiostro del Paradiso (Paradise
Cloister),** the thirteenth-century cloister that was once the cemetery
for the city's religious and political elite. From it, you can gain access
to the **crypt** containing the remains of St. Andrew. An interesting detail
is that his face is missing — it was donated to St. Andrew's in Patras,
Greece. Admission to the cloister is 5,000L ($2.70), and it's open daily
9 a.m. to 7 p.m. July to September, concerts are held in the cloister on
Friday nights.

The once-powerful republic was famous for its paper industry, and
paper from Amalfi was shipped all around Europe. This art has been
preserved in town, where one of the descendants of the ancient master
papermakers is still at his work: **Antonio Cavaliere** (Via Fiume; ☎ **089-
7871-954**). You can visit his workshop — complete with the traditional
equipment of the trade, where he still produces paper of an almost forgotten quality. The shop is open regular business hours. His products
are sold to the most exclusive paper shops in Italy and Europe. The

water for this craft still comes from the covered river that crosses town and was the key resource in the development of the paper industry in Amalfi.

If you follow the river out of town toward the hills (start at Piazza del Duomo and head up Via Genova), you can explore the **Valle dei Mulini,** the path stretching down the narrow valley of the river, along which the old paper mills that were the town's main economic resource are still visible. You can find out more details about the industry at the **Museo della Carta (Museum of Paper)** (Via Valle dei Mulini; ☎ 089-872-615), filled with antique presses and yellowing manuscripts. It's open Tuesday, Thursday, Saturday, and Sunday 9 a.m. to 1 p.m., and admission is 2,000L ($1.10).

Besides paper, Amalfi is famous today for its lemons. Unique in size, sweetness, flavor, and color, the lemons of Amalfi are exported as rare gems to markets around Italy. Here you can see them turned into the famous *limoncello,* a yellow-colored sweet lemon liqueur, but also into delicious confections like candied lemons, jams, and lemon ice cream.

Limoncello has a very nice taste, but few people can drink glasses of it. If you buy a bottle, consider that you can also use it to flavor cakes, cookies, and other sweet preparations.

Ravello

The only one of the major towns not on the coast, **Ravello** opens into a splendid valley with intensive cultivation — vineyards and lemons and other fruit grow on its steep terraced flanks. The town has a feeling of subdued elegance, the evidence of its magnificent past. Indeed, Ravello continued, after the fall of Amalfi, to be an important center for the commerce with the East during the thirteenth century. Celebrities and writers favor this town, and the reigning celeb of the moment is Gore Vidal, who purchased a villa as a writing retreat.

The eleventh-century **Duomo,** on Piazza Vescovado, has a beautiful portal from the twelfth century, a campanile from the thirteenth century, and interesting treasures in the crypt. The **Cappella di San Pantaleone (Chapel of St. Pantaleone),** the patron saint of Ravello, contains a relic of the saint (a cracked vessel with his blood, which miraculously fails to leak away); it's to the left of the main altar. The blood is a symbol of the saint's violent demise: He was beheaded in Nicomedia on July 27, 290. Ravello holds a festival on that day every year. The Duomo is open daily 8 a.m. to 7 p.m., and admission is free.

Also on Piazza Vescovado is the entrance to **Villa Rufolo** (☎ 089-857-657), founded in the eleventh century; though today it's a jumble of styles (from imitation Moorish to pretend Norman), you can still see memories of its past splendor. Among its illustrious guests was Richard Wagner, who is said to have composed an act of *Parsifal* during his residence here. The big attractions are the gardens, filled with flowers in spring and offering beautiful views over Salerno Bay. In summer, the villa is open daily 9 a.m. to 8 p.m. (winter to 6 p.m.), and admission is 5,000L ($2.70).

Going farther inland, you can reach the **Villa Cimbrone** (Via Santa Chiara 26; ☎ **089-857-459**), built in the nineteenth century by an eccentric Englishman over a pre-existing fifteenth-century villa. The views and the gardens are very beautiful, and it's well worth spending the night there (some of the rooms have been opened as a hotel accommodation — see "Where to Stay"). The villa is accessible only on foot after a somewhat steep walk of about 10 minutes. If you ring the bell at the entrance, a member of the staff lets you in and even takes you inside the building to admire the strange architecture. The villa is open daily 9 a.m. to 7 p.m., and admission is 6,000L ($3.25).

More cool things to see and do

Many people drive the Amalfi Coast and stop at only one or two of the towns, usually Amalfi itself or Positano. But the smaller towns and destinations are worth exploring, too. Here are a few recommendations:

✔ At 5 km (3.1 miles) west of Amalfi on SS163, the **Grotta di Smeraldo (Emerald Grotto)** is a good alternative to Capri's Blue Grotto. This cave is accessible only from the sea and costs 5,000L ($2.70), which includes the elevator from the road down to sea level and the boat ride to and inside the cave. From Amalfi, you can take the SITA bus toward Sorrento (ask the driver to stop at the grotto) or take a boat from the dock in the harbor (10,000L/$5 round-trip). The particularity of this grotto is its ancient formation of stalactites and stalagmites, which has been partially invaded by sea water. As a result, some of the formations are submerged, creating fantastic effects of light and shade. The boat takes you inside and around this bizarre world. It's open daily 9 a.m. to 4 p.m., weather permitting.

✔ Of course, the **Amalfi Coast** is a seaside resort and you can enjoy the beach. Amalfi has a nice sandy beach, but even better are the beaches at the small towns of Maiori and Minori, farther east. There you can sunbathe and swim in the blue **Mediterranean Sea.**

✔ At the southeastern end of the Amalfi Coast, the little town of **Vietri sul Mare** is on your way to the *autostrada* Salerno-Napoli and is worth the detour if you're a ceramics lover. Vietri is one of the famous Italian centers for artistic ceramics — with Deruta, Fienza, Sciacca, Santo Stefano, and Caltagirone — and the industry here is still very much alive. The streets are lined with ceramics of all kinds, characterized by bright colors and semigeometric patterns. Some of the shops sell products by different artists, but others are the marketplace of individual workshops, each with its individual pattern and colors. It's a perfect place to find a small gift for someone back home. We're especially fond of **D'Amore,** for the quality of his ceramics and the funny little goats that are his trademark and are imitated by many — or so he says.

Fast Facts: The Amalfi Coast

Country Code and City Code

The **country code** for Italy is **39**. The **city code** for the towns along the Amalfi Coast is **089**; use this code when calling from anywhere outside or inside Italy, even within the towns themselves (include the zero every time, even when calling from abroad).

Consulates and Embassies

See "Fast Facts: Naples" in Chapter 20.

Currency Exchange

You can change currency at banks in the three main towns, which also have ATMs.

Emergencies

Ambulance, ☎ **118**; Fire, ☎ **115**; Police, ☎ **113**; road assistance ACI, ☎ **116**.

Hospital

The **Ospedale Generale** is in Amalfi, 2 Localita Pogerola (☎ **089-830-065**).

Information

Each of the three main towns has a **tourist office**. The **Positano** office is on Via del Saraceno 4 (☎ **089-875-067**); it's open Monday to Friday 8:30 a.m. to 2 p.m. (in summer also Saturday 8:30 a.m. to noon. The **Amalfi** office is on Corso delle Repubbliche Marinare 19 (☎ **089-871-107**); it's open Monday to Friday 8 a.m. to 2 p.m. and Sat. 8 a.m. to noon. The **Ravello** office is on Via Santa Chiara 26 (☎ **089-857-096**); it's open Monday to Saturday 8 a.m. to 7 p.m. (to 8 p.m. in summer).

Mail

Ravello, Positano, and Amalfi each has an **Ufficio Postale** in the center of town.

Police

Call ☎ **113**; for the Carabinieri (other police), call ☎**112**.

Part VII

Sicily

The 5th Wave   By Rich Tennant

"I appreciate that our room looks out onto several baroque fountains, but I had to get up 6 times last night to go to the bathroom."

In this part . . .

"**Y**ou cannot get a true idea of Italy without seeing Sicily. Sicily is where you can find the key to everything." These words, which Goethe wrote in 1787, still hold true. Sicily is a more intense version of Italy, where things from the past are preserved with a magic vitality and hit you with strength and clarity. As you'll see from reading this part of the guide, visiting Sicily is a unique experience if you abandon yourself to the task.

In Chapter 23, we give everything you need to know to explore Sicily's capital, Palermo, southern Italy's largest art center. In Chapter 24, we recommend two very interesting destinations that you can easily visit as day trips from Palermo: Cefalù, a fishing port and lovely seaside resort, and Segesta, famous for its remarkable Doric temple. To round out Part VII, we guide you through the highlights of Taormina and the rest of this wonderful region, which is rich in art and attractions, in Chapter 25.

Chapter 23

Palermo

- -

In This Chapter

▶ Finding the part of Palermo that speaks to you

▶ Getting the best deal on lodging and the best meal

▶ Filling your time with activities that interest you

- -

*W*hy go to Sicily, you ask? Well, if you don't, you'll be missing out on a big chunk of Italy — bigger than Tuscany, bigger than Lombardy. In fact, Sicily is the largest of the Italian regions. The island's central position in the Mediterranean — Africa is only a day's sail away — has made it a strategic base since ancient times, and its rich volcanic soil has attracted colonizers and pillagers for just as long. No wonder Rome and Carthage used the island as a battleground. Though Sicily's northeast corner is separated from the mainland only by the sliver of the Straits of Messina, at its southernmost points it's farther south than Tunis.

The perfect word to describe Sicily is *unique* — unique architecture, unique cuisine, and a unique people distinct from the rest of the Italian nation.

Palermo is a busy modern port and is the political center of "recent" Sicily — meaning from about 1060 onward. The invasions of the Arabs and then of the Normans, who ruled from Palermo for centuries, brought about a cultural mix that's still apparent in the fabulous works of art that have been preserved and in the traditions that have been handed down. (The Sicilian Parliament meets in the building that was the Norman palace.) Palermo was severely damaged by earthquakes in the early twentieth century and was bombarded in World War II, and much of it seems never to have recovered. Although most visitors arrive here, you'll find it easier to understand and appreciate Palermo after having seen other parts of the island.

The capital of Sicily since Norman times, Palermo boasts some of Sicily's best art. Its churches alone are worth the visit, and its museums, in a region where museums are rather inadequate, are very good. Under a decaying facade, treasures wait for you, and a people bursting with energy and kindness are ready to help you enjoy your visit. Remember, though, that *respect* is the key word here, as well as *reserve* and *composure*.

Sicily

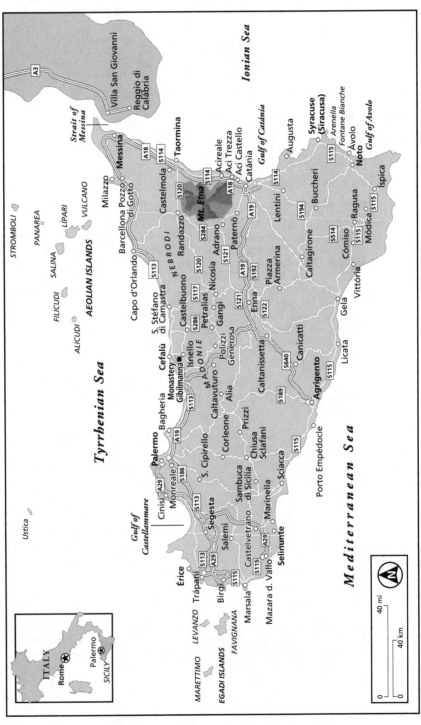

Palermo is a good starting point for exploring Sicily, especially if you're planning to take a guided tour. Indeed, tours start from here for each of the major attractions on the island. The other good starting point is Taormina (see Chapter 25).

Getting There

There are many ways to get to Sicily, but the best way, in our opinion, is to take the ferry.

By ferry

One of the newest and best ferries is the **SNAV SiciliaJet** (Via Giordano Bruno 84; ☎ **081-761-2348**; Fax 081-761-2141; Internet: www.snavali.com), which takes only four hours between Naples and Palermo. It runs once a day, leaving from Palermo around 9 a.m. and from Naples around 5:30 p.m. The one-way fare is 96,000L to 120,000L ($52 to $65) for adults depending on the season; a car with two adults is 257,000L to 409,000L ($139 to $221) depending on the car size and the season, plus 4,200L ($2.25) per person and 9,300L ($5) per car in harbor taxes. The boat has 200 car and bus slots and takes 800 passengers. Ticketing offices are in the harbors of Naples (☎ **081-761-2348**) and Palermo (☎ **091-611-8525**).

SNAV offers discounts with Avis car rental (10 percent off if the Avis rental was during the previous 48 hours, 20 percent off if the car is actually on the ferry). Taking the SNAV ferry also gives you discounts at the Astoria Palace Hotel in Palermo and the Grand Hotel Terminus in Naples.

The regular old-fashioned ferry run by **Tirrenia** (☎ **091-333-300** in Naples and 06-474-2041 in Rome) goes between Naples and Palermo overnight (10 hours) — a good deal because you save on a hotel for the night and don't use up daylight hours traveling. It's also cheaper: A one-way adult fare is 80,000L ($43) for a double cabin (with bunk beds, very comfortable); a car costs about 100,000L to 150,000L ($54 to $81). Note that Naples is about a two-hour train ride from Rome for about 30,000L ($16).

By air

Flying is less romantic than taking the ferry but is still an excellent way to get to Sicily. Remember, though, that you can't fly directly in and out of Italy from Sicily — you have to fly into Rome or Milan first. **Air Sicilia** (☎ **06-6501-1046**) offers excellent deals — about 250,000L ($135) round-trip on its daily flights from Rome to Sicily. **Alitalia** (☎ **1478-65643** or 06-65643) has several flights a day and is slightly more expensive at about 300,000L ($156). The flight lasts just over an hour. To find out about national departures, call ☎ **091-702-0302**.

Like Rome's Fiumicino, Palermo's airport, **Aeroporto Civile Punta Raisi** (☎ 091-591-414), is referred to by its location and not by its actual name, the Aeroporto Falcone Borsellino. The airport is open daily 8 a.m. to 11 p.m.

The bus company **Prestia & Comande** (☎ 091-580-457) runs the bus service between the airport and the Hotel Politeama and Stazione Centrale in Palermo. The bus runs every 30 minutes, and the fare is 6,500L ($3.50). To get to the airport in a hurry if you're traveling light, you can take a helicopter from **Elitaxi** (☎ 091-227-350 or 091-227-068), leaving from Viale Regione Siciliana 544. The cost is 55,000L ($30), double that if you have more than hand luggage. Regular helicopter flights are bunched in the early morning and the evening to correspond with the usual plane departures.

By train

The train (☎ 147-888-088 toll-free in Italy or 091-616-1806 or 091-616-7514) from Rome takes 11 to 13 hours and costs 70,000L to 120,000L ($38 to $65) per person, depending on whether it's a local or an express. A *cuccetta* (sleeping berth) runs 20,000L to 30,000L ($11 to $16). You don't save much, obviously, over the ferry, and the train takes longer. The train is put on a train ferry at Messina and continues on to Palermo. The train arrives at Palermo's **Stazione Centrale FS** (☎ 091-616-5914) on Piazza Giulio Cesare, very near the center of town.

By car

You don't really want to go to Sicily by car, but if you must, take **A1** from Rome to Caserta, **A30** from Caserta to Salerno, and **A3** from Salerno to Villa San Giovanni, where you take the *traghetto* (ferry) for Messina. When in Messina, pick up **A18** to Catania and then **A19** from Catania to Palermo. We don't recommend driving from Rome to Palermo, because the trip is a total of 1,050 km (651 miles). The ferry from Villa San Giovanni to Messina is cheap at 20,000L ($11) for the car, but when you add some tanks of gas at about $50 a pop and 10 or 11 hours of driving, we don't think it makes sense.

While in Palermo, you can park in the lot on Via Spinuzza, in front of the Teatro Massimo; it costs 2,000L ($1.10) per hour from 8 a.m. to 8 p.m., then free overnight. You can buy the access card to the lot in most bars. **AMAT** (☎ 091-690-2690) manages this lot.

Orienting Yourself in Palermo

Palermo is a seaside city, organized around its busy port. Although the modern town sprawls between the mountains and the sea, the historic center of interest to tourists is fairly concentrated; its neighborhoods reflect the various cultures that have dominated the city through history.

Palermo

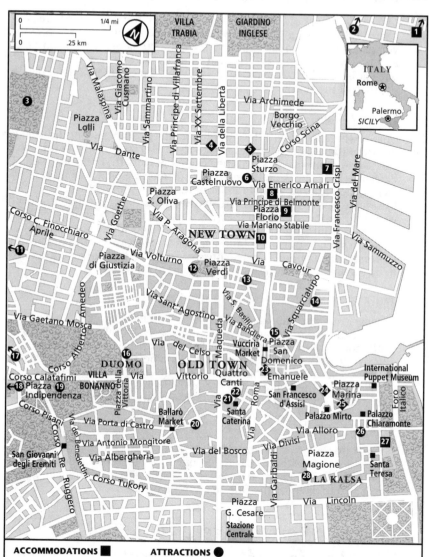

0   1/4 mi
0   .25 km

VILLA TRABIA

GIARDINO INGLESE

ITALY

Rome ✪

Palermo ✪
SICILY

Via Giacomo Cusmano
Via Malaspina
Via Sammartino
Via Principe di Villafranca
Via XX Settembre
Via della Libertà
Via Archimede
Borgo Vecchio
Corso Scina

Piazza Lolli
Via Dante
Piazza Castelnuovo
Piazza Sturzo
Via Emerico Amari
Via del Mare

Piazza S. Oliva
Via Principe di Belmonte
Piazza Florio
Via Mariano Stabile
Via Francesco Crispi

Corso C. Finocchiaro Aprile
Via Goethe
Via P. Aragona
NEW TOWN
Via Sammuzzo

Piazza di Giustizia
Via Volturno
Piazza Verdi
Via Cavour

Via Gaetano Mosca
Via Sant'Agostino
Via S. Basilio
Via S. Bandiera
Via Squarcialupo

Via del Celso
Vucciria Market
Piazza San Domenico
International Puppet Museum

DUOMO
VILLA BONANNO
Via della Vittoria
OLD TOWN
Vittorio
Quattro Canti
Emanuele
Piazza Marina
Foro Italico

Corso Calatafimi
Piazza Indipendenza
Corso Pisani
Via del Bosco
Via Porta di Castro
Ballarò Market
Santa Caterina
Via Roma
San Francesco d'Assisi
Palazzo Mirto
Palazzo Chiaramonte

San Giovanni degli Eremiti
Via Antonio Mongitore
Via Albergheria
Via Maqueda
Via Alloro
Via Divisi
Piazza Magione
Santa Teresa

Corso Tukory
Via Garibaldi
LA KALSA

Piazza G. Cesare
Stazione Centrale
Via Lincoln

ACCOMMODATIONS ■
Cristal Palace Hotel **8**
Grand Hotel et des Palmes **10**
Grand Hotel Villa Igiea **1**
Joli Hotel **9**
Jolly Hotel **27**
President Hotel **7**

DINING ◆
Capricci di Sicilia **5**
Casa del Brodo **23**
Gourmand's **4**
I Beati Paoli **25**
La Cambusa **24**

ATTRACTIONS ●
Catacombe dei Cappuccini **17**
Cattedrale (Duomo) **16**
Chiesa del Gesù
   (Casa Professa) **20**
Chiesa di Santa Maria
   dell'Ammiraglio
   (La Martorana) **21**
Fontana Pretoria **22**
Galleria Regionale Siciliana
   (Palazzo Abatellis) **26**
La Cuba **18**
La Kalsa **28**

La Zisa **11**
Monte Pellegrino and
   Santuario di Santa Rosalia **2**
Museo Archeologico Regionale **13**
Oratorio del Santissimo Rosario
   di San Domenico **15**
Oratorio di Santa Cita **14**
Palazzo dei Normanni and
   Cappella Palatina **19**
Teatro Massimo **12**
Teatro Politeama Garibaldi **6**
Villa Malfitano **3**

Palermo by neighborhood

The historic part of Palermo is where most of the attractions are concentrated. Although it's not too small, you can visit it on foot, provided you make a logical plan — as usual, it's best to avoid the up and down, east and west itineraries. The historic part can be divided into an older one (going back to the Arabian rulers) and a more recent one (built at the turn of the twentieth century).

The Old Town

This is where Palermo's development started. The heart of the old city lies from the old harbor, the **Cala,** to the **Palazzo dei Normanni,** the castle and royal residence of the various powers that reigned over Palermo (from the Arab Emirs to the current Regional Assembly of Sicily), along **Corso Vittorio Emanuele.** Cutting Corso Vittorio Emanuele at a right angle is **Via Maqueda,** the "new" avenue leading west to the modern part of the city. The crossing of these two arteries is the beautiful baroque square of the **Quattro Canti** (four corners). Here are such important monuments as **La Martorana,** the **Cattedrale (Duomo),** the famous **Vucciria** open-air market, the **Galleria Regionale della Sicilia,** and the Arab neighborhood of **La Kalsa.**

The New Town

Of lesser interest, this part of town was developed in the late nineteenth century. Important here are the **Teatro Massimo,** the **Teatro Politeama** (its full name is the Teatro Politeama Garibaldi, but it's usually shortened), and **Via Libertà** with its Liberty (Italian art nouveau) palaces. This is central Palermo's most pleasant area, very popular with locals — the Politeama is the rendezvous place for people of every age — and boasting boutiques and restaurants and hotels.

Monreale

A separate town yet so close it's almost a neighborhood, Monreale is to Palermo what Fiesole is to Florence, dominating the city from a beautiful hill. The great attraction here, sufficient alone to justify your whole trip to Sicily, is the **Duomo** with its cloister.

Street smarts: Where to get information after you arrive

The walk-in public office of the **Azienda Autonoma Provinciale per l'Incremento Turistico** is at Piazza Castelnuovo 34, across from the Teatro Politeama (☎ **091-583-847** or 091-605-8351; E-mail: aapit@gestelnet.it; Internet: www.aapit.pa.it). It's open Monday to Friday 8:30 a.m. to 2 p.m. and 2:30 to 6 p.m. and Saturday 8:30 a.m. to 2 p.m. You can also find **tourist booths** at the airport (☎ **091-591-698**) and at the train station (☎ **091-616-5914**), both open daily 9 a.m. to 6 p.m.

Getting Around Palermo

Palermo is an interesting city to discover on foot, and the only real safety problems are the purse snatchers (particulalry effective and dangerous ones operate from *motorini*, motorscooters) and pickpockets — be very careful, especially in the crowded Vucciria open-air market. Small backpacks are particularly attractive to these skilled thieves. This relative safety extends even to areas that by our standards may be a bit scary, such as the forlorn blocks with partially destroyed buildings — some by World War II bombings, others by earthquakes — that are visible in many parts of the old town.

When you're too tired to walk, you can easily take an **AMAT bus** (☎ 091-321-333), with single tickets costing 1,500L (80¢) and day tickets 5,000L ($2.70). Monreale is the one place where you really have to take a bus, unless you're traveling with a mule.

When you need to reach sights out of town, note that the *provincia* of Palermo is served by **AST** (☎ **091-688-2906**).

Taxis are also a good way to get around, especially considering the traffic and the heat that can make waiting for a bus uncomfortable. The basic charge for a taxi is 6,000L ($3.25), and then small increments are added for every minute or kilometer. For a radio taxi, call ☎ **091-225-455**, 091-512-727, or 091-682-5441.

We once got a taxi driver who awarded himself an inflation increase to 10,000L ($5) because "rates haven't been adjusted since 1991." To avoid such problems, confirm up front where you're going and what the base price is (a long trip obviously costs more than the basic fee).

Where to Stay

Because most of the sights are within walking distance of the center, it pays to have a central hotel. In addition, because tourism isn't as highly developed here as it is in other major centers in Italy of comparable importance, hotels are much more old-fashioned than what you may be used to. Modern conveniences and private baths are definitely not the norm. On Sicily, even more than anywhere else in Italy, family-run hotels tend to feel as if you stepped into someone's home. But things are changing.

For the reasons we just explained, if you're planning to pick a hotel that's not from our listing, remember that it doesn't pay to go for an el cheapo choice on Sicily.

The top hotels

Cristal Palace Hotel

$$ Politeama

Opened in 1990 as a member of the Hotels and Resorts Club, this central hotel occupies a converted bank building (a modern glass box but comfortable). The air-conditioned guest rooms have refrigerators/bars, hair dryers, and well-designed small baths. The furnishings are modern and streamlined (with an IKEA feeling). The hotel has a restaurant, and the breakfast buffet includes ham and cheese as well as the usual pastries.

Via Roma 477/D, 2 blocks northeast of the Teatro Politeama. ☎ *091-6112580. Fax 091-611-2589. Rack rates: 200,000L ($108) double, including buffet breakfast. AE, DC, MC, V.*

Grand Hotel et des Palmes

$$$ Via Roma

Once a private home, the Grand Hotel opened in 1874 and has since been the hotel to go to in central Palermo. Wagner finished writing his *Parsifal* here, and one of the guests in more recent times was Bill Clinton. The classically inspired lobby has marble floors, Greek columns, chandeliers, marble staircases, and art nouveau furnishings. Though the air-conditioned guest rooms can't match the level of the public spaces, they're well furnished and large. Meals are served in La Palmetta Restaurant, and the Sala degli Specchi (Hall of Mirrors) is used not only for receptions but also as the breakfast room — the breakfast is great, with eggs, meat, *cornetti* (Italian croissants), juices, and good coffee.

Via Roma 398, 4 blocks northeast of the Teatro Politeama. ☎ *091-583-933. Fax: 091-331-545. E-mail:* des-palmes@thi.it. *Rack rates: 350,000L ($189) double, including buffet breakfast. AE, DC, MC, V*

Grand Hotel Villa Igiea

$$$$ North of the port area

This is one of the best hotels not only in Palermo but also on the whole island. Housed in a former private villa on the outskirts of town, the Grand Hotel Villa Igiea is a masterpiece of the Sicilian Liberty (Italian art nouveau) architect Ernesto Basile, who also designed the furnishings. The spacious guest rooms are as glamorous as the public areas, and the hotel is surrounded by splendid terraced gardens overlooking the bay. The two restaurants feature local and regional cuisine; in summer, meals are served on the elegant terrace overlooking Palermo. Other features include a piano bar, a seawater pool, tennis courts, and a meeting center if you're bringing your entourage.

Salita Belmonte 43. ☎ *091-543-744. Fax: 091-547-654. E-mail:* villa-igea@ thi.it. *Bus: 139 to Villa Igiea. Parking: Free. Rack rates: 250,000–390,000L ($135–$211) double, including breakfast. AE, DC, MC, V.*

Joli Hotel

$ **Piazza Florio**

This modest hotel, on a quiet square just north of the port, has been renovating one floor after another, and by the time you read this, the Joli should have doubled its size to 30 rooms and added a bar. All the air-conditioned guest rooms have small but functional baths and private terraces; some have views of Monte Pellegrino, the mountain overlooking Palermo. Although the hotel is small, it offers a pleasant lounge for guests.

Via Michele Amari 11, 2 blocks southeast of the Teatro Politeama. ☎ *and fax* **091-611-1765** *or 091-611-1766. Parking: Free. Rack rates: 120,000L ($65) double. AE, DC, MC, V*

Runner-up accommodations

Jolly Hotel

$$ Foro Italico   This modern pleasant place is surrounded by a garden with a pool. Although the guest rooms are moderate in size, some have balconies. East of the harbor, near the train station; ☎ **091-616-5090**; Fax: 091-616-1441.

President Hotel

$$ Via Francesco Crispi   Across from the port where the ferries arrive, it was renovated in 1999. All the guest rooms have air-conditioning, and rates include a buffet breakfast served in the restaurant with sunny views of the port and mountains. Via Francesco Crispi 230, west of the harbor; ☎ **091-580-733**; Fax: 091-611-1588.

Where to Dine

Sicily has a unique cuisine, even for Italy, which has so many regional variations. You can find dishes like Italian-looking pasta with pistachio nuts and North African spices — the Sicilians perfected "multiculturalism" centuries ago. And because Sicily is an island, its cuisine is full of things from the sea.

Typical Sicilian dishes are *pasta con le sarde* (pasta with shredded fresh sardines), *caponata* (cubed eggplant with other vegetables, spiced and sautéed), *tonno con aglio e menta* (fresh tuna with garlic and mint), and fish dishes with *finocchietto* (small fresh fennel, a common herb). If you want only a sandwich, go for *focacce,* the typical Palermo sandwich. Inside you can have a variety of things, from the excellent *caciocavallo* (typical cheese) to fried spleen. Yes, spleen, plus a little lung as well to make it better. We tried it and it was okay if you're very hungry (it's definitely an acquired taste). Also excellent on the "fast food" side are *arancini* (deep-fried flavored rice balls) and *panelle* (chickpea fritters).

Sicilian desserts and pastries are famous. *Cassata* is a fabulous creation — the heart is ricotta mixed with sugar and candied fruit, which is covered with a layer of cake and then almond paste. Some say that *gelato* was invented in Palermo. Sicily presents you with not only good food but *interesting* food.

The top restaurants

Casa del Brodo

$$ Vucciria   Sicilian

This trattoria, opened in 1890, claims to be the oldest in Palermo. If you choose to have the *antipasto,* you'll select from a buffet with a large variety of traditional specialties, all freshly prepared. The fresh fish dishes are great, as are the traditional *primi (pasta alla Norma, pasta con le sarde,* and so on). The old-fashioned ambiance isn't a bit ruined by the air-conditioning. The restaurant is in a busy area of town and gets quite full at lunch.

Corso Vittorio Emanuele 175. ☎ 091-321-655. Reservations recommended on weekends. Bus: 104 to Quattro Canti or 105 to Corso Vittorio Emanuele, east of Via Roma. Secondi: 10,000–18,000L ($5–$10). MC, V. Open: Lunch and dinner Wed–Mon.

Gourmand's

$$$ Politeama Sicilian

One of the best restaurants in Palermo, Gourmand's attracts foreigners and less adventurous customers for its tamer cuisine and reasonable prices. The *antipasti* are excellent, as is the grilled fish. In addition to typical Sicilian specialties, the menu includes a choice of dependable Italian dishes like *risotto al salmone* (risotto with salmon).

Viale della Libertà 37/A. ☎ 091-323-431. Reservations recommended on weekends. Bus: 101 and 102 to Via della Libertà. Secondi: 14,000–28,000L ($8–$15). AE, DC, MC, V. Open: Lunch and dinner Mon–Sat.; closed Aug.

La Cambusa

$$ Piazza Marina Sicilian

Here you find excellent homemade-style typical fare. La Cambusa is very popular with the people of La Cala (the marina across the street) and other Palermitans, so come early — Sicilians eat at 9 or even 9:30 p.m. in summer — or be prepared to wait. Try the superb *pasta con le sarde* (pasta with sardines, fennel, and tomato sauce) or the *pasta alla carrettiera* (the Sicilian version of pesto sauce, with capers, almonds, and tomato) and the variety of fish *secondi.*

Piazza Marina 16. ☎ 091-584-574. Reservations recommended on weekends. Bus: 105 to Piazza Marina. Secondi: 10,000–18,000L ($5–$10). MC, V. Open: Lunch and dinner Tues–Sun.

Runner-up restaurants

Two excellent areas to find restaurants are the ones most popular with locals: Attracting younger crowds is the area around Piazza Marina, behind the recreational harbor of **La Cala;** the area around the **Teatro Politeama,** on Piazza Sturzo/Piazza Castelnuovo, is favored by slightly more mature customers. Two good examples:

Capricci di Sicilia

$$ Piazza Sturzo   In the more elegant part of the center, Capricci di Sicilia is an excellent restaurant offering typical recipes of the Sicilian tradition. Via Istituto Pignatelli 6, off Piazza Sturzo to the northwest of the Teatro Politeama; ☎ **091-327-777**.

I Beati Paoli

$$ Piazza Marina   Open only for dinner, this popular pizzeria has a lively young atmosphere. The menu also features a number of Sicilian specialties. Piazza Marina 50; ☎ **091-616-6634**.

Exploring Palermo

Palermo has a depth and breadth of sights to suit every taste. Just walking among the major sights (listed in this section) is fascinating in itself. You never know what you're going to stumble upon next as you stroll through this city, which has been the crossroads of the Mediterranean for centuries (and be sure to get an early start, especially if it's hot).

The top sights

Cattedrale (Duomo)

Palermo's Duomo was built in 1185 atop a mosque built atop a Byzantine church. In this mixed-up sandwich, some material was reused — in the portico is a column with an engraved inscription from the Koran (first on the left), an unusual feature for a Catholic church. In the fifteenth century, the south side became the main entrance, with a portico in Gothic-Catalan style. In the eighteenth century, the whole interior was redone in neoclassical style, and the lateral naves were added along with the dome. The apse is the original part of the church. While the outside is a magnificent Romanesque in warm, pale ochres, the inside is a shock of white and gray baroque. Look for the bas-reliefs by Vincenzo and Fazio Gagini on the altar and the *Madonna with Child* by Francesco Laurana in the seventh chapel of the left nave (Laurana's famous sculpture of Eleanora d'Aragona is in the Galleria Regionale Siciliana — see the description later in this chapter). The **imperial and royal tombs** include those of Frederick II and Roger II. The **Cappella di Santa Rosalia (Chapel**

of St. Rosalia) contains the saint's remains, which are carried through the streets in a procession every July (see "More cool things to see and do" later in this chapter).

Piazza della Cattedrale, on Via Vittorio Emanuele. ☎ *091-334-376. Admission: Free. Open: Mon-Sat 7 a.m.–7 p.m., Sun and holidays 8 a.m.–1:30 p.m. and 4–7 p.m.*

Chiesa del Gesù (Casa Professa)

Commonly called the Casa Professa, this is the first church in Sicily founded by the Jesuits. Its interior is rich in stuccowork by the Serpotta (famous seventeenth- and eighteenth-century Palermitan sculptors), and beautiful marble inlays in a large range of colors decorate the altar and walls. The original Renaissance church, in the form of a Latin cross (a nave and two short aisles), was designed by Giovanni Tristano in 1564. It was much changed in the following century by the Jesuit Natale Masuccio, who made it into one of the most ostentatious churches of the Sicilian baroque. A large part of the church was destroyed in 1943 but later restored.

Piazza Casa Professa, off Via Ponticello from Via Maqueda. ☎ *091-607-6111. Admission: Free. Open: Daily 7:30–11:30 a.m.; no visits during mass.*

Chiesa di Santa Maria dell'Ammiraglio (La Martorana)

This church was built by the admiral of Ruggero II, Giorgio di Antiochia, in 1143 but was transformed during later centuries. However, the original structure's beautiful **Byzantine mosaics** remain. The central scene depicts the heavenly hierarchy, with God at the apex of the dome and four archangels at his feet; in a bit of artistic politicking, a mosaic on the balustrade shows Roger II getting his crown directly from Christ and not from the pope. Other scenes are from the life of Mary. The name Martorana comes from the nearby convent, founded by the Martorana family. Tradition says that the nuns there invented the little marzipan fruits that today are a typical — and delicious — souvenir from Sicily. They still sell their original creations: delicate sculptures of bunches of grapes with each grape (made of almond paste) delicately painted with sugar and with stems made of candied orange peel covered in dark chocolate — a little expensive, but a treat for a king.

Piazza Bellini 3, off Via Maqueda, near the Quattro Canti. ☎ *091-616-1692. Admission: 4,000L ($2.15). Open: Mon–Sat 9:30 a.m.–1 p.m. and 3:30–7 p.m., Sun and holidays 8:30 a.m.–1 p.m.*

Duomo di Monreale

This twelfth-century Romanesque church in Monreale is one of the most breathtaking in existence. It may not be exceptional for its Norman exterior — the Duomo in Palermo is more interesting — but the interior is extraordinary. The church is decorated with 6,000 square meters (55,000 square feet) of fabulous **Byzantine school mosaics,** whose subjects come from the Old and New Testaments, with the stories of Noah,

Isaac, and Jacob most prominent. In the dome is a **Christ Pantocrator** (pictured with his fingers making the Greek symbol of his divine and human nature). The apse's decorations show an Islamic influence. The floors are of remarkable marble mosaics, and the bronze portals are masterpieces. Annexed to the church is the **cloister** from 1180, one of the most beautiful in Italy. It has 228 double columns, some with mosaic inlay and each with an individual pattern; the carved stone capitals are amazingly intricate renderings of scenes such as battles, the punishment of the damned, and stories of obscure meaning.

Piazza del Duomo in Monreale. ☎ 091-640-4413 or 091-640-4403 (cloister). Bus: 389 from Piazza Indipendenza, off the Palazzo dei Normanni, to Piazza del Duomo, running every 20 minutes. Admission: Duomo free, cloister 4,000L ($2.15). Open: Duomo daily 8 a.m.–6 p.m.; cloister Mon–Sat 9 a.m.–1 p.m. and 3–6:30 p.m., Sun and holidays 9 a.m.–12:30 p.m.

Fontana Pretoria

This magnificent sixteenth-century fountain was created for a Florentine villa, but when the villa's owner died, his son sold the fountain to the Palermo Senate. The nudes created a big scandal in town, and for a while it was called the "fountain of shame." The succession of concentric circular platforms are connected by stairways and balustrades. There are 4 basins on which 24 heads of monsters and animals face outward, 56 channels of water, 37 statues portraying mythological characters, and 4 large statues representing the rivers that fertilize the countryside around Palermo.

Piazza Pretoria, off the Quattro Canti, where Via Vittorio Emanuele crosses Via Maqueda.

Galleria Regionale Siciliana (Palazzo Abatellis)

In late Catalan Gothic style, the 1490 Palazzo Abbatellis houses the principal museum of Sicilian art from the thirteenth to the eighteenth century. The fifteenth-century *Triumph of Death* is a powerful and intriguing fresco that came from the hall of the 1330 Palazzo Sclafani (Piazza San Giovanni Decollato, off Piazza della Vittoria). A skeleton on horseback fires arrows at pleasure seekers, rich prelates, and other sinners while the poor and ill look on (the two artists who did the fresco painted themselves in this group). The faces are incredible and expressive; Picasso could have done the horse's head. Antonello da Messina's *Madonna Annunziata,* looking out from under a blue mantle, is also here; it displays Antonello's uncanny ability to portray more than one emotion at the same time. Francesco Laurana's *bust of Eleonora d'Aragona* is another masterpiece. These works are definitely worth the visit, even if many other pieces are of minor importance or in poor condition.

Via Alloro, near Piazza Marina. ☎ 091-616-4317. From Piazza Marina, cross the garden and take Via Quattro Aprile 2 blocks to Via Alloro; turn right and walk 2 blocks. Admission: 8,000L ($4.30). Open: Mon–Sat 9 a.m.–1:30 p.m. (Tues and Thurs also 3–7:30 p.m.), Sun 9 a.m.–12:30 p.m.

La Kalsa

One of the city's oldest neighborhoods (it was built by the Arabs as the emir's citadel), La Kalsa developed around **Piazza Magione,** southeast of **Piazza Marina.** The grandiose battle scene between Garibaldi and the Bourbons in the famous Visconti movie *Il Gattopardo* (*The Leopard*) was filmed on Piazza Magione. Piazza Marina is one of La Kalsa's main features, with its beautiful garden enclosed by elegant Liberty-style iron railings and graced by an impressive giant ficus. **Via Alloro** was the central street of La Kalsa, as you can see from the once elegant palaces lining the street. The nearby **Cala** is Palermo's original harbor.

Unfortunately, the rest of the neighborhood is quite grungy. Much of the Arabs' fine work was destroyed when the Spanish viceroys took over, adding their own architectural interpretations, and much of the later palazzi were damaged or destroyed by earthquakes and World War II and are mostly semi-abandoned. For an idea of what they looked like in their former splendor, visit the restored fifteenth-century **Palazzo Abbatellis,** seat of the Galleria Regionale Siciliana (see the description earlier in this chapter) and the early-twentieth-century **Palazzo Mirto** (Via Merlo 2; ☎ 091-616-4751); the latter is open Monday to Friday 9 a.m. to 1 p.m. and 3 to 7 p.m. and Saturday and Sunday 9 a.m. to 12:30 p.m., with a 4,000L ($2.15) admission. Among the neighborhood's churches, you may want to visit **Santa Teresa** (Piazza Kalsa; ☎ 091-616-1658), a good example of the irrepressible Sicilian baroque, and the thirteenth-century **San Francesco d'Assisi** (Piazza San Francesco d'Assisi, off Via Merlo; ☎ 091-616-2819), with a superb fourteenth-century portal and handsome carvings inside. Both churches are closed in the early afternoon.

Unless you're a diehard urbanite, check out La Kalsa during the daytime. Its dark alleys and decaying buildings can be intimidating at night.

Defined by Via Maqueda, Corso Vittorio Emanuele, Via Lincoln, and the sea.

La Zisa

Also called Castello della Zisa, this building dates from 1165-1167 and is more a home than a castle. The castle is known for its elegant columns and mosaics and may have belonged to an Arab noblewoman, Azisa, or may have been built for King Guglielmo I (William) using Arab techniques and named Al-Aziz, the Magnificent. The palace was surrounded by a park with an artificial lake in which the building was reflected (a few hundred years before the Taj Mahal) and with small rivers and ponds for fish. The surrounding garden has disappeared, and the building suffered partial collapse in 1971 and was then restored. The second floor opens on a beautiful courtyard. La Zisa also houses a collection of Islamic art, including the characteristic carved wooden screens known as *musciarabia.*

Piazza Guglielmo il Buono. ☎ *091-6520269. Bus: 124 to Zisa, from Via Ruggero Settimo. Admission: 4,000L ($1.15). Open: Mon–Sat 9 a.m.–1:30 p.m. and 3–6 p.m., Sun and holidays 9 a.m.–1 p.m.*

Monte Pellegrino and Santuario di Santa Rosalia

Rosalia is Palermo's patron saint. The young girl, niece of Guglielmo II, abandoned the riches of her royal family and took refuge in a cave on the mountain, where she prayed until her death (not unlike St. Francis, who also spurned his family's wealth in order to live a purer religious life). After her body was found, the cave became the site of a shrine/convent. An unforgettable view is offered from this 2,000-foot promontory — labeled by Goethe the most beautiful in the world — separating the bay of Palermo from the gulf of Mondello and its beaches. From its top, in good weather, you can see all the way to Etna and the Aeolian Islands. Toward the interior is a plain with beautiful villas. The flanks of Monte Pellegrino are filled with caves, some of which have Paleolithic carvings. The mountain is reached by Via Pietro Bonnano; the road to the top was finished only in the 1920s.

In the northeast area of Palermo. Bus: 812 from Piazza Sturzo, off the Teatro Politeama.

Museo Archeologico Regionale

This museum, built on the site of a monastery, is a good introduction to Sicily's ancient history. The best collections are on the ground floor, including major art finds from Greek sites in southern Italy and some Roman art (as you pass through the cloister, you see a collection of Roman objects, including pieces from Pompeii). Remains from Selinunte, the site of an ancient Greek colony on Sicily's southwestern tip and today much damaged by looters, have an important place in the display. The collection was begun during the nineteenth century when the first *metope* (part of the frieze) from the site were found. The **main salon** has important finds from several of the temples, including the famous head of Medusa. The **basement** houses a reconstruction of the clay decorations of the Temple "C," and in the **Sala Marconi** there's a partial reconstruction of the cornice moldings with lion heads from the Temple of Victory in Himera. There are beautiful bronze statues as well as a number of Etruscan and Phoenician objects.

Piazza Olivetti 24, between Via Roma and Via Maqueda, near Via Cavour. ☎ *091-611-6805. Admission: 8,000L ($4.30). Open: Daily 9 a.m.–1:30 p.m. (Tues and Fri also 3–6:30 p.m.), Sun and holidays 9 a.m.–1 p.m.*

Oratorio del Santissimo Rosario di San Domenico

Sicilian sculptor Giacomo Serpotta belonged to this small chapel (oratory); though he excelled in the use of marble and polychrome, he chose stucco to lavishly decorate the oratory from 1714 to 1717, making it his masterpiece. Another member of the oratory was Pietro Novelli, who painted many of the walls and ceilings. The painting on the altar is a masterpiece by Anthony van Dyck, a *Madonna del Rosario* commissioned during his stay in Palermo in 1624 but painted four years later in Genoa.

Via dei Bambinai 2, off Via Roma, between La Cala and Via Maqueda. Admission: Free. Open: Tues–Sat 9 a.m.–1 p.m., Mon–Fri 3–6 p.m.

Palazzo dei Normanni and Cappella Palatina

The seat of the Sicilian Parliament, this palazzo boasts foundations going back to Punic and Roman times. In the twelfth century, the Normans remodeled the palace, which had been the residence of the Arab Emir. It had four towers, of which only one remains today, the **Torre Pisana.** It was remodeled again in the sixteenth century to become the residence of the Spanish viceroy. The royal apartments are open to the public, but because of the parliamentary meetings, access is restricted (see details in the following paragraph). On the third floor is the **Sala di Ruggero,** originally Ruggero's bedroom, with mosaics representing hunting scenes and striking animals and plant forms. On the second floor is the famous **Cappella Palatina (Palatine Chapel),** with its impressive decorations. The chapel, started by Ruggero II in 1132, took over ten years to complete and is a harmony of masterwork from different cultures — Arab artisans made the inlaid wooden ceilings, Sicilians did the stonecutting, and the mosaics are Byzantine. The walls and dome are completely covered with rich mosaics representing scenes from the Old Testament (the nave), Christ's life (the southern transept), and scenes from the lives of Peter and Paul (the aisles). A particularly striking illustration of *Genesis* seems to show the creation of the world out of an energy field. The floors are typically Byzantine in style, with geometrical designs in marble of varied colors. Note by the entryway the monolithic (made out of a single piece of stone) candlestick, intricately carved and over 13 feet tall.

Piazza Indipendenza, off Corso Calatafimi, through the Porta Nuova, on the other side of Piazza della Vittoria. ☎ 091-696-1111. Admission: Free. Open: Cappella Palatina daily 9 a.m.–noon; royal apartments, call the Questura at ☎ 091-656-1737 to arrange a visit Mon, Fri, and Sat 9 a.m.–noon.

Teatro Massimo

Begun in 1875 but not completed until 1897, this building cost a fortune and was Italy's largest and most splendid theater at a time when Palermo didn't even have a good hospital. The theater is a masterpiece of Liberty style (Italian art nouveau) and was designed by Gian Battista and Ernesto Basile, the famous Sicilian father and son art nouveau stylists. The stage and backstage measure 1,280 square meters (12,000 square feet), the second largest in Europe after the Opéra Garnier in Paris. Its greatest marvel is a painted ceiling with 11 panels that open like flower petals to let heat escape from the interior during intermissions. The only change that has been made since the building's conception has been to lay a wood floor for acoustic reasons. The building was not only a theater but also a meeting place, and these rooms were used for important business and political meetings. The most famous is the Sala Pompeiana, at the level of the second loggia, where the men would meet; it's designed to have an echo so that the sound of voices would keep bouncing from wall to wall and not get out of the room and disturb the performance. After 23 years of closure for restoration, the theater reopened in 1997.

Piazza Verdi, west on Via Maqueda. ☎ 091-334-246 to make an appointment for a visit to the theater or 091-605-3315 for tickets. Admission: Free.

Villa Malfitano

This great Liberty-style villa lies within one of the city's most spectacular gardens. It was built in 1886 by Joseph Whitaker, who arranged to have trees shipped here from all over the world and planted around his villa. High society in Palermo flocked here for lavish parties, and royalty from Great Britain visited. The villa today is lavishly furnished with antiques and artifacts from all over the world. The **Sala d`Estata (Summer Room)** is particularly stunning, with trompe-l'oeil frescoes covering the walls and ceiling.

Via Dante 167. ☎ *091-681-6133. Admission: 5,000L ($3). Open: Mon–Fri 9 a.m.– 12:30 p.m.*

More cool things to see and do

The major sites of Palermo are stunning, but there's still much more to see and do — as well as things to eat. Here are a few recommendations:

✔ If you happen to be in Palermo in July, the **Festa di Santa Rosalia** (July 11–15) is an interesting event celebrating the anniversary of the discovery of the saint's remains many centuries after her death. Niece of Norman King Guglielmo II, Rosalia abandoned the palace for a cave on Monte Pellegrino (see the description earlier in this chapter) to live a life of prayer. During the terrible plague epidemic of 1624, her bones were found and brought down the mountain. As the procession bringing her remains traversed the city, the epidemic miraculously stopped (a good reason to keep celebrating her!). During the festival, a religious procession with a beautifully decorated, huge triumphal carriage carrying an orchestra wends through the town. There's also a spectacular candlelit procession up Monte Pellegrino to Santa Rosalia's cave. The end of the festival is marked by great fireworks.

✔ If you're into catacombs or just morbid, go to the **Catacombe dei Cappuccini** (Piazza Cappuccini; ☎ 091-212-117) to see 8,000 mummified bodies of aristocratic Sicilians and priests, still dressed in the costumes of their time. The catacombs were used as a burial spot, or rather a repository, for mummified remains until 1920. It's open Monday to Saturday 9 a.m. to noon and 3 to 5:30 p.m., with a 2,000L ($1.10) admission.

✔ The city has three much-visited traditional food markets, where fruits, vegetables, meat, and fish provide an explosion of colors and flavors. **La Vucciria,** whose name comes from the French word *boucherie* ("meat store"), is in La Kalsa and goes along Via Argenteria to Piazza Garraffello. The **Ballarò** is our preferred market — Palermo's oldest, running from Piazza Casa Professa to Corso Tukory toward Porta Sant'Agata. It's connected to the market of Casa Professa (selling shoes and secondhand clothes); this market was called the *mercato americano* because for a long time secondhand clothes came to Italy from the United States in huge bundles with everything from swimsuits to nightgowns to ski clothes and fur coats! Smaller and less lively, **Il Capo** covers Via

Carini and Via Beati Paoli, crossing Via Sant'Agostino and Via Cappuccinelle. The three markets are shown in blue on the free city map you find in hotels and at the tourist office. In all the markets, beware of *motorini* and their potential purse snatchers and pickpockets.

✔ **La Cuba** (Corso Calatafimi 100, inside the Caserma Tukory; ☎ 091-590-299), a dome surrounded by gardens, is a striking example of Arab and early Norman architecture. It was built by Guglielmo II in 1180 in the Park of Genoardo; its beauty was so famous that Boccaccio used it in the *Decameron*. The building is only one floor, organized around a central space with a star-shaped fountain. Today only the external walls and giant arches remain. It's open Monday to Saturday 9 a.m. to 1:30 p.m. and 3 to 6 p.m. and Sunday 9 a.m. to 1 p.m., with a 4,000L ($2.15) admission.

✔ If you fell in love with the work of Giacomo Serpotta, you should add to your schedule a visit to the **Oratorio di Santa Cita** (Via Valverde 3, off Via Squarcialupo, between Via Cavour and Via Roma, on the left of the church; ☎ 091-332-779). Famous for his stucco *putti* (cherubs), the Sicilian sculptor worked here between 1687 and 1718, creating a whole world of stucco figures and reliefs. The church is open Monday to Friday 3 to 5 p.m., and admission is free.

And on your left, the Palazzo dei Normanni: Seeing Palermo by guided tour

Palermo's city bus company, **AMAT** (Via Alfonso Borrelli 16; ☎ 091-350-415; Fax: 091-224-563; E-mail: amat.ced@ita.flashnet.it; Internet: www.ama.pa.it), offers seven sightseeing tours daily. All tours are bilingual, last 3½ hours, cost 20,000L ($11), and start at Via Mariano Stabile at the corner of Via Ruggero Settimo at 9 a.m. (a few have a second round at 3 p.m.). You can buy tickets from travel agencies and hotels, at the AMAT office, or directly on the bus. The entrance fees to attractions visited along the way aren't included. Tour 1 includes the Museo Archeologico, the Duomo, and the Cappella Palatina. Tour 6 includes La Zisa, the Catacombe dei Cappuccini, and the Duomo di Monreale. A longer itinerary of the historic center of Palermo and Monreale leaves daily at 9 a.m.

CST (Via A. Amari 124; ☎ 091-582-294; Fax: 091-582-218; 24-hour service at 0348-343-6104; E-mail: cstmail@tin.it; Internet: http://web.tin.it/cst) offers a 1-day tour of Palermo and Monreale for 40,000L ($22), leaving Saturdays at 9 a.m. It also offers a choice of day trips from Palermo to all other major destinations in Sicily: The trip to Etna/Taormina is 100,000L ($54), leaving Tuesdays at 7 a.m.; to Segesta/Erice/Trapani 70,000L ($38), leaving Sundays at 8 a.m.; and to Agrigento/Piazza Armerina 80,000L ($43), leaving Thursdays at 7:30 a.m.

Carriage tours of Palermo (☎ 0338-755-9021) leave from the following locations in town: Piazza Marina, Piazza San Domenico, Piazza

Massimo, Stazione Centrale SF, and Palazzo delle Aquile. The price is 50,000L ($27) per hour for a maximum of four people.

The city-sponsored organization **Palermo Open Doors** (☎ 091-350-415) offers free guided tours. On every weekend for a month (usually May), students accompany visitors around Palermo as guides. A shuttle bus is available to connect the sights. Call for an appointment.

Suggested 1-, 2-, and 3-day Sightseeing Itineraries

You can see the most impressive sights of Palermo in a day, but if you have time to stay a bit longer you can explore more of this fascinating city. The longer you tarry, the more it grows on you. Here we provide itineraries for visits ranging from one to three days.

If you have only 1 day

The best idea is to head straight for the **Palazzo dei Normanni** and its **Cappella Palatina.** Then you can continue with a visit to the **Duomo di Monreale** (the bus to Monreale is just outside the palazzo). Back in Palermo, you can stroll along Via Vittorio Emanuel through the **Quattro Canti** (the Renaissance square at the crossing with Via Maqueda) and **Piazza Pretoria;** if you have time, visit **La Martorana.** To end your day, have dinner in one of the restaurants on **Piazza Marina** at the edge of La Kalsa and take a post-dinner stroll to the nearby old harbor **La Cala.**

If you have 2 days

Start on the first day as in the one-day itinerary, but leave **La Martorana** for your second day. The second day, begin with **La Martorana** and then head to the **Oratori del Santissimo Rosario di San Domenico** for a full taste of Sicilian baroque. You can step inside **La Vucciria** and sample the offerings from the market before continuing. You can then head for the **Museo Archeologico Regionale** or the **Galleria Regionale Siciliana,** depending on your taste. End your day with an evening concert at the **Teatro Massimo** and dinner in the area of the **Teatro Politeama.**

If you have 3 days

Three days allow you to see most of the major sights. Use days one and two as described in the two-day itinerary and visit the **Galleria Regionale Siciliana** on the second day. This strategy allows you to see more of **La Kalsa** and to see the **Chiesa del Gesù.** On the third day, visit the **Museo Archeologico Regionale** in the morning, then continue with two remarkable examples of Norman-Arab architecture, **La Zisa** and **La Cuba.** End your day with a visit to **Monte Pellegrino** to enjoy the beautiful views over the city and the bay. Alternatively, take one of the **day trips** suggested in Chapter 24.

Shopping

Shopping isn't Palermo's strong suit, unless you're buying swordfish, tuna, or almond paste. The city has some of Italy's best open-air food markets (see "More cool things to see and do," earlier in this chapter), notable for the freshness and quality of their produce, and they offer some great deals. Alas, visitors can't take advantage of this fact: How are you going to explain to customs back home that pound of home-made Sicilian pesto or that bunch of dried red peppers? Of course, you can buy things for a picnic (great for one of the out-of-town excursions or for a snack in the gardens of Piazza Marina).

In terms of clothing, the center of town offers some nice shops — Palermitans are very keen on dressing up — with a somewhat different style than you find in other Italian cities but always quite refined. For the best shopping, try the streets south of the Politeama, especially **Via Ruggero Settimo** (which becomes **Via Maqueda**) and **Via Roma** and the smaller streets in between, such as **Via Principe di Belmonte.**

Regarding other typical Sicilian goods, besides the models of **Sicilian carts** and **puppets** that you find in stands at most tourist sites, Sicily is famous for its **pottery.** In Palermo you find works from the three Sicilian schools of Santo Stefano di Camastra, Caltagirone, and Sciacca. Try **Via E. Amari,** running from the Politeama to the port; it has a number of very reliable ceramic shops. **De Simone** has two shops, one at Via Gaetano Daita 13/B (☎ 091-584-876) and one at Via Principe de Scalea 698 (☎ 091-671-1005), where they also have their factory; **Verde Italiano** at Via Principe di Villafranca 42 (☎ 091-320-282) also has a shop and a factory you can tour.

Nightlife

Nightlife in Palermo has been picking up steadily after the dark years of the 1980s, when people were almost too afraid to walk the streets. Like all Italians, Sicilians like to eat out, especially at an outdoor terrace in the good season, as evening entertainment. Sicilians, especially young ones, love to dance, and Palermo is home to dozens of discos.

The performing arts

Opera and ballet performances take place in the **Teatro Politeama Garibaldi** (Piazza Ruggero VII; ☎ 091-605-3315). Like everything else in Sicily, tickets are reasonably priced at 30,000L to 40,000L ($16 to $22). The revived **Teatro Massimo** (Piazza Verdi; ☎ 091-605-3315 for tickets and schedules) also hosts concert and opera performances. The season runs from October to June.

Another interesting entertainment is the traditional **Teatro dei Pupi (Puppet Theater).** The Pupi became popular in the eighteenth century and, dressed in armor and bright-colored fabrics, tell tales of Orlando and the Paladins of France (who, however, think and act in a perfectly Sicilian way). They usually stage fights against the Saracens, in which the audience participates actively. A few decades ago Palermo boasted more than ten companies, but today the companies that are left perform only on request or on weekends in summer. The best is at the **Teatro Arte Cuticchio — Opera dei Pupi e Laboratorio** (Via Bara all'Olivella 95; ☎ **091-323-400**). November to June, shows are Saturday and Sunday at 5:30 p.m. and cost 10,000L ($5) adults and 5,000L ($2.70) children; the theater also contains a museum with a collection of pupi, machines, and special effects you can see for 2,000L ($1.10). In Monreale, there's the **Compagnia Munna** (Cortile Manin 15; ☎ **091-640-4542**), with shows Sundays at 5 p.m. for the same price.

Discos, bars, and pubs

A popular disco is **Il Cerchio** (Viale Strasburgo 312; ☎ **091-688-5421**) which is only open Fridays and Saturdays; two others are **Kandinsky** (Discesa Tonnara 4; ☎ **091-637-6511**) and **Dancing Club** (Viale Piemonte 16; ☎ **091-348-917**). If you want to have a drink in a piano bar, try **Escargot** (Via Generale Magliocco 15; ☎ **091-321-366**).

Pubs have also swept through Palermo (like other Italian cities) and have really funny names. Try **Hot Dog** (Piazza Amendola, four blocks west — up — of the Teatro Politeama; ☎ **091-328-756**), **Kovacs** (Via della Libertà 6; ☎ **091-611-5151**), or **The Navy** (Via della Cala 46, off the marina; ☎ **091-323-032**) for a good beer.

A more Italian trend are the *enoteche,* the Italian answer to an English pub. Very popular all over Italy, they're places where you can sample some nice wine and have a light snack — sometimes a real dinner. A good one of these *enoteche* is **Ai Vini d'Oro** (Piazza Nascé 11; ☎ **091-585-647**).

Fast Facts: Palermo

Country Code and City Code

The **country code** for Italy is **39**. The **city code** for Palermo is **091**; use this code when calling from anywhere outside or inside Italy, even within Palermo itself (include the zero every time, even when calling from abroad).

Currency Exchange

You can find **exchange booths** in the airport and scattered around town, especially in the center. You can also exchange currency at the many banks in town or use their ATMs.

Doctors

The **Guardia Medica Turistica** (emergency doctor for tourists) is at ☎ **091-532-798**.

Embassies and Consulates

The **U.S. Consulate** is at Via Vaccarini 1 (☎ **091-305-857**) and the **U.K. Consulate** is at Via Cavour 117 (☎ **091-326-412**); for other embassies and consulates, see "Fast Facts: Naples" in Chapter 20 and "Fast Facts: Rome" in Chapter 12.

Emergencies

Ambulance, ☎ **118**; Red Cross Ambulance, ☎ **091-306-644**; Fire, ☎ **115**; Polizia Stradale (Road Police), ☎ **091-656-9111**.

Hospital

The **Ospedale Civico** is at Via Carmelo Lazzaro (☎ **091-606-2207** or 091-606-2207).

Information

The **Azienda Autonoma Provinciale per l'Incremento Turistico** is at Piazza Castelnuovo 34, across from the Teatro Politeama (☎ **091-583-847** or 091-605-8351; E-mail: aapit@gestelnet.it; Internet: www.aapit.pa.it).

Pharmacy

Several pharmacies are open at night in Palermo. Among the most central are **Farma Taxi** (Via Libertà 54; ☎ **091-309-8098**) and **Farmacia Pensabene** (Via Mariano Stabile, off Teatro Massimo; ☎ **091-334-482**).

Police

Call ☎ **113**; for the Carabinieri, call ☎ **112**.

Rest Rooms

Museums have public toilets. The best bet for a rest room is often to go to a nice-looking cafe (though you'll have to buy something, like a cup of coffee).

Safety

Palermo's historic districts are quite safe except for the pickpockets and purse snatchers on *motorini:* They concentrate in tourist areas, public transportation, and crowded open-air markets like the Vucciria.

Smoking

Smoking is allowed in cafes and restaurants and is very common. Unfortunately for non-smokers, it's almost impossible to find a restaurant with a no-smoking area, though some are beginning to appear.

Taxes

Palermo has no local tax. Other taxes are always included in the prices quoted. You can get a refund of the 19 percent **IVA (value-added tax)** for purchases above 300,000L ($160). See Chapter 4.

Transit/Tourist Assistance

The 24-hour **tourist assistance hotline** is toll-free ☎ **167-234-169**. You can call ☎ **147-888-088** daily 7 a.m. to 9 p.m. for the FS, the state railroad.

Weather Updates

For forecasts, the best bet is to watch the news on TV (you can't just call to get weather forecasts). On the Web, you can check meteo.tiscalinet.it.

Web Sites

Try the city's own Web site, www.comune.palermo.it (although much of the information is in Italian, you can find all kinds of info on the city).

Chapter 24

Side Trips from Palermo

● ●

In This Chapter

▶ Visiting Greek ruins in Segesta

▶ Basking in the Mediterranean sea in Cefalù

● ●

*Y*ou can reach many interesting places as day trips from Palermo. In this chapter we describe two of the closest and best: one choice for those who are thirsty explorers of antiquity and another for those who like a mix that includes some more epicurean pleasures.

Viewing a Remarkable Doric Temple in Segesta

Segesta contains one of the best preserved Doric temples in existence and is set in wonderful surroundings. It was the most important town in this part of Sicily in ancient times and was long in conflict with Athens and Syracuse. Segesta was allied to Carthage but was sacked by the Siracusans and later fell into the hands of the Romans. The origin of the people who founded Segesta is a mystery, however; known as the Elyminians, they may have been related to the Trojans and came to Sicily in the thirteenth century B.C. Small enough to be visited in half a day, Segesta is a perfect break from Palermo and a trip farther back in time.

Getting there

One **train** per day leaves at 6:42 a.m. from Palermo and stops at Segesta Tempio; the return train comes through around 1 p.m. The trip from Palermo lasts about 45 minutes and costs 9,000L ($4.90). You then have to walk about 20 minutes uphill to get to the temples. If this sounds awfully early to get up to see ruins, consider that the temperatures in Sicily are on a level with those of North Africa. In the hot months, many people do nothing but stay inside with the shutters closed to block out the heat for most of the afternoon.

Segesta is about 75 km (47 miles) from Palermo. If you're **driving**, take **A29** to Trapani/Mazara del Vallo and stay on the branch that goes to Trapani; Segesta is the first exit.

The bus company **Segesta** (☎ **091-616-7919**) has a regular service between Segesta and Palermo. During the theater season (see "Teatro Greco," later in this chapter), **Noema Viaggi** (Via di Marzo 13; ☎ **091-625-4221**) runs special buses to the sight, costing 8,500L ($4.30).

Taking a tour

A number of companies organize excursions to Segesta from Palermo. A good one is **CST** (Via A. Amari 124; ☎ **091-582-294**; Fax: 091-582-218; 24-hour service at 0348-343-6104; E-mail: cstmail@tin.it; Internet: http://web.tin.it/cst). It offers a tour of Segesta, Erice, and Trapani for 70,000L ($38), leaving Palermo at 8 a.m on Sundays.

Seeing the sights

Little remains of Segesta today, but what's left is worth seeing. On a beautiful — and unfortunately steep — hill rise the two symbols of Greek culture: a temple and a theater.

Tempio Greco

An impressive sight amid the greenery, the Doric temple is on the top of the hill, commanding a superb vista over the countryside. Built in the fifth century B.C., the temple was never quite finished (no roof was built and the columns weren't fluted), but it still stands and is exceptionally well preserved. Its 36 columns are still topped by the entabulature with two fronts. All the parts are smooth, without decorations.

Teatro Greco

Near the temple, on the side of the hill, is this third-century B.C. theater, the site of classical performances in summer. The season alternates yearly with the one in the Greek theater of Syracuse (see Chapter 25); dramas are performed in Segesta in odd-numbered years. During the season, special buses run from Palermo (see "Getting There," earlier in this chapter). Contact the **Istituto Nazionale del Dramma Antico** (Corso G. Matteotti 29, 96100 Siracusa; ☎ **0931-67-415** or 1478-82-211 toll free in Italy) for a schedule of the events or call Palermo's tourist office (see Chapter 23).

Soaking Up Rays in the Seaside Resort of Cefalù

Just a few miles from Palermo, **Cefalù** is a popular day trip. Young people from the capital like to come here for a romantic dinner by the sea or a day at the beach. The reverse is also true, and young people from Cefalù like to go for a wild night in Palermo. A small fishing village today transformed into a quiet seaside resort, Cefalù has many an attraction to offer (you may recognize it if you saw the Oscar-winning film *Cinema Paradiso*), such as its splendid location and its cathedral.

Getting there

Frequent **trains** run to Cefalù from Palermo (about once an hour); the trip lasts about an hour and costs 6,000L ($3.25).

Cefalù is 81 km (51 miles) from Palermo. If you have a **car,** take **A20** toward Bagheria, Termini Imerese, and Messina and get off at the exit for Cefalù. Alternatively, take the coastal *strada statale* **SS113**, panoramic but narrow and much slower.

Seeing the sights

Dominated by the **Rocca** (clifftop fort), Cefalù has been famous for its beauty since Greek times. It was graced by nature with a nice sandy beach, scenic rocks, and a promontory, and the Normans made it over in splendid style. Roger II survived a terrible storm at sea and promised to build a cathedral that would be visible from the sea — he built it at Cefalù, where he landed after the storm. The best views are from the cliff. If you have some time and dare the steep ascent, the Rocca is just above the village, surrounded by walls. Within the same complex is the **Tempio di Diana (Temple of Diana)** — so called by the locals and probably built in the second century B.C.

Duomo

Begun in 1131, the cathedral is a perfect fusion of Norman architecture, Arab craftsmanship and art, and Byzantine principles. After a period of abandonment, it was restored in 1240 and reconsecrated in 1267. Inside, the church is dominated by the golden mosaics, particularly the one in the apse: a beautiful example of a Byzantine **Christ Pantocrator.** Outside, the imposing facade is typically Norman and characterized by two powerful towers. Note that the dress code is strictly enforced: no bare legs above the knee or bare shoulders are allowed (luckily they sometimes very kindly hand out shawls).

Piazza del Duomo, off Corso Ruggero. ☎ *0921-922-021. Admission: Free. Open: Daily 8:30 a.m.–noon and 3:30–6:30 p.m.*

Lavatoio Medievale

Another interesting sight is the medieval washing place, fed by a rich spring flowing from the mountains. It was an important meeting place in medieval times, but the spring was used since time immemorial. Sailors (going back to the Phoenicians) have always stopped here to get water.

Off Via Vittorio Emanuele, indicated by a sign. Admission: Free. Open: Daily sunrise to sunset.

Museo Mandralisca

This museum is not really worth the detour, even though it has the famous **Ritratto di Ignoto,** the portrait of a man smiling an almost drunken grin, by Antonello da Messina,. The painting is currently displayed so inaccessibly that you get a better view from a postcard. The rest of the collection is odd: very detailed displays of Greek ceramics, stuffed birds and mammals of the region, and many paintings in poor condition.

Via Mandralisca 13. ☎ *0921-21-547. Admission: 5,000L ($2.70). Open: Daily 9:30 a.m.–12:30 p.m. and 4–6 p.m.*

Where to stay

Cefalù is a popular seaside resort, so it has many hotels. If you want to stop for a dip, the beach is beautiful and easily accessible. If you're on a driving tour of Sicily, Cefalù may be a convenient place to stop, swim, and rest. If you decide to stay over rather than continue, the Hotel Villa Belvedere is one good place to stay without paying spa prices.

Hotel Villa Belvedere

$ **Cefalù**

The hotel is just a walk away from the beach and from the town, it has a nice outdoor terrace, and parking is free. The guest rooms are simple and clean, with all the basics.

Via dei Mulini 13. ☎ *0921-21-593. Fax: 0921-21-845. Parking: Free. Rack rates: 90,000–180,000L ($49–$97) double. No credit cards accepted.*

Where to dine

The town has many restaurants from which to choose. One of the nicest is Lo Scoglio Ubriaco.

Lo Scoglio Ubriaco

$ **Cefalù   Sicilian/Pizza**

This restaurant has a great terrace overlooking the sea and the "drunken rock" after which it's named. One of the myths explaining the origin of the name says that a ship carrying wine broke apart on that rock, while another says that the shape of the rock makes it seem as if it moves when you stare at it, therefore inducing the impression that you're drunk. The staff explained this legend to us after an excellent dinner — the place serves pizza and typical Sicilian fare — and some great local wine. The rock moved, indeed.

Via Bordonaro 2. ☎ *0921-423-370. Secondi: 12,000–25,000L ($7–$14). Open: Lunch and dinner Tues–Sun.*

Chapter 25

Taormina and the Rest of Sicily

• •

In This Chapter

▶ Touring Taormina

▶ Viewing the past and present in Syracuse

▶ Visiting the Valley of the Temples in Agrigento

• •

*I*nhabited from prehistoric times, Sicily has always been a coveted — and conquested — land. The Sicani and Siculi (the people of Italic origin who gave the name to the island) traded with the Phoenicians, who established colonies along the coast. The Phoenicians shared the island with the Greeks during the eighth century B.C., but the Greeks eventually took over and Sicily became a shining center for their art and philosophy. The Carthaginians, Romans, and Byzantines followed, each leaving their mark on Sicily's culture.

The Arabs landed in 827 and ruled Sicily for more than two centuries but in 1060 were displaced by the Normans, who established a feudal kingdom and reigned until they were eclipsed in favor of the French dynasty of the d'Angió. After only 20 years of this government, a revolution started in Palermo (the 1282 Vespri Siciliani) and ended French power, opening a short period of political autonomy under the local feudal families (particularly the Chiaramonte). The increasing Spanish influence brought Sicily under the Spanish Crown in 1415 (first Aragona, and later the Bourbons, who ruled from 1735 until the unification of Italy in 1860).

Sicily has been shaped, culturally and physically, by each of its rulers. The ancient ruins (Phoenicians sites, Greek amphitheaters and temples, Roman theaters, and villas) mingle with stern Norman palaces and cathedrals, softened and embellished by decorations and details of Byzantine and Arab art. No complete Arab building remains — the 500 mosques that existed under their rule were destroyed — but they left a permanent mark with the introduction of citrus fruits, which is one of the symbols of Sicily.

The arts exploded during the Renaissance, and Sicily offers some of Italy's most splendid examples of baroque architecture. After decades of neglect and the ravages of World War II, most of these jewels are in bad need of repair, and luckily, a slow process of recuperation has started, bringing glory back to some major examples of Sicilian architecture.

What's Where?: Sicily and Its Major Attractions

Sicily is roughly triangular in shape, with one corner — the city of Messina — almost touching the boot of Italy. And it feels like a mini-continent, with mountains, beautiful beaches, central agricultural plains, and the giant volcano Etna. We already talked about the region's capital **Palermo** (see Chapter 23), on the northern shore of the island.

On the eastern shore, near **Etna** and south of Messina, is **Taormina,** founded by Andromachus in 358 B.C. This Greek city-state changed hands many times during the millennium after its founding (and was sacked by Arabs and Normans) before it sank into obscurity for several hundred years. However, tourists like the famous German writer Goethe rediscovered it in the eighteenth and nineteenth centuries. Taormina backed the Romans in the Punic Wars, which resulted in a glorious period between the third century B.C. and the end of the Roman Empire. The **Teatro Greco-Romano (Greco-Roman Theater)** that remains is one of the great archaeological treasures of the island. Taormina makes an excellent starting point for visiting the rest of the region, so much so that many travel agencies are based in Taormina and offer guided tours to most destinations in Sicily. (See "And on your left, Etna: Seeing Taormina's environs by guided tour," for more information.)

South of Taormina and close to the island's southeast corner is **Siracusa (Syracuse),** an ancient Greek colony that once rivaled the great cities of the mother country (like Athens). The island on which Syracuse began, **Ortigia,** was the home of Calypso, who kept Odysseus captive for seven years. The Corinthians founded Syracuse in the eighth century B.C. Like the rest of Sicily, the city was swept up in the Punic Wars between Rome and Carthage, but despite the genius of Archimedes, who died in the Roman siege, it wound up on the losing side. Syracuse's **Zona Archeologica (Archaeological Zone)** contains two theaters and the quarries where stone was excavated to build all the monuments in town. The city's beautiful harbor, perfectly positioned to trade with and control the eastern and western Mediterranean, has seen many tyrants (like Dionysius I) and invaders come and go. Today Syracuse is a beautiful stone city shimmering somewhat sleepily by the sea (the summer heat is unbelievable). Nearby is the unique baroque city of **Noto.**

Between Syracuse and Agrigento, along the southern shore of Sicily, is a vast and mainly agricultural area. Dominating the southern shore, **Agrigento** was another important Greek city, one of the most beautiful of the ancient world. (The Greek poet Pindar admired it deeply.) Agrigento reached great heights in art and culture in the third century B.C. and saw its fortunes wax and wane with those of the Roman Empire. The **Valle dei Templi (Valley of the Temples),** where the ancient city once stood, is one of the most dramatic classical ruins anywhere in the Mediterranean. Farther up the hill from the ruins stands modern Agrigento, a small town that most visitors bypass.

Seeing Taormina and Its Ideal Vista

Taking its name from Monte Taurus, the cliff dominating the sea over **Taormina,** this small town was a forgotten medieval village until the end of the eighteenth century, when the art academies of Europe suddenly celebrated it as the "ideal vista." Indeed, Taormina is a unique panorama, with the sea on one side and snow-capped Etna smoking on the other.

Taormina is actually the second town built at this location. In the fifth century B.C., Dionysius I of Syracuse destroyed the first, Naxos (today the seaside resort of Giardini Naxos), which lies below near the water. The residents prudently moved to the top of the cliffs, though that didn't save them from further invasions. Taormina flourished during the Roman period and received the coveted status of Roman colony under Augustus. After the empire ended, the city of Taormina declined and was twice laid waste by the Arabs. Roger II took over the city in 1078 for the Normans.

Today, Taormina counts about 10,000 residents and 900,000 visitors per year, which averages about 2,500 visitors per day. Consider that 80 percent of these visitors are non-Italians and that this figure includes only those visitors who stay overnight, while many others just pass through for the day. Therefore, you may find it odd that Taormina was a haunt of Greta Garbo, who "wanted to be alone." However, Taormina isn't a stranger to wealth and glamour, with many magnificent villas and famous visitors past and present.

Getting there

You can get to Taormina via **train,** from Palermo (with one change in Messina), as well as from Catania and Syracuse (direct, no change). The ride from Palermo is approximately 4½ hours at 22,000L ($12), the ride from Catania is 50 minutes at 5,500L ($3), and the ride from Syracuse is 2¼ hours at 12,500L ($7).

Trains arrive at the **Stazione F.S. di Taormina** (Via Nazionale; ☎ 0942-51-026 or 0942-51-511), located a little down the hill, below Taormina's center, in Villagonia. From the station, you can catch a bus to the center of town every 15 to 45 minutes, depending on the season and hour of the day, for 2,500L ($1.35).

Taormina is 250 km (150 miles) from Palermo, 50 km (30 miles) from Catania, and 41 km (22 miles) from Messina. If you're **driving** from Catania or Messina, take the **A18** and exit at Taormina. From Palermo, the fastest route is **A19,** which runs briefly along the coast and then cuts cross-country to Catania, where you pick up A18. Taormina's center is pedestrian only, so you have to leave your car at the entrance of town. The best place to leave your car is just after the highway exit for Taormina, in the large city parking lot **Parcheggio Lumbi** at the base of the hill. A shuttle bus runs from the parking lot to town every few minutes. If your hotel has parking, then, obviously, you can park your car there.

Taormina

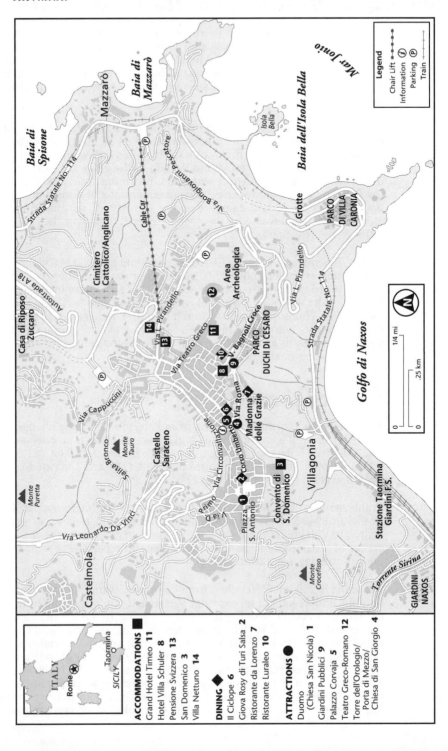

Legend

Chair Lift
Information *i*
Parking Ⓟ
Train

Mar Jonio

Baia di Spisone

Baia di Mazzarò

Mazzarò

Isola Bella

Baia dell'Isola Bella

Strada Statale No. 114

Via Bongiovanni Pescatore

Cable Car

Cimitero Cattolico/Anglicano

Casa di Riposo Zuccaro

Autostrada A18

Area Archeologica

Grotte

PARCO DI VILLA CARONIA

V. Bagnoli Croce

PARCO DUCHI DI CESARO

Via Pirandello

Via L. Pirandello

Strada Statale No. 114

Via Teatro Greco

Via Cappuccini

Salita Branco

Monte Tauro

Castello Saraceno

Monte Puretta

Golfo di Naxos

1/4 mi

.25 km

N

14

13

12

11

10

9

8

7

5 6

4

1 2

3

i

Via Roma

Madonna delle Grazie

Corso Umberto I

Via Circonvallazione

Primo V. ei D

Piazza S. Antonio

Convento di S. Domenico

Villagonia

Stazione Taormina Giardini F.S.

Monte Crocefisso

Torrente Sirina

Castelmola

GIARDINI NAXOS

Via Leonardo Da Vinci

ITALY
Rome ★
SICILY
Taormina ○

ACCOMMODATIONS ■
Grand Hotel Timeo **11**
Hotel Villa Schuler **8**
Pensione Svizzera **13**
San Domenico **3**
Villa Nettuno **14**

DINING ◆
Il Ciclope **6**
Giova Rosy di Turi Salsa **2**
Ristorante da Lorenzo **7**
Ristorante Luraleo **10**

ATTRACTIONS ●
Duomo
(Chiesa San Nicola) **1**
Giardini Pubblici **9**
Palazzo Corvaja **5**
Teatro Greco-Romano **12**
Torre dell'Orologio/
Porta di Mezzo/
Chiesa di San Giorgio **4**

The bus company **SAIS** (☎ **090-625-301**) runs a regular connection from Messina to Taormina. The trip takes 1½ hours and costs 6,000L ($3.25).

Getting around

The center of town is pedestrian only, but since Taormina is very small, the best — and only — way to get around is on foot. Of course, if you get tired or need to go a little farther then the city center, there are **taxis** that you can call (☎ **0942-51-150** or 0942-23-800). If you wish to reach your hotel by car you can, but remember that it's very difficult (indeed impossible) to find parking around town and that driving in the very narrow and steep streets of Taormina is tricky.

From the center of town starts the **funivia** (funicular; ☎ **0942-23-906**), which connects Taormina with the beach down below. There are runs every 15 minutes for 5,000L ($2.70) round-trip or 3,000L ($1.60) one-way. It runs until 3 a.m. in summer.

Where to stay

Grand Hotel Timeo

$$$$$ **Centro**

The first hotel opened in Taormina dates back to the eighteenth century. This beautiful villa sits just below the Greek theater, surrounded by its own garden. As you'd expect for this kind of money, the guest rooms are spacious and come with every amenity, including large marble baths. Old-fashioned elegance is updated with modern comforts, and the hotel offers a private beach as well as a sophisticated restaurant and bar.

Via del Teatro Greco 59, just off the Greek theater. ☎ *0942-23-801. Fax: 0942-24-838. Parking: Free. Rack rates: 480,000–680,000L ($259–$368) double, including breakfast. AE, DC, MC, V.*

Hotel Villa Schuler

$$ **Centro**

Lovely gardens and terraces surround this moderately priced hotel, which is very close to Corso Umberto I (Taormina's main street). The good-sized guest rooms are attractively furnished, and many have balconies overlooking the sea. You can check out the hotel's library, 24-hour bar, and laundry facilities. On top of these perks, the hotel is a member of the Catena del Sole group: After you stay in one of this group's hotels, you receive a 10 percent discount at the second Catena del Sole group hotel in which you stay.

Piazzetta Bastione, off Via Roma. ☎ *0942-23-481. Fax: 0942-23-522. E-mail:* schuler@tao.it. *Parking: 15,000L ($8) in covered garage; free outside. Rack rates: 160,000L ($87) double, including breakfast. AE, DC, MC, V.*

Pensione Svizzera

$ **Centro**

This centrally located hotel offers decent guest rooms at a moderate price. It offers a few frills, such as breakfast in the lovely garden when the weather is good. Other pluses are that it's conveniently close to the beach, and the owners speak English and are very friendly.

Via Piradello 26, just off Porta Messina. ☎ *0942-23-790. Fax: 0942-625-906. Parking: Free for only five cars. Rack rates: 120,000L ($65) double, including breakfast. AE, DC, MC, V. Closed in Jan.*

San Domenico

$$$$$ **Centro**

In a converted monastery amid magnificent terraced gardens, the San Domenico was the second hotel built in Taormina and has long been the haunt of the rich and famous. The eclectically furnished guest rooms feature fine furniture from various Mediterranean lands, and the superb Bougainvillées restaurant serves regional specialties on the terrace with a breathtaking view. The hotel offers a piano bar and a conference center housed in the church of the original convent and also boasts a heated pool with a view.

Piazza San Domenico 5, south of the Duomo. ☎ *0942-23-701. Fax: 0942-625-506. Parking: 30,000L ($16). Rack rates: 500,000–700,000L ($270–$378) double, including breakfast. AE, DC, MC, V.*

Villa Nettuno

$ **Centro**

This small hotel is in an attractive villa that's near the center of Taormina and the *funivia* to the beach. The villa was built in 1860 and converted into a hotel in the 1950s. The furnishings are modest and modern, and some of the guest rooms feature terraces and ocean views.

Via Pirandello 23, just off Porta Messina. ☎ *0942-23-797. Fax: 0942-626-035. Parking: 8,000L ($4.30). Rack rates: 110,000L ($59) double, including breakfast. MC, V.*

Where to dine

Il Ciclope

$$$ **Centro** **Sicilian**

This busy trattoria is popular with visitors and Italians alike, serving hearty Sicilian food at relatively inexpensive prices for Taormina. Dishes include fish soup, calamari, and grilled fish, just to name a few. The *antipasti di mare* (seafood appetizers) are very tasty as well.

Corso Umberto 203. ☎ *0942-23-263. Reservations not accepted. Secondi: 18,000–30,000L ($10–$16). AE, MC, V. Open: Lunch and dinner Thurs–Tues; closed a month in Jan–Feb.*

Giova Rosy di Turi Salsa

$$$ **Centro** **Sicilian**

On Taormina's main street, this restaurant has been around for a long time but is still dependable. Among its specialties are *spiedini* (skewers) with shrimp and lobster and *pesce spada* (swordfish). You can request a table with a view of the Greco-Roman Theater.

Corso Umberto I 38. ☎ *0942-24-411. Reservations recommended. Secondi: 18,000–32,000L ($10–$17). AE, DC, V. Open: Lunch and dinner daily; closed Jan and Feb.*

Ristorante da Lorenzo

$$$ **Centro** **Sicilian**

This excellent restaurant is a bit away from the thick crowds. It has a pleasant terrace, which is remarkable for an ancient tree that has given shade for 800 years, or so they say. The food lives up to the setting and includes fresh fish, an excellent *antipasto,* and such unusual dishes as *spaghetti ai ricci di mare* (spaghetti with sea urchins), considered a real delicacy by Italians.

Via Roma, near via Michele Amari. ☎ *0942-23-480. Reservations necessary. Secondi: 16,000–40,000L ($9–$22). AE, DC, MC, V. Open: Lunch and dinner Thurs–Tues; closed a month in Nov–Dec.*

Ristorante Luraleo

$$$ **Centro** **Sicilian**

The romantic atmosphere and the terrace help ensure a pleasant experience at this restaurant, which serves a variety of Sicilian specialties. You're always safe choosing the grilled fish if you don't want to try something more adventurous, like *risotto al salmone e pistacchi* (risotto with salmon and pistachios).

Via Bagnoli Croce 27. ☎ *0942-24-279. Reservations recommended. Secondi: 16,000–30,000L ($9–$22). DC, MC, V. Open: Summer lunch and dinner daily; winter lunch and dinner Thurs–Tues.*

Exploring Taormina

As reported by the first famous travelers in the eighteenth century, Taormina's main attraction is its location on a cliff, offering breathtaking views over the surrounding sea. Centuries of history, though, have left many other interesting sights, and we list the best.

The top sights

Taormina's central street, **Corso Umberto I** stretches between the town's two main gates, the **Porta Catania** and the **Porta Messina**. In the Middle Ages, the city shrank to the area comprised between the Porta Catania and the **Torre dell'Orologio (clock tower)**. Also called the Porta di Mezzo (Middle Gate), the Torre dell'Orologio was built during the early Middle Ages as the gate to the medieval village. After its partial destruction, the clock tower was rebuilt in 1679 and is attached to the **Chiesa di San Giorgio** with its seventeenth-century baroque facade. During the Renaissance, the city started expanding again. However, it has reoccupied the whole hourglass-shaped area of the Greek city only in modern times. Along Corso Umberto are some of Taormina's most interesting monuments, such as the **Palazzo dei Duchi di Santo Stefano (Palace of the Dukes of St. Stephen),** the best preserved of the town's Norman buildings, and the **Chiesa di Sant'Agostino (Church of St. Augustine),** the sixteenth-century church opening on its nice square, **Largo IX Aprile**, above the sea. The church is today closed to worship and used as the town library.

Duomo (Chiesa San Nicola)

Built in the twelfth century in a Latin cross plan, this church was later remodeled. The central portal dates from 1633, while the lateral portals date from the fifteenth and sixteenth centuries, respectively. Half a dozen monolithic pink marble columns — the fish-scale decoration on their capitals recalls Sicily's maritime tradition — hold up the nave. In front of the Duomo is the beautiful baroque **Fontana Monumentale,** built in 1635 with two-legged female centaurs.

Piazza del Duomo, just off Corso Umberto. Admission: Free. Open: Daily for mass, usually early morning and early evening.

Palazzo Corvaja

This palazzo consists of three structures built between the eleventh and fifteenth centuries, around a pre-existing Arab structure (probably a fortress). The center of the palace is the cubic tower built by the Arabs. During the fourteenth century, the crenellated structure and beautiful entrance staircase were added to the tower. And in the fifteenth century, the right wing was built to serve as the meeting place for the Sicilian Parliament. This palazzo also houses the tourist office on the ground floor.

Piazza Santa Caterina off Corso Umberto. ☎ 0942-23-243. Admission: Free. Open: Mon–Sat 8 a.m.–2 p.m. and 4–7 p.m.

Teatro Greco-Romano

With a capacity of 5,000 people, this theater carved out of rock is second in Sicily only to Syracuse's (see further in this chapter) in size and importance. It's the best preserved of all Greek and Roman theaters in Italy. Unusual for a Greek theater, the backdrop scene was a fixed structure: It represented a two-story house, part of which is still visible. As was the case for many buildings of antiquity, part of the theater's materials were taken to build other buildings, in this case by the Arabs and Normans. During its glory days, the walls of the theater (only a portion in the back remains) were covered with marble and frescoes. Although the theater was Greek in origin, the Romans modified it for gladiator battles. For example, a tunnel connected the cellar of the Roman arena with the out-side; the orchestra of the theater was enlarged and closed off by a high podium in order to protect spectators. The theater is famous for the summer performances held there (see "Nightlife").

Via del Teatro Greco. ☎ *0942-23-220. Admission: 4,000L ($2.15). Open: Tues–Sun 9 a.m. to 2 hours before sunset.*

More cool things to see and do

Many visitors come to Taormina only for a day. If you have more time to spend in the city, check out these other events and sights:

- ✔ If you're in Taormina during summer, enjoy the **Taormina Arte,** a festival of cinema, theater, music, ballet, and video started in 1983. Included are shows at the Teatro Greco-Romano (see the listing under "Exploring Taormina," earlier in this chapter). For the sched-ule, contact Taormina Arte (*Via Pirandello 31, 98039 Taormina;* ☎ **0942-21-142;** Fax: 0942-23-348). You can also get info from the **tourist office** (Azienda Autonoma di Soggiorno e Turismo, Palazzo Corvaja, 98039 Taormina; ☎ **0942-23-243**; Fax: 0942-24-941) or the **Comune di Taormina–Assessorato Turismo** (Piazza Municipio, 98039 Taormina; ☎ **0942-610-218;** Fax: 0942-610-216).

- ✔ Just below Corso Umberto, lower on the hillside on Via Bagnoli Croce, the **Giardini Pubblici (Public Gardens)** were built by Miss Florence Trevelyan, who arrived in 1882, fell in love with the town, and bought a piece of land sloping toward the sea. She worked at transforming the land into a garden, training and employing local workers as gardeners. Taorminians were fond of her, and when she died in 1902, they threw flowers at her passage in the funeral procession. Her will forbade her heirs from building or industrially cultivating the land. Within the gardens, she designed and built the **Victorian Follies** — bizarre structures like toy houses built with red bricks and light-colored stone containing inlaid archaeo-logical materials.

- ✔ By the sea below Taormina lies the town of **Mazzarò,** with its beautiful beach and restaurants featuring fish. It's easy to reach by *funicular* from Taormina. In front of Mazzarò is the **Isola Bella (Beautiful Island)** with its marine grottoes.

- ✔ If you have the time, take a day trip to visit the great **Etna,** which dominates the background of Taormina. Europe's biggest and most active volcano is 3,300 m (10,000-plus feet) tall and growing. Vulcanologists have charted its eruptions back to the Middle Ages and even to ancient eruptions, which were usually far more dra-matic and catastrophic. Though these mega-eruptions ceased cen-turies ago, Etna's littlest grumbles and oozings from its vents can wipe out vast areas and human settlements. The 1669 eruption not only took out some of the not-so-close-by town of Catania (amazingly, the deposits by the side of the highway south of town look as if they were made yesterday) but also extended the coastline about a kilometer (more than half a mile) into the sea. Many of Etna's eruptions, including some of the most violent, didn't originate from the snow-capped summit but from dozens of vents and secondary craters that mark the sides of this giant. And, Etna isn't all lava and debris; parts of its north slopes are covered with a soaring conifer forest that took root in the rich soil.

The easiest way to visit Etna is to take an organized tour from Taormina (see "And on your left, Etna: Seeing Taormina's environs by guided tour"). However, if you have a car, you can go by yourself. From Taormina, follow the directions for Linguaglossa and then Zafferana, where you take the small winding road to the Rifugio Sapienza. If you're starting from Catania, follow the directions to Belpasso and then Nicolosi, where you take another windy road up to the Rifugio Sapienza, from which you can take a cable car to the summit.

Climbing Etna is more regulated than it used to be since a group of tourists were killed by a sudden explosion several years ago. If you want to see the craters up close and personal, you need an authorized guide. Book one at **Guide Alpine Etna Sud** (☎ **095-791-4755**).

✔ In the mountains above Taormina are the unique **Gole dell'Alcantara (Gorges of the Alcantara River),** a series of gorges carved by one of Italy's coldest rivers. Taking an organized trip from Taormina (see "And on your left, Etna: Seeing Taormina's environs by guided tour") is the best way to see them. If you want to drive, take the Catania-Messina SS114 in the direction of Catania and get off at the Giardini exit for SS185 (right, going inland), in the direction of Francavilla. After the small town of Gaggi, the road turns left (leaving at your right the road for Graniti) and arrives at the Gole dell'Alcantara. You can park in the large parking lot by the **Bar-Restaurant Meeting** (☎ **0942-985-010**). The site is open daily 9 a.m. to 5 p.m., but access is restricted during winter. Admission is 3,500L ($1.90). The climb takes about an hour but it isn't difficult; you're liable to get wet, so wear a swimsuit or other proper clothing (you can rent a wetsuit on-site); the site supplies rubber boots.

And on your left, Etna: Seeing Taormina's environs by guided tour

Because Taormina is so small, there are no tours of the village itself. However, excellent tours depart from the town for some of the other major attractions in Sicily.

SAT Sicilian Airbus Travel (Corso Umberto 73; ☎ **0942-24-653;** Fax: 0942-21-128; Internet: www.tao.it/sat; E-mail: sat@tao.it) offers some good tours of Etna, including a nice bus-and-jeep sunset tour on Tuesdays and Thursdays for 84,000L ($45). This tour leaves at 3:30 p.m. in June and July and at 2:30 p.m. in August and September. The company also offers a day trip to Etna, leaving Mondays at 8:30 a.m. for 35,000L ($19). It includes only the bus and the guide for the trekking, but you can arrange a tour by jeep if you desire. This company also

Other Sicilian favorites

Sicily is a large island, and in addition to the major sights there are many minor ones. Here we provide a selection of further destinations, from ancient ruins to other islands off the Sicilian coast.

Aeolian Islands: These seven volcanic islands lie to the northeast of Sicily. Their natural beauty attracts snorkelers and scuba-divers as well as sun worshipers who come to lie on the volcanic black-sand beaches. Lipari is the largest and most developed of the Aeolian islands; Stromboli is the farthest from the Sicilian coast and also the most volcanically active; Vulcano, on the other hand, is the closest and is known for its therapeutic mud baths.

Catania: Lying 52 km (32 miles) south of Taormina, Catania is known as the "Baroque City." When a 1693 earthquake leveled the town, the townspeople decided to rebuild their city in the baroque style. The reconstruction took the entire eighteenth century to complete.

Egadi Islands: Just a few miles off Sicily's west coast are the Egadi Islands — Levanzo, Favignana, and Marettimo. The attraction of these islands is their peace and quiet, Paleolithic cave drawings, and clear waters.

Erice: Erice is 97 km (60 miles) from Palermo and lies on the slope of Mt. Erice. It's one of Europe's best-preserved medieval towns, with picturesque (and steep) cobblestone streets, narrow twisted alleys, and lots of tourists.

Selinunte: Selinute, 122 km (76 miles) southwest of Palermo, has some evocative ruins in its archaeological park, though they can't compare with the far more intact ruins of Agrigentum (see later in this chapter). There are seven temples in varying degrees of preservation and decay; most date from the fifth and sixth century B.C.

Tràpani: A coastal town 103 km (64 miles) southwest of Palermo, Tràpani is close to northern Africa, whose hot winds blow across a narrow stretch of the Mediterranean. There's a charming historic district (you can avoid the modern sprawl around it), and it's also one of the less visited parts of Sicily.

organizes tours to Agrigento and the Valle dei Templi for 62,000L ($34), leaving at 6.30 a.m. on Tuesdays and Thursdays, as well as to Syracuse for 55,000L ($30), including Ortigia and the Archaeological Zone, leaving at 7:30 a.m. on Mondays and Thursdays.

CST (Corso Umberto 99–101; ☎ **0942-626-088;** Fax: 0942-23-304; 24-hour service 0348-343-6104; Internet: http://web.tin.it/cst; E-mail: csttao@tin.it) also offers good Etna tours. You can choose a basic one for 35,000L ($19) or a tour including also ascent by cable car and jeep for 65,000L ($35), departing on Tuesdays and Thursdays at 8:15 a.m. CST's Etna sunset tour is 84,000L ($45) and leaves on Mondays and Wednesdays at 3:45 p.m. June to August and at 3:15 p.m. September to October. The company also runs tours to the Gole dell'Alcantara for 30,000L ($16), Wednesdays and Saturdays at 8:15 a.m.; to Agrigento for 62,000L ($34), Tuesdays at 6:15 a.m.; and to Syracuse for 55,000L ($30), Wednesdays and Fridays at 7:30 a.m.

Fast Facts: Taormina

Country Code and City Code

The **country code** for Italy is **39**. The **city code** for Taormina is **0942**; use this code when calling from anywhere outside or inside Italy, including within Taormina. (Include the zero every time, even when calling from abroad.)

Currency Exchange

There are banks with ATMs on Corso Umberto, just before the Porta Messina to the north. You can also find banks in Giardini Naxos, the town next to Taormina.

Emergencies

Ambulance, ☎ **118**; Fire, ☎ **115**; road assistance ☎ **116**; *pronto soccorso* (first aid), ☎ **0942-625-419**.

Hospital

The **Ospedale Sirina** is on Piazza San Francesco di Paola (☎ **0942-53-745**).

Information

The **tourist office** is inside the beautiful Palazzo Corvaja on Piazza Santa Caterina off Corso Umberto to the west (Azienda Autonoma di Soggiorno e Turismo, Palazzo Corvaja, 98039 Taormina; ☎ **0942-23-243**; Fax: 0942-24-941). Hours of operation are Monday to Saturday 8 a.m. to 2 p.m. and 4 to 7 p.m.

Pharmacy

Visit **Dr. Verso** at Piazza IX Aprile 1 (☎ **0942-625-866**).

Mail

The **Ufficio Postale** (post office) is on Piazza Medaglie d'Oro (☎ **0942-23-010**).

Police

Call ☎ **113**; for the Carabinieri (other police force), call ☎ **112**.

Enjoying Syracuse and Its Archaeological Zone

The island of Ortigia sticks out into the large natural harbor of **Siracusa (Syracuse)** as if designed to be a fortress city. This geographical feature wasn't lost on the Greek colonists from Corinth who settled on Ortigia in the eighth century B.C. Although Greek colonies were never subservient to the hometowns of the settlers, Syracuse rose to become the Mediterranean's greatest power under its forceful tyrants (particularly Dionysius I). However, during the Punic Wars, Syracuse was caught between a rock and a hard place — the Romans and the Carthaginians. The Roman siege lasted two years, and in 215 B.C. they finally overwhelmed the city, despite the clever devices Archimedes, the city's most famous son, constructed to thwart them and their siege engines.

Syracuse's glory days ended more than 1,000 years ago. Since then, it's been battered by invaders — from the Saracens to the Nazis to the Allied bombs of 1943 — but its Archaeological Zone miraculously survived. Today, Syracuse is a small, busy modern center, while the original island of Ortigia has an indescribable, uncanny feeling — or maybe it's the blinding light off the water and the heat of the sun.

You can easily visit Syracuse in one day, but there's enough to do for an overnight stay, especially if you plan to visit nearby Noto.

Getting there

To get to Syracuse from Catania, you can take advantage of the frequent direct **train** service (the trip takes about 1½ hours). However, from Taormina and Palermo, you usually must transfer in Catania, and from Agrigento, you need to change in Ragusa. The ride from Taormina is about 2 hours at 12,500L ($7), the ride from Palermo takes 5 to 7 hours at 25,000L ($14), and the ride from Agrigento 6 hours at 26,000L ($14). Syracuse's train station **(Stazione FS)** is on the west side of town; it is approximately a 20-minute walk from there to either Ortigia or the Archaeological Zone. From the train station, city buses connect to the main sights.

Syracuse is 259 km (162 miles) from Palermo, 154 km (96 miles) from Messina, and 218 km (136 miles) from Agrigento. If you're **driving** from Palermo, take **A19** to Catania, where this road ends. Follow the signs for Syracuse and take **SS114,** also labeled **E14** on European maps. From Agrigento, a highway is under construction but not yet completed; until it is, you'll have to take the state road **SS115,** which is picturesque but a long haul — about 5 hours.

If you're driving south from Catania to Syracuse, exercise caution on the stretch (about 21 km/13 miles) where it reduces to a two-lane road that's much too small for the amount of traffic on it. You really have to pay attention to who's passing whom in both directions. Avoid it at night if at all possible.

Getting around

The island of **Ortigia,** connected to the modern town of Syracuse by a bridge, is where the city began and is still its heart. Most of the ancient ruins on the island were displaced by or incorporated into the baroque city that developed there, particulary after the 1693 earthquake. Ortigia is a small area that you can easily tour on foot. Most of the tourist sights are on Ortigia, except for the Archaeological Zone (see the next paragraph).

On the edge of Syracuse's modern part is the **Zona Archeologica (Archaeological Zone).** The city bus system connects Ortigia to this zone. In between the zone and Ortigia lies some of modern Syracuse. Most buses stop at Piazza Archimede, the heart of Ortigia; in Largo XXV Luglio, just before the bridge to the mainland; and on Corso Umberto, which runs between the bridge to Ortigia and the train station.

Where to stay

Forte Agip

$$$ **Archaelogical Park**

A modern hotel near the amphitheaters, the Forte Agip offers all the modern comforts, including air-conditioning (a godsend after May). The guest rooms are plain but have contemporary furnishings. The restaurant is popular with locals and serves good fish dishes.

Via Teracati 30–32. ☎ ***0931-463-232.*** *Fax: 0931-67-115. Parking: Free. Rack rates: 240,000L ($130) double, including buffet breakfast. AE, DC, MC, V.*

Gran Bretagna

$ **Ortigia**

This small hotel has the great advantage of being on Ortigia, the main historic center of town, and it's very popular with Italian and foreign tourists alike. The guest rooms are basic but comfortable; however, only half of them have private baths.

Via Savoia 21. ☎ ***0931-68-865.*** *Rack rates: 100,000–120,000L ($54–$65) double, including breakfast. No credit cards accepted.*

Hotel Bella Vista

$$ **Center**

In the modern section of Syracuse, the Bella Vista is a well-kept family-run hotel. The furniture in the bright guest rooms is modern, and many rooms offer balconies with ocean views. The hotel restaurant, reserved for guests, serves tasty Sicilian fare. The Bella Vista is a member of the Catena del Sole group, which means that after you've stayed in one of the group's hotels, you receive a 10 percent discount for the second one in which you stay.

Via Diodoro Siculo 4. ☎ ***0931-411-355.*** *Fax: 0931-37-927. Internet:* www. sistemia.it/bellavista. *E-mail:* bellavista@sistemia.it. *Parking: Free. Rack rates: 94,000–150,000L ($51–$81) double, including breakfast. AE, MC, V.*

Where to dine

Gambero Rosso

$$$ **Corso Umberto   Sicilian**

In an old tavern near the harbor, this restaurant is known for its seafood and has a terrace overlooking the port. Try the *cannelloni* (tubes of pasta filled with fish or meat, cooked in the oven with a sauce and cheese, in the manner of lasagna) or one of the fish soups.

Via Eritrea 2, on the right after the bridge leaving Ortigia. ☎ *0931-68-546. Reservations recommended. Secondi: 15,000–30,000L ($8–$16). AE, DC, MC, V. Open: Lunch and dinner Fri–Wed.*

Ristorante Jonico

$$$ Latomia dei Cappuccini   Sicilian

On the main street running along the coast north of Ortigia, this elegant place overlooks the sea. The roof garden serves pizza, and down below is the upscale dining room. The seafood is particularly good, such as the *antipasto misto* and the *pesce spada alla pizzaiola* (swordfish in tomato-and-garlic sauce). You can also choose from a large selection of home-made pastas too.

A Rutta e Ciauli, Riviera Dionisio II Grande 194, just off Piazza dei Cappuccini. ☎ *0931-65-540. Reservations recommended. Secondi: 18,000–30,000L ($10–$16). AE, MC, V. Open: Lunch and dinner Wed–Mon.*

Ristorante Rossini

$$$ Ortigia   Sicilian

This intimate restaurant, run by a renowned chef, offers a menu based mainly on seafood prepared in both traditional and imaginative ways. One specialty is *pesce alla stimpirata,* which creatively combines mint, garlic, and olive oil with fish. More familiar Sicilian-style preparations include roasted swordfish. The buffet *antipasto* is excellent.

Via Savoia 6. ☎ *0931-24-317. Reservations recommended. Secondi: 18,000–30,000L ($10–$16). AE, DC, MC, V. Open: Lunch and dinner Wed–Mon.*

Exploring Siracusa

You can easily visit Syracuse on foot, and there are some beautiful strolls, whether by the harbor or amid the ancient ruins. But beware of the sun in the hotter months — walking around the ruins at high noon will quickly exhaust and dehydrate you. Also keep in mind that the old town of Syracuse on the island of Ortigia is made of stone, though you can find a little more shade here than in the Archaeological Zone.

The top sights

Museo Archeologico Regionale Paolo Orsi

This is the best archaeological museum in Sicily. The well-organized large collection covers every time period, from prehistoric objects to an extensive Hellenistic collection from Syracuse's heyday. The most famous single piece is the second-century B.C. **Venus Anadyomene** that — though headless — powerfully evokes the birth of the goddess from the sea. The pre-Greek vases are lovely too. Other collections relate to the cities of Naxos, Lentini, Zancle, and Megara Iblea.

In the gardens of the Villa Landolina, Viale Teocrito 66, near the Zona Archeologica.
☎ *0931-464-022. Bus: 4, 5, 12, or 15 to Viale Teocrito. Admission: 8,000L ($4.30).*
Open: Tues–Sat 9 a.m.–1 p.m. and 3:30–6:30 p.m., Mon 3:30–6:30 p.m.

Ortigia

This is the island in Syracuse's harbor that is the heart of the historic city. At the end of the nineteenth century, Ortigia was still all there was of Syracuse; the land side contained only the rail station and the Greek ruins. The mainland part of Syracuse has changed much since, but not Ortigia. As you cross the Ponte Nuovo, the first ruin you see is the **Tempio di Apollo (Temple of Apollo),** built in the sixth century B.C.; it is now just a few columns. If you walk up Via Savoia, you come to the **Porta Marina,** from which you can enter the old town. Farther along the stone border of the harbor is the **Fonte Aretusa (Aretusa Fountain),** where the nymph of classic mythology allegedly turned into a spring. From here, turn left and head to the center of Ortigia to see the seventh-century **Duomo,** Piazza del Duomo, built on the remains of a Greek temple to Athena (Minerva for the Romans) and including 12 of the temple's columns; it's open daily 8 a.m. to noon and 4 to 7 p.m. with free admission. Head down toward the tip of Ortigia to the thirteenth-century **Palazzo Bellomo,** Via Capodieci 14, which houses the **Galleria Regionale** (☎ **0931-69-617**); its main claim to fame is Antonello da Messina's famous *Annunciation.* The museum is open Monday to Saturday 9 a.m. to 1:30 p.m. and Sunday 9 a.m. to 12:30 p.m., with an admission cost of 8,000L ($4.30).

Off Largo XXV Luglio by the Ponte Nuovo.

Zona Archeologica

The Archaeological Zone contains two theaters and the quarries from which stone was excavated to build all the monuments in town. Actually a giant sculpture because it's carved out of the rock on the hillside, the **Teatro Greco (Greek Theater),** from the fifth century B.C., is a beautiful example of an ancient theater. The tunnels you see in the stage area aren't original; they were dug later by the Romans so they could use the theater for their blood sports. At the back of the theater are Byzantine tombs and a fountain to which water was brought by the Greeks from 40 km (25 miles) away via a system of aqueducts.

In even-numbered years, the theater comes to life again when ancient dramas by Greek authors are presented as they were 2,500 years ago. Contact the **Istituto Nazionale del Dramma Antico** (Corso G. Matteotti 29, 96100 Siracusa; ☎ **0931-67-415** or 1478-82-211 toll-free in Italy), which sponsors the plays. Tickets are 30,000L to 70,000L ($11 to $38). Call or write to the institute for information on programs and dates.

On the other side of the hill is the **Latomia del Paradiso (stone quarry).** What you see is a huge hole covering many acres, with a few pillars sticking up and giant stones scattered here and there. The central pillar held up the roof of the quarry, and the big blocks of stone were once the roof, which collapsed in the 1693 earthquake. One of the excavated caves, the **Grotta dei Cordari (Grotto of the Ropemakers),** was used in later centuries for ropemaking; it has been closed for years for safety reasons. After descending into the quarry, you can visit **Orecchio di Dionisio (Dionysius's Ear),** a deep, very tall pitch-black cave. The story that Dionysius used the cave to eavesdrop on conversations is a myth; the painter Caravaggio was said to have given the cave its name (perhaps he made up the story, too). Nearby is another important structure, the **Anfiteatro Romano (Roman Amphitheater),** built during the reign of Augustus and partially carved from the rock. Like other Roman theaters, it was used for life-and-death battles between humans as well as animals and was sometimes flooded and filled with crocodiles and other friendly creatures for water fights.

What you see today is only the bottom story — try to imagine how it looked when the top of the theater reached the present height of the surrounding trees. Holy Roman Emperor Charles V is the bad guy of many stories about Italy, and Syracuse is no exception. He did more damage than the earthquake and is responsible for turning this theater into a quarry. During his North African campaigns, he destroyed much of the Roman ruins for material to build fortifications.

Via Augusto, near the intersection of Corso Gelone and Viale Teocrito. ☎ 0931-66-206. Bus: 4, 5, or 6 to Parco Archeologico. Admission: 4,000L ($2.15). Open: Daily 9 a.m. – 2 hours before sunset.

More cool things to see and do

Here are a few sights just outside Syracuse:

✔ To the north of the city, the **Forte (Fort) di Eurialo** is a masterpiece of Greek military defensive architecture, connected to walls running far up into the hills behind Syracuse and protecting the land side of the city. The fort has four powerful towers and a network of subterranean passages where cavalry could gather for an attack. You can reach it driving north on Riviera Dionisio il Grande toward Catania or take the 9, 10, or 11 bus from the modern city center. The fort is open Monday to Saturday 9 a.m. to two hours before sunset and Sunday 9 a.m. to 2 p.m., and admission is 4,000L ($2.15).

✔ Only 32 km (20 miles) south of Syracuse is the famous town of **Noto,** a wonderful example of Sicilian baroque. It was reduced to rubble by the 1693 earthquake that destroyed the whole southeast of Sicily, but the town's notables decided to rebuild it 10 miles south of its original location. The reconstruction happened very rapidly — in about 45 years — and the result was a town remarkably uniform in style. Faithful to pure baroque standards, Noto was built on a regular street grid. Many important Sicilian artists contributed to the reconstruction. Carvings of grotesque animals and figures support the balconies, and the whole town is built in golden-yellow stone. Noto underwent a restoration that started in 1997. The **tourist office,** where you can also get a map of the town, is in the center at Piazza XIV Maggio (☎ 0931-573-779); summer hours are daily 9 a.m. to 1 p.m. and 3:30 to 6:30 p.m.; winter hours are Monday to Saturday 8 a.m. to 2 p.m. and 3:30 to 6:30 p.m.

Fast Facts: Syracuse

Country Code and City Code

The **country code** for Italy is **39**. The **city code** for Syracuse is **0931**; use this code when calling from anywhere outside or inside Italy. Add the codes even when calling within Syracuse itself, and include the zero every time, even when calling from abroad.

Emergencies

Ambulance, ☎ **118**; Fire, ☎ **115**; Road assistance ☎ **116**.

Information

The **tourist office** maintains two booths, one at Piazza San Sebastiano (☎ **0931-67-710**)

and one at the Zona Archeologica (Via Augusto); both are open Monday to Saturday 8:30 a.m. to 2 p.m. and 4:30 to 7:30 p.m. in summer (3:30 to 6:30 p.m. in winter).

Mail

The **Ufficio Postale** (post office) is on Piazza Riva della Posta 15, to the left of the main bridge in Ortigia (☎ **0931-68-973**). It's open Monday to Friday 8:10 a.m. to 6:30 p.m. (Saturday to 1 p.m.).

Police

Call ☎ **113**; for the Carabinieri (other police force), call ☎ **112**.

Discovering Agrigento and the Valley of the Temples

Agrigento was founded in 581 B.C. on a gentle slope toward the sea shaped as a natural amphitheater and protected by two hills and two rivers. A prosperous city in antiquity, it was progressively abandoned during the decline of the Roman Empire. The Arabs and then the Normans later occupied the site, and the population moved up the hill to the current site of town. During the thirteenth and fourteenth centuries, the feudal Chiaramonte family promoted the construction of walls around the town, as well as numerous churches and monasteries.

You can easily visit Agrigento in one day as a day trip from Palermo. However, it also makes a good base for exploring some other interesting sights, such as Syracuse and Segesta.

Getting there

Eleven **trains** a day run from Palermo to Agrigento; the trip takes 1½ hours and costs about 12,000L ($6). The trip from Syracuse is 6 hours, with a change in Ragusa, costing about 26,000L ($14). Agrigento's rail station is the **Stazione Centrale** (Piazza Guglielmo Marconi; ☎ **0922-725-669**).

The company **Licata** (Via XXV Aprile 142, 92100 Agrigento; ☎ **0922-401-360**) runs a **bus** from Palermo's airport to Agrigento daily at 11:30 a.m. and 8 p.m.; the trip takes about 2½ hours and costs around

12,000L ($6). **Omnia** (Via Ragazzi del '99 10, 92100 Agrigento; ☎ 0922-596-490) runs four buses daily between Palermo and Agrigento, which take approximately 2 hours and cost about 12,000L ($6).

Agrigento is 126 km (79 miles) from Palermo by regular road or 180 km (112 miles) by *autostrada*, 191 km (119 miles) from Taormina, and 218 km (136 miles) from Syracuse. If you're driving from Palermo, take **A19** to Caltanissetta, and then follow the directions to Agrigento and take **SS640** for the remaining 60 km (37 miles). If you don't mind narrower roads, you can take **SS121/189** all the way from Palermo to Agrigento, which is shorter. To Agrigento from Syracuse, you take a scenic five-hour drive on **SS115** (E45 and E931); follow the directions for Noto, Ragusa, Gela, and Agrigento. From Taormina, take **A18** to Catania, then **A19** to Caltanissetta, then **SS640** to Agrigento.

Getting around

Agrigento isn't very big, so you can easily visit it on foot. The Valle dei Templi (see "The top sights," later in this section) is 3 km (2 miles) south of the center, and **city buses** connect the valley with the train station in Agrigento (nos. 8 to 11). For a **taxi,** call ☎ **0922-21-899** or 0922-26-670.

The archaeological area where the temples are located is quite wide and — as is often the case — there are very few trees. Remember to bring very comfortable shoes, a hat, sunscreen, and at least a quart of water per person. If you're planning to visit only as a day trip, we recommend that you pack a picnic lunch to eat near the ruins — it's a nice spot, and you'll have more time to visit.

Where to stay

Hotel Belvedere

$ Agrigento

If you travel by public transportation or prefer to stay in town, the Belvedere is conveniently behind Piazza Vittorio Emanuele near the station. The exterior isn't the most beautiful we've ever seen, but the hotel is well run and comfortable. It offers basic guest rooms, which aren't large but are adequate given the price.

Via San Vito 20, not far from the train station. ☎ *0922-20-051. Parking: Free. Rack rates: 50,000–100,000L ($27–$54) double, including breakfast. No credit cards accepted.*

Hotel Costazzurra

$$ San Leone

If you're going to stay in Agrigento, why not stay near the beach and swim in the beautiful water? Only 2.5 km (1.4 miles) from the Valle dei Templi, this hotel is modern, and, although you won't get antique charm, you get air-conditioning, a restaurant, and a bar. The spacious guest rooms are furnished in modern Mediterranean style, with bright white walls and well-appointed baths. The Costazzurra is a member of the Catena del Sole group, which means that after you've stayed in one of its hotels, you receive a 10 percent discount at the next group hotel in which you stay.

Via delle Viole 2, off Viale dei Giardini in San Leone (off SS115 toward the sea from the Valle dei Templi). ☎ *0922-411-222. Fax: 0922-414-040. E-mail:* holiday@ infoservizi.it. *Parking: Free. Rack rates: 110,000–160,000L ($59–$87) double, including breakfast. AE, MC, V.*

Hotel Kaos

$$$ Caos

This hotel was originally a *casale* (farm) but was completely transformed into a major resort with all modern conveniences (including wheelchair accessibility). The huge grounds include a courtyard, fountains, a giant pool, tennis courts, gardens, and terraces with palm trees. The air-conditioned guest rooms are modern and comfortable; there's a bar and a good restaurant in addition to the hotel's other features. The Kaos is only minutes by car from the Valle dei Templi.

Via Pirandello, in Caos (off SS115 to the right going to Porto Empedocle from the Valle dei Templi). ☎ *0922-598-622. Fax: 0922-598-770. Parking: Free. Rack rates: 220,000–240,000L ($119–$130) double, including breakfast. AE, DC, MC, V.*

Hotel Villa Athena

$$$ Valle dei Templi

This hotel — with all the modern comforts, including an open-air pool — is right in the Valle dei Templi. Housed in an eighteenth-century villa, the Athena is comparable to the Kaos but offers a little classier atmosphere. The guest rooms are large and airy, with reproduction or modern furniture. You can eat outdoors with a view of the Temple of Concorde (see later in this chapter).

Via dei Templi 35 (off SS115 toward the Valle dei Templi). ☎ *0922-596-288. Fax: 0922-402-180. Parking: Free. Rack rates: 300,000L ($162) double, including breakfast. AE, DC, MC, V.*

Where to dine

The cuisine of Agrigento is heavily based on seafood, which is similar to the rest of Sicily. A distinction of Agrigento, however, is that it's at the center of the almond-growing industry, so almonds are used in a variety of preparations.

Le Caprice

$$$$ Valle dei Templi   Sicilian

Although expensive, this is *the* restaurant in Agrigento. Locals come for special celebrations, and visitors gather to sample the delicious seafood and numerous specialties and to enjoy the typical Sicilian *antipasto* buffet. The *involtini di pesce spada* (stuffed swordfish) is superb.

Strada Panoramica dei Templi 51. ☎ *0922-26-469. Reservations necessary. Secondi: 20,000–32,000L ($11–$17). AE, DC, MC, V. Open: Lunch and dinner Sat.–Thurs.; closed two weeks in July.*

Ristorante Corte degli Sfizi

$$ Agrigento   Sicilian

In this small restaurant and pizzeria, you can get excellent pasta dishes (including some traditional Sicilian specialties) and pizzas at very moderate prices. It's a popular place at night, particularly with a young crowd.

Corte Contarini, Via Atenea 3, just left from the train station. ☎ *0922-595-520. Reservations recommended on weekends. Secondi: 8,000–16,000L ($4.30–$9). No credit cards accepted. Open: Lunch and dinner Tues–Sun.*

Ristorante Il Casello

$$$ Valle dei Templi   Sicilian

Near the Valle dei Templi, this restaurant that doubles as a pizzeria offers well-prepared Sicilian fare, including a variety of traditional dishes like *pasta alla Norma* (with eggplant, tomato, and ricotta) and grilled fish.

Viale Emporium 1, just off SS115 in the direction of San Leone and the sea. ☎ *0922-26-208. Reservations not necessary. Secondi: 15,000–25,000L ($8–$14). AE, MC, V. Open: Lunch and dinner Thurs–Tues.*

Exploring Agrigento

Agrigento is most famous for its ancient Greek temples, but it has several other sights worth seeing. They cover the area's history from the decline of the ancient town to its rebirth in later centuries. There's also a house museum related to Agrigento's most famous son, playwright Luigi Pirandello.

The top sights

Chiesa di San Nicola

Built in the twelfth century, this church is the first sight you encounter descending to the Valle dei Templi from Agrigento and offers a perfect view over the temples. Inside, at the center of the second chapel, is the famous third-century *Sarcofago di Fedra,* one of the most gracious examples of Greek sculpture, evoking the myth of Phaedra and Ippolyte (a sad story of unrequited love in which the rejected Phaedra is delirious while Ippolyte goes hunting; he is killed in an accident).

Contrada San Nicola, Via dei Templi, Zona Archeologica. Bus: 8, 9, 10, or 11 from Agrigento's train station. Admission: Free. Open: Daily 8 a.m.–1 p.m.

Museo Archeologico Regionale

This museum contains a large collection of Greek artifacts, many of which were found during the excavations in Agrigento. Besides the ample collection of Greek vases, an interesting piece is one of the Telamons (human figures supporting a structure) from the Tempio di Giove (see description under the Valle dei Templi listing), which is in much better shape than the one on the ground at the temple.

Contrada San Nicola, Via dei Templi, Zona Archeologica. ☎ 0922-401-565. Bus: 8, 9, 10, or 11 from Agrigento's train station. Admission: 8,000L ($4.30). Open: Daily 8 a.m.–1 p.m.

Valle dei Templi

The **Valley of the Temples** is the reason that most people come to Agrigento, and it's the most impressive Greek ruin outside Greece. It covers a large area, so you need about three hours to see everything (excluding the museum).

You won't find shade near the largest of the temples, so you definitely need a hat and sunscreen. Many books recommend that you see the valley at sunrise or sunset; this is indeed dramatic, but at sunset there isn't time to see everything before dark. However, the temperature at this time is cooler, which reduces your risk of sunstroke in summer.

If you're coming from Agrigento, Via dei Templi brings you to **Piazzale Posto di Ristoro,** the large parking lot with several vendors and a bar (Posto di Ristoro, or rest stop) at the **Porta Aurea,** a gate in the Greek walls of ancient Agrigento. This is the center of the archaeological zone, with the three best-conserved temples on one side (Tempio di Ercole, Tempio della Concordia, and Tempio di Giunone) and the Tempio di Giove and Tempio dei Dioscuri and the river on the other.

The massive **Tempio di Giove (Temple of Jove or Zeus)** was built to celebrate the gratitude of the people of Agrigento for their 480–479 B.C. victory over the Carthaginians at Himera. One of the largest temples of antiquity, the Tempio di Grove covered approximately 68,000 square feet and was 108 feet tall. Each of the columns rose 55.4 feet and measured 13.8 feet at the base. The Telamons — also called Atlases (human figures supporting a structure) — probably alternated with columns. Each of these giants measured 25 feet high, and one is now lying flat on the ground.

The Greek temple

The Greek temple was conceived as the habitation of a god and always opened to the east because the god's statue had to look at the rising sun (symbol of the beginning of light and life) and never the sunset (symbol of the night and death). Over a high rectangular platform with steps, the classic temple has a perimeter of columns and an inside wall enclosing three rooms: the *pronaos* (entrance), the *naos* (the cell with the statue of the god), and the *opistodomos* (where the treasure, the votive gifts, and the archives of the temple were kept). In fact, temples were so sacred that citizens used to leave their valuables there, thus using them as safes.

The **Tempio di Castore e Polluce (Temple of Castor and Pollux)** is believed to have been built in 480–460 B.C. to honor Castor and Pollux (the twin sons of Leda, queen of Sparta, and Jupiter), protectors of athletes, hospitality, and sailors in difficulty. Of the 34 columns, only 4 remain standing (at the corner of the temple), and they were restored in the nineteenth century. Nearby are the few remains of the **Tempio di Vulcano**.

The **Tempio di Ercole (Temple of Hercules)** is one of the most beautiful temples. Hercules was highly revered in Sicily and particularly in Agrigento; god of strength, he was thought to free people from nightmares and unwanted erotic stimuli. The largest of the temples on this side, it occupied an area of about 22,000 square feet. Only nine columns are standing, and they were raised by the generosity of the English Captain Hardcastle in the 1920s. The columns were painted white to simulate marble, and the cornice was decorated in red, blue, and turquoise; there was also a rich decoration of sculptures.

The **Tempio della Concordia (Temple of Concordia),** built around 430 B.C., is remarkably well preserved, because in A.D. 597, it was transformed into a church. Twelve arches were opened in the walls of the temple, and the space between the columns was walled in to make it a church with three naves. These alterations were reversed in 1743 when the temple was declared a national monument and restored. It's one of the best conserved temples of this period, together with the one of Hera in Paestum (see Chapter 22) and the Theseion in Athens.

Juno (Hera), the mother goddess, was the protectress of marriage and fertility. The 450–440 B.C. **Tempio di Giunone (Temple of Juno or Hera)** has 34 columns (6–×–13) and a maximum height of 15.31 meters (50.2 feet). If you visit this monument, note there's a tree just below the temple!

Piazzale dei Templi/Posto di Ristoro, at the crossroad with SS115 Siracusa–Trapani. ☎ *0922-497-235. Bus: 8, 9, 10, or 11 to the Posto di Ristoro. Admission (ticket booth is at the entrance for the Tempio di Giove): 4,000L ($2.15). Open: Tempio di Giove archaeological area, daily 8:30 a.m.–6:30 p.m. in summer (open til 5:30 p.m. in winter); Tempio della Concordia archaeological area, daily 8:30 a.m.–10:30 p.m. in summer (til 9:30 p.m. in winter). The town of Agrigento makes a point to keep the* *area open at sunset, when the Valle dei Templi is at its best; however, as everywhere in Italy, closing times may vary, so check with the tourist office near the entrance.*

More cool things to see and do

Agrigento has more to offer. Here are a couple more things you may want to check out:

✔ Held in February, the **Sagra del Mandorlo in Fiore (Festival of the Almond Flowers)** was first held in 1938 as a celebration of spring — symbolized by the almond tree in blossom — accompanied by traditional dances and songs. Immediately successful, it was continuously improved, and today the week-long festival features folklore groups from around Sicily as well as from the rest of Italy and neighboring countries. Other events include painting shows, research meetings, cinema, and a market of almond products.

✔ The **Casa di Pirandello** (Contrada Caos; ☎ **0922-511-102**) is the house where the writer was born in 1867. The house contains the author's memorabilia, and his ashes are buried under a pine on the property. Luigi Pirandello received the Nobel Prize for Literature in 1934. In works such as *Six Characters in Search of an Author,* he explored the theme of the mask that everyone must wear to have a role in society. To visit, take the no. 11 bus. The house is open Monday to Saturday 9 a.m. to 1:30 p.m. and Monday to Friday 3 to 5:45 p.m. Admission is 4,000L ($2.15).

And on your left, the Valle dei Templi: Seeing Agrigento by guided tour

You can take guided tours of the Valley of the Temples from both Palermo and Taormina. From Taormina, **SAT Sicilian Airbus Travel** (Corso Umberto 73; ☎ **0942-24-653**; Fax: 0942-21-128; Internet: www.tao.it/sat; E-mail: sat@tao.it) organizes tours to the Valle dei Templi for 62,000L ($34), leaving at 6.30 a.m. on Tuesdays and Thursdays. Check out Chapter 23 for tours departing from Palermo.

Fast Facts: Agrigento

Country Code and City Code

The **country code** for Italy is **39**. The **city code** for Agrigento is **0922;** use this code when calling from anywhere outside or inside Italy, even within Agrigento. Make sure that you include the zero every time, even when calling from abroad

Currency Exchange

There's an **exchange office** at Piazzale Posto di Ristoro, Valle dei Templi, near the tourist booth.

Emergencies

Ambulance ☎ **118** or 0922-401-344; Fire ☎ **115**; road assistance ☎ **116**; *pronto soccorso* (first aid), ☎ **0922-492-485**.

Hospital

The **Ospedale San Giovanni di Dio** is on Via Rupe Atenea (☎ 0922-492-111).

Information

The main tourist office is **AAPIT** (Viale della Vittoria 255; ☎ 0922-401-352 or 0922-20-454; Fax 0922-35-185). There's also an **AAPIT branch** on Piazzale Posto di Ristoro, at the entrance to the Valle dei Templi (☎ 0922-20-391). Both are open Monday to Friday 8:30 a.m. to 1:45 p.m. and 4 to 7 p.m.

Mail

The **Ufficio Postale** (post office) is on Piazza Vittorio Emanuele, to the left of the Stazione Centrale (☎ 0922-26321). It's open Monday to Friday 8:10 a.m. to 7:40 p.m.

Police

Call ☎ 113; for the Carabinieri (other police force), call ☎ 112.

Part VIII
The Part of Tens

The 5th Wave   By Rich Tennant

"So far you've called a rickshaw, a unicyclist, and a Zamboni. I really wish you'd learn the Italian word for taxicab."

In this part . . .

*T*his part is a list, a resource, and a reminder. Here you can find tips to help you make the most of your vacation. Think you can make do in Italy knowing only 10 Italian words? Believe it or not, it's possible, and in Chapter 26 we give you a few words that help you converse with the natives. In Chapter 27, we give you a choice of wonderful books (beside this one) that'll get you excited about your trip before you go. And in Chapter 28, we recommend some of the most affordable and best craft buys in Italy, which make wonderful small gifts for friends or yourself.

Chapter 26

Non Capisco: The Top Ten Expressions You Need to Know

- -

In This Chapter

▶ Using salutations

▶ Asking questions

▶ Learning life savers

- -

Traveling in a country where you don't know the language can be intimidating, but trying to speak the language can be amusing, at the very least. Local people often appreciate it if you at least make the effort. And you'll find that Italian is a fun language to try to speak.

Per Favore (per fa-voe-ray)

Meaning "please," this is the most important phrase you can learn. With it you can make useful phrases such as *"Un caffè, per favore"* ("A coffee, please") and *"Il conto, per favore"* ("The bill, please"). There's no need for verbs, and it's perfectly polite!

Grazie (gra-tziay)

This means "thank you"; if you want to go all out, use *grazie mille* (*mee*-lay), meaning "a thousand thanks." Say it clearly and loudly enough to be heard — like when a bus stops for you though you weren't quite at the stop or it waited for you to run up to it, when you buy something, when you're given directions, whenever. It's always right and puts people in a good mood. *Grazie* also has some additional employment: Italians often use it as a way to say goodbye or mark the end of an interaction. It's particularly useful when you don't want to buy something from an insistent street vendor: Say *"Grazie"* and walk away.

Permesso (per-mess-ow)

Meaning "excuse me" (to request passage or admittance), this is of fundamental importance on public transportation. When you're in a crowded bus and need to get off, say loudly and clearly *"Permesso!"* and people will clear from your path. The same thing applies in supermarkets, trains, museums, and so on. Of course, you may be surrounded by non-Italians and the effect may be a little lost on them.

Scusi (scoo-sy)

This means "excuse me" (to say you're sorry after bumping into someone) and is more exactly *mi scusi*, but the simple form is the most used. Again it's a most useful word in any crowded situation. You'll note that Italians push their way through a narrow passage with a long chain of *"Scusi, permesso, mi scusi, grazie, permesso. . . ."* It's very funny to hear. *Scusi* has another important use: It's the proper beginning to attract somebody's attention before asking a question. Say *"Scusi?"* and the person will turn toward you in benevolent expectation. Then it's up to you.

Buon Giorno (bwon djor-know) and Buona Sera (bwon-a sey-rah)

Buon giorno ("good day") and its sibling *buona sera* ("good evening") are of the utmost importance in Italian interactions. Italians always salute one another when entering or leaving a public place. Do the same, saying it clearly when entering a place. Occasionally, these words can also be used as forms of goodbye.

Arrivederci (ah-rree-vey-der-tchy)

This is the appropriate way to say goodbye in a formal occasion — in a shop, in a bar or restaurant, or to friends. If you can say it properly, people will like it very much: Italians are aware of the difficulties of their language for foreigners. You'll hear the word **ciao** (chow), the familiar word for goodbye, used among friends (usually of the same age). It's considered quite impolite to use it with someone you don't know.

Dov'è (doe-vay)

Meaning "where is," this is useful to ask for directions. Since the verb is included, you just need to add the thing you're looking for: *"Dov'è il Colosseo?"* ("Where is the Colosseum?") or *"Dov'è la stazione?"*

("Where is the train station?"). Of course you need to know the names of monuments in Italian, but don't worry! We always give you the Italian names first in this book. It makes things much easier once you're there!

Quanto Costa? (quahnn-tow koss-tah?)

Meaning "how much does it cost?" this is of obvious use all around Italy for buying all kinds of things, from a train ticket to a trinket.

Che Cos'è? (kay koss-ay?)

Meaning "what is it?" this is useful for buying things, particularly food. But it could also be useful in museums and other circumstances. But then the problem remains to understand the answer.

Non Capisco (nonn kah-peace-koh)

This means "I don't understand." There's no need to explain this one: Keep repeating it and Italians will try more and more imaginative ways to explain things to you.

Chapter 27

Ten (or so) Authors to Help You Understand More about Italy

In This Chapter

▶ Reading the classics

▶ Enjoying a romantic read

▶ Reliving Italy's past adventures

There are thousands of books you could read in preparation for your trip to Italy. Here's a varied selection of great books of various kinds from different periods. A lot of them are actually light reading that will put you in the mood while taking a break!

Polybius

Polybius was a Greek hostage in Rome for 16 years in the second century B.C., during which he wrote his *Histories* (reprint Regnery/Gateway 1987 as *Polybius on Roman Imperialism* or Penguin 1980 as *The Rise of the Roman Empire*) to explain "by what means and under what kind of constitution, almost the whole inhabited world was conquered and brought under the dominion of the single city of Rome, and that, too, within a period of not quite fifty-three years" (219–167 B.C.).

Robert Graves

Graves's two novels *I, Claudius* (1934; Vintage Books 1989) and the sequel *Claudius the God* (1934; Penguin Books 1989) are a highly entertaining way to learn about the glory and decadence of Imperial Rome. You can also buy or rent the 1970s BBC TV series to see for yourself just who did what to whom.

Eric Newby

Newby was a British soldier during World War II and was made a prisoner of war in Italy. He captures the spirit of the land and people in the vivid and romantic *Love and War in the Apennines* (Lonely Planet 1999), in which he recounts how he escaped and was hidden by Italians (one of whom he fell in love with and later married).

Tacitus

This classical author's *Annals* is one of our primary sources of information — and lurid stories — about the early emperors, including Augustus, Tiberius, Caligula, and Nero. Published in the Penguin classics series as *The Annals of Imperial Rome* (1956) and reprinted many times since.

Giorgio Vasari

Painter, architect, and (literally) Renaissance man, Giorgio Vasari is best known for *Lives of the Most Eminent Painters and Sculptors* (1550; expanded 1568), commonly referred to as *Lives of the Painters*. Although *The Lives. . .* have been criticized for inaccuracy, they're a foundational work of art history and contain much interesting information about the great painters of the Renaissance, some of whom were the author's personal friends. The Oxford edition (1998) is one of the many abridgments in translation of this huge work.

Benvenuto Cellini

This talented Florentine sculptor/goldsmith painted himself as a larger-than-life figure in his famous *Autobiography* (1728; Penguin 1999). It doesn't matter what lies he told about himself — the book presents a vivid picture of Renaissance Italy. Among those whom it influenced was Goethe (see listing in this chapter), who translated it into German.

Edward Gibbon

If you read 25 pages a day, it'll take you only about 4 months to get through Gibbon's *History of the Decline and Fall of the Roman Empire* (begun in 1776), one of the monuments of English prose (a less monumental Penguin abridged version [1983] is available in paperback). Gibbon described history as "little more than the crimes, follies, and misfortunes of mankind," and he gives you 13 centuries worth, up until the collapse of the Empire and the founding of the Holy Roman Empire.

Novel works

Besides the works listed in this chapter, you may want to read one or two of the following novels set at least partially in Italy:

- ✔ *The Agony and the Ecstacy* by Irving Stone
- ✔ *Christ Stopped at Eboli* by Carlo Levi
- ✔ *A Death in Venice* by Thomas Mann
- ✔ *The Innocents Abroad* by Mark Twain
- ✔ *Roman Tales* and *The Woman of Rome* by Alberto Moravia
- ✔ *A Room with a View* and *Where Angels Fear to Tread* by E. M. Forster
- ✔ *The Talented Mr. Ripley* by Patricia Highsmith
- ✔ *Vittorio the Vampire* by Anne Rice
- ✔ *The Volcano Lover* by Susan Sontag

Goethe

Johann Wolfgang von Goethe was the first great modern literary visitor to Italy; his *Italian Journey* (1816; Penguin Books 1992) embodies his profound love of the country and culture and recounts his varied travels.

Henry James

Henry James lived most of his life in Europe and contributed travel pieces on art and culture to *Harper's* and other journals. Some of these essays are collected in *Italian Hours* (1907; Penguin 1995). The pieces on Venice are particularly good. You may also want to read his novella *The Aspern Papers* (1888; Wordsworth 1999), set in Venice.

D. H. Lawrence

Lawrence wrote several books about Italy, including *The Sea and Sardinia* (1921) and *Etruscan Places* (1927); a selected edition, *D. H. Lawrence and Italy*, has been published by Penguin (1997).

Ignazio Silone

Silone was an important socialist writer who had to go into exile during Mussolini's reign. *Bread and Wine* (*Pane e Vino;* 1937; New American Library 1988) is a vivid novel set during the Fascist period — a modern classic.

Giuseppe Lampedusa

Lampedusa was actually Giuseppe Tomasi, prince of Lampedusa. His novel *The Leopard* (*Il Gattopardo*; 1958; Pantheon 1991) is about the effect on a noble Sicilian family of Garibaldi's invasion and the war to unify Italy as a state. It was made into a tremendous film by Luchino Visconti, starring Burt Lancaster.

Mary McCarthy

Critic/novelist Mary McCarthy, author of *The Group* (1963; Harcourt Brace 1963), also wrote entertaining nonfiction works about the places in Italy she loved: *Venice Observed* (1956; Harcourt Brace 1989) and *The Stones of Florence* (1959; Harcourt Brace 1989).

Karl Ludwig Gallwitz

Gallwitz's recent *Handbook of Italian Renaissance Painters* (1999) gives you an at-a-glance guide to 1,200 Italian painters; it also has some nice reproductions, brief essays on the major schools of painting, and some weird charts that show who influenced whom. You might want to peruse it before you go if you're really into art — it's softcover and not very thick, so you might even bring it along.

Chapter 28

From Lace to Glass: The Top Ten (or so) Affordable Craft Specialties of Italy

. . . .

In This Chapter

▶ Buying souvenirs for the home

▶ Giving unique gifts

▶ Treating yourself

. . . .

*T*here are lots of fabulous things to buy in Italy, from Murano chandeliers to Armani suits. But if you don't feel like spending $800 or $8,000, there are a lot of craft items (we exclude mass-produced things like shoes, though of high quality) you can buy that'll remind you of your trip and bring beauty to your home (or the home of a relative or friend). We don't even go into the food specialties, because many may not be importable to your country and most are sold in gourmet specialty stores worldwide.

Blown Glass from Murano

A Murano chandelier can cost thousands — and you need to have the place and the taste for it — but one of the smaller trinkets from this Venetian lagoon island can be very affordable and attractive. Small colored animals are popular, and you can also find small dishes and paperweights (in England they used to call these lumps "end of day" glasses, and they're collectible). You can go directly to the island itself, but for small pieces it's easier to just check out the numerous shops in Venice (see Chapter 18).

Embroideries from Florence

Although the craft is disappearing, you can still find hand-embroidered items for sale in specialized shops in Florence (see Chapter 14). The larger items — such as tablecloths and bedsheets — are very expensive, but you can buy very nice placemats, centerpieces, and handkerchiefs. They can make elegant inexpensive gifts.

Handmade Paper from Amalfi

Paper has been a traditional industry in Italy for centuries, and in Amalfi you can still find artisans making their paper as in the Middle Ages, but with innovation. If you like writing, you'll have to buy a few of these beautiful sheets of paper (see Chapter 22).

Hand-Painted Pottery from Sicily

The Sicilian centers of Caltagirone, Santo Stefano, and Sciacca make colorful objects well worth bringing home, and they're very different in style from the pottery in the other Italian schools. You don't need to go to the actual towns at the three corners of this large island, however; shops in Palermo have great collections (see Chapter 23). Here too it's easy to find small objects that make good affordable gifts.

Marbleized Paper from Venice or Florence

This special technique for decorating paper was invented in Italy. Both Florentine and Venetian craftspeople claim paternity of this difficult art, but you don't need to decide: There are beautiful products — slightly different in style — in the two cities (see Chapter 14 for Florence and Chapter 18 for Venice). You can choose from diaries, notebooks, and other stationery.

Pottery from Vietri

A small vase or little dish from Vietri on the Amalfi Coast (see Chapter 22) will be a fine souvenir for yourself and a welcome gift for friends. The array of pieces to chose from is enormous, and the sunny colors of the typical geometric hand-painted decorations make you happy just looking at them. The terra cotta is generically of high quality, and if you choose a dish or compact vase, it'll travel very well. We even brought home a large cake dish in a hard suitcase without a problem.

Presepio from Naples

Carving figurines for the *presepio* (nativity scene), an Italian tradition related to Christmas, is an ancient art in Naples (see Chapter 20). They can be carved in wood or made out of plaster but are always brightly colored. The traditional ones can be quite big — even life-size — but you can find much smaller ones. They have very baroque looks and colors — like bringing a small Renaissance painting home with you.

Prints from Rome

Beautifully executed prints and engravings, usually of classic subjects — monuments, landscapes, ruins with sheep and figures — have been traditionally manufactured in Rome (see Chapter 12). You can find some valuable antique ones but also some very nice reproductions from old engraving plates. Without a frame, they're quite affordable, can be easily transported, and make excellent gifts for your art-lover friends.

Swimsuits from Positano

For some reason — probably because it's the most exclusive seaside resort on the Amalfi Coast — in Positano you'll find the best and most colorful swimsuits anywhere (see Chapter 22). They make very welcome gifts.

Appendix

Quick Concierge

● ●

Italy Facts at Your Fingertips

Automobile Club

Contact the Automobile Club d'Italia (ACI) at
☎ **06-4477** for 24-hour information and assistance. For road emergencies in Italy, dial
☎ **116**.

American Express

The Rome office is at Piazza di Spagna 38
(☎ **06-676-41**; Metro: Line A to Spagna); the
Florence office is at Via Dante Alighieri 22R
(☎ **055-50-981**); and the Venice office is at
Salizzada San Moisè, 1471 San Marco
(☎ **041-520-0844**).

ATMs

ATMs are available everywhere in the centers of towns. Most banks are linked to the
Cirrus network. If you require Plus, your best
bet is the BNL (Banca Nazionale del Lavoro).

Business Hours

Normal **banking hours** are Monday to Friday
8:30 a.m. to 1 or 1:30 p.m. and 2 or 2:30 to 4
p.m. Banks are closed Saturday and Sunday.
Merchant hours are the same, except they
don't reopen in the afternoon until 4 p.m., and
they then stay open til 7 or 7:30 p.m. Food
stores are usually closed all Thursday afternoon; all other shops close Monday morning.
Some supermarkets and some stores are
open longer hours, don't close at lunchtime,
and are also open Sundays.

Currency Exchange

You can find very good exchange bureaus
(marked cambio/change/wechsel) at airports
and at major train stations. Otherwise, there
are exchange offices in most towns and concentrated near the major attractions.

Customs

U.S. citizens can bring back $400 worth of
merchandise duty-free. You can mail yourself $200 worth of merchandise per day and
$100 worth of gifts to others — alcohol and
tobacco excluded. You can bring on the
plane 1 liter of alcohol and 200 cigarettes or
100 cigars. The $400 ceiling doesn't apply to
artwork or antiques (antiques must be 100
years old or more). You're charged a flat rate
of 10 percent duty on the next $1,000 worth
of purchases. Make sure that you have
your receipts handy. Agricultural restrictions
are severely enforced: no fresh products,
no meat products, no dried flowers, and
other foodstuffs are allowed only if they're
canned or in sealed packages. For more
information, contact the **U.S. Customs
Service**, 1301 Constitution Ave. (P.O. Box
7407), Washington, DC 20044 (☎ **202/
927-6724**) and request the free pamphlet
Know Before You Go, which is also available
on the Web at www.customs.ustreas.
gov/travel/kbygo.htm.

Canadian citizens are allowed a $500 exemption and can bring back duty-free 200 cigarettes, 2.2 pounds of tobacco, 40 imperial ounces of liquor, and 50 cigars. In addition, you're allowed to mail gifts to Canada from abroad at the rate of Can$60 a day, provided they're unsolicited and don't contain alcohol or tobacco (write on the package "Unsolicited Gift, Under $60 Value"). Declare all valuables on the Y-38 form before your departure from Canada, including serial numbers of valuables that you already own, such as expensive foreign cameras. You can use the $500 exemption only once a year and only after an absence of seven days. For more information write for the booklet *I Declare*, issued by Revenue Canada, 2265 St. Laurent Blvd., Ottawa K1G 4KE (☎ 613-993-0534).

There's no limit on what **U.K. citizens** can bring back from an E.U. country, as long as the items are for personal use (this includes gifts), and the necessary duty and tax has already been paid. However, Customs law sets out guidance levels. If you bring in more than these levels, you may be asked to prove that the goods are for your own use. Guidance levels on goods bought in the E.U. for your own use are 800 cigarettes, 200 cigars, 1 kg smoking tobacco, 10 liters of spirits, 90 liters of wine (of this not more than 60 liters can be sparkling wine), and 110 liters of beer. For more information, contact HM Customs & Excise, Passenger Enquiry Point, 2nd Floor Wayfarer House, Great South West Road, Feltham, Middlesex, TW14 8NP (☎ 0181-910-3744; from outside the U.K. 44-181-910-3744), or consult their Web site at www.open.gov.uk.

Australian citizens are allowed an exemption of A$400 or, for those under 18, A$200. Personal property mailed back home should be marked "Australian Goods Returned" to avoid payment of duty. On returning to Australia, you can bring in 250 cigarettes or 250 grams of loose tobacco, and 1,125 ml of alcohol. If you're returning with valuable goods you already own, such as foreign-made

cameras, you should file form B263. A helpful brochure, available from Australian consulates or Customs offices, is *Know Before You Go*. For more information, contact Australian Customs Services, GPO Box 8, Sydney NSW 2001 (☎ 02-9213-2000).

New Zealand citizens have a duty-free allowance of NZ$700. If you're over 17, you can bring in 200 cigarettes, 50 cigars, or 250 grams of tobacco (or a mix of all three if their combined weight doesn't exceed 250 grams); plus 4.5 liters of wine and beer, or 1.125 liters of liquor. New Zealand currency doesn't carry import or export restrictions. Fill out a certificate of export, listing the valuables you're taking out of the country. (That way, you can bring them back without paying duty.) You can find the answers to most of your questions in a free pamphlet available at New Zealand consulates and Customs offices: *New Zealand Customs Guide for Travelers, Notice no. 4*. For more information, contact **New Zealand Customs**, 50 Anzac Ave., P.O. Box 29, Auckland (☎ 09-359-6655).

Doctors

Contact any of the embassies and consulates to get a list of English-speaking doctors (see later in this listing and the "Fast Facts" sections in the chapters on the larger cities). In Palermo, contact the Guardia Medica Turistica (emergency doctor for tourists) at ☎ 091-532-798.

Electricity

Electricity in Italy is 220 volts. To use your appliances, you need a transformer. Remember that plugs are different too: The prongs are round, so you also need an adapter. You can buy an adapter kit in many electronics stores.

Embassies and Consulates

Rome is the capital of Italy and therefore the seat of all the embassies and consulates, which maintain a 24-hour referral service for emergencies: United States (☎ 06-46741), Canada (☎ 06-445-981), Australia (☎ 06-852-721),

New Zealand (☎ 06-440-2928), United Kingdom (☎ 06-7-482-5441), Ireland (☎ 06-697-9121). For more information on embassies and consulates around Italy, see the "Fast Facts" sections in the chapters on the larger cities.

Emergencies

For an ambulance, call ☎ 118; for the police, call ☎ 113; for the Carabinieri (other police force), call ☎ 112; for the fire department, call ☎ 115; for road emergencies, call ☎ 116 (road emergencies and first aid of the Italian Automobile Club).

Information

See "Where to Get More Information," later in this listing.

Language

Italians speak Italian. You can survive with very little knowledge of the Italian language (see Chapter 26 and the glossary later in this Appendix), especially because Italians are very friendly and ready to help foreigners in difficulty. However, you'll greatly enhance your experience if you master more than a dozen basic expressions. A good place to start your studies is *Italian For Dummies* (IDG Books)!

Liquor Laws

There are no liquor laws in Italy. However, there are laws against disturbing the *quiete pubblica* (public quiet) — getting drunk and loud in the streets and so on. Italians consider public drunkenness disgraceful, and though they love wine, they very much frown upon drinking to excess. You can buy alcohol in all supermarkets and grocery stores, open usually 9 a.m. to 1 p.m. and 4 to 7 p.m.

Mail

Each town has at least one post office, usually in the center. Mail in Italy is notoriously unreliable but getting better. In fact, many tourists in Rome prefer to use the Vatican post office while they're visiting St. Peter's (same price as other Italian post offices). A

postcard or letter to the U.S. costs 1,300L (70¢), to Australia and New Zealand 1,400L (76¢), and to the U.K. and Ireland 800L (43¢). For valuable packages, use a private carrier like UPS or DHL. Technically, you're supposed to mail international mail either inside the post office or in one of the *blue international mail boxes,* not the red ones that you see everywhere. However, if you use a red mailbox, your mail will probably still reach its destination.

Maps

You can find free good maps at information booths. If you want something more detailed, you can buy one at a newsstand or kiosk.

Newspapers and Magazines

All the newspaper kiosks in the center of major cities carry the *International Herald Tribune,* European issues of *Time,* and usually *The Economist* and *Financial Times.*

Pharmacies

Pharmacies are open on a rotation schedule, so there's always a pharmacy *di turno* (on call). Ask your hotel to find the closest open pharmacy for you.

Rest rooms

You can find rest rooms in public buildings like train stations and airports and at major sights. You can also use rest rooms in bars and cafes, but because these are for patrons (and not a public service), buy something before you ask. A glass of bottled water (*acqua minerale*) is the cheapest. Some cities offer public toilets, which are marked with a "WC" sign. For these, travel with a supply of 500L coins in case there's an attendant, and bring your own toilet paper in case the rest room is out.

Safety

Italy is very safe, not considering petty theft. Pickpockets abound in tourist areas, public transportation, and crowded open-air markets. Bag snatchers on motor scooters are less frequent than they used to be, and Palermo is the only city where they're still common. Keeping your bag on the wall side of a sidewalk or between you and your companion is a good rule to follow, however. Likewise, there are areas of poverty where a wealthy-looking tourist with an expensive camera might be mugged after dark. (Seedy areas are often behind rail stations.)

Smoking

Smoking is allowed in cafes and restaurants and is very common. Unfortunately for non-smokers, finding a restaurant with a separate no-smoking area is virtually impossible.

Taxes

Italy doesn't have a local tax, and other ta xes are always included in the prices quoted. You can get a refund of the 19 percent IVA (value-added tax) for purchases costing more than 300,000L ($160). See "Keeping a Lid on Hidden Expenses" in Chapter 4 for details.

Telephone

All public pay phones in Italy take a *carta telefonica* (telephone card), which you can buy at a *tabacchi* (tobacconist; marked by a sign with a white T on a black background), bar, or newsstand. The cards are precharged with value (5,000L/$2.70, 10,000L/$5, or 15,000L/$8). Tear off the perforated corner, stick the card in the phone, and you're ready to go. A few phones, usually inside bars, still take coins, but someone else who also forgot to buy a card is always using that one when you're in a hurry.

To call Italy from abroad, dial the **international access code, 011;** and then Italy's **country code, 39;** and then the **city code** for the city you're calling (06 for Rome, 055 for Florence, 041 for Venice, and so on); and then the regular phone number. Note that in 1998, city codes became permanent parts of all phone numbers, so you must include them for every call.

A local call in Italy costs 200L (11¢). To **make a call within Italy,** dial the city code of the city that you're calling (even if you're in that town) and then the phone number. To **make an international call from Italy,** dial 00, the country code of the country that you're calling (1 for the United States and Canada, 44 for the United Kingdom, 353 for Ireland, 61 for Australia, 64 for New Zealand), and then the phone number. Make sure that you have a high-value *carta telefonica* before you start; your 5,000L won't last long when you call San Diego at noon. Lower rates apply on Sundays and other days after 11 p.m. and before 8 a.m.

The best option for calling home, though, is using your own calling card linked to your home phone. For AT&T, dial ☎ **172-1011;** for MCI, dial ☎ **172-1022;** and for Sprint, dial ☎ **172-1877.** To access these numbers, however, you still must put in a 200L coin or a *carta telefonica.* You can also use these numbers to make collect calls. To make a collect call to a country other than the United States, dial ☎ **170.** Directory assistance for calls within Italy is a free call: Dial ☎ **12.** International directory assistance is a toll call: Dial ☎ **176.** Remember that calling from a hotel is convenient but usually very expensive.

Time Zone

In terms of standard time zones, Italy is six hours ahead of eastern standard time in the United States. Daylight saving time goes into effect in Italy each year from the end of March to the end of September.

Tipping

Tipping is customary as a token of appreciation as well as a polite gesture. A 15 percent service charge is usually included in your restaurant bill (check the menu when you order). You also must tip bellhops who carry your bags (about 2,000L/$1.10 per bag), while cab drivers get a small tip like waiters in those restaurants where service is already included (about 5 percent).

Transit/Tourist Assistance

You can call ☎ **147-888-088** (toll free in Italy) daily 7 a.m. to 9 p.m. for information on trains. In Rome, the tourist hotline is ☎ **06-3600-4399**. For 24-hour assistance, call the tourist hotline ☎ **167-234-169**.

Weather Updates

For forecasts, your best bet is to watch the news on TV (there's no "weather number" for the telephone as there is in the U.S.). On the Internet, check meteo.tiscalinet.it.

Toll-Free Numbers and Web Sites for Airlines, Car-Rental Agencies, and Hotel Chains

Airlines that fly to Italy and in Italy

Air Canada

☎ 888-247-2262

www.aircanada.ca

Air France

☎ 800-237-2747

www.airfrance.com

Air New Zealand

☎ 800-737-000

www.airnz.com

Air One

☎ 06-488-800 or 478-48-880 toll-free in Italy

www.flyairone.it

Air Sicilia

☎ 06-6501-1046

Alitalia

☎ 800-223-5730 in the U.S.; ☎ 800-361-8336 in Canada; ☎ 0990-448-259 in the U.K. and 020-7602-7111 in London; ☎ 1300-653-747 or 1300-653-757 in Australia; ☎ 06-65643 in Italy or 1478-65-643 toll-free in Italy

www.alitalia.it or alitaliausa.com

American Airlines

☎ 800/433-7300

www.americanair.com

British Airways

☎ 800-AIRWAYS (800-247-9297) in the U.S.

www.british-airways.com

Canadian Airlines International

☎ 800-426-7000

www.cdnair.ca

Cathay Pacific

☎ 131-747 toll-free in Australia or 0508-800454 in New Zealand

www.cathaypacific.com

Continental Airlines

☎ 800-525-0280

www.flycontinental.com

Delta Airlines

☎ 800-241-4141

www.delta-air.com

KLM

☎ 800-374-7747

www.klm.nl

Lufthansa
☎ 800-645-3880
www.lufthansa-usa.com

Meridiana
☎ 06-874-081 or 199-111-333 in Italy
www.meridiana.it

Qantas
☎ 13-13-13
www.qantas.com

TWA
☎ 800-221-2000
www.twa.com

United
☎ 800-538-2929
www.ual.com

US Airways
☎ 800-428-4322
www.usairways.com

Car-rental companies that operate in Italy

AutoEurope
☎ 800-334-440 toll-free in Italy or
800-223-5555 in the U.S.
www.autoeurope.com or www.sbc.it

Avis
☎ 06-41-999 in Italy or 800-331-1212 in
the U.S.
www.avis.com

Europe by Car
☎ 800-223-1516 in the U.S.
www.europebycar.com

Europcar
☎ 800-014-410 toll free in Italy or
06-6501-0879
www.europcar.it

Hertz
☎ 199-112-211 in Italy or 800-654-3001
in the U.S.
www.hertz.com

Kemwel
☎ 800-678-0678 in the U.S.
www.kemwel.com

National/Maggiore
☎ 1478-67-067 toll-free in Italy or
800-227-7368 in the U.S. www.maggiore.it

Hotel chains in Italy

Best Western
☎ 800-780-7234 in the U.S. and Canada,
☎ 0800-39-31-30 in the U.K., ☎ 131-779 in
Australia, ☎ 0800-237-893 in New Zealand;
www.bestwestern.com or www.
bestwestern.it

Hilton Hotels
☎ 800-HILTONS;
www.hilton.com

Holiday Inn
☎ 800-HOLIDAY;
www.holiday-inn.com

Jolly Hotels
☎800-017-703 toll free in Italy, ☎ 800-
221-2626 toll free in the U.S., ☎ 800-247-1277
toll-free in New York state, ☎ 800-237-0319
toll-free in Canada, ☎ 0800-731-0470 toll-free
in the U.K.
www.jollyhotels.it

ITT Sheraton

☎ **800-325-3535**

www.sheraton.com

Sofitel

☎ **800-SOFITEL** in the U.S. and Canada, ☎ **020-8 283-4570** in the U.K., ☎ **02-2951-2280** in Italy, ☎ **800-642-244** in Australia, ☎ **0800-44-44-22** in New Zealand; www.sofitel.com or

www.accor-hotels.it/sofitel.htm. (Sofitel is part of the giant Accor group, representing 3,400 hotels in several chains. You can connect to all of them through ☎ **800-221-4542** in the U.S. and Canada and ☎ **0208-283-4500** in the U.K.; www.accor.com)

Where to Get More Information

Visitor information

There are **Italian National Tourist Board (ENIT)** offices in the following cities (they're all open Monday to Friday 9 a.m. to 5 p.m.):

- ✔ **New York** (630 Fifth Ave., Suite 1565, New York, NY 10111; ☎ **212-245 -5095** or 212-245-4822; Fax: 212-586-9249; E-mail: enitny@bway.net)

- ✔ **Chicago** (500 N. Michigan Ave., Suite 2240, Chicago, IL 60611; ☎ **312-644- 0996;** Fax: 312-644-3019; E-mail: enitch@italiantourism.com)

- ✔ **Los Angeles** (12400 Wilshire Bld., Suite 550, Los Angeles, CA 90025; ☎ **310-820-2977** or 310-820-1898; Fax: 310-820-6357)

- ✔ **Montreal** (1 place Ville Marie, Suite 1914, Montreal, H3B 2C3 Quebec; ☎ **514-866- 0975** or 514-866-7669; Fax: 514-392-1429; E-mail: initaly@ican.net)

- ✔ **London** (1 Princes St., London, WIR 9AY; ☎ **020-7408-1254** or 020-7355-1438; Fax: 020-7493-6695; E-mail: enitland@globalnet.co.uk)

For more information about specific destinations, you can contact the following:

- ✔ **APT Roma** (Via Parigi 5, 00100 Roma; ☎ **06-4889-9255**)

- ✔ **APT Firenze** (Via A. Manzoni, 16, 50121, Firenze; ☎ **055-23-320;** Fax: 055-234-6286)

- ✔ **APT Venezia** (Castello 4421, 30100 Venezia; ☎ **041-529-8711;** Fax: 041-523-0399)

- ✔ **APT Napoli** (Piazza dei Martiri 58, 80100 Napoli; ☎ **081-405-311**)

- ✔ **APT Palermo** (Piazza Castelnuovo 35, 90141 Palermo; ☎ **091-586-122;** Fax: 091-582-788; Internet: www.aapit.pa.it; E-mail: aapit@gestelnet.it)

For 24-hour assistance call the **tourist hotline** at ☎ **167-234-169**. For assistance to pilgrims after the end of the Jubilee, you can contact **Peregrinatio Ad Petri Sedem** (Piazza Pio XII,4 Vaticano; ☎ **06-6988-4896**; Fax: 06-6988-5617; E-mail: peregrinatio@jubilee-2000.va)

Crawling the Web

Italy in general

The following sites provide a variety of cultural and visitor information:

- ✔ **ABC's of Italy** (www.italiaabc.com). This is a good site for cultural details on the country. It's comprehensive and also offers good links and hotel listings.

- ✔ **Dolce Vita** (www.dolcevita.com). The site is all about style — as it pertains to fashion, cuisine, design, and travel. Dolce Vita is a good place to stay up to date on trends in modern Italian culture.

- ✔ **FS On-line** (www.fs-on-line.com). This official site of the Italian rail system gives you station descriptions, train timetables, and ticket costs for Italy. (This site can help you find practical information to help you organize your trip.)

- ✔ **In Italy Online** (www.initaly.com). This extensive site helps you find all sorts of accommodations (country villas, historic residences, convents, and farmhouses) and includes tips on shopping, dining, driving, and viewing art.

- ✔ **Italian Tourist Web Guide** (www.itwg.com). Each month, this site recommends new itineraries for art lovers, nature buffs, wine enthusiasts, and other Italiophiles. It features a searchable directory of accommodations, transportation tips, and city-specific lists of restaurants and attractions.

- ✔ **Italy Hotel Reservation** (www.italyhotel.com). With almost 10,000 listings solely for Italy, this functional site is an ideal place to research and reserve lodgings.

- ✔ **ItalyTour.com** (www.italytour.com). Check out this vast directory for coverage of the arts, culture, business, tours, entertainment, restaurants, lodging, media, shopping, sports, and major Italian cities. See photo collections and videos in the "Panorama" section.

- ✔ **Sharelook Italy** (www.sharelook.it). At this site, you find some information (historical and cultural) on most destinations in Italy, plus some tourist links (hotels and restaurants).

- ✔ **Welcome to Italy** (www.wel.it). This site is a good source for all kinds of visitor info about Italy — from cultural (monuments and history) to practical (hotels and restaurants) to curiosities.

Rome

- ✔ **Ancient Sites** (www.ancientsites.com/users/COCCIEIUS-CAESAR). At this private site, you can see a reconstruction of ancient Rome.

- ✔ **Christus Rex** (www.christusrex.org). You can find lots of information, including updated opening hours of the Cappella Sistina, as well as a photo tour of the Vatican and its art treasures, at this unrelentingly religious site.

- ✔ **Enjoy Rome** (www.enjoyrome.com). Maintained by a private company, this site promotes the company's walking tours in Rome, Florence, and Venice as well as guided trips to Pompeii.

- ✔ **Roma Preview** (www.romapreview.it). Although mostly in Italian, this site is a great source for all the latest happenings in Rome and gives an excellent schedule of cultural events.

- ✔ **Rome Guide** (www.romeguide.it). Here you find a lot of historic information about Rome's monuments as well as a number of tourist links.

- ✔ **The Rome Page** (www.comune.roma.it). Under "Cultura" at the city's official Web site, you can find all the galleries and museums, as well as lists of hotels and restaurants. Though mostly everything is in Italian, you can get phone and fax numbers and addresses.

- ✔ **The Vatican** (www.vatican.va). This is the official site of the Holy See, where you can find lots of multilingual information about the Vatican.

- ✔ **Virtual Rome** (www.Virtualrome.it). Find a lot of visitor information as well as lots of pictures and interesting links at this site.

- ✔ **Welcome to Rome** (www.welcomerome.it). Here's another site with tourism in mind, and you can find interesting itineraries to discover the Eternal City.

Florence, Tuscany, and Umbria

- ✔ **About Pisa** (www.comune.pisa.it). This official site of the city is quite well done, with good info and links.

- ✔ **Assisi** (www.comune.assisi.pg.it). This is the official site of the city of Assisi. Although it's mostly in Italian, you can find a lot of information about the city as well as other good links.

- ✔ **Chianti DOC Marketplace** (www.chianti-doc.com). Taste a bit of Chianti's flavor at this site before traveling to the famous wine region. Take a quick online course in grape producing and Chianti Classico wines. You can also take a peek at Alitalia flight schedules and get information on booking vacation rentals in Chianti or Siena.

- **Chianti Net** (www.chiantinet.it). Self labeled as "the original site of Chianti," this site provides a lot of info and links about the region, including restaurants, shops, and places to stay.

- **Firenze By Net** (www.mega.it/florence). Updated weekly for news and notices about concerts and dance recitals, this site also lets you explore the art scene by clicking on the museum map, and then switching to the monument version for both the city and surrounding regions, including Chianti.

- **The Florence Page** (www.comune.firenze.it). Under "Turismo" at Florence's official site, you can find all the galleries and museums and lists of hotels and restaurants. Though mostly everything is in Italian, you can get phone and fax numbers and addresses.

- **The Heart of Tuscany** (www.nautilus-mp.com/tuscany/index.html). For each of five major art towns in Tuscany, this site provides a historic overview, photos, maps, an events calendar, and a shopping guide. You can also find details on a range of accommodations, some of which take reservations online.

- **Know It All: Know Tuscany** (www.knowital.com). As the name suggests, this travel guide seems to know it all about lodging, dining, and wine in the Italian region of Tuscany.

- **Lucca** (www.comune.lucca.it). The official site of the city gives lots of info, which is also available in English.

- **Pisa Online** (www.pisaonline.it). If English is your language of choice, you'll be happy to find this site, chock-full of useful details.

- **Your Way to Florence** (www.arca.net/florence.htm). If you're going to Florence to see its magnificent works of art, first take a peek at this site, which is a combined tour guide and art history lesson that includes a glossary of art terms. The site provides hotel reviews and city news as well.

Venice and the Veneto

- **Carnival of Venice** (www.carnivalofvenice.com/uk). Find out what's afoot for the *Carnevale* celebration in the city of gondolas. You can also find information about transportation, city services, and other basics. Also see www.doge.it, which offers a modest amount of information about hotels and happenings.

- **Meeting Venice** (www.meetingvenice.it). Intended for both leisure and business travelers, this guide to the magical city provides a calendar of events, weather forecasts, a hotel search, and brief descriptions of hundreds of eating places.

- **Padova Guide** (www.padovanet.it). In English and Italian, this is an excellent source of info on Padua.

- **Venezia** (`www.provincia.venezia.it/aptve`). In addition to listings of events, sights, and suggested itineraries, this official tourist board site piles on scores of pages of hotel descriptions.

- **The Venice Page** (`www.comune.venezia.it`). The official site of the city, the Venice Page is also available in English and is chock-full of information.

- **Venice World** (`www.veniceworld.com`). This site lists links to Venice's accommodations, centers for the arts, nightclubs, restaurants, sporting events, travel agencies, Internet service providers, transportation, schools, newspapers, and so forth.

- **Verona: City of Art and History** (`www.intesys.it/Tour/Eng/Verona.html`). Don't let the Montagues and Capulets bog you down; there's a lot more to do in Verona than reenact the scene at Juliet's balcony. For suggestions, peruse some itineraries here, where tours are based on historic themes like Roman Verona, Verona as a city-state, Austrian Verona, and the city's churches and monasteries.

Naples, the Amalfi Coast, and Capri

- **Amalfi and the Amalfi Coast** (`www.starnet.it/italy/incostam.htm`). While promoting the lemon liqueur (limoncello) and stained glass produced on the Amalfi Coast, this site provides a map and a photo-illustrated historic overview of each of the region's little cities and villages.

- **Capri Online** (`www.caprionline.com`). This site boasts enticing beach-filled photographs and descriptions of seafood dishes and luxury lodgings. A profile showcases a local artist and his miniature ceramic replica of Capri. You can look through the directory of hotels, ranked by stars, or download free travel brochures and maps.

- **Naples in Virtual Reality** (`ww2.webcomp.com/virtuale/us/napoli/movie.htm`). This site gives you a good idea of what you can see in Napoli. The virtual reality tour shows Piazza del Plebiscito, Il Maschio Angioino, the Galleria Umberto I, and other great artifacts. Visiting this site is almost like being in Naples.

- **Napoli Napoli** (`www.napolinapoli.it`). This site is about style — it's the insiders' site on Naples with a lot of information about the city's culture and interesting articles. It also has plenty of useful links.

- **Pompeii Forum Project** (`pompeii.virginia.edu`). The University of Virginia and the National Endowment for the Humanities explore urban history and design in an unearthed Pompeii. Their site is full of cool photos, educational information, and even some virtual-reality segments and video clips.

Sicily

- ✔ **Etna Decade Volcano (www.geo.mtu.edu/~boris/ETNA.html).** Learn all you want to know about one of the world's most active volcanoes, which has been erupting in Sicily since about 1500 B.C. The site offers spectacular (and alarmingly recent) photographs, fact and figures, maps, weather forecasts, and a geology lesson or two.

- ✔ **The Palermo Page (www.comune.palermo.it).** This is the official site of the city of Palermo. Although a lot of it is in Italian, this is a good source of information on cultural and tourist events.

- ✔ **Sicily Region (www.sicily.infcom.it).** Follow this site's ready-made itineraries to see the many treasures lurking in Palermo in the forms of parks, cathedrals, great works of art, and nightlife. If you'd prefer to make your own plans, no problem. This site is overflowing with info about Sicilian culture, events, transportation, lodging, public services, and businesses.

Molto Italiano: A Basic Vocabulary

You can't become fluent in Italian in one day, but you can still learn enough to get by without much trouble. Below are the few essential words that will make things a lot easier for you during your vacation.

Useful words

English	Italian
Excuse me	Permesso ("per-*mess*-ow")
Goodbye	Arrivederci ("ah-rree-vey-*der*-tchy")
Hello (Good day)	Buon giorno ("bwon *djor*-know")
Hello (Good evening)	Buona sera ("bwon-a *sey*-rah")
Please	Per favore ("per fa-*voe*-ray")
Sorry	Scusi ("*scoo*-sy")
Thank you	Grazie ("*gra*-tziay")
Where is . . .	Dov'è. . . ("doe-*vay*")

Useful expressions

English	Italian
A coffee, please	Un caffè, per favore ("oon ka-*ffay* per fa-*vo*-e-ray")
How much does it cost?	Quanto costa? ("*quahnn*-tow *koss*-tah?")
I don't understand	Non capisco ("Nonn kah-*peace*-koh")
The bill, please	Il conto, per favore ("eel *kon*-tow per fa-*vo*-e-ray")

English	Italian
What is it?	Che cos'è? ("kay koss-*ay?*")
Where is the Coliseum?	Dov'è il Colosseo? ("doe-*vay* eel ko-low-*ssay*-o?")
Where is the train station?	Dov'è la stazione? ("doe-*vay* lah stah-*tziow*-nay?")

Numbers

1	uno ("*oo*-no")
2	due ("*doo*-ay")
3	tre ("tray")
4	quattro ("*kwa*-troh")
5	cinque ("*cheen*-kway")
6	sei ("say")
7	sette ("*set*-tay")
8	otto ("*oht*-toh")
9	nove ("*no*-vay")
10	dieci ("dee-*ay*-chee")
11	undici ("*oon*-dee-chee")
12	dodici ("*doe*-dee-chee")
13	tredici ("*tray*-dee-chee")
14	quattordici ("kwa-*tor*-dee-chee")
15	quindici ("*queen*-dee-chee")
16	sedici ("*say*-dee-chee")
17	diciassette ("dee-chay-*set*-tay")
18	diciotto ("deech-*oht*-toh")
19	diciannove ("deechay-*nno*-vay")
20	venti ("*vehn*-ti")
100	cento ("*chen*-toh")
1,000	mille ("*meel*-leh")

For prices, refer to the numbers above and add *mila*, the suffix for thousands, since the price will be in lira. For example: 5,000 *cinquemila* ("cheenkway-*mee*-lah") and 6,000 *seimila* ("say-*mee*-lah").

Knowing Your Apse from Your Ambone: A Glossary of Architectural Terms

Apse: Semi-circular recess, topped by a dome or an arch. In Christian churches, the half-rounded extension behind the main altar; Christian tradition dictates that the apse be placed at the eastern end of an Italian church, the side closest to Jerusalem. In Italian, apse is *abside*.

Architrave: The main beam (usually on top of columns) that supports the roof or an upper floor.

Atrium: Courtyard in the center of an ancient Roman house; the term also applies to the covered portico before a Christian church.

Baldachin or **baldaquin** (also **ciborium**): A canopy, suspended or on pillars, usually placed above the altar of a church or a throne. In Italian, a baldachin is a *baldacchino*.

Baptistry: A separate building or a separate area in a church where the rite of baptism is held. The word comes from the Greek and means "bathing place" (in Italian, *battistero*).

Bas-relief: A flat sculpture in which the carved figures project slightly from the surface.

Basilica: Originally, this word meant *royal palace;* the meaning then extended to include any rectangular building, divided into three aisles by rows of columns and with an apse at the end. In ancient Rome, this architectural form was frequently used for places of public assembly and law courts. Later, Roman Christians adopted the form for their churches. The word now refers principally to the seven churches of Rome that were founded by Emperor Constantine, the first Roman Christian emperor. A few others have been given this title also, namely the churches housing the remains of certain saints, such as the Basilica di San Francesco in Assisi.

Caldarium: The steam room of an ancient Roman bath.

Campanile: The bell tower, often detached, of a church.

Capital: The top of a column, often carved.

Chancel: The section of the church containing the altar and reserved to priests and choir; it's usually separated by a railing and often raised. The chancel is also referred to as the *choir* (in Italian, *coro*).

Cloister: A covered walk around a courtyard or a garden in a convent or a monastery; the inner side opens toward the center with windows or arches and columns. The Italian word for cloister is *chiostro*.

Cornice: The decorative projection at the top of a wall, before the ceiling or roof, which is often molded.

Cupola: Dome.

Duomo: Cathedral, the main church of a town that has a bishop.

Entablature: The part above the column; it includes the architrave, the frieze, and the cornice. In Greek temples it supported the roof.

Forum: The religious, commercial, and political center of a Roman town. It's usually the site of the city's most important temples and civic buildings.

Frieze: The decorated part of the entablature above the architrave.

Greek cross: The plan of a church; the Greek cross has arms of equal length.

Latin cross: The plan of a church; the Latin cross has one long arm (the nave) crossed by a short one.

Loggia: Roofed balcony or gallery.

Nave: The largest and longest section of a church, usually devoted to sheltering and/or seating worshipers and often divided by aisles.

Naos: In a Greek temple, the room where the image of the god was kept. See also **Pronaos.**

Opistodomos: The part of a Greek temple where treasure, votive gifts, and the temple archives were kept. It was the most remote room in the temple, behind the statue of the god.

Palazzo: A palace or public building, or a *casa signorile* (large house of a noble family).

Piano Nobile: The floor of a residential palazzo (usually the second floor) containing the reception and public rooms; this is where the family entertained.

Pieve: A term used in the Middle Ages for a parish church in central and northern Italy. The word came from Latin *plebs* and also referred to the people and the community. Because it was the main church of the area, the pieve was often fortified.

Portico: A porch, usually crafted from wood or stone.

Pronaos: The entrance to a Greek temple, in front of the room where the image of the god was kept (*naos*).

Putto (plural *putti*): A figure of a small child, cherub, or cupid often seen in Italian Renaissance and baroque art. Famous are the putti of Serpotta, the Sicilian baroque sculptor of Palermo.

Stucco: Plaster composed of sand, powdered marble, water, and lime, either molded into statuary or applied in a thin layer to surfaces.

Thermae: Roman public baths, often including a natural hot spring. The Italian word is *terme*.

Travertine: The stone from which ancient and Renaissance Rome were built; this stone is known for its hardness, light coloring, and tendency to be pitted or flecked with black or rusty brown.

Tympanum: The half-rounded space above the portal of a church, whose semicircular space usually showcases a sculpture.

From Antipastto Zuppa Inglese: A Glossary of Italian Menu Terms

Abbacchio: Lamb. Usually roasted or baked.

Agnolotti: A fresh crescent-shaped pasta stuffed with a mix of chopped meat, spices, vegetables, and cheese; when prepared in rectangular versions, the same combination of ingredients is identified as *ravioli*.

Al cartoccio: A method of baking fish or vegetables in a parchment envelope with onions, parsley, and herbs.

Amaretti: Crunchy and sweet almond-flavored macaroons.

Amaro: A bitter liqueur, usually served as an after-dinner drink.

Anguilla: Eel.

Antipasto: Served at the beginning of a meal (before the pasta), antipasto may include slices of cured meats, seafood (especially shellfish), and cooked and seasoned vegetables.

Aperitivo: A drink before a meal; the drink can be alcoholic (a glass of wine, a mild cocktail, or a Campari) or an *analcolico* (non-alcoholic), sweet-bitter beverage.

Aragosta: Lobster.

Arancina or **arancino:** A rice ball, fried in oil, with a crunchy crust (usually made of egg and bread crumbs).

Arrosto: Roasted meat.

Baccalà: Dried and salted codfish.

Bistecca: Steak, usually grilled.

Bocconcini: Literally meaning "small mouthful," it can refer to small bite-sized mozzarella or little rolled up pieces of veal.

Bollito misto: Assorted boiled meats served on a single platter.

Braciola: Pork chop.

Bresaola: Air-dried spiced beef.

Bruschetta: Toasted bread, heavily seasoned with olive oil and garlic, and often topped with a variety of things, particularly tomatoes.

Bucatini: Large hollow spaghetti.

Cacciucco alla livornese: Seafood stew.

Caciotta: A firm, mild sheep-milk (sometimes mixed with cow-milk) cheese very common in central Italy.

Calzone: A pizza dough pocket, usually filled with ham, mozzarella, and tomato.

Cannelloni: A square of fresh pasta dough, filled with meat and cheese or fish, and then baked with a tomato and bechamel (white) sauce.

Cappelletti: Literally "little hats," they are filled fresh pasta.

Carciofi: Artichokes.

Carpaccio: Raw beef, sliced paper thin and served with olive oil, shavings of parmesan cheese, and sometimes arugula.

Cassata: A Sicilian dessert combining layers of sponge cake, sweetened ricotta cheese, and candied fruit, covered with almond paste.

Cena: Dinner; it's often a smaller meal when eaten in the home, though more extensive when eaten in a restaurant.

Contorno: Side dish of vegetables or potatoes.

Cornetto: Italian croissant, sweeter than its French counterpart and less oily, often filled with cream or jam

Costoletta alla milanese: Deep-fried veal cutlet.

Cozze: Mussels.

Crostata: Homemade dessert similar to the Linzer Torte; it's a thick, sweet crust layered with jam; sometimes with cream or sweet ricotta.

Fagioli: Beans.

Fagiolini: Green beans.

Fave: Fava beans.

Fegato: Liver, usually calves' liver.

Filetti di baccalà: Salt cod, battered and deep fried.

Fiori di zucca: Flowers of zucchini, battered, deep fried, and filled with a small piece of mozzarella and anchovy.

Focaccia: A flatbread; a cousin of Neapolitan pizza. Around Florence, focaccia is thick, soft, and white, and sometimes made with olives. In the far south, it's made from potato-based dough, often garnished with onions and tomato.

Frittata: Italian omelet.

Fritto misto: A deep-fried medley of small fish, shrimp, and squid.

Fusilli: Spiral-shaped pasta.

Gelato (produzione propria): Ice cream (homemade).

Gnocchi: Dumplings made from potatoes (*gnocchi alla patate*) and usually served with a tomato and parmesan sauce. *Gnocchi alla romana* are semolina dumplings covered with butter and grated Parmesan and toasted in the oven.

Gorgonzola: One of the most famous blue-veined cheeses of Europe, it's strong, creamy, and aromatic.

Granita: Frozen coffee, lemonade, or almond milk; when made with coffee, it's usually served with whipped cream.

Grappa: Wine-based brandy.

Insalata di frutti di mare: Seafood salad (usually including shrimp and octopus) seasoned with vinegar or lemon, olive oil, and herbs.

Involtini: Thinly sliced beef, veal, or pork rolled and stuffed.

Lonza: Cured morsels of pork filet encased in sausage skins and served in slices.

Minestrone: A chunky vegetable soup with red beans, olive oil, and sometimes short pasta, served with parmigiano.

Mortadella: A pork cold cut from Bologna, with pistacchio nuts that become soft after curing. It's the ancestor of baloney (sometimes spelled bologna).

Mozzarella: A non-fermented fresh cheese; the original is made from the milk of a buffalo (*mozzarella di bufala*), but the most common type is made from cow milk.

Osso buco: Sliced beef or veal shank slowly braised until tender.

Pancetta: Cured pork belly. Pancetta is the Italian bacon. When rolled into a cylinder and sliced, it's called *pancetta arrotolata*.

Pane: Bread.

Panettone: A bell-shaped, sweet yellow-colored cake with raisins and candied fruit; a Christmas specialty.

Panna: Heavy cream (usually whipped).

Pansotti: Pasta stuffed with greens, herbs, and cheeses, usually served with a walnut sauce.

Pappardelle: A kind of fresh pasta, short and wide, often served with hare sauce.

Peperoncino: Red hot pepper.

Peperoni: Green, yellow, or red sweet peppers. (Don't confuse this term with pepperoni.)

Parmigiano: Parmesan, the hard and salty yellow cheese usually grated over pastas and soups but also eaten alone. The best is *parmigiano Reggiano*.

Pesce: Fish.

Pesto: A flavorful green sauce made from basil leaves, parmigiano, garlic, marjoram, and pinoli (pine nuts).

Piccata: Thin slice of veal sauteed; you can get it *al marsala* (in a marsala wine sauce) or *al limone* (in a lemon sauce).

Piselli: Peas; often *al prosciutto* (cooked with strips of ham).

Pizzaiola: A tomato-and-oregano sauce.

Polenta: Firm-cooked cornmeal, usually served with sausages and stews.

Pollo: Chicken.

Pranzo: Lunch; frequently the big meal of the day — although progressively less so — which is eaten between noon and 2:30 p.m.

Prima colazione: Breakfast; in Italy it's often eaten on the run between 8 and 9:30 a.m.

Primo or **primo piatto (plural *primi*):** The "first plate" of a meal, usually pasta or rice.

Prosciutto: Cured hind leg of a pig. The best is from Parma and tastes very sweet.

Ragu: Meat-and-tomato sauce.

Ricotta: A soft fresh cheese made from cow or sheep milk.

Risotto: Rice, first sautéed, and then simmered with a variety of seasonings. The result is a sticky rice.

Salame: Salami; you can find this meat in a variety of sizes, textures, and flavorings, depending on the region.

Salsa verde: "Green sauce," made from capers, anchovies, lemon juice and/or vinegar, and parsley.

Salsiccia: Sausage (usually fresh); it's served grilled or stewed.

Saltimbocca: Veal layered with prosciutto and sage, folded and held together with a toothpick; its name literally translates as "jump in your mouth" — a reference to its tart and savory flavor.

Salvia: Sage.

Scaloppine: Thin slices of veal coated in flour and sautéed in butter or oil.

Secondo or **secondo piatto (*plural secondi*):** The "second plate," or main course, usually consisting of meat or fish.

Semifreddo: A frozen dessert of ice cream with sponge cake.

Seppia: Cuttlefish (a kind of squid); food preparers use its black ink for flavoring in certain sauces for pasta and also in risotto dishes.

Sogliola: Sole (a delicate white fish).

Spaghetti: A long, round, thin pasta, variously served: *alla bolognese* (with ground meat, mushrooms, peppers, and so on), *alla carbonara* (with bacon, black pepper, and eggs), *al pomodoro* (with tomato sauce), *al sugo/ragù* (with meat sauce), and *alle vongole* (with clam sauce).

Spiedini: Grilled skewers, usually of meat.

Stufato: Stew.

Suppli: An *arancina* (see listing earlier in this list) with tomato added and a piece of mozzarella inside.

Tagliatelle: Flat egg noodles.

Tiramisù: A dessert containing layers of *mascarpone* (a creamy fresh cheese), coffee, and rum-soaked lady fingers.

Toast: Pronounced "tost." This isn't your usual toast — in Italy it's a grilled cheese sandwich with ham.

Tonno: Tuna.

Tortelli: Pasta dumplings stuffed with ricotta and greens.

Tortellini: Similar to *agnolotti* and *cappelletti* (see listings, earlier in this section).

Trenette: Thin noodles served with pesto sauce and potatoes.

Trippa: Beef tripe (stomach lining).

Vermicelli: Very thin spaghetti.

Vino: Wine; Vino is *rosso* (red) or *bianco* (white). House wine is usually sold by the liter, half liter, and quarter liter (*un litro, un mezzo litro,* and *un quarto litro*).

Vitello tonnato: Cold sliced veal covered with tuna-fish sauce.

Zabaglione/zabaione: Egg yolks whipped into the consistency of a custard, flavored with marsala; served as eggnog or ice cream dessert.

Zampone: Pig's foot stuffed with spicy seasoned pork, boiled and sliced, served usually with lentils for Christmas.

Zuccotto: A liquor-soaked sponge cake, molded into a dome and layered with chocolate, nuts, and whipped cream.

Zuppa inglese: Liquor-soaked sponge cake layered with custard.

Fare Game: Choosing an Airline

Travel Agency: _____ Phone: _____

Agent's Name: _____ Quoted Fare: _____

Departure Schedule & Flight Information

Airline: _____ Airport: _____

Flight #: _____ Date: _____ Time: _____ a.m./p.m.

Arrives in: _____ Time: _____ a.m./p.m.

Connecting Flight (if any)

Amount of time between flights: _____ hours/mins

Airline: _____ Airport: _____

Flight #: _____ Date: _____ Time: _____ a.m./p.m.

Arrives in: _____ Time: _____ a.m./p.m.

Return Trip Schedule & Flight Information

Airline: _____ Airport: _____

Flight #: _____ Date: _____ Time: _____ a.m./p.m.

Arrives in: _____ Time: _____ a.m./p.m.

Connecting Flight (if any)

Amount of time between flights: _____ hours/mins

Airline: _____ Airport: _____

Flight #: _____ Date: _____ Time: _____ a.m./p.m.

Arrives in: _____ Time: _____ a.m./p.m.

Notes

Making Dollars and Sense of It

Expense	Amount
Airfare	
Car Rental	
Lodging	
Parking	
Breakfast	
Lunch	
Dinner	
Baby-sitting	
Attractions	
Transportation	
Souvenirs	
Tips	
Grand Total	

Notes

Sweet Dreams: Choosing Your Hotel

Enter the hotels where you'd prefer to stay based on location and price. Then use the worksheet below to plan your itinerary.

Hotel	Location	Price per night

Sweet Dreams: Choosing Your Hotel

Enter the hotels where you'd prefer to stay based on location and price. Then use the worksheet below to plan your itinerary.

Hotel	Location	Price per night

Places to Go, People to See, Things to Do

Enter the attractions you would most like to see. Then use the worksheet below to plan your itinerary.

Attractions	Amount of time you expect to spend there	Best day and time to go

Places to Go, People to See, Things to Do

Enter the attractions you would most like to see. Then use the worksheet below to plan your itinerary.

Attractions	Amount of time you expect to spend there	Best day and time to go

Menus & Venues

Enter the restaurants where you'd most like to dine. Then use the worksheet below to plan your itinerary.

Name	*Address/Phone*	*Cuisine/Price*

Menus & Venues

Enter the restaurants where you'd most like to dine. Then use the worksheet below to plan your itinerary.

Name	Address/Phone	Cuisine/Price

Going "My" Way

Itinerary #1

☐ _____
☐ _____
☐ _____
☐ _____

Itinerary #2

☐ _____
☐ _____
☐ _____
☐ _____

Itinerary #3

☐ _____
☐ _____
☐ _____
☐ _____

Itinerary #4

☐ _____
☐ _____
☐ _____
☐ _____

Itinerary #5

☐ _____
☐ _____
☐ _____
☐ _____

Itinerary #6

☐ _____
☐ _____
☐ _____
☐ _____

Itinerary #7

☐ _____
☐ _____
☐ _____
☐ _____

Itinerary #8

☐ _____
☐ _____
☐ _____
☐ _____

Itinerary #9

☐ _____
☐ _____
☐ _____
☐ _____

Itinerary #10

☐ _____
☐ _____
☐ _____
☐ _____

Itinerary #11

❑ _____
❑ _____
❑ _____
❑ _____

Itinerary #12

❑ _____
❑ _____
❑ _____
❑ _____

Itinerary #13

❑ _____
❑ _____
❑ _____
❑ _____

Itinerary #14

❑ _____
❑ _____
❑ _____
❑ _____

Itinerary #15

❑ _____
❑ _____
❑ _____
❑ _____

Notes

Notes

Notes

Index

• G •

IDG BOOKS WORLDWIDE BOOK REGISTRATION

We want to hear from you!

Visit **http://my2cents.dummies.com** to register this book and tell us how you liked it!

- Get entered in our monthly prize giveaway.

- Give us feedback about this book — tell us what you like best, what you like least, or maybe what you'd like to ask the author and us to change!

- Let us know any other *For Dummies®* topics that interest you.

Your feedback helps us determine what books to publish, tells us what coverage to add as we revise our books, and lets us know whether we're meeting your needs as a *For Dummies* reader. You're our most valuable resource, and what you have to say is important to us!

Not on the Web yet? It's easy to get started with *Dummies 101®: The Internet For Windows® 98* or *The Internet For Dummies®* at local retailers everywhere.

Or let us know what you think by sending us a letter at the following address:

For Dummies Book Registration
Dummies Press
10475 Crosspoint Blvd.
Indianapolis, IN 46256

BESTSELLING BOOK SERIES